HANDBOOK OF SPECIAL EDUCATION RESEARCH, VOLUME II

Divided into two volumes, the *Handbook of Special Education Research* provides a comprehensive overview of critical issues in special education research. Volume II addresses research-based practices, offering a deep dive into tiered systems of support and advances in interventions and assessments, as well as socially, emotionally, culturally, and linguistically relevant practices. Each chapter features considerations for future research and implications for fostering continuous improvement and innovation. Essential reading for researchers and students of special education, this handbook brings together diverse and complementary perspectives to help move the field forward.

Christopher J. Lemons is Associate Professor of Special Education in the Graduate School of Education at Stanford University, USA.

Sarah R. Powell is Associate Professor in the Department of Special Education at the University of Texas at Austin, USA.

Kathleen Lynne Lane is the Roy A. Roberts Distinguished Professor in the Department of Special Education and Associate Vice Chancellor for Research at the University of Kansas, USA.

Terese C. Aceves is Chair of the Department of Specialized Programs in Professional Psychology in the School of Education at Loyola Marymount University, USA.

HANDBOOK OF SPECIAL EDUCATION RESEARCH, VOLUME II

Research-Based Practices and Intervention Innovations

Edited by Christopher J. Lemons, Sarah R. Powell, Kathleen Lynne Lane, and Terese C. Aceves

NEW YORK AND LONDON

Cover image: Getty Images/piranka

First published 2022
by Routledge
605 Third Avenue, New York, NY 10158

and by Routledge
4 Park Square, Milton Park, Abingdon, Oxon, OX14 4RN

Routledge is an imprint of the Taylor & Francis Group, an informa business

© 2022 selection and editorial matter, Christopher J. Lemons, Sarah R. Powell, Kathleen Lynne Lane, and Terese C. Aceves; individual chapters, the contributors

The right of Christopher J. Lemons, Sarah R. Powell, Kathleen Lynne Lane, and Terese C. Aceves to be identified as the authors of the editorial material, and of the authors for their individual chapters, has been asserted in accordance with sections 77 and 78 of the Copyright, Designs and Patents Act 1988.

All rights reserved. No part of this book may be reprinted or reproduced or utilised in any form or by any electronic, mechanical, or other means, now known or hereafter invented, including photocopying and recording, or in any information storage or retrieval system, without permission in writing from the publishers.

Trademark notice: Product or corporate names may be trademarks or registered trademarks, and are used only for identification and explanation without intent to infringe.

Library of Congress Cataloging-in-Publication Data
A catalog record for this book has been requested

ISBN: 978-0-367-74271-3 (hbk)
ISBN: 978-0-367-70892-4 (pbk)
ISBN: 978-1-003-15688-8 (ebk)

DOI: 10.4324/9781003156888

Typeset in Bembo
by Apex CoVantage, LLC

This volume is dedicated to Marty Kaufman. He exemplified being a rigorous empiricist, conducting special education research to directly improve the lives of children and adolescents with disabilities, and being a fearless leader for the Division of Research and our broader field. Thank you, Marty. We hope this volume will inspire the next generation of researchers to follow in his steps.

CONTENTS

1 Research-Based Practices and Intervention Innovations   1
Christopher J. Lemons, Sarah R. Powell, and Kathleen Lynne Lane

2 Comprehensive, Integrated, Three-Tiered (Ci3T) Models of Prevention: Prioritizing Integrated Systems   4
Kathleen Lynne Lane, Wendy Peia Oakes, Mark Matthew Buckman, and Holly M. Menzies

3 Treatment Integrity and Social Validity in Tiered Systems: Using Data to Inform Implementation Efforts   19
Mark Matthew Buckman, Kathleen Lynne Lane, and Wendy Peia Oakes

4 Reading Achievement and Growth Mindset of Students With Reading Difficulties or Reading Disabilities: Contemporary Research and Implications for Research and Practice   31
Stephanie Al Otaiba, Jeannie Wanzek, Mai Zaru, Rachel Donegan, Dayna Russell Freudenthal, Jennifer Stewart, Brenna Rivas, Christopher J. Lemons, and Yaacov Petscher

5 Well-Being of Educators Working in Tiered Systems   43
Wendy Peia Oakes, Kathleen Lynne Lane, David James Royer, Holly M. Menzies, and Nelson C. Brunsting

6 Leveraging Working Conditions to Improve the Quality and Effectiveness of the Special Education Teacher Workforce   56
Michelle M. Cumming, Elizabeth Bettini, Nelson Brunsting, and Sharde Theodore

Contents

7   Advances in Interventions for Students With Reading Difficulties   71
    Nathan H. Clemens, Alexis N. Boucher, and Katherine O'Donnell

8   Considerations for Choosing and Using Screeners for Students
    With Disabilities   83
    Yaacov Petscher and Marissa Suhr

9   Paraprofessionals' Perceptions of Job-Related Supports, Challenges, and
    Effectiveness   97
    *Sally K. Fluhler, Christopher J. Lemons, Yasmina E. Haddad, Casey
    Chauvin, Guy Martin, Lauren LeJeune, and Emily Gurwitz*

10 Writing Instruction for Students With Disabilities (and Other Struggling
    Writers): Current Research and Implications for Research and Practice   110
    Erin FitzPatrick, Robin Parks Ennis, and Debra McKeown

11 Mathematics Interventions for Students Experiencing Mathematics Difficulty   125
    Sarah R. Powell and Samantha E. Bos

12 Mathematics Assessments for Students Experiencing Mathematics Difficulty   138
    *Erica S. Lembke, Jessica Rodrigues, Stacy Hirt, Jiyung Hwang,
    and Elizabeth R. Thomas*

13 Evidence-Based, Culturally Responsive Interventions to Improve
    Academic Outcomes for English Learners With Reading Difficulties   150
    Catherine Richards-Tutor and Emily J. Solari

14 Academic Strategies for At-Risk Students in Urban Schools   163
    Phillip J. Belfiore

15 Advances in the Use of Technology and Online Learning to Improve
    Outcomes for Students With Disabilities   178
    Sean J. Smith, Maggie A. Mosher, and K. Alisa Lowrey

16 Enhancing the Social Lives of Students With Disabilities: Effective
    Practices and Improved Outcomes   190
    Erik W. Carter, Hilary E. Travers, and Michael Tuttle

17 Theoretically and Empirically Supported Intensive Interventions for
    Students' Social-Emotional and Behavior Needs   203
    *Eric Alan Common, Kathleen Lynne Lane, Wendy Peia Oakes,
    and Katie S. Austin*

Contents

18 The Behavioral, Academic, and Social Engagement (BASE) Model of
    Social Inclusion   220
    Thomas W. Farmer, Heartley B. Huber, David L. Lee,
    Jill V. Hamm, and Brittany Sterrett

19 Multilingual Learners: Testing, Assessment, and Evaluation   233
    Julie Esparza Brown and Terese C. Aceves

20 Teaching Children How to Play: More Than Just a Context   247
    Erin E. Barton and Justin Lane

21 Addressing the Whole Youth: Characteristics and Evidence-Based
    Practices and Programs for Systems-Involved Youth   260
    Kristine Jolivette, Skip Kumm, Sara Sanders, and Sarup R. Mathur

22 Bully Prevention and Social and Emotional Learning: Impact on Youth
    With Disabilities   272
    Nikita McCree, Monica Romero, Stephanie Hopkins,
    Lindsey Mirielli, and Chad A. Rose

Index   *291*

1
RESEARCH-BASED PRACTICES AND INTERVENTION INNOVATIONS

Christopher J. Lemons, Sarah R. Powell, and Kathleen Lynne Lane

"Necessity is the mother of invention" is an oft-quoted proverb—in this volume, we aim to shift that proverb slightly and say that "Necessity is the mother of intervention." Special education researchers are devoted to designing, evaluating, and scaling effective interventions to improve academic, behavioral, and social outcomes for children and adolescents with disabilities, their family members, and the educators who support them. In Volume II of this *Handbook of Special Education Research*, authors highlight critical areas of special education research and outline what we currently know about effective interventions and where special education researchers should go next to enhance the effectiveness of our interventions. Our hope is that this volume will inspire the next generation of special education researchers to be innovative in terms of methodology, intervention design, and intervention focus to ensure that special educators and family members are well prepared to support children and adolescents with disabilities from early childhood through transition so they enter the postsecondary world on the firmest foundation for success.

Overview

Authors of chapters in this volume focus on a diverse set of issues that are critical to enhancing outcomes for students with or at risk of disability. Lane and colleagues (Chapter 2) provide an overview, explaining how Ci3T models are a broadening of Multitiered System of Supports (MTSS) to address the integration of academic, behavioral, and social-emotional domains for all learners—including students receiving special education services. Buckman and colleagues (Chapter 3) identify how the measurement and use of treatment integrity and social validity data are foundational to the implementation of tiered systems, describe how extant research has addressed these concepts, and provide recommendations to the field for advancing the collection and use of these data within tiered systems.

Al Otaiba and colleagues (Chapter 4) highlight the current state of research regarding relations between mindset-related constructs and reading achievement and describe the effects of interventions on mindset and reading achievement for students with reading difficulties and disabilities.

Oakes and colleagues (Chapter 5) examine the theoretical and empirical support for the well-being of educators working within tiered systems and provide an overview of the research on the well-being of teachers who work in tiered systems and implications for treatment integrity and teacher efficacy.

Cumming and colleagues (Chapter 6) describe mechanisms by which working conditions affect the capacity of the special education teacher workforce, discuss how working conditions contribute to special education teachers' experiences and outcomes, and consider how working conditions affect the capacity of educational systems to meet their obligations to students.

Clemens and colleagues (Chapter 7) focus on the two most common forms of reading difficulties: word-level reading and reading comprehension. They review best practices in reading interventions, identify shortcomings in the knowledge base, and review contemporary research. Petscher and colleagues (Chapter 8) describe five core considerations one should minimally look at when choosing a screener and five core considerations expressed as questions for using a screener.

Fluhler and colleagues (Chapter 9) highlight the current state of research focused on supporting paraprofessionals and highlight a study conducted to explore paras' perceptions of job-related supports, challenges, and their experiences and effectiveness after participating in a professional development study.

FitzPatrick and colleagues (Chapter 10) highlight the current state of research focused on writing instruction for students receiving intervention supports through MTSS or special education, and they provide implications for practitioners.

Powell and Bos (Chapter 11) review recent mathematics intervention research, discuss the evidence base of practices for design and delivery of mathematics intervention for students who are experiencing mathematics difficulty, and present pathways for improving mathematics intervention research and practice. Lembke and colleagues (Chapter 12) share information about best practices in mathematics assessment for students with the most intensive needs. The authors describe best practices for screening and progress monitoring, share information on using and creating high-quality diagnostic materials in mathematics, and provide an overview of data-based decision making centered on using mathematics assessment data to make better instructional decisions.

Richards-Tutor and Solari (Chapter 13) focus on reading interventions for students who are English learners with reading difficulties. The authors provide data on the current state of achievement and practices used for English learners, review evidence-based practices for English learners, and discuss tenets of culturally responsive and sustaining practices, focusing on how these can be used in tandem with effective interventions practices to potentially positively affect outcomes for English learners.

Belfiore (Chapter 14) focuses on students enrolled in our largest urban school districts who continue to underperform same grade-level peers and who are therefore more likely to face disciplinary sanctions. The author provides strategies rooted in applied behavior analysis to help reconstruct and maintain an equitable public education playing field for this group of learners.

Smith and colleagues (Chapter 15) highlight the current state of research focused on using technology and online learning to improve outcomes for students with disabilities and provide implications for practitioners and parents, and outline goals for the next decade of research, focusing using technology to support students with disabilities.

Carter and colleagues (Chapter 16) address six primary outcome areas that can be addressed within social-focused interventions in schools, review ten research-based interventions that can contribute to noticeable changes in the social outcomes of students, and offer recommendations for practice and research related to the social dimensions of schooling.

Common and colleagues (Chapter 17) examine theoretical and empirical support for two intensive interventions to support students' behavioral and social needs: functional assessment-based interventions and individualized de-escalation plans. The authors examine the development of and theoretical and empirical support for each practice and discuss the breadth and scope of rigorous research undergirding each intervention's foundation.

Farmer and colleagues (Chapter 18) focus on the social inclusion of students with disabilities from a dynamic-ecological systems perspective in which the whole child is viewed in context. The authors present the Behavioral, Academic, and Social Engagement model as a classroom management framework aimed at aligning the strengths and needs of specific students with social opportunities and experiences that promote their social adaptation and inclusion in the classroom society and provide considerations for integrating individual and peer support interventions within the model.

Esparza Brown and Aceves (Chapter 19) focus on the fair assessment of multilingual learners with an aim at ensuring equitable and effective instruction and decision making for students often from marginalized communities. The authors highlight current research, identifying the continuum of assessment practices used in schools and the key considerations when assessing multilingual students, describe formative assessments and their use by collaborative teams, and examine the use of summative assessments with diverse populations.

Barton and Lane (Chapter 20) focus on play—a critical, early milestone that contributes to the learning and development of young children in multiple ways. The authors provide a description of play in young children, a rationale for teaching play to all children and particularly children with disabilities, and an overview of evidence-based practices for teaching play to all children.

Jolivette and colleagues (Chapter 21) focus on systems-involved youth who are more likely to present with multiple and complex social, emotional, behavioral, and educational needs than their peers in public education settings. They review interventions that focus on equity and equality through the delivery of social-emotional, mental health, educational, behavioral, and trauma-informed programming, which can increase with intensity to meet each youth's needs.

McCree and colleagues (Chapter 22) focus on the critical issue of bullying involvement, which disproportionately affects students with disabilities. The authors outline the intersection of social-emotional learning (SEL) and bully prevention, provide guidance on embedding SEL within an MTSS framework to address school-based bullying, address data collection and evaluation of school-based bully prevention systems, and highlight interventions that are promising for all youth, with a direct emphasis on students with disabilities.

In Closing

In 2021, Adam Grant, an organizational psychologist at The Wharton School, published a book titled *Think Again*. In the text, he argues that one key to success is having the ability to question previously held assumptions and to embrace an approach of mental flexibility. He argues that approaching problems like a scientist—being objective, data based, and curious—leads to more effective solutions to challenges. It is in this spirit that we have pulled together the contributions to this volume. We as special education researchers are scientists at heart. Our hope is that as you read the chapters, you will embrace the suggestions provided by the authors to evaluate your current thinking and to consider whether thinking again about the content, design, measurement, delivery, and ways of supporting special educators could lead to the next breakthroughs in special education research and improve the ability of schools to meet the individualized needs of students with disabilities.

Reference

Grant, A. (2021). *Think again: The power of knowing what you don't know*. Viking.

2
COMPREHENSIVE, INTEGRATED, THREE-TIERED (Ci3T) MODELS OF PREVENTION

Prioritizing Integrated Systems

Kathleen Lynne Lane, Wendy Peia Oakes, Mark Matthew Buckman, and Holly M. Menzies

Reflecting on the past 30 years, we have had the privilege of serving as paraprofessionals, general education teachers, special education teachers, behavior specialists, and administrators in the K-12 educational system from California to New York and several states in between (Lane, Buckman, et al., 2020). Some of us experienced firsthand several reforms devoted to improving students' educational outcomes. In the 1980s, the refer–test–place model of meeting students' needs reigned (Walker, Severson, et al., 2014). With Public Law 94.142 newly in effect (the Education for All Handicapped Children's Act, 1975), general education teachers provided instruction and support, usually without specialized training, within the context of their general education classroom. When the discrepancy between a student's academic achievement and their grade-level placement became too great or if students' behavioral or social-emotional issues were too disruptive, students would likely be referred to determine special education eligibility (Walker et al., 1995). In short, if students did not "fit" within the scope of the general education community, they were referred, tested, and often placed elsewhere if special education services were warranted.

Over time, this refer–test–place model was replaced with a new model from the field of school psychology: refer–consult–intervene (Bergan & Kratochwill, 1990). This was an improvement over the more exclusionary approach to support, as it focused on a collaborative problem-solving paradigm (Lloyd et al., 1991). In this case, when students struggled academically, behaviorally, or socially, general education teachers would work with a pre-referral intervention team to decide on how to address a student's needs, with the goal of avoiding special education placement if unwarranted. The team engaged in a data-informed, four-step process: problem identification, problem analysis, treatment implementation, and treatment evaluation (Bergan & Kratochwill, 1990). General education teachers implemented interventions, often focusing on adjustments to instruction and classroom management practices (Lane, Mahdavi, et al., 2003). Yet too often these interventions fell short, given limited attention to important issues such as treatment integrity (measuring the degree to which the intervention design was implemented as planned; Buckman et al., this volume), social validity (social significance of the goals, social acceptability of treatment procedures, and social importance of effects; Wolf, 1978), and generalization and maintenance (broadening and lasting effects). Some critics of the pre-referral intervention process suggested this well-intended process was only serving to delay special education services (Rock & Zigmond, 2001).

Teachers attempted a range of instructional, behavioral, and social supports for students with the aid of the pre-referral intervention process. If interventions did not yield desired shifts in student performance, the student was often referred to and determined eligible for special education services. These placements tended to be restrictive (e.g., self-contained classrooms) and *still* did not yield the hoped-for improvements, academically or otherwise (e.g., social skills, behavioral excesses and deficits; Lane, Wehby, et al., 2005a, 2005b; Mattison et al., 2002).

Throughout this problem-solving process, the general education teacher served as the gatekeeper of additional supports (Lane, 2003, 2007). If a teacher did not notice a concern and initiate steps to seek input, students for whom the general education experience was insufficient were overlooked. This was incredibly unfortunate, given the importance of early detection and treatment before learning, behavior, and social skills challenges become intractable and lead to long-term difficulty. In short, well-intended efforts left much to be desired, which was particularly troubling given the large percentage (approximately 20%) of school-age youth who struggled with emotional and behavioral disorders (EBDs) in the form of mild-to-moderate externalizing (e.g., aggression, defiance) and internalizing (e.g., shy, anxious) behaviors—most of whom would not qualify for special education services due to emotional disturbances (EDs, 1%; Individuals with Disabilities Education Improvement Act, 2004). The general education community was tasked with managing learning and behavioral challenges, with many teachers reporting feeling ill-prepared to meet this charge (The New Teacher Project, 2013).

In this chapter, we discuss inquiry related to the value of one comprehensive system of support to meet students' multiple needs (e.g., academic, behavioral, and social) in an effective, efficient, integrated system—the comprehensive, integrated, three-tiered (Ci3T) model of prevention. Following a historical view of tiered systems, we provide a brief review of the current research base for Ci3T, implications for practitioners, and implications for researchers.

Historical Context: A Shift to a System of Supports

Fortunately, in 1996 Hill Walker and colleagues recognized a different path forward to meet the learning, behavioral, and social needs of all students—including those with and at risk for EBD. Rather than waiting for students to fail and then providing supports, Walker et al. (1996) brought a system-of-care model from the mental health field into the educational community. This was the beginning of a tiered system of supports: one system, many supports, with an emphasis on using systematic screening data to detect accurately which students needed strategies, practices, or programs beyond the efforts designed for all students (i.e., Tier 1). As part of this important work, the education field began the important shift from viewing challenges as "within child" deficits to seeing challenges as system-level issues. As part of this initial introduction to a systems view, each school—and later district—would design a coordinated tiered system featuring evidence-based strategies, practices, and programs at each level of prevention: Tier 1 (for all students), Tier 2 (for some students), and Tier 3 (for a few students), with all students—including those receiving special education services—accessing each level of support according to individual needs (Lane, Buckman, et al., 2020).

This shift served as the basis for positive behavior intervention and supports (PBIS), which was theoretically grounded in applied behavior analysis (Horner & Sugai, 2015). As part of this system, adults established clear expectations. Then, these agreed-upon expectations were taught, modeled, practiced, and reinforced using behavioral analytic principles (e.g., behavior-specific praise; Royer et al., 2017). Tiered logic was also the foundation of response to intervention (RTI; Fuchs et al., 2012), focused primarily on academic domains: initially on reading skills and later mathematic skills.

As school leaders shifted to a system-level approach to prevent and respond to learning and behavioral challenges, they frequently developed two separate systems in their buildings: one for behavioral needs (PBIS) and a second for academic needs (RTI). Recognizing the value of tiered systems, but needing to focus also on efficiencies, Multi-Tiered System of Supports (MTSS) emerged. This approach attempted to bring systems for reading, mathematics, and behavior together into a single model. An incremental training model emerged that started with reading, then added mathematics, and finally behavior. Although likely not intentional, this approach tended to result in a perpetually siloed approach to meeting students' multiple needs without fully integrating systems and practices (McIntosh & Goodman, 2016). Furthermore, this formulation did not address an equally important domain: students' social and emotional well-being. Interconnected systems framework (ISF; Barrett et al., 2012) is an integrated tiered system focusing on meeting students' behavioral and mental health needs—a positive direction, but one with limited emphasis on academic performance. The Ci3T model of prevention (Lane et al., 2010) offers one integrated system addressing academic, behavior (PBIS), and social and emotional well-being using validated curricula. Ci3T inquiry first began in 1996 (Lane & Menzies, 2003), inspired by the initial introduction of tiered systems by Walker et al. (1996) and the emphasis on social skills emphasized in a now-classic book by Walker et al. (1995): *Antisocial Behavior in School: Strategies and Best Practices*.

Schools can now design their own Ci3T model of prevention using the fully manualized Ci3T professional learning process (Lane, Oakes, Cantwell, et al., 2018; see figure on ci3t.org), with the full scope of professional learning materials for a six-part series (three full days and alternating three 2-hour sessions held after school) freely available on www.ci3t.org/build. In brief, Ci3T leadership teams include the principal, two general education teachers, one special education teacher, another person at their discretion (e.g., school psychologist, interventionist), a parent, and the parent's child (who attends sessions three and five held after school). Ci3T leadership teams collaborate over the course of a full academic year to develop a Ci3T model with the full scope of evidence-based strategies, practices, and programs at Tiers 1, 2, and 3. As part of this manualized building process, Ci3T leadership teams construct a series of Ci3T blueprints: (a) Primary (Tier 1) Prevention Plan, (b) Reactive Plan, (c) Expectation Matrix, (d) Assessment Schedule, (e) Secondary (Tier 2) Intervention Grid, and (f) Tertiary (Tier 3) Intervention Grid with input from the full faculty and staff using a data-informed, iterative process. Specifically, faculty and staff provide input on what students need to know to be successful in all key settings using the School-wide Expectation Matrix for Specific Setting Survey (SESSS: Lane et al., 2010) which is used to construct the Expectation Matrix. Then, following session 4, faculty and staff review a full draft of the Ci3T Primary (Tier 1) Prevention Plan, Reactive Plan, Expectation Matrix, and Assessment Schedule, providing social validity input using the Primary Intervention Rating Scale (PIRS; Lane, Robertson, et al., 2002). Information regarding stakeholder views of the goals, procedures, and outcomes is used to inform plan revisions, with the revised plan reviewed using a second social validity tool, the Ci3T Primary Plan: Feedback Form (Lane, 2002). The output from this Ci3T Professional Learning series is a fully developed Ci3T model of prevention, ready for implementation the following academic year.

Purpose

In this chapter, we discuss inquiry related to Ci3T implementation, focused on the value of one comprehensive system of support to meet students' multiple needs (e.g., academic, behavioral, and social) in an effective, efficient, integrated system. Following this historical view of tiered systems, we provide a brief review of the current research base, implications for practitioners, and implications for researchers.

Current State of Ci3T Research

Our research team has had the honor of working within this Ci3T model since the late 1990s, collaborating with more than 100 schools from across several states and geographic regions. As part of our collaborative, programmatic lines of inquiry, we have engaged with our valued school and district partners in a series of studies related to the design, implementation, and evaluation of Ci3T as an integrated system for addressing students' academic, behavioral, and social learning domains (Lane, 2017).

Ci3T inquiry features a series of descriptive, experimental, and psychometric studies. For example, early inquiry involved small-scale descriptive studies of Tier 1 efforts (Lane & Menzies, 2003, 2005), and single-case design studies examining the effectiveness of Tier 2 supports focused on early literacy (Lane, Wehby, et al., 2002) and social skills (e.g., Lane, Wehby, et al., 2003). As the model was refined and interest in Ci3T expanded across the United States, inquiry also expanded in breadth and depth. For example, additional studies involving single-case methodology were conducted to further examine academic interventions at Tier 2 for reading instruction (e.g., Lane, Little, et al., 2007) and writing instruction (e.g., Little et al., 2010), as well as Tier 3 supports such as functional assessment-based interventions (FABIs; Germer et al., 2011; Majeika et al., 2011). In addition, we conducted experimental inquiry using rigorous experimental designs (e.g., randomized control trials [RCTs]) to examine the effects of academic and social skills interventions at Tier 2 (e.g., Lane, Harris, et al., 2011; Kalberg et al., 2012; Robertson & Lane, 2007), as well as large-scale psychometric studies of systematic screening efforts in Ci3T models (e.g., Lane, Oakes, Ennis, et al., 2013).

In this section, we provide a brief overview of inquiry conducted to date, featuring (a) the development of effective practices to support installation and sustainability of Ci3T and (b) evaluation of effective practices to support teacher installation and sustainability of Ci3T.

Developing Effective Practices to Support Installation and Sustainability of Ci3T

As mentioned, our research team is committed to collaborative, respectful, and ethical inquiry as part of practitioner–researcher partnerships (see Walker, Forness, et al., 2014). In this section, we provide information about a few funded and unfunded projects illustrating the development of effective practice to support installation and sustainability of Ci3T: Ci3T Partnerships (Tier 1). Project WRITE (Tier 2), Empowering Teachers (Tier 2), Project FUNCTION (Tier 3), Project SCREEN (free-access screening tool), and most recently Project ENHANCE (on-demand "enhanced" professional learning resources). These projects serve as representative illustrations of how we have collaborated to design, implement, and evaluate Ci3T models to effectively and efficiently (a) prevent the development of learning and behavioral challenges and (b) respond when challenges arise using evidence-based practices at each level of prevention (Lane, 2017).

Ci3T Partnership: Tier 1 Efforts

Collectively, all Ci3T inquiry is theoretically grounded in applied behavior analysis and implementation sciences. We contend that context has a key role in shaping productive and positive instructional environments for all learners. In the early years of our practitioner–researcher partnership projects, partners explored Tier 2 and Tier 3 supports, without first ensuring implementation of Tier 1 efforts. Yet we felt strongly that Tier 2 and 3 practices would be more effective and generalize more easily when they built on Tier 1 practice. This would give students participating in higher-intensity supports the opportunity to have their new skills reinforced beyond the training setting (Lane & Beebe-Frankenberger, 2004).

Through the years, three key lessons learned regarding Ci3T implementation emerged. First, we have established an empirical link between social validity and treatment integrity.

Specifically, school-site averages of social validity ratings from faculty and staff during the Ci3T Professional learning series (conducted before implementation) indicated higher levels of integrity for Tier 1 implementation by those who rated the Ci3T plan as more socially valid compared to those who rated it less socially valid (Lane, Kalberg, et al., 2009).

Second, multiple studies have documented positive shifts in student performance. For example, descriptive studies indicated schools implementing their Ci3T plan demonstrated decreases in the overall level of behavioral risk for students as measured by systematic screening tools (e.g., Lane, Kalberg, et al., 2008; Lane, Menzies, Oakes, et al., 2012). Furthermore, a series of studies conducted in K-12 consistently indicated that students' falling internalizing and externalizing behavior screening scores predicted year-end academic performance (e.g., reading measures, GPA, course failures), as well as performance on social and behavioral measures (e.g., office discipline referrals [ODRs], suspensions, self-control skills; Ennis et al., 2012; Lane, Kalberg, et al., 2008; Lane, Oakes, Ennis, et al., 2013; Oakes et al., 2010). Third, we have learned teachers fare well in Ci3T models of prevention, experiencing lower levels of burnout and a higher sense of self-efficacy relative to national norms (Oakes et al., 2021; Oakes et al, this volume).

One important feature of these and other Ci3T studies is that the questions of interest are developed in partnership between practitioners and researchers: To what extent are Tier 1 procedures for teaching, reinforcing, and monitoring put in place as planned (treatment integrity)? How do teachers view the goals, procedures, and outcomes (social validity)? To what degree are screening procedures implemented and sustained? How are students—and teachers—faring when Ci3T is implemented as planned? What additional professional learning needs do teachers have during initial and full installation?

After building a Ci3T model of prevention, the structures and system are developed not only to examine the impact of Tier 1 efforts (e.g., Lane, Kalberg, et al., 2008) but to explore the utility of additional evidence-based, strategies, practices, and programs at Tier 2 and Tier 3, as specified in a school's Secondary (Tier 2) Intervention Grid and Tertiary (Tier 3) Intervention Grids from their Ci3T implementation manuals (e.g., Lane, Oakes, Menzies, Oyer, et al., 2013). Perhaps H. Menzies (personal communication, 2013) expressed it best, "the models become fertile ground for additional research: you have established rapport, you have grown their capacity through previous collaboration, they trust you, they see and have experienced the benefits of a research collaboration." Next we highlight additional lessons learned.

Project WRITE

As part of an Institute of Education Sciences (IES)-funded development and innovation grant, *The Effects of Strategy and Self-Regulation Instruction on Students' Writing Performance and Behavior: A Preventative Approach*, we conducted experimental studies at Tier 1 and Tier 2 using group and single-case designs to explore the impact of self-regulated strategy development (SRSD) for writing on students' engagement and writing skills (e.g., Lane, Harris, et al., 2011; Little et al., 2010). This project was situated in five schools in one district implementing Ci3T K-12. In conversations with elementary principals, they indicated a desire to focus on "writing next," following a multiple-year project enhancing reading instruction. As part of Project WRITE, inquiry began with a series of single-case design studies at Tier 2, with an emphasis on how to modify and adapt procedures to meet the needs of students who also demonstrated challenging behaviors (e.g., internalizing and externalizing issues), as well as limited writing skills. In addition to gleaning information on how to refine the intervention (e.g., not sharing baseline data with students until after they began to show increases in writing targets), results suggested a functional relation between the introduction of SRSD and improvements in writing performance.

Next, we conducted two RCTs using this adapted process, first as a Tier 2 support (Lane et al., 2011) and then as a Tier 1 support (Harris et al., 2012). Results of the first RCT testing SRSD as a Tier 2 support indicated students receiving SRSD instruction in writing essays and stories exhibited statistically significant increases in writing quality and composition relative to students in the control condition (Lane, Harris, et al., 2011). For the second RCT, the initial plan was to have research assistants lead instruction at Tier 1. Yet with permission from IES and the institutional review board, we revised the protocol to have general education teachers lead instruction. The change was made in response to teachers' interest in learning more about the strategy that had worked so effectively with students requiring Tier 2 supports. This shift in procedures illustrates the priority placed on collaborative—and methodologically rigorous—inquiry.

Empowering Teachers With Low-Intensity Supports

During our regularly scheduled district meetings conducted as part of *Project Support and Include* (a state technical assistance project examining Ci3T training and implementation), several conversations focused on how to empower educators (certificated and classified) to increase students' engagement and minimize disruptions. Essentially, how could teachers use PBIS during instruction? And how could these strategies be learned, implemented, and evaluated with limited university supports? To explore these questions, we collaborated with partners to conduct a series of unfunded studies as part of *Empowering Teachers with Low-Intensity Strategies to Support Instruction*. This project had three objectives: (a) to design, implement, and evaluate research-based, low-intensity supports implemented as Tier 2 practices by teachers in authentic educational settings preK-12 with limited university support; (b) provide in-service teachers remote support in learning more about feasible, effective strategies to integrate into instruction (e.g., behavior-specific praise, precorrection, instructional choice, and increased opportunities to respond); and (c) provide experiences for university students to engage in school-based inquiry.

As part of university- and district-approved procedures, we used single-case design methodology to examine issues of treatment integrity; impact on student performance; and social validity from teacher, parent, and student perspectives. For example, one teacher was interested in exploring the utility of instructional choice to support her students during writing instruction, a time when some students were not particularly engaged in this inclusive first-grade classroom. This Ohio-based educator collaborated with research team members from Kansas and Arizona to test two types of choices: within-task choices (e.g., choice of writing tool—pencil or pen) and across-task choices (e.g., choice of writing task—a story about or letter to a character; Lane, Royer, et al., 2015). While the intervention was implemented by the teacher with the whole class, she used screening data to determine which students had Tier 2 needs in terms of writing and behavior. After obtaining parent permission and student assent for two of the three students, she began the process of collecting additional data for just these students, using momentary time sampling procedures to examine their performance during the different choice activities and using a component checklist to measure treatment integrity. Results indicated instructional choice conditions were implemented with fidelity, yielding a functional relation between instructional choices conditions and increases in engagement during writing and decreases in disruption for one student. Yet a functional relation was not established for the second student. Nonetheless, all stakeholders viewed instructional choice as a useful and acceptable intervention.

These early studies served as foundational inquiry for an IES Early Career Development and Mentoring Grant led by R. Ennis, *Empowering Teachers with Low Intensity Strategies to Support Instruction II*. The project extended this inquiry examining how such strategies—particularly instructional choice—could affect students with and at risk for EBD in K-3 in general education settings (e.g., Ennis et al., 2020).

Project FUNCTION

In addition, Ci3T inquiry included an emphasis on understanding the function of behavior to assist students with the most intensive intervention needs—Tier 3 supports—within the context of an unfunded project, Project FUNCTION (Lane, Oakes, & Cox, 2012). As with Tier 2 and low-intensity support inquiry, we collaborated with district and school partners to explore feasible and effective approaches for conducting FABI (Umbreit et al., 2007).

After securing university and district approvals, we established a practitioner–researcher partnership in which graduate students learned a systematic approach to design, implement, and evaluate FABI under the guidance of university professors, while providing support to local preK-12 schools implementing Ci3T. In brief, teams of graduate students had the opportunity to develop their intervention skills while supporting local districts in an apprenticeship model, similar to a surgical training model: read one, watch one, do one. The FABI process was manualized into a five-step process (Table 2.1; see www.ci3t.org/FABI for implementation step checklists, instructional videos, and other resources) for sustainability and scalability.

As part of Project FUNCTION, students learned how to conduct methodologically rigorous inquiry, while respectfully meeting the multiple needs of students requiring substantially more than Tier 1 or Tier 2 supports. In these studies, the primary research questions were as follows: (a) To what extent were FABIs implemented by in-service teachers as planned (treatment integrity)? (b) To was extent was a functional relation established between the introduction of FABI and changes in students' target behavior (e.g., engagement)? (c) To what extent did teachers, families, and students view the intervention goals, procedures, and outcomes as acceptable and useful (social validity)?

Study results suggested the FABI process could be implemented with integrity, yield desired changes in students' performance, and provide a socially acceptable intensive intervention within authentic educational settings (preK-12; Germer et al., 2011). Furthermore, studies examining the professional learning process suggested in-service educators could collaborate as a team (e.g., school-site general education and special education teachers, school psychologists, social workers, principals) to learn this process. In addition, results of descriptive and experimental studies indicated educators' knowledge, confidence, and perceived usefulness of the FABI concepts improved by engaging in a practice-based, professional learning series (Common et al., 2020; Lane, Oakes, Powers, et al., 2015; Oakes et al., 2018).

Over the course of these projects and other Ci3T inquiry, we also conducted qualitative and quantitative inquiry to learn how teachers fared in these models (see Oakes et al. this volume), as well as how implementation efforts could be refined and enhanced. For example, as part of an IES Researcher Practitioner Partnership grant we learned three particular areas in need of refinement to facilitate Ci3T implementation: (a) on-boarding of new and development of continuing district- and school-level leaders; (b) data-informed professional learning for all stakeholders (e.g., classified and certified staff, families, community members) on how to meet students' academic, behavioral, and social needs; and (c) accessing and interpreting multiple data sources to inform instruction, with an emphasis on systematic screening (Menzies et al., 2020). Given financial and time constraints typical

Table 2.1 Functional Assessment-Based Interventions (FABI) Implementation Steps

Step	Description
1	Determining which students need a FABI
2	Conducting the functional assessment and determining the hypothesized function
3	Collecting baseline data
4	Designing the intervention
5	Testing the intervention

in most districts, durable, on-demand, flexible, free-access professional learning resources would facilitate training in each area.

Evaluating Effective Practices to Support Teacher Installation and Sustainability of Ci3T

As discussed, this collective Ci3T inquiry from 1996 to 2019 established positive, productive, playing fields for joint inquiry. In addition, we understand the professional learning needed to assist school and district leaders in moving from design to sustained implementation of their respective Ci3T models. For example, one of our partner districts had several shifts in leadership during the first five years of Ci3T design and implementation (eight new principals [K-12] and four superintendents, including interim leaders). While the district did an impressive job of sustaining their Ci3T models, they realized that newly hired leaders and teachers needed on-demand professional learning resources to provide timely, practical, and compelling instruction on the rationale and structures for an integrated tiered system. Also, tools were needed to bolster ongoing professional learning for faculty and staff to deepen their knowledge as they continued to use academic and behavior screening data to inform instruction. Many conversations focused on how to sustain the data-informed approach to professional learning characteristic of Ci3T and how to support professional learning for teachers at various stages in their learning.

Project ENHANCE: Enhancing Ci3T Implementation

Fortunately, IES also prioritized an emphasis on the design, implementation, and evaluation of integrated tiered systems, resulting in the iMTSS Network grant request for applications. As part of Enhancing Ci3T: Project ENHANCE (84.325N), we are now engaging in an iterative design process to create on-demand modules to assist leaders with the knowledge and practices needed to lead sustained implementation, use of student screening data (Oakes et al., 2014), integration of new initiatives, and ongoing evaluation of Ci3T models with attention to sustainability (Strickland-Cohen et al., 2014).

As part of Project ENHANCE (2019–2024), we spent the first year collaborating with five districts from three geographic regions (West Coast, Midwest, and East Coast) currently implementing Ci3T to learn about their ongoing professional learning needs to support installation and sustainability. These 28 schools represented a range of implementers, with some Ci3T leadership teams serving in schools in the first year of implementation and others serving in schools with more than five years of implementation experience. We conducted a series of three studies focused on leadership, screening, and building capacity using surveys, semi-structured interviews, and focus groups. While we are currently in the final stages of data analyses, preliminary results provided direction for eight modules to be developed and tested 2020–2024 (see Table 2.2).

Table 2.2 Project ENHANCE: Proposed Module Topics

Focus Area	Proposed Module Topic
Leadership	Setting Up for Success
	Mapping Your Professional Learning Plans
	Building Capacity and Sustainability
Building Capacity	Creating Positive, Productive, Safe Learning Environments
	Responding Respectfully to Challenging Behavior
	Understanding the "Hows and Whys" of Behavior to Support Change
Screening	Selecting and Installing Behavior Screeners
	Screening Using Data

One unique feature of Ci3T relative to other tiered systems is the use of data-informed professional learning (Lane, Carter, et al., 2015; Oakes, Lane, et al., 2021). Just as data are used to make instructional decisions (e.g., academic and behavior screening data, ODRs, attendances, nurse visits), data are used to inform implementation efforts—including professional learning needs.

For example, when building this model, Ci3T leadership teams acquire knowledge regarding the importance of—and practical methods for—monitoring (a) treatment integrity at each level of prevention (Tier 1, 2, and 3) to determine the degree each is implemented as designed; (b) social validity for each level of prevention (including Tier 1) to understand stakeholders' views regarding intervention goals, procedures, and outcomes; and (c) student performance through the use of reliable, valid systematic screenings in academic and behavioral domains to inform instruction. A priority is placed on supporting Ci3T leadership teams in selecting and installing systematic academic and behavior screening tools to inform instruction, with attention on how to analyze these data in connection with other data collected as part of regular school practices (e.g., attendance, ODRs; Sherod et al., 2020). First, data are examined for the school as a whole and then by grade levels or department levels to examine overall student performance. Next, data are examined at the classroom level to inform the use of low-intensity supports (e.g., behavior-specific praise, active supervision, instructional choice, precorrection, and increased opportunities to respond) for classes with more than 20% of students scoring in the moderate-risk range (Lane, Menzies, Ennis, et al., 2018). Finally, these data are used at the individual student level to connect students to evidence-based practices at Tier 2 and Tier 3 (e.g., Kalberg et al., 2012).

During implementation, Ci3T leadership teams continue to access and offer professional learning. They work with Ci3T district leaders as part of regularly scheduled professional learning sessions (typically five 2- to 3-hour sessions held over the course of the academic year) to engage in data-informed decision making. Sessions focus on using treatment integrity, social validity, and student-level data to (a) guide professional learning experiences for faculty and staff and (b) inform instructional decisions for students. For example, in the early years of Ci3T inquiry, district leaders and Ci3T leadership teams had questions about the reliability, validity, and utility of screening tools within their particular context that were voiced in social validity surveys, faculty and staff meetings, and in Ci3T leadership team meetings. As such, we partnered with multiple districts and technical assistance providers across the United States to explore the psychometric properties of screening tools (e.g., Oakes et al., 2010). As mentioned, this body of evidence indicated behavior screening scores predict academic performance across the K-12 continuum (e.g., reading measures, GPA, course failures) in addition to performance on social and behavioral measures (e.g., ODRs, suspensions, self-control skills; e.g., Ennis et al., 2012; Oakes et al., 2010). Yet questions remained, leading to Project SCREEN.

Project SCREEN

Current inquiry is under way as part of Project SCREEN (an IES-funded measurement project) to conduct additional psychometric studies, with attention to bias analyses, to determine if screening scores function differently for various groups of students (e.g., sex, disability status, race, and ethnicity). The focus of Project SCREEN is a free-access screening tool: the Student Risk Screening Scale for Internalizing and Externalizing (SRSS-IE; Drummond, 1994; Lane & Menzies, 2009). This work will complement commercially available screening tools (e.g., Social Skills Improvement System—Social Emotional Learning; Elliott & Gresham, 2017; BASC-3 Behavioral and Emotional Screening System, Kamphaus & Reynolds, 2015; and Systematic Screening for Behavior Disorders,

SSBD; Walker, Severson, et al., 2014) by ensuring that a no-cost screening is an option for all schools and districts, particularly for those with economic barriers.

Projects ENHANCE and SCREEN offer but two illustrations of inquiry currently in progress to offer guidance in implementing and sustaining Ci3T. These lessons, along with lessons from the overall iMTSS Network projects, hold promise for establishing effective and feasible next steps for practitioners and researchers alike when installing and sustaining integrated tiered systems such as Ci3T. In the next section, we offer initial considerations for practitioners and researchers. Given the priority placed on collaborative inquiry, we present these considerations to be acted upon in partnership.

Implications for Practitioners and Future Research

As illustrated earlier, Ci3T inquiry is grounded in applied behavior analytic principles and implementation sciences, with a commitment to positive, productive, respectful, collaborative inquiry. As we consider tiered system inquiry, we have learned it typically requires two to three years of high-fidelity implementation before shifts in student performance occur (McIntosh & Goodman, 2016). As such, it is essential for educational leaders and researchers to recognize implementation is a long-term commitment.

Develop Practitioner–Researcher Collaborative Lines of Inquiry

It is important to develop programmatic lines of inquiry and companion structures to deepen understanding of any integrated, tiered system (e.g., MTSS, ISF, Ci3T). In the illustrations earlier, we highlighted studies spanning multiple decades to demonstrate how methodologically rigorous inquiry—funded and unfunded—can be mutually beneficial to practitioners and researchers. The professional learning components of these projects have often involved practice-based professional learning for in-service and preservice teachers (e.g., Common et al., 2020; Grossman & McDonald, 2008; Harris et al., 2012; Lane, Barton-Arwood, et al., 2007; Lane, Oakes, Powers, et al., 2015).

As part of this effort to support teachers in installing and sustaining evidence-based strategies, practices, and programs at each level of prevention, as well as the overall system, we encourage researchers to commit to long-term, programmatic inquiry with practitioner partners. Studying integrated systems is complex—practically and methodologically, taking years of carefully inquiry. To be frank, researchers must commit to collaborative inquiry that facilitates sustainability of the important lessons learned.

Conduct Professional Learning for Effective and Efficient Use of Data for Instructional Decisions

An essential feature of this inquiry is creating clarity about the necessity of data-informed professional learning for all teachers, with careful attention to the "hows and whys" of core components of valid inference-making activities (Datnow & Hubbard, 2015). As teachers continue to explore what works, for whom, and under what conditions, they need to be knowledgeable and confident in core practices such as assessing and using multiple data sources, social validity, treatment integrity, and student performance at each level of prevention. For example, when designing Tier 1, 2, and 3 efforts, teachers need deep knowledge and skill sets to answer questions such as: (a) Are stakeholders (e.g., students, families, fellow colleagues) comfortable with the goals, procedures, and outcomes (social validity)? (b) Are strategies, practices, and programs implemented as planned (treatment integrity)?

(c) When implemented as planned, does the strategy, practice, or program yield the desired change in student performance (e.g., academic, behavior, and/or social learning domains)?

Some would contend procedures for monitoring are more research-related than practitioner-related; however, this is not the case. For example, a teacher requires reliable, valid, easy-to-access screening data to know which students have higher-than-average internalizing issues and/or lower-than-average oral reading fluency scores. In addition, this same teacher must be confident Tier 1 efforts are implemented as planned in their building, grade level, and classroom so they can accurately communicate with colleagues and parents. A teacher cannot suggest to a parent their child needs more intensive support if they are not certain the student has had the benefit of Tier 1 academic, behavioral, and social instruction as planned. For a classroom teacher to deliver effective instruction and attend to issues of equity and access, school-wide data systems must be nimble. Good decision making about instruction is reliant on accurate, useful, and easily accessible data.

Use Data to Determine Responsive Professional Learning Offerings

Similarly, reliable data must be readily available to determine the professional learning necessary to inform high-quality implementation at each level of prevention: Tier 1, 2, and 3. If school-wide data suggest a student would benefit from Direct Behavior Ratings (Chafouleas et al., 2009; a validated Tier 2 intervention noted in the school's Ci3T Secondary [Tier 2] Intervention Grid), teachers need high-quality, on-demand professional learning resources to learn how to implement this intervention and determine how effective it is for a particular student. Similarly, if school-wide data indicate a student needs additional support in written expression, and SRSD for writing (Harris et al., 2008) is listed as a Tier 2 option in the school's Secondary (Tier 2) Intervention Grid, the teacher again needs access to high-quality, on-demand professional learning resources to learn how to implement this strategy and examine how effective it is for improving a student's written expression.

In sum, we are hopeful we have provided concrete illustrations for meeting these lofty goals. Moreover, we are hopeful these illustrations offer insight as to how teachers and other educators (e.g., instructional coaches, behavior specialists, and technical assistance providers) can participate with sufficient intensity to eventually take ownership of the strategies, practices, and programs explored with their university partners to ultimately expand their own capacity (Cook & Tankersley, 2013; Desimone, 2009).

At this time in history—the COVID-19 era—inquiry on how to best use integrated, tiered systems to meet students' academic, behavioral, and social learning is perhaps more important than ever. As practitioners turn to the scientific community for answers about how to pivot to and away from remote, in-person, and hybrid instruction to keep students and school personnel safe, we urge researchers to lean in to respectful, mutually beneficial partnerships (Lane, Cabell, & Drew, 2021).

Summary

Our Ci3T research team is highly committed to respectful, responsible, and ethical inquiry. We certainly have room to grow; however, we believe collaborative, long-term inquiry is essential for long-term health of educational systems (see Table 2.3 for additional readings and resources). We extend our sincere gratitude to education leaders (e.g., Yudin, 2014) and agencies (e.g., IES) who encourage and support exploring the design, implementation, evaluation, and sustainability of integrated tiered systems of supports such as Ci3T. It is through these priorities that we have learned lessons important to practitioners and researchers alike: (a) establishing shared goals to focus inquiry and (b) learning how to use treatment integrity and social validity from stakeholders to shape instructional experiences for students, as well as professional learning experiences for adults.

Table 2.3 Additional Readings and Resources

Source	Item
Website	www.ci3t.org/
	www.pbis.org/
	https://intensiveintervention.org/
	https://iris.peabody.vanderbilt.edu/
	www.thinksrsd.com/
	Functional Behavioral Assessment and Positive Interventions: What Parents Need to Know https://osepideasthatwork.org/node/123
	https://ies.ed.gov/ncee/wwc/EvidenceSnapshot/667
Readings	Lane, K. L., Oakes, W. P., Menzies, H. M., Buckman, M. M., & Royer, D. J. (2020). Systematic screening for behavior: Considerations and commitments to continued inquiry. Practice brief available via ci3t.org/screening
	Lane, K. L., Menzies, H. M., Ennis, R. P., & Bezdek, J. (2013). School-wide systems to promote positive behaviors and facilitate instruction. *Journal of Curriculum and Instruction*, 7(1), 6–31. Available via www.joci.ecu.edu/

References

Barrett, S., Eber, L., & Weist, M. (Eds) (2012). *Advancing education effectiveness: Interconnecting school mental health and school-wide positive behavior support*. Monograph. University of Oregon. https://greatlakesequity.org/resource/advancing-education-effectiveness-interconnecting-school-mental-health-and-school-wide

Bergan, J., & Kratochwill, T. (1990). *Behavioral consultation and therapy*. Plenum Press.

Chafouleas, S. M., Riley-Tillman, T. C., & Christ, T. J. (2009). Direct behavior rating (DBR) an emerging method for assessing social behavior within a tiered intervention system. *Assessment for Effective Intervention*, 34(5), 195–200. https://doi.org/bnjb6t

Common, E. A., Lane, K. L., Oakes, W. P., Schellman, L. E., Shogren, K., Germer, K. A., & Quell, A. E. (2020). Building site-level capacity for functional assessment-based interventions: Outcomes of a professional learning series. *Manuscript in review*.

Cook, B. G., & Tankersley, M. (2013). *Effective practices in special education*. Pearson.

Datnow, A., & Hubbard, L. (2015). Teachers' use of assessment data to inform instruction: Lessons from the past and prospects for the future. *Teachers College Record*, 117(4), 1–26.

Desimone, L. M. (2009). Improving impact studies of teachers' professional development: Toward better conceptualizations and measures. *Educational Researcher*, 38, 181–199.

Drummond, T. (1994). *The student risk screening scale (SRSS)*. Josephine County Mental Health Program.

Elliott, S. N., & Gresham, F. (2017). *Social skills improvement system (SSiS)—Social emotional learning*. PsychCorp Pearson Education.

Ennis, R. P., Lane, K. L., & Oakes, W. P. (2012). Score reliability and validity of the Student Risk Screening Scale: A psychometrically sound, feasible tool for use in urban elementary school. *Journal of Emotional and Behavioral Disorders*, 20, 241–259.

Ennis, R. P., Lane, K. L., Oakes, W. P., & Flemming, S. C. (2020). Empowering teachers with low-intensity strategies to support instruction: Implementing across-activity choices in 3rd grade reading. *Journal of Positive Behavioral Interventions*, 22(2), 78–92. https://doi.org/10.1177/1098300719870438

Fuchs, D., Fuchs, L. S., & Compton, D. L. (2012). Smart RTI: A next-generation approach to multilevel prevention. *Exceptional Children*, 78, 263–279.

Germer, K. A., Kaplan, L. M., Giroux, L. N., Markham, E. H., Ferris, G., Oakes, W. P., & Lane, K. L. (2011). A function-based intervention to increase a second-grade student's on-task behavior in a general education classroom. *Beyond Behavior*, 20, 19–30.

Grossman, P., & McDonald, M. (2008). Back to the future: Directions for research in teaching and teacher education. *American Educational Research Journal*, 45, 184–205.

Harris, K. L., Lane, K. L., Graham, S., Driscoll, S., Wilson, K., Sandmel, K., . . . Schatschneider, C. (2012). Practice-based professional development for self-regulated strategies instruction in writing: A randomized controlled study. *Journal of Teacher Education*, 63, 103–119.

Harris, K. R., Graham, S., Mason, L., & Friedlander, B. (2008). *Powerful writing strategies for all students*. Brookes.

Horner, R. H., & Sugai, G. (2015). School-wide PBIS: An example of applied behavior analysis implemented at a scale of social importance. *Behavior Analysis in Practice, 8*(1), 80–85. https://doi.org/10.1007/s40617-015-0045-4

Individuals with Disabilities Education Improvement Act of 2004, Pub. L. No. 20 U.S.C. 1400 et seq. (2004).

Kalberg, J. R., Lane, K. L., & Lambert, W. (2012). The utility of conflict resolution and study skills interventions with middle school students at risk for antisocial behavior: A methodological illustration. *Remedial and Special Education, 22*, 23–38. https://doi.org/10.1177/0741932510362514

Kamphaus, R. W., & Reynolds, C. R. (2015). *Behavior assessment system for children-third edition (BASC-3): Behavioral and emotional screening system (BESS)*. Pearson.

Lane, K. L. (2002). *Ci3T primary plan: Feedback form*. www.ci3t.org/measures

Lane, K. L. (2003). Identifying young students at risk for antisocial behavior: The utility of "teachers as tests". *Behavioral Disorders, 28*, 360–389.

Lane, K. L. (2007). Identifying and supporting students at risk for emotional and behavioral disorders within multi-level models: Data driven approaches to conducting secondary interventions with an academic emphasis. *Education and Treatment of Children, 30*, 135–164.

Lane, K. L. (2017). Building strong partnerships: Responsible inquiry to learn and grow together TECBD-CCBD keynote address. *Education and Treatment of Children, 40*(4), 597–618. https://doi.org/10.1353/etc.2017.0026

Lane, K. L., Barton-Arwood, S. M., Spencer, J. L., & Kalberg, J. R. (2007). Teaching elementary school educators to design, implement, and evaluate functional assessment-based interventions: Successes and challenges. *Preventing School Failure, 51*(4), 35–46.

Lane, K. L., & Beebe-Frankenberger, M. E. (2004). *School-based interventions: The tools you need to succeed*. Allyn & Bacon.

Lane, K. L., Buckman, M. M., Oakes, W. P., & Menzies, H. M. (2020). Tiered systems and inclusion: Potential benefits, clarifications, and considerations. In J. M. Kauffman (Ed.), *On educational inclusion: Meanings, history, issues, and international perspectives* (pp. 85–106). Routledge Taylor & Francis.

Lane, K. L., Cabell, S. Q., & Drew, S. V. (2021). A productive scholar's guide to respectful, responsible inquiry during the COVID-19 pandemic: Moving forward. *Journal of Learning Disabilities, 54*(5), 388–399. https://doi.org/10.1177/00222194211023186

Lane, K. L., Carter, E., Jenkins, A., Magill, L., & Germer, K. (2015). Supporting Comprehensive, Integrated, Three-Tiered Models of Prevention in schools: Administrators' perspectives. *Journal of Positive Behavior Interventions, 17*, 209–222.

Lane, K. L., Harris, K., Graham, S., Driscoll, S. A., Sandmel, K., Morphy, P., Hebert, M., House, E., & Schatschneider, C. (2011). Self-regulated strategy development at tier-2 for second-grade students with writing and behavioral difficulties: A randomized control trial. *Journal of Research on Educational Effectiveness, 4*, 322–353. https://doi.org/10.1080/19345747.2011.558987

Lane, K. L., Kalberg, J. R., Bruhn, A. L., Driscoll, S. A., Wehby, J. H., & Elliott, S. (2009). Assessing social validity of school-wide positive behavior support plans: Evidence for the reliability and structure of the Primary Intervention Rating Scale. *School Psychology Review, 38*, 135–144.

Lane, K. L., Kalberg, J. R., Bruhn, A. L., Mahoney, M. E., & Driscoll, S. A. (2008). Primary prevention programs at the elementary level: Issues of treatment integrity, systematic screening, and reinforcement. *Education and Treatment of Children, 31*, 465–494. https://doi.org/10.1353/etc.0.0033

Lane, K. L., Little, M. A., Rhodes, J. R., Phillips, A., & Welsh, M. T. (2007). Outcomes of a teacher-led reading intervention for elementary students at-risk for behavioral disorders. *Exceptional Children, 74*, 47–70.

Lane, K. L., Mahdavi, J. N., & Borthwick-Duffy, S. A. (2003). Teacher perceptions of the prereferral intervention process: A call for assistance with school-based interventions. *Preventing School Failure, 47*, 148–155.

Lane, K. L., & Menzies, H. M. (2003). A school-wide intervention with primary and secondary levels of support for elementary students: Outcomes and considerations. *Education and Treatment of Children, 26*, 431–451. www.jstor.org/stable/42899771

Lane, K. L., & Menzies, H. M. (2005). Teacher-identified students with and without academic and behavioral concerns: Characteristics and responsiveness to a school-wide intervention. *Behavioral Disorders, 31*, 65–83.

Lane, K. L., & Menzies, H. M. (2009). *Student risk screening scale for early internalizing and externalizing behavior (SRSS-IE). Screening scale*. www.ci3t.org/screening

Lane, K. L., Menzies, H. M., Ennis, R. P., & Oakes, W. P. (2018). Effective low-intensity strategies to enhance school success: What every educator needs to know. *Beyond Behavior, 27*, 128–133. https://doi.org/10.1177/1074295618799044

Lane, K. L., Menzies, H. M., Oakes, W. P., & Kalberg, J. R. (2012). *Systematic screenings of behavior to support instruction: From preschool to high school*. Guilford Press.

Lane, K. L., Oakes, W. P., Cantwell, E. D., & Royer, D. J. (2018). *Building and installing comprehensive, integrated, three-tiered (Ci3T) models of prevention: A practical guide to supporting school success (v. 1.2)*. KOI Education.

Lane, K. L., Oakes, W. P., & Cox, M. L. (2012). Functional assessment-based interventions: A university-district partnership to promote learning and success. *Beyond Behavior, 20*, 3–18.

Lane, K. L., Oakes, W. P., Ennis, R. P., Cox, M. L., Schatschneider, C., & Lambert, W. (2013). Additional evidence for the reliability and validity of the Student Risk Screening Scale at the high school level: A replication and extension. *Journal of Emotional and Behavioral Disorders, 21*, 97–115. https://doi.org/10.1177/1063426611407339

Lane, K. L., Oakes, W. P., & Menzies, H. M. (2010). *Schoolwide expectations survey for specific settings*. www.ci3t.org/measures

Lane, K. L., Oakes, W. P., Menzies, H. M., Oyer, J., & Jenkins, A. (2013). Working within the context of three-tiered models of prevention: Using school wide data to identify high school students for targeted supports. *Journal of Applied School Psychology, 29*, 203–229. https://doi.org/10.1080/15377903.2013.778773

Lane, K. L., Oakes, W. P., Powers, L., Diebold, T., Germer, K., Common, E. A., & Brunsting, N. (2015). Improving teachers' knowledge of functional assessment-based interventions: Outcomes of a professional development series. *Education and Treatment of Children, 38*(4), 93–120. https://doi.org/10.1353/etc.2015.0001

Lane, K. L., Robertson, E. J., & Wehby, J. H. (2002). *Primary intervention rating scale*. www.ci3t.org/measures

Lane, K. L., Royer, D. J., Messenger, M. L., Common, E. A., Ennis, R. P., & Swogger, E. D. (2015). Empowering teachers with low-intensity strategies to support academic engagement: Implementation and effects of instructional choice for elementary students in inclusive settings. *Education and Treatment of Children, 38*, 473–504. https://doi.org/10.1353/etc.2015.001

Lane, K. L., Wehby, J. H., Little, M. A., & Cooley, C. (2005a). Academic, social, and behavioral profiles of students with emotional and behavioral disorders educated in self-contained classrooms and self-contained schools: Part I—Are they more alike than different? *Behavioral Disorders, 30*, 349–361.

Lane, K. L., Wehby, J. H., Little, M. A., & Cooley, C. (2005b). Students educated in self-contained classes and self-contained schools: Part II—How do they progress over time? *Behavioral Disorders, 30*, 363–374.

Lane, K. L., Wehby, J. H., Menzies, H. M., Gregg, R. M., Doukas, G. L., & Munton, S. M. (2002). Early literacy instruction for first-grade students at-risk for antisocial behavior. *Education and Treatment of Children, 25*, 438–458.

Lane, K. L., Wehby, J., Menzies, H. M., Doukas, G. L., Munton, S. M., & Gregg, R. M. (2003). Social skills instruction for students at risk for antisocial behavior: The effects of small-group instruction. *Behavioral Disorders, 28*, 229–248.

Little, M. A., Lane, K. L., Harris, K., Graham, S., Brindle, M., & Sandmel, K. (2010). Self-regulated strategies development for persuasive writing in tandem with schoolwide positive behavioral support: Effects for second grade students with behavioral and writing difficulties. *Behavioral Disorders, 35*, 157–179.

Lloyd, J., Kauffman, J., Landrum, T., & Roe, D. (1991). Why do teachers refer pupils for special education: An analysis of referral records. *Exceptionality, 2*, 115–126.

Majeika, C. E., Walder, J. Pl., Hubbard, J. P., Steeb, K. M., Ferris, G. J., Oakes, W. P., & Lane, K. L. (2011). Improving on-task behavior using a functional assessment-based intervention in an inclusive high school setting. *Beyond Behavior, 20*, 55–66.

Mattison, R. E., Hooper, S. R., & Glassberg, L. A. (2002). Three-year course of learning disorders in special education students classified as behavioral disorder. *Journal of the American Academy of Child & Adolescent Psychiatry, 41*, 1454–1461. https://doi.org/10.1097/00004583-200212000-00017

McIntosh, K., & Goodman, S. (2016). *Integrating multi-tiered systems of support: Blending RTI and PBIS*. Guilford Press.

Menzies, H. M., Lane, K. L., Oakes, W. P., Royer, D. J., Cantwell, E. D., Common, E. A., & Buckman, M. M. (2020). Elementary teachers' perceptions of a Comprehensive, Integrated, Three-tiered model of prevention. *Remedial and Special Education*. https://doi.org/10.1177/0741932519896860

The New Teacher Project. (2013). *Perspectives of irreplaceable teachers: What America's best teachers think about teaching*. https://tntp.org/publications/view/retention-and-school-culture/perspectives-of-irreplaceable-teachers-best-teachers-think-about-teaching

Oakes, W. P., Lane, K. L., Cox, M., & Messenger, M. (2014). Logistics of behavior screenings: How and why do we conduct behavior screenings at our school? *Preventing School Failure, 58*, 183–190.

Oakes, W. P., Lane, K. L., Royer, D. J., Buckman, M. M., Common, E. A., Allen, G. E., & Cantwell, E. D. (2021). Supporting the installation of comprehensive, integrated, three-tiered (Ci3T) models of prevention: Educator perspectives. *Manuscript in review*.

Oakes, W. P., Schellman, L. E., Lane, K. L., Common, E. A., Powers, L., Diebold, T., & Gaskill, T. (2018). Improving educators' knowledge, confidence, and usefulness of functional assessment-based interventions: Outcomes of professional learning. *Education and Treatment of Children, 41*(4), 533–565.

Oakes, W. P., Wilder, K., Lane, K. L., Powers, L., Yokoyama, L., O'Hare, M. E., & Jenkins, A. B. (2010). Psychometric properties of the Student Risk Screening Scale: An effective tool for use in diverse urban elementary schools. *Assessment for Effective Intervention, 35*, 231–239.

Robertson, E. J., & Lane, K. L. (2007). Supporting middle school students with academic and behavioral concerns within the context of a three-tiered model of support: Findings of a secondary prevention program. *Behavioral Disorders, 33*, 5–22.

Rock, M. L., & Zigmond, N. (2001). Intervention assistance: Is it substance or symbolism?. *Preventing School Failure: Alternative Education for Children and Youth, 45*(4), 153. https://doi.org/161.10.1080/10459880109603330

Royer, D. J., Lane, K. L., Cantwell, E. D., & Messenger, M. (2017). A systematic review of the evidence base for instructional choice in k-12 settings. *Behavioral Disorders, 42*, 89–107. https://doi.org/10.1177/0198742916688655

Sherod, R., Oakes, W. P., Lane, K. L., & Lane, K. S. (2020, May). *Tips for communicating with your community about systematic screening*. Center on PBIS, University of Oregon. www.pbis.org

Strickland-Cohen, M. K., McIntosh, K., & Horner, R. H. (2014). Sustaining effective practices in the face of principal turnover. *Teaching Exceptional Children, 46*(3), 18–24.

Umbreit, J., Ferro, J. B., Liaupsin, C. J., & Lane, K. L. 2007. *Functional behavioral assessment and function-based intervention: An effective, practical approach*. Prentice-Hall.

Walker, H. M., Colvin, G., & Ramsey, E. (1995). *Antisocial behavior in school: Strategies and best practices*. Brooks/Cole.

Walker, H. M., Forness, S. R., & Lane, K. L. (2014). Design and management of scientific research in applied school settings. In B. Cook, M. Tankersley, & T. Landrum (Eds.). *Advances in learning and behavioral disabilities* (Vol. 27, pp. 141–169). Emerald.

Walker, H. M., Horner, R. H., Sugai, G., Bullis, M., Spragues, J. R., Bricker, D., & Kaufman, M. J. (1996). Integrated approaches to preventing antisocial behavior patterns among school-age children and youth. *Journal of Emotional and Behavioral Disorders, 4*, 194–209.

Walker, H. M., Severson, H. H., & Feil, E. G. (2014). *Systematic screening for behavior disorders (SSBD) technical manual: Universal screening for PreK—9* (2nd ed.). Pacific Northwest Publishing.

Wolf, M. M. (1978). Social validity: The case for subjective measurement or how applied behavior analysis is finding its heart. *Journal of Applied Behavior Analysis, 11*, 203–214.

Yudin, M. (2014). *PBIS: Providing opportunity*. A keynote address presented at the National PBIS Leadership Forum. Keynote Address presented at the PBIS Building Capacity & Partnerships to Enhance Educational Reform.

3
TREATMENT INTEGRITY AND SOCIAL VALIDITY IN TIERED SYSTEMS

Using Data to Inform Implementation Efforts

Mark Matthew Buckman, Kathleen Lynne Lane, and Wendy Peia Oakes

Educational systems require systematic structures to support the diverse learning needs of all students. School leaders are increasingly looking to tiered systems to provide this structure. Tiered systems, typically represented by a three-tiered pyramid, involve implementation of prevention and intervention efforts across multiple tiers. Interventions at higher tiers become increasingly intensive and are provided to students demonstrating more significant needs. Researchers have conceptualized various formulations of these systems, which often emphasize specific domains. For example, Response-to-Intervention (RTI) was introduced as an alternative means of identifying students with reading disabilities and framework for providing academic interventions (Fuchs, 2003), whereas School-wide Positive Behavioral Interventions and Supports (SW-PBIS) provides a framework for teaching students prosocial behaviors and implementing intensive behavioral interventions for students who engage in challenging behavior (Sugai & Horner, 2002). Recent iterations of tiered systems emphasize integration of multiple domains. For example, the Comprehensive, Integrated Three-tiered (Ci3T) Model of Prevention exemplifies an integrated approach to support students' academic, behavioral, and social emotional needs (Lane, Oakes, et al., 2019).

The underlying theme unifying these various approaches is an investment in prevention and use of data-informed decision-making to detect students requiring interventions at the earliest possible juncture (McIntosh & Goodman, 2016). The base of tiered systems, here referred to as primary (Tier 1) prevention, involves implementation of practices intended to proactively support development of students' skills and reduce the likelihood that challenges will negatively impact students' educational achievement. Ideally, primary (Tier 1) prevention efforts involve implementation of evidence-based practices (EBPs; Lane, Oakes, et al., 2019). EBPs are practices shown to be effective across multiple rigorous research studies (Cook et al., 2009). Selecting EBPs provides confidence that students will be more likely to experience desired outcomes, thus likely decreasing the proportion of students experiencing difficulty at school. Yet it is expected that some students will need additional support despite participating in evidence-based prevention efforts. For these students, educators collaborate to implement evidence-based secondary (Tier 2) and/or tertiary (Tier 3) interventions. To determine which students may require Tier 2 or Tier 3 interventions, educators utilize multiple sources of data. For example, curriculum-based measures for reading and math serve as academic screeners and are administered to all students three times per year. Review of these data indicate which students are not on a trajectory to meet expected end-of-year benchmarks and require intervention. Similarly, educators complete systematic behavior screening to identify which students exhibit patterns of behavior indicative of risk for externalizing (e.g., disruptive, aggressive) or internalizing (e.g., shy, anxious) behaviors (Oakes et al., 2017). Using these data sources alongside other information, such as office discipline referrals, attendance, or course failures, educators may conclude that the current level of prevention is insufficient to meet that student's level of need and connect them to a Tier 2 or Tier 3 intervention.

The logic and structure of tiered systems hold promise for improving school and student outcomes. Experimental and quasi-experimental studies of SW-PBIS, for example, have demonstrated reductions in suspensions and expulsions (Bradshaw et al., 2010; Gage et al., 2018), increases in perceived school safety (Horner et al., 2009), and small improvements in academic outcomes (Gage et al., 2017; Horner et al., 2009). Similarly, reviews of specific Tier 2 and Tier 3 interventions focused on academic and behavioral outcomes indicate availability of a multitude of efficacious supports for students at elevated risk in one or more domain (Common et al., 2017; Gersten et al., 2017). However, the promise of tiered systems may not be fully realized without careful attention to how these systems and their constituent interventions are actually implemented. It has long been recognized that educational innovations often look quite different from their conception when used in the real world (Hall et al., 1975). To that end, in this chapter we describe two critical sources of programmatic data—treatment integrity and social validity—and illustrate how they can be used to inform efforts to implement tiered systems. First, we offer a brief overview of these concepts including their definitions and origins in educational research. Then, we describe the current state of research on their usage in the context of tiered systems. Lastly, we share implications for practitioners and researchers regarding use of these data to optimize implementation efforts to support educators and students.

Treatment Integrity and Social Validity: Historical Context

The historical origins of treatment integrity and social validity in educational research can be traced to the field of Applied Behavior Analysis (ABA). In a seminal article, Baer et al. (1968) articulate foundational principles of ABA, emphasizing the application of a scientific approach to understanding and shaping socially important behaviors with a goal of improving the lives of individuals and the societies in which they live. Two necessities arose from these underlying values of ABA, one technical and one humanistic. The technical necessity was accurate measurement, an essential component of any scientific pursuit. Early applied behavioral research had well-established approaches for measuring dependent variables, typically direct measurement of a target behavior to be increased or decreased. Researchers less frequently measured independent variables, the procedures used to effect a change in the dependent variable. Peterson and colleagues described this as a "curious double standard" (1982, p. 478), one that threatened the reliability and validity of research findings. Measuring the integrity with which interventionists carried out procedures related to the independent variable increased confidence that findings reflected the relative effectiveness of the intervention rather than idiosyncrasies related to how the independent variable was carried out. This concept has been subsequently described as treatment integrity, or the extent to which interventions are implemented as intended (Gresham, 1989).

With respect to the humanistic element of applied research, tenets provided by Baer et al. (1968) suggested empiricism alone was insufficient. The goal of improving quality of life grounded applied research in philosophy as much as science, with necessary attention paid to questions such as: "What behaviors are important for one to lead a good, fulfilled life?" Wolf (1978) expanded upon this line of thinking by defining social validity, a concept providing the essential link between scientific empiricism and humanistic values. Social validity refers to the views of stakeholders—a group consisting of all those involved in applied research, including participants, their families, the researcher, the interventionists, and potentially others—as they related to three underlying aspects of any intervention: social significance of the goals, social acceptability of the procedures, and social importance of the outcomes. Wolf emphasized that, although data related to social validity could not inform causal conclusions (e.g., the intervention caused behavior to increase), it provided invaluable insight into how those involved experienced and valued the intervention related to its goals, procedures, and outcomes. He argued these insights had important implications for applied research, as they likely mediated whether treatments would be used and sustained.

Educational researchers have largely embraced the importance of both treatment integrity and social validity. In the field of special education, for example, researchers have developed quality indicators (QIs) to assist in evaluating the rigor of studies as part of the process of identifying EBPs. QIs published by the Council for Exceptional Children (CEC, 2014) include indicators related to both treatment integrity and social validity, demonstrating the significance of their roles in conducting and evaluating research. Yet despite the emphasis placed on these constructs, a lineage of literature reviews suggests these data are not collected and reported at a frequency commensurate with their importance (e.g., Gresham, 1989; Gresham et al., 1993). Recently, Hagermoser Sanetti and colleagues (2011) conducted a systematic literature review of school psychology journals from 1995 through 2008 and found only half (50.2%) of 223 reviewed studies reported treatment integrity data. Social validity data are also sparsely reported. Clarke and Dunlap (2008) reviewed intervention studies published from 1999 to 2005 in three journals related to special education. Reporting of social validity data was relatively low across all journals, ranging from 31% of studies reporting social validity in the *Journal of Positive Behavioral Interventions and Supports* to 3% in the *Journal of Applied Behavior* (2008). Based on these findings from the early 2000s, it is clear there is room for growth in increasing collection and reporting of this critical information in educational research. Additionally, these data serve important roles in applied settings, given their importance for intervention selection (i.e., social validity) and drawing valid inferences evaluating intervention effectiveness (i.e., treatment integrity, Lane et al., 2020).

Current State of Research

When considered in the context of tiered systems, issues related to treatment integrity and social validity take on heightened importance. The premise of tiered systems involves educators assessing student progress as an indicator of whether a more intensive intervention is warranted. When students do not respond to lower-level prevention efforts (e.g., Tier 1), educators connect students to Tier 2 or Tier 3 supports. In doing so, they are making judgements about whether strategies, practices, or programs used as part of Tier 1 are sufficient for a specific student, and when they are deemed ineffective or insufficient, they select and implement new or more intensive versions of those practices.

In this way, the work of educators within tiered systems mirrors the work of applied researchers. If treatment integrity is not assessed at each level of prevention, educators hazard making erroneous decisions such as determining Tier 1 is insufficient without first determining Tier 1 is implemented with integrity. Similarly, without consideration of social validity from multiple perspectives, decision-makers risk reliance on practices poorly aligned with goals valued by students and/or their families (i.e., socially unimportant goals). Alternatively, educators themselves may struggle to implement practices due to infeasible procedures or perceived ineffectiveness (i.e., socially unimportant outcomes). Thus, treatment integrity and social validity are integral data sources to support implementation and decision-making within tiered systems. In the next section, we examine current research related to each of these constructs in the context of tiered systems. We attend to the extent to which these constructs are reported in the literature, the measures used, and areas for further development, beginning with treatment integrity.

Treatment Integrity in Tiered Systems

A fundamental premise of tiered systems is that students participating in Tier 2 or Tier 3 interventions require these supports because Tier 1 instruction is by itself insufficient to meet their educational needs. To make valid decisions in this regard, it is essential to consider treatment integrity of Tier 1 instruction to ensure students truly had access to prevention efforts. It is therefore heartening that the movement to adopt tiered systems is associated with widescale collection of treatment integrity. In 2018, of the over 27,000 schools in the United States implementing SW-PBIS, more than 15,000 collected treatment integrity data and submitted it to the National Center on PBIS (McIntosh, 2019). This represents a substantial movement toward embracing the use of treatment integrity data to support implementation. However, questions remain as to how these data are used for decision-making, such as confirming whether students have access to Tier 1 implemented with integrity.

Several reviews of intervention research taking place within tiered systems provide insights into these questions. Hill and colleagues (2012) examined studies of Tier 2 reading interventions implemented in the context of RTI. They found researchers assessed treatment integrity of Tier 2 interventions in 21 of 22 studies (95.45%). Despite near unanimous inclusion of treatment integrity of Tier 2 interventions, Hill et al. noted researchers did not consistently report treatment integrity of Tier 1, with only 8 of 22 studies (36.36%) providing treatment integrity of the core (Tier 1) reading program. The authors posit this as a concern. Namely, they argued the absence of this information makes it difficult to evaluate whether students truly require Tier 2 interventions or are "casualties of poor instruction" (p. 121). A review by Bruhn and colleagues (2014) came to similar conclusions when examining studies of Tier 2 interventions in the context of multitier models of behavioral prevention. Of 28 studies reviewed, 27 (96.43%) included treatment integrity data for the Tier 2 intervention but only 12 (42.86%) included treatment integrity data for Tier 1. Like Hill et al. (2012), Bruhn and colleagues (2014) argued for the importance of Tier 1 treatment integrity data as a mechanism for making accurate decisions about the need for more intensive intervention. Additionally, the authors noted that when Tier 1 data were reported, they tended to be in an aggregate form. Specifically, studies reported treatment integrity at the school-wide level, which made it challenging to determine whether specific students had access to Tier 1 within their classrooms. Therefore, beyond ensuring that treatment integrity data are collected across the tiers, consideration of *how* these data are collected is necessary, as this may affect how they are used.

A multitude of approaches to measuring treatment integrity in tiered systems exist, with much diversification occurring relative to the kind of tiered system examined. In their review, Hill et al. (2012) found fidelity of academic Tier 1 instruction in RTI was often monitored through feedback and coaching rather than formal measurement. The benefit of this approach is potential efficiency and cost savings (e.g., completing direct observations may be time and resource intensive). Furthermore, using feedback as a method for monitoring treatment integrity allows for a classroom-specific approach aimed at increasing and/or sustaining fidelity. Unfortunately, in the absence of a formal measurement process, it is difficult to make reliable decisions regarding whether Tier 1 is implemented with sufficient integrity.

In contrast, several published measures exist for assessing fidelity of behavioral-focused systems such as SW-PBIS. Recently, the Tiered Fidelity Inventory (TFI; Algozzine et al., 2014) has become a widely used assessment tool for measuring treatment integrity of SW-PBIS (McIntosh, 2019). The TFI includes three protocols, one for assessing each of the three tiers of SW-PBIS. School leadership teams complete the protocols, preferably alongside an external coach (e.g., a district, researcher, or technical assistance provider). Protocols consist of a series of questions covering essential features, including teaming (e.g., leadership), specific practices related to each tier (e.g., teaching behavior expectations, implementation of interventions with documented evidence of effectiveness), and evaluation (e.g., use of data to monitor outcomes). As they reflect and respond, leadership teams refer to a variety of data sources, including permanent products (e.g., meeting agendas), walkthrough data (consisting of brief interviews asked of students and staff), and school-wide data (e.g., systematic screening, historical data).

The benefit of utilizing a published measure such as the TFI to assess treatment integrity is the opportunity to produce a reliable estimate of the degree to which SW-PBIS is implemented with fidelity. Indeed, extant research on TFI provides an exemplary illustration of inquiry to explore the reliability and validity of such measures. For example, McIntosh et al. (2017) conducted a multi-pronged study to assess content validity, reliability, and usability of the TFI. The authors received input on the measure from researchers and expert SW-PBIS implementers, which informed revisions and clarifications to the measure. Next, the authors conducted a usability and reliability study. Participants indicated the measure was practical to complete, and repeated measurements at a two-week interval produced consistent measurements (test-retest coefficient = 0.99). Lastly, the authors undertook a large-scale validation study involving 789 schools from a geographically diverse sample. Results showed measurements were internally consistent (alpha coefficients ranging from 0.87 to 0.98 across subscales) and correlated at least moderately with other established measures of SW-PBIS. Notably, scores from the TFI correlated strongly with scores on other SW-PBIS measures when school leadership teams completed the TFI with an external coach, suggesting involvement of the coach increased reliability (McIntosh et al., 2017).

Bolstered by strong evidence for the psychometric adequacy of tools such as the TFI, these measures provide a strong basis for making decisions about the functioning of the school-wide system. For example, the TFI is intended for use by school leaders in creating action plans to improve and sustain implementation of core features of each tier. Through this action planning step, which is data informed, school leaders have a mechanism from which to participate in an ongoing evaluation and refinement of their school-wide system.

Although there are a great number of strengths in the current approaches to assessing treatment integrity within tiered systems, there are also some notable areas requiring further development. First, there is a need to increase collection of treatment integrity data for academic components of tiered systems. Exemplar studies exist illustrating how implementation can be monitored across the tiers of academic instruction (Algozzine et al., 2012; VanDerHeyden et al., 2007). However, extant reviews suggest that, although procedures for monitoring treatment integrity such as coaching and feedback are used in some cases, collection of quantifiable fidelity data is not routine (Hill et al., 2012). As implementation of tiered systems evolve, utilizing treatment integrity data as part of decision-making processes represents a critical area of emphasis (Lane et al., 2020). Having quantifiable data across learning domains (e.g., academic, behavior, social) will support these efforts.

Similarly, a notable limitation of commonly used approaches for assessing treatment integrity of SW-PBIS is that they tend to rely on aggregate, school-wide measurement. As argued by Bruhn et al. (2014), aggregated data make it difficult to determine whether specific students have access to Tier 1. Treatment integrity data are important in making valid decisions regarding student responsiveness to Tier 1; therefore, availability of specific data reflecting treatment integrity within specific classrooms is necessary. It is not reasonable to assume implementation is happening in a parallel fashion across classrooms simply because school-wide implementation meets specified criteria (e.g., 80%; Buckman et al., in review). This suggests the need for a comprehensive framework for collecting and utilizing treatment integrity and other data to inform decision-making. Such a framework would include assessment of treatment integrity at the school-wide level using established measures and assessment of individual educators' implementation.

Measure	Aug	Sep	Oct	Nov	Dec	Jan	Feb	Mar	Apr	May
School Demographics										
Student Demographic Information	X	X	X	X	X	X	X	X	X	X
Screening Measures										
Behavior Screeners: SRSS-IE		X			X				X	
Academic Screeners: AIMSweb (reading and math)	X	X				X				X
Student Outcome Measures—Academic										
Unit assessments	X	X				X				X
State and district assessment								X	X	
Progress reports				X			X			X
Student Outcome Measures—Behavior										
Absences		X	X	X	X	X	X	X	X	
Tardies		X	X	X	X	X	X	X	X	
Office discipline referrals (ODRs)		X			X				X	
Counselor referrals	X	X	X	X	X	X	X	X	X	X
Nurse visits	X	X	X	X	X	X	X	X	X	X
Bullying referrals	X	X	X	X	X	X	X	X	X	X
Program Measures										
Social Validity—PIRS			X					X		
Tiered Fidelity Inventory (TFI)			X					X		
Ci3T Treatment Integrity (TSR)			X					X		
Direct observations			X					X		
Positive Action Treatment Integrity			X					X		

Figure 3.1 Sample Assessment Schedule Including Treatment Integrity and Social Validity
Note. SRSS-IE = Student Risk Screening Scale—Internalizing and Externalizing; Reprinted with permission from Lane, K. L., Oakes, W. P., Cantwell, E. D., & Royer, D. J. (2019). *Building and installing comprehensive, integrated, three-tiered (Ci3T) models of prevention: A practical guide to supporting school success (v1.3).* KOI Education.

An example of such a framework can be found embedded within the Ci3T model of prevention. School leaders develop a plan to monitor implementation using multiple measures, including at the level of individual educators through the Ci3T Treatment Integrity: Teacher Self-Report (Lane, 2009a; see Figure 3.1 for a sample assessment schedule). This is a survey distributed by school or district leaders to all faculty and staff and provides educator-level implementation data. Additionally, school leaders coordinate data collection using the Ci3T Treatment Integrity: Direct Observation tool (Lane, 2009b). This is administered during a 30-minute instructional period by either a trained school-based staff (e.g., instructional coach) or research personnel as part of ongoing research–practitioner partnerships (see Lane et al., this volume). The direct observation tool entails collecting data from both an outside observer and the educator who was observed. By assessing treatment integrity from multiple perspectives, school teams can increase confidence in the accuracy of decisions regarding implementation. For example, Lane and colleagues (2008) found educators tended to report higher levels of treatment integrity than outside observers. Identifying these disagreements may prove fruitful for identifying needs for professional learning to address potential misconceptions. For example, if educators report using behavior-specific praise but this is not observed by the outside observer, school leaders may plan for refresher trainings to assist staff in embedding this reinforcement strategy into instruction.

When building a comprehensive assessment framework for collecting data about implementation, an important additional consideration is assessing social validity. In the next section, we move to discussing social validity and how it has been assessed in the context of tiered systems.

Social Validity in Tiered Systems

The importance of social validity has been acknowledged since the initial conception of SW-PBIS, one of the earliest formulations of tiered systems. A fundamental philosophy of SW-PBIS is the merging of the scientific empiricism of ABA with humanistic values (Carr et al., 2002). Consideration of social validity provides a means to merge these values, particularly when social validity across multiple stakeholders (e.g., educators, families, students) is considered. Despite ongoing emphasis of this construct, research on SW-PBIS and other tiered systems has typically underreported information regarding social validity (Marchant et al., 2013). Nevertheless, several examples of social validity assessment within tiered systems are instructive for considering how these data can be used.

In one such example, Lane and colleagues (2009) examined the extent to which social validity data from schools implementing SW-PBIS predicted levels of treatment integrity. Prior to beginning implementation, faculty and staff from each school had the opportunity to share perceptions of their school's SW-PBIS plan by completing the Primary Intervention Rating Scale (PIRS; Lane et al., 2002). The PIRS measures social validity from the perspective of faculty and staff members regarding the Tier 1 plan (details about the PIRS are shared subsequently). Results indicated strong correlations between preimplementation social validity ratings and self-reported levels of treatment integrity in the first year of implementation. These findings are important as an illustration of the value of collecting social validity data during the planning (i.e., preimplementation) phase. By sharing drafted plans with faculty and staff and asking for input using a social validity measure, school leaders have the opportunity to apply data-informed decision-making as they design their tiered system. Specifically, school leaders can use these data to (a) identify whether the plan is likely to be implemented with fidelity, (b) shift their plans to be more socially valid if specific components are perceived as infeasible or unlikely to achieve desired outcomes, or (c) anticipate and make plans to address potential implementation challenges (e.g., low acceptability of procedures).

Similarly, Miramontes et al. (2011) collected social validity ratings from a varied sample of educators (e.g., teachers, administrators, related service personnel) from 35 schools implementing SW-PBIS and RTI. They analyzed correlations between participants' social validity responses and schools' level of treatment integrity using scores on the School-wide Evaluation Tool (SET; Sugai et al., 2001). Results included statistically significant correlations between school treatment integrity scores and participant responses to questions related to perceived positive outcomes, staff buy-in, satisfaction with universal (Tier 1) procedures, and satisfaction with supplemental (e.g., Tier 2) and intensive (e.g., Tier 3) goals. In sum, these findings provide further evidence of a relation between social validity of plans across the tiers and levels of treatment integrity. Gathering such data thus becomes a mechanism by which to predict and understand levels of fidelity, and thereby contributes helpful contextual information for interpreting these data. These findings reiterate the importance of creating socially valid implementation plans, particularly with respect to soliciting staff buy-in, establishing acceptable procedures, and utilizing practices educators perceive to be effective.

Given the value of social validity data with respect to implementation of tiered systems, consideration to how school leaders and researchers can collect these data is necessary. Research examples by Lane et al. (2009) and Miramontes et al. (2011) both utilized rating scale-based assessments. The PIRS, for example, contains 17 items rated on a six-point Likert-type scale and open-ended questions for which faculty and staff can provide narrative comments (e.g., "What would you change about this plan [components, design, implementation, etc.] to make it more student-friendly and educator-friendly?"). Preliminary inquiry suggests the PIRS is unidimensional and produces internally consistent scores (alpha coefficients = 0.97, 0.98, and 0.97 for scores from elementary, middle, and high school faculty and staff, respectively; Lane et al., 2009). Two versions of the measure are publicly available (Lane et al., 2002; see reference for access). One version is intended for administration prior to implementation; the other is intended for schools currently implementing. The difference between versions is the verb tense (i.e., "I would be willing to use this primary plan . . ." vs. "I am willing to use this primary plan . . ."). This formulation allows for collection and use of social validity data from initial adoption through initial and sustained implementation.

Although rating scale approaches to assessment are highly efficient and allow for collection of data across all faculty and staff, other methods may provide more nuanced information. For example, interviews and focus groups may provide in-depth understanding related to perceived successes and challenges. Frey and colleagues (2010) demonstrated this approach by conducting focus groups of SW-PBIS implementation in the context of early childhood programs. Their findings showed how focus group data can create a nuanced depiction of how educators perceive implementation efforts, such as illustrating high enthusiasm for some elements (i.e., socially important goals) but variable acceptability for others (e.g., socially acceptable procedures).

In addition to increasing and diversifying the collection and use of social validity data in the context of tiered systems, a major area for expansion and future consideration is integration of stakeholders beyond school staff members into measurement of social validity. Students, families, and community members are also critical school stakeholders. Sharing information about prevention and intervention efforts with these stakeholders and soliciting feedback related to the three aspects of social validity may provide insightful information to ensure systems are built in a manner to best serve students and achieve important educational outcomes. The possibility of gathering data from nonstaff members would expand the manner in which social validity data are treated. Specifically, extant research on social validity in tiered systems has emphasized the perspective of faculty and staff members, as presented in association with treatment integrity (e.g., social validity predicting treatment integrity). Examining social validity from the perspective of students and families may broaden the focus to also include alignment with student, family, and community values. Finding ways to expand social validity data collection to include more diverse stakeholders represents an important next step for the design, implementation, and evaluation of tiered systems.

Implications for Practitioners

As educational leaders continue to prioritize tiered systems as a preferred approach for meeting students' individual needs, it is clear that treatment integrity and social validity should feature prominently in these efforts. There are several important considerations for practitioners as they consider how to collect and use these data.

Formulate a Comprehensive Assessment Framework

First, it is critical that school leaders systematically formulate a comprehensive assessment framework as part of their plans for implementing a tiered system. Such frameworks include plans for collecting data reflecting student performance (e.g., systematic academic and behavior screening, attendance, and other school-wide data sources), as well as measures of implementation (e.g., treatment integrity and social validity). By mapping out a transparent, clearly defined plan for data collection as part of the design of a tiered system, school leaders can establish a strong, data-based foundation for decision-making (see Figure 3.1). This ensures a plan is in place to collect data necessary to ensure a student has benefit from Tier 1 and to connect students to supports as needed—which includes student performance as well as fidelity.

Select Valid and Reliable Measures

Additionally, when creating such a framework, care should be taken to select measures likely to produce valid and reliable measurements, such as the TFI if implementing SW-PBIS. School leaders may also seek to select multiple measures or data collection approaches. For example, a systems-level measurement such as the TFI may be selected, but school leaders may also seek out methods for collecting and using treatment integrity data at the classroom level to assess implementation of academic and/or behavioral components of the tiered systems. Such methods may include observation protocols aligned with specific components of the school plan, accompanied by opportunities to provide feedback and coaching. School leaders may also select diverse methods for assessing social validity. This can include surveys such as the PIRS (Lane et al., 2002) but may also incorporate brief interviews or focus groups. Furthermore, seeking input from multiple stakeholders, including school support staff, family and community members, and students, may provide useful information for planning and adjusting implementation plans to ensure they are socially valid.

Plan to Share and Use Data

Lastly, school leaders should also make plans for sharing and using data. In terms of sharing data, this may be done in the context of a program evaluation, as a mechanism for acknowledging the work put in by stakeholders to support students, and/or as a way to contextualize priorities for ongoing professional learning to support implementation. Sharing data with stakeholders can promote their active engagement in ongoing program evaluation efforts. Data sharing also substantiates that they have a voice in how implementation is carried out, particularly through the sharing of deidentified social validity information.

Regarding usage of data, school leaders should seek ways of making data available to those making tiered decisions for students, whether this be in the context of Tier 2 or Tier 3 intervention teams, professional learning communities, or individual educators making plans for their students. These data should be used as a means to reflect on the question: "Have students had consistent access to Tier 1?" If yes, then educators can confidently move forward with connecting students to Tier 2 or Tier 3 supports in an additive fashion, building off of the foundation of Tier 1. If Tier 1 is not consistently implemented, this provides important insights. Initial efforts may focus on increasing the integrity with which educators implement Tier 1 to ensure students have access to prevention practices and that a solid foundation exists from which to build on for Tier 2 and Tier 3. In this scenario, treatment integrity and social validity data prove useful for informing professional learning with the aim of improving, enhancing, or sustaining implementation efforts (Lane et al., 2020). To illustrate, treatment integrity data may indicate specific practices are underutilized. School leaders may respond by leading professional learning to reteach skills and reinvigorate enthusiasm, as well as a plan to reinforce educators who demonstrate these practices with fidelity. In this way, these data hold great practical utility for sustaining implementation of tiered systems over time.

Directions for Future Researchers

Although researchers in tiered systems have clearly prioritized treatment integrity and social validity in recent years, there are several areas for further development. First, regarding measures of treatment integrity, an important area for further development is the creation and validation of measurement systems to assess treatment integrity efficiently and accurately at the level of individual educators. Currently, the majority of fidelity tools are aimed at systems-level implementation. Such measures hold immense value and utility, particularly for identifying whether implementation is occurring with fidelity at the school-wide level. They prove less useful, though, when attempting to answer a question fundamental to tiered systems. Specifically, determining whether a student requires more than Tier 1 necessitates knowledge of whether that student has had consistent access to Tier 1 implemented with fidelity. This question can most appropriately be answered through some process of localized fidelity assessment (Buckman et al., in review). Furthermore, when data suggest an individual educator is struggling to implement Tier 1 with fidelity, it is vital to create mechanisms by which to support those educators. Thus, an area of emphasis is the creation of integrated suites of tools to assess treatment integrity, offer coaching and feedback, and provide targeted, self-directed professional learning to develop and refine skills. A challenge of this endeavor is that a multitude of tiered systems exist, with each school's implementation varying according to the practices and programs selected for use. Therefore, consideration of a framework that allows for customization while also retaining procedures for ensuring reliability is warranted.

Regarding social validity, the concept has been prioritized—particularly in the development of SW-PBIS—though not measured as often as one might expect given its status as a foundational component (Carr et al., 2002). Thus, an area for development is increasing the collection and reporting of these data, as well as considering how these data may act as a moderator of outcomes for students and the degree to which implementation is carried out and sustained. Additionally, advancing the inclusivity of social validity data collection is an important area for further research. Most work in this area has focused on the perceptions of school personnel. However, the perspectives of students, families, and community members are critical for consideration. This is particularly so as school leaders strive to become more responsive to the unique values of their communities. Utilizing feedback from more diverse stakeholders throughout the process of designing and implementing tiered systems stands to better align the goals, procedures, and planned-for outcomes of these systems to ensure they are best suited to meet the needs and expectations of those who they are designed to support.

Summary

In this chapter we focused on the importance of treatment integrity and social validity data within tiered systems of support, with detail instrumental to effective, data-informed decision-making efforts. We discussed how the measurement of treatment integrity and social validity and use of data are foundational to the implementation of tiered systems, described how extant research has addressed these concepts, and offered recommendations to the field for advancing the collection and use of these data within tiered systems. To guide continued conversations regarding this topic, we refer the reader to a multitude of free-access resources for assessing treatment integrity and social validity. Visit pbis.org, the website of the Center for Positive Behavioral Interventions & Supports, which contains a trove of information and measures such as the TFI under the *Tools* section of the site. Additionally, ci3t.org provides further free-access materials, including the PIRS social validity measure (Lane et al., 2002), an example of an educator-level assessment of treatment integrity, the Ci3T Treatment Integrity: Teacher Self-Report (Ci3T TI: TSR; Lane, 2009a), and resources to support educators in using these data. The Center on Multi-Tiered Systems of Supports at the American Institute of Research sponsors a website (mtss4success.org) containing guidance for collecting and using fidelity data, such as infographics about fidelity and rubrics for using coaching to increase treatment integrity.

References

Algozzine, B., Barrett, S., Eber, L., George, H., Horner, R., Lewis, T., Putnam, B., Swain-Bradway, J., McIntosh, K., & Sugai, G (2014). *School-wide PBIS tiered fidelity inventory*. OSEP Technical Assistance Center on Positive Behavioral Interventions and Supports. www.pbis.org.

Algozzine, B., Wang, C., White, R., Cooke, N., Marr, M. B., Algozzine, K., . . . Duran, G. Z. (2012). Effects of multi-tier academic and behavior instruction on difficult-to-teach students. *Exceptional Children, 79*(1), 45–64. https://doi.org/gbfhq6

Baer, D. M., Wolf, M. M., & Risley, T. R. (1968). Some current dimensions of applied behavior analysis 1. *Journal of Applied Behavior Analysis, 1*(1), 91–97. https://doi.org/bt77cr

Bradshaw, C. P., Mitchell, M. M., & Leaf, P. J. (2010). Examining the effects of schoolwide positive behavioral interventions and supports on student outcomes: Results from a randomized controlled effectiveness trial in elementary schools. *Journal of Positive Behavior Interventions, 12*(3), 133–148. https://doi.org/dqzv36

Bruhn, A. L., Lane, K. L., & Hirsch, S. E. (2014). A review of tier 2 interventions conducted within multitiered models of behavioral prevention. *Journal of Emotional and Behavioral Disorders, 22*(3), 171–189. https://doi.org/gcmc4r

Buckman, M. M., Lane, K. L., Common, E. A., Royer, D. J., Oakes, W. P., Allen, G. E., Lane, K. S., & Brunsting, N. (in review). Treatment integrity of primary (tier 1) prevention efforts in tiered systems: Mapping the literature. *Manuscript in review.*

Carr, E. G., Dunlap, G., Horner, R. H., Koegel, R. L., Turnbull, A. P., Sailor, W., . . . Fox, L. (2002). Positive behavior support: Evolution of an applied science. *Journal of Positive Behavior Interventions, 4*(1), 4–16. https://doi.org/fkmsbz

Clarke, S., & Dunlap, G. (2008). A descriptive analysis of intervention research published in the Journal of Positive Behavior Interventions: 1999 through 2005. *Journal of Positive Behavior Interventions, 10*(1), 67–71. https://doi.org/ftgvdg

Common, E. A., Lane, K. L., Pustejovsky, J. E., Johnson, A. H., & Johl, L. E. (2017). Functional assessment–based interventions for students with or at-risk for high-incidence disabilities: Field testing single-case synthesis methods. *Remedial and Special Education, 38*(6), 331–352. https://doi.org/gdcdrk

Cook, B. G., Tankersley, M., & Landrum, T. J. (2009). Determining evidence-based practices in special education. *Exceptional Children, 75*(3), 365–383. https://doi.org/gd23h9

Council for Exceptional Children. (2014). Standards for evidence-based practices in special education. *Teaching Exceptional Children, 46*(6), 206–212. https://doi.org/fp5c

Frey, A. J., Lee Park, K., Browne-Ferrigno, T., & Korfhage, T. L. (2010). The social validity of program-wide positive behavior support. *Journal of Positive Behavior Interventions, 12*(4), 222–235. https://doi.org/ffm9b8

Fuchs, L. S. (2003). Assessing intervention responsiveness: Conceptual and technical issues. *Learning Disabilities Research & Practice, 18*(3), 172–186. https://doi.org/bjgkdf

Gage, N. A., Lee, A., Grasley-Boy, N., & Peshak George, H. (2018). The impact of school-wide positive behavior interventions and supports on school suspensions: A statewide quasi-experimental analysis. *Journal of Positive Behavior Interventions, 20*(4), 217–226. https://doi.org/gfbj55

Gage, N. A., Leite, W., Childs, K., & Kincaid, D. (2017). Average treatment effect of school-wide positive behavioral interventions and supports on school-level academic achievement in Florida. *Journal of Positive Behavior Interventions, 19*(3), 158–167. https://doi.org/gbmksh

Gersten, R., Newman-Gonchar, R., Haymond, K. S., & Dimino, J. (2017). *What is the evidence base to support reading interventions for improving student outcomes in grades 1–3?* REL 2017–271. Regional Educational Laboratory Southeast.

Gresham, F. M. (1989). Assessment of treatment integrity in school consultation and prereferral intervention. *School Psychology Review, 18*(1), 37–50.

Gresham, F. M., Gansle, K. A., & Noell, G. H. (1993). Treatment integrity in applied behavior analysis with children. *Journal of Applied Behavior Analysis, 26*(2), 257–263. https://doi.org/b5wtmr

Hagermoser Sanetti, L. M., Gritter, K. L., & Dobey, L. M. (2011). Treatment integrity of interventions with children in the school psychology literature from 1995 to 2008. *School Psychology Review, 40*(1), 72–84. https://doi.org/f9ps

Hall, G. E., Loucks, S. F., Rutherford, W. L., & Newlove, B. W. (1975). Levels of use of the innovation: A framework for analyzing innovation adoption. *Journal of Teacher Education, 26*(1), 52–56. https://doi.org/d5r4s7

Hill, D. R., King, S. A., Lemons, C. J., & Partanen, J. N. (2012). Fidelity of implementation and instructional alignment in response to intervention research. *Learning Disabilities Research & Practice, 27*(3), 116–124. https://doi.org/frd9

Horner, R. H., Sugai, G., Smolkowski, K., Eber, L., Nakasato, J., Todd, A. W., & Esperanza, J. (2009). A randomized, wait-list controlled effectiveness trial assessing school-wide positive behavior support in elementary schools. *Journal of Positive Behavior Interventions, 11*(3), 133–144. https://doi.org/cg99xm

Lane, K. L. (2009a). *Ci3T treatment integrity: Teacher self-report form.* www.ci3t.org/measures

Lane, K. L. (2009b). *Ci3T Treatment Integrity: Direct observation tool.* www.ci3t.org/measures

Lane, K. L., Kalberg, J. R., Bruhn, A. L., Driscoll, S. A., Wehby, J. H., & Elliott, S. N. (2009). Assessing social validity of school-wide positive behavior support plans: Evidence for the reliability and structure of the Primary Intervention Rating Scale. *School Psychology Review, 38*(1), 135–144. https://doi.org/f9qb

Lane, K. L., Kalberg, J. R., Bruhn, A. L., Mahoney, M. E., & Driscoll, S. A. (2008). Primary prevention programs at the elementary level: Issues of treatment integrity, systematic screening, and reinforcement. *Education and Treatment of Children, 31*(4), 465–494. https://doi.org/frkn59

Lane, K. L., Menzies, H. M., Oakes, W. P., & Kalberg, J. R. (2020). *Developing a schoolwide framework to prevent and manage learning and behavior problems* (2nd ed.). Guilford Press.

Lane, K. L., Oakes, W. P., Cantwell, E. D., & Royer, D. J. (2019). *Building and installing comprehensive, integrated, three-tiered (Ci3T) models of prevention: A practical guide to supporting school success* (v1.3). KOI Education.

Lane, K. L., Robertson, E. J., & Wehby, J. H. (2002). *Primary intervention rating scale.* www.ci3t.org/measures

Marchant, M., Heath, M. A., & Miramontes, N. Y. (2013). Merging empiricism and humanism: Role of social validity in the school-wide positive behavior support model. *Journal of Positive Behavior Interventions, 15*(4), 221–230. https://doi.org/f5c6gj

McIntosh, K. (2019, October 3). *How do we support every student to be successful in school?* [Keynote address]. National PBIS Leadership Forum, Chicago, IL, United States. www.pbis.org/video/pbis-forum-2019-keynote-how-do-we-support-every-student-to-be-successful-in-school

McIntosh, K., & Goodman, S. (2016). *Integrated multi-tiered systems of support: Blending RTI and PBIS.* Guilford Publications.

McIntosh, K., Massar, M. M., Algozzine, R. F., George, H. P., Horner, R. H., Lewis, T. J., & Swain-Bradway, J. (2017). Technical adequacy of the SWPBIS tiered fidelity inventory. *Journal of Positive Behavior Interventions, 19*(1), 3–13. https://doi.org/f9qb8j

Miramontes, N. Y., Marchant, M., Heath, M. A., & Fischer, L. (2011). Social validity of a positive behavior interventions and support model. *Education and Treatment of Children, 34*(4), 445–468. https://doi.org/f9qd

Oakes, W. P., Lane, K. L., Cantwell, E. D., & Royer, D. J. (2017). Systematic screening for behavior in K-12 settings as regular school practice: Practical considerations and recommendations. *Journal of Applied School Psychology, 33*(4), 369–393. https://doi.org/f9qc

Peterson, L., Homer, A. L., & Wonderlich, S. A. (1982). The integrity of independent variables in behavior analysis. *Journal of Applied Behavior Analysis, 15*(4), 477–492. https://doi.org/fk485r

Sugai, G., & Horner, R. H. (2002). The evolution of discipline practices: School-wide positive behavior supports. *Child & Family Behavior Therapy, 24*(1–2), 23–50. https://doi.org/fhwspn

Sugai, G., Lewis-Palmer, T., Todd, A., & Horner, R. H. (2001). *School-wide evaluation tool.* University of Oregon.

VanDerHeyden, A. M., Witt, J. C., & Gilbertson, D. (2007). A multi-year evaluation of the effects of a response to intervention (RTI) model on identification of children for special education. *Journal of School Psychology, 45*(2), 225–256. https://doi.org/c8pbn9

Wolf, M. M. (1978). Social validity: The case for subjective measurement or how applied behavior analysis is finding its heart. *Journal of Applied Behavior Analysis, 11*(2), 203–214. https://doi.org/fj4vkr

4
READING ACHIEVEMENT AND GROWTH MINDSET OF STUDENTS WITH READING DIFFICULTIES OR READING DISABILITIES

Contemporary Research and Implications for Research and Practice

Stephanie Al Otaiba, Jeannie Wanzek, Mai Zaru, Rachel Donegan, Dayna Russell Freudenthal, Jennifer Stewart, Brenna Rivas, Christopher J. Lemons, and Yaacov Petscher

Despite the intent of the Every Student Succeeds Act of 2015 to improve academic performance by promoting evidence-based practices and multitiered systems of supports, less than a third of students with disabilities can read at even a basic level, which limits their success in other academic areas (National Center for Education Statistics, 2019). Thus, it may not be surprising that researchers have found that students with reading disabilities score lower in academic self-efficacy and motivation than peers without disabilities (Klassen, 2002; Lackaye & Margalit, 2006), which may limit their beliefs about their own efforts to improve, including engaging and persisting with reading tasks (Baird et al., 2009).

The purpose of this chapter is to summarize research that includes students identified as having reading difficulties or disabilities (Miciak & Fletcher, 2020) in order to better understand the relations among school-age (K-12) students' reading achievement and what Dweck and colleagues refer to as a growth mindset, or individuals' belief that their abilities can grow (e.g., Dweck, 2008; Yeager & Dweck, 2012). In our chapter, we use the term *mindset-related* or we use the term the study authors used to specify the construct. As we explain, mindset may include a constellation of related constructs, including attributions about effort (e.g., Weiner, 1985), motivation (e.g., Guthrie et al., 1998), and self-efficacy and self-concept (e.g., Bandura, 1977; Chapman & Tunmer, 2003). The chapter is not an exhaustive review, and given our focus, we did not incorporate self-regulated strategy instruction in reading (i.e., modeling, goal setting, and self-monitoring), but we refer readers to Berkeley and Larsen (2018) and Graham et al. (2014) for contemporary meta-analyses examining the effects of self-regulated reading comprehension strategy instruction and writing instruction for students with learning disabilities. We also limited our studies to those conducted in English within North America. First, we describe our theoretical framework for mindset-related constructs in relation to reading. Second, we summarize mindset-reading correlational research. Third, we synthesize a small but growing body of causal evidence for combining reading and mindset-related interventions on student performance in both domains. Finally, we discuss implications for research and practice and highlight some limitations and potential directions for future research.

Theoretical Framework

Given the complexity and lack of agreement about how to operationalize and measure psycho-social constructs (Duckworth & Yeager, 2015), our theoretical framework has several related strands. The first, and most proximal, strand is *growth mindset theory*, which suggests that individuals who believe that intelligence or academic success is malleable have stronger academic outcomes than those with a fixed mindset (e.g., Dweck, 2008). Students with a growth mindset are receptive to constructive feedback, learn from peer success, and adopt the idea that if they have not "yet" developed a skill, it can be developed with effort. Studies examining mindset in the general population have noted a growth mindset predicts better general academic performance for middle and high school students (e.g., Destin et al., 2019). Growth mindset has been adopted in many schools and organizations, but recent meta-analytic research suggests the relationship between mindset and academic outcomes might be smaller than some individual studies have reported (e.g., Costa & Faria, 2018 [ES = 0.07]; Sisk et al., 2018 [ES = 0.08]). However, Sisk et al.'s (2018) moderator analyses noted promising effects for students who were academically at risk (ES = 0.17) or were from low-socioeconomic status (SES) households (ES = 0.34). Given that students with reading difficulties or disabilities frequently experience failure, mindset theory suggests that training a growth mindset may be important, particularly since students receiving special education often demonstrate a more fixed mindset (Hartmann, 2013).

A second strand includes *attribution theory*, which posits that students attribute causes of their success to internal (e.g., innate reading ability or effort) or external sources (e.g., luck). Research suggests students with learning disabilities who attribute success to malleable internal sources demonstrate stronger gains in achievement, but are less likely than typically developing peers to attribute failure to a lack of effort rather than innate ability (e.g., Cox & Yang, 2012; Kistner et al., 1988; Tabassam & Granger, 2002). Research suggests that retraining students to attribute success to persistent effort and failure to insufficient effort may boost their motivation to use effective strategies (e.g., Robertson, 2000; Schunk & Cox, 1986; Shell et al., 1995).

A third related strand includes *motivation, and reading motivation theory* in particular (Morgan & Fuchs, 2007; Toste et al., 2020). Motivation is a multidimensional construct which includes extrinsic motivation (performing a task for external contingent rewards, such as grades) and intrinsic motivation (performing a task for enjoyment or personal improvement) (i.e., Conradi et al., 2014; Schiefele et al., 2012). In a recent meta-analytic review, Toste et al. (2020) reported a significant and moderate correlation ($r = 0.22$) between motivation and reading that was larger when samples included students with learning disabilities. However, some researchers report reading skills predict motivation (Hebbecker et al., 2019), whereas others report the inverse relationship (Park, 2011). There is also disagreement about whether motivation generally decreases across the grades (e.g., Lazowski & Hulleman, 2016), and if the association between reading and motivation starts early, and is consistent across time (e.g., Morgan & Fuchs, 2007).

The fourth strand includes *self-concept and self-efficacy theory* (e.g., Bandura, 1977; Chapman & Tunmer, 2003), or the belief that one has the ability to succeed in the face of challenges. Some researchers suggest self-concept is related to reading achievement (e.g., Quirk et al., 2009), but others caution this relation is small after accounting for earlier reading skill (e.g., Conradi et al., 2014). In a recent meta-analysis Unrau et al. (2018) examined the effect of interventions on reading that also focused on self-efficacy. Small but statistically significant positive increases (ES = 0.24) were reported that were stronger in elementary grades (ES = 0.53). Effects were similar for students with reading difficulties versus typical readers.

Relationships Among Mindset-Related Constructs and Reading Achievement for Students With Reading Difficulties or Disabilities

By the upper elementary level, students are expected to have learned to read, and instruction focuses more on comprehension and learning from reading, and so developing a mindset to overcome reading difficulties are foundational to success. We first summarize findings from two series of studies conducted by two research teams in upper elementary settings and then describe a study conducted in middle school. Cho and her colleagues conducted a series of three studies in the upper elementary grades. In their first study, Cho et al. (2015) examined self-efficacy of 165 students in fourth grade who had reading difficulties (defined as scoring below the 25th percentile in reading comprehension). Students with reading difficulties demonstrated lower overall self-efficacy than typical readers. Next, Cho et al. (2018) examined the associations among reading achievement and mindset-related constructs, including perceived competence, mastery goals (i.e., a focus on mastering tasks) and performance goals (a performance approach, defined as judging performance relative to other students vs. performance avoidance, defined as avoiding failure). Participants were 112 fourth- and fifth-grade students with reading difficulties (below the 25th percentile in word reading). The struggling readers with more positive perceptions of reading competence demonstrated stronger word reading and comprehension performance; this viewpoint had a positive moderating role that countered performance-avoidance goals. Somewhat surprisingly, struggling readers' mastery goals negatively predicted word reading, whereas the overall classroom mastery goal structure positively predicted reading comprehension, suggesting struggling readers may benefit from instructional environments that encourage a growth mindset.

In their third study, Cho et al. (2019) examined associations among reading comprehension, student mindset, mastery and performance goals, and engagement (self-report and teacher-rated). Participants included 107 fourth- and fifth-grade students with reading difficulties (below the 25th percentile in word reading). There was no direct effect of mindset on reading comprehension; rather the associations were mediated by mastery and performance-avoidance achievement goals. Students with a more fixed mindset were less likely to demonstrate mastery goals and more likely to avoid failure. Engagement was vital, entirely mediating the effect of mastery goals on reading comprehension. Cho et al. suggested struggling readers may benefit when reading instruction also supports engagement, motivation, mindset, and mastery goals.

Our own research team conducted a set of three studies, all in fourth grade, to inform psychometric issues for measuring mindset and its relation to reading. First, Petscher et al. (2017) explored whether general or reading-specific mindset items (Al Otaiba et al., 2015) were separate constructs when predicting reading comprehension. A majority of the 195 participating students had reading difficulties (below the 30th percentile for reading comprehension), and 7% had a disability. Students' general mindset was assessed using the *Mindset Assessment Profile* (*MAP*; Mindset Works, 2019), and their reading-specific mindset was assessed using the *Reading Mindset Measure* (Al Otaiba et al., 2015). We found a bifactor model with a global mindset factor and separate general and reading-specific mindset factors best explained the data, with both factors predicting reading comprehension achievement (controlling for initial word reading abilities). Global mindset was more strongly associated with reading comprehension for students with weaker reading comprehension skills; reading mindset was more strongly related to comprehension for those with stronger reading comprehension skills. The second study (Petscher et al., 2021) included a larger sample ($n = 431$) and focused only on *MAP*. A majority of students had reading difficulties, and 9% had a learning disability. We explored whether global mindset-related subgroups performed differently on standardized measures of word reading, vocabulary, and reading comprehension outcomes. Three factors best fit the data: growth mindset, fixed mindset, and effort. Students with a growth mindset and above-average effort (i.e., who believed their academic skills could improve with effort) showed the strongest reading performance. By contrast, students with more fixed mindset profiles had lower reading performance. In the third study, Tock et al. (2020) analyzed data from the Petscher et al. (2021) study and specifically focused on the psychometric properties of the *Reading Mindset Measure* (Al Otaiba et al., 2015). The measure predicted student reading comprehension scores above and beyond word reading. Students with low word reading who had a more positive reading mindset scored higher than those with more fixed mindsets.

The study with the oldest participating students in this review was conducted by Chapman et al. (2018), who examined the relations between self-perceptions and reading achievement among sixth-grade students with reading difficulties. They used a measure that asked students to report perceptions of their reading skills relative to peers, perceptions about messages from peers or teachers regarding their reading, perceptions about their learning and growth in reading (progress), and how reading made them feel. Researchers conducted a cluster analysis that categorized students into profiles: (a) average reader self-perception, (b) low reader self-perception, and (c) very low reader self-perception. Reading achievement did not significantly differentiate profiles, nor did disability status. Thus, these older struggling readers had variable reading self-perception that was not explained by their reading achievement or disability.

Effects of Reading and Mindset-Related Interventions for Students With Reading Difficulties or Disabilities

In this next section, we describe contemporary research examining the effects of interventions that included reading interventions and mindset-related interventions. To show the progress in developing and testing these interventions, we present studies in chronological order; these are subdivided into six studies in elementary and two in middle and high school settings.

Effects of Elementary-Grade Interventions

The oldest and most studied intervention was Concept Oriented Reading Instruction (CORI, e.g., Guthrie et al., 1998), a multicomponent reading program that includes supports for motivation, fluency, content knowledge, and reading comprehension. At least one CORI study reported disaggregated effects for students with reading difficulties; Guthrie et al. (2009) used a pretest-posttest quasi-experimental design and included 156 fifth-grade students. Those with reading difficulties scored at a 4.0 grade equivalent for reading comprehension. Schools were assigned to condition, with two CORI schools (n = 94 students in six classrooms) and one business as usual (BAU) school that provided traditional instruction (n = 62 students in three classrooms). CORI and BAU students performed similarly at pretest on all reading measures and had similar demographics. Research-trained school personnel provided students 12 weeks of daily 90-minute whole-group and small-group instruction (three to six students). The homogeneous groups who had reading difficulties focused on fluency practice, one-on-one word recognition and decoding instruction, and explicit inferencing lessons with science content. For all students, CORI motivational and mindset-related practices incorporated (a) student choice of texts and subtopics, (b) relevance to student experience, (c) success with trade books at the student's reading level, (d) peer collaboration, and (e) thematic units to support depth of knowledge. Students in the BAU condition also received 90 minutes of daily reading instruction. CORI students scored significantly higher than BAU students at posttest on reading comprehension (ES = 0.59), word recognition (ES = 0.87), and science content knowledge (ES = 1.59) and marginally higher on inferencing (ES = 0.54). There were no significant differences in motivation scores, which differed from previous studies of CORI, where effects on motivation and reading were more consistently observed. However, students with reading difficulties scored significantly lower than typical students on inferencing (ES = -1.12) and fluency measures (ES = -1.68). Moreover, there were no significant interactions with condition, revealing that for students with reading difficulties, CORI was not more effective than BAU. Strong correlations were observed between posttest reading and motivational variables (i.e., perceived difficulty and avoidance).

Nearly a decade after the Guthrie et al. study, Orkin et al. (2018) also combined a multicomponent reading intervention with mindset-like intrinsic motivation components. They examined the impact of a five-week (two hours daily) summer reading program that included both Wilson and RAVE-O reading interventions (Wilson, 2011; Wolf, 2010); participants were randomly assigned to an intrinsic motivation "treatment" condition or to a "control" condition that provided more typical extrinsic motivation (rewards and a token economy). The intrinsic treatment engaged students by building autonomy, sense of belonging, peer support, and other mindset-related activities. The 47 participants ranged from grades 2 to 4; 21 students had dyslexia, and 10 had a clinical diagnosis of anxiety or attention deficit hyperactivity disorder (ADHD). Most were White (84%), and all spoke English as a first language. Significant differences on posttest reading scores favored students in the intrinsic treatment condition (ES = 0.24), who also demonstrated increased engagement (ES = 0.37) and reduced avoidance behaviors (ES = 0.52).

Toste and her colleagues conducted a series of two studies that also examined the effects of reading interventions embedded with mindset-like training, including intrinsic motivation and attribution (Toste et al., 2017; Toste et al., 2019). Their first study included 59 students with reading difficulties in grades 3 to 4 nominated by their teachers and who screened in with word reading below the 37th percentile. Researchers randomly assigned students (within grade-level blocks) to one of two treatment conditions (multisyllabic word-reading intervention only or combined training) or to a BAU condition. Student ethnicity varied at the two schools, with a majority of students being Hispanic (68.5% and 95%) at both schools and other students being Black (11.5% and 1.5%), White (15% and 2.5%), or Other (5%). Most students received free and reduced lunch (FARL).

Research-trained interventionists worked with two to three students for 40 minutes three times per week for eight weeks. Both treatment conditions used the same explicit scripted reading intervention focusing on reading, blending, segmenting, and spelling for multisyllabic words, followed by repeated reading of connected text to apply these word-reading skills. In the reading plus mindset-related training condition, the aim was to increase student motivation and positive self-talk, or affirmations about effort. Interventionists modeled and scaffolded students in replacing negative with positive attributions. Students in the BAU condition received the same core reading instruction. Findings revealed students in both reading intervention conditions significantly outperformed students in the BAU condition on sight word efficiency (ES = 0.73). There were no significant differences on other reading measures, but moderate effect sizes favored both intervention conditions over BAU for timed phonemic decoding (ES = 0.31) and letter-word identification (ES = 0.29), and for untimed word attack (ES = 0.30). Students who received the combined reading and motivation intervention scored statistically higher than students in the reading-only condition on sentence comprehension (ES = 0.61). Students in both treatment conditions scored significantly higher than the BAU on a measure of reading attribution (*Reading Attribution Scale*, Berkeley et al., 2011), on their attributions for success and failure on internal (ability, effort, and strategy use) variables, and lower attributions for external variables (teacher assistance, luck, interest, or difficulty of task).

In their second study, Toste et al. (2019) replicated the same treatment conditions with slightly older students in grades 4 and 5 in three elementary schools. Schools identified low-performing students based on universal screening data, then researchers selected students who screened as performing below the 25th percentile on word reading. The 114 participating students were randomly assigned to one of two reading treatments (i.e., multisyllabic word-reading intervention with or without motivation training) or to a BAU control condition. The majority of participating students qualified for FARL; a majority were Hispanic (88.07%) and nearly a third (26.61%) were English learners (Els), which motivated the researchers to explore whether EL status moderated treatment effects. The intervention conditions were similar to their prior study—four times per week but with a longer dosage (40 sessions). Toste et al. introduced additional mindset-like aspects related to effort, goal setting, and identifying strengths linked to achieving reading goals. They included most measures from the prior study with some modifications. For example, they administered a proximal measure of the multisyllabic taught words. They substituted the *Reading Self-Concept Scale* (Chapman & Tunmer, 1999) for the *Reading Attribution Scale*. There were no significant differences between treatment groups. Findings revealed that students in both treatment conditions demonstrated significantly stronger gains relative to the BAU condition on the proximal reading measure (ES = 0.90), on most standardized measures of decoding (ES ranging from 0.17 to 0.43), spelling (ES = 0.25), and one measure of comprehension (ES = 0.26). These effects were similar for ELs, except that non-ELs demonstrated stronger growth on spelling. However, the differences in the *Reading Self-Concept Scale* were only significant for the attitude subscale, but surprisingly, this difference favored the control condition. Toste et al. noted that shifting intervention toward goal planning may have inadvertently made students more aware of their challenges and that students may not have had enough practice to see the fruits of their effort.

A recent study tested the feasibility of combining reading and a mindset-related intervention included students in grades 2 to 4 with reading difficulties and disabilities (Denton et al., 2020). This quasi-experimental study involved eight schools, with teachers randomly assigned to treatment ($n = 10$) or BAU ($n = 11$) conditions. Teachers in the two conditions differed—most treatment teachers were certified to teach special or elementary education, but most teachers in the BAU group were reading interventionists, and 18% were uncertified instructional aides. Students were initially identified by their classroom teachers as having reading difficulty; researchers included students with screening scores below the 25th percentile for word reading. The final sample included 43 students (23 treatment and 20 BAU), but notably students in the BAU had significantly higher pretest reading scores, and though not significant, there was a higher proportion of students with disabilities in the treatment condition. Treatment teachers implemented the intervention four days a week for a total of 26 weeks across two phases. Phase 1 focused on foundational reading skills (e.g., phonemic awareness, reading decodable texts, guided questions) and practice toward mastery; Phase 2 incorporated more advanced reading skills (multisyllabic words, oral reading fluency, and comprehension strategy instruction) and structured support for a growth mindset. In the BAU condition, teachers also provided students with supplemental intervention ($M = 81$ days; SD = 37) ranging from a structured dyslexia program, computerized word reading and fluency intervention, a fluency program, or a combination of these interventions. At posttest, there were no significant differences between conditions on standardized reading measures. In fact, small to moderate effects favored the BAU condition on passage comprehension (ES = –0.57) and fluency (ES = –0.46). However, when examining a subgroup of students diagnosed with dyslexia, there was a moderate effect favoring the treatment condition on sight-word efficiency (ES = 0.60). The qualitative analysis of the feedback researchers collected from treatment teachers indicated teachers reported positive effects of growth mindset training on student confidence and of teaching students to recognize negative self-statements and replace them with positive self-talk. It is important to interpret these findings with caution given pretreatment differences between conditions; replication is needed.

Another recent study with a larger sample size was conducted by Wanzek et al. (2020), who compared the effects of reading intervention alone, reading intervention plus a standalone mindset intervention, and a BAU condition on reading and mindset performance. Fourth-graders with reading difficulties were initially identified by their classroom teachers and were selected to participate if they scored below the 30th percentile on a word reading test. These 361 students were assigned to the three conditions using stratified random assignment within schools. Schools indicated 14% of students were identified with disability; 50% had specific learning disabilities, 14% had speech or language impairments, 10% had other health impairment, 2% had emotional/behavior impairment, 2% had autism, and the remainder were unspecified. Roughly half of participants were female (51%); 74% qualified for FARL. The sample was a majority minority sample, with nearly half (46%) identifying as Hispanic in ethnicity, and in terms of race, 42% identified as Black, 18% as White, 5% as American Indian, 1% as Asian, and the remaining students' schools did not report their race.

For the reading intervention in both treatment conditions, trained research staff provided small-group instruction reading intervention (three to five students) 45 minutes per day using a multi-component reading program focusing on phonics and a word reading structured literacy program (*Lindamood Phoneme Sequencing Program [LiPs]*; Lindamood & Lindamood, 2011). On average students received 73.5 sessions across the school year. For the reading plus mindset treatment condition, other staff provided a standalone mindset intervention, including teacher-led and online activities about growth mindset (*Brainology*; Mindset Works, Inc., 2016); this occurred in groups of four to seven students for 24 sessions scheduled twice weekly for 30 minutes. Schools provided some students with supplemental reading instruction, but no mindset training. Wanzek et al. (2020) used a multilevel structural equation analysis to account for students being nested in treatment groups and in schools that revealed similar effects favoring both treatment conditions relative to the BAU, demonstrating small effects for nonword reading (ES = 0.29 to 0.35), phonological processing (ES = 0.20 to 0.28), and reading comprehension (ES = 0.19 to 0.23). Future research may explore whether students would benefit if mindset intervention is explicitly embedded in the content area of reading. Moderation analyses revealed no differences based on initial characteristics, including reading achievement, mindset, or problem behavior.

Struggling Readers in Middle and High School

Berkeley et al. (2011) was an example of a relatively early study that examined the effects of brief reading comprehension strategy instruction with and without attribution retraining. Participants ($n = 59$) in middle and high school (grades 7 to 9) and were identified by their schools as having learning or other mild disabilities. A majority were boys (67.79%); most (76.27%) had a learning disability and the remainder had other health impairment (OHI). In terms of ethnicity, 49.15% were Black, 38.98% were Hispanic, and the remainder were White. Researchers stratified students by class and then randomly assigned them to two treatment conditions: reading comprehension strategy intervention or reading comprehension strategy intervention plus attribution retraining, or to a BAU comparison condition. The study involved a pretest-posttest design and also included a six-week maintenance posttest.

The interventionists included researchers and school staff who provided 12- to 30-minute intervention sessions over one month that included reading comprehension strategy lessons (i.e., setting the purpose for reading, previewing, background knowledge activation, self-questioning, summarizing, and strategy monitoring). The attribution retraining included explicit instruction to identify external and false attributions for success and failure (i.e., luck) and to replace these with internal attributions for success (i.e., use of the appropriate strategies). In the BAU comparison condition, school personnel used a reading fluency and comprehension training program that required students to monitor and graph their word reading fluency growth.

Findings revealed that students in the reading comprehension strategy group with or without attribution training significantly outperformed students in the BAU condition on a proximal reading summarization test (ES = 1.44 and 0.94, respectively), and no differences between treated conditions were seen. At the six-week delayed posttest, this pattern continued (ES = 1.21 and 0.71, respectively). Similar effects were found on a researcher-developed meta-comprehension strategy awareness test. Students in the reading comprehension strategy plus attribution retraining condition significantly outperformed students in both other conditions on the items on the reading success subscale (on a measure adapted from the *Reading Attribution Scale*; Shell et al., 1995) measured at posttest (ES = 1.01 relative to the comprehension-only and ES = 0.86 compared to the BAU conditions). At the delayed posttest, there remained a statistically significant difference only for the combined condition relative to the BAU (ES = 0.54). There were no significant differences at any time between conditions for the items on the reading failure subscale. An implication of the Berkeley et al. (2011) study was that older students with a learning disability or OHI benefited from comprehension strategy instruction and also benefited from attribution retraining in terms of reading success.

The most recent study involved a large sample of 514 adolescents (grades 6 to 8) identified with a reading disability (Lovett et al., 2020). The majority of students were White (51.2%); the remainder were Black, Hispanic, or Other (32%, 10.5%, and 6.3%, respectively). All students spoke English as a primary language. Students were matched on word reading and randomly assigned to condition; teachers provided interventions to small groups of four to eight students for a total of 125 hours (45 to 60 minutes a session). Students assigned to PHAST (Phonological and Strategy Training; Lovett et al., 2000) reading with a comprehension focus received additional comprehension training through reciprocal teaching (e.g., activate their schema, make predictions, construct questions, etc.) that fostered deep comprehension. Students assigned to reading with a fluency-focus condition received additional fluency training by providing multiple opportunities to engage and practice sounds, words, compound words, and reading texts. In both PHAST conditions, a mindset-like motivational feature was embedded to support self-efficacy and attributions for effort through dialogue and small-group interactions. Students assigned to the BAU condition received locally developed reading programs provided by special education teachers that incorporated decoding, reading comprehension, and writing skills, but with no additional motivational elements.

Lovett and colleagues (2020) reported both reading interventions were significantly more effective than the BAU, with a large mean effect size (across eight reading measures) of ES = 0.70). Researchers also reported a significant effect on sense of competence and attribution in favor of the two PHAST conditions (ES = 0.27 and ES = 0.38, respectively). Findings suggest that a multicomponent intervention that included reading and mindset-like motivational aspects was effective for older students with reading disabilities.

Implications and Next Steps for Research and Practice

The purpose of this chapter was to summarize the current research regarding relations between mindset-related constructs and reading achievement and to describe the effects of mindset-related and reading interventions for students with reading difficulties and disabilities on reading and mindset. We limited our review to interventions in English and to North America, which we thought would ease interpretations. However, we still encountered several challenges in comparing study findings related to differences in how researchers operationalized and measured mindset-like constructs (e.g., Duckworth & Yeager, 2015) and reading performance. For example, researchers categorized reading difficulties and disabilities differently across studies, although such differences are consistent with identification issues in the broader research and policy (e.g., Miciak & Fletcher, 2020). Several researchers used a brief standardized word reading screener to confirm risk, such as the Test of Word Reading Efficiency-2 (Torgesen et al., 2012). Using a common screener and more consistent measures might allow researchers to combine their relatively small data sets into larger databases (e.g., Daucourt et al., 2018). This would be helpful in the future, as many sample sizes in the current research base were relatively small, which precluded many researchers from conducting moderation analyses to build a much-needed better understanding of the importance of mindset-like constructs and their malleability and also an understanding of individual differences in response for students with disabilities.

There are several important implications for research and practice stemming from this that extend prior correlational research in the general population (e.g., Costa & Faria, 2018; Sisk et al., 2018). First, across several studies and grade levels (the majority of which focused on the mid-to-late elementary grades), students with reading difficulties or disabilities demonstrated lower mindset-related constructs, including a general or reading mindset, self-concept, self-efficacy, and motivation in reading, when compared to typical readers. Generally, these constructs were correlated to or predictive of reading achievement. An exception was that Chapman et al. (2018) reported that middle school students' reading self-perceptions were not related to reading achievement or to their disability status. To date, the studies of the relationship between mindset and reading outcomes for students with reading difficulties or disabilities have mostly been conducted at the upper elementary level. Research is needed to clarify the directionality of the relationships, if they can be identified earlier, and their short- vs. longer-term influence.

There are also important implications for research and practice related to intervention studies. The majority, six of the eight intervention studies, were conducted within elementary school grades with either trained school personnel or research staff providing small-group interventions. The intervention studies that we reviewed had relatively strong research designs: All but one study incorporated a randomized control trial, but many had relatively small sample sizes. These reading interventions included multiple reading components (word reading, fluency, comprehension). Encouragingly, when compared to a BAU, the effects of elementary-grade reading interventions with (and without) mindset-related components were generally positive, with small to moderate effects on standardized reading measures and moderate to large effects on proximal measures (with the exception of Denton et al., 2020 and Guthrie et al., 2009). In one of Toste et al.'s studies (2017), they also found a statistically significant difference between treatment conditions which favored reading plus mindset-related intervention, but only on a measure of sentence comprehension. In addition, Orkin et al. (2018) found significantly stronger reading and mindset-related performance (engagement and reduced avoidance) for students in a reading plus intrinsic motivation treatment than those who did not receive the intrinsic motivation. The two studies conducted with middle and high school students also provided two treatments in contrast to a BAU condition and reported significantly different reading achievement, with large effects favoring the treatment conditions. These effects persisted at a six-week delayed maintenance test (Berkeley et al., 2011) and at one-year follow-up (Lovett et al., 2020). Berkeley et al. reported significantly stronger mindset-related performance (i.e., attributions) for students in their reading comprehension strategy plus attribution condition than for students who did not receive the attribution training, which remained at the delayed posttest.

Future research is needed to replicate and extend this research base to determine whether mindset-related training adds value to the reading interventions and for whom this works best (students with disabilities, minority students). To date, mindset-related training was compared to reading-only intervention, or sometimes the mindset-related interventions differed, and only one study provided a standalone commercially available program (Wanzek et al., 2020). It is important to clarify mindset-like constructs and develop measures with stronger psychometric properties. Using common tools and common observation protocols to assess mindset-related constructs would also allow researchers to compare findings and to combine databases to include larger numbers of students identified with reading difficulties vs. reading disabilities. Furthermore, it is important to study early literacy and mindset interventions with younger students, before they experience failure, and to older students, who have reading disabilities.

Author Note

The research reported here was supported by the Institute of Education Sciences, U.S. Department of Education, through Grant R305A200397 and Grant R01HD091232 by the Eunice Kennedy Shriver National Institute of Child Health & Human Development of the National Institutes of Health. The opinions expressed are those of the authors and do not represent views of the institute or the U.S. Department of Education or the National Institutes of Health.

References

Al Otaiba, S., Rivas, B., Jones, F., Petscher, Y., & Wanzek, J. (2015). *Reading growth mindset*. Unpublished test, College of Education, Southern Methodist University, Dallas, TX.

Baird, G. L., Scott, W. D., Dearing, E., & Hamill, S. K. (2009). Cognitive self regulation in youth with and without learning disabilities: Academic self-efficacy, theories of intelligence, learning vs. performance goal preferences, and effort attributions. *Journal of Social and Clinical Psychology, 28*, 881–908.

Bandura, A. (1977). Self-efficacy: Toward a unifying theory of behavioral change. *Psychological Review, 84*(2), 191–215.

Berkeley, S., & Larsen, A. (2018). Fostering self-regulation of students with learning disabilities: Insights from 30 years of reading comprehension intervention research. *Learning Disabilities Research & Practice, 33*(2), 75–86

Berkeley, S., Mastropieri, M. A., & Scruggs, T. E. (2011). Reading comprehension strategy instruction and attribution retraining for secondary students with learning and other mild disabilities. *Journal of Learning Disabilities, 44*(1), 18–32.

Chapman, J. W., & Tunmer, W. E. (1999). Reading self-concept scale. In R. Burden (Ed.), *Children's self-perceptions* (pp. 29–34). NFER-Nelson.

Chapman, J. W., & Tunmer, W. E. (2003). Reading difficulties, reading-related self-perceptions, and strategies for overcoming negative self-beliefs. *Reading & Writing Quarterly, 19*(1), 5–24.

Chapman, L. A., Calhoon, M. B., & Krawec, J. (2018). Using cluster analysis to explore differences in the reader self-perceptions of adolescent struggling readers. *Middle Grades Research Journal, 12*(1), 39–50.

Cho, E., Lee, M., & Toste, J. R. (2018). Does perceived competence serve as a protective mechanism against performance goals for struggling readers? Path analysis of contextual antecedents and reading outcomes. *Learning and Individual Differences, 65*, 135–147.

Cho, E., Roberts, G. J., Capin, P., Roberts, G., Miciak, J., & Vaughn, S. (2015). Cognitive attributes, attention, and self-efficacy of adequate and inadequate responders in a fourth grade reading intervention. *Learning Disabilities Research & Practice, 30*(4), 159–170.

Cho, E., Toste, J. R., Lee, M., & Ju, U. (2019). Motivational predictors of struggling readers' reading comprehension: The effects of mindset, achievement goals, and engagement. *Reading and Writing, 32*(5), 1219–1242.

Conradi, K., Jang, B. G., & McKenna, M. C. (2014). Motivation terminology in reading research: A conceptual review. *Educational Psychology Review, 26*(1), 127–164.

Costa, A., & Faria, L. (2018). Implicit theories of intelligence and academic achievement: A meta-analytic review. *Frontiers in Psychology, 9*, 829.

Cox, C. B., & Yang, Y. (2012). Getting off on the wrong foot: Longitudinal effects of Hispanic students' stability attributions following poor initial test performance. *Learning and Individual Differences, 22*(1), 123–127.

Daucourt, M. C., Schatschneider, C., Connor, C. M., Al Otaiba, S., & Hart, S. A. (2018). Inhibition, updating working memory, and shifting predict reading disability symptoms in a hybrid model: Project KIDS. *Frontiers in Psychology, 9*, 238. https://doi.org/10.3389/fpsyg.2018.00238

Denton, C. A., Montroy, J. J., Zucker, T. A., & Cannon, G. (2020). Designing an intervention in reading and self-regulation for students with significant reading difficulties, including dyslexia. *Learning Disability Quarterly*, Advance online publication.

Destin, M., Hanselman, P., Buontempo, J., Tipton, E., & Yeager, D. S. (2019). Do student mindsets differ by socioeconomic status and explain disparities in academic achievement in the United States? *AERA Oopen, 5*(3).

Duckworth, A. L., & Yeager, D. S. (2015). Measurement matters: Assessing personal qualities other than cognitive ability for educational purposes. *Educational Researcher, 44*(4), 237–251.

Dweck, C. (2008). *Mindset: The new psychology of success*. Random House Digital, Inc.

Graham, S., Harris, K. R., & McKeown, D. (2014). The writing of students with learning disabilities, meta-analysis of self-regulated strategy development writing intervention studies, and future directions: Redux.

In H. L. Swanson, K. R. Harris, & S. Graham (Eds.), *Handbook of learning disabilities* (pp. 405–438). The Guilford Press.

Guthrie, J. T., McRae, A., Coddington, C. S., Lutz Klauda, S., Wigfield, A., & Barbosa, P. (2009). Impacts of comprehensive reading instruction on diverse outcomes of low- and high-achieving readers. *Journal of Learning Disabilities, 42*(3), 195–214.

Guthrie, J. T., Van Meter, P., & Hancock, G. (1998). Does concept-oriented reading instruction increase strategy use and conceptual learning from text? *Journal of Educational Psychology, 90*(2), 261–278.

Hartmann, G. M. (2013). *The relationship between mindset and students with specific learning disabilities* [Doctoral dissertation]. Humboldt State University.

Hebbecker, K., Förster, N., & Souvignier, E. (2019). Reciprocal effects between reading achievement and intrinsic and extrinsic reading motivation. *Scientific Studies of Reading, 23*(5), 419–436.

Kistner, J. A., Osborne, M., & LeVerrier, L. (1988). Causal attributions of learning-disabled children: Developmental patterns and relation to academic progress. *Journal of Educational Psychology, 80*(1), 82.

Klassen, R. (2002). A question of calibration: A review of the self-efficacy beliefs of students with learning disabilities. *Learning Disability Quarterly, 25*(2), 88–102.

Lackaye, T. D., & Margalit, M. (2006). Comparisons of achievement, effort, and self-perceptions among students with learning disabilities and their peers from different achievement groups. *Journal of Learning Disabilities, 39*(5), 432–446.

Lazowski, R. A., & Hulleman, C. S. (2016). Motivation interventions in education: A meta-analytic review. *Review of Educational Research, 86*(2), 602–640.

Lindamood, P. (2011). *Lindamood phonemic sequencing (LiPS) program*. Pro-Ed.

Lovett, M. W., Frijters, J. C., Steinbach, K. A., Sevcik, R. A., & Morris, R. D. (2020). Effective intervention for adolescents with reading disabilities: Combining reading and motivational remediation to improve outcomes. *Journal of Educational Psychology*. Advance online publication.

Lovett, M. W., Lacerenza, L., & Borden, S. L. (2000). Putting struggling readers on the PHAST track: A program to integrate phonological and strategy-based remedial reading instruction and maximize outcomes. *Journal of Learning Disabilities, 33*(5), 458–476.

Miciak, J., & Fletcher, J. M. (2020). The critical role of instructional response for identifying dyslexia and other learning disabilities. *Journal of Learning Disabilities, 53*(5), 343–353.

Morgan, P. L., & Fuchs, D. (2007). Is there a bidirectional relationship between children's reading skills and reading motivation? *Exceptional Children, 73*(2), 165–183.

National Center for Education Statistics., National Assessment of Educational Progress (Project), Educational Testing Service., & United States. (2019). *NAEP . . . reading report card for the nation and the states*. Washington, DC: National Center for Education Statistics, Office of Educational Research and Improvement, U.S. Dept. of Education.

Orkin, M., Pott, M., Wolf, M., May, S., & Brand, E. (2018). Beyond gold stars: Improving the skills and engagement of struggling readers through intrinsic motivation. *Reading & Writing Quarterly, 34*(3), 203–217.

Park, Y. (2011). How motivational constructs interact to predict elementary students' reading performance: Examples from attitudes and self-concept in reading. *Learning and Individual Differences, 21*(4), 347–358.

Petscher, Y., Al Otaiba, S., & Wanzek, J. (2021). Study of the factor structure, profiles, and concurrent validity of the mindset assessment profile tool for elementary students. *Journal of Psychoeducational Assessment, 39*(1), 74–88.

Petscher, Y., Al Otaiba, S., Wanzek, J., Rivas, B., & Jones, F. (2017). The relation between global and specific mindset with reading outcomes for elementary school students. *Scientific Studies of Reading, 21*, 376–391.

Quirk, M., Schwanenflugel, P. J., & Webb, M. Y. (2009). A short-term longitudinal study of the relationship between motivation to read and reading fluency skill in second grade. *Journal of Literacy Research, 41*(2), 196–227.

Robertson, J. S. (2000). Is attribution training a worthwhile classroom intervention for K—12 students with learning difficulties? *Educational Psychology Review, 12*(1), 111–134.

Schiefele, U., Schaffner, E., Möller, J., & Wigfield, A. (2012). Dimensions of reading motivation and their relation to reading behavior and competence. *Reading Research Quarterly, 47*(4), 427–463.

Schunk, D. H., & Cox, P. D. (1986). Strategic training and attributional feedback with learning disabled students. *Journal of Educational Psychology, 78*, 201–209.

Shell, D. F., Colvin, C., & Bruning, R. H. (1995). Self-efficacy, attribution, and outcome expectancy mechanisms in reading and writing achievement: Grade-level and achievement-level differences. *Journal of Educational Psychology, 87*(3), 386.

Sisk, V. F., Burgoyne, A. P., Sun, J., Butler, J. L., & Macnamara, B. N. (2018). To what extent and under which circumstances are growth mind-sets important to academic achievement? Two meta-analyses. *Psychological science, 29*(4), 549–571.

Tabassam, W., & Granger, J. (2002). Self-concept, attributional style and self-efficacy beliefs of students with learning disabilities with and without attention deficit hyperactivity disorder. *Learning Disability Quarterly, 25*, 141–151.

Tock, J. L., Quinn, J. M., Otaiba, S. A., Petscher, Y., & Wanzek, J. (2020). Establishing a reading mindset measure: A validation study. *Assessment for Effective Intervention*, Advance online publication.

Torgesen, J. K., Wagner, R. K., & Rashotte, C. A. (2012). *TOWRE-2 examiner's manual.* Pro-Ed.

Toste, J. R., Capin, P., Vaughn, S., Roberts, G. J., & Kearns, D. M. (2017). Multisyllabic word-reading instruction with and without motivational beliefs training for struggling readers in the upper elementary grades: A pilot investigation. *Elementary School Journal, 117*(4), 593–615.

Toste, J. R., Capin, P., Williams, K. J., Cho, E., & Vaughn, S. (2019). Replication of an experimental study investigating the efficacy of a multisyllabic word reading intervention with and without motivational beliefs training for struggling readers. *Journal of Learning Disabilities, 52*(1), 45–58.

Toste, J. R., Didion, L., Peng, P., Filderman, M. J., & McClelland, A. M. (2020). A meta-analytic review of the relations between motivation and reading achievement for K 12 students. *Review of Educational Research, 90*(3), 420–456.

Unrau, N. J., Rueda, R., Son, E., Polanin, J. R., Lundeen, R. J., & Muraszewski, A. K. (2018). Can reading self-efficacy be modified? A meta-analysis of the impact of interventions on reading self-efficacy. *Review of Educational Research, 88*(2), 167–204.

Wanzek, J., Otaiba, S. A., Petscher, Y., Lemons, C. J., Gesel, S. A., Fluhler, S., . . . Rivas, B. K. (2020). Comparing the effects of reading intervention versus reading and mindset intervention for upper elementary students with reading difficulties. *Journal of Learning Disabilities, 54*(3), 203–220.

Weiner, B. (1985). An attributional theory of achievement motivation and emotion. *Psychological review, 92*(4), 548.

Wilson, B. A. (2011). *Wilson reading system.* Wilson Language Training Corporation.

Wolf, M. (2010). *The RAVE-O program.* Longview, CO: Cambium/Sopris Learning.

Yeager, D. S., & Dweck, C. S. (2012). Mindsets that promote resilience: When students believe that personal characteristics can be developed. *Educational Psychologist, 47*(4), 302–314.

5
WELL-BEING OF EDUCATORS WORKING IN TIERED SYSTEMS

Wendy Peia Oakes, Kathleen Lynne Lane, David James Royer, Holly M. Menzies, and Nelson C. Brunsting

The retention of teachers is a complex issue with direct effects on the overall health of school systems. The well-being of teachers has critical implications for teacher retention (Billingsley & Bettini, 2019), school organizational health (Guin, 2004), and student learning outcomes (Hanushek et al., 2016; Ronfeldt et al., 2013). In this chapter, we discuss teachers' well-being within tiered systems. We define well-being to include a teacher's sense of efficacy, the belief in one's capabilities to affect positive outcomes (Bandura, 1993), and the ability to cope, which serves to mitigate effects of professional stressors (Herman et al., 2018). Retention, or stability, of teachers includes staying in the profession and at a school site.

We begin with an overview of implications of well-being on teacher retention and student learning. Next, we offer an overview of tiered systems with attention to how these systems provide support for educators' well-being and factors that lead to teacher burnout and turnover. We summarize research conducted to date and end with implications for the field related to promoting well-being for teachers working in tiered systems.

Teacher Well-Being, Stability, and Student Outcomes

Approximately 16% of teachers in the United States leave the profession each year, and 19% to 30% of teachers leave within the first five years; these rates are even higher for teachers in Title 1 schools; those in special education; and those in science, technology, engineering, and mathematics (STEM; Sutcher et al., 2016). Collectively, the financial strain on schools is more than $8 billion in replacement costs, with high-poverty schools further disadvantaged due to higher turnover rates (Carver-Thomas & Darling Hammond, 2017; Sutcher et al., 2016). In addition to the financial cost, lack of teacher stability makes it difficult for schools to provide consistently positive and effective learning environments.

General and special education teachers leave the profession due to a variety of school-level factors, including lack of perceived administrative support, limited influence on practices in their school, role ambiguity, student behavior and discipline practices, school culture, collegial relationships, lack of time for collaboration and planning, lack of decision-making power, poor experiences with professional development, lack of parental support or involvement, and low availability of resources (Brunsting et al., 2014; Geiger & Pivovarova, 2018; Ronfeldt et al., 2013; Sutcher et al., 2016). The perception of negative working conditions can be a precursor to stress causing physical illness, emotional burnout, and high absenteeism or low intent to stay (Bettini et al., 2020; Cumming et al., this issue; Hanushek et al., 2016). High levels of stress and burnout often lead to job dissatisfaction and, ultimately, turnover (Sutcher, 2016).

The organizational health of a school is negatively affected by higher teacher turnover because it frequently results in lower teacher quality, disruptions to school programs, lessened teacher collaborations, misfit of professional learning offerings and professional learning needs, low morale, and mistrust (Guin, 2004; Hanushek et al., 2016). Evidence suggests schools experiencing high turnover also experience disruption to the continuity of high-quality instructional experiences with a detrimental effect on student outcomes (McLeskey & Billingsley, 2008; Ronfeldt et al., 2013; Sutcher, 2016). For example, Guin (2004) found a significant negative correlation between teacher turnover and student achievement; elementary schools with higher turnover had lower student achievement in mathematics and reading. Similar findings in a large study conducted by Ronfeldt et al. (2013) indicated better mathematics and English language arts outcomes due to greater teacher stability.

Teachers with a strong sense of well-being are more likely to create a positive classroom climate that minimizes disruptions and conflict, values social and emotional learning such as expressing emotions in healthy ways and using problem-solving strategies, and achieves higher levels of student engagement and performance gains (Jennings & Greenberg, 2009). Teacher well-being contributes to constructive student–teacher relationships with substantial evidence of a positive influence on students' academic, behavior, and social-emotional outcomes (McGrath & Van Bergen, 2015; Roorda et al., 2011). Teacher well-being and positive student outcomes have a reciprocal relation—teachers are more likely to stay if they have the support and resources to positively affect their students' learning outcomes, and students are more likely to make positive gains when their school's workforce is stable with a high sense of efficacy (Ronfeldt et al., 2013). Therefore, promoting teachers' well-being holds promise for maintaining a stable workforce, healthy schools, and better student outcomes.

A Systems-Level Response

Tiered systems, such as positive behavioral interventions and supports (PBIS; Sugai & Horner, 2002) and the comprehensive, integrated, three-tiered (Ci3T) model of prevention (Lane et al., 2020; see Lane et al., this volume), feature a continuum of increasingly intensive supports in various domains, with Tier 1 efforts for all students, Tier 2 for some students, and Tier 3 for a few students with intensive needs. These coordinated, data-informed approaches to meeting students' multiple needs may offer a unique opportunity for enhancing teachers' well-being and school health (Lane et al., 2020). Ultimately, a healthy school system promotes the well-being of educators in addition to the academic, behavior, and social-emotional well-being of students. Initial evidence suggests teachers working in tiered systems may experience less burnout and improved efficacy. For example, the implementation of school-wide PBIS (SW-PBIS) is associated with improved school climate (e.g., commitment to students, positive feelings toward colleagues; Bradshaw et al., 2009) and may increase teacher efficacy while decreasing the risk for burnout and increasing retention (Kelm & McIntosh, 2012; Ross et al., 2012). Likewise, educators implementing Ci3T experienced lower levels of burnout (i.e., higher personal accomplishment and lower depersonalization) and high levels of efficacy with instructional strategies and classroom management compared to a national sample (Lane et al., 2021; Oakes et al., 2020). As district and school leaders adopt tiered systems, they could intentionally leverage the inherent possibilities tiered models offer for improving teacher well-being in order to further promote positive student outcomes.

Historical Context

Interest in teacher well-being and its implications for student learning were spurred in the 1970s by the release of a Rand report examining the effects of a district reading program that found school and teacher variables made a significant difference in students' reading gains (Armor et al., 1976). The top three factors in reading gains were teacher training in the use of materials to meet individual student needs, teacher efficacy, and an orderly classroom. Since that time, a wealth of research has been conducted to examine teacher well-being as it relates to student outcomes. Grounded in social cognitive theory (Bandura, 1993), efficacy is developed through multiple sources such as experiences and feedback. Strong efficacy increases the use of coping strategies, effort expended to achieve the desired outcomes, and persistence in the face of challenge, and minimizes defensiveness (Bandura, 1993). A teacher's locus of control (Rotter, 1966) contributes to efficacy: Teachers who believe they have control over outcomes have more confidence in their abilities. In the classroom, teachers with these dispositions show a willingness to implement new practices, including school reforms; persist in supporting students with learning and behavior difficulties; refrain from blaming students or families for student difficulties; and refer students for special education at lower rates (Soodak & Podell, 1993).

According to theory, teacher well-being both contributes to and is affected by student learning outcomes, and positive student outcomes reinforce teacher practices and effort (Burns et al., 2013). However, confidence in one's abilities is also dependent on having the knowledge, skills, and resources to affect the desired outcomes (Armor et al., 1976; Hanushek et al., 2016). With an evolving society come new challenges, such as full inclusion of students with disabilities in general education classrooms, growing numbers of multilingual learners, variability in school readiness, heterogenous student needs, and meeting students' social-emotional well-being and behavioral needs. Teachers address these challenges while under extraordinary pressure to achieve standardized academic gains for all students. Unfortunately, this has sometimes resulted in overreliance on punitive responses (Sugai & Horner, 2002). Fortunately, tiered systems, initially used in health prevention, were adapted for educational contexts (Walker et al., 1996). PBIS was incorporated into the Individuals with Disabilities Education Act (IDEA, 1997) as an approach for addressing the behavioral needs of students, and Response to Intervention was written into the 2004 IDEA reauthorization to better identify and respond to students with and at risk for learning disabilities (Fuchs et al., 2003).

Tiered systems shifted the responsibility for student learning and development from teachers solely to the larger educational system (district, school), with specified structures and practices that have the potential to contribute to teacher well-being (Brunsting et al., 2014; Sutcher et al., 2016). Tiered systems provide for a clear vision and purpose. They include several elements designed to comprehensively support all learners: an instructional approach to behavior with clearly stated expectations; opportunities for students to practice and receive reinforcement; use of evidence-based practices that meet the students' level of need; need identified and monitored through universal screening procedures; reliable and accurate school and student data sources; regular use of data for instructional planning; supports with increasing intensity to match student need; and ongoing, focused professional learning for the implementation of the systems and all curricular materials and strategies (Horner & Sugai, 2015; Lane et al., this issue). These systems required a shift in teachers' practice from working in isolation and bearing sole responsibility for all student outcomes to a highly collaborative, clearly articulated, data-rich systems approach and accountability. In recent years, a priority was placed on *integrated* systems that work in coordinated ways to address student needs across multiple domains: academic, behavioral, and social-emotional well-being (Institute of Education Sciences [IES], 2018; McIntosh & Goodman, 2016). Ci3T is one such model designed to comprehensively meet students' needs in all three domains (Lane et al., 2020; Lane & Menzies, 2003). Other examples include Multi-Tiered System of Supports (MTSS), integrating academic and behavioral domains (e.g., mathematics, reading, behavior), and the Interconnected Systems Framework, integrating comprehensive mental health supports and PBIS (Barrett et al., 2013).

Current State of Research

In this section, we offer a discussion of elements of tiered systems and how they contribute to educators' well-being. Then, we provide an overview of research on teacher well-being in tiered systems and implications for treatment integrity and teacher efficacy.

Developing Effective Practices to Support Teacher Well-Being in Tiered Systems

Several elements integral to tiered systems may address issues related to teacher well-being. In this section, we focus on the following: decision-making norms, structures for collaboration, use of data, and professional learning, as each may promote teacher efficacy and the ability to cope with the complex demands of teaching. If administrators and school leadership teams are intentional in the ways they facilitate these elements when installing tiered systems such as Ci3T, they have the opportunity to simultaneously address teacher well-being.

Decision-Making

Teachers' acceptance of a comprehensive reform or program is related to their degree of involvement in the decision-making related to its adoption (Datnow & Castellano, 2000). Decision-making enhances teacher autonomy, which in turn can affect job satisfaction and well-being. Ci3T is an example of a tiered system designed to maximize teacher involvement in its design and implementation. For example, a leadership team is created to guide installation and sustainability of the model. The team is made up of teachers and includes stakeholders such as parents, administrators, school staff, and other school personnel. The team systematically solicits faculty and staff input using established measures and builds a site-specific Ci3T model, sensitive to its local context, using this information (Lane et al., 2020). Decisions range from adoption of curricula, selection of screening measures, data-informed decision-making procedures for Tier 2 and 3 supports, and design of professional learning opportunities. While administrators provide critical leadership and resources, teachers' behaviors or actions are often the engine that drives the reform efforts.

However, teacher involvement cannot be pro forma. Datnow and Castellano (2000) examined the adoption of a comprehensive school reform, Success for All, and noted tensions that arose because of administrators' superficial solicitation of teacher participation. At the same time, a school-site principal's ability to communicate the importance and utility of a reform is crucial for teacher buy-in (Turnbull, 2002). Likewise, the administrator's ability to communicate a clear vision makes teachers feel supported in their work. In fact, teachers who report a lack of administrative support are more than twice as likely to leave compared to those who feel the administrator is supportive (Carver-Thomas & Darling-Hammond, 2017). A balance must be found in a co-constructed process between administrative leadership and vision (district and site levels) and authentic teacher participation in decision-making (Datnow & Castellano, 2000).

Structures for Collaboration

Collaborative structures such as leadership and grade/department-level teams or professional learning communities are foundational to tiered systems. Collaboration and collegial trust may serve as protective factors for teacher well-being (Geiger & Pivovarova, 2018). In addition to facilitating teacher participation, work completed in teams can efficiently enact school processes for addressing student needs. For example, grade-level teams may analyze student data to decide on specific Tier 2 or 3 interventions and provide peer support to implement interventions. Rather than a teacher needing to independently navigate these decisions or requesting a specialist provide services, teachers have a structure in which to work collaboratively and systematically to review screening and other data to identify and provide tiered supports for students who indicate need (Lane et al., 2020). Tiered systems support both autonomous and collaborative decisions, schools implementing Ci3T models have Tiered Intervention Grids that describe interventions and detail the data-informed process for making decisions about entering, monitoring, and exiting each intervention (Oakes et al., 2013). These structures build efficiencies so that teachers may look at their screening data alongside other sources of data collected as part of regular school practices (e.g., attendance, office discipline referrals [ODRs]) and move forward autonomously to swiftly connect students to needed supports or to work collaboratively with their colleagues to make these decisions. These clearly articulated plans specified in Secondary (Tier 2) and Tertiary (Tier 3) Intervention Grids empower teachers to work independently or as part of collaborative teams to efficiently, effectively connect students to evidence-based practices according to student needs. These options support autonomy in decision-making approaches and protect against feelings of isolation. Tasks such as collecting and analyzing student data, sharing evidence-based practices, choosing appropriate interventions and supports, and monitoring student progress can be implemented autonomously or collaboratively. The transparency of the range of supports offered and the availability of multiple colleagues who are familiar with Tier 1, 2, and 3 efforts may support autonomy and lessen the isolation that occurs in the teaching profession (predictors of teacher dissatisfaction; Ostovar-Nameghi & Sheikhahmadi, 2016). In addition to promoting collaboration, these structures provide efficiencies that, once in place (e.g., establishment of tiered supports, scheduled meeting times and tasks), may help manage the wide array of teacher responsibilities. Yet for collaboration to be worthwhile and sustainable, teachers need to see it is meaningful and believe it will result in positive outcomes for their students (Burns et al., 2013; Datnow & Park, 2018). Collaborative work can be demanding and difficult to structure, and results often are not immediate (Turnbull, 2002), so administrators must lay the groundwork by providing time, resources, and guidance to help teachers become productive collaborators.

Use of Data

Educators are expected to use data-informed processes fluently to improve educational outcomes (Farrell & Marsh, 2016). As part of the Ci3T model, schools collect treatment integrity (the degree to which the model is implemented as planned; Buckman et al., this issue) and social validity (stakeholders' perceptions of the procedures, goals, and intended outcomes; Wolf, 1978) data from all faculty and staff members twice per year to monitor system implementation (see Lane et al., this volume). In addition, they conduct systematic screening for academics and behavior three times per year (fall, winter, and spring; Lane et al., 2019) and analyze screening data along with other school data, such as attendance and ODRs, to inform decisions. Data analysis guides decision-making and instructional practice, as well as informs site-specific program improvement and professional learning topics. Teachers' use of data for instructional purposes has the potential to increase efficacy by strengthening their autonomy in decision-making and reinforcing their efforts by providing evidence of students' progress and achievement (Burns et al., 2013). It may also increase teachers' awareness of the importance of high-fidelity implementation through the use of treatment integrity data—if changes are not observed in student outcome measures, were programmatic elements in place (see Buckman et al., this volume)?

Once again, administrators and leadership teams need to consider a number of issues related to data use. First, school sites must determine which data are most valuable in guiding their decision-making processes (Farrell & Marsh, 2016). Ci3T Implementation Manuals include an Assessment Schedule to name each data source and timeline for its collection (Lane et al., 2020), creating transparency of data sources available for each student enrolled. Second, not all teachers are data literate, such as examining assessment data for patterns and trends that require instructional adjustments, as teacher preparation programs may not adequately teach this skill (Mandinach et al., 2015). Similarly, using assessment data to inform instruction is not as clear-cut as it may appear, and teachers require support and targeted professional development to use data for instructional planning (Datnow & Hubbard, 2016).

Professional Learning

Adequate training and professional learning opportunities are instrumental in facilitating teachers' participation in new practices and in improving treatment fidelity. This is particularly relevant during the first year of implementation (Turnbull, 2002), when teachers are at the same time experiencing the largest professional growth of their careers and are most likely to leave the profession (Sutcher et al., 2016). Teacher well-being is supported when they have the knowledge and skills to affect positive student outcomes (Armor et al., 1976; Brunsting et al., 2014). Therefore, a relevant and coherent professional learning plan that can flexibly adjust to specific roles and teachers' experience levels is needed (Guin, 2004). For example, Ci3T professional learning plans are informed by treatment integrity, social validity, and student progress data collected from the school site (Oakes et al., 2021).

Data may show teachers would benefit from information on installation of the model, knowledge of specific practices (e.g., positive behavioral support, teaching of the schoolwide social-emotional learning curricula, use of low-intensity strategies), or attending to treatment integrity, among others. There is substantial evidence that high-quality professional learning in data literacy, using assessment data for instructional planning, and working in teams to use data are important foci as well (Orland, 2015). Once again, making careful choices as to where to invest professional learning resources (i.e., time, materials, expertise, funds) will result in choices about professional learning that can support teacher well-being by preparing them to be more effective in improving student outcomes.

Evaluating Effective Practices to Support Teacher Well-Being in Tiered Systems

As districts adopt and implement tiered systems to address students' multiple needs, school leaders may benefit from understanding the implications of teacher well-being and indicators of burnout. This information can inform the selection of professional learning opportunities to promote teacher well-being, as well as teacher efficacy, when implementing reform efforts and using evidence-based practices to promote students' academic, behavioral, and social-emotional outcomes (Herman et al., 2018; Skaalvik & Skaalvik, 2007). While the implications of implementation of tiered practices and teacher well-being are not fully understood, initial studies show promising outcomes.

To date, studies have examined teacher efficacy and burnout within SW-PBIS (e.g., Kelm & McIntosh, 2012; Reinke et al., 2013; Ross et al., 2012) and Ci3T models of prevention (e.g., Lane et al., 2021; Oakes et al., 2021). Findings across studies indicated teachers working in tiered systems have higher levels of efficacy and lower levels of burnout (i.e., lower depersonalization, higher personal accomplishment). Emotional exhaustion persisted for these teachers, but studies indicated that even when teachers experience heightened levels of emotional exhaustion (stress), having coping strategies in place ameliorates some of the detrimental effects on student performance, particularly in terms of behavioral outcomes (Herman et al., 2018).

Elementary school teachers working in schools with high levels of SW-PBIS implementation fidelity reported a higher sense of efficacy compared to teachers at non–SW-PBIS schools within the same district (Kelm & McIntosh, 2012). Similarly, Ross and Horner (2007) examined data from 20 middle school teachers working in SW-PBIS schools. Treatment integrity levels were associated positively with teacher efficacy and were not associated with teacher stress. Ross and colleagues (2012) extended this inquiry with a larger sample ($N = 186$) of elementary school teachers. Findings indicated SW-PBIS treatment integrity scores were positively associated with teacher efficacy and negatively associated with burnout.

To further explore relations between implementation of tiered practices and teacher well-being within SW-PBIS schools, Reinke and colleagues (2013) examined data from 33 kindergarten through third-grade classrooms in three high-implementing schools using the following indicators: direct observations of student and teacher behaviors, teacher efficacy, emotional exhaustion as an indicator of burnout, and a measure of classroom practices. Teachers with a higher sense of efficacy in classroom management used general praise more often and had fewer student disruptions. Likewise, teachers with lower emotional exhaustion used higher ratios of positive-to-negative statements. Conversely, teachers reporting higher levels of emotional exhaustion experienced more disruptions and used harsh reprimands more often. These studies provided an important initial inquiry exploring the relation between PBIS and teacher well-being.

To extend this inquiry to integrated tiered models, Oakes and colleagues (2013) examined relations between Ci3T treatment integrity, social validity, efficacy, and burnout for 86 teachers from two middle schools in a Southern state at the end of their first year of Ci3T implementation. Teachers completed self-report measures of treatment integrity and social validity two times during the school year and efficacy and burnout measures at year end. Compared to national norms, teachers reported experiencing lower burnout (i.e., lower depersonalization and higher personal accomplishment) similar to findings by Ross et al., 2012. Teachers also reported slightly higher levels of emotional exhaustion. Higher teacher-reported treatment integrity scores predicted lower depersonalization. In terms of predicting teacher efficacy, neither treatment integrity nor social validity scores were significant.

Next, Oakes and colleagues (2021) examined data for 120 elementary teachers from 14 schools in one large school district in a Midwestern state in their second year of Ci3T implementation. Findings were similar to Oakes et al. (2013) with teachers having low levels of depersonalization and high levels of personal accomplishment, with significant favorable differences compared to a national sample. Again, teachers reported moderate to high levels of emotional exhaustion consistent with the national sample. For efficacy scores teachers reported small-to-medium magnitude favorable differences compared to the national sample in the areas of student engagement and instructional strategies and medium-to-large favorable differences for classroom management. For these teachers in their second year of implementation, spring treatment integrity and social validity scores predicted efficacy for student engagement. Treatment integrity scores predicted all three areas of teacher efficacy. For a similar look at middle and high school teachers, Lane et al. (2021) examined these same features for 82 secondary teachers from four middle and two high schools in the same district as Oakes et al. (2021). Findings were comparable to the elementary sample. Secondary teachers reported low depersonalization and high personal accomplishment, with more favorable scores compared to the national sample. Again, emotional exhaustion remained similar to the sample. In terms of efficacy, teachers' sense of efficacy for student engagement remained lower than for instructional strategies and classroom management, with the latter two above the sample mean. Ci3T treatment integrity scores were predictive of all three efficacy scales. Social validity scores were, again, not predictive of any efficacy or burnout outcomes.

Collectively, results from these studies provide evidence to suggest a positive relation between tiered model implementation and teachers' sense of efficacy and measures of burnout (Kelm & McIntosh, 2012; Lane et al., 2021; Oakes et al., 2021; Ross et al., 2012). Moreover, initial evidence suggests degree of implementation of practices related to prevention models (e.g., teaching behavior expectations, providing positive reinforcement) may be related to a greater sense of self-efficacy (Reinke et al., 2013). Additional inquiry is needed to examine these relations over time and as they relate to student outcomes when tiered models are fully installed and sustained in schools in varying geographic locales.

Herman and colleagues (2018) extended this line of inquiry to examine the potential influences of coping, as measured using a one-item scale (Eddy et al., 2019). Authors examined the stress and coping of 121 general education teachers and behavioral and academic outcomes for their students ($N = 1,817$). Teachers were located in nine schools in the Midwestern United States with students who had high levels of prosocial behavior and concentration (Herman et al., 2018). All participating schools were implementing district-wide PBIS with high levels of fidelity. Teachers completed four measures assessing their stress, coping, burnout, and sense of efficacy. Teachers also completed a student behavioral measure, and a standardized test of achievement was used to assess reading and mathematics performance. Four teacher profiles of stress and coping emerged: stressed/low coping (3% of teachers), stressed/moderate coping (30%), stressed/high coping (60%), and well adjusted (7%; i.e., low levels of stress). Results reported most teachers in these high-implementing PBIS schools indicated they had high levels of stress *and* coping. Next, researchers examined how student behavior and academic indicators varied according to teacher profile. Stressed/low coping teachers had significantly higher levels of student disruptions and concentration problems, lower levels of student prosocial behavior, and lower levels of student mathematics achievement. No significant differences were found for students' reading performance (Herman et al., 2018). Findings from this study indicate teacher well-being can be fostered through the use of strategies that contribute to coping skills. In addition, when teachers see the positive effects of their efforts, it contributes to their well-being (Burns et al., 2013; Guin, 2004). We contend elements of tiered systems facilitate coping by addressing issues related to burnout and leaving the field (Brunsting et al., 2014; Geiger & Pivovarova, 2018).

Implications for Practitioners

When school systems have structures and supports in place to positively affect teacher well-being, school communities, teachers, and students benefit from a more stable educator workforce. We offer the following considerations for school leaders as they put practices in place to nurture teacher well-being in tiered models.

Offer Onboarding for New Leaders

When new leaders join schools with tiered systems in place, onboarding activities to provide information about the tiered system will help them articulate a clear vision that incorporates their desired changes into the existing system (Menzies et al., 2020). Teachers are more likely to report positive job satisfaction when they have administrators who convey a clear vision and respect teachers' decision-making to influence practices within the system (Sutcher et al., 2016). Schools with tiered models have invested considerable time, thought, and changes in practice to implement these systems (Lane et al., 2020). It would be disheartening to teachers and staff for a new leader to come in and change the system or begin again without an understanding of the system currently in place. In a Ci3T model, schools have defined roles and responsibilities for all stakeholder groups clearly articulated in their Ci3T Implementation Manual, including those of administrators (Lane et al., 2020). Administrators' understanding of their teacher and staff expectations buoys their ability to meet those expectations and communicate when shifts in responsibilities may occur. The underlining asset is clear communication to alleviate role ambiguity between administrators and teachers.

Adopt and Install Data Systems

Teachers benefit from having feasible access to reliable and accurate data on the progress of their students. This allows teachers to make timely and independent decisions about instructional practices, as well as choose to collaborate with colleagues with shared understandings of Tier 1, 2, and 3 strategies, practices, and programs. In addition, teachers are able to engage in data-informed professional learning opportunities to make small shifts in their practice to better meet identified needs. Data also offer evidence of effectiveness, bolstering a teacher's sense of efficacy when improvements are made or providing data for goal setting when improvement is needed (Burns et al., 2013). Efficient and reliable data systems fortify teacher's knowledge of student progress to make appropriate instructional adjustments.

Provide Structures for Collaboration

It is important to provide a balance between autonomy and collaboration. Without collaborative structures, teachers, particularly those new to the profession or school, may feel isolated and be overwhelmed by a feeling of responsibility to meet all the needs of their students (Ostovar-Nameghi & Sheikhahmadi, 2016). Tiered systems lessen isolation by establishing common structures and practices for collaboration and facilitating teamwork. In a Ci3T model, each school has a Ci3T Implementation Manual specifying Tier 1, 2, and 3 offerings. Programmatic data (e.g., treatment integrity and social validity) are analyzed in conjunction with student-level data to inform the student and adult experience. For example, teams meet to discuss student-level data and have a common planning time for collaboration as part of the master schedule. They use management systems to access data across all classes, analyze data to look for patterns of concern to be addressed through Tier 1 efforts, and look for individual needs to be addressed through integrated Tier 2 or 3 interventions. In a Ci3T model, teams have an Assessment Schedule to know relevant available data sources and Tiered Intervention Grids to guide their consideration and selection of the most appropriate intervention (Lane et al., 2020). Structures also support autonomous efforts with improved communication with colleagues, as all teachers will have a shared understanding of interventions and data to make decisions. In these models, all teachers participate in professional learning and are learners in some areas (e.g., effective practices for increasing student engagement) and share their knowledge as experts in other areas (e.g., reading instruction; Oakes et al., 2020), allowing opportunities for the distribution of expertise. These structures can foster trusting collegial relationships through shared investment in student outcomes.

Attend to the Professional Learning Needs of Teachers

Studies of teacher efficacy in tiered models found treatment integrity data are predictive of teacher efficacy in the use of instructional strategies and classroom management (Lane et al., 2021). Therefore, investing in professional learning to promote the use of tiered practices with integrity may in turn promote teacher efficacy and minimize indicators of burnout. The whole system benefits when practices are in place to promote the well-being of all members of the school community (Geiger & Pivovarova, 2018; Guin, 2004).

Schools with high turnover often offer professional learning targeted at teachers with the least experience, and rightfully so; however, this can lead to a stagnated learning environment for experienced teachers (Guin, 2004). Providing a rich array of professional learning resources such as collaborative book studies or study groups, district workshops, webinars, brief "good practice" guides, and interactive self-paced learning modules (Common et al., 2021) allows teachers to deepen their professional knowledge through the choice of collaborative or individualized learning avenues accommodating preferences, interests, and varying levels of expertise.

Implications for Future Research

Particularly now, in response to the COVID-19 pandemic, there is an immediate need for additional inquiry to protect teacher well-being as they currently confront new demands of even greater proportion—how to keep themselves, their students, and their families healthy and safe—in addition to providing high-quality instruction in remote, hybrid, and in-person learning environments.

Fortunately, many teachers and educational leaders see the value of teachers' well-being and are using their tiered systems to support teachers and students alike.

As our review of the recent literature on teacher well-being in tiered systems shows, this line of inquiry is in its nascent stage. Continued inquiry should address how practices such as the recommendations we made in this chapter serve to promote high levels of treatment integrity in tiered systems, teacher well-being, and student outcomes. Current studies have primarily focused on the proximal outcomes of implementation integrity and teacher well-being (Oakes et al., 2021; Ross et al., 2012). Inquiry must be extended to distal outcomes, such as student academic, behavioral, and social-emotional outcomes; teacher persistence with students with learning and behavioral challenges; and teachers' persistence in implementing evidence-based practices with integrity even in the face of difficulty. Inquiry should continue to examine factors that promote retention of teachers to increase the stability and well-being of the education workforce, including teachers' perceptions of their working conditions (Cumming et al., this issue).

Summary

Through tiered models' promotion and support of a healthy school at the system level, educators may not only improve school climate, they support teacher efficacy while reducing burnout (see Table 5.1 for additional readings and resources). Providing data-informed professional learning in tiered models helps empower teachers with the knowledge, skills, and resources needed to strengthen their professional practice and sense of efficacy and belief they have control over the outcome of events (locus of control; e.g., provide student supports at the first sign of concern using data-informed procedures). This may lead to positive student outcomes, which in reciprocal fashion positively affect teacher well-being. With collegial trust and collaboration and strong administrative support, initial evidence suggests tiered models of prevention have the potential to support teacher well-being and reduce the percentage who leave the profession each year.

Table 5.1 Additional Readings and Resources

Item	*URL*
Comprehensive, Integrated Three-Tiered (Ci3T) Model of Prevention—website with open-access resources for designing, implementing, and evaluating Ci3T.	www.ci3t.org/
Midwest PBIS Network—resources for implementing PBIS and Interconnected Systems Framework (ISF)	www.midwestpbis.org/home
National Center on Positive Behavioral Interventions and Supports (PBIS)—website for open-access resources for designing, implementing, and evaluating PBIS.	www.pbis.org/
Honigsfeld, A., & Normeyer, J. (2020). Teacher collaboration during a global pandemic. *An Educational Leadership Special Report. A new reality: Getting report learning right*, 77, 47–50.	www.ascd.org/publications/educational-leadership/summer20/vol77/num10/Teacher-Collaboration-During-a-Global-Pandemic.aspx
The Collaborative for Academic, Social, and Emotional Learning (CASEL)—website with open access resources for social and emotional learning	https://casel.org/
Measure: Maslach, C., Jackson, S. E., & Schwab, R. L. (1996). *MBI—Educators Survey—MBI-ES*. Mind Garden.	www.mindgarden.com/
Measure: Dr. Tschannen-Moran's collection of efficacy measures (measure available in multiple languages)	https://wmpeople.wm.edu/site/page/mxtsch/researchtools

References

Armor, D., Conry-Oseguera, P., Cox, M., King, N., McDonnell, L., Pascal, A., Pauley, E., & Zellman, G. (1976). *Analysis of the school preferred reading program in selected Los Angeles minority schools*. Rand Corporation.

Bandura, A. (1993). Perceived self-efficacy in cognitive development and functioning. *Educational Psychologist, 28*, 117–148. https://doi.org/10.1207/s15326985ep2802_3

Barrett, S., Eber, L., & Weist, M. D. (2013). *Advancing education effectiveness: An interconnected systems framework for Positive Behavioral Interventions and Supports (PBIS) and school mental health*. Center for Positive Behavioral Interventions and Supports, University of Oregon Press.

Bettini, E., Cumming, M., O'Brien, K. M., Brunsting, N. C., Ragunanthan, M., Sutton, R., & Chopra, A. (2020). Predicting special educators' intent to continue teaching students with emotional/behavioral disorders in self-contained classes. *Exceptional Children, 86*, 209–228. https://doi.org/10.1177/0014402919873556

Billingsley, B., & Bettini, E. (2019). Special education teacher attrition and retention: A review of the literature. *Review of Educational Research, 89*(5), 697–744. https://doi.org/gf5czh

Bradshaw, C. P., Koth, C. W., Thornton, L. A., & Leaf, P. J. (2009). Altering school climate through school-wide positive behavioral interventions and supports: Findings from a group-randomized effectiveness trial. *Prevention Science, 10*, 100–115. https://doi.org/b5qh87

Brunsting, N. C., Sreckovic, M. A., & Lane, K. L. (2014). Special education teacher burnout: A synthesis of research from 1979 to 2013. *Education and Treatment of Children, 37*(4), 681–711. https://doi.org/10.1353/etc.2014.0032

Burns, M. K., Egan, A. M., Kunkel, A. K., McComas, J., Peterson, M. M., Rahn, N. L., & Wilson, J. (2013). Training for generalization and maintenance in RtI implementation: Front-loading for sustainability. *Learning Disabilities Research & Practice, 28*(2), 81–88. http://dx.doi.org/10.1111/ldrp.12009

Carver-Thomas, D., & Darling-Hammond, L. (2017). *Teacher turnover: Why it matters and what we can do about it*. Learning Policy Institute. https://learningpolicyinstitute.org/product/teacher-turnover-report

Common, E. A., Buckman, M. M., Lane, K. L., Oakes, W. P., Royer, D. J., Chafouleas, S. M., Briesch, A. M., & Sherod, R. L. (2021). Project ENHANCE: Assessing professional learning needs for implementing Comprehensive, Integrated, Three-tiered (Ci3T) prevention models. *Education and Treatment of Children, 44*, 125–144. https://link.springer.com/article/10.1007/s43494-021-00049-z

Datnow, A., & Castellano, M. (2000). Teachers' responses to Success for All: How beliefs, experiences, and adaptations shape implementation. *American Educational Research Journal, 37*(3), 775–799. https://doi.org/10.3102/00028312037003775

Datnow, A., & Hubbard, L. (2016). Teacher capacity for and beliefs about data-driven decision making: A literature review of international research. *Journal of Educational Change, 17*(1), 7–28. https://doi-org.ezproxy1.lib.asu.edu/10.1007/s10833-015-9264-2

Datnow, A., & Park, V. (2018). *Professional collaboration with purpose: Teacher learning towards equitable and excellent schools*. Routledge.

Eddy, C. L., Herman, K. C., & Reinke, W. M. (2019). Single-item teacher stress and coping measures: Concurrent and predictive validity and sensitivity to change. *Journal of School Psychology, 76*, 17–32. https://doi.org/10.1016/j.jsp.2019.05.001

Farrell, C. C., & Marsh, J. A. (2016). Metrics matter: How properties and perceptions of data shape teachers' instructional responses. *Educational Administration Quarterly, 52*(3), 423–462. https://doi.org/10.1177/0013161X16638429

Fuchs, D., Mock, D., Morgan, P. L., & Young, C. L. (2003). Responsiveness-to-intervention: Definitions, evidence, and implications for the learning disabilities construct. *Learning Disabilities Research & Practice, 18*(3), 157–171. https://doi.org/dv9jkr

Geiger, T., & Pivovarova, M. (2018). The effects of working conditions on teacher retention. *Teachers and Teaching, 24*(6), 604–625. https://doi.org/djwh

Guin, K. (2004). Chronic teacher turnover in urban elementary schools. *Education Policy Analysis Archives, 12*(42), 1–25. https://doi.org/10.14507/epaa.v12n42.2004

Hanushek, E. A., Rivkin, S. G., & Schiman, J. C. (2016). Dynamic effects of teacher turnover on the quality of instruction. *Economics of Education Review, 55*, 132–148. http://dx.doi.org/10.1016/j.econedurev.2016.08.004

Herman, K. C., Hickmon-Rosa, J., & Reinke, W. M. (2018). Empirically derived profiles of teacher stress, burnout, self-efficacy, and coping and associated student outcomes. *Journal of Positive Behavior Interventions, 20*(2), 90–100. https://doi.org/gf5d9w

Horner, R. H., & Sugai, G. (2015). School-wide PBIS: An example of applied behavior analysis implemented at a scale of social importance. *Behavior Analysis in Practice, 8*(1), 80–85. http://dx.doi.org/10.1007/s40617-015-0045-4

Individuals with Disability Education Act Amendments of 1997 [IDEA], Pub. L. No. 105-17 Stat. 37 (1997). https://www.congress.gov/105/plaws/publ17/PLAW-105publ17.pdf

Individuals with Disabilities Education Improvement Act, 20 U.S.C. § 1400 (2004).

Institute of Education Sciences. (2018). *Request for applications: Research networks focus on critical problems of policy and practice in special education* (CFDA 84.324N). U.S. Department of Education.

Jennings, P. A., & Greenberg, M. T. (2009). The prosocial classroom: Teacher social and emotional competence in relation to student and classroom outcomes. *Review of Educational Research, 79*(1), 491–525. https://doi.org/10.3102/0034654308325693

Kelm, J. L., & McIntosh, K. (2012). Effects of school-wide positive behavior support on teacher self-efficacy. *Psychology in the Schools, 49*(2), 137–147. https://doi.org/fxvt4s

Lane, K. L., & Menzies, H. M. (2003). School-wide intervention with primary and secondary levels of support for elementary students: Outcomes and considerations. *Education and Treatment of Children, 26*(4), 431–451.

Lane, K. L., Menzies, H. M., Oakes, W. P., & Kalberg, J. R. (2020). *Developing a schoolwide framework to prevent and manage learning and behavior problems* (2nd ed.). Guilford Press.

Lane, K. L., Oakes, W. P., Cantwell, E. D., Royer, D. J., Leko, M., Schatschneider, C., & Menzies, H. M. (2019). Predictive validity of Student Risk Screening Scale for Internalizing and Externalizing (SRSS-IE) scores in secondary schools. *Journal of Emotional and Behavioral Disorders, 27*(2), 86–100. https://doi.org/frds

Lane, K. L., Oakes, W. P., Royer, D. J., Menzies, H. M., Brunsting, N., Buckman, M. M., Common, E. A., Lane, N. A., Schatschneider, C., & Lane, K. S. (2021). Secondary teachers' self-efficacy during initial implementation of comprehensive, integrated, three-tiered models. *Journal of Positive Behavior Interventions, 23*(4), 232–244. https://doi.org/10.1177/1098300720946628

Mandinach, E., Friedman, J. M., & Gummer, E. (2015). How can schools of education help to build educators' capacity to use data? A systemic view of the issue. *Teachers College Record, 117*(4), 1–50. https://doi.org/10.1177/016146811511700404

McGrath, K. F., & Van Bergen, P. (2015). Who, when, why and to what end? Students at risk of negative student—teacher relationships and their outcomes. *Educational Research Review, 14,* 1–17. https://doi.org/10.1016/j.edurev.2014.12.001

McIntosh, K., & Goodman, S. (2016). *Integrated multi-tiered systems of support: Blending RTI and PBIS.* Guilford Press.

McLeskey, J., & Billingsley, B. S. (2008). How does the quality and stability of the teaching force influence the research-to-practice gap?: A perspective on the teacher shortage in special education. *Remedial and Special Education, 29*(5), 293–305. https://doi.org/bjtt2g

Menzies, H. M., Lane, K. L., Oakes, W. P., Royer, D. J., Cantwell, E. D., Common, E. A., & Buckman, M. M. (2020). Elementary teachers' perceptions of a Comprehensive, Integrated, Three-tiered model of prevention. *Remedial and Special Education.* Online first. http://dx.doi.org/10.1177/0741932519896860

Oakes, W. P., Cantwell, E. D., Lane, K. L., Royer, D. J., & Common, E. A. (2020). Examining educators' views of classroom management and instructional strategies: School-site capacity for supporting students' behavioral needs. *Preventing School Failure, 64*(1), 1–11. https://doi.org/10.1080/1045988x.2018.1523125

Oakes, W. P., Lane, K. L., Jenkins, A., & Booker, B. B. (2013). Three-tiered models of prevention: Teacher efficacy and burnout. *Education and Treatment of Children, 36*(4), 95–126. http://dx.doi.org/10.1353/etc.2013.0037

Oakes, W. P., Lane, K. L., Royer, D. J., Menzies, H. M., Buckman, M. M., Brunsting, N. C., Cantwell, E. D., Schatschneider, C., & Lane, N. A. (2021). Elementary teachers' self-efficacy during initial implementation of comprehensive, integrated, three-tiered models of prevention. *Journal of Positive Behavior Interventions, 23*(3), 93–105. https://doi.org/10.1177/1098300720916718

Orland, M. (2015). Research and policy perspectives on data-based decision making in education. *Teachers College Record, 117*(4), 1–10.

Ostovar-Nameghi, S. A., & Sheikhahmadi, M. (2016). From teacher isolation to teacher collaboration: Theoretical perspectives and empirical findings. *English Language Teaching, 9*(5), 197–205. http://dx.doi.org/10.5539/elt.v9n5p197

Reinke, W. M., Herman, K. C., & Stormont, M. (2013). Classroom-level positive behavior supports in schools implementing SW-PBIS: Identifying areas for Enhancement. *Journal of Positive Behavior Interventions, 15,* 39–50. https://doi.org/f4gq6h

Ronfeldt, M., Loeb, S., & Wyckoff, J. (2013). How teacher turnover harms student achievement. *American Educational Research Journal, 50*(1), 4–36. https://doi.org/dnb4

Roorda, D. L., Koomen, H. M. Y., Spilt, J. L., & Oort, F. J. (2011). The influence of affective teacher—student relationships on students' school engagement and achievement: A meta-analytic approach. *Review of Educational Research, 81*(4), 493–529. https://doi.org/dnb4

Ross, S. W., & Horner, R. H. (2007). Teacher outcomes of school-wide positive behavior support. *TEACHING Exceptional Children Plus, 3*(6). https://files.eric.ed.gov/fulltext/EJ967462.pdf

Ross, S. W., Romer, N., & Horner, R. H. (2012). Teacher well-being and the implementation of school-wide positive behavior interventions and supports. *Journal of Positive Behavior Interventions, 14*(2), 118–128. https://doi.org/10.1177/1098300711413820

Rotter, J. B. (1966). Generalized expectancies for internal versus external control of reinforcement. *Psychological Monographs, 80*, 1–28.

Skaalvik, E. M., & Skaalvik, S. (2007). Dimensions of teacher self-efficacy and relations with strain factors, perceived collective teacher efficacy, and teacher burnout. *Journal of Education Psychology, 99*, 611–625. http://dx.doi.org/10.1037/0022-0663.99.3.611

Soodak, L. C., & Podell, D. M. (1993). Teacher efficacy and student problem as factors in special education referral. *The Journal of Special Education, 27*(1), 66–81. http://dx.doi.org/10.1177/002246699302700105

Sugai, G., & Horner, R. (2002). The evolution of discipline practices: School-wide positive behavior supports. *Child & Family Behavior Therapy, 24*, 23–50. https://doi.org/fhwspn

Sutcher, L., Darling Hammond, L., & Carver-Thomas, D. (2016). *A coming crisis in teaching? Teacher supply, demand, and shortages in the U.S.* Learning Policy Institute.

Turnbull, B. (2002). Teacher participation and buy-in: Implications for school reform initiatives. *Learning Environments Research, 5*, 235–252. https://doi.org/10.1023/A:1021981622041

Walker, H. M., Horner, R. H., Sugai, G., Bullis, M., Sprague, J. R., Bricker, D., & Kaufman, M. J. (1996). Integrated approaches to preventing antisocial behavior patterns among school-age children and youth. *Journal of Emotional and Behavioral Disorders, 4*(4), 194–209. http://dx.doi.org/10.1177/106342669600400401

Wolf, M. M. (1978). Social validity: The case for subjective measurement or how applied behavior analysis is finding its heart. *Journal of Applied Behavior Analysis, 11*(2), 203–214. https://doi.org/10.1901/jaba.1978.11-203

6
LEVERAGING WORKING CONDITIONS TO IMPROVE THE QUALITY AND EFFECTIVENESS OF THE SPECIAL EDUCATION TEACHER WORKFORCE

Michelle M. Cumming, Elizabeth Bettini, Nelson Brunsting, and Sharde Theodore

Students with disabilities depend on special education teachers (SETs) to provide high-quality instruction and behavior management to meet their academic and social-emotional needs (Kauffman & Landrum, 2018); in turn, SETs depend on working conditions that aid them in fulfilling their roles and responsibilities (Cumming et al., 2020). The Individuals with Disabilities Education Improvement Act (IDEA, 2004) requires schools to provide students with research-supported services for their specific needs. For instance, students with emotional and behavioral disorders (EBDs) require highly effective behavior management practices (e.g., behavior contracts) to increase positive behaviors (Kauffman & Landrum, 2018), as well as evidence-based academic instruction that includes opportunities to respond and high rates of feedback (Common et al., 2020). These well-researched practices should inform the provision of school-based services, yet observational studies indicate SETs seldom enact effective practices with the frequency and intensity students require (e.g., Kurth et al., 2016; Wexler et al., 2018).

Working conditions present a potential lever by which leaders and policy makers could improve SETs' capacity to enact effective practices in service of students with disabilities (e.g., Billingsley et al., 2020). By working conditions, we mean SETs' perceptions of the context of their work, a manifestation of the school's organization in SETs' experiences (Billingsley et al., 2020). A growing body of research in educational leadership and policy highlights working conditions as a key contributor to the quality and effectiveness of the teacher workforce (e.g., Johnson et al., 2012), including the SET workforce (Bettini et al., 2016). For instance, administrative support and school culture are associated with student learning gains, as measured through value-added scores (Johnson et al., 2012), and working conditions contribute to improvements in teachers' effectiveness over time (e.g., Kraft & Papay, 2014). These findings have led to increasing interest in leveraging working conditions to improve the SET workforce, and thereby outcomes among students with disabilities (Billingsley et al., 2020).

Thus, our aim is to elaborate on mechanisms by which working conditions shape the quality and effectiveness of the SET workforce, as these can yield insights into how working conditions might be enhanced to better support SETs in providing effective services to students with disabilities. We first conceptualize and define SETs working conditions, provide an overview of the historical context for working conditions research, and highlight what is currently known about SETs' working conditions. We then describe extant research on how these conditions may affect students with disabilities. Finally, we provide implications for practice and research.

Conceptualizing and Defining Special Education Teachers' Working Conditions

To conceptualize working conditions, we rely on conservation of resources (COR) theory, which was developed by organizational researchers who posited that individuals pursue personal and organizational goals by strategically deploying their resources (e.g., Hobfoll et al., 2018). In COR theory, resources may be the objects, conditions, and characteristics an employee values or uses to fulfill their role (e.g., time, social capital; Halbesleben et al., 2014; Hobfoll et al., 2018). When the demands of their job are balanced with their resources, employees feel they can manage responsibilities and experience positive affective outcomes (e.g., commitment). Yet when they experience prolonged periods of high demands and low resources, the result is higher than optimal stress and reduced job commitment (Alarcon, 2011). Backed by meta-analyses, COR theory has explained burnout (i.e., a consequence of prolonged stress) across varied workplaces (Halbesleben, 2006; Hobfoll et al., 2018) and has also recently been used to explain SETs' attrition, intent to stay, and use of instructional practices (e.g., Cumming et al., 2020).

We define SETs' working conditions as including a variety of resources that SETs actively pursue and protect, as well as demands they are expected to meet. Based on prior research (e.g., Bettini et al., 2016), we posit salient demands include paperwork, instructional responsibilities, instructional grouping, paraprofessional supervision, and extra responsibilities (e.g., administrative tasks). These studies indicate SETs depend on three kinds of resources: (a) social resources (e.g., administrative support, collegial support, paraprofessional support, school culture, and autonomy); (b) informational resources (e.g., professional development [PD] and mentoring); and (c) logistical resources (e.g., planning time and curricular resources).

Ecological systems theory (Bronfenbrenner, 1992) posits various ecosystems (e.g., school, society, culture) interact with and influence each other to affect an individual's life and development. From this perspective, SETs' experiences of working conditions are a result of the characteristics of educational ecosystems. For example, SETs are assigned specific grades and subjects to teach, as well as planning time by administrators based on the school's structure and student needs, provided resources (e.g., curricula) based on district funding, and mandates based on policy. These, in turn, affect SETs' demands and resources, as well as their outcomes (Brunsting et al., 2014). Thus, SETs' demands and access to resources are shaped by characteristics and choices made at the classroom, school, district, and state levels.

Historical Context of Special Educators' Working Conditions

Researchers have examined SETs' working conditions for over 40 years, often rooted in addressing the critical shortage of qualified SETs and their persistently high attrition rates (Billingsley et al., 2020). The earliest studies began shortly after the passage of the P.L. 94–142, in 1975. Following passage of the first legal mandates for special education, SETs' roles rapidly evolved, dramatically changing their responsibilities, resources, and expectations for collaboration (Weatherley & Lipsky, 1977). During this period, the number of students with disabilities served in U.S. schools grew, increasing demand for SETs (Dewey et al., 2017). The result was a "severe, chronic, and pervasive" shortage of SETs (McLeskey & Billingsley, 2008, p. 295).

Over the last few decades, professional organizations (e.g., Council for Exceptional Children) and researchers have continued to highlight the need to improve SETs' working conditions (e.g., Kozleski et al., 2000), which they posited would reduce SET attrition, and thereby reduce shortages (Billingsley et al., 2020). Yet in the only study examining changes in SETs' working conditions over time (using nationally representative Schools and Staffing Survey data), Gilmour et al. (in press) determined demands increased significantly over time: SETs in 2016–2017 reported working more hours and serving larger caseloads than SETs in 1999–2000. However, SETs in 2016–2017 also reported stronger administrative support, cooperation with colleagues, and access to material resources than SETs in 1999–2000, indicating some improvements. While promising, improvements in access to certain resources may be inadequate, as evidenced by the ongoing SET shortage, with high attrition rates constituting a substantial contributor to the shortage (Goldhaber et al., 2018; Theobald et al., 2020). For example, Theobald et al. (2020) found only 40% of SETs who entered teaching in 2010 were still teaching 6 years later. Thus, substantial concerns about SETs' working conditions remain (Fowler et al., 2019).

Current State of Special Education Teachers' Working Conditions

SETs' current working conditions can fluctuate due to shifting social conditions, new policies, changing labor markets (Mason-Williams et al., 2020), and a number of personal and contextual factors (Scott et al., 2020). The factors that contribute to SETs' demands and resources includes but are not limited to (a) whether they serve in a high- or low-poverty school (Fall & Billingsley, 2011); (b) whether they work in rural or urban settings; (c) their service delivery model (Bettini et al., in revision); and (d) needs of students (Gilmour & Wehby, 2020). Focusing on recent studies, we review the current state of SETs' working conditions, highlighting demands and social, logistical, and informational resources.

Demands

SETs experience complex demands associated with their overlapping roles in (a) providing academic and behavioral instruction, (b) collaborating with colleagues, and (c) managing caseloads (Bettini et al., 2022). For example, to fulfill their instructional roles, SETs often teach smaller instructional groups (e.g., 10.38 students with individualized education program [IEPs], 12.66 including students with 504 plans; Giangreco et al., 2013) than general educators, but these groups tend to be highly heterogeneous, including students with varied instructional needs from varied grades (O'Brien et al., 2019). For instance, in a survey of 577 SETs from 221 districts in the United States, Leko et al. (2018) found SETs taught students who received services under, on average, 4.74 different disability labels, while SETs in O'Brien et al.'s (2019) survey reported being responsible for teaching 9 distinct subject/grade combinations. Consequently, SETs' responsibilities include planning lessons across many subject areas and grade levels, often in collaboration with many colleagues (Leko et al., 2018; O'Brien et al., 2019). Thus, SETs spend significant time on work responsibilities outside of work hours. For example, Bettini, Gilmour, et al. (2020) found the average SETs reported working more than 50 hours per week, far exceeding the contractual school day.

Social Resources

SETs depend on social resources, the supports provided by other educators (e.g., administrators, colleagues), school collective culture, and autonomy (the extent to which social context affords latitude to make decisions; Bettini et al., 2016; Billingsley et al., 2020). SETs often report moderate to high mean levels of administrator support (Albrecht et al., 2009; Bettini, Gilmour, et al., 2020; O'Brien et al., 2019), collegial support (Albrecht et al., 2009; Bettini, Gilmour, et al., 2020), and paraprofessional support (e.g., O'Brien et al., 2019). For example, in their 2017–2018 national survey, O'Brien et al. found SETs reported between half and most of their colleagues promoted a school culture supportive of students with disabilities. Further SETs perceived, on average, high levels of autonomy, reporting "a lot of control" over planning, teaching, and disciplining students (O'Brien et al., 2019). There is evidence, however, that SETs in higher poverty schools may experience weaker social resources (Fall & Billingsley, 2011), possibly due to higher personnel turnover (Béteille et al., 2012; Johnson et al., 2012), which could disrupt development of strong social support systems in schools (Simon & Johnson, 2015).

Informational Resources

SETs rely on formal PD and mentoring to receive timely and quality instructional guidance. However, in their national survey of SETs serving students with EBDs in self-contained settings, O'Brien et al. (2019) found that SETs reported participating in required PD fewer than one to three times per month, and, on average, they neither agreed nor disagreed with items representing indicators of PD quality, implying that they had limited access to PD and felt existing PD was mediocre. Similarly, in their survey of secondary SETs, Leko et al. (2018) determined SETs reported slightly fewer than 3 hours of PD focused on adolescents with disabilities, with less time devoted to literacy. No comparable recent data are available on rates of mentoring, though an analysis of a national sample of SETs from 1999 to 2000 revealed, encouragingly, that SETs in higher poverty districts (>39% students in poverty) had greater access to a formal mentoring program than SETs in lower poverty districts (Fall & Billingsley, 2011); however, these data are quite dated.

Logistical Resources

SETs rely on logistical resources, which include time for planning and material resources, to fulfill their responsibilities (Billingsley et al., 2020). In a national survey of SETs serving students with EBDs, SETs reported that they "seldom" to "sometimes" had adequate time to plan (O'Brien et al., 2019). These findings are perhaps unsurprising given that SETs spent, on average, 9.83 hours per week outside of their scheduled workday on planning and preparation (O'Brien et al., 2019). Similarly, in an earlier survey of SETs serving students with EBDs, the majority of SETs also rated their available time for paperwork as below satisfactory (Albrecht et al., 2009). Further, most SETs reported insufficient access to adequate curricular resources (Albrecht et al., 2009; O'Brien et al., 2019). In a nationally representative survey, SETs rated access to curricular resources slightly better, saying that they "somewhat agree" that they had necessary materials (Bettini, Gilmour, et al., 2020). Overall, although SETs indicate more positive experiences related to social resources, they continue to face high demands and weak logistical resources—substantial challenges to providing instruction and supports to students with disabilities.

Pathways Through Which Working Conditions Affect Students With Disabilities

COR theory (Hobfoll et al., 2018), ecological systems theory (Bronfenbrenner, 1992), and extant research highlight several pathways by which working conditions may affect students with disabilities via their SETs (Billingsley et al., 2020). First, working conditions affect SETs' opportunities to learn and enact effective practices, as well as their stress and burnout. By affecting individual SETs, working conditions can shape the quantity and quality of services they provide. Second, working conditions contribute to SETs' retention, thereby affecting (a) the size and quality of the SET workforce and (b) SETs distribution across schools, districts, and regions. By affecting who teaches where (e.g., high-poverty schools) and for how long (e.g., becoming experienced teachers), working conditions have the potential to increase the likelihood that students will be served by a well-qualified, experienced SET. These pathways are displayed in Figure 6.1, and we explain them in detail next.

Individual Effects

Working conditions shape individual SETs' experiences in their schools, including their opportunities to learn and enact effective practices (Bettini, Cumming, et al., 2020), as well as their stress and burnout (Brunsting et al., 2014; Cumming et al., 2020).

Opportunities to Learn and Enact Effective Practices

To effectively serve students with disabilities, SETs must know how to skillfully enact effective practices for academic instruction, behavior, social-emotional instruction, assessment, and collaboration (McLeskey et al., 2017). Thus, they need opportunities to learn (Brownell et al., 2010). In traditional preparation programs, SETs learn effective practices (Leko et al., 2015), but they still need opportunities to continue developing skill in using these practices throughout their careers. Further, opportunities to learn effective practices are insufficient without opportunities to enact those practices in service of students (Billingsley et al., 2020).

PD provided by the school or district is one of the most obvious working conditions intended to support SETs' learning (Billingsley et al., 2020). Though PD is an essential mechanism for developing skills, extant research indicates that access to multiple social and logistical resources may also shape SETs' learning and enactment of practices. First, researchers have learned that informal interactions with colleagues are a crucial source of teacher learning (e.g., Sun et al., 2017). For example, Sun et al. (2017), examining how teachers' instructional effectiveness (measured by students' standardized tests gains) changed over time, found the addition of a more effective teacher to a grade-level team resulted in "spillover" effects. When a highly effective teacher joined a team, other teachers became more effective, indicating teachers learn through team interactions (Sun et al., 2017). Although no large-scale studies have examined effects of interactions with colleagues on SETs' instructional effectiveness, extant studies confirm the importance of instructional interactions for SETs' instruction (Bettini et al., 2016). Further, collegial interactions may support SETs' opportunities to enact effective practices; for example, SETs in inclusive settings may depend on colleagues to ensure they have dedicated time with their students (Olson et al., 2016).

Second, extant research indicates school culture may play a crucial role in fostering positive interactions among teachers, such that teachers become more effective when they work in schools with positive and collaborative cultures (e.g., Ronfeldt et al., 2015). For example, Kraft and Papay (2014) determined new teachers became more effective (measured by students' achievement gains) over time, and their rate of growth was partly explained by their school's professional environment (a composite working conditions measure). There is no comparable research with SETs (Bettini et al., 2016), but case studies of inclusive schools suggest school culture is likely as important (e.g., McLeskey et al., 2014).

Third, curricular materials provide teachers guidance regarding academic content, how students learn content, and effective instructional practices to support learning (Ball & Cohen, 1996), with extant research indicating teachers may learn through interactions with curricular materials (e.g., Jackson & Makarin, 2016). For example, Jackson and Makarin (2016) conducted a randomized controlled trial evaluating how general educators' math instructional effectiveness changed in response to receiving lesson plans introducing new math content. Results were significant and meaningful,

Leveraging Working Conditions to Improve the Quality

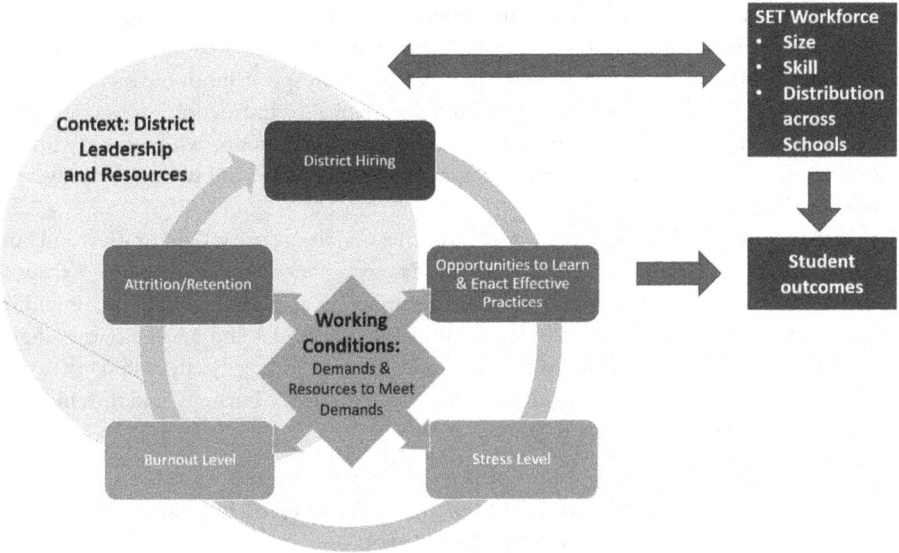

Figure 6.1 Mechanisms by Which SETs' Working Conditions May Contribute to Student Outcomes

with especially strong effects for teachers who were least effective initially. Though comparable studies have not been conducted with SETs, extant research indicates SETs may also learn new practices through curricular materials. For example, in a qualitative study, Siuty et al. (2018) found SETs who had access to research-based reading curricula were able to learn about and develop more accurate conceptions of their students' needs; further, curricula provided clear guidance on intensifying instruction, which led them to focus more on foundational skills than other SETs. Further, teachers often enact practices embedded in curricular materials, regardless of whether those practices align with what they know about effective instruction (e.g., Grossman & Thompson, 2008), suggesting quality curricular resources may support enactment of effective practices with students with disabilities.

Fourth, planning time may provide opportunities for SETs to enact effective practices by providing them dedicated time to examine goals, select or alter curricular materials, and make sense of student data (Bettini et al., 2016). Few studies have examined planning time, but extant research suggests it is important (Bettini et al., 2016). For example, Allinder (1996) examined factors differentiating SETs who enacted a newly learned practice with high vs. low fidelity; their ratings of planning time were the only significant differentiating factor, suggesting planning time may support integration of newly learned practices into SETs' instructional repertoires. Further, SETs report planning time contributes to their instruction (Bettini, Wang, et al., 2019) and that, without adequate planning time, they sometimes use instructional time for planning (Vannest et al., 2010). Thus, planning time may be essential for enacting effective practices.

Stress and Burnout

Working conditions may also contribute to negative affective outcomes for SETs, including stress and burnout (Bettini, Cumming, et al., 2020; Brunsting et al., 2014). Burnout is a condition characterized by emotional exhaustion, cynicism, and reduced sense of personal accomplishment, which occurs when prolonged stress exhausts one's resources to cope (Brunsting et al., 2014; Garwood et al., 2018). Burnout is associated with consequential educational processes (e.g., Oakes et al., 2020). For example, Wong et al. (2017) examined how burnout related to teaching quality and student outcomes among 79 SETs teaching students with autism spectrum disorders. They found SETs who experienced higher overall stress provided lower-quality instruction (as assessed by the Teacher Behavior Scale) and were less effective in engaging their students, while those who were more emotionally exhausted and demonstrated higher depersonalization had students who were less likely to achieve IEP goals.

Importantly, ample research indicates a range of working conditions are related to stress and burnout (e.g., Brunsting et al., 2014). For example, SETs may experience higher emotional exhaustion when they have inadequate planning time (Bettini, Cumming, et al., 2020), conflicting or ambiguous role expectations (Garwood et al., 2018), or insufficient collegial and administrative support (Zabel & Zabel, 2002). Thus, improving working conditions may indirectly affect students' experiences and outcomes by decreasing the likelihood SETs will experience burnout, and thus increasing the likelihood SETs will enact effective practices.

Size, Composition, and Distribution of the Special Education Teacher Workforce

Working conditions consistently predict attrition and intent to leave a career (Nguyen et al., 2020), including among SETs (Billingsley & Bettini, 2019). A robust and growing body of research conducted over the past 30 years consistently indicates that SETs who experience less supportive conditions (higher demands, weaker resources) are more likely to intend to leave and to actually leave teaching (Billingsley, 2004; Billingsley & Bettini, 2019). Prior studies indicate many working conditions are associated with intent to leave and/or attrition. Social resources (e.g., administrative support) have been examined more often than other working conditions; studies consistently find SETs are more likely to stay and to intend to stay when they experience supportive administrators, positive interactions with colleagues, and school cultures of collective responsibility for students with disabilities (Billingsley & Bettini, 2019). Other relevant working conditions include caseload characteristics (Gilmour & Wehby, 2020), paperwork (Albrecht et al., 2009), planning time (Bettini, Cumming, et al., 2020), and PD (Albrecht et al., 2009). Recent research suggests workload manageability—SETs' perceptions that they can manage demands with available resources—mediates relationships between working conditions and intent to leave, supporting the major tenets of COR theory (Bettini, Cumming, et al., 2020).

To our knowledge, no extant research has documented effects of SET attrition on students with disabilities (Billingsley & Bettini, 2019), but studies with general educators find significant effects. Ronfeldt et al. (2013) analyzed administrative data from the New York City school district, examining effects of teacher attrition on students' academic gains. They found that in grades with more turnover, students had significantly lower achievement compared to grades with lower turnover and compared to the same grade in a different year with lower turnover (Ronfeldt et al., 2013). McLeskey and Billingsley (2008) posited that these effects may be magnified among SETs, as their work involves collaboration with families and other educators; thus, when they leave, many collaborative relationships are disrupted, potentially amplifying the effects of their attrition.

In addition to direct effects on students, by contributing to SET attrition, working conditions are likely related to the (a) size, (b) composition, and (c) distribution of the SET workforce (Figure 6.1). First, attrition contributes to the shortage, which has been defined as "a shortage of fully qualified SETs who are willing to work for the wages we are able to pay and under the conditions we currently are able to provide in schools" (Mason-Williams et al., 2020, p. 56). Due to the shortage, administrators may struggle to replace SETs who leave. In 2016–2017, 38% of SETs worked in schools where administrators reported having a difficult-to-fill position (Gilmour et al., in review). Difficulties replacing SETs who leave may be magnified in high-poverty schools (Goldhaber et al., 2018), rural schools (Berry et al., 2011), and special education schools (Mason-Williams et al., 2017) and in positions serving students with certain disabilities (Berry et al., 2011), all of which tend to experience more substantial shortages. For example, Berry et al. (2011) surveyed 373 special education administrators in rural districts and found 72% reported problems filling vacancies for SETs who left, with particular difficulties replacing SETs serving students with autism, EBDs, severe/multiple disabilities, and sensory disabilities.

Second, the shortage, in turn, shapes the quality of the SET workforce, as administrators most often hire less experienced personnel to fill vacancies, a great concern given that teachers become more effective with more experience (e.g., Feng & Sass, 2013). Because of the ongoing shortage, a SET's decision to leave can place school leaders in the position of needing to hire less qualified personnel to replace them (Mason-Williams et al., 2020).

Third, higher-poverty schools often have more challenging working conditions due to resource disparities and, consequently, higher attrition (Simon & Johnson, 2015). Research with general educators indicates resulting patterns of attrition exacerbate teacher quality gaps between high- and low-poverty schools (Goldhaber et al., 2018). Goldhaber et al. used administrative data from two states to examine factors contributing to gaps in students' access to experienced teachers across advantaged versus disadvantaged schools. Over 10 years, discrepancies in rates of attrition from the profession explained about one-third of the disparity in students' access to experienced teachers across schools, while between-district transfers explained about one-third of the disparity, and within-district transfers explained near one-eighth of the disparity. SET turnover overall explained the majority of the disparity in students' access to experienced teachers.

Implications

National and State Policy

Policy initiatives have targeted the national shortage of qualified SETs since the inception of P.L. 94–142 in 1975 (Mason-Williams et al., 2020). Nationally, the Office of Special Education Programs (OSEP) has enacted many policies aimed at recruiting more SETs by, for example, funding teacher and leader training grants, as well as funding centers to support professional learning systems (e.g., teacher preparation, PD, evaluation) for SETs (e.g., Collaboration for Effective Educator Development, Evaluation, and Reform [CEEDAR] Center). At the state level, many states have created incentives to become SETs; for example, Hawaii currently offers $10,000 pay differentials to SETs (Hawaii DOE, 2020). Extant research suggests these efforts have yielded positive benefits (e.g., Feng & Sass, 2017).

However, we contend that these policies are likely incomplete if they do not also address SETs' working conditions (Billingsley et al., 2020). For example, salary incentives are effective at reducing attrition (Feng & Sass, 2017) and should be continued, yet they might induce a burned-out teacher to stay without addressing the causes of burnout, which could limit their utility for improving student outcomes. We recommend that state and national policy complement current policies with initiatives to improve SETs' working conditions.

We recognize that constructing policy to promote stronger working conditions poses a substantial challenge, as working conditions are multidimensional, deeply embedded within particular school and district organizations, and variable across schools and districts. For example, SETs in one district may experience challenges with school cultures that are hostile to inclusion of students with disabilities in general education, while SETs in a neighboring district may experience ample support for inclusion, but insufficient curricular materials for supporting foundational skill instruction. The policies needed in these two contexts would likely differ.

One potential state-level approach would be to systematically and regularly collect data on SETs' working conditions and use this data to target supports to districts to improve specific working conditions.[1] By administering a working conditions survey to all SETs in the state yearly, states could provide all districts with relevant data and share targeted assistance and PD with districts with especially concerning working conditions. Further, states could use the data generated to evaluate intended and unintended effects of other policy initiatives. Whereas prior policies have primarily targeted either recruitment or retention, such an initiative could affect every aspect of the system illustrated in Figure 6.1.

Teacher Educators

Given teacher educators' knowledge, expertise, and experience, teacher educators have a unique opportunity to support preservice SETs to understand and respond to the challenges of using effective practices in current school contexts (Billingsley et al., 2020). Research demonstrates that novice SETs encounter an unexpected range of extra responsibilities that they did not envision as core to their role, and they struggle to navigate these responsibilities within contexts that often do not provide the supports they may expect (Mathews et al., 2017). We encourage teacher educators to provide preservice SETs learning opportunities focused on navigating challenging working conditions and maintaining high instructional quality despite high demands and limited resources.

District and School Administrators

District leaders may leverage working conditions to support SETs in fulfilling their roles and responsibilities, and thereby improve the quality and effectiveness of the SET workforce. First, district administrators should consider collecting data to gain a clear understanding of working conditions SETs experience in their district. We encourage districts to administer yearly a reliable and valid measure(s) of SETs' working conditions, as well as conduct interviews (e.g., exit interviews) to gain insight into current and changing working conditions across the district. Second, we recommend district administrators use data to identify systemic challenges and strengths SETs experience within and across schools in their district. For example, administrators can examine the extent to which SETs in their district have adequate access to social, logistical, or informational resources and target these for improvement as needed. Based on their data, leaders may find they need to adjust district-wide policies (e.g., caseloads), practices (e.g., district PD), and/or funding (e.g., for curriculum) to better support SETs. Third, we suggest district leaders work closely with colleagues and school leaders to collaborate on how best to leverage working conditions. Because school leaders often have limited knowledge on how to lead special education (Petzko, 2008), district leaders may need to provide training, coaching, and support regarding SETs' working conditions.

We encourage school leaders to work closely with SETs to evaluate and improve how they proactively support SETs. For instance, school leaders may find SETs in their schools feel overwhelmed by the demands placed on them. Adding more paraprofessionals may seem like a feasible way to reduce demands, but past research has found that supervising paraprofessionals may constitute an additional demand (Bettini, Cumming, et al., 2020). Thus, administrators should collaborate with SETs to determine what resources will be most helpful for addressing demands. As a proactive approach, school leaders can ensure SETs have access to needed resources at the start of each school year. For example, administrators can ensure the school's master schedule provides collaborative planning opportunities and protected planning time. Similarly, leaders can ensure SETs have access to the same curricular resources as general educators, as well as access to remediated materials for varied student ability levels. Because school leaders' ability to create a supportive work environment may be limited by funding and district policies, we encourage them to actively engage with district leaders to obtain resources.

Special Education Teachers

Teachers play a critical role in promoting inclusion for students and shaping policy in their schools (Li & Ruppar, 2020). As such, SETs may be a powerful force for improving working conditions in their schools, as they can advocate for the resources they need to effectively serve their students (Bettini, Lillis, et al., 2021). We encourage SETs to document the challenges they experience and communicate these challenges to others in a position to help. For instance, if there is little access to formal mentoring, SETs can actively connect with others who have relevant expertise. SETs who have insufficient planning time or curricular resources can work with administration to communicate why these are important and to find solutions.

However, working conditions are unlikely to change immediately, and SETs who are experiencing stress and burnout should also engage in self-care, using research-based strategies to effectively manage stress (Ansley et al., 2016). Note, we concur with Valerio (2019), that "shouting 'self-care' at people who actually need community care is how we fail people," and we argue systemic improvements to working conditions are needed. Yet SETs cannot wait for systemic solutions for their well-being to be a priority. Ansley et al. (2016) highlighted several evidenced-supported stress-management activities (i.e., exercise, yoga, mindfulness). They recommend SETs use these strategies in the context of a self-directed stress management plan: (a) identify stress-related symptoms (e.g., high blood pressure, dread); (b) select strategies from each of the three stress-management areas (e.g., physical activity; relaxation; health functioning); (c) implement the plan; and (d) assess progress. By using a self-directed stress management plan, SETs can build stress management skills and potentially reduce school-related stress.

Future Research

Research on working conditions is a growing line of inquiry, and much research is needed. Most existing research does not disaggregate results by SET characteristics (e.g., disability served, service delivery model, race/ethnicity, gender; Billingsley et al., 2020), which limits our understanding of how working conditions may differ for different groups of SETs. Research examining differences in SETs' experiences of working conditions is needed.

Further, we recommend scholars measure all salient working conditions and examine relationships among them, as prior research (and COR theory) indicates they interact with one another in complex ways (Cumming et al., 2020). For example, SETs with stronger curricular resources may perceive planning time as more adequate because they have to spend less time finding and creating materials (Bettini, Cumming, et al., 2020). In a systematic review of studies measuring SETs' working conditions, Stark et al. (in review) found few studies measured all working conditions. Because SETs' outcomes result from the balance between their demands and resources to meet demands (Cumming et al., 2020), studies measuring the full range of working conditions are needed to fully understand how working conditions might be improved.

We encourage scholars to investigate how working conditions relate to a broader range of outcomes, including instructional practice, student outcomes, and implementation of interventions (Cumming et al., 2020). For example, scholars could explore how working conditions moderate enactment of practices learned in PD (Billingsley et al., 2020). Further, we encourage scholars to conduct studies on *how* to effectively change working conditions (Billingsley et al., 2020), as there are currently no working condition interventions for SETs.

Because research is only as strong as the validity of measures used, we urge researchers to develop a comprehensive, valid, and reliable working-conditions measure for SETs. Few extant measures comprehensively evaluate all salient working conditions, and prior validation work is limited (Stark et al., in review). For instance, the Study of Personnel Needs in Special Education (SPeNSE) is among the most comprehensive measures, but it omits most logistical resources (e.g., planning time), and psychometric properties beyond reliability are unexamined (Stark et al., in review). O'Brien et al.'s (2019) measure captures a range of demands and resources and has strong psychometric properties (Bettini, Cumming, et al., 2020), but it evaluates working conditions of SETs with students with EBDs in self-contained settings. A comprehensive measure, validated for all SETs, is needed.

Future working conditions research would also benefit from relying on more consistent theoretical foundations (Stark et al., in review). Prior scholars have used varied theoretical frameworks (e.g., social cognitive theory [Scott, 2012]; COR theory [Bettini, Gilmour, et al., 2020]). Using a shared framework (e.g., Figure 6.1) can support researchers in establishing a shared understanding of SETs' working conditions, as well as identify trends across studies.

Additional Readings and Resources

- IRIS Module: Teacher Retention: Reducing the Attrition of Special Education Teachers: https://iris.peabody.vanderbilt.edu/module/tchr-ret/
- Bettini, E., Cumming, M. M., Brunsting, N., McKenna, J. W., Schneider, C., Muller, B., & Peyton, D. (2020). Administrators' roles: Providing special educators opportunities to learn and enact effective reading practices for students with EBD. *Beyond Behavior*, *29*, 52–61.
- Billingsley, B., Bettini, E., Mathews, H. M., & McLeskey, J. (2020). Improving working conditions to support special educators' effectiveness: A call for leadership. *Teacher Education and Special Education*, *43*(1), 7–27. https://doi.org/10.1177/0888406419880353

Note

1 Nineteen states currently administer the New Teacher Center's Teaching, Empowering, Leading, and Learning (TELL) survey to all teachers in the state. However, TELL data are aggregated to the school level, and SETs' data cannot be disaggregated. The TELL administration indicates that such efforts are possible; potentially, a SET-specific survey could supplement current data systems.

References

Alarcon, G. M. (2011). A meta-analysis of burnout with job demands, resources, and attitudes. *Journal of Vocational Behavior*, *79*, 549–562. https://doi.org/10.1016/j.jvb.2011.03.007

Albrecht, S. F., Johns, B. H., Mounsteven, J., & Olorunda, O. (2009). Working conditions as risk or resiliency factors for teachers of students with emotional and behavioral disabilities. *Psychology in the Schools*, *46*(10), 1006–1022. https://doi.org/10.1002/pits.20440

Allinder, R. M. (1996). When some is not better than none: Effects of differential implementation of curriculum-based measurement. *Exceptional Children*, *62*(6), 525–535. https://doi.org/10.1177/001440299606200604

Ansley, B. M., Houchins, D., & Varjas, K. (2016). Optimizing special educator wellness and job performance through stress management. *Teaching Exceptional Children*, *48*(4), 176–185. https://doi.org/10.1177/0040059915626128

Ball, D. L., & Cohen, D. K. (1996). Reform by the book: What is: Or might be: The role of curriculum materials in teacher learning and instructional reform? *Educational Researcher*, *25*(9), 6–8. https://doi.org/10.2307/1177151

Berry, A. B., Petrin, R. A., Gravelle, M. L., & Farmer, T. W. (2011). Issues in special education teacher recruitment, retention, and professional development: Considerations in supporting rural teachers. *Rural Special Education Quarterly, 30*(4), 3–11. https://doi.org/10.1177/875687051103000402

Béteille, T., Kalogrides, D., & Loeb, S. (2012). Stepping stones: Principal career paths and school outcomes. *Social Science Research, 41*(4), 904–919. https://doi.org/10.1016/j.ssresearch.2012.03.003

Bettini, E. A., Crockett, J. B., Brownell, M. T., & Merrill, K. L. (2016). Relationships between working conditions and special educators' instruction. *The Journal of Special Education, 50*(3), 178–190. https://doi.org/10.1177/0022466916644425

Bettini, E. A., Cumming, M. M., O'Brien, K. M., Brunsting, N. C., Ragunathan, M., Sutton, R., & Chopra, A. (2020). Predicting special educators' intent to continue teaching students with emotional or behavioral disorders in self-contained settings. *Exceptional Children, 86*(2), 209–228. https://doi.org/10.1177/0014402919873556

Bettini, E. A., Gilmour, A. F., Williams, T. O., & Billingsley, B. (2020). Predicting special and general educators' intent to continue teaching using conservation of resources theory. *Exceptional Children, 86*(3), 310–329. https://doi.org/10.1177/0014402919870464

Bettini, E. A., Lillis, J., Stark, K., Brunsting, N., & Morris-Mathews, H. (2021). Special educators' experiences of interpersonal interactions in self-contained settings for students with emotional/behavioral disorders. *Remedial and Special Education*. https://doi.org/10.1177/07419325211022833.

Bettini, E., Morris-Mathews, H., Lillis, J., Meyer, K., Shaheen, T., Kaler, L., & Brunsting, N. C. (2022). Special educators' roles in inclusive schools. Invited chapter for J. McLeskey, F. Spooner, B. Algozzine, & N. L. Waldron (Eds.), *Handbook of Effective, Inclusive Elementary Schools: Research and Practice*. Routledge. https://www.routledge.com/Handbook-of-Effective-Inclusive-Elementary-Schools-Research-and-Practice/McLeskey-Spooner-Algozzine-Nancy-Waldron/p/book/9780367486778

Bettini, E., Wang, J., Cumming, M., Kimerling, J., & Schutz, S. (2019). Special educators' experiences of roles and responsibilities in self-contained classes for students with emotional/behavioral disorders. *Remedial and Special Education, 40*(3), 177–191. https://doi.org/10.1177/0741932518762470

Billingsley, B. S. (2004). Special education teacher retention and attrition: A critical analysis of the research literature. *The Journal of Special Education, 38*(1), 39–55. https://doi.org/10.1177/00224669040380010401

Billingsley, B. S., & Bettini, E. (2019). Special education teacher attrition and retention: A review of the literature. *Review of Educational Research, 89*(5), 697–744. https://doi.org/10.3102/0034654319862495

Billingsley, B. S., Bettini, E., Mathews, H. M., & McLeskey, J. (2020). Improving working conditions to support special educators' effectiveness: A call for leadership. *Teacher Education and Special Education, 43*(1), 7–27. https://doi.org/10.1177/0888406419880353

Bronfenbrenner, U. (1992). Ecological systems theory. In R. Vasta (Ed.), *Six theories of child development: Revised formulations and current issues* (pp. 188–249). Jessica Kingsley.

Brownell, M. T., Sindelar, P. T., Kiely, M. T., & Danielson, L. C. (2010). Special education teacher quality and preparation: Exposing foundations, constructing a new model. *Exceptional Children, 76*(3), 357–377. https://doi.org/0.1177/001440291007600307

Brunsting, N. C., Sreckovic, M. A., & Lane, K. L. (2014). Special education teacher burnout: A synthesis of research from 1979 to 2013. *Education and Treatment of Children, 37*(4), 681–711. https://doi.org/10.1353/etc.2014.0032

Common, E. A., Lane, K. L., Cantwell, E. D., Brunsting, N. C., Oakes, W. P., Germer, K. A., & Bross, L. A. (2020). Teacher-delivered strategies to increase students' opportunities to respond: A systematic methodological review. *Behavioral Disorders, 45*(2), 67–84. https://doi.org/10.1177/0198742919828310

Cumming, M. M., O'Brien, K. M., Brunsting, N. C., & Bettini, E. (2020). Special educators' working conditions, self-efficacy, and practices use with students with emotional/behavioral disorders. *Remedial and Special Education*. https://doi.org/10.1177/0741932520924121

Dewey, J., Sindelar, P. T., Bettini, E., Boe, E. E., Rosenberg, M. S., & Leko, C. (2017). Explaining the decline in special education teacher employment from 2005 to 2012. *Exceptional Children, 83*(3), 315–329. https://doi.org/10.1177/0014402916684620

Education for All Handicapped Children Act of 1975, Pub. L. No. 94-142.89 Stat. 773 (1975).

Fall, A. M., & Billingsley, B. S. (2011). Disparities in work conditions among early career special educators in high-and low-poverty districts. *Remedial and Special Education, 32*(1), 64–78. https://doi.org/10.1177/0741932510361264

Feng, L., & Sass, T. R. (2013). What makes special education teachers special? Teacher training and achievement of students with disabilities. *Economics of Education Review, 36*, 122–134. https://doi.org/10.1016/j.econedurev.2013.06.006

Feng, L., & Sass, T. R. (2017). The impact of incentives to recruit and retain teachers in "hard-to-staff" subjects. *Journal of Policy Analysis and Management, 37*, 112–135. https://doi.org/10.1002/pam.22037

Fowler, S. A., Coleman, M. R. B., & Bogdan, W. K. (2019). The state of the special education profession survey report. *TEACHING Exceptional Children, 52*(1), 8–29. https://doi.org/10.1177/0040059919875703

Garwood, J. D., Werts, M. G., Varghese, C., & Gosey, L. (2018). Mixed-methods analysis of rural special educators' role stressors, behavior management, and burnout. *Rural Special Education Quarterly, 37*(1), 30–43. https://doi.org/10.1177/8756870517745270

Giangreco, M. F., Suter, J. C., & Hurley, S. M. (2013). Revisiting personnel utilization in inclusion-oriented schools. *The Journal of Special Education, 47*(2), 121–132. https://doi.org/10.1177/0022466911419015

Gilmour, A., Nguyen, T., Redding, C., & Bettini, E. (in press). The shifting context of special education teachers' work and its relationship with retention. *Remedial and Special Education.*

Gilmour, A. F., & Wehby, J. H. (2020). The association between teaching students with disabilities and teacher turnover. *Journal of Educational Psychology, 112*(5), 1042–1060. https://doi.org/10.1037/edu0000394

Goldhaber, D., Quince, V., & Theobald, R. (2018). Has it always been this way? Tracing the evolution of teacher quality gaps in U.S. public schools. *American Educational Research Journal, 55*(1), 171–201. https://doi.org/10.3102/0002831217733445

Grossman, P. L., & Thompson, C. (2008). Learning from curriculum materials: Scaffolds for new teachers? *Teaching and Teacher Education, 24*(8), 2014–2026. https://doi.org/10.1016/j.tate.2008.05.002

Halbesleben, J. R. B. (2006). Sources of social support and burnout: A meta-analytic test of the conservation of resources model. *Journal of Applied Psychology, 91*(5), 1134–1145. https://doi.org/10.1037/0021-9010.91.5.1134

Halbesleben, J. R. B., Neveu, J.-P., Paustian-Underdahl, S. C., & Westman, M. (2014). Getting to the "COR": Understanding the role of resources in conservation of resources theory. *Journal of Management, 40*(5), 1334–1364. https://doi.org/10.1177/0149206314527130

Hobfoll, S. E., Halbesleben, J., Neveu, J. P., & Westman, M. (2018). Conservation of resources in the organizational context: The reality of resources and their consequences. *Annual Review of Organizational Psychology and Organizational Behavior, 5*(1), 103–128. https://doi.org/10.1146/annurev-orgpsych-032117-104640

Individuals with Disabilities Education Act of 2004, 20 U.S.C § 1400 (2004).

Jackson, C. K., & Makarin, A. (2016). Can online off-the-shelf lessons improve student outcomes? Evidence from a field experiment. *American Economic Journal: Economic Policy, 10*(3), 226–254. https://doi.org/10.3386/w22398

Johnson, S. M., Kraft, M. A., & Papay, J. P. (2012). How context matters in high-need schools: The effects of teachers' working conditions on their professional satisfaction and their students' achievement. *Teachers College Record, 114*(10), 1–39.

Kauffman, J. M., & Landrum, T. J. (2018). *Characteristics of emotional and behavioral disorders of children and youth* (11th ed.). Pearson.

Kozleski, E., Mainzer, R., & Deshler, D. (2000). Bright futures for exceptional learners: An agenda to achieve quality conditions for teaching and learning. *TEACHING Exceptional Children, 32*(6), 56–69. https://doi.org/10.1177/004005990003200608

Kraft, M. A., & Papay, J. P. (2014). Can professional environments in schools promote teacher development? Explaining heterogeneity in returns to teaching experience. *Educational Evaluation and Policy Analysis, 36*(4), 476–500. https://doi.org/10.3102/0162373713519496

Kurth, J. A., Born, K., & Love, H. (2016). Ecobehavioral characteristics of self-contained high school classrooms for students with severe cognitive disability. *Research and Practice for Persons with Severe Disabilities, 41*(4), 227–243. https://doi.org/10.1177/1540796916661492

Leko, M. M., Brownell, M. T., Sindelar, P. T., & Kiely, M. T. (2015). Envisioning the future of special education personnel preparation in a standards-based era. *Exceptional Children, 82*(1), 25–43. https://doi.org/10.1177/0014402915598782

Leko, M. M., Chiu, M. M., & Roberts, C. A. (2018). Individual and contextual factors related to secondary special education teachers' reading instructional practices. *The Journal of Special Education, 51*(4), 236–250. https://doi.org/10.1177/0022466917727514

Li, L., & Ruppar, A. (2020). Conceptualizing teacher agency for inclusive education: A systematic and international review. *Teacher Education and Special Education.* https://doi.org/10.1177/0888406420926976

Mason-Williams, L., Bettini, E., & Gagnon, J. (2017). Access to qualified special educators across elementary neighborhood and exclusionary schools. *Remedial and Special Education, 38*(5), 297–307. https://doi.org/10.1177/0741932517713311

Mason-Williams, L., Bettini, E., Peyton, D., Harvey, A., Rosenberg, M., & Sindelar, P. T. (2020). Rethinking shortages in special education: Making good on the promise of an equal opportunity for students with disabilities. *Teacher Education and Special Education, 43*(1), 45–62. https://doi.org/10.1177/0888406419880352

Mathews, H. M., Rodgers, J. D., & Youngs, P. Y. (2017). Sensemaking for beginning special educators: A systematic mixed studies review. *Teaching and Teacher Education, 67*, 23–36. https://doi.org/10.1016/j.tate.2017.05.007

McLeskey, J., Barringer, M.-D., Billingsley, B., Brownell, M., Jackson, D., & Ziegler, D. (2017). *High-leverage practices in special education.* Council for Exceptional Children & CEEDAR Center. http://ceedar.education.ufl.edu/portfolio/ccsc-2017-high-leverage-practice

McLeskey, J., & Billingsley, B. S. (2008). How does the quality and stability of the teaching force influence the research-to-practice gap? A perspective on the teacher shortage in special education. *Remedial and Special Education, 29*(5), 293–305. https://doi.org/10.1177/0741932507312010

McLeskey, J., Waldron, N. L., & Redd, L. (2014). A case study of a highly effective, inclusive elementary school. *The Journal of Special Education, 48*(1), 59–70. https://doi.org/10.1177/0022466912440455

Nguyen, T. D., Pham, L. D., Crouch, M., & Springer, M. G. (2020). The correlates of teacher turnover: An updated and expanded meta-analysis of the literature. *Educational Research Review, 31*, 100355. https://doi.org/10.1016/j.edurev.2020.100355

Oakes, W. P., Lane, K. L., Royer, D. J., Menzies, H. M., Buckman, M. M., Brunsting, N., Cantwell, E. D., Schatschneider, C., & Lane, N. A. (2020). Elementary teachers' self-efficacy during initial implementation of comprehensive, integrated, three-tiered models of prevention. *Journal of Positive Behavior Interventions.* https://doi.org/10.1177/1098300720916718

O'Brien, K. M., Brunsting, N. C., Bettini, E., Cumming, M. M., Ragunathan, M., & Sutton, R. (2019). Special educators' working conditions in self-contained settings for students with emotional or behavioral disorders: A descriptive analysis. *Exceptional Children, 86*(1), 40–57. https://doi.org/10.1177/0014402919868946

Olson, A., Leko, M. M., & Roberts, C. A. (2016). Providing students with severe disabilities access to the general education curriculum. *Research and Practice for Persons with Severe Disabilities, 41*(3), 143–157. https://doi.org/10.1177/1540796916651975

Petzko, V. (2008). The perceptions of new principals regarding the knowledge and skills important to their initial success. *NASSP Bulletin, 92*(3), 224–250. https://doi.org/10.1177/0192636508322824

Ronfeldt, M., Loeb, S., & Wyckoff, J. (2013). How teacher turnover harms student achievement. *American Educational Research Journal, 50*(1), 4–36. https://doi.org/10.3102/0002831212463813

Ronfeldt, M., Owens Farmer, S., McQueen, K., & Grisson, J. A. (2015). Teacher collaboration in instructional teams and student achievement. *American Educational Research Journal, 52*(3), 475–514. https://doi.org/10.3102/0002831215585562

Scott, L. A. (2012). Teacher self-efficacy with teaching students to lead IEP meetings: A correlation study on administration support. *Journal on Educational Psychology, 5*(3), 9–20. http://dx.doi.org/10.26634/jpsy.5.3.1655

Scott, L. A., Brown, A., Wallace, W., Powell, C., Cormier, C. J. (2020). If we're not doing it, then who? A qualitative study of Black special educators' persistence. *Exceptionality.* https://doi.org/10.1080/09362835.2020.1850453

Simon, N. S., & Johnson, S. M. (2015). Teacher turnover in high-poverty schools: What we know and can do. *Teachers College Record, 117*(3), 1–36.

Siuty, M. B., Leko, M. M., & Knackstedt, K. M. (2018). Unraveling the role of curriculum in teacher decision making. *Teacher Education and Special Education, 41*(1), 39–57. https://doi.org/10.1177/0888406416683230

Stark, K., Bettini, E., Cumming, M., O'Brien, K., Brunsting, N., Huggins, C., Shaheen, T., & Binkert, G. (in review). A systematic review of the measurement of special educators' working conditions. *Review of Educational Research.*

Sun, M., Loeb, S., & Grissom, J. A. (2017). Building teacher teams: Evidence of positive spillovers from more effective colleagues. *Educational Evaluation and Policy Analysis, 39*(1), 104–125. https://doi.org/10.3102/0162373716665698

Theobald, R., Goldhaber, D., Naito, N., & Stein, M. (2020). *The special education teacher pipeline: Teacher preparation, workforce entry, and retention* (Working Paper No. 231–0220). National Center for Analysis of Longitudinal Data in Education Research.

Valerio, N. (2019, March 24). Shouting 'self-care' at people who actually need community care is how we fail people. [Status update]. Facebook. https://m.facebook.com/story.php?story_fbid=10156721251245568&id=665010567

Vannest, K. J., Soares, D. A., Harrison, J. R., Brown, L., & Parker, R. I. (2010). Changing teacher time. *Preventing School Failure. 54*(2), 86–98. https://doi.org/10.1080/10459880903217739

Weatherley, R., & Lipsky, M. (1977). Street-level bureaucrats and institutional innovation: Implementing special education reform. *Harvard Educational Review*, *47*(2), 171–197. https://doi.org/10.17763/haer.47.2.v870r1v16786270x

Wexler, J., Kearns, D. M., Lemons, C. J., Mitchell, M., Clancy, E., Davidson, K. A., Sinclair, A. C., & Wei, Y. (2018). Reading Comprehension and Co-Teaching Practices in Middle School English Language Arts Classrooms. *Exceptional Children*, *84*(4), 384–402. https://doi.org/10.1177/0014402918771543

Wong, V. W., Ruble, L. A., Yu, Y., & McGrew, J. H. (2017). Too stressed to teach? Teaching quality, student engagement, and IEP outcomes. *Exceptional Children*, *83*(4), 412–427. https://doi.org/10.1177/0014402917690729

Zabel, R. H., & Zabel, M. K. (2002). Burnout among special education teachers and perceptions of support. *Journal of Special Education Leadership*, *15*(2), 67–73

7
ADVANCES IN INTERVENTIONS FOR STUDENTS WITH READING DIFFICULTIES

Nathan H. Clemens, Alexis N. Boucher, and Katherine O'Donnell

The consequences of reading difficulties are significant. Reading difficulties are associated with school dropout, unemployment, and delinquency (Reynolds & Ou, 2004; Wagner et al., 2005), all of which are a burden to lives and society. Learning disabilities comprise the largest group of students eligible for special education services (33%; National Center for Education Statistics, 2021), and 80% of these individuals demonstrate difficulties in reading (Society for Neuroscience, 2004). Reading difficulties are common among students with or at risk for disabilities in other areas such as attention, behavior, and autism (e.g., Brown et al., 2013; Morgan et al., 2008; Rabiner et al., 2000). A continued focus on intervention for students with reading difficulties is necessary for students, their families, and society as a whole.

Current practices in reading intervention center on the use of explicit instruction and opportunities to individualize instruction based on students' needs. Explicit instruction refers to (a) segmenting complex skills, (b) teacher modeling and demonstration, (c) systematically fading supports and prompts, (d) providing opportunities for students to respond to and receive feedback, and (e) creating purposeful practice opportunities (Hughes et al., 2017). Supported opportunities to read are critical; reading practice with immediate affirmative or corrective feedback are key to developing efficient word recognition (Ehri & Saltmarsh, 1995), and reading experience builds vocabulary and background knowledge necessary for comprehension (Cain & Oakhill, 2011). Ongoing data collection (i.e., progress monitoring) either informs when effective interventions should continue or signals when ineffective programs should be adjusted to improve students' rates of growth (Danielson & Rosenquist, 2014; D. Fuchs et al., 2014).

In this chapter, we focus specifically on interventions in the two primary areas in which reading difficulties occur: word reading and reading comprehension. For each area, we first discuss common practices and research-based intervention approaches. Then, we discuss advances and innovations in interventions, driven by recent research, that show promise for targeting unmet needs for students with reading disabilities. All intervention approaches are applicable to students identified with a learning disability in reading, students considered to be at risk for such identification, or students with disabilities or identification in other areas who experience co-occurring difficulties in reading.

Word-Level Reading Difficulties

Learning to read individual words with accuracy and efficiency represents a primary hurdle for a developing reader (Adams, 1990). Indeed, word-level reading difficulties (WLRDs) are the most commonly occurring form of reading difficulty, and individuals with an identified disability in this area (i.e., dyslexia, specific learning disability in basic reading) represent the largest subgroup of the reading disability population (Torgesen, 2004). Common estimates of the prevalence of dyslexia fall in the range of 3% to 7% of the total student population. Many more students have WLRDs that have not been formally identified, and WLRD commonly co-occurs with attention deficit hyperactivity disorder (ADHD), behavior disorders, and mathematics difficulties (Fletcher et al., 2018).

One of the most commonly observed characteristics among students with WLRDs is a deficit in phonemic awareness—the ability to perceive and manipulate the smallest sound units of speech (i.e., phonemes) within words (Melby-Lervåg et al., 2012; Snowling, 1995). Phonemic awareness allows a child to segment a word into its component phonemes, blend phonemes together to form a word, or alter one or more phonemes in a word to create a new word. Phonemic awareness is important because it (a) facilitates connecting speech sounds to printed letters (i.e., letter-sound knowledge; the "alphabetic principle"), which provides the essential foundation for decoding, and (b) affords the ability to use phonemic segmenting and blending to decode (read) and encode (spell) words (Ehri, 2020; Melby-Lervåg et al., 2012).

WLRD may also occur due to insufficient instruction in foundational reading skills in the primary years of schooling. In addition to direct instruction, a developing reader requires numerous supported opportunities to read. Among students with attention and behavior disorders, low motivation to read or behaviors that interfere with instruction may be associated with disrupted and inconsistent opportunities to learn. Regardless of whether WLRDs are the result of an underlying disability, inadequate instruction, or insufficient opportunities to read, there are little differences in how to best intervene.

Practices, Advances, and Next Steps in Word-Level Reading Interventions

Research has consistently supported the use of explicit phonics instruction, which directly and unambiguously teaches the connections between letters and sounds and how to use that information to read and spell words, for teaching beginning readers and students with WLRDs (Ehri et al., 2001; Ehri, 2020; Wanzek et al., 2018). Instruction in phonemic awareness is an inherent part of phonics instruction, and effective practices emphasize phoneme segmenting and blending within word decoding and spelling activities (Adams, 1990; Bus & IJzendoorn, 1999; Ehri, 2020). Repeated opportunities to read words, with teacher support and feedback, are necessary to bind letter strings to pronunciations in increasingly larger units (Ehri, 2020), which allows words to be read with little conscious effort (i.e., automaticity). Word-level automaticity is a primary driver of text-reading fluency (Jenkins et al., 2003), and strategies for building text-reading fluency have most often utilized repeated reading of text (Stevens et al., 2017).

Although much has been learned about effective strategies and practices for students with WLRDs, unmet needs remain. For starters, a sizeable portion of students do not respond adequately to interventions that are effective for most students (e.g., Austin et al., 2017). Second, intervention studies for students with WLRDs have observed that pseudoword decoding and reading accuracy tend to be more amenable to intervention, but weaker and less consistent effects have been observed for reading real words and text with fluency (Flynn et al., 2012; Torgesen et al., 2001). Scholars have investigated ways to enhance existing practices and to explore new directions for targeting WLRD.

Teaching a Set of Decoding Strategies and How to Flexibly Apply Them

Theory and research have examined the gap that must be bridged between a pronunciation derived by individual letter sounds to how the word is pronounced correctly (i.e., its "standard pronunciation"). To ultimately read word like *listen* as "lissen" and not "liss-ten," the reader must learn to reconcile the information provided by its letter sounds—its *spelling pronunciation*—with its standard pronunciation. This connection requires flexibility on the part of the reader, referred to as "set for variability" (Venezky, 1999; Tunmer & Chapman, 2012), or an intermediary step (Elbro & de Jong, 2017) in decoding. Skills in adjusting word pronunciations are powerful predictors of general reading skills (Steacy et al., 2019) and may be underdeveloped among students with reading difficulties (Kearns et al., 2016). Compton et al. (2014) argued that traditional word-reading interventions (a) tend to emphasize a letter-by-letter word attack approach that may not adequately build students' consolidation of letters into larger spelling units that is necessary for efficient word recognition and (b) do not provide students with sufficient exposure to variable spelling pronunciations that are inherent in an opaque orthography like English.

Promoting students' set for variability and their ability to navigate variable spelling pronunciations can be built into interventions. Lovett and colleagues' multicomponent intervention, Triple Focus (Lovett et al., 2017), involved teaching five word identification strategies and training students to apply them flexibly when they encounter an unknown word: (a) sounding out; (b) reading by rime/analogy (e.g., "if I know best, I can read crest"); (c) "peeling off" to isolate prefixes or suffixes and the root word and reading the parts together as a whole word; (d) vowel alert in which students are taught to apply alternative pronunciations for vowel sounds (e.g., first try oo as in look, then try oo as in boot, read when a word makes sense); and (e) the SPY strategy to find smaller words within larger words, as in compound words like "cupcake." Statistically significant and sizable effect sizes ($d = 0.59$ to 1.39) were observed for students with WLRD in grades 1 to 3 favoring the Triple Focus group on measures of reading accuracy, word-reading efficiency, decoding efficiency, reading fluency, spelling, and reading comprehension. To be clear, the Triple Focus program also included instruction in vocabulary, reading fluency, and reading comprehension; therefore, it is not clear what component was most responsible for reading improvement. Nevertheless, the approach is an example of how "phonics" intervention can be designed to equip students with a versatile set of word-reading strategies, including those that support flexible pronunciations while decoding.

Considering Statistical and Probabilistic Learning

Statistical learning refers to skill and knowledge acquisition that is driven by the recognition of patterns and probabilistic sequences within and across stimuli. The human brain learns from experience; we are highly tuned to recognize patterns and associate things that either do or do not tend to occur together. Statistical learning offers explanations for how children can acquire language without formal instruction.

Phonics instruction helps students learn to read many types of words, but the irregularities of an orthography like English means that phonics instruction alone is not entirely sufficient. Scholars have argued that perceiving underlying statistical regularities of spelling patterns in words may explain the ability for skilled readers to read tens of thousands of words, some of which have variable spelling-sound connections, without instruction on each one (Arciuli, 2018; Mano & Kloos, 2018). The idea is that typically developing readers, through repeated exposure to words, implicitly build an understanding of how the pronunciation of letter combinations can be influenced by their position in a word (e.g., gh in ghost vs. laugh) or surrounding letters (e.g., ea in bead vs. learn). Essentially, they begin to recognize the statistical regularities of the English spelling system. Correlational evidence indicates that readers are highly sensitive to the frequency with which letter patterns recur and their position within words (Chetail, 2017), which has been observed even among older preschoolers (but not younger, less experienced children; Mano & Kloos, 2018). Steacy et al. (2020) found that, compared with typically developing readers, students with WLRDs had more difficulty attending to letters and units of letters within words, which likely negatively affects their ability to learn context-dependent pronunciations of lower-frequency letters and letter combinations.

The implications of this work are that interventions for WLRDs could be adjusted to draw students' attention to statistical regularities in letter patterns and pronunciations. But how can that be applied in interventions? Because statistical learning requires considerable exposure to stimuli, one of the primary ways is to make sure that students have ample opportunities to read a variety of texts and word types, with continuous feedback and support from a teacher. Interventions might also include strategies that promote flexible decoding strategies, such as the "vowel alert" approach (Lovett et al., 2017; Steacy et al., 2016), or other strategies that teach students to evaluate a pronunciation derived from their knowledge of letter-sound correspondence and adapt or adjust pronunciations when needed to yield a word they recognize (e.g., Dyson et al., 2017; Savage et al., 2018). Strategies that systematically expose students to different types of spelling patterns and teach students to pay greater attention to letter combinations, their positions within words, and their relation to other letters in a process to "problem-solve" decoding may help draw greater attention to the statistical regularities of the spelling system.

Better Alignment of Core Instruction and Supplemental Intervention

Traditionally, supplemental reading interventions included programs and strategies that, although often not contradictory to core instruction, have not been strategically aligned. More recent trends involve systematically aligning intervention with core reading instruction, which may increase the effectiveness of instruction in both settings. The Enhanced Core Reading Instruction (ECRI; Fien et al., 2015) is one such example. In addition to making core reading instruction more systematic and more explicit and increasing student practice opportunities, ECRI includes a supplemental small-group intervention in which instruction focuses specifically on skills and content that will be taught in core instruction *the following day*. Essentially, intervention provides preteaching of key skills, which is designed to help students benefit more from core instruction. Studies have observed benefits of ECRI intervention on students' word reading, pseudoword decoding, and reading fluency (Baker et al., 2015; Fien et al., 2020; Smith et al., 2016).

Systematic Integration of Semantic Information Within Word Reading Interventions

A traditional focus of interventions for students with WLRDs emphasizes phonics: establishing and strengthening connections between word spellings (orthographic representations) and pronunciations (phonological representations). This is certainly important. However, connectionist perspectives of reading acquisition suggest that, although orthographic to phonological connections are the primary way that word reading is initially acquired, semantic (i.e., vocabulary, morphological) knowledge may enhance word reading skills, especially for words that are less phonetically regular and more complex (Seidenberg, 2017).

Can teaching the meanings of words targeted in decoding instruction improve acquisition and retention of those words? Correlational evidence indicates that knowing the meaning of words helps elementary students correct word reading mispronunciations (e.g., Kearns et al., 2016) and that word-specific semantic information may be particularly helpful in reading multisyllabic words (Kearns & Al Ghanem, 2019). Steacy and Compton (2019), with first- and second-graders at risk for reading disabilities, found irregular words with greater imageability (i.e., words that are more likely to elicit a clear mental image, such as "brain") were more likely to be read accurately and learned faster than irregular words that were less imageable (e.g., "choice"), especially for students with lower initial word-reading skill.

Intervention research is more equivocal. Some studies have found that integrating semantic information within decoding instruction did not benefit word reading outcomes, although others have found that including semantic information improved word reading accuracy or fluency (see Austin et al., in press, for a review). Austin and colleagues utilized a within-subjects design of fourth- and fifth-graders with WLRDs in which one set of words was taught focused on decoding alone and another set of words was taught by integrating word-meaning instruction with decoding. Results indicated statistically significant differences and large effect sizes in students' posttest word reading accuracy ($d = 0.74$) and fluency ($d = 0.84$) for words in which meaning instruction was integrated with decoding instruction compared to words targeted with decoding instruction alone. Notably, Austin et al. targeted words that were primarily multisyllabic and low-frequency; thus, semantic information may have been particularly beneficial for helping students link spellings to pronunciations over decoding instruction alone.

Scholars have argued that teaching morphological information (i.e., spelling units within words that hold meaning, such as affixes and roots) may support struggling readers in reading complex words when phonics rules are less applicable (Carlisle & Kearns, 2017; Reed, 2008). As summarized by Kirby and Bowers (2017), several reviews of research on the effects of morphological instruction have observed moderate to strong effects favoring morphology instruction on students' word reading, and effects tend to be stronger for students with reading difficulties.

Rethinking Reading Fluency Intervention

Stevens et al. (2017) observed that "repeated reading" (i.e., reading the same passage three to four times per session) has been a commonly implemented strategy for targeting reading fluency. However, their review revealed that the largest effects are observed on the passages the students practiced. Fewer studies examined effects on measures of generalized reading fluency, and those that did observed much lower or negligible effects on generalized measures. Alternatively, scholars have observed that "wide" or "continuous" reading, which involves reading a continuous passage for the same amount of time as a student would spend repeatedly reading a shorter section of text, offers equivalent or greater benefits in students' reading skills (Ardoin et al., 2016; O'Connor et al., 2007). Another variation was investigated by Reed et al. (2019), who found that students who read three different passages that had a high proportion of overlapping words demonstrated significantly stronger gains in reading fluency compared to students who repeatedly read the same passages. Effects were stronger for lower-achieving readers. These results can be interpreted in line with perspectives on statistical learning: Exposure to a broader corpus of words and the same words in varying contexts may improve word recognition and skill generalization. Another advantage of continuous reading (compared to repeated reading) is that it reduces the boredom of reading the same passage multiple times, which may improve implementation for students who are unmotivated to read.

Reading Comprehension Difficulties

Although less common than WLRDs, reading comprehension is the other primary area in which reading difficulties occur. The notion of *specific* reading comprehension difficulties assumes that students' word- and text-reading skills are accurate and efficient enough to not pose a barrier to reading comprehension, an assumption that is met less often than many practitioners and researchers realize given the high prevalence of problems with word reading in middle and secondary grades (e.g., Brasseur-Hock et al., 2011). Nevertheless, a subgroup of students remains who experience significant difficulties understanding text despite seemingly adequate word reading skills. Difficulties specific to reading comprehension tend to emerge later than WLRDs and appear to be commonly associated with underdeveloped language and background knowledge necessary for supporting comprehension (Cain & Oakhill, 2006; Catts et al., 2012), and attentional processes needed to continuously maintain a coherent mental representation of text (Arrington et al., 2014). Students with a history of speech-language disability are at risk for reading comprehension difficulties (Catts et al., 2012), as are students with ADHD or behavior disorders given the high rates of co-occurrence with learning disabilities, underlying language difficulties, and other factors that impede reading (Hollo et al., 2014; Miller et al., 2013).

Practices, Advances, and Next Steps in Reading Comprehension Intervention

Research syntheses and meta-analyses have identified several aspects associated with larger effect sizes in improving reading comprehension (Berkeley et al., 2010; Edmonds et al., 2009; Scammacca et al., 2015; Solis et al., 2012; Swanson et al., 2014). Strategy instruction, with an emphasis on questioning techniques, self-monitoring of comprehension, and main idea/summarizing strategies, has been the most commonly studied and associated with moderate to large effect sizes. Other intervention foci that have evidence for benefits on reading comprehension include inference making (Elleman, 2017), vocabulary (Elleman et al., 2009), and knowledge of text structure (Hebert et al., 2016).

Reading comprehension interventions have tended to demonstrate stronger effects on proximal, researcher-developed measures compared to outcomes on standardized tests (e.g., Scammacca et al., 2015). Although these differential effects have much to do with the challenges of adequately measuring reading comprehension (Clemens & D. Fuchs, 2021), improving reading comprehension interventions has been the subject of research and conjecture in recent years. One overarching consideration is a view of reading comprehension less as a discrete "skill" and more the outcome of a successful orchestration of multiple skill and knowledge sources (Catts & Kamhi, 2017). This perspective is reflected in recent directions in reading comprehension interventions.

Emphasis on Building Language and Background Knowledge

Linguistic comprehension and background knowledge form the bedrock of reading comprehension, (Kintsch, 1988; Perfetti & Stafura, 2014). Recent perspectives on reading comprehension interventions advocate for a stronger emphasis on building language skills and background knowledge important for understanding a wide variety of texts (Barth & Elleman, 2017; Catts & Kamhi, 2017; Compton et al., 2014; Elleman & Compton, 2017; Silverman et al., 2020). Calls for building students' word and world knowledge are not new notions; reading comprehension interventions have long included components targeting these aspects. However, there has been increasing focus on these aspects as core intervention features.

VOCABULARY

There are few skills more important for reading comprehension than vocabulary knowledge. Even when all words in a passage are decoded correctly, if as few as 3% of word meanings are unknown, comprehension can be significantly impaired (Schmitt et al., 2011). For students with reading difficulties, low vocabulary knowledge is a common characteristic in elementary through secondary grades (Brasseur-Hock et al., 2011; Clemens et al., 2017). Vocabulary knowledge has been a common component in reading comprehension interventions (Scammacca et al., 2015), but more recent perspectives have considered how to emphasize vocabulary knowledge more strategically to support reading comprehension (Elleman & Compton, 2017). For instance, Swanson et al. (2017) trained teachers to implement stronger reading comprehension instruction within social studies classes, in which a primary aspect of the intervention was teaching vocabulary relevant for passages students were about to read and reviewing the vocabulary terms after reading. Of particular importance for students as they advance through grade levels is their knowledge of academic vocabulary—words that are less common in everyday speech but more common in academic writing, and therefore important for understanding and learning from print. In addition to targeting new word meanings, vocabulary instruction should target words that have different or multiple meanings in their academic texts than the meanings with which students may be more familiar.

BACKGROUND KNOWLEDGE AND INTEGRATION WITHIN CONTENT AREA CLASSES

Background knowledge has been recognized as an important component of reading comprehension for some time (Kintsch, 1988), but more recently, scholars have called for greater attention to building background knowledge in interventions for struggling readers. Background knowledge is important for making inferences (Kendeou et al., 2016), which are critical for text comprehension because authors rarely provide every detail needed to understand a text. Systematic reviews indicate that strategies aimed at helping students build and integrate background knowledge with events and details in the text are associated with improved general and inferential reading comprehension among struggling readers (Elleman, 2017; Hall, 2016). Instruction that builds students' knowledge and integrates it with inference-making instruction appears to be a particularly promising approach. For example, Barth and Elleman (2017) implemented an intervention to improve inferential reading comprehension with struggling readers in grades 6 to 8. A primary focus of the intervention was on teaching content knowledge (in this case, of ancient Egypt) and how to integrate it to make inferences while reading. At posttest, students in the treatment group significantly outperformed students in a control group (who received school-designed intervention) on a proximal measure of content knowledge ($ES = 1.47$) and a standardized test of reading comprehension ($ES = 0.46$). Effects on a test of inferential reading comprehension were not statistically significant, but the effect size was appreciable (0.36).

Background knowledge is intertwined with vocabulary knowledge (Ahmed et al., 2016). Having "knowledge" about a topic often depends on having a strong understanding of the terminology used in that domain. For instance, learning about an ecosystem involves learning terms such as biotic, abiotic, carnivore, herbivore, photosynthesis, consume, interact, and depend. This reciprocal relationship means that identifying important vocabulary and terminology for upcoming text helps establish background knowledge that will support students' comprehension. Interventionists can also expand vocabulary instruction to integrate background knowledge by including key phrases, events, or concepts relevant to a topic in which students will read about. In addition to teaching key knowledge and vocabulary, instruction should support students' integration of *relevant* background knowledge with information from the text (and avoiding discussion of irrelevant information), as struggling readers are often less able to suppress activation of irrelevant knowledge, which negatively affects their comprehension (De Beni & Palladino, 2000; Gernsbacher & Faust, 1991).

Integrating reading comprehension instruction within content-area classes (i.e., science, social studies/history) for students in late elementary through secondary grades can effectively situate reading comprehension in classes where students are expected to build new knowledge from text. Reviews indicate that reading interventions implemented in these contexts can be highly effective in improving both knowledge and reading comprehension (McCulley & Osman, 2015; Swanson et al., 2014). A distinct advantage of situating reading interventions within content-area classes, like science or social studies, is that it helps to focus vocabulary and knowledge-building instruction on the texts students read, which reinforces the role of reading comprehension as a knowledge-building and knowledge-integration process.

More Strategic and Judicious Use of Comprehension Strategies

Reading comprehension "strategies" refer to techniques aimed at improving reading comprehension such as main-idea identification, prediction, graphic organizers, self-monitoring, and questioning.

Reading comprehension strategies have been very common in intervention research and in practice (Ness, 2011; Scammacca et al., 2015) and are often perceived as a default approach when the idea of "reading comprehension intervention" is considered. However, scholars have recommended a more careful consideration of reading comprehension strategy instruction. Elleman and Compton (2017) argued that although comprehension strategy instruction is an important component of intervention, it should not be implemented at the expense of instruction in language and background knowledge. Strategies will not be effective in improving reading comprehension if vocabulary and background knowledge are inadequate. Care should also be taken to ensure that strategies, such as completing graphic organizers or extended discussion about text prediction, do not take inordinate time me away from students' opportunities to read.

Continuing to Address Word-Level Difficulties During Comprehension Instruction

Our last "advance" is more of a reminder. Too often, it seems that interventions for students with "reading comprehension" difficulties lose sight of the frequency with which struggling readers across all grade levels have persistent difficulties with word reading. Several studies have demonstrated that even across middle and secondary grades, struggling readers are likely to demonstrate difficulties with accuracy and fluency in word and text reading (Brasseur-Hock et al., 2011; Cirino et al., 2013; Clemens et al., 2017). Many researchers and practitioners may underestimate the negative effect that word-reading errors can have on reading comprehension; even 90% accuracy (i.e., one error for every 10 words) can have a significant negative effect on reading comprehension and motivation to read (Rodgers et al., 2018). As text difficulty and complexity increase across grade levels, students will read words that are longer, more complex, and unfamiliar. Intervention aimed at ultimately improving reading comprehension should take care to address word reading, and perhaps even seek to root out any underlying word-reading difficulties that were previously unnoticed.

Implications for Practitioners

For students with WLRDs, the primary implications from recent research pertain to considering how explicit phonics instruction can be augmented by (a) equipping students with a set of decoding strategies and the ability to flexibly apply them; (b) considering ways to strategically expand the corpus of words students read in supported practice opportunities to include words that deviate from phonics rules and standard pronunciations; and (c) systemically and consistently integrating word meaning instruction within word reading instruction. Overall, these aspects are aimed at fostering a skill set that allows for expanded ways of connecting spellings to pronunciations, perhaps resulting in the development of more durable and generalizable word reading skills over time.

For interventions aimed at improving reading comprehension, implications from recent work indicate that while reading comprehension strategy instruction should continue, it should be used judiciously and should not come at the expense of instruction that improves language (especially vocabulary) and builds background knowledge or sacrifices students' opportunities to read. Language- and knowledge-building efforts should increase in emphasis, and intervention should target students' ability to integrate new knowledge within strategically selected texts that reinforce inference-making and forming connections within and across texts. Intervention for reading comprehension should also not lose sight of the high prevalence of word-reading deficits among struggling readers, even for students in middle and secondary grades.

Conclusions

Much has been learned about improving word reading and text comprehension skills for students that struggle in reading. However, there are several areas in which research can continue to innovate toward identifying intervention strategies that are maximally effective. Continued research is needed to identify instruction and practice strategies that promote generalizable, efficient word recognition skills for students with WLRDs. Reading fluency remains a difficult skill to improve, and research is needed to determine if the answer lies in providing more opportunities to read over longer periods of time, or if interventions can find ways to better foster word-level automaticity that facilitates text reading fluency. For students with reading comprehension difficulties, research should investigate ways to flexibly tailor interventions that strategically balance vocabulary and knowledge building components with strategy instruction. Finally, although extensive work has established the importance of explicit instruction for all aspects of reading, researchers should critically evaluate the benefits of teacher-directed instruction relative to extensive, high-quality opportunities for reading practice.

Author Note

Authorship of this chapter was supported in part by grants from the U.S. Department of Education, Institute for Education Sciences, Grants R324N180018 and R324A20029. The opinions expressed in this chapter are those of the authors and do not represent the views of the Institute of Education Sciences or the U.S. Department of Education.

The authors declare no conflicts of interest in the authorship of this chapter.

References

Adams, M. J. (1990). *Beginning to read: Thinking and learning about print*. MIT Press.

Ahmed, Y., Francis, D. J., York, M., Fletcher, J. M., Barnes, M., & Kulesz, P. (2016). Validation of the direct and inferential mediation (DIME) model of reading comprehension in grades 7 through 12. *Contemporary Educational Psychology, 44–45*, 68–82.

Arciuli, J. (2018). Reading as statistical learning. *Language, Speech, and Hearing Services in Schools, 49*, 634–643.

Ardoin, S. P., Binder, K. S., Foster, T. E., & Zawoyski, A. M. (2016). Repeated versus wide reading: A randomized control design study examining the impact of fluency interventions on underlying reading behavior. *Journal of School Psychology, 59*, 13–38.

Arrington, C. N., Kulesz, P. A., Francis, D. J., Fletcher, J. M., & Barnes, M. A. (2014). The contribution of attentional control and working memory to reading comprehension and decoding. *Scientific Studies of Reading, 18*(5), 325–346.

Austin, C. R., Vaughn, S. R., Clemens, N. H., Pustejovsky, J. E., & Boucher, A. N. (in press). The relative effects of integrating word reading and word meaning instruction compared to word reading instruction alone on the accuracy, fluency, and word meaning knowledge of 4th-5th grade students with dyslexia. *Scientific Studies of Reading*. https://www.tandfonline.com/doi/abs/10.1080/10888438.2021.1947294

Austin, C. R., Vaughn, S., & McClelland, A. M. (2017). Intensive reading interventions for inadequate responders in grades K—3: A synthesis. *Learning Disability Quarterly, 40*(4), 191–210.

Baker, S. K., Smolkowski, K., Chaparro, E. A., Smith, J. L., & Fien, H. (2015). Using regression discontinuity to test the impact of a tier 2 reading intervention in first grade. *Journal of Research on Educational Effectiveness, 8*(2), 218–244.

Barth, A. E., & Elleman, A. (2017). Evaluating the impact of a multistrategy inference intervention for middle-grade struggling readers. *Language, Speech, and Hearing Services in Schools, 48*(1), 31–41.

Berkeley, S., Scruggs, T. E., & Mastropieri, M. A. (2010). Reading comprehension instruction for students with learning disabilities, 1995—2006: A meta-analysis. *Remedial and Special Education, 31*(6), 423–436.

Brasseur-Hock, I. F., Hock, M. F., Kieffer, M. J., Biancarosa, G., & Deshler, D. D. (2011). Adolescent struggling readers in urban schools: Results of a latent class analysis. *Learning and Individual Differences, 21*(4), 438–452.

Brown, H. M., Oram-Cardy, J., & Johnson, A. (2013). A meta-analysis of the reading comprehension skills of individuals on the autism spectrum. *Journal of Autism and Developmental Disorders, 43*(4), 932–955.

Bus, A. G., & Van IJzendoorn, M. H. (1999). Phonological awareness and early reading: A meta-analysis of experimental training studies. *Journal of Educational Psychology, 91*(3), 403.

Cain, K., & Oakhill, J. (2006). Profiles of children with specific reading comprehension difficulties. *British Journal of Educational Psychology, 76*(4), 683–696.

Cain, K., & Oakhill, J. (2011). Matthew effects in young readers: Reading comprehension and reading experience aid vocabulary development. *Journal of Learning Disabilities, 44*(45), 431–443.

Carlisle, J. F., & Kearns, D. M. (2017). Learning to read morphologically complex words. In K. Cain, R. Parrila, & D. Compton (Eds.), *Theories of reading development* (p. 191). John Benjamins.

Catts, H. W., Compton, D., Tomblin, J. B., & Bridges, M. S. (2012). Prevalence and nature of late-emerging poor readers. *Journal of Educational Psychology, 104*(1), 166.

Catts, H. W., & Kamhi, A. G. (2017). Prologue: Reading comprehension is not a single ability. *Language, Speech, and Hearing Services in Schools, 48*(2), 73–76.

Chetail, F. (2017). What do we do with what we learn? Statistical learning of orthographic regularities impacts written word processing. *Cognition, 163*, 103–120.

Cirino, P. T., Romain, M. A., Barth, A. E., Tolar, T. D., Fletcher, J. M., & Vaughn, S. (2013). Reading skill components and impairments in middle school struggling readers. *Reading and Writing, 26*(7), 1059–1086.

Clemens, N. H., & Fuchs, D. (2021). Commercially developed tests of reading comprehension: Gold Standard or Fools Gold? *Reading Research Quarterly*.

Clemens, N. H., Simmons, D., Simmons, L. E., Wang, H., & Kwok, O. M. (2017). The prevalence of reading fluency and vocabulary difficulties among adolescents struggling with reading comprehension. *Journal of Psychoeducational Assessment, 35*(8), 785–798.

Compton, D. L., Miller, A. C., Elleman, A. M., & Steacy, L. M. (2014). Have we forsaken reading theory in the name of "quick fix" interventions for children with reading disability? *Scientific Studies of Reading, 18*(1), 55–73.

Danielson, L., & Rosenquist, C. (2014). Introduction to the TEC special issue on data-based individualization. *TEACHING Exceptional Children, 46*(4), 6–12.

De Beni, R., & Palladino, P. (2000). Intrusion errors in working memory tasks: Are they related to reading comprehension ability? *Learning and Individual Differences, 12*(2), 131–143.

Dyson, H., Best, W., Solity, J., & Hulme, C. (2017). Training mispronunciation correction and word meanings improves children's ability to learn to read words. *Scientific Studies of Reading, 21*(5), 392–407.

Edmonds, M. S., Vaughn, S., Wexler, J., Reutebuch, C., Cable, A., Tackett, K. K., & Schnakenberg, J. W. (2009). A synthesis of reading interventions and effects on reading comprehension outcomes for older struggling readers. *Review of Educational Research, 79*(1), 262–300.

Ehri, L. C. (2020). The science of learning to read words: A case for systematic phonics instruction. *Reading Research Quarterly, 55*(S1), S45–S60.

Ehri, L. C., Nunes, S. R., Stahl, S. A., & Willows, D. M. (2001). Systematic phonics instruction helps students learn to read: Evidence from the National Reading Panel's meta-analysis. *Review of Educational Research, 71*(3), 393–447.

Ehri, L.C., & Saltmarsh, J. (1995). Beginning readers outperform older disabled readers in learning to read words by sight. *Reading and Writing, 7*(3), 295–326.

Elbro, C., & De Jong, P. F. (2017). Orthographic learning is verbal learning. In K. Cain, D. Compton, & R. Parrila (Eds.), *Theories of reading development* (pp. 169–189). John Benjamins Press.

Elleman, A. M. (2017). Examining the impact of inference instruction on the literal and inferential comprehension of skilled and less skilled readers: A meta-analytic review. *Journal of Educational Psychology, 109*(6), 761–781.

Elleman, A. M., & Compton, D. L. (2017). Beyond comprehension strategy instruction: What's next? *Language, Speech, and Hearing Services in Schools, 48*(2), 84–91.

Elleman, A. M., Lindo, E. J., Morphy, P., & Compton, D. L. (2009). The impact of vocabulary instruction on passage-level comprehension of school-age children: A meta-analysis. *Journal of Research on Educational Effectiveness, 2*(1), 1–44.

Fien, H., Nelson, N. J., Smolkowski, K., Kosty, D., Pilger, M., Baker, S. K., & Smith, J. L. M. (2020). A conceptual replication study of the enhanced core reading instruction MTSS-Reading model. *Exceptional Children, 87*(3), 265–288.

Fien, H., Smith, J. L. M., Smolkowski, K., Baker, S. K., Nelson, N. J., & Chaparro, E. (2015). An examination of the efficacy of a multitiered intervention on early reading outcomes for first grade students at risk for reading difficulties. *Journal of Learning Disabilities, 48*(6), 602–621.

Fletcher, J. M., Lyon, G. R., Fuchs, L. S., & Barnes, M. A. (2018). *Learning disabilities: From identification to intervention* (2nd ed.). Guilford Press.

Flynn, L. J., Zheng, X., & Swanson, H. L. (2012). Instructing struggling older readers: A selective meta-analysis of intervention research. *Learning Disabilities Research & Practice, 27*(1), 21–32.

Fuchs, D., Fuchs, L. S., & Vaughn, S. (2014). What is intensive instruction and why is it important? *Teaching Exceptional Children, 46*(4), 13–18.

Gernsbacher, M. A., & Faust, M. E. (1991). The mechanism of suppression: A component of general comprehension skill. *Journal of Experimental Psychology: Learning, Memory, and Cognition, 17*(2), 245–262.

Hall, C. S. (2016). Inference instruction for struggling readers: A synthesis of intervention research. *Educational Psychology Review, 28*(1), 1–22.

Hebert, M., Bohaty, J. J., Nelson, J. R., & Brown, J. (2016). The effects of text structure instruction on expository reading comprehension: A meta-analysis. *Journal of Educational Psychology, 108*(5), 609–629.

Hollo, A., Wehby, J. H., & Oliver, R. M. (2014). Unidentified language deficits in children with emotional and behavioral disorders: A meta-analysis. *Exceptional Children, 80*(2), 169–186.

Hughes, C. A., Morris, J. R., Therrien, W. J., & Benson, S. K. (2017). Explicit instruction: Historical and contemporary contexts. *Learning Disabilities Research & Practice, 32*(3), 140–148.

Jenkins, J. R., Fuchs, L. S., Van Den Broek, P., Espin, C., & Deno, S. L. (2003). Sources of individual differences in reading comprehension and reading fluency. *Journal of Educational Psychology, 95*(4), 719–729.

Kearns, D. M., & Al Ghanem, R. (2019). The role of semantic information in children's word reading: Does meaning affect readers' ability to say polysyllabic words aloud? *Journal of Educational Psychology, 111*(6), 933–956.

Kearns, D. M., Rogers, H. J., Koriakin, T., & Al Ghanem, R. (2016). Semantic and phonological ability to adjust recoding: A unique correlate of word reading skill? *Scientific Studies of Reading, 20*(6), 455–470.

Kendeou, P., McMaster, K. L., & Christ, T. J. (2016). Reading comprehension: Core components and processes. *Policy Insights from the Behavioral and Brain Sciences, 3*(1), 62–69.

Kintsch, W. (1988). The role of knowledge in discourse comprehension: A construction-integration model. *Psychological Review, 95*(2), 163–182.

Kirby, J. R., & Bowers, P. N. (2017). Morphological instruction and literacy. In K. Cain, D. Compton, & R. Parrila (Eds.), *Theories of reading development* (pp. 437–457). John Benjamins Press.

Lovett, M. W., Frijters, J. C., Wolf, M., Steinbach, K. A., Sevcik, R. A., & Morris, R. D. (2017). Early intervention for children at risk for reading disabilities: The impact of grade at intervention and individual differences on intervention outcomes. *Journal of Educational Psychology, 109*(7), 889–914.

Mano, Q. R., & Kloos, H. (2018). Sensitivity to the regularity of letter patterns within print among preschoolers: Implications for emerging literacy. *Journal of Research in Childhood Education, 32*(4), 379–391.

McCulley, L. V., & Osman, D. J. (2015). Effects of reading instruction on learning outcomes in social studies: A synthesis of quantitative research. *The Journal of Social Studies Research, 39*(4), 183–195.

Melby-Lervåg, M., Lyster, S. A. H., & Hulme, C. (2012). Phonological skills and their role in learning to read: A meta-analytic review. *Psychological Bulletin, 138*(2), 322–352.

Miller, A. C., Keenan, J. M., Betjemann, R. S., Willcutt, E. G., Pennington, B. F., & Olson, R. K. (2013). Reading comprehension in children with ADHD: Cognitive underpinnings of the centrality deficit. *Journal of Abnormal Child Psychology, 41*(3), 473–483.

Morgan, P. L., Farkas, G., Tufis, P. A., & Sperling, R. A. (2008). Are reading and behavior problems risk factors for each other? *Journal of Learning Disabilities, 41*(5), 417–436.

National Center for Education Statistics (2021). Students with disabilities. Available: https://nces.ed.gov/programs/coe/indicator/cgg

Ness, M. (2011). Explicit reading comprehension instruction in elementary classrooms: Teacher use of reading comprehension strategies. *Journal of Research in Childhood Education, 25*(1), 98–117.

O'Connor, R. E., White, A., & Swanson, H. L. (2007). Repeated reading versus continuous reading: Influences on reading fluency and comprehension. *Exceptional Children, 74*(1), 31–46.

Perfetti, C., & Stafura, J. (2014). Word knowledge in a theory of reading comprehension. *Scientific Studies of Reading, 18*(1), 22–37.

Rabiner, D., Coie, J. D., & Conduct Problems Prevention Research Group. (2000). Early attention problems and children's reading achievement: A longitudinal investigation. *Journal of the American Academy of Child & Adolescent Psychiatry, 39*(7), 859–867.

Reed, D. K. (2008). A synthesis of morphology interventions and effects on reading outcomes for students in grades K—12. *Learning Disabilities Research & Practice, 23*(1), 36–49.

Reed, D. K., Zimmermann, L. M., Reeger, A. J., & Aloe, A. M. (2019). The effects of varied practice on the oral reading fluency of fourth-grade students. *Journal of School Psychology, 77*, 24–35.

Reynolds, A. J., & Ou, S. (2004). Alterable predictors of child well-being in the Chicago longitudinal study. *Children and Youth Services Review, 26*(1), 1–14.

Rodgers, E., D'Agostino, J. V., Kelly, R. H., & Mikita, C. (2018). Oral reading accuracy: Findings and implications from recent research. *The Reading Teacher, 72*(2), 149–157.

Savage, R., Georgiou, G., Parrila, R., & Maiorino, K. (2018). Preventative reading interventions teaching direct mapping of graphemes in texts and set-for-variability aid at-risk learners. *Scientific Studies of Reading, 22*(3), 225–247.

Scammacca, N. K., Roberts, G., Vaughn, S., & Stuebing, K. K. (2015). A meta-analysis of interventions for struggling readers in grades 4–12: 1980–2011. *Journal of learning disabilities, 48*(4), 369–390.

Schmitt, N., Jiang, X., & Grabe, W. (2011). The percentage of words known in a text and reading comprehension. *The Modern Language Journal, 95*(1), 26–43.

Seidenberg, M. (2017). *Language at the speed of sight: How we read, why so many can't, and what can be done about it*. Basic Books.

Silverman, R. D., Johnson, E., Keane, K., & Khanna, S. (2020). Beyond decoding: A meta-analysis of the effects of language comprehension interventions on K–5 students' language and literacy outcomes. *Reading Research Quarterly, 55*, S207–S233.

Smith, J. L. M., Nelson, N. J., Fien, H., Smolkowski, K., Kosty, D., & Baker, S. K. (2016). Examining the efficacy of a multitiered intervention for at-risk readers in grade 1. *The Elementary School Journal, 116*(4), 549–573.

Snowling, M. J. (1995). Phonological processing and developmental dyslexia. *Journal of Research in Reading, 18*(2), 132–138.

Society for Neuroscience. (2004). *Dyslexia: What brain research reveals about reading*. www.ldonline.org/article/10784/.

Solis, M., Ciullo, S., Vaughn, S., Pyle, N., Hassaram, B., & Leroux, A. (2012). Reading comprehension interventions for middle school students with learning disabilities: A synthesis of 30 years of research. *Journal of Learning Disabilities, 45*(4), 327–340.

Steacy, L. M., & Compton, D. L. (2019). Examining the role of imageability and regularity in word reading accuracy and learning efficiency among first and second graders at risk for reading disabilities. *Journal of Experimental Child Psychology, 178*, 226–250.

Steacy, L. M., Elleman, A. M., Lovett, M. W., & Compton, D. L. (2016). Exploring differential effects across two decoding treatments on item-level transfer in children with significant word reading difficulties: A new approach for testing intervention elements. *Scientific Studies of Reading, 20*(4), 283–295.

Steacy, L. M., Petscher, Y., Elliott, J. D., Smith, K., Rigobon, V. M., Abes, D. R., . . . Compton, D. L. (2020). The Effect of Facilitative Versus Inhibitory Word Training Corpora on Word Reading Accuracy Growth in Children with Dyslexia. *Learning Disability Quarterly*, 0731948720938684.

Steacy, L. M., Wade-Woolley, L., Rueckl, J. G., Pugh, K. R., Elliott, J. D., & Compton, D. L. (2019). The role of set for variability in irregular word reading: Word and child predictors in typically developing readers and students at-risk for reading disabilities. *Scientific Studies of Reading, 23*(6), 523–532.

Stevens, E. A., Walker, M. A., & Vaughn, S. (2017). The effects of reading fluency interventions on the reading fluency and reading comprehension performance of elementary students with learning disabilities: A synthesis of the research from 2001 to 2014. *Journal of Learning Disabilities, 50*(5), 576–590.

Swanson, E., Hairrell, A., Kent, S., Ciullo, S., Wanzek, J. A., & Vaughn, S. (2014). A synthesis and meta-analysis of reading interventions using social studies content for students with learning disabilities. *Journal of Learning Disabilities, 47*(2), 178–195.

Swanson, E., Wanzek, J., Vaughn, S., Fall, A. M., Roberts, G., Hall, C., & Miller, V. L. (2017). Middle school reading comprehension and content learning intervention for below-average readers. *Reading & Writing Quarterly, 33*(1), 37–53.

Torgesen, J. K. (2004). Lessons learned from research on interventions for students who have difficulty learning to read. In P. McCardle & V. Chhabra (Eds.), *The voice of evidence in reading research* (pp. 355–382). Brookes Pub.

Torgesen, J. K., Alexander, A. W., Wagner, R. K., Rashotte, C. A., Voeller, K. K., & Conway, T. (2001). Intensive remedial instruction for children with severe reading disabilities: Immediate and long-term outcomes from two instructional approaches. *Journal of Learning Disabilities, 34*(1), 33–58.

Tunmer, W. E., & Chapman, J. W. (2012). Does set for variability mediate the influence of vocabulary knowledge on the development of word recognition skills? *Scientific Studies of Reading, 16*(2), 122–140.

Venezky, R. L. (1999). *The American way of spelling: The structure and origins of American English orthography*. Guilford Press.

Wagner, M., Newman, L., Cameto, R., Garza, N., & Levine, P. (2005). *After high school: A first look at the post-school experiences of youth with disabilities. A report from the National Longitudinal Transition Study-2 (NLTS2)*. SRI International.

Wanzek, J., Stevens, E. A., Williams, K. J., Scammacca, N., Vaughn, S., & Sargent, K. (2018). Current evidence on the effects of intensive early reading interventions. *Journal of Learning Disabilities, 51*(6), 612–624.

8
CONSIDERATIONS FOR CHOOSING AND USING SCREENERS FOR STUDENTS WITH DISABILITIES

Yaacov Petscher and Marissa Suhr

Introduction

Universal screening is a strategy used in many aspects of life to provide a current indicator of some type of presently unknown, future outcome. Screening practices are familiar to us in doctor offices where vitals such as blood pressure, temperature, and family history are taken to inform the potential likelihood for current or future disease. For those who are accustomed to airline travel, airport security screens all passengers to prevent negative outcomes. Screening is also done in supermarkets where avocados, watermelons, and grapes are sometimes pressed, tapped, or tasted to gauge the level of freshness to estimate early risk for food rot. In education, states across the United States in the last 20 years have passed universal screening legislation as a polemic against wait-to-fail service delivery models where reading, math, or writing interventions may not occur until students fail key state outcomes in grade 3.

The broad goal of universal screening can often become challenging to localize in state and district contexts as a function of the intersection between how the definition of the construct of interest (e.g., dyslexia) is defined (Miciak & Fletcher, 2020) and how policy varies across states in what components should be measured in a screening process (Gearin et al., 2021). When considering dyslexia, there is no shortage of definitions, including those from the U.S. First Step Act (Cassidy, 2019), the International Dyslexia Association (IDA; Lyon et al., 2003), the British Dyslexia Association (BDA, 2007), and the World Health Organization (WHO, 2013). Despite some commonalities in the etiology and symptomatology for dyslexia, there are sufficient differences that could manifest in the way policy is created about what should be assessed in universal screening for dyslexia risk. Indeed, Gearin et al. (2021) conducted a document of state dyslexia legislation and found that states vary in the definition of dyslexia used for universal screening of dyslexia risk (i.e., 33 of 50 states recognize the IDA definition, 12 did not recognize a definition, and 5 recognized an alternative to IDA); the required grades in screening for dyslexia risk (i.e., 13 states use kindergarten to grade 3, 6 states use kindergarten to grade 1, 5 states use kindergarten to grade 2, 2 states use kindergarten only, 1 state uses grade 1 only); and the construct(s) that should be assessed in universal screening for dyslexia risk (i.e., 23 different targets across word reading, written expression, phonological memory, oral language, comprehension, rapid naming, onset rime, and family history).

With an inconsistent application of definitions and requirements for universal screening for dyslexia risk, special educators may understandably be confused about how one should go about choosing a screener and using a screener in one's local context to understand who is at risk for future low educational outcomes. The purpose of this chapter is to provide a set of core considerations one may use when evaluating screeners for a host of special education classifications—those that may guide choosing a screener and those that may support using a screener. The five core considerations we outline here are (a) defining the population of interest, (b) scope of the assessment, (c) reliability of scores, (d) validity of scores, and (e) classification accuracy of scores.

Core Considerations for Choosing a Screener

Defining the Population of Interest

Defining the population of interest should be informed by the etiology and symptomatology related to the primary exceptionality one is interested in screening for risk in. Taking the earlier example, simply using a descriptor of *children with dyslexia* for screening is a necessary but insufficient start. A developmental aspect of the population has been identified (i.e., children), as has the outcome (i.e., dyslexia) that separates one group of individuals from another (e.g., children with dyslexia vs. children with language disorders). However, *children with dyslexia* as a population is lacking specificity for the age range of the population and the expected symptomatology associated with the outcome. A close correspondence between what is developmentally appropriate in content for measurement and the identified outcome safeguards against poor assessment decision-making, such as screening for dyslexia risk in preschool-age children with a nonword fluency assessment or administering a letter name fluency task to fifth-grade students. Choosing a definition for the population of interest should be done carefully, with attention to how the population is described in the relative completeness of its symptomatology, etiology, and persistence over time (Tonnessen, 1997).

Scope of Assessment

Choosing a screener should include an evaluation of scope coverage—such as *what* is assessed and *how* it is assessed. Evaluation should minimally include attention to (a) the alignment among the population of interest definition, the measurement outcome used to separate the population of interest from the remaining population (e.g., what risk is being screened *for*; Keenan & Meenan, 2014), and what is measured by the screener (e.g., what risk is being screened *by*; Glover & Albers, 2007); (b) whether the screener is applicable to the local context based on its measurement of automaticity in skills (e.g., time limited in curriculum-based measurement) or accuracy only in skills (e.g., fixed-item or computer adaptive accuracy measures); and (c) the extent to which single or multiple assessments should be combined (e.g., Compton et al., 2010).

Population of Interest–Screener–Outcome Alignment

Alignment among how the population of interest is operationally defined (e.g., students with a specific reading comprehension deficit; S-RCD), how a measurement outcome distinguishes the population of interest from the remaining population (e.g., performance <10th percentile of standardized reading comprehension assessment), and what is measured by the screener (e.g., silent reading efficiency and comprehension, multiple choice reading comprehension, or maze reading) is important, as not all screener and outcome assessments are created equally.

To illustrate, even where reading comprehension assessments, such as the Gray Oral Reading Test (GORT), Qualitative Reading Inventory–3 (QRI), Woodcock-Johnson Passage Comprehension–3 (WJPC), and Peabody Individual Achievement Test (PIAT), are viewed as standardized, norm-referenced tests of reading comprehension, individuals who are identified as having poor comprehension skills may vary according to which measure may be used. In a sample of 995 children, Keenan and Meenan (2014) found that for those students achieving at the lowest 10% of the distribution of each assessment, only 39% to 56% of students were consistent across pairs of the assessment. That is, when categorizing students at or below the 10th percentile of the WJPC, only 39% of those students were found to be at or below the 10th percentile of the GORT.

Not only may variability exist in who gets identified as having S-RCD based on which outcome measure is used, but so, too, can the interplay between outcome and screener. Cutting and Scarborough (2006) found that the amount of variance explained in reading comprehension varied when using the same measures of decoding and oral language as independent variables but different standardized reading comprehension–dependent variables. When using the Weschler Individual Achievement Test, 72% of the variance was explained by the decoding and oral language predictors compared with 67% in the Gates-MacGinitie Reading Comprehension Test and 49% in the GORT. The way a stimulus is designed to measure reading skills in the screener and the outcome assessment is critical to understand when evaluating screening assessments for the intended population, as there are important implications for who is identified as being at risk based on the alignment among the population of interest, the outcome, and the studied screener.

Speed–Power Assessments

Research on trade-offs between speed-based assessments, such as curriculum-based measurements (CBMs) that measure speed and accuracy (i.e., fluency assessments), and power-based assessments, such as computer adaptive assessments (CAA), is very much in its infancy. CBMs in reading have long been used for universal screening due to the brevity in administration and psychometric properties of reliability and validity (Petscher et al., 2013). Computer adaptive measures have more recently permeated the screening landscape, as they are more often reliable for more individuals than fixed-item assessments at the individual level (Wainer et al., 2000) and leverage accuracy-based performance without regard to automaticity (Van der Linden & Glas, 2000). An important consideration for CAAs is that they can provide individual-level precision estimates such that the reliability of scores is known for each test taker, whereas in CBM, this property is assumed to be fixed for all. An implication for screening is that an advantage of CAA compared to CBM lies in the former's ability to maximize student-level reliability that may then yield larger possible correlations and classification accuracy.

Direct comparisons in the predictive utility of CBM versus CAA are limited. Shapiro et al. (2015) examined differential predictions of AIMSweb Mathematics CBM and the STAR-Math CAA to the Pennsylvania System of School Assessment (PSSA). Bivariate correlations between AIMSweb Concepts and Applications and the PSSA were $r = 0.61$, 0.24, and 0.49 in each of grades 3, 4, and 5, respectively, compared to the AIMSweb Computation-PSSA correlations of $r = 0.61$, 0.75, and 0.74 and the STAR-Math-PSSA correlations of $r = 0.82$, 0.88, and 0.70. Although no correlation contrast test was applied to these estimates, and one must take respective screener assessment content development, foci, and screener-outcome alignment into account, one may surmise that a potential explanatory mechanism for a stronger correlation of STAR-Math to PSSA is that the CAA produces student-level precision estimates, allowing for the possibilities of estimating larger correlations. As more CAAs are commercially available for screening, greater attention is needed to their utility for universal screening in intended populations of interest.

Univariate or Multivariate Screening

The extent to which one or more screeners are useful for screening or evaluating broader reading risk is not a new discussion. A critical goal in the screening process is to ensure that overidentification and underidentification rates are minimized so that more accurate screening results may be observed. One cannot simultaneously minimize both types of errors, as it is a trade-off that test-makers make as to which of the types of errors is prioritized to minimize. Previous research has noted that univariate screening produces too many false positives (e.g., Johnson et al., 2009; Johnson et al., 2010). Conversely, research into multiple-screener methods reveals that multivariate screening models, such as two-stage screening (Compton et al., 2006; Compton et al., 2010), four-step screening (Gilbert et al., 2012), and hybrid model approaches (Schatschneider et al., 2016), can yield greater classification accuracy and longitudinal stability of classification by not only leveraging multiple screening assessments but also including measures of estimated growth on the screeners.

In one of only a few existing screening studies for language impairment risk or dyslexia compared to typical word reading, Adlof et al. (2017) found that a combined battery of word reading and listening comprehension was approximately equal in discriminatory power of identification (i.e., area under the curve [AUC] = 0.79) over using only word reading (AUC = 0.78) in risk for language impairment for a group of second-grade students. Moreover, risk of dyslexia was not improved by a combined battery (AUC = 0.85) compared to using only word reading (AUC = 0.86). The idea of combining multiple screeners has led to the creation of multiple risk calculators such as Catts et al. (2001), who provided an algorithm that leveraged five kindergarten measures to estimate the probability of risk in second grade. Petscher et al. (2016) created a risk calculator (i.e., the Earlier Assessment for Reading Success [EARS]) using multiple curriculum-based measures to predict longitudinal risk in reading comprehension and language. In both of these risk calculators, the AUC for the probabilistic score, as well as the sensitivity and specificity at cut-points of the probabilistic score, were higher with combined measures than using single measurement (Catts & Petscher, in press).

In addition to considering the merit of using multiple, direct measures of reading skills in a screener, it is possible that using multiple measures from multiple informants may improve classification accuracy. Compton et al. (2012) used a battery of student-level universal screening measures, Tier 1 and Tier 2 progress monitoring data, and standardized tests of word reading and listening comprehension, along with teacher ratings of student attention and behavior and tutor ratings of attention and behavior of students in Tier 2, to evaluate how much data were necessary for screening for nonresponse to instruction or intervention across tiers. Results showed that adding both Tier 1 progress monitoring and teacher ratings improved AUC from 0.88 in a model with only screeners to 0.92 with added measurements. However, it is unclear the extent to which teacher ratings served as the active ingredient in moving the AUC compared to the progress monitoring data, especially in light of research that shows the unique value of slopes in predicting outcomes above benchmark status measures (e.g., Kim et al., 2010; Schatschneider et al., 2008; Yeo et al., 2012; Zumeta et al., 2012).

There is a tension in the process of univariate or multivariate screening that is important to acknowledge. Screeners are typically developed with individual tasks, administered as individual assessments, and have cut-point recommendations for who is at risk based on the individual assessments. The decision as to whether a univariate or multivariate set of scores should be used should be informed by how well those individual assessment scores may be combined in a meaningful way that collectively can improve screening beyond the utility of the individual measures. Especially when multiple-informant ratings are considered, it is important to empirically test the incremental change in classification accuracy to ascertain the value of ratings beyond direct measurement of skills.

Reliability

The most basic definition of reliability is the consistency of a set of scores for a measure, yet this definition may be deceptively simplistic in the context of psychometrics due to the number of ways it can be estimated. Different forms of the reliability of scores are often reported for screeners, including one or more combinations of internal consistency, alternate form, test–retest, split-half, and inter-rater. Careful evaluation of the *type* and *magnitude* of the reliability of the screener's scores is necessary, as not all forms of reliability are created equal.

Internal Consistency

Internal consistency can be roughly defined as how well a set of item-level scores from an assessment correlate with each other. The importance of this form of reliability is that one is able to quickly gauge the coherence of items for a screener and then view its potential impact on correlation and classification accuracy (see previous section on speed–power assessments). Recent discussions in the measurement literature have debated the merit of reliability estimators (e.g., Cronbach's alpha) with some arguing that alpha should be disregarded due to easy-to-meet methodological assumptions (e.g., NcNeish, 2017) and others providing evidence that under simulated conditions alpha yields accurate population reliability values (Edwards et al., 2021). When reporting estimates of internal consistency via Cronbach's alpha or alternative statistics such as omega total, Coefficient H, or the greatest lower bound, the ideal is for internal consistency to minimally exceed 0.80 for research purposes and 0.90 for clinical decision-making (Nunnally & Bernstein, 1994).

Alternate Form Reliability

Also referred to as parallel form reliability, screener technical reports frequently include alternate form reliability, which is defined as the consistency of scores (i.e., the correlation) between two different versions of the same test. This form of reliability can be useful for characterizing the feasibility of using different forms across groups of individuals or within a group across multiple waves of data collection. A strength in reporting alternate form reliability is that when its evidence is strong, the use of alternate forms allows practitioners to guard against practice effects or exposure effects (i.e., the likelihood of an individual to get an item right because of previous exposure to the same stimulus). A potential weakness of alternate form reliability is that the threshold for acceptable levels should be high to ensure that individual difference performances across forms are due to actual ability changes and not form effects. For example, an alternate form reliability of 0.70 might suggest a strong correlation, but it also suggests significant nonoverlap in measurement, as a 0.70 estimate translates to only 49% shared variance in scores between two forms. Similarly, alternate form reliability of 0.90 points to very high overlap in the scores, but nearly 20% of the variance between the forms is unexplained. This proportion of unexplained variance does not by itself point to a fatality in form equivalence, but speaks to a broader contextual issue that has emerged in the last decade of screening research related to *if*, *when*, and *how* to adjust for lack of equivalence across forms of assessments (e.g., Francis et al., 2008).

Test–Retest Reliability

The longitudinal consistency of scores is frequently reported where the screener is given at two short-interval time points. Where retest reliability can be useful is in the very short time frame of administration (e.g., one week) to demonstrate that the relative rank ordering of scores does not change over time. Two limitations of this form of reliability are temporal and growth-expectation factors. The former refers to the amount of space that occurs for test–retest reliability; a review of many screeners that have been evaluated by the National Center on Intensive Intervention's academic screening tool chart shows examples of retest spacing of one week, two weeks, and four weeks. The greater the amount of spacing between testing occasions, the more that maturation effects influence the strength of the correlation. In a related manner, the theoretical expectation for growth is also critical for evaluating test–retest. That is, beyond considering the retest spacing, does a researcher expect individuals in the sample to differentially change over the one-week, two-week, or four-week period? To the extent that individual differences change over time, a low retest reliability may reflect such an expectation.

Split-Half Reliability

Split-half reliability tests for how well one portion of the screener (e.g., odd items) correlates with another portion of the screener (e.g., even items). Although this form of reliability can provide a proxy for alternate form reliability, it is also limited due to the possibility of the manipulation of how the halves are constructed in order to achieve optimal estimates (Chakrabartty, 2013).

Inter-Rater Reliability

A final form of reliability worth evaluating is inter-rater reliability, and this is the consistency of scores on a particular behavior between two or more raters. Inter-rater reliability is key when validating scores from observation tools such as teacher ratings of student behaviors (Anastopoulos et al., 2018) or observer ratings of oral language skills (Connor, 2019). Even within the context of direct student assessment, inter-rater reliability can be useful in understanding the extent to which differences among students in screener scores are due to administration or scoring errors. Cummings et al. (2014) evaluated the relation between examiner errors in scoring oral reading fluency probes and found that 16% of the variance in scores was due to examiner differences. Such findings underscore the potential importance of calibrating administrations of screeners to reduce scoring errors and misidentification.

The interplay among reliability types in choosing screeners is balance and purpose for evaluating reported statistics based on the need for each type. If one were to take a set of indexes, such as Social Security number, date of birth, and height, collected data would likely demonstrate excellent test–retest reliability but poor internal consistency (McCrae et al., 2011). Conversely, an assessment of stress or anxiety might have good internal consistency and poor test–retest reliability. The choice of which forms of reliability are most important for a screener is inextricably tied to the scope of the assessment. Curriculum-based measdurement (CBM) screeners operate as time-limited assessments and do not report information at the item level—hence, estimates of internal consistency are not available. Instead, CBMs typically report alternate form and test–retest reliability. Computer adaptive assessment (CAA) screeners operate with inherent equivalence across forms (i.e., all items are calibrated to the same scale). Accordingly, CAA reliability tends to be reported via marginal reliability (akin to internal consistency) and test-retest reliability.

Validity

Forms of validity evidence are vast to the point that we may be able to provide an alphabetized and nonexhaustive sample of forms of validity that includes conclusion, concurrent, construct, content, convergent, criterion, discriminant, ecological, etiological, external, face, factor, hypothesis, in situ, internal, nomological, predictive, translational, treatment, and washback.

Validity is simply concerned with the extent to which something measures what it purports to measure. A word reading test should measure word reading and not receptive vocabulary. An historical perspective of validity was that three independent forms of validity existed (i.e., content, criterion, and construct validity) and could be readily interchanged (Messick, 1995). Content validity is primarily established by the consistency of expert judgments that test content is related to its described use. A classical definition of criterion validity is the simple correlation between a test score and an outcome score, and construct validity is concerned with the interpretation and use of scores (Messick, 1995). Messick (1989) sought to reconceptualize all forms of validity as forming a cohesive, unified framework of *construct* validity. This framework includes the six areas that should be evaluated to measure a test, including a screener's construct validity.

Content

Evidence for content validity includes characterizations of the content's relevance, the overall representativeness of the content (e.g., test items or stimuli), and the quality of the test items or stimuli. This form of validity is especially important when one is building an assessment, such as a screener, and is relevant to the *scope of the assessment* previously described because it provides a foundation by which score interpretations can be defended. That is, a domain that has been evaluated for content validity via the domain's definitions, item representation, and domain relevance allow for interpretations and score use to be parsimoniously developed and defended (Sireci, 1998).

Substantive

A general perspective of substantive validity is that this form is established by describing the theoretical rationales that explain consistency in one's response to test items. Tasks such as rater judgment of items relative to an established taxonomy (Rovinelli & Hambleton, 1976), rater judgment of the extent to which a particular knowledge base or skill is essential to successful item completion (Lawshe, 1975), or calculating the proportion of raters who assign an item to its theorized content (Anderson & Gerbing, 1991) have all been used to provide evidence of substantive validity.

Structural

Structural aspects of validity are concerned with how well the structure of the assessment aligns with the construct domain and can be tested via quantitative methods such as exploratory or confirmatory factor analysis.

Generalizability

The interpretation of scores and how well they generalize across tasks, samples, and time points reflects the generalizability aspect of validity. It may be ascertained by a description of what the defined population and boundaries for that population are; the sample representativeness in the conducted study to validate the assessment; the employed design, data collection measures, procedures, and analyses within the validation study; a review of potential biases (e.g., sample selection bias or information bias) and confounds; and studies of replication.

External

External validity is concerned with quantitative evidence, including convergent, discriminant, and predictive forms of validity. Convergent validity measures the degree to which scores that should be related are in fact related to each other. For example, a measure of uppercase alphabet letter knowledge should be strongly correlated with a measure of lowercase alphabet letter knowledge, and a researcher-developed measure of receptive vocabulary should be moderately to strongly correlated with a standardized measure of receptive vocabulary like the Peabody Picture Vocabulary Test. Discriminant validity is characterized by how unrelated scores from two domains should be when they are expected to be unrelated. For example, a measure of alphabet letter knowledge should not be correlated with one's intake of sugar-sweetened beverages. Predictive validity is the longitudinal association between a test score at one time point and another test score at a later time point.

Consequential

One of the more hotly debated forms of validity is consequential validity (Cizek et al., 2008), and in the area of screening for dyslexia risk, it is unsurprising that this should be a hallmark of evaluating screeners. Due to the confluence of accountability testing, screening legislation, individualized education program (IEP) provision, and instructional and intervention supports for at-risk readers, there is a burden on screener developers and users to carefully take stock of implications of at-risk and not-at-risk classifications on screeners, specifically pertaining to what happens when correct decisions and decision errors occur. It is key that that score labels (e.g., high risk, moderate risk, low risk) are accurate and precise descriptors of what is being assessed (Messick, 1989) and that assessment developers and test users clearly describe as well as possible the potential and actual consequences of using a selected screener.

Classification Accuracy

The language around classification accuracy and the process by which students are correctly or incorrectly identified as at risk is diverse in the same ways as reliability and validity. Classification accuracy is a form of concurrent and predictive validity that looks at how a sample of individuals falls into one of two outcome groups (i.e., within an educational context, those who perform at or above a cut point on an outcome and those who perform below a cut point on a screener). In the medical literature, the classic two outcome groups are those who are noted as failing the outcome or passing the outcome based on two screener groups (i.e., at risk or not at risk on the screen).

As depicted in Table 8.1, four cells characterize student performances on the screen and outcome measure: Cell A individuals are called *True Positives*, as these are individuals who were identified as at risk on a screener and performed below the set threshold on the outcome (e.g., below the 20th percentile of a standardized reading test); Cell B individuals are called *False Positives*, as they were classified as at risk on the screener but ultimately performed at or above the set threshold on the outcome (e.g., above the 20th percentile of a standardized reading test); individuals in Cell C are *False Negatives*, as they were identified as not at risk on the screener and performed below the set threshold on the outcome; and Cell D are the *True Negative* individuals who were not at risk on the screener and performed at or above the set threshold on the outcome. Stated more conceptually from a medical perspective, true positives are the actual sick people who are correctly identified as sick from a screener; true negatives are the actual healthy people who are correctly identified as healthy from a screener; false positives are people who are actually healthy that a screener says are sick; and false negatives are people who are actually sick that a screener says are healthy. These cell counts may be used to compute further classification accuracy indices such as sensitivity, specificity, negative and positive predictive values, and overall correct classification.

Table 8.1 Sample 2 × 2 Contingency Table

Screen	Outcome	
	Fail	*Pass*
At Risk	A: True Positive	B: False Positive
Not At Risk	C: False Negative	D: True Negative

The sensitivity of a screener is the proportion of individuals who are correctly identified as having the outcome (e.g., performing <20th percentile) and is computed by Cell A/(Cell A + Cell C). Specificity of a screener is the proportion of individuals who are correctly identified as *not* having the outcome (e.g., performing >= 20th percentile) and is computed by Cell D/(Cell D + Cell B). It is often desirable to have sensitivity and specificity > 0.80, yet it may be difficult to achieve this given the competing nature of increasing sensitivity at the cost of specificity and vice versa (see Streiner, 2003 for an overview). Positive and negative predictive values are properties of the screener that indicate the accuracy of the cut points on the screener based on all who are identified as at risk on the screener (positive predictive value) or all those who are identified as not at risk on the screener (negative predictive value).

Core Considerations for Using Screeners

The data that come from screeners should not be divorced from the context where they are intended to be used. It is important, therefore, that as an individual or group is looking at the core considerations of the screeners themselves, a core set of questions should be addressed that will support effective use of screeners in the local context (National Center on Intensive Interventions, 2019).

Who Should be Present to Help Choose a Screener?

This question may be asked during the entire process of prescreener evaluation, screener selection, and data use coming from the screener. No one person should be tasked with the documentation of screener assets, screener selection, or how to use the data to support data-based decision-making. Practitioners, teachers, school social workers, and school administrators all have valuable input as to how scores can be used to provide services, the relative ease of explaining scores to parents/caregivers, and the resources needed to administer and support ongoing use of the screener. Thus, when choosing a screening tool and interpreting screening data, decisions should be made by a team of individuals that represents these varied skill sets and perspectives. Identifying the varied skill sets and perspectives to choose a tool will provide a broader framework of consideration.

What Are Our Needs and Priorities?

Each locale where a screener is to be used is unique. Applying a one-size-fits-all framework to using scores means that aspects of the locale, such as the prevalence of students with disabilities, are lost. When pulling a team together, the collective can look at the development and prioritization of needs. When determining priorities, teams should ask themselves what questions they expect the data to answer (e.g., which students have risk for dyslexia?) and what decisions they expect to make using the data (e.g., assigning students to intervention supports). The availability of reading, math, behavior, writing, social-emotional learning screeners, and direct assessment or informant measurement necessitates careful consideration of screening priorities across grades, content areas, and exceptionalities. Moreover, the local service delivery model should be considered as a primary means, where possible, for remediation. For example, widespread state and district adoption of Multi-Tiered Systems of Support in Reading (MTSS-R; Balu et al., 2015) and dyslexia screening requirements (Gearin et al., 2021) has led to broad implementation of dyslexia screening processes in schools whereby students may then be served through Tier 2 or Tier 3 interventions (Miciak & Fletcher, 2020). In these contexts, practitioners may then use screening data to predict risk, assign students to supplemental or intensive supports, and evaluate the effectiveness of their school's instruction and intervention supports.

What Do Our Data Say?

Many, if not most, screeners include basic score types that are indicative of normative-based or criterion-based performance. Percentile ranks based on their screener score indicate how well an individual performed in relation to other students in a comparison, or normative, population. This rank ordering can help practitioners evaluate the percentage of individuals with disabilities in their locale compared to national proportions. For example, a school with 20% of students at or below the tenth percentile would be roughly double the population expectation (i.e., 10% of students normatively perform at or below the tenth percentile), indicating a greater base rate of risk. Percentile ranks may support practitioners in deciding which students to prioritize for supplemental or intensive reading support. Screeners also often use a benchmark-type score that assigns a risk category based on a score interval that each child's screener score falls into (e.g., at risk, some risk, low risk). In preventative model frameworks such as MTSS/RTI, the normative expectation is that ~80% of students should be considered low risk and thus benefit from general classroom instruction, ~15% of students will require additional short-term services, and ~5% of students will need intensive services to meet grade-level expectations. The alignment between screener benchmarks of risk levels and instructional support will not fit neatly in all locales, and thus the "Who should be present?" question has special relevance to understanding how to best balance available resources for intervention and services with the proportion of students who are at various risk categories, especially in light of vulnerability factors and inequities that exist and play into identification and services (e.g., Fien et al., 2021; Schelbe et al., 2021).

One limitation of screener scores is that they often do not include longitudinal, aggregate calculations to inform locale-based performance over time. That is, ongoing screening during the school year will support teachers and practitioners to look at how a student is changing over time. Individual student growth curves can support individual student remediation. Individual locales can certainly look at how the percentage of students who are low risk changes from one administration period to the next; however, this approach loses the nuance of accounting for baseline performance. For example, a school may show that 20% of students were at "some risk" during initial fall screening and 15% were at "some risk" during winter screening, where a 5% decrease in risk was observed. This type of data inference does not take into account how the baseline set of students in each category at the initial fall screening spread across the categories at the winter screening. Here we re-introduce two types of indices that were used across a number of states during the *Reading First* program: Effectiveness of Core Instruction (ECI) and Effectiveness of Intervention (EI).

Effectiveness of Core Instruction

The ECI is an index that shows the percentage of students who were categorized as "low risk" or a comparable "on grade-level" category who continued to perform at a level that was categorized as "low risk" at the next mid-year assessment. This index then communicates how well the core instruction or its implementation is facilitating the instructional needs of the students such that they maintain grade-level performance. The ECI is calculated in the following manner: (1) Count the number of students whose fall screening score was at a "low risk" or comparable "on grade-level" category. (b) Using that number of students, count the number of students who were at that same category at the winter screening assessment. (c) Divide the number of students from part (b) by the number of students from part (a). Suppose there are ten students who are "low risk" at the fall and eight of those ten students were "low risk" at winter, then the ECI = 8/10 = 80% such that 80% of students who were low risk at the fall remained low risk at the winter.

Effectiveness of Intervention

The EI communicates to teachers and practitioners how the initial grouping of students in "some risk" or "at risk" categories at the fall resulted in improvements the following screening period. Two specific EI scores can be computed from the fall screening data that track how the "some risk" and "at risk" students respond. An Effectiveness of Intervention–Strategic (EI-S) index calculates the proportion of students in a "some risk" category from the fall screening period that moved to a "low risk" category in the winter. The steps to computing the EI-S are similar in concept to the ECI: (a) Count the number of students who were at "some risk" at the fall. (b) Using that number of students, count the number of students who were at a "low risk" category at the winter screening assessment. (c) Divide the number of students from part (b) by the number of students from part (a). A larger value reflects a higher proportion of students moving from "some risk" to "low risk" from fall screening to winter screening. The Effectiveness of Intervention–Intensive (EI-I) index calculates the proportion of students in an "at risk" category from the fall screening period that moved to *either* a "some risk" or "low risk" category in the winter. The steps to computing the EI-I are: (a) Count the number of students who were "at risk" at the fall. (b) Using that number of students, count the number of students who were *either* at "some risk" or "low risk" category in the winter. (c) Divide the number of students from part (b) by the number of students from part (a). A larger value reflects a higher proportion of students moving from "at risk" to a lower level of risk from fall screening to winter screening.

The ECI and EI indices allow teachers and practitioners to leverage their benchmark data in news ways to support decision-making that considers both initial status and change over time. Other resources, indices, and considerations exist to support leveraging screening data over time (e.g., Bailey et al., 2017).

Who Should We Talk To?

A final consideration worth mentioning is determining who else should be included to support interpretation and use of scores in a locale. Where the first question is geared toward bringing together a diversity of locale-based personnel, this question is aimed at broadening that circle on an as-needed basis for questions or support. Test vendors can be a good starting place for asking technical questions related to core considerations outlined in the first section of this chapter. The National Center on Intensive Interventions (NCII; https://intensiveintervention.org/), National Center for Systemic Improvement (NCIS; https://ncsi.wested.org/), and National Center on Improving Literacy (NCIL; https://improvingliteracy.org/) are each committed to providing resources and assistance pertaining to screening. NCII maintains a clearinghouse of independently reviewed academic and behavior screening tools with ratings provided on technical quality and information on administration. NCSI provides universal, targeted, and intensive technical assistance to states and districts to teach and reinforce data literacy and research-informed practices with a goal of maximizing improvement for students with disabilities. NCIL provides tools and resources on improving literacy, understanding universal screening, and providing implementation toolkits to support literacy practices for families and schools.

In addition to these organizations, scientists can be tapped to support localization of screening and how to use data, and are generally eager to partner with practitioners. As greater calls from scientists to scientists are made for a "team science" approach (Petscher et al., 2020; Solari et al., 2020; Terry et al., 2021), team-ups of practitioners and scientists can result in a pursuit of greater good for child development in education and overall human flourishing.

Where Should We Be Going?

It is fairly uncontroversial to say that screening is a useful mechanism by which individuals who are at risk for future, poor educational outcomes are identified. Complexities in a screening process may arise when sifting through and weighing the many core considerations for choosing a screener. Here we have offered starting points that practitioners may use to navigate a process to help organize the conversations that should occur at each locale where screening is conducted. Through careful detailing of the defined population of interest, how screeners are validated, and the technical quality of scores from the screener, practitioners may engage in meaningful conversations both interior to the locale and with outside partners such as scientists to help choose and use the most appropriate screener to support learning.

Yet even as we take stock of *some* of these considerations, it is worth reflecting on present realities and new opportunities that may be on the horizon to advance screening methods and practices. Threshold models for screening, which are rooted in the medical model, have been advocated by VanDerHeyden (2013) to identify a test threshold and a treatment threshold to inform decision-making according to the empirical, probabilistic risks and benefits of administering a screener and when to provide interventions. Emerging methodologies from Klingbeil et al. (2019, 2020) and Wagner et al. (2020) have advocated for Bayesian models to use better informed likelihoods for both prevalence and screening measures. In addition, researchers have studied the extent to which the inclusion of statistical moderation between scores in a multivariate screener model can improve classification accuracy. Petscher and Catts (2021) found that the AUC improved from 0.88 when using main effects of letter sounds, teacher ratings of child behavior, and parental measurement of adverse childhood experiences to AUC = 0.96 by including pairwise interactions among the scores.

Beyond the methodologies of how to estimate scores to be used in screening, it is critical to be cognizant of the assumptions we make in our use of screening scores. We often assume that teachers and practitioners have the core knowledge, experiences, and cultural competence to serve *all* students. The evidence base of what is effective instruction or intervention may be insufficient when considering students who attend high-poverty schools, students with disabilities, students who are dual language learners, and students of color (Petscher & Patton Terry, in press) thus, there are ecological considerations that should be part of the conversation about how tools are created (e.g., digital tools may not be accessible or usable in all locations) or used (e.g., embedded speech recognition may be biased in its scoring based on linguistic variability). These and other conditions should be examined as we move forward in making screening, interventions, and education equitable for all students.

Funding Note

This work was funded in part by the National Center on Improving Literacy and the Chan Zuckerberg Initiative. A portion of the materials here were used in the appendix of a non-peer reviewed report: Petscher, Y., Fien, H., Stanley, C., Gearin, B., Gaab, N., Fletcher, J. M., & Johnson, E. (2019). *Screening for Dyslexia*. improvingliteracy.org.

References

Adlof, S. M., Scoggins, J., Brazendale, A., Babb, S., & Petscher, Y. (2017). Identifying children at risk for language impairment or dyslexia with group-administered measures. *Journal of Speech, Language, and Hearing Research, 60*(12), 3507–3522.

Anastopoulos, A. D., Beal, K. K., Reid, R. J., Reid, R., Power, T. J., & DuPaul, G. J. (2018). Impact of child and informant gender on parent and teacher ratings of attention-deficit/hyperactivity disorder. *Psychological Assessment, 30*(10), 1390–1394.

Anderson, J. C., & Gerbing, D. W. (1991). Predicting the performance of measures in a confirmatory factor analysis with a pretest assessment of their substantive validities. *Journal of Applied Psychology, 76*(5), 732–740.

Bailey, T., Ruedel, K., & Petscher, Y. (April, 2017). *Data analysis strategies for using general outcome measures to evaluate program impact*. Paper presented at the Annual Council for Exceptional Children Convention, Boston, MA.

Balu, R., Zhu, P., Doolittle, F., Schiller, E., Jenkins, J., & Gersten, R. (2015). *Evaluation of response to intervention practices for elementary school reading.* NCEE 2016–4000. National Center for Education Evaluation and Regional Assistance.

British Dyslexia Association. (2007). *Definition of dyslexia.* www.actiondyslexia.co.uk/view-article/Defining-Dyslexia.

Cassidy, B. (2019). *Cassidy urges full implementation of First Step Act dyslexia screening.* www.cassidy.senate.gov/newsroom/press-releases/cassidy-urges-full-implementation-of-first-step-act-dyslexia-screening.

Catts, H., Fey, M. E., Zhang, X., & Tomblin, J. B. (2001). Estimating the risk of future reading difficulties in kindergarten children: A research-based model and its clinical implementation. *Language, Speech & Hearing Services in Schools, 32*(1), 38–50.

Catts, H. W., & Petscher, Y. (in press). A cumulative risk and resilience model of dyslexia. *Journal of Learning Disabilities.* https://edarxiv.org/g57ph/

Chakrabartty, S. N. (2013). Best split-half and maximum reliability. *IOSR Journal of Research & Method in Education, 3*(1), 1–8.

Cizek, G. J., Rosenberg, S. L., & Koons, H. H. (2008). Sources of validity evidence for educational and psychological tests. *Educational and Psychological Measurement, 68*(3), 397–412.

Compton, D. L., Fuchs, D., Fuchs, L. S., Bouton, B., Gilbert, J. K., Barquero, L. A., . . . Crouch, R. C. (2010). Selecting at-risk first-grade readers for early intervention: Eliminating false positives and exploring the promise of a two-stage gated screening process. *Journal of Educational Psychology, 102*(2), 327.

Compton, D. L., Fuchs, D., Fuchs, L. S., & Bryant, J. D. (2006). Selecting at-risk readers in first grade for early intervention: A two-year longitudinal study of decision rules and procedures. *Journal of Educational Psychology, 98*(2), 394.

Compton, D. L., Gilbert, J. K., Jenkins, J. R., Fuchs, D., Fuchs, L. S., Cho, E., . . Bouton, B. (2012). Accelerating chronically unresponsive children to tier 3 instruction: What level of data is necessary to ensure selection accuracy? *Journal of Learning Disabilities, 45*(3), 204–216.

Connor, C. M. (2019). Using technology and assessment to personalize instruction: Preventing reading problems. *Prevention Science, 20*(1), 89–99.

Cummings, K. D., Biancarosa, G., Schaper, A., & Reed, D. K. (2014). Examiner error in curriculum-based measurement of oral reading. *Journal of School Psychology, 52*(4), 361–375.

Cutting, L. E., & Scarborough, H. S. (2006). Prediction of reading comprehension: Relative contributions of word recognition, language proficiency, and other cognitive skills can depend on how comprehension is measured. *Scientific Studies of Reading, 10*(3), 277–299.

Edwards, A. A., Joyner, K. J., & Schatschneider, C. (2021). A simulation study on the performance of different reliability estimation methods. *Educational and Psychological Measurement, 81*(6), 1089–1117.

Fien, H., Chard, D. J., & Baker, S. K. (2021). Can the evidence revolution and Multi-Tiered Systems of Support improve education equity and reading achievement? *Reading Research Quarterly, 56*, S105–S118.

Francis, D. J., Santi, K. L., Barr, C., Fletcher, J. M., Varisco, A., & Foorman, B. R. (2008). Form effects on the estimation of students' oral reading fluency using DIBELS. *Journal of School Psychology, 46*(3), 315–342.

Gearin, B., Petscher, Y., Stanley, C., Nelson, N. J., & Fien, H. (2021). Document analysis of state dyslexia legislation suggests likely heterogeneous effects on student and school outcomes. *Learning Disability Quarterly*, 0731948721991549.

Gilbert, J. K., Compton, D. L., Fuchs, D., & Fuchs, L. S. (2012). Early screening for risk of reading disabilities: Recommendations for a four-step screening system. *Assessment for Effective Intervention, 38*(1), 6–14.

Glover, T. A., & Albers, C. A. (2007). Considerations for evaluating universal screening assessments. *Journal of School Psychology, 45*(2), 117–135.

Johnson, E. S., Jenkins, J. R., & Petscher, Y. (2010). Improving the accuracy of a direct route screening process. *Assessment for Effective Intervention, 35*(3), 131–140.

Johnson, E. S., Jenkins, J. R., Petscher, Y., & Catts, H. W. (2009). How can we improve the accuracy of screening instruments? *Learning Disabilities Research & Practice, 24*(4), 174–185.

Keenan, J. M., & Meenan, C. E. (2014). Test differences in diagnosing reading comprehension deficits. *Journal of Learning Disabilities, 47*(2), 125–135.

Kim, Y. S., Petscher, Y., Schatschneider, C., & Foorman, B. (2010). Does growth rate in oral reading fluency matter in predicting reading comprehension achievement? *Journal of Educational Psychology, 102*(3), 652.

Klingbeil, D. A., Van Norman, E. R., & Nelson, P. M. (2020). Using interval likelihood ratios in gated screening: A direct replication study. *Assessment for Effective Intervention*, 1534508420953894.

Klingbeil, D. A., Van Norman, E. R., Nelson, P. M., & Birr, C. (2019). Interval likelihood ratios: Applications for gated screening in schools. *Journal of School Psychology, 76*, 107–123.

Lawshe, C. H. (1975). A quantitative approach to content validity. *Personnel Psychology, 28*(4), 563–575.

Lyon, G. R., Shaywitz, S. E., Shaywitz, B. A. (2003). A definition of dyslexia. *Annals of Dyslexia, 53*, 1–14.

McCrae, R. R., Kurtz, J. E., Yamagata, S., & Terracciano, A. (2011). Internal consistency, retest reliability, and their implications for personality scale validity. *Personality and Social Psychology Review, 15*(1), 28–50.

McNeish, D. (2018). Thanks coefficient alpha, we'll take it from here. *Psychological methods, 23*(3), 412.

Messick, S. (1989). Validity. In R. L. Linn (Ed.), *Educational measurement* (3rd ed., pp. 13–103). New York: Macmillan.

Messick, S. (1995). Validity of psychological assessment: Validation of inferences from persons' responses and performances as scientific inquiry into score meaning. *American Psychologist, 50*(9), 741.

Miciak, J., & Fletcher, J. M. (2020). The critical role of instructional response for identifying dyslexia and other learning disabilities. *Journal of Learning Disabilities, 53*(5), 343–353.

National Center on Intensive Interventions. (2019). *Tool chart users guide*. Washington, DC: American Institutes for Research.

Nunnally, J. C., & Bernstein, I. H. (1994). *Psychometric theory* (McGraw-Hill Series in Psychology) (Vol. 3). New York: McGraw-Hill.

Petscher, Y., Cabell, S. Q., Catts, H. W., Compton, D. L., Foorman, B. R., Hart, S. A.,. . Wagner, R. K. (2020). How the science of reading informs 21st-century education. *Reading Research Quarterly, 55*, S267–S282.

Petscher, Y., & Catts, H. (2021). *Screening for dyslexia: Intersections among cognitive, linguistic, and biopsychosocial factors*. https://doi.org/10.6084/m9.figshare.14611308

Petscher, Y., Cummings, K. D., Biancarosa, G., & Fien, H. (2013). Advanced (measurement) applications of curriculum-based measurement in reading. *Assessment for Effective Intervention, 38*(2), 71–75.

Petscher, Y., & Patton Terry, N. (in press). Cross-cultural considerations for screening and identification. In N. Gaab, L. Siegel, A Linzarini, & R. Merkley (Eds.), *Learning differences/exceptional learner*. UNESCO MGIEP.

Petscher, Y., Truckenmiller, A., & Zhou, C. (2016). *The earlier assessment for reading success* [EARS; Web application software]. Tallahassee, FL: Florida State University.

Rovinelli, R. J., & Hambleton, R. K. (1976, April 19–23). *On the use of content specialists in the assessment of criterion-referenced test item validity*. Paper presented at the Annual Meeting of the American Educational Research Association, 60th, San Francisco, California.

Schatschneider, C., Wagner, R. K., & Crawford, E. C. (2008). The importance of measuring growth in response to intervention models: Testing a core assumption. *Learning and Individual Differences, 18*(3), 308–315.

Schatschneider, C., Wagner, R. K., Hart, S. A., & Tighe, E. L. (2016). Using simulations to investigate the longitudinal stability of alternative schemes for classifying and identifying children with reading disabilities. *Scientific Studies of Reading, 20*(1), 34–48.

Schelbe, L., Pryce, J., Petscher, Y., Fien, H., Stanley, C., Gearin, B., & Gaab, N. (2021). *Dyslexia in the context of social work: Screening and early intervention*. https://psyarxiv.com/v6fzu/.

Shapiro, E. S., Dennis, M. S., & Fu, Q. (2015). Comparing computer adaptive and curriculum-based measures of math in progress monitoring. *School Psychology Quarterly, 30*(4), 470.

Sireci, S. G. (1998). The construct of content validity. *Social Indicators Research, 45*(1–3), 83–117.

Solari, E. J., Terry, N. P., Gaab, N., Hogan, T. P., Nelson, N. J., Pentimonti, J. M.,. . Sayko, S. (2020). Translational science: A road map for the science of reading. *Reading Research Quarterly, 55*, S347–S360.

Streiner, D. L. (2003). Diagnosing tests: Using and misusing diagnostic and screening tests. *Journal of Personality Assessment, 81*(3), 209–219.

Terry, N. P., Petscher, Y., Gaab, N., & Hart, S. (2021). Researchers translating the science of reading: Widening the lens of translational science through team science. *The Reading League Journal, 2*(1), 46.

Tonnessen, F. E. (1997). How can we best define "dyslexia"? *Dyslexia, 3*, 78–92.

VanDerHeyden, A. M. (2013). Universal screening may not be for everyone: Using a threshold model as a smarter way to determine risk. *School Psychology Review, 42*(4), 402–414.

Van der Linden, W. J., & Glas, C. A. (Eds.). (2000). *Computerized adaptive testing: Theory and practice*. Dordrecht: Kluwer Academic.

Wagner, R. K., Zirps, F. A., Edwards, A. A., Wood, S. G., Joyner, R. E., Becker, B. J., Liu, G., & Beal, B. (2020). The prevalence of Dyslexia: A new approach to its estimation. *Journal of Learning Disabilities, 53*(5), 354–365.

Wainer, H., Dorans, N. J., Flaugher, R., Green, B. F., & Mislevy, R. J. (2000). *Computerized adaptive testing: A primer*. Routledge.

World Health Organization. (2013). *The ICD-10 classification of mental and behavioral disorders: Clinical descriptions and diagnostic guidelines*. Author.

Yeo, S., Fearrington, J. Y., & Christ, T. J. (2012). Relation between CBM-R and CBM-mR slopes: An application of latent growth modeling. *Assessment for Effective Intervention, 37*(3), 147–158.

Zumeta, R. O., Compton, D. L., & Fuchs, L. S. (2012). Using word identification fluency to monitor first-grade reading development. *Exceptional Children, 78*(2), 201–220.

9

PARAPROFESSIONALS' PERCEPTIONS OF JOB-RELATED SUPPORTS, CHALLENGES, AND EFFECTIVENESS

Sally K. Fluhler, Christopher J. Lemons, Yasmina E. Haddad, Casey Chauvin, Guy Martin, Lauren LeJeune, and Emily Gurwitz

In 2017, slightly more than 6 million children and adolescents received special education services in public schools in the United States. These students were educated by 389,456 special education teachers and 458,676 paras (U.S. Department of Education, 2020). The number of paras who support students with disabilities has increased substantially over the past decade (i.e., 390,000 full-time equivalent paras a little more than a decade prior (U.S. Department of Education, 2008). This change in special educator staffing trends clearly highlights the need to understand the best ways to provide professional development (PD) and ongoing coaching to paras.

Paras are special education support staff who most commonly have a high school diploma or have additional education such as credit hours from an institution of higher education, or an associate's or bachelor's degree (National Center for Education Statistics, 2007; Brock & Anderson, 2020). Many paras have also received supplemental training in the form of school district–provided PD. Carter et al. (2009) found that 97% of paras included in their study reported providing one-on-one instruction to students with disabilities. Other responsibilities often identified include small-group or large-group instruction, clerical tasks, data collection or observation, recess or lunch supervision, and supporting the special education teacher in delivering instruction (Carter et al., 2009; Giangreco et al., 2005; Fisher & Pleasants, 2011). Further, when paras are used to fulfill supplemental instructional roles, this can assist special education teachers in maximizing their primary instructional time with students with disabilities (Causton-Theoharis et al., 2007).

Due in part to school districts' increased reliance on paras to support students with disabilities, the Every Student Succeeds Act (ESSA, 2015) outlined the expectation that paras would demonstrate competence by either (a) having completed a minimum of two years of study at an institution of higher education (i.e., an associate's degree) or (b) having demonstrated meeting rigorous standards of knowledge and skill as indicated by a formal state or local assessment (e.g., ParaPro Assessment; Educational Testing Service, n.d.). ESSA also outlines appropriate roles for paras indicating that they can be appropriately used to provide one-on-one instruction, assist with classroom management, or provide instructional support services under the direct supervision of a teacher (ESSA, 2015).

Based on the number of paras currently employed in public schools, it is clear they are essential school personnel who can assist students with disabilities in obtaining individualized education program (IEP) goals through a free and appropriate public education (FAPE) as outlined in the

Individuals with Disabilities Education Act (IDEA, 2004). However, previous studies have suggested that paras typically receive minimal preservice training (Breton, 2010; Brock & Carter, 2015; Giangreco et al., 2001) and, when it is provided, in-service training is typically focused on compliance and managing challenging behavior (Fisher & Pleasants, 2011; Reddy et al., 2021). The purpose of this chapter is to provide a review of current research focused on supporting paras, to highlight outcomes from a research study in which we provided ongoing PD and coaching to paras who were delivering reading and math interventions to students with intellectual and developmental disabilities (IDDs), and to outline implications for current practice and future research.

Current State of Research

Several research teams have explored responsibilities of and PD for paras. For example, Giangreco et al. (2001) reviewed literature from 1991 to 2000 pertaining to the types of supports paras provided to students with disabilities. The authors found that para job descriptions are too often vaguely defined with unclear expectations, leading to confusion in job responsibilities. Further, and perhaps unsurprisingly, the roles and responsibilities of paras varied widely and frequently included responsibilities for which paras were not adequately trained (e.g., required to support students with complex support needs, assigned as a primary instructor to students with disabilities with limited supervision).

Brock and Anderson (2020) reviewed experimental studies published between 2012 and 2019 in which the efficacy of training paras who work with students with IDDs was evaluated. The authors found that the number of experimental studies focused on para training has increased over time (c.f., Brock & Carter, 2013), with an average of three to six studies being published each year between 2013 and 2019. Brock and Anderson (2020) also found that recent research further supports the idea that paras can be effectively trained to deliver high-quality instruction. The authors also identified several characteristics of effective training for paras, including the use of performance feedback, implementation checklists, modeling, planning, and role play. The authors suggested that para training can be delivered effectively through group in-person, online, or online/in-person hybrid formats. Paras in the included studies focused on systematic instruction, function-based interventions, video modeling and prompting, peer support interventions, and social network interventions. The authors highlighted that the diversity of interventions delivered by paras in the included studies is encouraging, as the responsibility of paras for providing supports to students with disabilities appears to be increasing (Brock & Anderson, 2020).

Study Context

Given the increased expectation that paras provide instructional supports to students with disabilities and the requirement within the 2017 Request for Applications from the Institute of Education Science's National Center for Special Education Research that research proposals had to focus on outcomes of teachers and other instructional personnel, our research team proposed and received funding for an efficacy trial to evaluate PD designed to enhance paras' knowledge and skill related to delivering a reading or math intervention to elementary and middle school students with IDD (https://ies.ed.gov/funding/grantsearch/details.asp?ID=2209). In the domain of reading, we had two PD conditions. The first, traditional reading-focused PD (T-PD), provided paras with basic training on the reading intervention combined with ongoing weekly PD sessions in which they reviewed intervention videos with an instructional coach (i.e., a university employee who was providing ongoing support). Paras were also given weekly goals and support. The second PD condition, an enhanced reading-focused PD (E-PD), extended T-PD by adding further training modules and coaching focused on a deeper understanding of reading development, explicit instruction, and behavior management. In a sense, we designed the E-PD condition to help paras understand the "why" behind the instructional practices we asked them to use and to broaden their skill set beyond the scripted reading intervention. The third condition, designed as a business-as-usual control (BAU) condition for the reading conditions, provided training and support to paras in the domain of intensive math intervention. The efficacy trial was designed to have three cohorts of para-student pairs who would each engage in the study across two full academic years of intervention.

The coaching model used in both reading conditions included ongoing weekly support provided by instructional coaches, which included performance feedback, the development and monitoring of targeted goals and support, and opportunities for modeling components of the intervention. Each week, instructional coaches watched at least one recorded intervention session for each para. The coaches focused on adequate fidelity of implementation, areas in which improvement could be made, and positive feedback in areas where implementation had improved in relation to previous feedback. During coaching sessions, instructional coaches started by providing specific praise statements about the positive instructional behaviors observed in the video. Next, coaches provided feedback on the fidelity of intervention by identifying up to three specific implementation steps that could be improved upon. In these instances, the instructional coaches provided explicit guidance on how to improve implementation (i.e., modeling a step, directing a para to a specific portion of a training video). Coaching sessions also provided opportunities to discuss data regarding student progression through the intervention. In cases where students were not responding as well as intended, the instructional coach discussed ideas to enhance responses (e.g., motivation strategies, behavior management). Coaches then discussed priority goals and action items for the para to work on before their next coaching session. The instructional coach finished the coaching session by reiterating positive feedback and providing encouragement to continue working to enhance intervention delivery. Paras in the E-PD condition were also provided time to discuss the content of the additional training modules they watched with their instructional coach. Due to being the BAU condition, coaching for paras in the math condition followed the same model for the reading conditions with the exception of setting priority goals each week and follow-up with a related email.

During the spring of 2020 the COVID-19 pandemic disrupted project activities, including paras' delivery of intervention and our ability to collect a majority of our student assessment data. Due to the disruption of planned activities, our research team decided that we had a unique opportunity to conduct a set of qualitative interviews with participating paras to ask about their experiences and roles in schools, prior training and preparation, and experiences in the larger project. We anticipated the responses from the participating paras could inform our ongoing research project and current practice and could potentially highlight future research needs.

The overall research questions for the qualitative interviews were:

1. How do paras describe their job experiences, including challenges?
2. What PD opportunities have paras received?
3. What supports have been provided to paras by their supporting teachers?
4. What were paras' experiences in the study, including motivation for participating, experience engaging in the study, and challenges?
5. How do paras perceive the impacts of the study on themselves and their students?

Method

Participants

During March 2020, 55 paras were engaged with the larger efficacy trial. All were invited via email to participate in the qualitative interviews; 47 paras across three states in the South and

Southwest regions of the United States agreed to participate. The interviews were conducted using Zoom (Zoom Video Communications, Inc., 2020). Regardless of their ability to complete required research project requirements due to school closures, we provided paras with the originally intended stipend of $600 for engaging in the larger study and requested their participation in the interview in lieu of missed intervention sessions. Of the 47 paras interviewed, the majority were female ($n = 45$; 96%). In terms of educational backgrounds, paras had received a high school diploma ($n = 8$; 17%); completed an associate's degree ($n = 6$, 13%); received trade, tech, or vocational training ($n = 3$; 6%); received some undergraduate credits ($n = 15$; 32%); completed their undergraduate studies ($n = 13$, 28%); and completed some postgraduate credits ($n = 2$, 4%). The paras were Black ($n = 8$; 17%), White ($n = 37$; 79%), and Asian ($n = 1$; 2%). Nine percent of the interventionists reported their ethnicity as Hispanic. The paras were equivalently divided across treatment conditions (T-PD = 16, E-PD = 16, BAU = 15).

Interview Procedures

Interviews were conducted by instructional coaches. Interviews were semi-structured and consisted of 14 or 15 questions (E-PD had one additional condition-related question). Interview durations ranged from 6 minutes to 93 minutes. All interviews were transcribed by instructional coaches.

Coding Procedures

Development of the coding procedures was an iterative process. First, three members of the research team reviewed one randomly chosen transcript to begin the development of codes to represent paras' responses to interview questions. Second, the research team met to review initial codes and came to a consensus regarding the initial draft of the codebook. Third, two members of the research team used the initial draft codebook to code three additional transcripts. Following the coding of each individual transcript, the team met again to come to a consensus on a revised version of the coding procedures. In this process, modifications were made to the codebook, and previously coded transcripts were recoded as necessary. Two researchers coded seven transcripts prior to establishing a finalized codebook for training and reliability.

Next, researchers trained a third coder to use the codebook and code transcripts. The training consisted of an hour-long orientation to the codes, codebook, and the coding process. The third coder reached at least 90% reliability on a gold standard transcripts in order to code independently; 31% of the total transcripts ($n = 14$) were coded for reliability. Reliability was determined using a procedure proposed by Kurasaki (2000) in which after two coders independently code the same transcript, the lead coder selects one coded unit (one line in the transcript) and compares all codes within the following 9 lines for a total of 10 coded lines of the transcript. The lead coder chose a starting line within the first 10 lines of the transcript, compared codes for 10 lines, then chose another chunk for reliability after 30 lines of the transcript. For example, the lead coder would code lines 7 to 17 for reliability, and then lines 47 to 57, and so on until the end of the transcript. The three coders met weekly to independently code transcripts and to come to a consensus on any additional edits that were needed in coding procedures and the codebook. The codebook was updated after each meeting, and previously coded transcripts were recoded as necessary. Once all transcripts were fully coded, a database in which all coded transcripts were represented was created. The database reflected each code that appeared in each transcript at least one time. This database allowed researchers to determine broad themes and trends in the coded data. Results are reported as percentages of paras who made statements reflecting a specific code.

Results

The first few questions of the interview asked paras about their overall jobs and experiences as paras. Participating paras reported being satisfied with their job ($n = 42$; 89.36%) and having positive relationships with school personnel and students ($n = 35$; 74.47%). Paras reported serving in numerous roles in the school, including providing one-on-one support ($n = 10$; 21.28%), assisting teachers ($n = 4$; 8.51%), and providing small ($n = 3$; 6.38%) and large ($n = 2$; 4.26%) group instruction. Positively, only a small number ($n = 6$; 12.77%) of paras reported being dissatisfied in their current position.

However, paras did report challenges with their job. The majority of paras reported that challenges in their positions were student related ($n = 25$; 53.19%), with a small percentage reporting that challenges in their positions were related to adult interactions (i.e., teacher, school staff, parents) ($n = 4$; 8.51%). Many paras reported challenges in their job due to various job characteristics ($n = 21$; 44.68%). These job characteristics included but were not limited to being constantly busy, having little downtime, providing support in inclusive settings, sudden changes in responsibilities or schedules, and large caseloads. Eighteen paras reported other challenges to their job (38.30%); these other challenges were comments made by only one para and could not be grouped with other coding categories (e.g., needing a substitute, feeling bad for student situations, lack of parental support, lack of pay). Many paras reported feeling underprepared for their positions ($n = 16$; 34.04%) or reported feeling a lack of respect, value, and/or equality in their position ($n = 13$; 27.66%). Some paras reported that even though they had challenges in their positions, they still expressed positive reactions or responses to the challenges ($n = 13$; 27.66%), and only one para expressed a negative response to the challenges of their position (2.13%).

We asked paras about the PD and training they had received prior to participating in our PD study. Paras reported they received prior PD related to instruction content ($n = 5$; 10.64%), behavior management ($n = 12$; 25.53%), nonspecified PD ($n = 29$; 61.70%), or PD that was in another area ($n = 7$; 14.89%). However, a slight majority ($n = 26$; 55.32%) of paras indicated a lack of prior PD or training. A few paras made comments that specified positive ($n = 4$; 8.51%) or negative ($n = 4$; 8.51%) responses to previously provided PD. Paras also made comments referring to the time of year or frequency of the PD that has been provided ($n = 18$; 38.30%).

Many paras reported that prior to the start of the larger efficacy trial, they received teacher support ($n = 19$; 42.22%). Specifically, 14 paras reported receiving support with materials (31.11%), 6 paras reported receiving support in skill development (13.33%), and 5 paras reported receiving personal or social and emotional support (11.11%) from their teachers. A smaller but meaningful number of paras ($n = 9$; 20%) reported a lack of prior support from their teachers or feeling neutral about prior supports ($n = 4$; 8.89%). Paras who reported feeling neutral about prior supports did not report a specific lack of support but also did not report feeling supported in a specific way (e.g., were provided with supports but also, they did not ask for support). The majority of paras ($n = 30$; 66.67%) made comments that indicated they felt supported, whereas a smaller number ($n = 5$, 11.11%) specifically indicated they did not feel support from their teachers.

The remaining questions of the interview pertained to the paras' participation and experiences in our PD study, beginning with their motivation to participate in the study. The overwhelming majority of paras reported that helping one particular student or students in general was their motivation for participating in the larger research project ($n = 37$; 78.72%). Many paras were motivated by the possibility for self-improvement (i.e., learning, developing new skills, improving skills, new techniques) ($n = 19$; 40.43%). Other sources of motivation for participation were being encouraged by a teacher, school administrator or other school personnel ($n = 11$; 23.40%), having general interest in the project based on the project description ($n = 9$; 19.15%), being told to participate by school personnel ($n = 2$; 4.26%), and being motivated by the compensation that was provided for participation ($n = 1$; 2.13%).

When asked about their experiences engaging in the study as a whole, overall paras reported having positive experiences with the larger research project (reading = 25; 78.13%; math = 13; 100%). Specifically, paras mentioned positive experiences with the training (reading = 8; 25%; math = 5; 38.46%), the curriculum used (i.e., the reading or math curriculum) (reading = 19; 59.38%; math = 10; 76.92%), their instructional coach (reading = 9; 28.13%; math = 6; 46.15%), and student outcomes (reading = 21; 65.63%; math = 10; 76.92%). All of the paras in the reading conditions mentioned they would continue to use the materials provided during the study in the future ($n = 32$; 100%), and nearly all paras in the math condition would continue use the research project materials ($n = 14$; 93.33%). Given the structure of the PD models used in the study, we asked paras about the ongoing instructional coach support provided. The majority of paras in both reading and math conditions reported that the feedback and coaching was the most helpful support provided by the instructional coaches (reading = 24; 75%; math = 11; 73.33%). Interestingly, paras reported the other most helpful support provided by the instructional coaches was social and emotional support, again across both conditions (reading = 17; 53.13%; math = 7; 46.67%). Other helpful supports that were commonly reported included motivation and encouragement provided (reading = 11; 34.38%; math = 4; 26.67%), supports for skill development (reading = 9; 28.13%; math = 2; 13.33%), and the instructional coach's responsiveness (reading = 10; 31.25%; math = 6; 40%).

Paras also reported on challenges in meeting the project expectations; reported challenges pertained to both implementation of the intervention and recording and uploading intervention sessions. Unsurprisingly, one of the most common challenges mentioned by paras across study conditions was challenges with having the time to implement (reading = 46.88%; math = 8; 53.33%). Many paras mentioned challenges with other school responsibilities (e.g., substituting in other classrooms in school, providing support to students other than the target student, inflexibility of schedules, abrupt schedule changes) that prevented implementation of the intervention (reading = 19; 59.38%; math = 11; 73.33%). The majority of paras in both reading and math conditions reported that student-related challenges were a barrier to intervention implementation (reading = 17; 53.13%; math = 7; 46.67%). Other challenges that were reported were challenges with the availability of physical space for intervention (reading = 7; 21.88%; math = 3; 20%), challenges with technology used (reading = 2; 6.25%; math = 4; 26.67%), and intrapersonal challenges (e.g., feeling self-conscious about being recorded, being evaluated via recording, self-doubt in general; reading = 6; 18.75%; math = 6; 40%).

The last part of our interview asked paras about the changes they noticed in themselves and their students as a result of participation in our PD study. Overall paras reported they noticed gains in knowledge and skill (reading = 23; 71.88%; math = 8; 53.33%) and their overall effectiveness as a para (reading = 21; 65.53%; math = 7; 46.67%). Paras also noticed social and emotional changes (reading = 9; 28.13%; math = 6; 40%), which included changes in their self-confidence, patience, happiness, and general understanding of and responsiveness to students' social-emotional state. A small portion of paras also mentioned changes in the relationships they had with either their student, teacher, and/or school staff as a result of participation in the larger research project (reading = 4; 12.50%; math = 3; 20%). Unfortunately, there were a small number of paras who specifically stated a lack of noticeable change (reading = 3, 9.38%; math = 1, 6.67%).

Paras were also asked to report on changes they noticed in their students as a result of participating in the larger research project. The majority of the paras in the reading conditions noticed gains in their students' reading skills ($n = 20$; 62.50%). The majority of the paras in the math condition noticed gains in their students' math skills ($n = 9$, 60%). Paras made statements regarding changes in their students' behavior (reading = 8; 25%; math = 4; 26.67%) and social and emotional skills. Overwhelmingly, the majority of paras noticed changes in their students' social and emotional skills (reading = 19; 59.38%; math = 12;, 80%). Social and emotional changes included reported changes in students' confidence, enjoyment of the intervention, eagerness or willingness to participate in intervention sessions, and excitement about intervention. Many paras reported other changes in their students, such as changes in their students' conversational skills, communication, and that the project was a positive experience in general for their student (reading = 11; 34.38%; math = 6; 40%). Paras also shared that other people who interact with their student reported changes in the student as well (reading = 17; 53.13%; math = 9; 60%). Unfortunately, a small number of paras indicated a lack of noticeable change in their student (reading = 3; 9.38%; math = 1; 6.67%).

Discussion

Our research team was evaluating PD designed to enhance paras' knowledge and skill related to delivering an intensive reading or math intervention through a randomized controlled trial. In the spring of 2020, when the COVID-19 pandemic halted our project activities, we conducted a set of qualitative interviews with 47 participating paras. The purpose of this qualitative study was to ask paras about their experiences and roles in schools, the training supports provided to them, and their experience and perceived outcomes while participating in our PD research study.

Job Experience

When asked about their experiences as paras, it is encouraging that most paras reported having job satisfaction and positive relationships with school-related personnel and students. Of paras who reported statements about the specific roles they performed, providing one-on-one support to students with disabilities was the most frequently mentioned role. This reflects the findings from Carter et al. (2009), reporting that 97% of the studied paras reported providing one-on-one instruction to students with disabilities. Additionally, the other specific roles mentioned reiterate previous research (Brock and Anderson, 2020; Carter et al., 2009; Giangreco et al., 2005; Fisher & Pleasants, 2011) and the general job description in ESSA.

Some paras made statements of job dissatisfaction using terms of wanting "more" from their jobs. For example, Ms. Pine described her experience of being a para as, "We don't do a lot of things like we're not included and stuff and some of the paraprofessionals they like that, like they just want to come in and do stuff. But it's really, I just want to be like, I want to matter." Paras also reported feelings of lack of respect, value, or equality. Ms. Pine described her feelings of lack of respect and equality as, "It's been fine, but it really pushed me to want to be a teacher more because a lot of times I feel and it's not the people I work with, they don't mean it, but it's like 'you're not a teacher.' So, you matter but not really kind of feeling." It is possible that these findings are related. Paras reported wanting to "matter" or wanting their ideas to be heard, which can seemingly lead to job dissatisfaction when one feels as if they are not being heard or respected. Although not related to our specific research questions, many paras expressed their appreciation for being able to participate in the PD study and having a study that focused on them, providing supports for them.

Several paras reported feeling underprepared for their job. This could be due to various reasons, including the vague job descriptions that vary across schools and districts or being asked to perform roles and responsibilities without proper or sufficient training. Studies have found that the majority of training provided to paras is considered "on-the-job" training, which can vary in quality, be spontaneous, and lead to feelings of being underprepared (Carter et al., 2009; Riggs & Mueller, 2001; Steckelberg et al., 2007).

Professional Development

Paras reported a lack of training and lack of preparedness for their positions prior to engaging in the larger research project. Although this is not novel—for example, Giangreco et al. (2001) found para job descriptions were often vaguely defined with unclear expectations—it does indicate the continued need to support paras, provide adequate training opportunities, and clearly define the roles and responsibilities of the position. Of the training paras participated in, most were very general. Of the targeted PD opportunities reported, specific behavior management training was the most frequently identified. This could be an indication of the primary focus of the defined roles for these paras. It also may relate to the fact that paras most frequently identified student-related behavioral challenges as their primary concern—in other words, schools may provide this type of focused PD because it is the most urgent need for paras.

A small number of paras reported receiving PD and training related to instructional content ($n = 5$; 10.64%). This is somewhat concerning, as the most frequently mentioned role that paras were serving in was providing one-on-one instruction. To provide high-quality one-on-one instruction, paras need training and preparation in the specific areas of instruction they are providing. There seems to be a disconnect between the paras' reported role and the preparation for that role with supportive instructional content PD. If paras are likely to fulfill one-on-one instructional roles, they should be provided with training and preparation to do so properly (with content-specific training) while being supervised by a certified special education teacher.

Related to this concern is the "elephant in the room" of poor pay for paras. Frequently, paras are not involved in beginning-of-school-year PD due to limited school district budgets, and the hourly pay paras in most districts receive is incredibly insufficient for the difficulty and importance of their job. In the larger PD project, there were multiple times when paras expressed stress, frustration, and unhappiness due to delays with project-related honorariums. One para was crying when she contacted her instructional coach because she was counting on the stipend to pay a cellular phone bill—and the university's delay in processing put her in financial distress. Clearly, we need to reconsider our policies and pay procedures to better support these critical members of the educator workforce.

Supports Provided by Teachers

Although many paras reported that their supervising teachers provided support to them, a small portion of paras reported feeling a lack of support or being neutral about support received. Those who reported neutral feelings indicated they had not asked for support for a variety of reasons. This finding is interesting because a part of a special education teacher's role is to provide support for paras, yet some paras may not be asking for support because they believe their supervising teacher to be too busy to provide it. This may indicate a lack of communication between teachers and paras regarding roles and responsibilities. Additionally, it may indicate the realities that special educators are too busy to adequately support their paras (Brock & Anderson, 2020), that special educators receive too little training on how to support paras (Riggs & Mueller, 2001), and that paras have not been provided with self-advocacy training to allow them to raise their voice when they have support needs. The need to enhance the collaborative relationships between special educators and paras remains a key priority for school districts.

Of the supports paras reported receiving from teachers, the most frequent type mentioned was in the area of instructional materials (e.g., teachers provide paras with resources needed to deliver instruction). In contrast, less than a quarter of paras mentioned receiving support in skill development. While teachers should be providing the appropriate instructional materials to their paras, they should also be providing support with skill development. The Council for Exceptional Children's standards for initial special educator preparation delineate that special educators should be able to "provide guidance and direction to paraeducators, tutors, and volunteers" (Council for Exceptional Children, 2020). While this notion does make sense (i.e., special educators should provide guidance to the paras in their classroom), it does raise questions about whether special educators are adequately trained to provide this support, whether they are provided ample time to give such support, and whether there are other district-level staff who could or should ensure that paras are adequately prepared for and supported in their role as education support staff for students with disabilities. Some clarity around the specific responsibilities that special educators have in ensuring the paras under their supervision are prepared would be useful in giving guidance to teachers, paras, and district staff.

PD Research Study Experience

It is encouraging that, overall, paras reported having positive experiences with the larger research project thus far, both those paras in the reading conditions and math condition. Some paras mentioned specific components of the research project that contributed to the positive experience. The paras in the reading conditions mentioned positive student outcomes most frequently as a reason for their positive experience. Paras also mentioned the curriculum, their instructional coach, and the training provided as other reasons for a positive experience. Similarly, the paras in the math condition mentioned both positive student outcomes and the curriculum most frequently, followed by their instructional coach, and then the training. This supports the paras' expression of appreciation for providing training and support that is targeted just for them.

It is not surprising that having positive student outcomes is a frequently mentioned positive experience regardless of treatment condition because it indicates that paras want their students to be successful. This also reflects our findings from the paras' reported motivation for participating in our larger research project—helping or supporting students ($n = 37$; 78.72%). It is also positive to know that paras had positive experiences with the curriculum provided and used.

In alignment with the finding that participants had overall positive experiences with instructional coaches, most paras mentioned the feedback and coaching as the most helpful support, with social and emotional supports as the second most helpful. It is possible that paras appreciated having a person checking in on their progress throughout the intervention and having an additional person to talk to. This could also contribute to the high reports of feeling socially and emotionally supported by their instructional coaches. Having an instructional coach and reporting feelings of social and emotional support could be an indication that paras felt respected and that their voices mattered. Paras expressed gratitude for the responsiveness of their instructional coaches and made statements about how quickly instructional coaches would respond to texts and emails; these, too, could reflect the feeling that paras matter and that the instructional coaches in the study were there to support them at any time.

We asked paras in all of the study conditions to implement intervention four times per week, yet found that, on average, paras delivered intervention two times a week. Accordingly, the most common challenge that paras reported in meeting project expectations was not having enough time to implement the intervention. Nearly half of paras in both reading and math conditions reported this as a barrier, despite the differences between intervention time per session (reading = ~45 minutes, math = ~30 minutes). This "time" barrier could be related to the other most common challenge of having other school responsibilities that pulled them away from being able to implement the intervention in the desired dosage. This challenge is, unfortunately, not surprising given previous research detailing the various duties and responsibilities that paraprofessionals have throughout the day (Brock & Anderson, 2020; Carter et al., 2009; Giangreco et al., 2005; Fisher & Pleasants, 2011). Although such responsibilities may be included in the broader job description, paras frequently get pulled from their primary job of providing support to students with disabilities to provide support or fill positions elsewhere in the school. This is important to keep in mind when planning for para research studies.

Effectiveness Following PD Research Study

The results from asking paras about the changes they noticed in themselves as a result of participation in the study are both positive and anticipated. Our primary aim of training paras to implement instruction was to affect growth in knowledge and skill. The reported changes in overall effectiveness is encouraging as well. These statements reflected participants' perceived ability to apply what they learned through training and implementation to other students they serve.

There was a small, yet notable difference in the percentage of paras in the reading and math conditions who reported social and emotional changes. A greater percentage of paras in the math condition reported changes in their social and emotional skills as compared to the reading conditions. Paras in the reading conditions received goals and specific feedback related to their knowledge, skills, and overall effectiveness, and thus, may have attended more closely to changes in these areas. On the other hand, paras in the math condition did not receive goal-related feedback, which may have resulted in them more broadly considering the types of changes they experienced.

Unfortunately, there were a small number of paras who specifically stated a lack of noticeable change in themselves. The interviews occurred while our PD study was in its second year; some paras had been a part of the study for over a year, while others had just joined the project weeks before COVID halted our research activities. Without more specific research on how long it takes for paras to notice changes in themselves, some participants might not have been exposed to the training long enough to note changes. Additionally, some paras joined our study with strong skills and foundational knowledge about interventions, which could also explain the lack of notable changes.

The results from asking paras about the changes in their students based on content area gains were expected. This is encouraging and important because the overall job of a para is to support their student with a disability in any skills, content-specific or social and emotional. However, there were a small number of paras who specifically stated a lack of noticeable change in their students. This could be a result of duration of participation in the larger research study at the time of the interview. Additionally, it may be possible student progress was relative to the student's skills at pretest. For example, paras who were paired with students who had lower initial skills may have observed those students' skills progressing at a slower rate compared to other students the para had contact with throughout their day.

Limitations

There are several limitations to take into consideration for this study. First, paras interviewed for this study volunteered to participate in the larger research project and the subsequent interview. It is possible the paras who chose to participate represent an atypical subset of paras. Second, instructional coaches who had a relationship with the paras conducted the interviews. Although this procedure may have supported interviewer–interviewee rapport, it could also have led to potential bias in responding, especially regarding the interview questions about instructional coach support. Third, the interviews occurred while many paras were in the initial or middle phases of the larger study—thus, findings could have been different had all paras completed two full years of participation.

Implications for Practitioners

The results of this study make it clear that paras can be incredibly effective members of the special education team. However, their roles and responsibilities need to be clearly defined. Administrators and special educators need to work with paras to define roles and responsibilities. Next, a plan for

Coaching Form

Name: _____ Intervention: _____ Student(s): _____ Date: _____

Section 1: Positive Feedback	
Start the meeting on a positive note. Write at least 3 specific praise statements about positive instructional behaviors you observed.	
1. 2. 3.	Meeting Notes
Section 2: Intervention Implementation and Student Data	
Write down notes about how the para implemented the intervention, elements that were implemented well, and areas where there is an opportunity for growth. These statements can focus on instructional delivery, student(s) engagement, and behavior management during the lesson. In addition, include notes on student data (if applicable). Review this section, including student data, prior to moving into Section 3.	
	Meeting Notes
Section 3: Priority Goals and Action items	
Based on the information you wrote in Section 2, write up to three priority goals to improve intervention implementation. For each, also provide an actionable item to support the para in meeting the goal. For example, you may provide a model of implementation, or you may direct the para to a resource that they can access independently.	
1. 2. 3.	Meeting Notes
Section 4: Wrap Up	
Close the meeting on a positive note (Ex. 1 really appreciate all the work you are doing with _____.) Plan for your next meeting/observation (date, time, group, etc.)	
1. 2.	Next meeting/observation

Figure 9.1 Sample Feedback and Coaching Form

initial training and ongoing coaching needs to be developed and implemented. In our study, the ongoing feedback was a feature most paras reported as being beneficial. Following guidance from Brock and Anderson (2020), this PD should include modeling, use of an implementation checklist, and ongoing feedback. Additionally, based on our findings, ensuring that the special educator also provides emotional supports, encouragement, and praise will likely be beneficial. Figure 9.1 is an adapted model of the form instructional coaches in our study used to provide ongoing feedback, and it could be used by special educators to structure postobservation feedback sessions. Finally, a majority of special educators report being unprepared to support paras in their charge (Sobeck et al., 2021). Clearly PD provided to preservice and in-service special and general educators needs to drastically increase the amount of training time spent on this topic.

Implications for Future Research

Based on our findings, we believe there are several promising avenues for future research. First, as our sample is relatively small, replicating and extending upon our study would be important. Second, based on paras' reported needs for additional training and support, research that explores the most effective and efficient models for delivery to paras is critical—for example, is expecting the special educator to be the primary resource for the para more or less effective than providing district-level support (e.g., a train-the-trainer model)? Third, we need a clearer understanding of the amount of support that paras need to be successful. In our PD study, we provide once-a-week feedback. We need to understand if this is sufficient, too much, or too little—and perhaps it varies based on the para's skill level. Research in this area will help us tailor PD and coaching to individual para's needs. Fourth, exploring optimal scheduling structures and caseloads would be useful, as paras frequently expressed concerns of not having sufficient time to be effective and being consistently redirected during their workday. Fifth, it is clear that individual student behavior challenges do drive paras' concerns about their abilities to be effective interventionists. Additional research on effective methods to increase paras' behavior management skills would be helpful. Finally, research focused on determining the most effective method to train preservice and in-service special and general educators would broaden our understanding of how to prepare educators to effectively support paras. We encourage current and future researchers to continue to explore these critical areas that have the potential to enhance the effectiveness of paras in helping students with disabilities meet IEP goals to optimize their success as they enter postsecondary settings.

Additional Readings and Resources

- Special Issue: Current Status and Future Directions for Training and Supporting Paraprofessionals in the Schools, *Psychology in the Schools*, Volume 58, Issue 4. Available at https://onlinelibrary.wiley.com/toc/15206807/2021/58/4
- Working with Paraprofessionals: A Resource for Educators of Students with Disabilities from the Texas Education Agency available at https://projects.esc20.net/upload/shared/20984_Paraprofessional_English_Updated_508.pdf

Author Note

The research described in this article was supported by Grant R324A190240 from the Institute of Education Science with the U.S. Department of Education. Nothing in the article necessarily reflects the positions or policies of the funding agencies, and no official endorsement by them should be inferred.

References

Breton, W. (2010). Special education paraprofessionals: Perceptions of preservice preparation, supervision, and ongoing development training. *International Journal of Special Education, 25*(1), 34–45. https://eric.ed.gov/?id=EJ890564

Brock, M. E., & Anderson, E. J. (2020). Training paraprofessionals who work with students with intellectual and developmental disabilities: What does the research say? *Psychology in the Schools, 58*(4), 702–722. https://doi.org/10.1002/pits.22386

Brock, M. E., & Carter, E. W. (2013). A systematic review of paraprofessional-delivered educational practices to improve outcomes for students with intellectual and developmental disabilities. *Research and Practice for Persons with Severe Disabilities, 38*, 211–221. https://doi.org/10.1177/154079691303800401

Brock, M. E., & Carter, E. W. (2015). Effects of a professional development package to prepare special education paraprofessionals to implement evidence-based practice. *The Journal of Special Education, 49*(1), 39–51. https://doi.org/10.1177/0022466913501882

Carter, E. W., O'Rourke, L., Sisco, L. G., & Pelsue, D. (2009). Knowledge, responsibilities, and training needs of paraprofessionals in elementary and secondary schools. *Remedial and Special Education, 30*(6), 344–359. https://doi.org/10.1177/0741932508324399

Causton-Theoharis, J. N., Giangreco, M. F., Doyle, M. B., & Vadasy, P. F. (2007). The "Sous-Chefs" of literacy instruction. *TEACHING Exceptional Children, 40*(1), 56–62. https://doi.org/10.1177/004005990704000107

Council for Exceptional Children. (2020). *Initial preparation standards: Standard 6.6*. https://exceptionalchildren.org/standards/initial-special-education-preparation-standards

Educational Testing Service. (n.d.). *ParaPro Assessment*. www.ets.org/parapro/

Every Student Succeeds Act, 20 U.S.C § 6301 (2015). www.congress.gov/114/plaws/publ95/PLAW-114publ95.pdf

Fisher, M., & Pleasants, S. L. (2011). Roles, responsibilities, and concerns of paraeducators: Findings from a statewide survey. *Remedial and Special Education, 33*, 287–297. https://doi.org/10.1177/0741932510397762

Giangreco, M. F., Edelman, S. W., Broer, S. M., & Doyle, M. B. (2001). Paraprofessional support of students with disabilities: Literature from the past decade. *Exceptional Children, 68*, 45–63. https://doi.org/10.1177/001440290106800103

Giangreco, M. F., Yuan, S., McKenzie, B., Cameron, P., & Fialka, J. (2005). "Be careful what you wish for . . .": Five reasons to be concerned about the assignment of individual paraprofessionals. *TEACHING Exceptional Children, 37*(5), 28–34. https://doi.org/10.1177/004005990503700504

Individuals with Disabilities Education Act (IDEA), 20 U.S.C. § 1400 (2004).

Kurasaki, K. S. (2000). Intercoder reliability for validating conclusions drawn from open-ended interview data. *Field Methods, 12*, 179–194. https://doi.org/10.1177/1525822X0001200301

National Center for Education Statistics. (2007). *Description and employment criteria of instructional paraprofessionals* (Issue Brief). U.S. Department of Education, Institute of Education Sciences, National Center for Education Statistics. https://nces.ed.gov/pubs2007/2007008.pdf

Reddy, L. A., Alperin, A., & Glover, T. A. (2021). A critical review of the professional development literature for paraprofessionals supporting students with externalizing behavior disorders. *Psychology in the Schools, 58*(4), 742–763. https://doi.org/10.1002/pits.22381

Riggs, C. G., & Mueller, P. H. (2001). Employment and utilization of paraeducators in inclusive settings. *The Journal of Special Education, 35*(1), 54–62. https://doi.org/10.1177/002246690103500106

Sobeck, E. E., Douglas, S. N., Chopra, R., & Morano, S. (2021). Paraeducator supervision in pre-service teacher preparation programs: Results of a national survey. *The Journal of Special Education, 49*(1), 669–685. https://doi.org/10.1002/pits.22383

Steckelberg, A. L., Vasa, S. F., Kemp, S. E., Arthaud, T. J., Asselin, S. B., Swain, K., & Fennick, E. (2007). A Web-based training model for preparing teachers to supervise paraeducators. *Teacher Education and Special Education, 30*(1), 52–55. https://doi.org/10.1177/088840640703000106

U.S. Department of Education. (2008). *33rd annual report to Congress on the implementation of the Individuals with Disabilities Education Act, 2011: Special Education teachers and paraprofessionals employed to serve students ages 6 through 21 under IDEA, Part B*. https://www2.ed.gov/about/reports/annual/osep/2011/parts-b-c/33rd-idea-arc.pdf

U.S. Department of Education. (2020). *42nd annual report to Congress on the implementation of the Individuals with Disabilities Education Act, 2020: Special Education teachers and paraprofessionals employed to serve students ages 6 through 21 under IDEA, Part B*. https://sites.ed.gov/idea/files/42nd-arc-for-idea.pdf

Zoom Video Communications, Inc. (2020). *ZOOM cloud meetings* (Version 4.6.9)

10
WRITING INSTRUCTION FOR STUDENTS WITH DISABILITIES (AND OTHER STRUGGLING WRITERS)

Current Research and Implications for Research and Practice

Erin FitzPatrick, Robin Parks Ennis, and Debra McKeown

In 2003, the National Commission on Writing framed writing as "The Neglected 'R'" and published a 44-page report detailing the need for a writing revolution if American education were to ever "realize its potential as an engine of opportunity and economic growth" (p. 3). That is, nearly two decades ago, the case was made for greater focus on writing in school. A decade later, the case was revisited set to the backdrop of the widespread adoption of the Common Core State Standards with a hopeful final thought that

> although [the standards] do not ensure positive change, they do create a window of opportunity for such a change to occur if they lead educators, administrators, and policymakers to reevaluate current practices, abandoning less effective methods in favor of more constructive ways of teaching writing.
>
> *(Kopke et al., 2014)*

Nearly a decade later, once again, we take up the pen to make the case that broadly, writing needs to be a greater focus in our nation's schools, and specifically, students with disabilities are being negatively affected by a lack of focus on written communication (NAEP, 2011).

It is a challenge to overstate the value of a perceptible, transferable, expressive means of communication in a democratic society. Barriers such as socioeconomic class, geography, scheduling, and disabilities can create separation that keeps us from engaging with one another. Writing, due to its transportable and asynchronous nature, can overcome these barriers and permit entree to these venues. This is particularly important for communities, such as students with disabilities, because writing is a tool used to advocate on one's own behalf in public spaces. These may be the spaces of school (e.g., presenting learning; Graham & Hebert, 2011), society (e.g., communicating across distance to maintain relationships; Bazerman, 2016), or politics (e.g., self-advocacy; Kissel et al., 2019). For instance, Kissel and colleagues (2019) explained how student victims of the shooting in Parkland, Florida, whose lives were threatened and whose peers' lives were taken during a school shooting, used writing and persuasion to effect change on a national level. It is imperative that high-quality writing instruction is made available to students with disabilities—a marginalized population whose needs are often made known through the voices of others and thus may be overlooked or inadequately addressed and who have found better life outcomes with higher degrees of self-determination and self-advocacy (e.g., Rowe et al., 2015). Thus, it follows that lack of or poor writing instruction—the systematic removal of a powerful tool to improve social and economic mobility—particularly for the nation's most vulnerable learners, is a civil rights crisis of modern times.

Writing Performance of Students With Disabilities

Beyond the social and political charges for teaching writing effectively, schools are legally required to demonstrate ambitious goals and adequate support for all learners (Every Student Succeeds Act, 2015). The most recently released national writing assessments in the United States indicated that nearly three-fourths of students and 95% of students with disabilities in elementary, middle, and high school failed to meet proficiency in writing (NAEP, 2002, 2011).

Writing is a complex competence that requires simultaneous application of multiple skills and cognitive processes (De La Paz et al., 1998; Graham et al., 2018a; Hayes, 1996). Research has consistently demonstrated that students with disabilities perform lower than their typically developing peers in writing (Gage et al., 2014; Graham et al., 2005; Reid et al., 2004). Particular challenges for these students include ineffective ideation, planning, organization, transcription, and revising (De La Paz et al., 1998; Garcia-Sanchez & Fidalgo-Redondo, 2006; Graham, 2006a; Graham et al., 2005), as well as limited sentence- and word-level skills such as spelling, grammar, and punctuation (Graham, Collins, et al., 2017). These students often demonstrate a lack of genre knowledge, which consequently results in lower-quality and less complete essays (Graham et al., 2005). Students with disabilities also face challenges with self-regulation, which directly affects their performance in the complex and cognitively demanding task of writing (Alevriadou & Giaouri, 2015; Bak & Asaro-Saddler, 2013; Gage et al., 2014).

In this chapter, we will review prevailing theoretical lenses that support the current work being done in the field of writing. Then, we consider the historical context of writing instruction. Next, we explore the current state of research considering methodological designs and findings and their implications for both research and practice. Finally, we close the chapter with additional readings and free or low-cost resources to support practitioners.

Theoretical Support

In 1986, Juel, Griffith, and Gough proposed the Simple View of Writing, claiming that writing is made of spelling and ideation (i.e., the formation of ideas and concepts). They based the model on longitudinal early literacy data and recognized complexity within each aspect. Informed by brain scan studies, Berninger and Winn (2006) developed the Not-So-Simple-View of Writing, which reflected a deeper understanding of the contribution of working memory and attention to writing effectively, in addition to spelling and ideation.

Most writing intervention research in special education is grounded in cognitive theories of writing, which do little to address the social, cultural, and historic influences on writing development. Sociocultural theories do not adequately capture the neurological processes of becoming a literate writer (Graham, 2018). In 2018, Graham put forth a new model of writing—Writer(s)-Within-Community—that situates the cognitive process of writing development within a social context. As we learn to write, experiences are affected by the community in which we are learning such as government mandates (e.g., standardized writing tests), teacher direction (e.g., prompts), and collaborators (e.g., peer feedback). Flower and Hayes (1980) proposed a model of the writing process, which included the "task environment" and recognized that environmental or social motivations affect writers and the text they produce. Graham, though, elucidates and complicates our understanding of the social context in ways others have not, offering his model as another perspective to further understanding of the writing process and development. Graham (2018) proposes that writing is social and is situated in specific contexts, bound by membership, characteristics, and resources—both tangible and cognitive—of its participants, as well as the history of the writing community and the created identities, roles, and ways of interacting with one another. Moreover, the Writer(s)-Within-Community model establishes participants as both writers and audience members to emphasize the communicative power of the written word to achieve authentic purposes. Moving forward, writing researchers will need to be even more theoretically inclusive by allowing the work to be informed by critical theory, social-cultural theory, social justice theory, and other approaches that situate the psychological processes within the complex context of culture, history, and race in the United States.

What Works in Writing Instruction

Historically, research on writing instruction has been less robust than research in the area of reading (Troia, 2007). Initial research focused on students' written products rather than the process they used to develop their writing (Poplin et al., 1980). As writing research developed, focus on other areas has risen to the forefront (Graham & Harris, 2009). First, understanding the writing process is essential, including planning, writing (drafting), and revising. Struggling writers may experience difficulty in one of more areas of writing, and intervention research addressing individual phases, as well as the entire process, has yielded positive outcomes (e.g., Harris et al., 2011). A second area of focus is students' understanding of writing, including genre knowledge, which has been found to be predictive of writing performance (Graham, 2006b). Third, the mechanics of writing, including spelling, handwriting, grammar, sentence construction, and related tasks, affect composition (Graham et al., 2012a); instruction in these areas is needed, but must be provided within the context of composing when possible. A final area of research refers to students' motivation and self-efficacy to write. Given the varying components discussed earlier, it is not surprising that students with disabilities often lack motivation to write (Graham et al., 2001; Graham, Kiuhara, et al., 2017).

More recently, the What Works Clearinghouse (WWC) has published two practice guides in the area of writing instruction for both elementary (Graham et al., 2012a) and secondary students (Graham et al., 2016). These practice guides, supported by the Institute of Education Sciences, provide best practices for educators in a targeted area, with recommendations supported by research and developed in conjunction between the WWC and an expert panel.

In the writing practice guide by Graham and colleagues (2012a), they outlined four recommendations for elementary students, with evidence that was minimal, moderate, or strong to support the practice. Recommendation 1 involves providing *daily time for students to write*, as research has demonstrated that daily practice engaged in the writing process results in improved writing performance. While the expert panel agreed on the importance of this practice, there is only minimal evidence supporting this recommendation, as few studies have explicitly evaluated the effect of extended time spent writing (e.g., Berninger et al., 2006). Recommendation 2 involves teaching students to (a) *use the writing process for* (b) *a variety of purposes*. Both of these elements have strong evidence for improving writing outcomes (Graham et al., 2012a). Much of this research is founded upon the use of the self-regulated strategy development (SRSD) framework to explicitly teach the writing process specific to targeted writing genres (e.g., Graham et al., 2012b). SRSD is a recursive instructional framework consisting of six stages, which provides students with a strong common foundation of knowledge, modeling, scaffolded instruction, feedback, and strategic instruction to manage the process and metacognitive variables that affect complex academic learning such as writing.

Recommendation 3 involves teaching students to be *fluent with the component skills of the writing process, including handwriting, spelling, sentence construction, and word processing*. There is moderate evidence to support the utility of this recommendation; numerous studies have demonstrated the need for the development of these basic skills to improve writing outcomes (e.g., Denton et al., 2006), with findings suggesting that instruction within context is most beneficial (e.g., Saddler et al., 2008). Finally, Recommendation 4 involves creating *an engaging writing community*. While there is only minimal evidence to support this recommendation, participating in activities such as peer revision and writing workshops can have positive effects on student outcomes (e.g., Graham et al., 2012b; MacArthur et al., 1991).

In 2016, Graham and colleagues outlined three recommendations for writing instruction for secondary students. Recommendation 1 involves (a) explicitly teaching appropriate writing strategies and (b) using the Model-Practice-Reflect instruction cycle to teach the writing process. There is strong evidence for both components of this recommendation with research that documents the utility of teaching explicit strategies aligned with the targeted genres of writing (e.g., Festas et al., 2015). The second component involves modeling ("I do"—teachers model), practice ("we do"—students practice with a teacher or peer), and reflect ("you do"—students evaluate their own writing; Pressley & Harris, 2006; Rupley et al., 2009). Research using this approach evaluated the gradual release of responsibility using targeted strategy instruction (e.g., Kim et al., 2011). Recommendation 2 involves integrating writing and reading to emphasize key writing elements, as reading and writing share cognitive processes that can be co-developed: meta-knowledge, domain knowledge, text features, and procedural knowledge (Graham et al., 2016). This recommendation has moderate evidence to support its use, with researchers evaluating the impact of teaching academic vocabulary and test structures to support students' reading and writing (e.g., Leseaux et al., 2014). Recommendation 3 involves using student writing assessments to inform instruction and feedback. There is only minimal evidence for this recommendation, as most studies did not directly assess the impact of informal assessment alone, but authors determined that giving students time to write and reflect on feedback for making revisions improved their writing performance (e.g., Kim et al., 2011).

Since the publication of these two WWC writing guides, additional research in these areas has further solidified these recommended practices; this will be discussed in the Current State of Research section to follow. It is also noteworthy that many of these recommendations are addressed in the intervention, SRSD, an evidence-based practice for writing instruction (Harris et al., 2016). SRSD uses explicit instruction for strategy acquisition and self-regulation (i.e., goal setting, self-monitoring, self-instruction, self-reinforcement) into one cohesive framework that involves six stages: developing background knowledge, discussing the strategy, modeling the strategy, memorizing the strategy, supporting the strategy, and independent practice (Harris et al., 2008). In 2017, the WWC evaluated SRSD single-case design studies to determine if SRSD is a practice for improving the performance of students with specific learning disabilities, identifying ten studies meeting single-case design standards including 43 students ages 7 to 16. Of these studies, nine (17 experiments) focused on writing achievement, with 88% of studies demonstrating positive and 0% demonstrating negative effects. In the area of writing achievement, SRSD met WWC criteria for having potentially positive effects, meaning that there is strong evidence of a positive effect with no overriding contrary evidence (WWC, 2017).

Current State of Research

A review of writing research in the past five years (2016–2021) produces an impressive array of work being done by dedicated researchers, far more than could be highlighted in this chapter. Our major foci in this chapter are findings that extend recommendations from the two WWC practice guides focused on writing instruction. This section is focused on integrating reading and writing instruction; writing instruction in content areas; wide use of technology, including feedback and intelligent tutoring systems; supporting students with emotional and behavioral challenges; and using writing for self-advocacy toward improved life outcomes.

Reading and Writing Integration

Meta-analyses (e.g., Graham & Hebert, 2011) have explored the impact of reading interventions on writing performance and writing interventions on reading performance. In 2011, Graham and Hebert evaluated the impact of writing instruction on reading. They learned that writing skill instruction (e.g., sentence structure), increasing the time for writing (e.g., five minutes at the end of each class period), and writing about material (e.g., summarizing) enhanced reading comprehension. These findings rested primarily on systematic interventions rather than typical writing instruction found in school settings. Thus, to further explore this, Coker and colleagues (2018) evaluated the effects of typical writing instruction on students' reading achievement with 391 first-grade students across 50 classrooms. Coker et al. (2018) learned that students' writing practice positively affected reading achievement. They also learned that explicit composing instruction and opportunities to engage in composing explained student performance in reading beyond that which can be accounted for with students' baseline reading achievement and ongoing reading instruction. Evaluating the inverse, in 2018, Graham and colleagues published a meta-analysis of reading interventions and their impact on writing. As Graham et al. hypothesized, teaching reading strengthened writing performance with regard to overall quality, words written, and spelling, and the impact was sustained across time.

Recent research with upper elementary struggling writers (i.e., students who had failed the state writing assessment and scored below the 25th percentile on a standardized measure of writing but had not or had not yet been identified with disabilities) explored the integration of SRSD instruction, including both close reading—a method of engaging deeply with the text, including reading carefully, with the author's purpose in mind, noting essential facts and ideas, rereading to self-monitor comprehension, asking questions, considering details, highlighting relevant content, and notetaking—and persuasive writing (Harris et al., 2019). At the end of the SRSD intervention focused on close reading and persuasive writing, students' writing improved in overall quality, including more genre elements (e.g., topic, reasons, explanations) and in the complexity of their planning. Two other studies (FitzPatrick & McKeown, 2020, 2021)—one with eight fifth-grade students with learning disabilities and other teacher-identified struggling writers, and the other with six middle school students with disabilities in a special education classroom—explored writing in the informational genre after reading two source texts based on common science topics. In both studies, students demonstrated improvement in holistic quality, number of included genre elements, and strategy use. Both teachers and students also found the intervention to hold high social validity. Building on what is already known about integrating reading and writing, researchers are continuing to explore impact on various populations in various settings to maximize student performance.

Content Area Writing

Writing instruction continues to be paired with content area instruction (e.g., instruction in mathematics or science), and based on meta-analyses, most often across the full range of learners, including those with disabilities. In 2020, Graham and colleagues published a meta-analysis of 56 experiments conducted with students from grades 1 through 12 that evaluated if students' writing about science, social studies, and mathematics content improved their learning in the related area. They determined writing in response to content increased learning in all evaluated content areas (mathematics, social studies, and science) and across all evaluated grade levels; effects were not moderated by the unique features of the instruction, activities, or assessment (Graham et al., 2020).

Recently, researchers have found success marrying explicit writing instruction with content area instruction to meet the needs of various learners. Garwood and colleagues (2019) taught a science teacher in a residential treatment facility to implement SRSD for persuasive writing in science content to 11 secondary students with complex trauma and identified with emotional and/or behavioral disorders. Results indicated growth in persuasive genre parts (e.g., topics, reasons, explanations) and writing quality across all students. Combining content area writing as well as technology, Hitchcock and colleagues (2016) tested a technology-based writing intervention called TeenACE for writing. The TeenACE intervention included multimedia technology (i.e., PowerPoint) used to plan and write integrated with SRSD for writing. In this study, classroom teachers implemented the instruction with 46 culturally and linguistically diverse students in grades 5 through 8 in rural schools in Hawaii where 75% of students qualified for free or reduced lunch. General and special education students learned to write science reports that included multimedia (e.g., photos, video). Students learned to research, take notes, organize information, draft, record themselves reading the draft, listen to the recording, evaluate, and revise. Results showed significant growth in science report writing.

Technology

A significant portion of writing occurs on electronic devices; email, texts, messaging, and posting on social media are all forms of written communication. This section focuses on recent research that has used technology to support students' writing efforts. The use of speech-to-text, or speech recognition, has been a tool in special education for more than 20 years, allowing learners to use their voices to create written works. Across time, the technology has improved, making it a more reliable and accurate recording medium. Speech recognition allows students to circumvent spelling and transcription difficulties. It may also prevent a loss of ideas that can occur during the mechanical process of writing because speaking aloud is more efficient and allows students to focus on the more complex aspects of writing (Gardner, 2008).

One of the most recent studies integrating technology and writing was conducted by Smith and colleagues (2020). The team taught three Grade 6 teachers to implement SRSD for persuasive writing; students with disabilities, including learning disabilities, attention disorders, emotional and behavioral disorders, intellectual disabilities, and autism, participated alongside their general education peers. Students learned to use two technology tools: Inspiration, a digital brainstorming app, and Co-Writer, a speech-to-text and text-to-speech app that includes word prediction and incorporated dictionaries. Teachers delivered the SRSD lessons while incorporating the use of the planning and prediction tools. Results showed a significant increase in the number of words written, spelled correctly, and correct writing sequence.

Technology-Based Feedback

Wilson and colleagues (2014) examined the results of automated feedback on student writing to determine impact on writing outcomes. Through automated feedback, students receive critique and notes on a variety of topics that may improve their writing such as organization, ideation, sentence structure, vocabulary, and grammar. Results indicated revisions in response to automated feedback improved writing outcomes, but the outcomes dissipated over time. The authors suggest that for students with disabilities and other struggling writers, feedback offered through automatic evaluation tools may need to be paired with high-quality writing instruction to achieve desired results. In another study, Wilson (2017) examined growth in students' writing performance when they were offered feedback through automatic essay evaluation; students with disabilities initially wrote lower-quality essays but improved faster, eventually performing comparatively to typically developing peers after multiple revisions. Wilson (2017) determined that school quality and technology access moderated student performance.

An approach showing promise for improving student revising behavior is asynchronous audio feedback. Students with disabilities do not revise their work in a substantive manner (e.g., McKeown et al., 2020). Explicit revision interventions can lead to increases in writing quality (e.g., McKeown et al., 2015). Asynchronous audio feedback has been tested with middle school students with emotional or behavioral disorders in a residential facility (McKeown et al., 2015) and with elementary-aged struggling writers (McKeown et al., 2020). In each study, teachers were taught to use an iPad app, Notability, to record systematic audio feedback in response to student first drafts. Students then listened to the feedback and made revisions to their drafts. Each study resulted in an increase in overall writing quality when comparing first drafts to revised drafts, and both teachers and students found the intervention effective.

Intelligent Tutoring

Some researchers are testing the use of an adaptable web-based tutor to support SRSD writing instruction. The program is called We Write and was developed in 2018 by Wijekumar, Harris, Graham, McKeown, and Owens. Working with a programming team, the researchers developed integrated web-based writing lessons that students engaged with following teacher-led instruction. The lessons provide a variety of check-ins, student demonstrations, and quizzes and offer immediate feedback on student performance. If students fail to demonstrate mastery, skill instruction is repeated until mastery is achieved. The computer lessons included review, independent practice, feedback, and lesson extensions that shore up foundations and strengthen skills. A waitlisted randomized controlled trial was conducted with 36 grades 3 through 5 teachers (18 intervention, 18 control) in inclusive classrooms. Initial data analysis shows that the program, composed of teacher-led and computer-based lessons, has had a positive impact on student writing outcomes.

Writing and Students With Motivation and Self-Regulation Challenges

Given the complex nature of writing (i.e., its incorporation of many subskills), it can be a challenge, as struggling writers face issues of motivation and self-regulation. Likewise, many students with emotional and behavioral disorders possess comorbid language deficits that affect their written expression and abilities. For this reason, students with behavioral challenges may find it particularly difficult to develop writing skills (Mason et al., 2010). Writing research with this population of students has overwhelmingly addressed writing and behavior simultaneously to facilitate student success (Ennis & Jolivette, 2014b). Writing instruction yields itself to the use of various instructional strategies to support students' academic and behavioral success, such as the use of choices (e.g., presenting students with a choice of what to write about, where to write, or what modality to draft their responses), high-probability request sequences (e.g., allowing students to engage in more preferred tasks such as a discussion about writing or writing with a partner prior to writing independently to build behavioral momentum for the difficult task), or using increased opportunities to respond to increase academic engagement (e.g., allow students to brainstorm ideas during the planning process or involve students in detailing steps of the writing process during teacher modeling; Ennis, 2015).

It is essential that all students are able to participate in high-quality writing instruction. Students served in alternative educational settings, including residential facilities and juvenile justice settings, often fail to receive high-quality, evidence-based instruction, as a significant focus is placed upon behavioral remediation. However, recent research has demonstrated that writing instruction, in particular SRSD, can have a positive impact on writing performance of students served in these settings when implemented with fidelity and simultaneously with behavioral supports (Ennis et al., 2014; Garwood et al., 2019). This work has also demonstrated that teachers in these settings can implement evidence-based writing practices with high fidelity.

Writing for Self-Advocacy

The final topic of current research we have chosen to address is particularly well-suited to both writing and students with disabilities. It expands on the suggestion that writing be used for varied, meaningful purposes—in these cases, self-advocacy. Cuenca-Carlino and colleagues (2019) trained a special education teacher and paraprofessional to teach nine high school students argumentative writing using SRSD; students then wrote essays to self-advocate during their transition meetings. Jozwik and Cuenca-Carlino (2020) explained how to use SRSD writing instruction to support writing development of English language learners with learning disabilities in rural settings to promote self-advocacy skills. Both studies resulted in improved student writing and awareness of how to actively advocate for themselves.

Implications for Practitioners

In this chapter, we have outlined several key practices for implementing effective writing instruction with a variety of students with disabilities. We encourage practitioners to seek professional development on any areas in which they are not currently confident supporting the needs of students with disabilities. We offer the following suggestions.

Implement Evidence-Based Practices

Whenever possible, teachers should seek to implement evidence-based practices in the classroom (IDEA, 2004). Evidence-based practices can be found at several of the online resources listed at the end of the chapter, including the WWC, IRIS Modules, and the CEEDAR Center. Many practitioner journals are designed to support teacher implementation of evidence-based practices, such as *Teaching Exceptional Children*, *Beyond Behavior*, *Intervention in School and Clinic*, and *Preventing School Failure*. Most of these journals are freely available to teachers through state library exchanges.

Teachers may also seek out practice-based professional development (PBPD) in evidence-based practices of the area of writing. PBPD focuses on development of content knowledge, pedagogy, collaboration, and the *practice* of newly learned skills in an environment with expert feedback. Six characteristics of PBPD include (a) working with colleagues, (b) personalized support in response to teachers' instructional context, (c) expert assessment and feedback, (d) explicit modeling and opportunities for performance, (e) identical materials that will be used in the classroom, and (f) guidance in differentiating for various contexts/situations (Ball & Cohen, 1999; Harris et al., 2012). Researchers have demonstrated that following PBPD, teachers offer evidence-based practices with high fidelity and social validity for the professional development experience (e.g., FitzPatrick & McKeown, 2020).

Prioritize Student Time for Writing

Datchuk et al. (2020) analyzed 18 single-case studies, and they learned that writing achievement gradually increases over time. Many writing researchers have reported the acquisition of complex skills such as writing taking more time to teach and to learn, requiring extensive practice (Ennis & Jolivette, 2014a; McKeown et al., 2016). It can be difficult for teachers to prioritize adequate time for writing instruction. We encourage teachers to set up time in their schedule for daily quick writes to engage students in the writing process on a regular basis (e.g., Ciullo et al., 2021). In addition, plan times for extended units of study in writing to provide explicit instruction using strategies for targeted genres of writing (e.g., persuasive, informational). We encourage teachers to use texts as examples, but also to model the cognitively demanding task of writing themselves, so students can experience the challenges and successes of applying a strategy to be successful.

Assessment and Feedback

As discussed, an important part of writing instruction is assessment of student writing and provision of timely expert feedback (Graham et al., 2012b). It is essential that teachers involve students in the evaluation of their own writing (e.g., graph genre elements, count academic vocabulary words) and discuss ways students can make improvements. The simple acts of self-evaluation and goal setting can have a profound impact on student writing performance in addition to other interventions.

Reinforce the Intersection of Reading and Writing Instruction

The intersection between reading and writing instruction is clear, and the instruction of both is only strengthened separately when addressed together (Graham, 2020). From the reciprocity between phonics and spelling to the interplay between reading comprehension and writing within a genre, there is a written, expressive communication skill for nearly every receptive communication skill students learn. Reinforcing those connections improves both reading and writing.

Implications for Researchers

The field has a strong foundation of what works, broadly, in writing instruction (e.g., Graham et al., 2012a). We have not yet found a reliable method to make this work broadly available to teachers. Writing is often not included in our preservice teaching programs (Brindle et al., 2016), and there is not a packaged curriculum that offers ease of access for teachers. No single writing intervention will sustain a comprehensive writing program. Writing is complex, and writing instruction must also be complex. Much like reading instruction, preparing teachers to offer high-quality writing instruction will require funding, time allocated for both ongoing professional development and implementation with students, and working across multiple theoretical foundations.

Scaling Up

Additionally, as writing interventions mature, the field must move toward scaling up interventions. For example, while not a panacea or a complete writing curriculum, SRSD is recognized as the writing intervention with the strongest effect sizes, and its effectiveness has been demonstrated across contexts, students, and disabilities (e.g., Harris et al., 2019). This evidence base makes it a candidate for scaling up. Most of the early studies of SRSD were conducted with researchers as implementers, but since around 2008, researchers have most often been putting SRSD in the hands of teachers, which means the experiments are a test of the effectiveness of professional development *and* the writing instruction. Conducting research on a large scale requires systems-level designs and long-term considerations for sustainability and feasibility. Writing researchers must continue to consider implementation science and the complex factors of conducting sound science in the unpredictable context of schools in ways that are minimally disruptive and considerate of all who are in the school settings. As other types of writing instruction develop an evidence base, it will be necessary to scale up those interventions as well.

Design Considerations

Randomized controlled trials are expensive, and researchers often fail to adequately meet the quality indicator for these studies to adequately describe participant demographics in a way that allows for delineation of data for specific groups (e.g., students with disabilities, Graham et al., 2018b). Single-case and quasi-experimental studies are the most common experimental designs used to evaluate student writing performance (Graham et al., 2012b; Rogers & Graham, 2008). Another practical way researchers may analyze the effects of tiered interventions within school settings is through the use of regression discontinuity designs (RDDs; Thistlewaite & Campbell, 1960). RDDs use a forcing variable at a set cut score to identify students requiring intervention (Jacob et al., 2012), such as 20% of students requiring Tier 2 or 3 interventions. This allows all students identified as needing an intervention to participate in the intervention without the need for a waitlist or control group. The intervention is determined to be effective if there is a significant discontinuity (change) in the regression lines on the posttest. The WWC (2014) recognizes RDD as a quasi-experimental design that can be used to support strong causal inferences. Despite the validity and feasibility of RDD for use with students with and at risk for disabilities, they have not been widely used within the special education literature either, including writing intervention research (Ryoo & Pullen, 2017). Future researchers should explore this design when implementing academic interventions within a Multi-tiered System of Supports (MTSS) framework.

The U.S. Department of Education (2019) reported that 67.35% of students with disabilities are served in general education classrooms more than 80% of the day and an additional 18.86% are served in these settings 40% to 79% of the day. Thus, it is reasonable that larger, more complicated studies of writing will occur in general education settings and include students with various disabilities, as this is where many receive writing instruction. When this occurs, it is imperative researchers report the performance of the subgroup to inform the field.

Future Research

Future research should consider expanding standardized assessments of writing, including the creation and validation of new assessments to evaluate various writing tasks (e.g., early writing skills, writing from multiple source texts across grade levels) and aspects (e.g., motivation, self-efficacy, mindset). Researchers should apply recent findings with automated essay scoring tools used in general education settings to students with disabilities to evaluate them for the ability to design larger trials for students with disabilities more efficiently.

Future research should focus on continuing to test potentially effective interventions while considering how those interventions can be integrated into the current curriculum and school day. Students would also benefit from more experience in applying their writing skills to issues that can positively affect their own lives and that of others (e.g., self-advocacy, activism). Teachers consistently report being overwhelmed and being asked to do more with less, and thus, participating in research, understandably, is not always a priority (e.g., McKeown et al., 2019). Interventions that address teacher needs and barriers to implementation, that include administrative involvement, and that are informed by multiple theories, including those related to systematic racism and the use of writing to effect change, will be critical to moving writing research forward.

Additional Readings and Resources

Practice Guides

Elementary Writing, https://ies.ed.gov/ncee/wwc/PracticeGuide/17
Secondary Writing, https://ies.ed.gov/ncee/wwc/PracticeGuide/22

IRIS Modules

Improving Persuasive Writing Performance, https://iris.peabody.vanderbilt.edu/module/pow/
Written Expression Grades 2–5: Case Study Unit, https://iris.peabody.vanderbilt.edu/wp-content/uploads/pdf_case_studies/ics_writex.pdf

Websites

SRSD Writing to Learn, https://srsdonline.org/
CEEDAR Center, https://ceedar.education.ufl.edu/cems/writing/
What Works Clearinghouse, https://ies.ed.gov/ncee/wwc/
Intervention Central, www.interventioncentral.org/
Reading Rockets, www.readingrockets.org
Kaizena, www.kaizena.com

References

Alevriadou, A., & Giaouri, S. (2015). The impact of executive functions in the written language process: Some evidence from children with writing disabilities. *Journal of Psychologists and Counselors in Schools, 25*, 24–37. https://doi.org/10.1017/jgc.2015.3

Bak, N., & Asaro-Saddler, K. (2013). SRSD for students with emotional behavioral disorders. *Beyond Behavior, 22*(3), 46–53. https://doi.org/10.1177/107429561302200307

Ball, D. L., & Cohen, D. K. (1999). Developing practice, developing practitioners: Toward a practice-based theory of professional education. In L. Darling-Hammond & G. Sykes (Eds.), *Teaching as a learning profession: Handbook for policy and practice* (pp. 3–31). Jossey-Boss.

Bazerman, C. (2016). What do sociocultural studies of writing tell us about learning to write? In C. A. MacArthur, S. Graham, & J. Fitzgerald (Eds.), *Handbook of writing research* (2nd ed., pp. 11–23). Guilford Press.

Berninger, V., Rutberg, J., Abbott, R., Garcia, N., Anderson-Youngstrom, M., Brooks, A., & Fulton, C. (2006). Tier 1 and tier 2 early intervention for handwriting and composing. *Journal of School Psychology, 44*(1), 3–30. https://doi.org/10.1016/j.jsp.2005.12.003

Berninger, V. W., & Winn, W. D. (2006). Implications of advancements in brain research and technology for writing development, writing instruction, and educational evolution. In C. A. MacArthur, S. Graham, & J. Fitzgerald (Eds.), *Handbook of writing research* (pp. 96–114). The Guilford Press.

Brindle, M., Graham, S., Harris, K. R., & Hebert, M. (2016). Third and fourth grade teacher's classroom practices in writing: A national survey. *Reading and Writing: An Interdisciplinary Journal, 29*, 929–954. https://doi.org/10.1007/s11145-015-9604-x

Coker, D. L., Jennings, A. S., Farley-Ripple, E., MacArthur, C. A., & Graham, S. (2018). The type of writing instruction and practice matters: The direct and indirect effects of writing instruction and student practice on reading achievement. *Journal of Educational Psychology, 110*(4), 502–517. https://doi.org/10.1037/edu0000232

Cuenca-Carlino, Y., Mustian, A. L., Allen, R. D., & Whitley, S. F. (2019). Writing for my future: Transition-focused self-advocacy of secondary students with EBD. *Remedial & Special Education, 40*(2), 83–96. https://doi.org/10.1177/0741932517751212

Ciullo, S., Mason, L. H., Judd, L., McKenna, J. W., & Brigham, F. J. (2021). Persuasive quick-writing about text: Intervention for students with learning disabilities. *Behavior Modification, 45*(1), 122–146. https://doi.org/10.1177/0145445519882894

Datchuk, S. M., Wagner, K., & Hier, B. O. (2020). Level and trend of writing sequences: A review and meta-analysis of writing interventions for students with disabilities. *Exceptional Children, 86*(2), 174–192. https://doi.org/10.1177/0014402919873311

De La Paz, S., Swanson, P., & Graham, S. (1998). The contribution of executive control to the revising by students with writing and learning difficulties. *Journal of Educational Psychology, 90*(3), 448–460. https://doi.org/10.1037/0022-0663.90.3.448

Denton, P., Cope, S., & Moser, C. (2006). The effects of sensorimotor-based intervention versus therapeutic practice on improving handwriting performance in 6- to 11-year-old children. *American Journal of Occupational Therapy, 60*(1), 16–27. https://doi.org/10.5014/ajot.60.1.16

Ennis, R. P. (2015). Simultaneously addressing academic and behavioral needs of students with and at-risk for E/BD using self-regulated strategy development. *Beyond Behavior, 24*, 3–9. https://doi.org/10.1177/107429561502400102

Ennis, R. P., Harris, K. R., Lane, K. L., & Mason, L. H. (2014). Lessons learned implementing self-regulated strategy development with students with emotional and behavioral disorders in alternative educational settings. *Behavioral Disorders, 40*, 68–77. https://doi.org/10.17988/0198-7429-40.1.68

Ennis, R. P., & Jolivette, K. (2014a). Using SRSD for persuasive writing to increase the writing and self-determination skills of students with E/BD in health class. *Behavioral Disorders, 40*, 26–36. https://doi.org/10.17988/0198-7429-40.1.26

Ennis, R. P., & Jolivette, K. (2014b). Existing research and future directions for self-regulated strategy development with students with and at-risk for E/BD. *Journal of Special Education, 48*, 32–45. https://doi.org/10.1177/0022466912454682

Every Student Succeeds Act of 2015, Pub. L. No. 114–95 § 114, Stat. 1177 (2015–2016).

Festas, I., Oliveira, A. L., Rebelo, J. A., Damião, M. H., Harris, K., & Graham, S. (2015). Professional development in self-regulated strategy development: Effects on the writing performance of eighth grade Portuguese students. *Contemporary Educational Psychology, 40*, 17–27. https://doi.org/10.1016/j.cedpsych.2014.05.004

FitzPatrick, E., & McKeown, D. (2020). Meeting the needs of middle school writers in a special education classroom: SRSD for the informational genre citing text-based evidence. *Education and Treatment of Children, 43*, 71–84. https://doi.org/10.1007/s43494-020-00006-2

FitzPatrick, E. & McKeown, D. (2021). Writing from multiple source texts: SRSD for fifth grade learners in inclusive settings. *Learning Disabilities Research and Practice, 37*(2), 188–200. https://doi.org/10.1111/ldrp.12257

Flower, L., & Hayes, J. (1980). The cognition of discovery: Defining a rhetorical problem. *College Composition and Communication, 31*(1), 21–32. https://doi.org/10.2307/356630

Gage, N., Wilson, J., & MacSuga-Gage, A. (2014). Writing performance of students with emotional and/or behavioral disabilities. *Behavioral Disorders, 40*, 3–14. https://doi.org/10.17988/0198-7429-40.1.3

Garcia-Sanchez, J. N., & Fidalgo-Redondo, R. (2006). Effects of two types of self-regulatory instruction programs on students with learning disabilities in writing products, processes, and self-efficacy. *Learning Disability Quarterly, 29*, 181–211. https://doi.org/10.2307/30035506

Gardner, T. J. (2008). Speech recognition for students with disabilities in writing. *Physical Disabilities: Education and Related Services, 26*(2), 43–53.

Garwood, J. D., Werts, M. G., Mason, L. H., Harris, B., Austin, M. B., Ciullo, S., Magner, K., Koppenhaver, D. A., & Shin, M. (2019). Improving persuasive science writing for secondary students with emotional and behavioral disorders educated in residential treatment facilities. *Behavioral Disorders, 44*(4), 227–240. https://doi.org/10.1177/0198742918809341

Graham, S. (2006a). Strategy instruction and the teaching of writing: A meta-analysis. In C. MacArthur, S. Graham, & J. Fitzgerald (Eds.), *Handbook of writing research* (pp. 187–207). Guilford Press.

Graham, S. (2006b). Writing. In P. Alexander & P. Winne (Eds.), *Handbook of educational psychology* (pp. 457–478). Lawrence Erlbaum.

Graham, S. (2018). A revised writer(s)-within-community model of writing. *Educational Psychologist, 53*(4), 258–279. https://doi.org/10.1080/00461520.2018.1481406

Graham, S. (2020). The sciences of reading and writing must become more fully integrated. *Reading Research Quarterly, 55*(S1), S35–S44. https://doi.org/10.1002/rrq.332

Graham, S., Bollinger, A., Booth Olson, C., D'Aoust, C., MacArthur, C., McCutchen, D., & Olinghouse, N. (2012a). *Teaching elementary school students to be effective writers: A practice guide* (NCEE 2012–4058). National Center for Education Evaluation and Regional Assistance, Institute of Education Sciences, U.S. Department of Education.

Graham, S., Bruch, J., Fitzgerald, J., Friedrich, L., Furgeson, J., Greene, K., Kim, J., Lyskawa, J., Olson, C. B., & Smither Wulsin, C. (2016). *Teaching secondary students to write effectively* (NCEE 2017–4002). National Center for Education Evaluation and Regional Assistance (NCEE), Institute of Education Sciences, U.S. Department of Education.

Graham, S., Collins, A., & Rigby-Wills, H. (2017). Writing characteristics of students with learning disabilities and typically achieving peers: A meta-analysis. *Exceptional Children, 83*(2), 199–218. https://doi.org/10.1177/0014402916664070

Graham, S., & Harris, K. R. (2009). Almost 30 years of writing research: Making sense of it all with The Wrath of Khan. *Learning Disabilities Research, 24*, 58–68. https://doi.org/10.1111/j.1540-5826.2009.01277.x

Graham, S., Harris, K. R., & Larsen, L. (2001). Prevention and intervention of writing difficulties for students with learning disabilities. *Learning Disabilities Research & Practice, 16*(2), 74–84.

Graham, S., Harris, K. R., & Mason, L. (2005). Improving the writing performance, knowledge, and self-efficacy of struggling young writers: The effects of self-regulated strategy development. *Contemporary Educational Psychology, 30*, 207–241. https://doi.org/10.1016/j.cedpsych.2004.08.001

Graham, S., & Hebert, M. (2011). Writing to read: A meta-analysis of the impact of writing and writing instruction on reading. *Harvard Educational Review*, *81*(4), 710–744. https://doi.org/10.17763/haer.81.4.t2k0m13756113566

Graham, S., Kiuhara, S. A., Harris, K. R., & Fishman, E. (2017). The relationship between strategic behavior, motivation, and writing performance with young, developing writers. *Elementary School Journal*, *118*, 82–104. https://doi.org/10.1086/693009

Graham, S., Kiuhara, S. A., & MacKay, M. (2020). The effects of writing on learning in science, social studies, and mathematics: A meta-analysis. *Review of Educational Research*, *90*(2), 179–226. https://doi.org/10.3102/0034654320914744

Graham, S., Liu, X., Aitken, A., Ng, C., Bartlett, B., Harris, K. R., & Holzapfel, J. (2018a). Effectiveness of literacy programs balancing reading and writing instruction: A meta-analysis. *Reading Research Quarterly*, *53*(3), 279–304. https://doi.org/10.1002/rrq.194.

Graham, L., Liu, X., Bartlett, B., Ng, C., Harris, K. R., Aitken, A., Barkel, A., Kavanaugh, C., & Talukdar, J. (2018b). Reading for writing: A meta-analysis of the impact of reading interventions on writing. *Review of Educational Research*, *88*(2), 243–284. https://doi.org/10.3102/0034654317746927

Graham, S., McKeown, D., Kiuhara, S., & Harris, K. R. (2012b). A meta-analysis of writing instruction for students in the elementary grades. *Journal of Education Psychology*, *104*, 879–896. https://doi.org/10.1037/a0029185

Harris, K. R., Graham, S., Fiske, S. T., Murphy, K., Mayer, R., Worrell, F., Levine, F., & Newcombe, N. (2016). Self-regulated strategy development in writing: Policy implications of an evidence-based practice. *Policy Insights from the Behavioral and Brain Sciences*, *3*(1), 77–84. https://doi.org/10.1177/2372732215624216

Harris, K. R., Graham, S., MacArthur, C., Reid, R., & Mason, L. (2011). Self-regulated learning processes and children's writing. In D. H. Schunk & B. Zimmerman (Eds.), *Handbook of self-regulation of learning and performance*. Taylor & Francis.

Harris, K. R., Graham, S., Mason, L., & Friedlander, B. (2008). *Powerful writing strategies for all students*. Brookes.

Harris, K. R., Lane, K. L., Graham, S., Driscoll, S. A., Sandmel, K., Brindle, M., & Schatschneider, C. (2012). Practice-based professional development for SRSD in writing: A randomized controlled study. *Journal of Teacher Education*, *63*, 103–119. https://doi.org/10.1177/0022487111429005

Harris, K. R., Ray, A., Graham, S., & Houston, J. (2019). Answering the challenge: SRSD instruction for close reading of text to write to persuade with 4th and 5th grade students experiencing writing difficulties. *Reading & Writing*, *32*(6), 1459–1482. https://doi.org/10.1007/s11145-018-9910-1

Hayes, J. R. (1996). A new model of cognition and affect in writing. In M. Levy, & S. Ransdell (Eds.), *The science of writing* (pp. 1–27). Erlbaum.

Hitchcock, C. H., Rao, K., Chuan, C. C., & Yuen, J. W. L. (2016). TeenACE for science using multimedia tools and scaffolds to support writing. *Rural Special Education Quarterly*, *35*(2), 10–23. https://doi.org/10.1177/875687051603500203

Individuals with Disabilities Education Act, 20 U.S.C. § 1400 (2004)

Jacob, R. T., Zhu, P., Somers, M.-A., & Bloom, H. (2012). *A practical guide to regression discontinuity*. MDRC. https://www.mdrc.org/publication/practical-guide-regression-discontinuity

Jozwik, S., & Cuenca-Carlino, Y. (2020). Promoting self-advocacy through persuasive writing for English Learners with learning disabilities. *Rural Special Education Quarterly*, *39*(2), 82–90. https://doi.org/10.1177/8756870519892883

Juel, C., Griffith, P. L., & Gough, P. B. (1986). Acquisition of literacy: A longitudinal study of children in first and second grade. *Journal of Educational Psychology*, *78*, 243–255. https://doi.org/10.1037/0022-0663.78.4.243

Kim, J., Olson, C., Scarcella, R., Kramer, J., Pearson, M., van Dyk, D., & Land, R. (2011). A randomized experiment of a cognitive strategies approach to text-based analytical writing for mainstreamed Latino ELLs in grades 6 to 12. *Journal of Research on Educational Effectiveness*, *4*, 231–263. https://doi.org/10.1080/19345747.2010.523513

Kissel, B. T., Whittingham, C. E., Tropp Laman, T., & Miller, E. T. (2019). Student activists and authors: Contemporary youth voices as classroom texts. *English Journal*, *108*(4), 76–82.

Kopke, R. A., Hawkins, L. K., Troia, G. A., & Olinghouse, N. G. (2014). The neglected "R" in a time of Common Core. *The Reading Teacher*, *67*(6), 445–453. https://doi.org/10.1002/trtr.1227

Leseaux, N. K., Kieffer, M. J., Kelley, J. G., & Harris, J. R. (2014). Effects of academic vocabulary instruction for linguistically diverse adolescents: Evidence from a randomized field trial. *American Educational Research Journal*, *51*(6), 1159–1194. https://doi.org/10.3102/0002831214532165

MacArthur, C. A., Schwartz, S., & Graham, S. (1991). Effects of a reciprocal peer revision strategy in special education classes. *Learning Disabilities Research and Practice*, *6*(4), 201–210.

Mason, L. H., Kubina, R. M., Valasa, L. L., & Cramer, A. M. (2010). Evaluating effective writing instruction for adolescent students in an emotional and behavior support setting. *Behavioral Disorders*, *35*, 140–156. https://doi.org/10.1177/019874291003500205

McKeown, D., Brindle, M., Harris, K. R., Graham, S., & Collins, A. A. (2016). Illuminating growth and struggles using mixed methods: Practice-based professional development and coaching for differentiating SRSD instruction in writing. *Reading and Writing: An Interdisciplinary Journal, 29*, 1105–1140. https://doi.org/10.1007/s11145-016-9627-y

McKeown, D., Brindle, M., Harris, K. R., Sandmel, K., Steinbrecher, T., Graham, S., Lane, K., & Oakes, W. (2019). Teachers' voices: Understanding effective practice-based professional development for elementary teachers on SRSD in writing. *American Educational Research Journal, 56*, 753–791. https://doi.org/10.3102/0002831218804146

McKeown, D., FitzPatrick, E., Ennis, R., & Potter, A. (2020). Writing is revising: Improving student writing through individualized asynchronous audio feedback. *Education and Treatment of Children, 43*, 35–48. https://doi.org/10.1007/s43494-020-00004-4

McKeown, D., Kimball, K., & Ledford, J. (2015). Effects of asynchronous audio feedback on the story revision practices of students with emotional/behavioral disorders. *Education and Treatment of Children, 38*, 541–564. https://doi.org/10.1353/etc.2015.0020

National Center for Education Statistics. (2002). *National assessment of educational progress: Writing assessment.* Institute of Education Sciences, U.S. Dept. of Education.

National Center for Education Statistics. (2011). *National Assessment of Educational Progress: Writing assessment.* Institute of Education Sciences, U.S. Dept. of Education.

Poplin, M., Gray, R., Larsen, S., Banikowski, A., & Mehring, T. (1980). A comparison of the components of written expression abilities in learning disabled and non-disabled students at three grade levels. *Learning Disability Quarterly, 3*, 46–53. https://doi.org/10.2307/1510674

Pressley, M., & Harris, K. R. (2006). Cognitive strategies instruction: From basic research to classroom instruction. In P. A. Alexander & P. H. Winne (Eds.), *Handbook of educational psychology* (pp. 265–286). Lawrence Erlbaum.

Reid, R., Gonzalez, J. E., Nordness, P. D., Trout, A., & Epstein, M. H. (2004). A meta-analysis of the academic status of students with emotional/behavioral disturbances. *Journal of Special Education, 38*, 130–143. https://doi.org/10.1177/00224669040380030101

Rogers, L., & Graham, S. (2008). A meta-analysis of single subject design writing intervention research. *Journal of Educational Psychology, 100*, 879–906. https://doi.org/10.1037/0022-0663.100.4.879.

Rowe, D., Alverson, C., Unruh, D., Fowler, C., Kellems, R., & Test, D. (2015). A Delphi study to operationalize evidence-based predictors in secondary transition. *Career Development and Transition for Exceptional Individuals, 38*(2), 113–126. https://doi.org/10.1177/2165143414526429

Rupley, W. H., Blair, T. R., & Nichols, M. D. (2009). Effective reading instruction for struggling readers: The role of direct/explicit instruction. *Reading & Writing Quarterly, 25*, 125–138. https://doi.org/10.1080/10573560802683523

Ryoo, J. H., & Pullen, P. C. (2017). Regression discontinuity design for longitudinal data, cross-sectional data, and intervention research. In J. Kauffman, D. P. Hallahan, & P. C. Pullen (Eds.), *Handbook of special education* (2nd ed., pp. 137–150). Taylor & Francis. https://doi.org/10.4324/9781315517698-13

Saddler, B., Behforooz, B., & Asaro, K. (2008). The effects of sentence-combining instruction on the writing of fourth-grade students with writing difficulties. *The Journal of Special Education, 42*, 79–90. https://doi.org/10.1177/0022466907310371

Smith, S. J., Lowrey, K., Rowland, A. L., & Frey, B. (2020). Effective technology supported writing strategies for learners with disabilities. *Inclusion, 8*(1), 58–73. https://doi.org/10.1352/2326-6988-8.1.58

Thistlewaite, D., & Campbell, D. (1960). Regression discontinuity analysis: An alternative to the ex-post facto experiment. *Journal of Educational Psychology, 51*, 309–317. https://doi.org/10.1037/h0044319

Troia, G. A. (2007). Research in Writing Instruction: What We Know and What We Need to Know. In M. Pressley, A. K Billman, K. H Perry, K. E. Reffitt, & J. M. Reynolds (Eds), *Shaping literacy achievement: Research we have, research we need* (pp. 129–156). Guilford Press.

U.S. Department of Education. (2019). *Number and percent of students ages 6 through 21 served under IDEA, Part B, by educational environment and state.* https://www2.ed.gov/programs/osepidea/618-data/static-tables/index.html#partb-cc

What Works Clearinghouse, Institute of Education Sciences, U.S. Department of Education. (2014). *Standards handbook version 4.0.* https://ies.ed.gov/ncee/wwc/Docs/referenceresources/wwc_standards_handbook_v4.pdf

What Works Clearinghouse, Institute of Education Sciences, U.S. Department of Education. (2017, November). *Students with a specific learning disability intervention report: Self-regulated strategy development.* https://whatworks.ed.gov/

Wijekumar, K., Harris, K. R., & Graham, S., McKeown, D., Lei, P. W., & Meyer, B. J. F. (2018). *Efficacy trial: We-Write teacher led & computer-supported intervention, 4th- & 5th-grade students.* Institute of Education Sciences (CFDA No: 84.305A; Award: R305A180212)

Wilson, J., Olinghouse, N. G., & Andrada, G. N. (2014). Does automated feedback improve writing quality? *Learning Disabilities: A Contemporary Journal, 12*(1), 93–118.

Wilson, W. (2017). Associated effects of automated essay evaluation software on growth in writing quality for students with and without disabilities. *Reading & Writing, 30*(4), 691–718. https://doi.org/10.1007/s11145-016-9695-z

11
MATHEMATICS INTERVENTIONS FOR STUDENTS EXPERIENCING MATHEMATICS DIFFICULTY

Sarah R. Powell and Samantha E. Bos

Mathematics is a challenging subject for many students. In 2019, only 41% of fourth-grade, 34% of eighth-grade, and 25% of 12th-grade students demonstrated proficiency in critical mathematics content. Thus, there is significant demand for effective mathematical instruction and interventions to address students' needs (National Center for Education Statistics, 2019). Students experiencing mathematics difficulty (MD) include students who are formally diagnosed with a specific learning disability, as well as those who are never formally identified but who still struggle in mathematics. Without targeted interventions, many students experiencing MD will continue to struggle in mathematics throughout their educational career and after graduation (Martin et al., 2013; Nelson & Powell, 2018a).

Students across both elementary and secondary grades who experience MD can benefit from systematic and targeted mathematics interventions (Chodura et al., 2015; Jitendra et al., 2018; Stevens et al., 2018). Response to intervention (RTI) and Multitiered Systems of Support (MTSS) offer two frameworks for identifying students who experience MD and providing necessary support services. Within these systems, students for whom quality Tier 1 (i.e., general education) instruction is insufficient can receive small-group, targeted Tier 2 support. Within Tier 2, students receive evidence-based mathematics intervention with continual progress monitoring to determine the effectiveness of Tier 2 for improving mathematics performance (Schumacher et al., 2017). Within the RTI and MTSS frameworks, students experiencing MD who require additional support participate in Tier 3 (Fuchs et al., 2018). In Tier 3, students often receive similar interventions as within Tier 2 but with greater intensity and individualization.

In this chapter, we focus on the design and delivery of mathematics intervention for students experiencing MD. We focus on intervention efforts provided within Tier 2 and 3 but understand that many intervention components also have proven effective for teaching students without MD (Zhang & Xin, 2012). We provide a practical guide for educators and an overview of strengths and gaps in the literature base for researchers.

Initially, we offer suggestions for designing effective mathematics interventions. Then, we discuss the delivery of mathematics intervention by outlining a brief overview of key intervention components, examples of current research utilizing each component, and the evidence base supporting each component. We conclude with a discussion about multicomponent interventions and limitations in the research base, and we provide suggestions for future research over the next decade.

Design of Mathematics Intervention

In this section, we discuss how to design mathematics intervention for students experiencing MD. Several steps are required prior to the actual implementation of Tier 2 or 3 intervention for students experiencing MD. First, educators or researchers must determine the critical mathematics content that students need to learn. The focus of Tier 2 or 3 intervention should reflect the foundational mathematics knowledge for which students did not reach proficiency levels in Tier 1. As described by the National Council of Teachers of Mathematics (2006), students need to develop a strong foundation with number, operations, and algebraic reasoning with whole numbers and rational numbers, as well as skill in geometry and measurement. The significant need to develop students' foundational skills explains why the majority of mathematics interventions focus on operations or problem-solving (Powell, Doabler, et al., 2020; Stevens et al., 2018). Educators need to assess students to determine their mathematical strengths and gaps in knowledge and then use this information to develop a scope and sequence of critical content (Powell et al., 2013).

After identifying the critical mathematics content, educators or researchers need to determine the most appropriate evidence-based practices for teaching the critical mathematics content. An evidence-based practice has high-quality research to support its use (Cook & Cook, 2013). In the area of mathematics, we encounter two types of evidence-based practices. Educators may use evidence-based interventions that are packaged programs or those that include all materials necessary to implement the intervention (Clarke et al., 2014; Fuchs et al., 2016). Educators also may use evidence-based strategies, such as using manipulatives to teach mathematics (Satsangi et al., 2016) or building fluency with incremental rehearsal techniques (McVancel et al., 2018). Evidence-based strategies often are used within packaged evidence-based interventions but also can be applied in isolation without an evidence-based intervention.

After determining the critical mathematics content and identifying the most appropriate evidence-based practices for teaching the content, educators or researchers need to construct the instructional platform. The instructional platform consists of the set of evidence-based practices that will be used during every Tier 2 or 3 mathematics intervention session. After reviewing numerous syntheses about mathematics intervention, we identified five components with an evidence base to include in an instructional platform: explicit instruction, precise mathematical language, multiple representations, fluency, and word-problem solving. We discuss each of these components in the following section.

Delivery of Mathematics Intervention

In this section, we focus on five components with an evidence base that educators should consider when delivering mathematics intervention (Codding et al., 2011; Cook et al., 2020; Dennis, Sharp, et al., 2016; Ennis & Losinski, 2019; Gersten et al., 2009; Hwang et al., 2019; Jitendra et al., 2018; Powell, Doabler, et al., 2020; Stevens et al., 2018). We selected to highlight these five components because they all have a strong evidence base for their use within mathematics intervention (Fuchs, Bucka, et al., 2021). Researchers should include these practices when designing interventions for research teams or educators to implement. In each subsection, we describe the component and its importance, the implementation of the component, and the research support for the component.

Explicit Instruction

What Is It and Why Is It Important?

Explicit instruction is a structured and direct method of instructional delivery that is educator-driven and includes purposeful and scaffolded teaching of critical content to develop students' independent learning (Archer & Hughes, 2011). Described as the bedrock of academic interventions, including mathematics interventions, explicit instruction serves as a highly effective method for increasing mathematical outcomes for students experiencing MD (Gersten et al., 2009). Although multifaceted, explicit instruction includes several elements that generally can be grouped within three main stages: modeling, practice, and support.

Teaching With Explicit Instruction

The cornerstone of explicit instruction occurs during the modeling stage. High-quality modeling includes well-planned explanations of the material using precise mathematical language and multiple examples to develop students' understanding. Clear and concise explanations and demonstrations of the mathematical topic with purposeful examples develop students' understandings of the mathematical concepts (Alfieri et al., 2011). The use of planned examples and nonexamples helps students refine their understanding of mathematical topics (Parmar & DeSimone, 2006).

The next stage of explicit instruction includes students' practice. The two primary forms of practice include scaffolded, educator-driven guided practice, and then independent practice. During guided practice, educators should be mindful of students' potential misconceptions and provide immediate, specific, and corrective feedback to address any misunderstandings or errors. As students develop greater confidence and understanding, educators should transition students towards independent practice. Independent practice is appropriate when students are able to complete activities with a high degree of accuracy and serves to support long-term retention of procedures and concepts (Archer & Hughes, 2011).

Throughout both modeling and practice stages, there are a series of supporting practices educators should embed into their explicit instruction to ensure high-quality student learning. Throughout all modeling and practice, educators and students should use precise and specific mathematical language (Riccomini et al., 2015). During the modeling and practice stages, educators also should elicit frequent responses and provide students with multiple opportunities to respond and verbalize their mathematical thinking (Doabler et al., 2015). Providing immediate and specific corrective feedback proves critical for helping students develop the correct procedural and conceptual mathematics knowledge (Hattie & Timperley, 2007). Finally, to maximize the dosage, educators should maintain a brisk pace by preparing examples and materials and studying intervention material prior to lessons.

What Does the Research Say?

Explicit instruction frequently is cited as an effective method for improving the mathematical outcomes of students across kindergarten through 12th-grade classrooms (Gersten et al., 2009; Jitendra et al., 2018). In addition, both students experiencing MD and students without MD have benefitted from instruction that is explicitly delivered (Gersten et al., 2009). Explicit instruction continues to serve as a fundamental component of many mathematics interventions (Fuchs, Bucka, et al., 2021).

Mathematical Language

What Is It and Why Is It Important?

All students are learners of the language of mathematics. Students may use mathematics language to speak and listen about mathematics or to read and write within mathematics. One critical aspect of mathematics language is *mathematics vocabulary*. Students often experience difficulty with mathematics vocabulary because of the sheer volume of terms. For example, in first grade, students may need to learn over 100 mathematics vocabulary terms (Powell & Nelson, 2017); in seventh grade, students may interact with over 450 different mathematics vocabulary terms (Hughes et al., 2020). Furthermore, students may mistake a mathematics term with a term from general English (e.g., *difference* with subtraction versus *difference* between two countries), confuse terms with different mathematical meanings (e.g., *base* of a figure versus *base* with an exponent), lack experience with terms used in mathematics (e.g., *hypothenuse*), and confuse homophones (e.g., *sum* versus *some*; Rubenstein & Thompson, 2002). Students experiencing MD demonstrate greater difficulty with understanding mathematics vocabulary than peers without MD (Forsyth & Powell, 2017).

Teaching Mathematical Language

The research base for focusing on mathematics language remains limited, but we can provide several suggestions. First, practice is essential (Petersen-Brown et al., 2019). Students need exposure to new vocabulary and practice recognizing terms and their definitions. Second, Riccomini et al. (2015) suggested explicitly teaching unfamiliar mathematics vocabulary, whereas embedded mathematics vocabulary within mathematics intervention may aid in the learning of mathematics vocabulary. Third, reading books aloud with students (i.e., read-alouds or dialogic reading) supports their mathematics vocabulary learning, especially those who are very young (Hassinger-Das et al., 2015; Purpura et al., 2017). Fourth, students may benefit from developing mathematics vocabulary knowledge through graphic organizers (Bruun et al., 2015), vocabulary grids (Marin, 2018), or playing games (Riccomini et al., 2015). Although these suggestions prove useful, the evidence base for such practices needs to be expanded.

What Does the Research Say?

The majority of research related to mathematics vocabulary has explored how students answer questions about mathematics vocabulary. Such investigations have occurred at the early elementary (Powell & Nelson, 2017), late elementary (Powell et al., 2017), and middle school grades (Hughes et al., 2020). Across studies, many students, especially those experiencing MD, have difficulty responding to questions about mathematics vocabulary (Forsyth & Powell, 2017). Interestingly, researchers have identified limited differences between dual-language learners experiencing MD and non-dual-language learners experiencing MD (Powell, Berry, et al., 2020). In terms of effective interventions for students experiencing MD, the area of mathematics vocabulary remains severely underresearched, with only a few studies targeted at students experiencing MD (e.g., Hassinger-Das et al., 2015). We recommend more researchers focus on the teaching of mathematics vocabulary in isolation, as well as embedded within interventions.

Multiple Representations

What Is It and Why Is It Important?

Multiple representations refers to the integration of concrete manipulatives, pictorial representations (e.g., drawings, pictures, or graphs), and abstract notation to demonstrate mathematical concepts. The use of multiple representations also is referred to as the CRA (concrete–representational–abstract) or CSA (concrete–semi-concrete–abstract) model. Many students experiencing MD struggle to develop a foundational number sense or conceptual understandings of more advanced mathematical concepts, such as algebra (Satsangi et al., 2016; Strickland, 2017). By including concrete manipulatives and pictorial representations alongside the abstract notation, students are better able to ground their understanding and acquire the fundamental knowledge related to numbers and mathematics.

Teaching With Multiple Representations

Concrete representations often are called manipulatives, as they allow students the opportunity to pick up and manipulate the pieces as they construct their mathematical understandings. Some of the most popular concrete representations include two-color counters, geoboards, Base-10 blocks, fraction tiles, and Algeblocks (Bouck & Park, 2018); however, educators may use a variety of commonplace items as well, including cups and beans, buttons, or even snack items. The key to using concrete representations is to align mathematical concepts to the manipulatives. For example, if an intervention is designed to teach positive and negative fractions, a number line would serve as a more effective manipulative than fraction tiles.

Pictorial representations include a two-dimensional representation of the three-dimensional concrete manipulative. As the name suggests, pictorial representations often involve pictures or drawings of the concrete representations, such as red and yellow circles to represent red and yellow two-color counters. Pictorial representations also can include graphs, tables, or graphic organizers. Pictorial representations may be presented virtually (Bouck et al., 2020; Satsangi et al., 2016; Shin et al., 2017). Pictorial representations can be introduced before, after, or while using concrete manipulatives, as no hierarchy exists among the three representations. If students cannot use manipulatives on high-stakes tests, teachers should encourage the use of pictorial and/or abstract representations.

Abstract representations refer to the Arabic numerals and mathematical symbols that students must interpret to solve mathematical problems. When students use concrete and pictorial representations, the abstract notation also should be included to ensure students are able to transfer the conceptual understanding and recognize the abstract form as representative of the mathematical concept. To allow for ease of manipulating more advanced mathematical knowledge, students must develop a strong number sense and ability to understand abstract mathematics.

What Does the Research Say?

A strong research base exists to support the use of multiple representations in the elementary grades (Flores et al., 2014; Mancl et al., 2012; Peltier, Morin, et al., 2020; Tournaki et al., 2008), as well as the effectiveness of both in-person and virtual manipulatives when working with students in the secondary grades (Jitendra, Nelson, et al., 2016; Namkung & Bricko, 2021; Peltier, Morin, et al., 2020; Satsangi & Bouck, 2015; Strickland & Maccini, 2012). Often, educators use multiple representations in tandem with other effective components of mathematics interventions, such as explicit instruction (e.g., Bryant et al., 2011; Clarke et al., 2014; Fuchs et al., 2013). The use of multiple representations serves as a powerful tool in helping students to develop both conceptual and procedural understanding of mathematics.

Fluency With Facts and Computation

What Is It and Why Is It Important?

In mathematics, fluency with mathematics facts and computation is foundational to solving mathematics problems in the domains of number and operations, place value, geometry, measurement, algebra, and statistics. Fluency often refers to immediate recall of mathematics facts. For example, a student should know, especially after second grade, that 8 plus 7 equals 15 without using fingers or counting strategies. Fluency with mathematics facts makes all multidigit computation easier. Students experiencing MD often demonstrate limited recall of mathematics facts compared to students without MD (Burns et al., 2015; Cirino et al., 2015). Similarly, students experiencing MD struggle with computation (Fuchs et al., 2009; Martin et al., 2013). Deficits in either or both of these areas slows mathematical processing, makes most tasks in mathematics more difficult, and leads to challenges with complex mathematics problems (Riccomini et al., 2017; Vukovic et al., 2014).

Teaching Fluency and Computation

Our definition of *fluency facts* refers to the 390 mathematics facts in addition, subtraction, multiplication, and division. Addition facts ($n = 100$) have single-digit addends (e.g., $1 + 4 = 5$; $9 + 8 = 17$), and subtraction facts ($n = 100$) have single-digit minuends and differences (e.g., $8 - 5 = 3$; $14 - 7 = 7$). Multiplication facts ($n = 100$) feature single-digit factors (e.g., $3 \times 8 = 24$; $8 \times 7 = 56$), and division facts ($n = 90$) have single-digit divisors and quotients ($8 \div 2 = 4$; $45 \div 9 = 5$). To help students experiencing MD increase fact fluency, teachers and researchers should consider explicit instruction on the concepts of the operations, as well as activities that aid with memorization (Codding et al., 2011). Activities with an evidence base include taped problems (Bliss et al., 2010), cover-copy-compare (Becker et al., 2009), incremental rehearsal (McVancel et al., 2018), and technology-based practice (Burns et al., 2012).

Our definition of *computation* refers to multidigit addition, subtraction, multiplication, and division of whole numbers, as well as operations with rational numbers including fractions and decimals. Students experiencing MD often make more mistakes with computation than students without MD, with common errors including using the incorrect operation (i.e., adding when the problem has a multiplication symbol), miscalculation (i.e., solving 8 plus 4 as 13), or errors related to place value (i.e., regrouping; Nelson & Powell, 2018b). With computation, explicit instruction on the conceptual understanding of the problem proves as important as practicing the procedural algorithm (Fuchs et al., 2008).

What Does the Research Say?

Authors have conducted most research on fact and computational fluency in the elementary grades because students learn addition and subtraction in the early elementary grades and multiplication and division in the late elementary grades. As suggested by Gersten et al. (2009), students experiencing MD should receive brief fluency practice during every session of mathematics intervention. With both facts and computation, preteaching—especially with the use of multiple representations (Watt et al., 2016), explicit modeling (Fuchs et al., 2008), and practice (Dennis et al., 2015)—leads to improvement in student fact and computation outcomes.

Word-Problem Solving

What Is It and Why Is It Important?

For students to demonstrate their mathematics competency, especially on chapter and unit tests, as well as high-stakes tests, students must set up and solve word problems. In fact, over 95% of high-stakes mathematics items involve word-problem solving (Powell, Namkung, et al., in press). Beyond tests, students need to develop proficiency with problem-solving to engage in mathematics in and outside of the classroom (National Governors Association Center for Best Practices and Council of Chief State School Officers, 2010). Students experiencing MD have difficulty with word-problem solving more often than students without MD (Fuchs, Seethaler, et al., 2021; Griffin et al., 2018; Kingsdorf & Krawec, 2014).

Teaching Word-Problem Solving

Fortunately, researchers have identified several efficacious practices for improving the word-problem outcomes for students experiencing MD. One practice involves the use of a meta-cognitive strategy to guide students through the problem-solving process. For example, Montague et al. (2011) and her team developed a seven-step process (Read, Paraphrase, Visualize, Hypothesize, Estimate, Compute, and Check). Freeman-Green et al. (2015) taught students to SOLVE: Study the problem, Organize the facts, Line up a plan, Verify your plan with action, and Evaluate your answer. Another practice focuses on using graphic organizers to organize the information presented in word problems. van Garderen (2007) helped students experiencing MD solve word problems via diagrams, and Xin (2008) assisted students with word-problem solving through the use of several graphic organizers focused on multiplicative word-problem schemas.

Another effective practice related to word-problem solving is instruction on recognizing word-problem schemas (Cook et al., 2020). A schema is a common structure that allows students to recognize a word problem as being similar to previously solved word problems. Word-problem schema instruction has demonstrated positive results for students experiencing MD in the early elementary grades with additive schemas (Fuchs, Seethaler, et al., 2021; Peltier, Sinclair, et al., 2020; Powell et al., 2015) and in the late elementary and middle school grades with multiplicative schemas (Jitendra & Star, 2011; Xin & Zhang, 2009). Often, educators provide instruction of the schemas through the use of multiple representations (Flores et al., 2016) or explicit instruction (Powell, Berry, et al., 2021). Enhanced anchored instruction also has demonstrated positive word-problem outcomes for students experiencing MD. During enhanced anchored instruction, students use technology to learn problem-solving in authentic contexts (Bottge et al., 2004).

What Does the Research Say?

In the elementary grades, authors of numerous studies have reported increased word-problem performance for students experiencing MD after participation in word-problem intervention (Alghamdi et al., 2020; Fuchs et al., 2014). Researchers have demonstrated similar positive effects at middle school (Bottge et al., 2004; Krawec et al., 2012) and high school (Dennis, Knight, et al., 2016). For example, Dennis, Knight, et al. (2016) worked with 11th-grade students experiencing MD and implemented an intervention package with a meta-cognitive strategy used within a graphic organizer. Students also used various representations (i.e., drawings of bar models) to represent different word problems. This intervention package led to improved word-problem performance for all students. Across studies, educators implemented word-problem intervention for sustained periods of time (e.g., at least 10 weeks with three sessions per week), and educators often used a mix of strategies (e.g., meta-cognitive strategies with a focus on schemas or explicit instruction with graphic organizers).

Research Gaps and Recommendations for the Next Decade

The field of mathematics interventions for students experiencing MD is rapidly developing a research base to support the efficacy of critical components, including explicit instruction, mathematical language, multiple representations, fluency and computation practice, and word-problem solving. However, a great deal remains unknown regarding the unique role each of these components plays in developing students' mastery of mathematical concepts.

Multicomponent Interventions

The majority of mathematics interventions include several evidence-based components, especially explicit instruction, mathematical language, and multiple representations. As a result, determining the unique contribution of each remains difficult (Gersten et al., 2009). Because each evidence-based practice contributes to mathematical learning in different ways, it is difficult and largely unfeasible to test components in isolation. For example, testing an intervention without including mathematically precise language would be challenging and likely result in poor teaching. With the development of more sophisticated statistical modeling, researchers do not have to sacrifice the inclusion of evidence-based components; however, the components must be described at a high level of detail to ensure statisticians can tease apart the unique contributions of each.

Opportunities for Future Research

Despite the developing research base to support mathematics interventions, many questions remain unanswered regarding the best ways to help students experiencing MD. As noted, the majority of mathematics interventions include multiple components that potentially increase student outcomes. Questions emerge regarding the effects of individual components of interventions, such as the role of word-problem solving alone, as well as specific questions about the most effective versions of each component. For example, in examining the evidence base for multiple representations, Jitendra, Nelson, et al. (2016) determined multiple representations were effective in improving student outcomes, but it was unclear which element or combination of elements led to the most improved student outcomes. Additional research is needed to determine the most effective elements of each evidence-based practice and whether these components vary across different populations of students at different grade levels.

In addition to determining critical elements of evidence-based interventions, researchers need to develop culturally responsive interventions that address the challenges of a wide variety of students experiencing MD (e.g., Shumate et al., 2012). As the United States becomes a more diverse nation, interventions must support the needs of culturally and linguistically diverse learners, especially those experiencing MD (Doabler et al., 2016). These students also benefit from a focus on mathematical language and explicit instruction, but may require additional culturally relevant teaching examples to support their learning (Kim, 2017).

Furthermore, students' mathematics learning trajectories tend to slow as students enter upper elementary and middle school, which creates greater challenges for developing interventions that will lead to significant changes in learning (Wei et al., 2013). As students progress through the grades, mathematical concepts become more abstract, and students are expected to fluently manipulate numbers that reflect both depth and breadth of conceptual knowledge. Such tasks prove especially challenging for students experiencing MD (Geary et al., 2012; O'Shea et al., 2017). Interventions focused on developing secondary students' mathematical knowledge are greatly needed, as limited research has been conducted with students in middle and high school. Importantly, students in these later grades often require greater supports than students in elementary grades (Jitendra et al., 2018).

Finally, as students are expected to learn mathematics in new ways that reflect social and cultural shifts, interventions must adapt to reflect those changes. For example, most students experiencing MD currently receive their mathematical instruction in the general education classroom under inclusion models where co-educators are expected to address the needs of students experiencing MD, as well as their typically achieving peers during the same class time (National Center for Education Statistics, 2019). Future interventions should be malleable enough to support students experiencing MD, as well as their peers without MD, in an inclusion setting. In addition to receiving educational supports within an inclusion model, many students are receiving mathematics instruction via online platforms or with the assistance of technology. Interventions should take advantage of the online or virtual opportunities available as many schools increase internet access to students.

In developing mathematics interventions, future researchers will be able to contribute to the robust research conducted over the past two decades; however, the challenges that educators experience in supporting students' mathematics development will remain immense and complex. As researchers and educators continue to develop a more sophisticated understanding of the specific needs of students experiencing MD, as well as the most effective components for addressing those needs, they will be better equipped to increase the mathematics performance and overall success of all students.

References

Alfieri, L., Brooks, P., Aldrich, N., & Tenebaum, H. (2011). Does discovery-based instruction enhance learning? *Journal of Educational Psychology, 103*, 1–18. https://doi.org/10.1037/a0021017

Alghamdi, A., Jitendra, A. K., & Lein, A. E. (2020). Teaching students with mathematics disabilities to solve multiplication and division word problems: The role of schema-based instruction. *ZDM Mathematics Education, 52*, 125–137. https://doi.org/10.1007/s11858-019-01078-0

Archer, A. L., & Hughes, C. A. (2011). *Explicit instruction: Effective and efficient teaching*. The Guilford Press.

Becker, A., McLaughlin, T., Weber, K. P., & Gower, J. (2009). The effects of copy, cover and compare with and without additional error drill on multiplication fact fluency and accuracy. *Electronic Journal of Research in Educational Psychology, 7*(2), 747–760. https://doi.org/10.25115/ejrep.v7i18.1368

Bliss, S. L., Skinner, C. H., McCallum, E., Saecker, L. B., Rowland-Bryant, E., & Brown, K. S. (2010). A comparison of taped problems with and without a brief post-treatment assessment on multiplication fluency. *Journal of Behavioral Education, 19*, 156–168. https://doi.org/10.1007/s10864-010-9106-5

Bottge, B. A., Heinrichs, M., Mehta, Z. D., Rueda, E., Hung, Y.-H., & Dannker, J. (2004). Teaching mathematical problem solving to middle school students in math, technology education, and special education classrooms. *Research in Middle Level Education, 27*(1), 1–17. https://doi.org/10.1080/19404476.2004.11658161

Bouck, E. C., Long, H., & Park, J. (2020). Using a virtual number line and corrective feedback to teach addition of integers to middle school students with developmental disabilities. *Journal of Developmental and Physical Disabilities, 33*(1), 99–116. https://doi.org/10.1007/s10882-020-09735-z

Bouck, E. C., & Park, J. (2018). A systematic review of the literature on mathematics manipulatives to support students with disabilities. *Education and Treatment of Children, 41*(1), 65–106. https://doi.org/10.1353/etc.2018.0003

Bruun, F., Diaz, J. M., & Bykes, V. J. (2015). The language of mathematics. *Teaching Children Mathematics, 21*(9), 530–536. https://doi.org/10.5951/teacchilmath.21.9.0530

Bryant, D. P., Bryant, B. R., Roberts, G., Vaughn, S., Pfannenstiel, K. H., Porterfield, J., & Gersten, R. (2011). Early numeracy intervention program for first-grade students with mathematics difficulties. *Exceptional Children, 78*(1), 7–23. https://doi.org/10.1177/001440291107800101

Burns, M. K., Kanive, R., & DeGrande, M. (2012). Effect of a computer-delivered math fact intervention as a supplemental intervention for math in third and fourth grades. *Remedial and Special Education, 33*(3), 184–191. https://doi.org/10.1177/0741932510381652

Burns, M. K., Ysseldyke, J., Nelson, P. M., & Kanive, R. (2015). Number of repetitions required to retain single-digit multiplication math facts for elementary students. *School Psychology Quarterly, 30*(3), 398–405. https://doi.org/10.1037/spq0000097

Chodura, S., Kuhn, J.-T., & Holling, H. (2015). Interventions for children with mathematical difficulties: A meta-analysis. *Zeitschrift für Psychologie, 223*, 129–144. https://doi.org/10.1027/2151-2604.a000211

Cirino, P. T., Fuchs, L. S., Elias, J. T., Powell, S. R., & Schumacher, R. F. (2015). Cognitive and mathematical profiles for different forms of learning difficulties. *Journal of Learning Disabilities, 48*(2), 156–175. https://doi.org/10.1177/0022219413494239

Clarke, B., Doabler, C. T., Smolkowski, K., Baker, S. K., Fien, H., & Cary, M. S. (2014). Examining the efficacy of a Tier 2 kindergarten mathematics intervention. *Journal of Learning Disabilities, 49*(2), 152–165. https://doi.org/10.1177/0022219414538514

Codding, R. S., Burns, M. K., & Lukito, G. (2011). Meta-analysis of mathematics basic-fact fluency interventions: A component analysis. *Learning Disabilities Research and Practice*, *26*(1), 36–47. https://doi.org/10.1111/j.1540-5826.2010.00323.x

Cook, B. G., & Cook, S. C. (2013). Unraveling evidence-based practices in special education. *The Journal of Special Education*, *47*(2), 71–82. https://doi.org/10.1177/0022466911420877

Cook, S. C., Collins, L. W., Morin, L. L., & Riccomini, P. J. (2020). Schema-based instruction for mathematical word problem solving: An evidence-based review for students with learning disabilities. *Learning Disability Quarterly*, *43*(2), 75–87. https://doi.org/10.1177/0731948718823080

Dennis, M. S., Knight, J., & Jerman, O. (2016). Teaching high school students with learning disabilities to use model drawing strategy to solve fraction and percentage word problems. *Preventing School Failure*, *60*(1), 10–21. https://doi.org/10.1080/1045988x.2014.954514

Dennis, M. S., Sharp, E., Chovanes, J., Thomas, A., Burns, R. M., Custer, B., & Park, J. (2016). A meta-analysis of empirical research on teaching students with mathematics learning difficulties. *Learning Disabilities Research and Practice*, *31*(3), 156–168. https://doi.org/10.1111/ldrp.12107

Dennis, M. S., Sorrells, A. M., & Falcomata, T. S. (2015). Effects of two interventions on solving basic fact problems by second graders with mathematics learning disabilities. *Learning Disability Quarterly*, *39*(2), 95–112. https://doi.org/10.1177/0731948715595943

Doabler, C. T., Baker, S. K., Kosty, D., Smolkowski, K., Clarke, B., Miller, S. J., & Fien, H. (2015). Examining the association between explicit mathematics instruction and student mathematics achievement. *Elementary School Journal*, *115*(3), 303–333. https://doi.org/10.1086/679969

Doabler, C. T., Nelson, N. J., & Clarke, B. (2016). Adapting evidence-based practices to meet the needs of English learners with mathematics difficulties. *Teaching Exceptional Children*, *48*(6), 301–310. https://doi.org/10.1177/0040059916650638

Ennis, R. P., & Losinski, M. (2019). Interventions to improve fraction skills for students with disabilities: A meta-analysis. *Exceptional Children*, *85*(3), 367–386.

Flores, M. M., Hinton, V. M., & Burton, M. E. (2016). Teaching problem solving to students receiving tiered interventions using the concrete-representational-abstract sequence and schema-based instruction. *Preventing School Failure*, *60*(4), 345–355.

Flores, M. M., Hinton, V. M., & Strozier, S. D. (2014). Teaching subtraction and multiplication with regrouping using the concrete-representational-abstract sequence and strategic instruction model. *Learning Disabilities Research and Practice*, *29*(2), 75–88. https://doi.org/10.1080*1045988x.2016.1164117

Forsyth, S. R., & Powell, S. R. (2017). Differences in the mathematics-vocabulary knowledge of fifth-grade students with and without learning difficulties. *Learning Disabilities Research and Practice*, *32*(4), 231–245. https://doi.org/10.1111/ldrp.12144

Freeman-Green, S. M., O'Brien, C., Wood, C. L., & Hitt, S. B. (2015). Effects of the SOLVE strategy on the mathematical problem solving skills of secondary students with learning disabilities. *Learning Disabilities Research and Practice*, *30*(2), 76–90. https://doi.org/10.1111/ldrp.12054

Fuchs, L. S., Bucka, N., Clarke, B., Dougherty, B., Jordan, N. C., Karp, K. S., & Woodward, J. (2021). *Assisting students struggling with mathematics: Intervention in the elementary grades*. U.S. Department of Education.

Fuchs, L. S., Fuchs, D., & Malone, A. S. (2018). The taxonomy of intervention intensity. *Teaching Exceptional Children*, *50*(4), 194–202. https://doi.org/10.1177/0040059918758166

Fuchs, L. S., Geary, D. C., Compton, D. L., Fuchs, D., Schatschneider, C., Hamlett, C. L., DeSelms, J., Seethaler, P. M., Wilson, J., Craddock, C. F., Bryant, J. D., Luther, K., & Changas, P. (2013). Effects of first-grade number knowledge tutoring with contrasting forms of practice. *Journal of Educational Psychology*, *105*(1), 58–77. https://doi.org/10.1037/a0030127

Fuchs, L. S., Powell, S. R., Cirino, P. T., Schumacher, R. F., Marrin, S., Hamlett, C. L., Fuchs, D., Compton, D. L., & Changas, P. C. (2014). Does calculation or word-problem instruction provide a stronger route to pre-algebraic knowledge? *Journal of Educational Psychology*, *106*(4), 990–1006. https://doi.org/10.1037/a0036893

Fuchs, L. S., Powell, S. R., Hamlett, C. L., Fuchs, D., Cirino, P. T., & Fletcher, J. M. (2008). Remediating computational deficits at third grade: A randomized field trial. *Journal of Research on Educational Effectiveness*, *1*(1), 2–32. https://doi.org/10.1080/19345740701692449

Fuchs, L. S., Powell, S. R., Seethaler, P. M., Cirino, P. T., Fletcher, J. M., Fuchs, D., Hamlett, C. L., & Zumeta, R. O. (2009). Remediating number combination and word problem deficits among students with mathematics difficulties: A randomized control trial. *Journal of Educational Psychology*, *101*(3), 561–576. https://doi.org/10.1037/a0014701

Fuchs, L. S., Schumacher, R. F., Long, J., Namkung, J., Malone, A. S., Wang, A., Hamlett, C. L., Jordan, N. C., Siegler, R. S., & Changas, P. (2016). Effects of intervention to improve at-risk fourth graders' understanding, calculations, and word problems with fractions. *The Elementary School Journal, 116*(4), 625–651. https://doi.org/10.1086/686303

Fuchs, L. S., Seethaler, P. M., Sterba, S. K., Craddock, C., Fuchs, D., Compton, D. L., Geary, D. C., & Changas, P. (2021). Closing the word-problem achievement gap in first grade: Schema-based word-problem intervention with embedded language comprehension instruction. *Journal of Educational Psychology, 113*(1), 86–103. https://doi.org/10.1037/edu0000467

Geary, D. C., Hoard, M. K., Nugent, L., & Bailey, D. H. (2012). Mathematical cognition deficits in children with learning disabilities and persistent low achievement: A five-year prospective study. *Journal of Educational Psychology, 104*(1), 206–223. https://doi.org/10.1037/a0025398

Gersten, R., Chard, D. J., Jayanthi, M., Baker, S. K., Morphy, P., & Flojo, J. (2009). Mathematics instruction for students with learning disabilities: A meta-analysis of instructional components. *Review of Educational Research, 79*(3), 1202–1242. https://doi.org/10.3102/0034654309334431

Griffin, C. C., Gagnon, J. C., Jossi, M. H., Ulrich, T. G., & Myers, J. A. (2018). Priming mathematics word problem structures in a rural elementary classroom. *Rural Special Education Quarterly, 37*(3), 150–163. https://doi.org/10.1177/8756870418772164

Hassinger-Das, B., Jordan, N. C., & Dyson, N. (2015). Reading stories to learn math: Mathematics vocabulary instruction for children with early numeracy difficulties. *The Elementary School Journal, 116*(2), 242–264. https://doi.org/10.1086/683986

Hattie, J., & Timperley, H. (2007). The power of feedback. *Review of Educational Research, 77*(1), 81–112. https://doi.org/10.3102/003465430298487

Hughes, E. M., Powell, S. R., & Lee, J.-Y. (2020). Development and psychometric report of a middle school mathematics vocabulary measure. *Assessment for Effective Intervention, 45*(3), 226–234. https://doi.org/10.1177/1534508418820116

Hwang, J., Riccomini, P. J., Hwang, S. Y., & Morano, S. (2019). A systematic analysis of experimental studies targeting fractions for students with mathematics difficulties. *Learning Disabilities Research and Practice, 34*(1), 47–61. https://doi.org/10.1111/ldrp.12187

Jitendra, A. K., Lein, A. E., Im, S., Alghamdi, A. A., Hefte, S. B., & Mouanoutoua, J. (2018). Mathematical interventions for secondary students with learning disabilities and mathematics difficulties: A meta-analysis. *Exceptional Children, 84*(2), 177–196. https://doi.org/10.1177/0014402917737467

Jitendra, A. K., Nelson, G., Pulles, S. M., Kiss, A. J., & Houseworth, J. (2016). Is mathematical representation of problems an evidence-based strategy for students with mathematics difficulties? *Exceptional Children, 83*(1), 8–25. https://doi.org/10.1177/0014402915625062

Jitendra, A. K., & Star, J. R. (2011). Meeting the needs of students with learning disabilities in inclusive mathematics classrooms: The role of schema-based instruction on mathematical problem-solving. *Theory Into Practice, 50*, 12–19. https://doi.org/10.1080/00405841.2011.534912

Kim, S. A. (2017). *Culturally responsive mathematics interventions for culturally and linguistically diverse students.* In E. C. Lopez, S. G. Nahari, & S. L. Proctor (Eds.), *Handbook of multicultural school psychology: An interdisciplinary perspective* (pp. 135–156). Routledge/Taylor & Francis Group.

Kingsdorf, S., & Krawec, J. (2014). Error analysis of mathematical word problem solving across students with and without learning disabilities. *Learning Disabilities Research and Practice, 29*(2), 66–74. https://doi.org/10.1111/ldrp.12029

Krawec, J., Huang, J., Montague, M., Kressler, B., & Melia de Alba, A. (2012). The effects of cognitive strategy instruction on knowledge of math problem-solving processes of middle school students with learning disabilities. *Learning Disability Quarterly, 36*(2), 80–92. https://doi.org/10.1177/0731948712463368

Mancl, D. B., Miller, S. P., & Kennedy, M. (2012). Using the concrete-representational-abstract sequence with integrated strategy instruction to teach subtraction with regrouping to students with learning disabilities. *Learning Disabilities Research and Practice, 27*(4), 152–166. https://doi.org/10.1111/j.1540-5826.2012.00363.x

Marin, K. A. (2018). Routinizing mathematics vocabulary: The vocab grid. *Mathematics Teaching in the Middle School, 23*(7), 395–398. https://doi.org/10.5951/mathteachmiddscho.23.7.0395

Martin, R. B., Cirino, P. T., Barnes, M. A., Ewing-Cobbs, L., Fuchs, L. S., Stuebing, K. K., & Fletcher, J. M. (2013). Prediction and stability of mathematics skill and difficulty. *Journal of Learning Disabilities, 46*(5), 428–443. https://doi.org/10.1177/0022219411436214

McVancel, S. M., Missall, K. N., & Bruhn, A. L. (2018). Examining incremental rehearsal: Multiplication fluency with fifth-grade students with math IEP goals. *Contemporary School Psychology, 22*(3), 220–232. https://doi.org/10.1007/s40688-018-0178-x

Montague, M., Enders, C., & Dietz, S. (2011). Effects of cognitive strategy instruction on math problem solving of middle school students with learning disabilities. *Learning Disability Quarterly, 34*(4), 262–272. https://doi.org/10.1177/0731948711421762

Namkung, J. M., & Bricko, N. (2021). The effects of algebraic equation solving intervention for students with mathematics learning difficulties. *Journal of Learning Disabilities, 54*(2), 111–123. https://doi.org/10.1177/0022219420930814

National Center for Education Statistics. (2019). *The nation's report card.* www.nationsreportcard.gov/

National Council of Teachers of Mathematics. (2006). *Curriculum focal points for prekindergarten through Grade 8 mathematics.* Author.

National Governors Association Center for Best Practices & Council of Chief State School Officers. (2010). *Common Core State Standards mathematics.* Authors.

Nelson, G., & Powell, S. R. (2018a). A systematic review of longitudinal studies of mathematics difficulty. *Journal of Learning Disabilities, 51*(6), 523–539. https://doi.org/10.1177/0022219417714773

Nelson, G., & Powell, S. R. (2018b). Computation error analysis: Students with mathematics difficulty compared to typically achieving students. *Assessment for Effective Intervention, 43*(3), 144–156. https://doi.org/10.1177/1534508417745627

O'Shea, A., Booth, J. L., Barbieri, C., McGinn, K. M., Young, L. K., & Oyer, M. H. (2017). Algebra performance and motivation differences for students with learning disabilities and students of varying achievement levels. *Contemporary Educational Psychology, 50,* 80–96. https://doi.org/10.1016/j.cedpsych.2016.03.003

Parmar, R. S., & DeSimone, J. R. (2006). Facilitating teacher collaboration in middle school mathematics classrooms with special-needs students. In M. Montague and A. Jitendra (Eds.), *Teaching mathematics to middle school students with learning difficulties* (pp. 154–174). Guilford Press.

Peltier, C., Morin, K. L., Bouck, E. C., Lingo, M. E., Pulos, J. M., Scheffler, F. A., Suk, A., Mathews, L. A., Sinclair, T. E., & Deardorff, M. E. (2020). A meta-analysis of single-case research using mathematics manipulatives with students at risk or identified with a disability. *The Journal of Special Education, 54*(1), 3–15. https://doi.org/10.1177/0022466919844516

Peltier, C., Sinclair, T. E., Pulos, J. M., & Suk, A. (2020). Effects of schema-based instruction on immediate, generalized, and combined structured word problems. *The Journal of Special Education, 54*(2), 101–112. https://doi.org/10.1177/0022466919883397

Petersen-Brown, S., Lundberg, A. R., Ray, J. E., Dela Paz, I. N., Riss, C. L., & Panahon, C. J. (2019). Applying spaced practice in the schools to teach math vocabulary. *Psychology in the Schools, 56*(6), 977–991. https://doi.org/10.1002/pits.22248

Powell, S. R., Berry, K. A., Fall, A.-M., Roberts, G., Fuchs, L. S., & Barnes, M. A. (2021). Alternative paths to improved word-problem performance: An advantage for embedding pre-algebraic reasoning instruction within word-problem intervention. *Journal of Educational Psychology, 113*(5), 898–910. https://doi.org/10.1037/edu0000513

Powell, S. R., Berry, K. A., & Tran, L. M. (2020). Performance differences on a measure of mathematics vocabulary for English Learners and non-English Learners with and without mathematics difficulty. *Reading and Writing Quarterly: Overcoming Learning Difficulties, 36*(2), 124–141. https://doi.org/10.1080/10573569.2019.1677538

Powell, S. R., Doabler, C. T., Akinola, O., Therrien, W. J., Maddox, S. A., & Hess, K. E. (2020). A synthesis of elementary mathematics interventions: Comparisons of students with mathematics difficulty with and without comorbid reading difficulty. *Journal of Learning Disabilities, 53*(4), 244–276. https://doi.org/10.1177/0022219419881646

Powell, S. R., Driver, M. K., Roberts, G., & Fall, A.-M. (2017). An analysis of the mathematics vocabulary knowledge of third- and fifth-grade students: Connections to general vocabulary and mathematics computation. *Learning and Individual Differences, 57,* 22–32. https://doi.org/10.1016/j.lindif.2017.05.011

Powell, S. R., Fuchs, L. S., Cirino, P. T., Fuchs, D., Compton, D. L., & Changas, P. C. (2015). Effects of a multitier support system on calculation, word problem, and pre-algebraic learning among at-risk learners. *Exceptional Children, 81*(4), 443–470.

Powell, S. R., Fuchs, L. S., & Fuchs, D. (2013). Reaching the mountaintop: Addressing the Common Core Standards in mathematics for students with mathematics difficulties. *Learning Disabilities Research and Practice, 28*(1), 38–48. https://doi.org/10.1177/0014402914563702

Powell, S. R., Namkung, J. M., & Lin, X. (in press). An investigation of using keywords to solve word problems. *The Elementary School Journal.* https://doi.org/10.1086/717888

Powell, S. R., & Nelson, G. (2017). An investigation of the mathematics-vocabulary knowledge of first-grade students. *The Elementary School Journal, 117*(4), 664–686. https://doi.org/10.1086/691604

Purpura, D. J., Napoli, A. R., Wehrspann, E. A., & Gold, Z. S. (2017). Causal connections between mathematical language and mathematical knowledge: A dialogic reading intervention. *Journal of Research on Educational Effectiveness, 10*(1), 116–137. https://doi.org/10.1080/19345747.2016.1204639

Riccomini, P. J., Smith, G. W., Hughes, E. M., Fries, K. M. (2015). The language of mathematics: The importance of teaching and learning mathematical vocabulary. *Reading and Writing Quarterly, 31*(3), 235–252. https://doi.org/10.1080/10473569.2015.1030995

Riccomini, P. J., Stocker Jr., J. D., & Morano, S. (2017). Implementing an effective mathematics fact fluency practice activity. *Teaching Exceptional Children, 49*(5), 318–327. https://doi.org/10.1177/0040059916684053

Rubenstein, R. N., & Thompson, D. R. (2002). Understanding and supporting children's mathematical vocabulary development. *Teaching Children Mathematics, 9*, 107–112. https://doi.org/10.5951/tcm.9.2.0107

Satsangi, R., & Bouck, E. C. (2015). Using virtual manipulative instruction to teach the concepts of area and perimeter to secondary students with learning disabilities. *Learning Disability Quarterly, 38*(3), 174–186. https://doi.org/10.1177/0731948714550101

Satsangi, R., Bouck, E. C., Taber-Doughty, T., Bofferding, L., & Roberts, C. A. (2016). Comparing the effectiveness of virtual and concrete manipulatives to teach algebra to secondary students with learning disabilities. *Learning Disability Quarterly, 39*(4), 240–253. https://doi.org/10.1177/0731948716649754

Schumacher, R. F., Zumeta Edmonds, R., & Arden, S. V. (2017). Examining implementation of intensive intervention in mathematics. *Learning Disabilities Research and Practice, 32*(3), 189–199. https://doi.org/10.1111/ldrp.12141

Shin, M., Bryant, D. P., Bryant, B. R., McKenna, J. W., Hou, F., & Ok, M. W. (2017). Virtual manipulatives: Tools for teaching mathematics to students with learning disabilities. *Intervention in School and Clinic, 52*(3), 148–153. https://doi.org/10.1177/1053451216644830

Shumate, L., Campbell-Whatley, G. D., & Lo, Y. (2012). Infusing culturally responsive instruction to improve mathematics performance of Latino students with specific learning disabilities. *Exceptionality, 20*, 39–57. https://doi.org/10.1080/09362835.2012.640905

Stevens, E. A., Rodgers, M. A., & Powell, S. R. (2018). Mathematics interventions for upper elementary and secondary students: A meta-analysis of research. *Remedial and Special Education, 39*(6), 327–340. https://doi.org/10.1177/0741932517731887

Strickland, T. K. (2017). Using the CRA-I strategy to develop conceptual and procedural knowledge of quadratic expressions. *Teaching Exceptional Children, 49*(2), 115–125. https://doi.org/10.1177/0040059916673353

Strickland, T. K., & Maccini, P. (2012). The effects of the concrete-representational-abstract integration strategy on the ability of students with learning disabilities to multiply linear expressions within area problems. *Remedial and Special Education, 34*(3), 142–153. https://doi.org/10.1177/0741932512441712

Tournaki, N., Bae, Y. S., & Kerekes, J. (2008). Rekenrek: A manipulative used to teach addition and subtraction to students with learning disabilities. *Learning Disabilities: A Contemporary Journal, 6*(2), 41–59. https://doi.org/10.1177/00222194030360050601

van Garderen, D. (2007). Teaching students with LD to use diagrams to solve mathematical word problems. *Journal of Learning Disabilities, 40*(6), 540–553. https://doi.org/10.1177/00222194070400060501

Vukovic, R. K., Fuchs, L. S., Geary, D. C., Jordan, N. C., Gersten, R., & Siegler, R. S. (2014). Sources of individual differences in children's understanding of fractions. *Child Development, 85*(4), 1461–1476. https://doi.org/10.1111/cdev.12218

Watt, S. J., & Therrien, W. J. (2016). Examining a preteaching framework to improve fraction computation outcome among struggling learners. *Preventing School Failure, 60*(4), 311–319. https://doi.org/10.1080/1045988x.2016.1147011

Wei, X., Lenz, K. B., & Blackorby, J. (2013). Math growth trajectories of students with disabilities: Disability category, gender, racial, and socioeconomic status differences from ages 7 to 17. *Remedial and Special Education, 34*(3), 154–165. https://doi.org/10.1177/0741932512448253

Xin, Y. P. (2008). The effect of schema-based instruction in solving mathematics word problems: An emphasis on prealgebraic conceptualization of multiplicative relations. *Journal for Research in Mathematics Education, 39*(5), 526–551. http://doi.org/10.5951.jresemathceduc.39.5.0526

Xin, Y. P., & Zhang, D. (2009). Exploring a conceptual model-based approach to teaching situated word problems. *The Journal of Educational Research, 102*(6), 427–441. https://doi.org/10.3200/joer.102.6.427-442

Zhang, D., & Xin, Y. P. (2012). A follow-up meta-analysis for word-problem-solving interventions for students with mathematics difficulties. *The Journal of Educational Research, 105*, 303–318. https://doi.org/10.1080/00220671.2011.627397

12
MATHEMATICS ASSESSMENTS FOR STUDENTS EXPERIENCING MATHEMATICS DIFFICULTY

Erica S. Lembke, Jessica Rodrigues, Stacy Hirt, Jiyung Hwang, and Elizabeth R. Thomas

While assessment in education often comes under fire for taking away from instructional time (e.g., Cobb, 2003), it should be viewed as a critical component to inform instruction. Particularly for students experiencing mathematics difficulty (i.e., those who have been identified as at risk in mathematics based on academic performance or those identified with a specific learning disability in mathematics), assessment is crucial to help teachers understand areas that students have mastered and the areas in which students continue to experience difficulty. Identifying specific areas of difficulty, and providing targeted intervention, are important parts of a data-based individualization (DBI) model that has become more prominent in the literature in the last decade (e.g., Lemons et al., 2017), primarily through work done by the National Center for Intensive Intervention (NCII). DBI is a model that helps teachers intensify instruction for their students (see Figure 12.1). This intensification means that data is utilized to narrow in on specific skills, and then the current intervention is refined, modified, or adapted to improve the instructional routine for a student. Data collection continues so that teachers can see how intensification affects student learning.

Primary assessment types used in a mathematics DBI model include screening, progress monitoring, and diagnostic assessment. Figure 12.2 illustrates how the three types of assessments fit together to create a comprehensive picture of how a student is performing in mathematics. In this figure, universal screening is the overarching umbrella for identifying students at risk, and then routine progress monitoring and diagnostic assessment are paired together for documenting student response to instruction or intervention and determining what modifications are needed. Next, we discuss each of these assessment types and how they work together within a Multi-Tiered System of Supports (MTSS) framework in where DBI is used across Tiers 2 and 3 to help teachers make decisions about tier movement and intensification of instruction.

Mathematics Screening

In the DBI model, teachers can use mathematics universal screening measures to assess students' response to universal instruction, identify students who require additional support in mathematics, and provide broad information about the intensity of the supports required (Clemens et al., 2016; Ketterlin-Geller et al., 2019). Screening assessments are important because students at risk in mathematics are likely to continue to perform poorly in later years if appropriate intervention is not provided (Jordan et al., 2009). To quickly identify students who may be at risk, researchers recommend that measures be technically adequate, brief, easy to administer, and administered at regular time points during the school year (Gersten et al., 2012).

Mathematics Assessments for Students

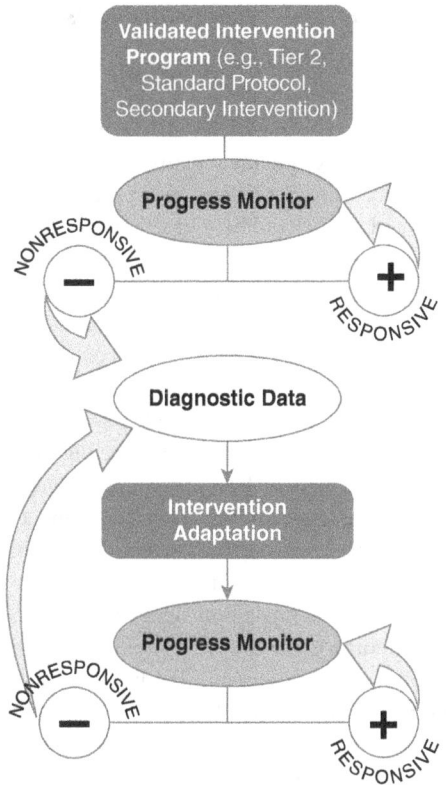

Figure 12.1 Overview of the DBI Process (NCII, 2013)

Source: National Center on Intensive Intervention [NCII]. (2013). Data-based individualization: A framework for intensive intervention. Washington, DC: Office of Special Education, U.S. Department of Education. Retrieved from www.intensiveintervention.org/sites/default/files/DBI_Framework.pdf

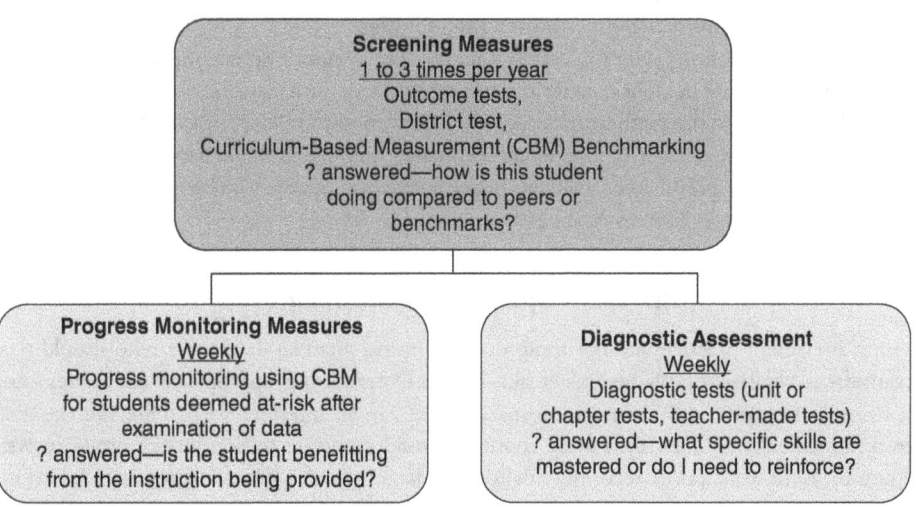

Figure 12.2 Assessments in a Mathematics DBI Model

Types of Screening Measures

Many mathematics screening measures in the primary grades focus on one of four components of numeracy: (a) strategic counting, (b) magnitude comparison, (c) retrieval of arithmetic facts, or (d) ability to solve simple word problems (Gersten et al., 2012). A reliable screening measure of arithmetic facts, for example, could be used to quickly identify students who are at risk for later difficulties related to number sense more broadly. Yet limitations of such measures include that they do not provide a full diagnostic profile and may yield lower predictive accuracy than screeners that assess a broader range of mathematics content (Geary et al., 2012).

A second approach to screening measures is to assess multiple aspects of mathematical competence rather than a measure focused on a single skill. Secondary screening measures tend to take this approach; for example, the Measures of Academic Progress (MAP) covers (a) computation and problem-solving; (b) number sense; (c) geometry; (d) measurement; (e) data, statistics, and probability; and (f) algebraic concepts (Northwest Evaluation Association, 2017). Multiple proficiency measures would theoretically give a clearer picture of mathematics performance and may have slightly higher predictive validity, but because of the range of concepts, they tend to be lengthier and less efficient (e.g., Clemens et al., 2016). Seethaler and Fuchs (2010) compared a single proficiency measure and a multiple proficiency measure in the fall and spring of kindergarten; findings suggested that both screening approaches produced similarly accurate outcomes and good predictive utility of future conceptual mathematics difficulties. Rodrigues et al. (2019) assessed the accuracy of single proficiency measures as well as multiple proficiency screeners focused on fractions for fourth-grade students. Findings supported the use of a combination of measures as the most accurate screener of risk status (Rodrigues et al., 2019). Moreover, researchers may improve the efficiency and practicality of a combination of measures by reducing the total number of items on the measure (Purpura et al., 2015; Rodrigues et al., 2019).

A third approach to screening is to align the screening measure to curriculum standards, referred to as curriculum-based assessment (CBA; Gersten et al., 2012). A type of CBA that is characterized by brief, easy administration and strong technical adequacy is curriculum-based measurement (CBM; VanDerHeyden et al., 2017). CBMs are standardized, efficient, and lend themselves well to informing instructional decisions. However, because CBMs typically sample knowledge and skills students will learn over the coming school year, scores tend to be very low initially and may lead to inaccurate classification of students as at risk (VanDerHeyden et al., 2017). The data are nevertheless valuable for showing incremental growth over a school year.

A few key considerations when selecting a technically adequate screening measure include the measure's content-related evidence, criterion-related evidence, and classification accuracy. Content-related evidence refers to the mathematics content (knowledge and skills) measured, criterion-related evidence refers to how accurately the screener predicts performance on later outcome measures (Ketterlin-Geller et al., 2019), and classification accuracy is the degree to which a screener accurately classifies students at risk (Clemens et al., 2016).

Research Gaps and Recommendations

Screening assessment practices are not foolproof, and using them to determine who should receive intervention is challenging (Klingbeil et al., 2019). Determining appropriate cut scores, single-point-in-time measures, and classification inaccuracies can all interfere with achieving the goal of screening (Clemens et al., 2016). Future research should continue to conduct rigorous analysis of screening measures to support recommendations of diagnostically accurate screeners. Additionally, researchers can explore ways of shortening screening measures to make them more efficient and practical for the classroom (e.g., Rodrigues et al., 2019). A final recommendation for future research is increased attention on the development and analysis of screeners at the secondary level.

Progress Monitoring

Monitoring of individual student academic progress has long been an important aim within the field of special education (Deno, 1985). The purpose of progress monitoring in the DBI model is to evaluate students' response to instruction on a regular basis and to provide feedback about students' performance that allows teachers to make timely and ongoing decisions about student learning (Deno, 2005; Jung et al., 2018). Specifically within the DBI model, evidence suggests that when progress monitoring is used to evaluate response to intensified intervention and instructional adaptations for students with mathematics difficulties, students show significant improvements in their mathematical performance (e.g., Stecker et al., 2008).

Types of Progress Monitoring Measures and Development of CBMs

One common tool for progress monitoring is a general outcome measurement (GOM; Deno, 1997), a formative assessment tool that evaluates a student's growth and skill development over time and reflects the student's overall competence in the annual curriculum. GOM includes CBM, which is considered a primary method of progress monitoring, as well as mastery measurement. CBM is a simple, quick, easy-to-administer, reliable, and valid set of measurement procedures that teachers can use to frequently and repeatedly measure students' growth in the foundational skills of reading, mathematics, spelling, and written expression.

In general, CBM research can be described within a three-stage continuum (Fuchs, 2004). Stage 1 research involves examining technical adequacy of measures as robust static indicators. This research focus is on the reliability and criterion validity of the measures and the extent to which scores can predict future performance or achievement (e.g., Foegen& Deno, 2001; Jitendra et al., 2014 ; Montague et al., 2010). Stage 2 research explores the technical characteristics of the slope generated by continuous progress monitoring data. Research at this stage examines the extent to which slopes are reflective of student growth in the content area (e.g., Clarke and Shinn, 2004 ; Foegen, 2000; Shapiro et al., 2005). Stage 3 research includes studies examining the instructional utility of the measures. These practical studies investigate whether teachers' instructional decisions and instruction adaptations based on their use of the measures results in improved student achievement.

Mathematics Progress Monitoring and Student Achievement

Research demonstrates that teachers' use of CBM data supports the mathematics achievement of students with and at risk for mathematics difficulties. At the elementary level, Bryant et al. (2011) examined the effects of early numeracy intervention with frequent progress monitoring for first-grade students with mathematics difficulties. Findings suggested that the students in the treatment group whose teacher made instructional adaptations based on the progress monitoring data outperformed students in the comparison group. A study conducted with middle school students with mathematics learning difficulty found that teachers' use of progress monitoring (i.e., Algebra Progress Monitoring Tool) with ongoing coaching improved students' performance on several algebra outcome measures (Powell et al, 2020). Progress monitoring has also affected positive changes in students' algebra learning at the secondary level (e.g., Foegen, 2008). Moreover, Calhoon and Fuchs (2003) examined the effects of a peer tutoring intervention and mathematics CBM to promote mathematics competence among secondary students with mathematics disabilities. The results showed that the intervention and CBM improved students' computation mathematics skills significantly more than students in the control group.

Research Gaps and Recommendations

Several gaps in the research literature regarding effective use of progress monitoring can inform directions for future research. Studies have primarily focused on Stage 1 or Stage 2, which are the prerequisite steps for conducting Stage 3. An increased focus on Stage 3 research that evaluates teachers' instructional adaptations as a function of CBM can help move the field forward by highlighting specific instructional decisions that affect students' mathematics achievement. Relatedly, only few mathematics measures (e.g., MBSP Computation, Algebra Progress Monitoring) have evidence supporting use of progress monitoring data to improve student achievement for students experiencing mathematics difficulties. Finally, while some work regarding progress monitoring tools has been conducted at the high school level (e.g., Calhoon & Fuchs, 2003), the literature would benefit from additional research that focuses on specific content domains for these upper grades such as geometry.

Diagnostic Assessment

Diagnostic measures are the glue that binds the assessment model together for a student. These measures, whether more formal or teacher developed, provide information on mathematics skills in terms of what a student has and has not mastered. Questions posed during diagnostic assessment seek to answer the following questions: Why is a student underperforming? What are the student's correct conceptualizations or understandings of the content? What are the student's persistent misconceptions and errors? What content and/or instructional design features should be included in the intervention for this student?

Types of Diagnostic Measures

Common diagnostic measures in mathematics include limited formal measures like the Diagnostic Online Mathematics Assessment (DOMA) and a more expansive list of informal measures like error analysis, interviews, teacher-made measures, quizzes, exit slips, and common formative assessments developed at the grade or district level. The DOMA (published by Let's Go Learn, Inc., via Seton Testing Services) is an online comprehensive diagnostic assessment. The DOMA-Pre-Algebra is an adaptive test that adjusts the item difficulty, item selection, and content based on students' responses to efficiently diagnose middle school students' strengths and weaknesses in 14 algebra-readiness constructs. Algebra-readiness concepts assessed align with the expectations specified by the National Council for Teachers of Math.

Informal measures like error analysis, Error analysis, for example, is one way to utilize student work samples to determine types and patterns of errors in student problem-solving. Teachers give students a small set of specific problems that focus on similar content (e.g., two-digit plus two-digit problems with regrouping) and ask the student to solve the problems on paper, as the teacher observes. The student takes as much time as they need, and for added information, the teacher might have the student talk aloud as they go through the steps in solving the problem. Following completion of the problem set, the teacher scores the items and then works to identify the error types. Error types might include slips, which are random errors, or bugs, which are persistent errors. The teacher should determine the type of error for each computation procedure, determine if it is persistent or not, and then find out why the student is making the error; augment with questions to find out why a student is making the error and under what types of questions/problems. Errors might include random responding, computation errors, lining up problems incorrectly, regrouping errors, basic fact errors, or using the wrong strategy. After the teacher determines what the error patterns are, reteaching or intervention can be applied as part of error correction, followed by working out examples of those same problem types.

Teacher-made assessments like quizzes, exit slips (short questions or problems given at the end of class to affirm mastery of content), or common formative assessments (CFAs) are part of many teachers' daily repertoire. These types of assessments are helpful, as they provide very immediate information related to the skills that were just taught. A teacher can make timely changes to instruction based on this feedback or follow up with individual students who need additional practice.

Research Gaps and Recommendations

Research on diagnostic assessments in mathematics is more limited than in the areas of screening and progress monitoring. Ketterlin-Geller and Yovanoff describe a variety of diagnostic assessments and review literature in their 2009 paper, but little work has been done to study diagnostic assessments specifically. One practical challenge with diagnostic assessments is the time that it takes to create the assessments. Other than those that are already created (like the DOMA), most diagnostic assessments are teacher created. Many districts have teacher teams spend hours in the summer to create common formative assessments that are aligned with the district grade-level mathematics standards. Or school teams create assessments that can be used for each mathematics unit. Individual teachers might develop the quizzes and exit slips that align with their mathematics units. Creation of diagnostic assessments can be time consuming, and more research could be done to identify less time-consuming methods of development.

Another research gap that could be examined related to diagnostic assessments is making certain that administration, scoring, and usage are consistent. If assessments are not administered in the same way each time, with the same time limitations and same directions, results will vary as a result of the assessment rather than as a result of student performance. Data analysis can also be a challenge. If teams or individual teachers are collecting the data but are not entering the data and visually examining it during their meetings, the utility of the data might be lost.

However, if these challenges can be overcome, the information diagnostic data can provide a critical link in determining next steps to intensify instruction for individual students.

Using Assessment Data to Inform Decisions

Using the assessment data collected to problem-solve about student concerns in data teams is perhaps one of the most important steps in the DBI process (McMaster et al., 2020). Following several weeks of intervention implementation and data collection, a team of administrators, educators, and special services personnel meet to discuss each student's progression. While collecting data is important, using the data is most critical. Too often, data are collected, but then never utilized.

Individual teachers can look at a student's progress monitoring data to make decisions about how the student is progressing, but meeting with colleagues or in small teams is a much more effective and collaborative approach. As teams meet (either grade-level teams, content teams, or school-wide teams), they discuss student progress by examining graphed data, what instruction and intervention are currently occurring, and whether a change needs to be made. A change in instruction might be warranted, if, for example, the trend of a student's data is falling below the goal line that was set utilizing the end-of-year benchmarks or norms. The team then determines what type of instructional change should be made. This might be a slight refinement of the current programming or a more substantive change. This is the point at which intensification of intervention might occur. The team discusses the evidence that supports potential changes, who will support the teacher as he or she makes this change, and when the team will reconvene to discuss a student's response to the intervention.

Decision-making typically involves comparing the student's progress monitoring data trend to the goal that was set as a result of initial screening. Following a minimum of four weeks of weekly data collection, graphed data are visually examined. If the trend of the student's progress monitoring data is below the goal line, an instructional change is needed. If the trend of the data is the same as the goal or very similar, the current instructional routine is continued. If the trend of the data is above the goal line, the current instruction is continued, but if this positive trend continues, the level of support or intensification of the intervention can be lessened over time. This decision-making process continues throughout the year as the teacher implements the DBI process with each student.

Case Example

This section illustrates the DBI process and mathematics assessments in a contextualized action research case study. Specifically, the case study examines the DBI model, mathematics assessments, and instructional decisions for a graduate student implementing action research for a student with intensive mathematics needs.

Mrs. Smith

Mrs. Smith is a sixth-grade pre-algebra teacher at Rock Middle School in a large suburban community in the Midwest. Mrs. Smith is taking a graduate-level course in mathematics assessment at the local university. One of her course assignments is to implement an action research project investigating assessment practices (i.e., screeners, progress monitoring, and diagnostic assessments) for a student in her sixth-grade classroom experiencing mathematics difficulties.

Mrs. Smith decides to screen all students in her sixth-grade class with a district universal screener (i.e., STAR Math) to identify those at risk for or with mathematics difficulties. She plans to use the universal screening data to drive decision-making. When analyzing the data, she asks:

- Are any students at risk or underperforming?
- Which students need interventions?
- What degree of intensity of intervention is needed?

Mrs. Smith understands that universal screening data are not intended to provide diagnostic information. When interpreting universal screeners, she knows that when assessment scores go down, the risk for difficulty in mathematics goes up.

Mrs. Smith analyzes the universal screening data and identifies three students in need of intervention based on their scores on the screening and how these scores compare to the national norms for STAR. She notes that none of the students are currently receiving specialized instruction through an individual education plan (IEP). After further examination, she determines that one student may be in need of intensive intervention. This student not only has screening data that places her at risk compared to peer data at this time point but for the previous two screening points. In addition, it appears that this student has been receiving some progress monitoring for the past few months and that the trajectory of progress monitoring scores compared to her goal is low.

Mrs. Smith shares deidentified student data with her mathematics assessment course instructor to help her select a student who would be a good fit for her action research project. Mrs. Smith's instructor agrees that the screener identifies three students with or at risk of a mathematics difficulty. The instructor encourages her to pilot the action research mathematical assessments with a student with consistent attendance and positive behavior in order to specifically focus on academics.

Mrs. Smith narrows her student participant to a sixth-grade female student (Taylor) exhibiting mathematics difficulty according to the district-wide universal STAR diagnostic screening

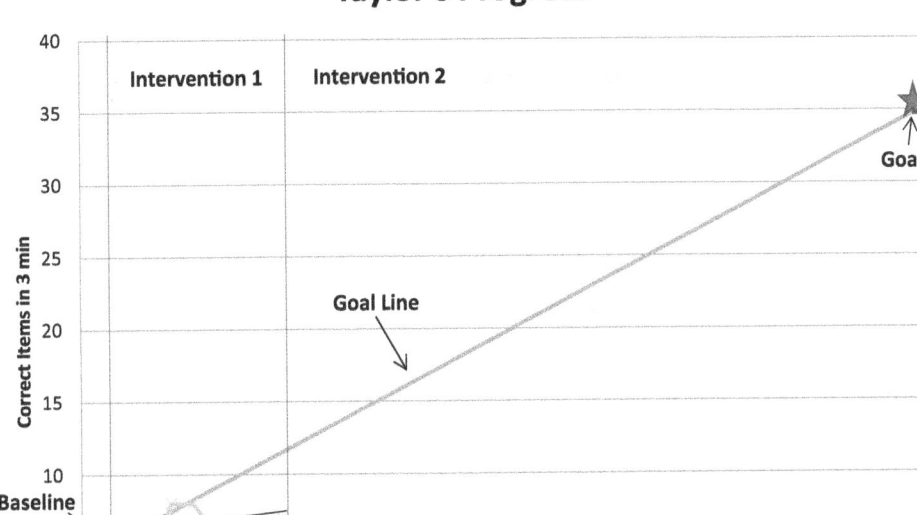

Figure 12.3 Implementing DBI Step 1 and Step 2

Note. This figure represents baseline data utilizing a validated curriculum-based measurement (CBM) (i.e., computerized system) (Step 1), an identified goal based on baseline benchmark(s) (Step 2).

assessment tool. For the past three months in Mrs. Smith's mathematics class, Taylor has been a part of a small group that is receiving additional practice on a validated, computer-based intervention three times per week for 20 minutes each session.

When reflecting and discussing Taylor's case history, Mrs. Smith considered the following guiding questions:

- What are Taylor's academic challenges?
- What academic interventions has Taylor received?
- What are Taylor's academic outcomes after she received the academic interventions?

Mrs. Smith then uses the five key steps to implementing DBI to guide her in the decision-making process (Figure 12.1).

First, Mrs. Smith establishes that a Tier 2 validated intervention program is in place (Step 1). Second, she selects a progress monitoring assessment that will provide frequent assessment data (Step 2). Mrs. Smith decides that Taylor will complete a weekly algebra progress monitoring measure on the computer. She sets a goal for Taylor using established benchmarks from the computerized system and the median baseline score (Figure 12.3). Mrs. Smith then graphs weekly scores and examines the data to see if Taylor is benefiting from the instruction and intervention being delivered.

After two 8-week cycles of data collection, Mrs. Smith is ready to make decisions based on Taylor's responses to the intervention (Step 3; Figure 12.4). She finds that Taylor's progress is suggesting nonresponsiveness to the intervention efforts based on the decision-making rules.

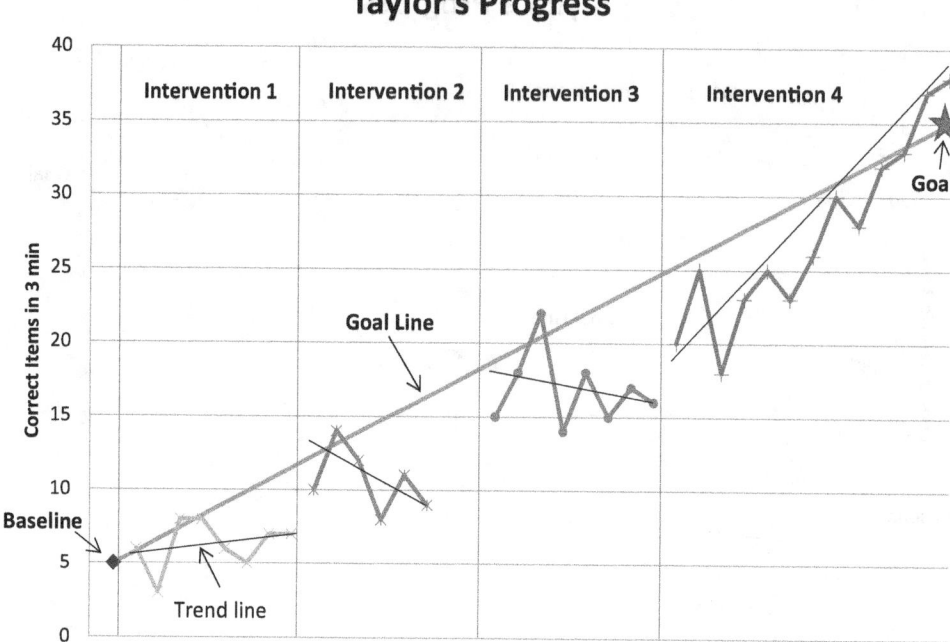

Figure 12.4 Implementing DBI Steps 3, 4, and 5

Note. This figure represents decisions based on responses to the intervention(s) and instructional changes based on the student's response to the intervention Included are the ongoing progress monitoring data points (Step 3), and trend lines based on the data points (Step 4).

Mrs. Smith's decision-making rule for these data is that if the trend of the data is below the goal line after six to eight data points, she will implement an instructional change. Mrs. Smith moves to the next steps in the process. She has learned in her mathematics assessment coursework to base decision-making on student responsiveness. Based on the progress monitoring data, Mrs. Smith will either:

1. Continue the Tier 2 program with progress monitoring;
2. Collect diagnostic data;

Given that Taylor has not been responsive to Tier 2 instruction, Mrs. Smith knows that she needs to make a change in the intervention she is providing. Her first step is to collect some additional diagnostic data to determine where Taylor's skill deficits are. She might use the DOMA or conduct a math interview, for instance, to determine where patterns are. She might also use error analysis from Taylor's work samples.

Based on the error analysis from Taylor's recent work samples and her patterns of errors on the computerized progress monitoring, Mrs. Smith determines that she needs to build in more fluency practice using fractions and also incorporate fraction practice using visual representations (Step 4). Mrs. Smith decides to try to deliver this to Taylor and a small group of other students during the 20-minute intervention time instead of the computerized instruction.

Mrs. Smith continues to monitor Taylor's progress (Step 5) and continues to use her decision-making rules. She compares the trend line to the goal line and makes a change in intervention as needed. As the end of the school year approaches, Taylor's progress indicates that she is on track and has exceeded her goal line for two data points. Mrs. Smith will think about program needs to be put in place when considering Taylor's instruction for seventh grade.

In summary, the case study provides a sample of one teacher's progress through the steps of the DBI model to intensify instruction for Taylor. Using the three mathematics assessment types discussed in this chapter equipped Mrs. Smith with critical data to inform instructional decisions.

Future Research and Practical Implications

While the research on mathematics assessment for students who are at risk has expanded considerably in the past two decades, there are still areas of need both in terms of research and practical implications. First, there is still work to be done to determine best practices for mathematics assessment at the secondary level. There is less research on mathematics universal screening measures and practices in secondary grades in the United States; however in a survey of response to intervention (RTI) practices, 90% of middle schools reported using universal screening data in mathematics, suggesting this is an area where further study is needed (Prewett et al., 2012). Klingbeil et al. (2019) conducted a screening study in a large middle school and found that a cost-effective approach that maintains diagnostic accuracy is to use the preceding year's state test scores with locally determined cut points. Taken with previous research on the viability of using these data as a screening measure and the lack of broadly available, technically adequate, secondary screening measures, the use of local cut scores warrants future research (Nelson et al., 2016; VanDerHeyden et al., 2017).

Continuing to inform district and building leadership about mathematics assessments, how to select them, and best practices in implementation should be a focus. District decisions about assessments affect all classrooms, teachers, and most importantly, students. Administrators should be provided the information and resources they need to make the best possible decisions.

Given the changes that have occurred in educational delivery and demands on teachers since the COVID pandemic, additional consideration should be given to the development of high-quality measures that can be administered in a timely fashion via computer or web technology. Screening, progress monitoring, and diagnostic assessments readily available to be administered via web technology will be a time saver for teachers and will allow for flexibility when time does not allow for paper-based administration. Particularly in secondary settings, this is important, as many of our students with intensive mathematics needs are receiving a great portion of their instruction in general education classrooms. So having tools that are easy to access will provide a greater opportunity for teachers to continue to assess these students and use the data in a timely manner.

As we consider the different modes of assessment in mathematics and how this is integrated with instruction, intervention, and intensification, continued support needs to be provided for teachers to navigate all of the information they have available. Data-based individualization should be at the forefront of support that teachers receive.

References

Bryant, D. P., Bryant, B. R., Roberts, G., Vaughn, S., Pfannenstiel, K. H., Porterfield, J., & Gersten, R. (2011). Early numeracy intervention program for first-grade students with mathematics difficulties. *Exceptional Children, 78*(1), 7–23. https://doi.org/10.1177/001440291107800101

Calhoon, M. B., & Fuchs, L. S. (2003). The effects of peer-assisted learning strategies and curriculum-based measurement on the mathematics performance of secondary students with disabilities. *Remedial and Special Education, 24*(4), 235–245. https://doi.org/10.1177/07419325030240040601

Clarke, B., & Shinn, M. R. (2004). A preliminary investigation into the identification and development of early mathematics curriculum-based measurement. *School Psychology Review, 33*, 234–248. https://doi.org/10.1080/02796015.2004.12086245

Clemens, N. H., Keller-Margulis, M. A., Scholten, T., & Yoon, M. (2016). Screening assessment within a multi-tiered system of support: Current practices, advances, and next steps. In Handbook of response to intervention (pp. 187–213). Springer. https://doi.org/10.1007/978-1-4899-7568-3_12

Cobb, C. (2003). Effective instruction begins with purposeful assessments. *The Reading Teacher, 57*(4), 386.

Deno, S. L. (1985). Curriculum-based measurement: The emerging alternative. *Exceptional Children, 52*, 219–232. https://doi.org/10.1177/001440298505200303

Deno, S. L. (1997). Whether thou goest . . . Perspectives on progress monitoring. In J. W. Lloyd, E. J. Kameenui, & D. Chard (Eds.), *Issues in educating students with disabilities* (pp. 77–99). Erlbaum.

Deno, S. L. (2005). Problem-solving assessment. In R. Chidsey-Brown (Ed.), *Problem-solving based assessment for education intervention* (pp. 10–38). New York, NY: Guilford Press.

Foegen, A. (2000). Technical adequacy of general outcome measures for middle school mathematics. *Diagnostique, 25*, 175–203. https://doi.org/10.1177/073724770002500301

Foegen, A. (2008). Algebra progress monitoring and interventions for students with learning disabilities. *Learning Disability Quarterly, 31*(2), 65–78. https://doi.org/10.2307/20528818

Foegen, A., & Deno, S. L. (2001). Identifying growth indicators for low-achieving students in middle school mathematics. *The Journal of Special Education, 35*, 4–16. https://doi.org/10.1177/002246690103500102

Fuchs, L. S. (2004). The past, present, and future of curriculum-based measurement research. *School Psychology Review, 33*(2), 188–192. https://doi.org/10.1080/02796015.2004.12086241

Geary, D. S., Hoard, M. K., Nugent, L., & Bailey, D. H. (2012). Mathematical cognition deficits in children with learning disabilities and persistent low achievement: A five-year prospective study. *Journal of Educational Psychology, 104*(1), 206–223. https://doi.org/10.1037/a0025398

Gersten, R., Clarke, B., Jordan, N. C., Newman-Gonchar, R., Haymond, K., & Wilkins, C. (2012). Universal screening in mathematics for the primary grades: Beginnings of a research base. *Exceptional Children, 78*(4), 423–445. https://doi.org/10.1177/001440291207800403

Jitendra, A. K., Dupuis, D. N., & Zaslofsky, A. F. (2014). Curriculum-based measurement and standards-based mathematics: Monitoring the arithmetic word problem-solving performance of third-grade students at risk for mathematics difficulties. *Learning Disability Quarterly, 37*(4), 241–251. https://doi.org/10.1177/0731948713516766

Jordan, N. C., Kaplan, D., Ramineni, C., & Locuniak, M. N. (2009). Early math matters: Kindergarten number competence and later mathematics outcomes. *Developmental Psychology, 45*(3), 850. https://doi.org/10.1037/a0014939

Jung, P. G., McMaster, K. L., Kunkel, A. K., Shin, J., & Stecker, P. M. (2018). Effects of data-based individualization for students with intensive learning needs: A meta-analysis. *Learning Disabilities Research & Practice, 33*(3), 144–155. https://doi.org/10.1111/ldrp.12172

Ketterlin-Geller, L. R., Shivraj, P., Basaraba, D., & Schielack, J. (2019). Universal screening for algebra readiness in middle school: Why, what, and does it work? *Investigations in Mathematics Learning, 11*(2), 120–133. https://doi.org/10.1080/19477503.2017.1401033

Ketterlin-Geller, L. R., & Yovanoff, P. (2009). Diagnostic assessments in mathematics to support instructional decision making. *Practical Assessment, Research, and Evaluation, 14*(1), 16.

Klingbeil, D. A., Maurice, S. A., Van Norman, E. R., Nelson, P. M., Birr, C., Hanrahan, A. R., . . . Lopez, A. L. (2019). Improving mathematics screening in middle school. *School School Psychology Review, 48*(4), 383–398. https://doi.org/10.17105/SPR-2018-0084.V48-4

Lemons, C. J., Sinclair, A. C., Gesel, S., Gruner Gandhi, A., & Danielson, L. (2017). *Supporting implementation of data-based individualization: Lessons learned from NCII's first five years*. National Center on Intensive Intervention.

McMaster, K. L., Lembke, E. S., Shin, J., Poch, A. L., Smith, R. A., Jung, P.-G., Allen, A. A., & Wagner, K. (2020). Supporting teachers' use of data-based instruction to improve students' early writing skills. *Journal of Educational Psychology, 112*(1), 1–21. https://doi.org/10.1037/edu0000358.

Montague, M., Penfield, R. D., Enders, C., & Huang, J. (2010). Curriculum-based measurement of math problem solving: A methodology and rationale for establishing equivalence of scores. *Journal of School Psychology, 48*(1), 39–52. https://doi.org/10.1016/j.jsp.2009.08.002

National Center on Intensive Intervention [NCII]. (2013). *Data-based individualization: A framework for intensive intervention*. Office of Special Education, U.S. Department of Education. www.intensiveintervention.org/sites/default/files/DBI_Framework.pdf

Nelson, P. M., Van Norman, E. R., & Lackner, S. K. (2016). A comparison of methods to screen middle school students for reading and math difficulties. *School Psychology Review, 45*(3), 327–342. https://doi.org/10.17105/spr45-3.327-342

Northwest Evaluation Association. (2017). *Linking the Wisconsin Forward Exam to NWEA MAP tests*. www.nwea.org/resources/wisconsin-linking-study/

Powell, S. R., Lembke, E. S., Ketterlin-Geller, L. R., Petscher, Y., Hwang, J., Bos, S. E., . . . Hopkins, S. (2020). Data-based individualization in mathematics to support middle school teachers and their students with mathematics learning difficulty. *Studies in Educational Evaluation, 69,* 100897. https://doi.org/10.1016/j.stueduc.2020.100897

Prewett, S., Mellard, D. F., Deshler, D. D., Allen, J., Alexander, R., & Stern, A. (2012). Response to intervention in middle schools: Practices and outcomes. *Learning Disabilities Research & Practice, 27*(3), 136–147. https://doi.org/10.1111/j.1540-5826.2012.00359.x

Purpura, D. J., Reid, E. E., Eiland, M. D., & Baroody, A. J. (2015). Using a brief preschool early numeracy skills screener to identify young children with mathematics difficulties. *School Psychology Review, 44*(1), 41–59. https://doi.org/10.17105/SPR44-1.41-59

Rodrigues, J., Jordan, N. C., & Hansen, N. (2019). Identifying fraction measures as screeners of mathematics risk status. *Journal of Learning Disabilities, 52*(6), 480–497. https://doi.org/10.1177/0022219419879684

Seethaler, P. M., & Fuchs, L. S. (2010). The predictive utility of kindergarten screening for math difficulty. *Exceptional Children, 77*(1), 37–59. https://doi.org/10.1177/001440291007700102

Shapiro, E. S., Edwards, L., & Zigmond, N. (2005). Progress monitoring of mathematics among students with learning disabilities. *Assessment for Effective Intervention, 30*(2), 15–32. https://doi.org/10.1177/073724770503000203

Stecker, P. M., Fuchs, D., & Fuchs, L. S. (2008). Progress monitoring as essential practice within response to intervention. *Rural Special Education Quarterly, 27*(4), 10–17. https://doi.org/10.1177/875687050802700403

VanDerHeyden, A. M., Codding, R. S., & Martin, R. (2017). Relative value of common screening measures in mathematics. *School Psychology Review, 46*(1), 65–87. https://doi.org/10.1080/02796015.2017.12087608

13
EVIDENCE-BASED, CULTURALLY RESPONSIVE INTERVENTIONS TO IMPROVE ACADEMIC OUTCOMES FOR ENGLISH LEARNERS WITH READING DIFFICULTIES

Catherine Richards-Tutor and Emily J. Solari

Inequities in our schools and school systems have long existed. It is well documented that students with disabilities, students of color, and students who are culturally and linguistically diverse, including English learners, suffer the greatest inequities in our schools (Office of Civil Rights, 2016). The COVID-19 pandemic that has affected and continues to affect schools has highlighted these inequities, and students with disabilities who are culturally and linguistically diverse are likely to have suffered some of the greatest losses in services due to lack of opportunities for quality instruction, technology, and other resources, such as parents being home to support their instruction (Council of the Great City Schools, 2020). Existing evidence suggests that students with disabilities require direct and explicit instruction in content areas, and they also require intensive instruction, meaning that the quantity and dosage of instructional time are important. The pandemic has made it difficult for teachers to adequately address the instructional needs of these students.

The English learner population is one that largely lives in poverty; recent data suggest that 60% of English learners live below federal guidelines for poverty; recent data also suggest that the COVID-19 pandemic has exacerbated these conditions (Center for American Progress, 2021). Further, the nation is experiencing a reckoning with deep-rooted racism, which while important and necessary, burdens marginalized students, like English learners, and their families differentially (Syetaz et al., 2020). It is to this end that we suggest the importance of considering how teachers and other school practitioners can implement culturally responsive and sustaining teaching practices in conjunction with evidence-based practices for reading instruction.

Legal and professional standards have established the importance of evidence-based instruction for all children with special needs, including those with identified disabilities and who are categorized as English learners (IDEA, 2004; Council for Exceptional Children, 2015). However, the research base on how to serve this group—children who are both English learners and identified as having a reading disability or reading difficulties—is not particularly robust. The number of studies that demonstrate efficacy in instruction approaches specific to English learners with disabilities compared to non-English learners is relatively small.

This chapter proposes that special education researchers and practitioners consider how academic interventions specific to reading could be implemented rigorously while also implementing culturally responsive teaching practices, thus garnering more effective interventions for English learners. We situate the discussion throughout the chapter within the Multi-Tiered Systems of Support (MTSS) model, specifically centering on Tier 2 and Tier 3 interventions. First, we outline the current state of academic achievement and instructional practices for English learners. Next, we review the most recent research (the past five years) that has implemented evidence-based reading interventions with English learners who have reading difficulties and describe the key tenets of culturally responsive teaching practices and how these can overlay elements of effective intervention for English learners with reading difficulties. Finally, we share recent work out of the Office of Special Education Model Demonstration Projects that incorporates both evidence-based reading intervention and culturally responsive and sustaining practices. The chapter ends with implications for practice and future research.

Current State of Academic Achievement and Practice for English Learners

Approximately 5 million students in the United States are English learners, and of these 3.8 million identify as Hispanic—over 76.5% (USDE, 2020). The most prevalent language spoken by English learners is Spanish, with 74.8% reporting it as their home language. Nationally, 10% of the students who receive special education services are also English learners (National Council on Disabilities, 2018), although this varies widely by state. For example, in California, 23% of students were English learners in 2015–2016, but 31% of English learners are identified as having a disability; in West Virginia only 7 % of students who are English learners also receive special education services.

Further, national-level data suggest that current practices are not improving reading outcomes for English learners and English learners who have disabilities. The existing data suggest that compared to their peers, these students perform significantly worse on reading-related measures across grade levels (Solari et al., 2014). Recent national-level data (NAEP, 2019) indicate that only 10% of English learners scored proficient in fourth-grade reading as compared to 39% of non-English learners, and in eighth grade, 4% of English learners are proficient compared to 36% of non-English learners. The discrepancy in reading achievement between English learners and non-English learners has not increased in recent years, but, importantly, our instructional efforts in schools have *not* decreased this achievement gap over the past three decades. For students with disabilities, these gaps are similar. In fourth grade just 12% of students with disabilities are proficient in reading compared to 39% of students without disabilities, and in eighth grade a similar pattern exists with 9% proficient compared to 37% of students without disabilities. Similarly, for students with disabilities, we are not making progress toward closing the achievement gap.

The majority of English learners in U.S. schools have been served through our school systems since kindergarten and yet are not considered to be proficient in English. These students are often designated as "long-term English learners" (LTELs), and as we develop practices and consider academic outcomes, we must think about the needs of these students, many of whom are in our secondary schools (Hanover Research, 2017). In California, 82% of English learners in secondary schools are LTELs. Typically, these students are fully bilingual and have mastered spoken English; however, their academic literacy skills are not as well developed (Hanover Research). Data have indicated that LTELs have particularly poor trajectories, such as graduation rates well below non-English learners and English learners who have become proficient (Huang et al., 2016). For example, in Arizona, only 49% of LTELs graduated from high school, while their peers graduated at a rate of 85% for non-English learners, 81% for long-term proficient English learners, and 67% for recently redesignated English learners. For these English learners, the opportunity gaps are wide and often have been further hampered by current practices used in schools. Research suggests that LTEL often do not receive the English language supports necessary, at times receive a narrowed curriculum that does not provide the full range of subject matter, and are enrolled in inappropriate courses because of misidentified or unidentified learning disabilities (Huang et al.). While little data exist on LTELs who have disabilities, we know that there are confounding factors that may create further opportunity gaps and therefore greater academic achievement gaps.

Current State of Intervention Research

In this section we review the current state of intervention research for English learners with reading difficulties and disabilities. We highlight the intervention research for English learners that has been conducted over the last five years, focusing on reviews of the literature, randomized control trials, quasi-experimental designs, and single-subject studies. Next, we discuss the tenets of culturally responsive and sustaining pedagogies (CRSPs) and how these tenets can overlay the elements of effective intervention. Finally, we share work from the model demonstration projects that focus on MTSS for English learners that aligns effective intervention with CRSP.

Effective Intervention Practices to Support English Learners

Several empirical studies and meta-analyses have shown that reading interventions that align with the scientifically based reading instruction have a positive impact on students who are English learners with reading difficulties (e.g., Baker et al., 2018; Richards-Tutor et al., 2015). These reviews indicated that systematic, explicit reading intervention in small groups for about 20 to 40 minutes a day is effective. However, these reviews provide less clarity, given the small number of studies and variations across studies, regarding the specific content of the intervention (i.e., prepackaged intervention vs. researcher developed, include all reading skills vs. just one or two). While previous reviews of the literature have indicated that explicit instruction for English learners in early reading skills generally yield improvement in known skills necessary for early reading success (e.g. phonemic awareness, phonics, and reading fluency), relatively few studies attend to students' growth on vocabulary and reading comprehension (Baker et al.; Ludwig et al.; Richards-Tutor et al., 2015; Richards-Tutor et al., 2016). While we know the importance of the foundational reading skills, we also know that vocabulary development and reading comprehension are critical aspects for English learners' overall academic achievement.

Reviews of the literature have also noted that the majority of intervention studies focus on younger English learners in kindergarten through about third grade, with relatively few studies focused on students at the upper elementary and secondary levels (Baker et al., 2018; Ludwig et al., 2019; Richards-Tutor et al., 2015). The lack of existing reading intervention research at the secondary level is concerning, as we know that the overall goal of reading is for students to comprehend what they read, not just to read words efficiently and accurately. More research is needed to better understand the full developmental trajectory of reading comprehension development for English learners, from preschool to adolescents and adulthood.

In our search for research articles published in the last five years (2015–2020) that focused on reading interventions for English learners, we found 20 peer-reviewed studies. Of the 20 intervention studies, only 4 met our criteria >50% English learners and at least two measures of reading (Baker et al., 2016; Castro-Olivo et al., 2018; Vaughn et al., 2016; Williams & Vaughn, 2019). Only two of these four met the criteria of one positive effect size. We highlight the four studies (Baker et al., 2016; Vaughn et al., 2016; Williams & Vaughn, 2019) in Table 13.1. In the following section we discuss specific features from these four intervention studies and features from some of the

Table 13.1 Intervention Studies 2015–2020

Study	Participant Description	Methodology	Intervention	Literacy Skills Included	Critical Teaching Methods	Instructional Features for English Learners	Outcomes Effect Size
Baker et al., 2016	First grade, Spanish or dual whole-group instruction, 100% Spanish-speaking English learners, below benchmark in pseudo-word reading and oral reading fluency (ORF)	Rank-ordered then randomly assigned	Transition lessons, project developed, 30 minutes, five days per week for 12 weeks	PA, phonics, word reading, vocabulary, sentence reading	Explicit instruction, scaffolding, multiple opportunities to respond, corrective feedback,	Making explicit what is transferrable and not transferable from English to Spanish, explicit instruction in academic language to facilitate learning of skills	Nonsense word reading ORF Reading achievement Bilingual verbal ability Proximal reading measures Effects sizes not reported, no significant differences between groups for any measures
Castro-Olivo et al., 2018	Kindergarten, Three English learners, Spanish-speaking (N = 3)	Multiple baseline, single subject	First steps to success (behavior component), culturally adapted plus direct instruction literacy, three days per week 20 minutes	Oral language/vocabulary, PA, phonics	Model-lead-test	Teacher training on best practices for working with Latino families using ecology validity model, student interactions took place in a bilingual or Spanish setting depending on preference.	Phoneme Segmentation (DIBELS) Nonsense Word Reading (DIBELS), Effect sizes not reported. Small to modest gains were made on NWF

(Continued)

Table 13.1 (Continued)

Study	Participant Description	Methodology	Intervention	Literacy Skills Included	Critical Teaching Methods	Instructional Features for English Learners	Outcomes Effect Size
Vaughn et al., 2016	Ninth and tenth graders far below grade level in reading, 89% English learners, 12% special education,	RCT	Reading Intervention for Adolescents (RIA)	REWARDS Secondary and collaborative strategic reading, word study, fluency, vocabulary, comprehension (with three semesters focused on vocabulary and comprehension)	Explicit instruction, collaborative reading, strategy instruction	Collaboration and interaction, focus on academic vocabulary, connection to content area learning	Word Reading (TOWRE) Sight Word = −0.02 Phonemic decoding = 0.06 Vocabulary (GMRT-4 = 0.00; proximal = 0.41) Comprehension (GMRT-4 = −0.9 and TOS-REC = 0.18)
Williams & Vaughn, 2019	Ninth-grade English learners with learning disabilities	RCT-4 groups RIA, RIA+DO, DO only, or BAU	RIA	REWARDS secondary and collaborative strategic reading, word study, fluency, vocabulary, comprehension (with three semesters focused on vocabulary and comprehension)	Explicit instruction, collaborative reading, strategy instruction, science and SS topics	Collaboration and interaction, focus on academic vocabulary, connection to content area learning	Word Reading (TOWRE) Sight Word = 0.08 Phonemic decoding = 0.18 Vocabulary (GMRT-4 = −0.10; proximal = 0.41*) Comprehension (GMRT-4 = 0.02) and TOS-REC = 0.14)

studies that did not meet our criteria but that we see as potentially useful in designing interventions for English learners.

The results of the four studies that met our criteria did not positively affect standardized measures of reading achievement. Despite this, there are valuable lessons to be learned from these studies. The first is that in the Baker et al. (2016), Vaughn et al. (2016), and Williams and Vaughn (2019) studies, researchers used proximal, researcher-developed measures of reading as well as more distal standardized measures. While in the Baker study there were not significant differences on the proximal measures, the intervention was relatively short in duration, and therefore the dosage of the intervention may not have been sufficient to detect improvement in reading scores. In the Vaughn et al. study and the Williams and Vaughn study, the intervention did affect student growth on the proximal measure of vocabulary. The use of more proximal measures that are more closely aligned with intervention content is helpful to understanding if the intervention is effective.

It is encouraging to see that there were several studies conducted with older students in the past five years given that many of our secondary English learners are LTELs and have different needs than English learners in the lower grades. Of the 20 studies we initially found 11 were conducted with students fourth grade and older. In the studies in Table 13.1, two involve high school students: the Vaughn et al. study and Williams and Vaughn study. As stated previously, results indicated that students only made growth on the proximal measure of vocabulary. Both studies used collaborative strategic reading as the base for the intervention. While the gains were small on reading measures beyond the proximal vocabulary measure, interventions that combine elements of direct instruction and collaborative peer learning may be prove to be effective intervention elements for English learners.

Another potential addition to interventions for English learners is motivational strategies. In the initial search for studies to include in this review, there were several studies that examined motivation to read (e.g., Barber et al., 2015; Toste et al., 2019). While positive reinforcement is a motivational strategy and a hallmark of explicit instruction practices, it would behoove us to think critically about other motivational strategies that engage students in intervention in ways that are meaningful to them. Of course, motivating topics are useful, and we may want to look at social studies and science curricula to help us determine engaging topics (e.g., Barber et al.). We may also consider type of texts, hands-on learning approaches, and working collaboratively as motivational strategies.

Using Culturally Responsive and Sustaining Practices in Intervention

The majority of intervention practices used in these studies, and intervention studies in general, are grounded in cognitive and behavioral theories of learning (e.g., Skinner, Bandura). Elements of sociocultural theories of learning are also relevant to student achievement (Vygotsky, 1978). Language and culture are important tenets of sociocultural theories of learning; however, this theory and these tenets have not been used widely to develop academic interventions or used often in research with students with disabilities. Culturally responsive and sustaining pedagogies (Ladson-Billings, 1995; Gay, 2000; Paris, 2012) as a framework are grounded in sociocultural theories and have the potential to provide the special education field with additional insight and guidance in the development of reading interventions, particularly for English learners. CRSP is not a set or checklist of practices that teachers "do," but a body of beliefs and values about teaching and learning and about students, families, and communities (Howard, 2020). CRSP encourages and supports teachers to value students' cultural and linguistic resources and see these as assets or capital to build from, all the while emphasizing increased student academic achievement (Howard, 2020). One important element of CRSP is that student experiences, prior knowledge, and interest are utilized to support instruction, rather than concentrating on child-level deficits or difficulties. CRSP (as well as sociocultural theory in general) posits that culture influences a child's learning, development, and cognition, and therefore culture should inform

Table 13.2 Critical Features of Culturally Responsive Teaching

Feature	Description	Relevance to Interventions
Instructional engagement	Engaging students by using students' culture, home language, and lived experiences.	Using students' home language during intervention to build connections between home language and English; collaborative pairs or groups that are carefully selected considering students' strengths.
Cultural, language, and racial identity	Culture, language, and race shape students' identity and affect learning.	Providing students responsive feedback in a way that considers their cultural and linguistic preferences.
Multicultural awareness	Critical reflection of one's own identity, cultural values, beliefs, and biases providing greater self-awareness and therefore greater awareness of others.	Modeling and observing is a practice for teaching and learning in many cultures; reflect on intervention instruction frequently to examine student response and any unconscious bias in intervention delivery or feedback or decisions.
High expectations	Communicating clear and specific expectations to students and belief that all students are capable of learning.	Provide necessary scaffolds to ensure students meet expectations; provide students supports in home language and point out similarities and differences between home language and English.
Critical thinking	Integrating higher-order thinking and critical inquiry with student cultural and linguistic experiences.	Balance teaching of basic reading skills with higher-level comprehension skills and vocabulary depth of development; allow students to further explore key vocabulary and the main ideas of passages that are directly relevant to their lives and communities.
Social justice	Foster student agency through accessing cultural capital and identifying structural inequities.	Materials and text tied to students' cultures and their communities and reflect the diverse student population of the school; use an interest inventory to get student input and their interests in topics for text and materials.

Source: (Aceves & Orosco, 2014)

instructional practices (Hammond, 2014). Teaching through a culturally relevant lens has the potential to "empower students intellectually, socially, emotionally, and politically by using cultural referents to impart knowledge, skills, and attitudes" (Ladson-Billings, 1994, p. 19). There are several key features of CRSP. Table 13.2 provides each feature, a definition, and a description of how this feature is relevant to intervention. Aceves and Orosco (2014) describe each of these elements in more detail and also provide information on the evidence base of these features.

Conceptualizing the tenets of CRSP as pedagogical principles that overlie explicit instruction used in Tier 2 and Tier 3 interventions may prove useful in our ability to adapt and modify current interventions and develop new ones that meet the academic needs of English learners (see Figure 13.1). If the school systems, school site, and individual teachers and staff understand the school community, consider individual student strengths and preferences related to culture and language, and build connections with their students, this will permeate all tiers of instruction and

Evidence-Based, Culturally Responsive

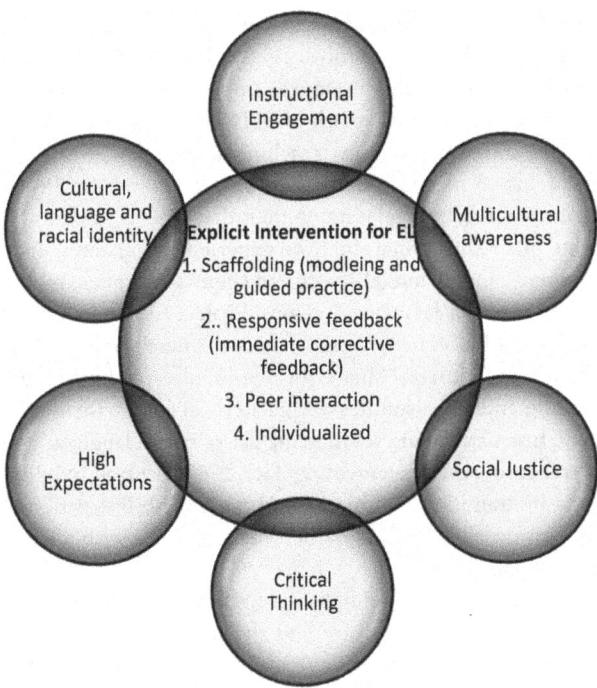

Figure 13.1 Overlaying CRSP on the Critical Elements of Intervention

decision-making within MTSS models. Several elements of CRSP should be considered in MTSS models at each tier: evidence-based instructional strategies to support English learners, teaching that sees a student's first language as an asset, building social connections among students and with the teacher, and having a deep understanding of students' multiple identities, i.e., race, culture, ethnic, and social identities, including disability (Linan-Thompson et al., 2018).

In the studies we reviewed in this chapter there were elements of CRSP in the intervention studies. For example, in the Baker et al. 2016 study, the intervention did include a focus on academic vocabulary and explicit teaching of language that was transferrable across languages. These elements of the intervention are aligned with CRSP by building connections between students' home language and English and also by teaching high-level academic vocabulary. In the two studies focused on high school students (Vaughn et al., 2016; Williams &Vaughn, 2019), the intervention included collaboration with peers. CRSP posits that student engagement can be enhanced by collaboration with peers that considers individual student strengths, and we know from research that English learners benefit from peer interaction (e.g., Echevarria et al., 2018; Sáenz et al., 2005). The Castro-Olivo et al. (2018) study incorporated teacher training on collaborating with Latino families, which also aligns with student engagement and alignment with students' cultures and identities. Additional studies that did not meet our criteria included motivational strategies that have the potential to facilitate instructional engagement to move students towards more autonomy.

Merging Evidence-Based Interventions and CRSP

Although research explicitly examining the effectiveness of CRSP for English learners within Tier 2 and Tier 3 interventions and/or within MTSS structures is in its infancy, a number of promising model demonstration research projects are developing, implementing, and evaluating MTSS models for English learners: Project Elite2 at UT Austin, Project Ellipses at American Institutes for Research, and Project Lee at Portland State University (Multitiered Systems of Supports for English Learners, 2020). Project Elite has already developed, implemented, and evaluated MTSS for K-3 English learners and is now completing the work of MTSS models for grades 3 to 5 English learners. The project focuses on culturally responsive teaching across tiers of instruction. While the project has not yet examined Tier 3 specifically, the Tier 2 interventions for Project Elite includes six important principles that use CRSP: (a) relevant content that reflects students cultural and linguistic backgrounds; (b) students' prior knowledge and lived experiences; (c) active and equitable participation; (d) high-quality linguistic input; and (e) structured language practice, high-quality instructional discourse, and instruction in all four language domains. Project LEE is working to enhance existing Tier 2 interventions using the PLUSS framework to meet the needs of English learners. Elements of the PLUSS framework include (a) preteaching critical vocabulary and priming background knowledge, (b) language modeling and opportunities for practice, (c) using visuals and graphic organizers, (d) systematic and explicit instruction, and (e) strategic use of native language and teaching for transfer. Project ELLIPSES is focusing on implementing Tier 2 intervention in bilingual schools in third to fifth grades as students are transitioning from Spanish to English instruction. This project focuses on Tier 2 interventions that develop English learners' reading skills with a emphasis on vocabulary, academic language, and oral language.

These model demonstration projects highlight the need for English learners to have instruction that is evidence-based and culturally responsive and the importance of developing oral language so that English learners can access both general education and special education curriculum. The projects also provide a roadmap for how CRSP is a foundation for an MTSS model in schools that serve English learners and is relevant across all tiers of instruction, including Tier 2 and Tier 3 interventions. The individual interventions within the MTSS models that are grounded in CRSP are analyzed for efficacy within the model and in the context of schools that serve English learners—merging evidence-based interventions with CRSP.

Implications for Practitioners

Special education has not historically utilized a CRSP lens as a driving feature in the development of academic interventions. The work in special education instead has developed and implemented explicit instruction models that were originally intended for monolingual English-speaking students. Subsequently, some researchers have applied these evidence-based practices with English learners to determine their efficacy with this population of students. It is possible that these design approaches need to shift to better meet the needs of English learners. An alternative approach would be to utilize the CRSP framework as an overlay to explicit instruction models to develop and or modify and adapt existing interventions for a given group of students. To implement this type of approach, it would also require training teachers and other school staff who deliver interventions using CRSP and to really know the students whom they serve so that they can tailor an intervention to meet their needs.

Thorius and Graff (2017) provide an example of how practitioners can use evidence-based interventions within the CRSP framework. The authors discuss how to extend the Peer Assisted Learning Strategies (PALS) intervention (Fuchs et al., 1997) to meet the needs of culturally, linguistically, and racially diverse learners. The authors suggest that while the main target in instruction is to improve discrete reading skills, it is also possible to connect the intervention to students' social and cultural identities, which has the potential to be more effective. For example, teachers could specifically choose texts that better reflect the lived experiences of their students. The materials used in the intervention could also be adjusted to "look" like students in a diverse classroom (see also Aceves & Orosco, 2014). Finally, as teachers assess and interpret assessment data, it is necessary for them to ask reflective questions about their own biases and the biases of various assessments and their practices as a facilitator during PALS.

Self-regulated strategy development (SRSD, Graham & Harris, 1989) is another evidence-based intervention that shows promise when used with English learners (Jozwik et al., 2019). The study did not meet our criteria, since it did not include two reliable and valid measures of reading. However, this single-subject study showed promise in English learners' strategy use and reading comprehension accuracy, both proximal measures of the intervention. SRSD promotes student autonomy through teaching independent reading strategies and also promotes collaboration with peers, both of which are elements of teaching that align with CRSP features.

In special education we are masters of individualized instruction and getting to know our students' strengths and needs. These are two important elements that are absolutely critical as we move forward in implementing interventions. The elements of explicit instruction—modeling, responsive feedback, and scaffolding—are necessary. However, it is also important to consider how we are using collaborative instructional models and providing students opportunities to engage in text to further vocabulary and reading comprehension. Further, we must be intentional about how we select texts and topics that are relevant to our English learners' lived experiences.

Implications for Future Research

At first glance the results of our search are a bit discouraging—we have been working now for several decades on effective interventions for English learners, and it seems we rarely get positive effects for more than early literacy skills in grades K-3. However, if we use these results to propel us forward in thinking differently about how we design interventions in a way that is culturally responsive and also how we design studies to examine for whom and under what conditions they work, it is possible that more progress will be made. There is potential that studies that implement evidence-based reading practices in tandem with implementation of culturally responsive pedagogies may be particularly important with older students. Better understanding how motivate students to engage in reading can be incorporated into academic interventions and needs further study. Additionally, there are several implications for future research based on the review of the intervention literature over the past five years and the CRSP literature.

Schools are complex ecosystems, and the context of intervention does affect the efficacy of interventions—it is important for the field to concentrate efforts on better understanding these contexts and how they affect student learning and achievement. We rarely discuss in our studies the context of schools beyond the content we are adding to the already complex school ecosystem. It is critical that the field better understand and describe the school context and complex sets of policies, teacher knowledge, and existing curricula when reporting study findings. This has potential to help researchers better understand what is effective, "with whom, by whom and in what contexts"—words our colleague, Janette Klingner, said years ago that continue to resonate (Klingner & Edwards, 2006, p. 110). If teachers in a school are trained in CRSP and use practices that reflect this, are interventions more effective for English learners? If students feel a sense of belonging in a school because they are respected and schools see students' cultures and lived experiences as assets, is this reflected in interventions and the outcomes of these interventions? Mixed-methods designs can help us understand evidence-based practices delivered within a larger framework like CRSP because the qualitative aspects of the research can allow us to examine the context in which the evidence practices are delivered. Mixed-methods designs may be one way to better understand the context of the schools in which the interventions are delivered in order to better understand student outcomes from individual interventions. Mixed-methods designs could also help us understand other individual factors such as motivation and self-concept of reading to help us better understand the impact of our interventions and who the interventions affect.

Research practice partnerships (RPPs; Coburn et al., 2013) may also prove useful as a tool for designing interventions and the implementation of these services for English learners in authentic school settings. RPPs are collaborations, usually long term, developed between practitioners within schools and districts and researchers that investigate problems of practice and work to improve these schools and districts. The work is intended to be mutually beneficial and comes directly from problems of practice identified by practitioners in collaboration with their research partners (Coburn et al., 2013). These partnerships have the potential for greater impact on practice because they are designed with the specific educational contexts in mind (Coburn & Penuel, 2016), and a focus on the specific context affects decision-making through research design, implementation, and use of data (Tseng, 2012). For intervention studies for English learners, RPPs have the potential for developing interventions based on the contexts of the particular schools and the needs of the English learners, and therefore are likely to produce better outcomes for these students. There is the potential that schools are more likely to continue to implement an intervention once a research study is concluded if they have a stake in the development and if they are involved in the research process.

Finally, it will be important for the field to examine other elements of our methodology, such as having greater than 50% of the students as English learners, including both proximal and distal outcome measures, as well as multiple outcome measures and studying interventions for both younger and older English learners. When we initially searched for studies that included participants who were English learners, we found many studies that did not meet our criteria but did provide the field with new directions for research, as many of these studies went beyond measuring only specific reading skills but examined students' self-concept of reading, motivation, and strategy use. There also may be more we need to understand regarding motivation and reading for English learners and the role of students' cultural identities that may be useful in developing more effective interventions. These areas of research may prove useful especially for older English learners, who are likely long-term English learners and may have different needs than younger English learners.

Conclusion

While we are making progress in the amount of research that is focused on English learners, we are not making the progress needed to really advance the educational opportunities and achievement of these students, particularly those who are English learners and also have reading difficulties. We know as a field that explicit instruction is fundamental to effective practices for students with learning disabilities. How do we take evidence-based practices (e.g., PALS or SRSD) and frame them in a culturally responsive and sustaining way and then test them in school context and examine those contexts? How do we develop new and effective interventions that really meet the needs of students who are English learners? Given the pandemic and the amount of lost learning opportunities that are likely to have happened, this could not be more urgent.

Additional Readings and Resources

CEEDAR Innovation Configuration-Culturally Responsive Teaching
https://ceedar.education.ufl.edu/wp-content/uploads/2014/03/IC-Cult-Resp.pdf
CEEDAR Innovation Configuration-Evidenced-based Practices for English Learners
https://ceedar.education.ufl.edu/wp-content/uploads/2016/11/EBP-for-english-learners.pdf
Multitiered Systems of Support for English Learners" Model Demonstration Research sponsored by the Office of Special Education Programs, U.S. Department of Education www.mtss4els.org
National Center on Intensive Intervention-Video with Dr. Alba Ortiz
https://intensiveintervention.org/resource/why-it-important-ensure-instruction-and-interventions-are-culturally-responsive

References

Aceves, T. C., & Orosco, M. (2014). *Culturally responsive teaching (Document No. IC-2)*. Retrieved from University of Florida, Collaboration for Effective Educator, Development, Accountability, and Reform Center website: http://ceedar.education.ufl.edu/tools/innovation-configurations/

Baker, D. L., Burns, D., Kame'enui, E. J. PhD, Smolkowski, K., & Baker, S. K. (2016). Does supplemental instruction support the transition from Spanish to English reading instruction for first-grade English learners at risk of reading difficulties. *Learning Disability Quarterly, 39*, 226–239.

Baker, D. L., Richards-Tutor, C., Sparks, A., & Canges, R. (2018). Review of single subject research examining the effectiveness of interventions for at risk English learners. *Learning Disabilities Research & Practice, 33*, 64–74.

Barber, A. T., Buehl, M. M., Kidd, J. K., Sturtevant, E. J., Nuland, L. R., & beck, J. (2015). Reading engagement in social studies: Exploring the role of a social studies literacy intervention on reading comprehension, reading self-efficacy, and engagement in middle school students with different language backgrounds. *Reading Psychology, 36*, 31–85.

Castro-Olivo, S., Preciado, J., Le, L., Marciante M., & Garcia, M. (2018). The effects of culturally adapted version of First Steps to Success for Latino English language learners: Preliminary pilot study. *Psychology in the Schools, 55*, 36–49.

Center for American Progress. (2021). *Latinos face disproportionate health and economic impacts from COVID-19*. www.americanprogress.org/issues/economy/reports/2021/03/05/496733/latinos-face-disproportionate-health-economic-impacts-covid-19/

Coburn, C. E., & Penuel, W. R. (2016). Research-practice partnerships in education: Outcomes, dynamics, and open questions. *Educational Researcher, 45*, 48–54.

Coburn, C. E., Penuel, W. R., & Geil, K. (2013). *Research-practice partnerships at the district level: A new strategy for leveraging research for educational improvement*. William T. Grant Foundation.

Council for Exceptional Children. (2015). *What every special educator must know: professional ethics and standards*. CEC.

Council of the Great City Schools. (2020). *Supporting English learners in the COVID-19 crisis*. www.cgcs.org/cms/lib/DC00001581/Centricity/domain/35/publication%20docs/CGCS_ELL%20and%20COVID_web_v2.pdf

Echevarria, J. E., Vogt, M. E., & Short, D. (2018). *Making content comprehensible for English learners: The SIOP model*. Pearson.

Fuchs, D., Fuchs, L. S., Mathes, P. G., & Simmons, D. (1997). Peer-assisted learning strategies: Making classrooms more responsive to diversity. *American Educational Research Journal, 34*(1), 174–206.

Gay, G. (2000). *Culturally responsive teaching theory, research, and practice*. Teachers College Record.

Graham, S., & Harris, K. R. (1989). A components analysis of cognitive strategy training: Effects on learning disabled students' compositions and self-efficacy. *Journal of Educational Psychology, 87*, 353–361.

Hammond, Z. (2014). *Culturally responsive teaching and the brain: Promoting authentic engagement and rigor among culturally and linguistically diverse students*. Thousand Oaks: Corwin Press.

Hanover Research. (2017). *Effective interventions for long term English learners*. https://portal.ct.gov/-/media/SDE/ESSA-Evidence-Guides/Effective_Interventions_for_Long-Term_English_Learners

Howard, T. C. (2020). *Why race and culture matter in schools: Closing the achievement gap in America's classrooms*. Teacher's College Press

Huang, M., Haas, E., Zhu, N., & Tran, L. (2016). *High school graduation rates across English learner student subgroups in Arizona* (REL 2017–205). U.S. Department of Education, Institute of Education Sciences, National Center for Education Evaluation and Regional Assistance, Regional Educational Laboratory West. http://ies.ed.gov/ncee/edlabs.

Individuals with Disabilities Education Improvement Act [IDEA], 20 U.S.C. §§ 1400 et seq. (2004).

Jozwik, S. L., Yojanna Cuenca-Carlino, Y. Mustian, A. M., & Douglas, K. H. (2019). Evaluating a self-regulated strategy development reading-comprehension intervention for emerging bilingual students with learning disabilities, *Preventing School Failure, 63*, 121–132

Klingner, J. K., & Edwards, P. A. (2006). Cultural considerations with response to intervention models. *Reading Research Quarterly, 41*(1), 108–117.

Ladson-Billings, G. (1994). *The dreamkeepers: Successful teachers of African American children*. Jossey-Bass.

Ladson-Billings, G. (1995). Toward a theory of culturally relevant pedagogy. *American Educational Research Journal, 32*, 465–491.

Linan-Thompson, S., Lara-Martinez, J. A., & Cavazos, L. O. (2018). Exploring the intersection of evidence-based practices and culturally and linguistically responsive practices. *Intervention in School and Clinic, 54*(1), 6–13.

Ludwig, C., Guo, K., & Georgiou, G. K. (2019). Are reading interventions for English language learners effective? A meta-analysis. *Journal of Learning Disabilities, 52*, 220–231

Multitiered System of Supports for English Learners. (2020). *Meeting the needs of English learners with and without disabilities: Brief 2, Evidence-based Tier 2 intervention practices for English learners.* U.S. Office of Special Education Programs.

NAEP. (2019). https://nces.ed.gov/nationsreportcard/data/

National Council on Disabilities. (2018). *English learners and students from low income families.* https://ncd.gov/sites/default/files/NCD_EnglishLanguageLearners_508.pdf

Office of Civil Rights. (2016). *A first look.* https://www2.ed.gov/about/offices/list/ocr/docs/crdc-2013-14.html

Paris, D. (2012). Culturally sustaining pedagogy: A needed change in stance, terminology, and practice. *Educational Researcher, 41*, 93–97.

Richards-Tutor, C., Aceves, T., & Reese, L. (2016). *Evidence-based practices for English Learners* (Document No. IC-18). Retrieved from University of Florida, Collaboration for Effective Educator, Development, Accountability, and Reform Center website: https://ceedar.education.ufl.edu/wp-content/uploads/2016/11/EBP-for-english-learners.pdf

Richards-Tutor, C., Baker, D. L., Gersten, R., Baker, S., & Smith, J. M. (2015). The effectiveness of reading interventions for English learners: A research synthesis. *Exceptional Children, 82, 144–169.*

Sáenz, L. M., Fuchs, L. S., & Fuchs, D. (2005). Peer-assisted learning strategies for English language learners with learning disabilities. *Exceptional Children, 71*(3), 231–247. https://eric.ed.gov/?id=EJ696976

Solari, E. J., Petscher, Y., & Folsom, J. S. (2014). Differentiating literacy growth of ELL students with LD from other high-risk subgroups and general education peers: Evidence from grades 3–10. *Journal of Learning Disabilities, 47*, 329–348.

Syetaz, M. V., Coyne-Beasley, T., Trent, M., Wade, R., Ryan, M. H., Kelley, M., & Chulani, V. (2020). The traumatic impact of racism and discrimination on young people and how to talk about it. In K. R. Ginsberg and Z. B. Ramirez McClain (Eds.), *Reaching teens: Strength-based, trauma-sensitive, resilience-building communication strategies rooted in positive youth development.* American Academy of Pediatrics. www.seattlechildrens.org/globalassets/documents/clinics/diversity/the-traumatic-impact-of-racism-and-discrimination-on-young-people-and-how-to-talk-about-it.pdf

Thorius, K. A., & Graff, C. S. (2017). Extending peer-assisted learning strategies for racially, linguistically, and ability diverse learners. *Intervention in School and Clinic 2018, 53*, 163–170.

Toste, J. R. Capin, P., Williams, K. J., Cho, E., & Vaughn, S. (2019). Word reading intervention with and without motivational beliefs training for struggling readers. *Journal of Learning Disabilities, 52*, 45–58.

Tseng, V. (2012). *Partnerships: Shifting the dynamics between research and practice.* William T. Grant Foundation

U.S. Department of Education, National Center for Education Statistics. (2020). The Condition of Education 2020 (2020–144), English Language Learners in Public Schools.

Vaughn, S., Martinez, L. R., Williams, K. J., & Miciak, J. (2016). Efficacy of a high school extensive reading intervention for English learners with reading difficulties. *Journal of Educational Psychology, 111*, 373–386.

Vygotsky, L. S. (1978). *Mind in society: The development of higher psychological processes.* Harvard University Press.

Williams, K. J., & Vaughn, S. (2019). Effects of an intensive reading intervention for ninth-grade English learners with learning disabilities. *Learning Disability Quarterly 2020, 43*, 154–166.

14
ACADEMIC STRATEGIES FOR AT-RISK STUDENTS IN URBAN SCHOOLS

Phillip J. Belfiore

While recent reports provided by the Institute of Educational Sciences (IES) indicate some progress in closing the K-12 urban/national academic achievement gap in mathematics and reading, students enrolled in urban public schools continue to underperform according to national standards for proficiency (National Center for Education Statistics, 2019). For example, the National Assessment of Educational Progress (NAEP) data from the 2019 Trial Urban District Assessment (TUDA) reported that fourth- and eighth-grade students' performance in reading and mathematics continues to fall below grade-level academic proficiency when compared to NAEP public school data nationwide (National Center for Education Statistics, 2019). To participate in TUDA, an urban district must meet the following guidelines: (a) have at least 250,000 residents, (b) include 50% or more minority students districtwide or in the grade level, and (c) include 50% or more students eligible for the free and reduced-price lunch program districtwide or in the grade level. In 2019, the TUDA measured student performance data in 27 of the largest urban districts in the United States, reporting that only 27% of students in the fourth grade and only 26% of students in the eighth grade met the NAEP proficiency standard in reading, while 34% of students in the fourth grade and only 27% of students in the eighth grade met the NAEP proficiency standard for mathematics (National Center for Education Statistics, 2019). This gap of academic achievement is greater, and in some cities growing, when disaggregating the overall urban district NAEP results by eligibility for the National School Lunch Program in these largest urban districts (National Center for Education Statistics, 2019).

In this chapter, I focus on academic strategies for at-risk students enrolled in urban schools. First, I describe difficulties at-risk students encounter in school settings. Then, I provide recommendations to address the academic needs of at-risk students by introducing strategies that (a) alter the classroom environment and (b) increase positive classroom regard, reinforcement, and resilience. Lastly, I provide a summary of recommendations for academic instruction for at-risk students in urban districts.

Academics and Discipline for At-Risk Students

In response to the reported chronic academic underachievement in high-poverty (i.e., eligible for the National School Lunch Program) urban schools, educational leaders, administrators, and researchers suggested numerous variables that may place students enrolled in these schools at risk for academic failure. Variables include neighborhood poverty, a lack of cultural responsiveness in teacher preparation programs and cultural relevance in curriculum and instruction, undercertified or noncertified teaching staff, sociofamilial factors, teacher misperceptions and low expectations, environmental conditions and chronic student illness, high teacher turnover, child maltreatment, poor instructional choices, and low-level or watered-down curricula (Belfiore et al., 2005; Banks, 2015; Black & Krishmakumar, 1998; Blanchett et al., 2005; Edmin, 2012; Fantuzzo et al., 2012; McKinney et al., 2005; Warren, 2002).

Additionally, students who experience difficulty with academics, whether identified with special needs or not, oftentimes engage in behaviors nonconducive for learning (e.g., noncompliance, verbal outbursts, defiance, aggression, passive resistance; Fantuzzo et al., 2012; Lee et al., 2008). Gregory et al. (2010) reported that students with a history of low academic achievement residing in high-poverty neighborhoods were at greater risk for school-based disciplinary sanctions as a result of engaging in these *nonschool* behaviors. Nonschool behaviors allow students to escape the unpleasantness of an academic environment (i.e., repeated lack of success when presented with and engaging in academic tasks and activities) that more often than not results in continued school-based failure. This may be especially true for students enrolled in high-poverty urban schools where limited academic success and support occur year over year (Gregory et al., 2010; Noltemeyer & Mcloughlin, 2010). Research showed students receiving disciplinary sanctions (e.g., suspensions, office disciplinary referrals, school expulsions) were more likely to be male, Black, identified as at risk for academic failure, receiving special education services, and come from lower socioeconomic environments (Bradshaw et al., 2010; Gregory et al., 2010; Gregory & Weinstein, 2008; Simmons-Reed & Cartledge, 2014; Skiba et al., 2008). Noltemeyer and Mcloughlin (2010) reported that Black students disproportionately received disciplinary sanctions (expulsions, suspensions, alternative placements, emergency removals), and those practices are most frequently utilized in high-poverty urban school districts. Interestingly, Skiba (2014) summarized that no data exist linking out of school suspensions and expulsions with reduced school disruption or improved school climate, rather, disciplinary removal has a negative effect on student outcomes. Disproportionate use of school disciplinary practices may contribute greatly to the academic achievement gap observed in high-poverty urban schools (Gregory et al., 2010). In fact, it seems counterproductive to remove academically struggling students from school following displays of noncompliant behavior because doing so results in fewer academic opportunities for those students who would benefit the most from them.

For students enrolled in high-poverty urban schools two gaps exist: (a) a gap in academic success (*fewer* students enrolled in high-poverty urban schools are reaching levels of academic proficiency when compared to same-grade-level peers enrolled in nonurban, low-poverty schools) and (b) a gap in school-based disciplinary sanctions (*more* students enrolled in high-poverty urban schools receive disciplinary sanctions when compared to same-grade-level peers enrolled in nonurban, low-poverty schools (National Center for Education Statistics, 2019; Noltemeyer & Mcloughlin, 2010). A lack of academic success often results in removal from academic opportunity. This is especially troubling if the behaviors associated with school removal have a functional relation with a less-than-equitable academic environment. An alternative behavioral explanation would begin from the position that students experiencing limited academic success may be engaging in behaviors nonconducive to learning as a result of repeated academic failures (i.e., increased punishment) and lack of school support and few academic successes (i.e., decreased reinforcement). A logical first step is to alter a classroom environment using evidence-based strategies.

Alter the Classroom Environment Using Evidence-Based Strategies

Many students in high-poverty urban schools are experiencing academic failure. Strategically, educators should look to themselves and those environmental variables they have some control over (i.e., physical classroom space, teacher and staff behavior, curriculum, and instruction) as a priority for building a climate of academic success and positive regard for all students.

From a behavior analytic approach, all voluntary behavior is learned and maintained through interactions with the social and physical environment, and those behavior–environment interactions can be described as positive and negative reinforcement contingencies (Peterson & Neef, 2020). Behaviors are strengthened or maintained by accessing something (positive reinforcement contingencies) and/or by removing or avoiding something (negative reinforcement contingencies).

For example, if a teacher repeatedly presents David and several of his second-grade classmates with a reading assignment above their current reading level, resulting in multiple reading errors, no story comprehension, little interest, and poor quiz scores, while being provided little teacher instructional support, feedback, or encouragement, David and his classmates may engage in noncompliance in the form of a verbal outbursts, crying, or repeated doodling while ignoring the teacher's instructional request. If those behaviors result in David and his classmates avoiding the assignment (e.g., David is asked to leave the room) or the teacher removing the required reading assignment, then the student's noncompliant behavior may be negatively reinforced by the teacher's consequential actions. Furthermore, the next time the class is preparing for reading instruction (an aversive situation usually ending in more failure), David and his classmates may exhibit similar noncompliant behaviors to continue to avoid or remove the reading assignment. In this case the curricular mismatch of required reading above the appropriate instructional level (i.e., aversive environmental situation) may have set the occasion for increased noncompliant behaviors. This, in turn, may result in increased disciplinary sanctions, reducing much-needed access to effective instructional time, materials, and support for David and his classmates.

David and his classmates may experience academic failure, not because of a lack of intellectual ability, but because of a lack of engagement, brought on by instruction delivered at the inappropriate level resulting in few opportunities for positive reinforcement of academic behaviors (Payne et al., 2007). Changing the course for at-risk students in high-poverty urban schools involves restructuring an educational environment that (a) fosters academic success while decreasing the academic aversive and (b) increases positive classroom regard, reinforcement, and resilience.

Foster Academic Success and Decrease the Academic Aversive: Educational Planning

Given the example of David and his second-grade classmates, an alternative approach may begin with conducting a curriculum-based assessment (CBA) to accurately determine the instructional oral reading level (correct words per minute [CWPM]) for each student in the second-grade classroom. Not all second-grade students may be reading at the same instructional level. Providing reading materials at each second-grade student's instructional level (40 to 60 CWPM; four or fewer errors) is the first step to avoiding the mismatch and increasing academic success. Alternatively, continuing to provide reading materials at a frustration level (fewer than 40 CWPM; more than four errors) maintains the mismatch, repeating academic failure.

In addition, if the teacher is aware David and other second-graders experience difficulty with reading, providing additional instructional support, instructional feedback, and culturally relevant text may be warranted. In this behavior analytic alternative, we have begun to arrange the educational environment to increase academic success for David and his classmates, while decreasing the aversiveness of the classroom environment. Following the CBA, David and his classmates would now be reading culturally relevant text at an instructional level where most words are known, resulting in increased fluency, comprehension, and content interest, as well as more positive teacher feedback. If the educational environment is less aversive, resulting in more academic successes for David and his classmates, it is less likely they will engage in noncompliant behaviors when presented with educational stimuli. Why escape something positive?

Table 14.1 SMART Assessment Guidelines

Specific Student Response: _____
Specific Discriminative Stimulus (S^D): Prompt _____

Procedural Steps

1. Create a pool of academic items (40–50 items); basic mathematics computation or basic literacy as the academic priority for the student(s).
2. Determine the specific student(s) response; will the student(s) *(select one)*
   a. Respond verbally (student states word or letter or states answer to math problem)
   b. Respond by writing (student writes the word or letter or writes answer to math problem)
3. Determine the discriminative stimulus (S^D) or prompt; will the instructor *(select one)*
   a. Present flashcard and say "What is the word/answer?" Wait three seconds before next flashcard.
   b. Hand out written worksheet and say "Please complete the worksheet." Allow student enough time to complete worksheet.
   c. Ask student to "Write the word ___." Wait five to ten seconds before the next word.
4. Conduct two or three assessment sessions.
5. Construct three equal instructional sets of unknown academic items (e.g., words, letters, or mathematic problems not answered or answered incorrectly during each of the two or three assessment sessions). Each set should have the same number of unknown items (6–10), for a total of 18–30 total unknown items.
   OUTCOME: From this initial assessment, create three equal (in number and difficulty) sets of unknown items that will serve as the dependent variable.

Source: Adapted from Belfiore & Lee, 2018

Curriculum-Based Assessment

The first planning strategy to avoiding a curricular mismatch is to conduct a CBA. *Curriculum-based assessment* can be described as a method of frequently evaluating a student's academic level within a specific curriculum content (e.g., oral reading fluency, sight word reading, letters/sounds recognition, written expression, mathematics computation), using that classroom content material as the basis for the assessment (Payne et al., 2007), and later, for individualized academic instruction. The results of an initial CBA (e.g., CWPM when conducting an oral reading CBA, percentage correct digits when conducting a mathematics computation CBA) provide an accurate instructional level from which instruction can begin.

For example, the first step in the Supplemental Mathematics and Reading Tutoring (SMART) program, developed in collaboration with a high-poverty K-8 urban charter school, is to conduct a CBA to determine unknown academic items (see Table 14.1). Before individualized instruction for two elementary-grade students, Mucci et al. (2018) conducted a mathematics CBA using a sampling of basic computations, including single-digit addition (e.g., 4 + 5), single-digit subtraction (e.g., 9 − 7), and single-digit multiplication (e.g., 4 × 7). Results from the initial CBA showed student mastery of addition and subtraction facts, as well as single-digit multiplication resulting in a one-digit product (e.g. 2 × 2; 3 × 2; 1 × 5), but not multiplication resulting in a two-digit product (e.g., 4 × 8; 6 × 7). We conducted a second CBA to identify known and unknown single-digit multiplication facts with two-digit products. Results from the second assessment yielded 21 (for student one) and 24 (for student two) unknown multiplication facts. Those unknown facts were then divided into three smaller instructional sets, equated for difficulty and total number of facts per set (Mucci et al., 2018). During intervention, the teachers taught one instructional set at a time until mastery. Using CBA results is fundamental for determining the individualized academic level to begin instruction (Payne et al., 2007), and individualized instruction is the centerpiece for differentiated instruction.

Assessing Student Preferences

Whereas a CBA is an essential academic planning strategy, *assessing student history and preference* is a necessary planning strategy for teachers to understand whom they teach, the lived experience of their students, and the student's community. Assessing student preferences requires teachers to learn how to listen to their students and not minimize them (Freire, 1998). Preferences and life experiences of each child may vary over a school year, so teachers should conduct preference assessments at the start of every grading quarter. Asking students about what they read, listen to, watch, believe in, interact with, are proud of, and like best about school provides a dialogical opportunity between teacher and student. Assessing student preferences in this way begins to build a culturally relevant context for the teacher. This context can be used to augment the academic curriculum (e.g., printed text, writing prompts, mathematics word problems) and classroom contingencies.

Classwide Expectations

A third strategy for planning for academic success is creating a set of *classwide expectations*. Classwide expectations should operate like rule-governed behavior, behaviors controlled by verbal and written antecedent stimuli. Classwide rules or expectations should follow several simple guidelines. First, describe expectations as clear, concise, observable behaviors (e.g., "We walk in our classroom"). If the classroom must follow districtwide expectations that are not readily observable (e.g., "Respect your classmate"), then specific behavioral examples of "respect" must be provided. Second, describe expectations in positive terms, such as what to do (e.g., "We walk in the classroom," not "No running"). Stating expectations as what not to do allows the students multiple opportunities for an alternative response (e.g., walking, skipping, hopping). Lastly, allow students a voice in the construction of expectations. Giving students a voice of what is to be expected in the classroom increases the likelihood students will engage in the expected behaviors, as well as monitor the behavior of others in the classroom. Other strategies that may increase the likelihood students will engage in the expected classroom behaviors include (a) explicitly teaching examples and nonexamples of classwide expectations as any other academic behavior to be mastered, (b) using modeling and role-playing, and (c) explaining to families about the student behaviors expected in the classroom. Establishing high behavioral expectations for all students sets a foundation for a safe, positive classroom environment and one that sets consistent boundaries.

Self-Management

A final educational planning strategy is *self-management*. The most researched self-management strategy, self-monitoring, is a procedure whereby a student self-observes, then self-records occurrences and nonoccurrences of a target behavior (Cooper et al., 2020). When working with a student diagnosed with attention deficit hyperactivity disorder and exhibiting noncompliant classroom behaviors, Blicha and Belfiore (2013) determined incomplete homework assignments resulted in a loss of recess time, and a loss of recess time resulted in increased noncompliant behaviors. Upon further assessment, incomplete homework was not a result of a limited academic skill set, but a lack of organizational skills. The student did not bring home all required materials and assignments, resulting in all assignments not completed the following day. An intervention of a simple self-monitoring checklist for required homework materials and assignments, as well as an automated antecedent prompt to initiate the checklist, resulted in 100% homework completion during every session of intervention, as well as during a five-month follow-up session (Blicha & Belfiore, 2013).

Table 14.2 Classwide Self-Monitoring Homework Checklist

	YES	NO	COMMENTS
Name			Date
Teacher			
1. Is all homework in my folder?			
2. Do I have a pencil?			
3. BEGIN homework			
4. Is all homework completed?			
5. Did someone check my homework?			Initials: _____
6. Is all homework back in my folder?			
7. When homework is complete, what is the TITLE and AUTHOR of the book I am going to read now? TITLE: AUTHOR:			

Self-monitoring strategies may also be implemented classwide. When working with an after-school club in a K-8 urban charter school, we developed a classwide homework checklist to increase the likelihood daily homework would be completed as required, with homework never leaving the school. On the days the after-school club was in session, teachers completed homework folders for each student enrolled, so that upon entering the after-school club, students would pick up their individual homework folder. Inside each folder was the homework checklist (see Table 14.2). During snack, students would open folders and complete their checklist and homework. One caveat to this classwide self-monitoring checklist was the planned transition from homework completion to independent reading (Table 14.2, Step 7). To reduce student uncertainty during activity transition, as well as to address the fact that students all completed homework at varied times, once students completed homework, the checklist required students to select a book at their independent reading level, copy the author and title, and begin silent reading.

If at-risk students with a history of academic failure are more likely to receive school-based disciplinary sanctions (Noltemeyer & Mcloughlin, 2010), and if from a behavioral perspective I suggest student academic failure is a result of a curricular mismatch and not an intellectual inability to succeed, then a first remedial step is to plan curricular conditions where success is forthcoming and failure is less likely. Outcomes of education planning include identifying (a) student instructional levels, (b) student preferences and culturally relevant content, (c) a set of shared classwide expectations, and (d) individual and classwide self-monitoring strategies. Educational planning sets the stage for behavioral-based academic instructional strategies.

Foster Academic Success and Decrease the Academic Aversive: Academic Instructional Strategies

Academic instructional strategies are effective and efficient when they are teacher-directed and delivered to students in a small-group format (Kim & Axelrod, 2005). Teacher-directed, small-group instruction is most effective and most efficient when student grouping is based on instructional level

(Kim & Axelrod, 2005). For example, if as a result of CBA, the oral reading instructional level is determined for the fourth-grade class at 70 to 100 CWPM with fewer than seven errors, those students reading 70 to 100 CWPM with fewer than seven errors at the 2.5 grade instructional level are grouped together, those students reading 70 to 100 CWPM with fewer than seven errors at the 3.0 reading level are grouped together, and those students reading 70 to 100 CWPM with fewer than seven errors at the 3.5 instructional level are grouped together. In this example, the fourth-grade class has three reading groups at three different reading levels, but each student is reading at their instructional level.

Teacher-Directed Instruction

Once small groups are in place, *teacher-directed instruction* can begin with each small group of students. In general, teacher-directed instruction prioritizes (a) increasing student academic response opportunities, (b) increasing class engagement on academic task, and (c) increasing teacher-delivered corrective feedback, while (d) targeting fluency, maintenance, and generalization of the acquired skill in the context of culturally relevant materials. Over the years, research has shown that teacher-directed instruction has been successful in increasing student academic performance across age, academic subject areas, and disability (e.g., Carroll et al., 2015; Engelmann et al., 1988; Mucci et al., 2018; Sener & Belfiore, 2017).

In general, the goal of any teacher-directed instructional strategy is to increase academic success, and in doing so, reducing the aversiveness of the academic instructional environment. Table 14.3 provides a procedural checklist for small-group instruction as step two of the SMART program (Belfiore & Lee, 2018). This includes increasing daily opportunities to practice (including errorless learning and discrimination trials), providing corrective feedback, increasing time on task through novel discrimination strategies (e.g., racetrack, modified board games, mnemonics), and interspersing known with unknown items (e.g., ratio; one known/one to two unknown).

The SMART program uses a simple two-component, teacher-directed instruction format: errorless learning trials followed by discrimination learning trials (Belfiore & Lee, 2018; Mucci et al., 2018). Following a CBA, three equal sets of unknown academic items (e.g., mathematics facts, sight words, letter names/sounds) are created (see Table 14.1). During intervention, the teacher introduces the first set of unknown items. Each instructional set usually contains eight to ten unknown academic items, and intervention is only introduced to the first instructional set until responding to that set reaches 100% accuracy during daily assessment of all academic items. Once 100% accuracy is observed for the first set, the teacher introduces the second instructional set. Once 100% accuracy is observed for the second set, the teacher introduces the third, and final, instructional set. Daily morning instruction runs 10 to 15 minutes, while daily afternoon assessment of all items runs 5 to 10 minutes (see Table 14.3).

The first component of the SMART teacher-directed instruction is errorless learning. Errorless learning trials allow students to first hear and see the correct academic response paired with the controlling discriminative stimuli (S^D), then require the students to immediately repeat the correct academic response in the presence of the controlling S^D, followed by positive reinforcement in the form of labeled teacher praise. Errorless learning trials increase academic success because students see and hear the correct response (simultaneous prompts) paired with the S^D before they respond, maximizing correct student responding in the presence of the S^D. For example, each errorless trial may begin with the teacher placing the printed *c-a-t* flashcard on the table in front of the group while simultaneously stating the correct response, "c-a-t, the word is cat." The students repeat the correct response "c-a-t, cat," followed by instructional feedback from the teacher, "excellent, the word is cat." In the SMART program, errorless trials are repeated two to three times for each unknown item in the set that is receiving instruction.

Table 14.3 SMART Teacher-Directed Instruction Guidelines

Procedural Steps
1. Determine materials needed (e.g. flashcards, game boards)
2. Design interventions that (check each line):
    a. _____ Increase daily opportunities to practice (including errorless learning)
    b. _____ Provide corrective feedback
    c. _____ Increase time on task through a novel discrimination strategy (e.g., flashcards, board games)
    d. _____ Intersperse known items with unknown items (ratio; one known/one to two unknown)
3. Graph and report daily student assessment data using Excel data sheet to faculty supervisor

Y/N	Begin teaching Set A until 100% mastery, then begin teaching Set B, then Set C

1. Student is sitting across from instructor
2. Instructor states what we are going to do: "Let's practice and then play a game"

I. Errorless Learning/Simultaneous Trials, Using flashcards

3. Instructor delivers S^D (e.g., placing the *c-a-t* flashcard and saying "the word is cat" or placing the $3+4=7$ flashcard and saying "$3+4=7$")
4. Student repeats the problem and answer verbally (e.g. "c-a-t spells cat" or "$3+4 = 7$")
5. Instructor delivers feedback (e.g., "yes, c-a-t spells cat" or "yes, $3+4=7$")
6. Instructor presents next flashcard until all flashcards for the set are completed
7. Instructor shuffles flashcard from the set
8. Instructor repeats errorless procedures two more times (each item is practiced **three times**)
9. When the third cycle ends, instructor says "thank you for helping"

II. Discrimination Training Trials. Using instruction "game" (e.g., racetrack, board game, cover-copy-compare, mnemonics)

10. Instructor places "RACETRACK" in front of the student and explains rules
11. Instructor uses a pointer, pointing to the *start* space
12. Instructor asks the student if they are ready to start; once the student signals that they are ready, the teacher will say, "*On your mark, get set, go!*" starts the stop watch, and points to the first space with a math problem.
13. Corrective feedback. Student has five seconds to state the answer.
    a. If correct student response, teacher responds "yes, $4+3=7$"
    b. If incorrect student response, teacher responds "no, $4+3=7$." Student repeats correctly.
    c. If no student response within the five seconds, teacher responds "$4+3=7$." Student repeats correctly.
14. Instructor moves pointer to next space and repeats corrective feedback (see step 13), following each student response to the SD.
15. When pointer moves to finish, stop stopwatch, tell student the time, and repeat a second cycle of racetrack, reminding the student: "Let's see if you can beat your last time." (each item is practiced two **times**)
16. When the second cycle ends, instructor tells the student the time to complete the track, and says "thank you for helping"

Source: Adapted from Belfiore & Lee, 2018

The second instructional component of the SMART teacher-directed instruction is discrimination trials. Discrimination trials require students to provide the correct answer (e.g., "the word is cat.") when presented only with the controlling S^D (e.g., the printed *c-a-t* flashcard on the table). Teacher corrective feedback follows every student response. Discrimination trials do not provide

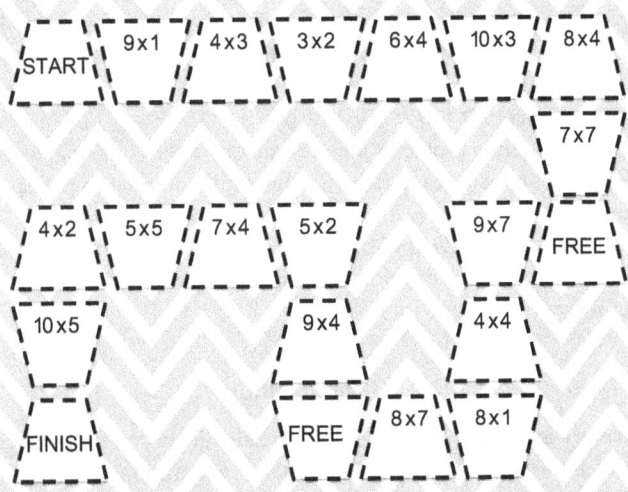

Figure 14.1 Racetrack for Set A
Source: Mucci et al., 2018

the student with the correct response prior to the student responding. In the SMART program, discrimination trials are always embedded into a novel game. For example, Mucci et al. (2018) constructed a multiplication racetrack board containing 21 total spaces: 2 free spaces, 1 start space, 1 finish space, 3 spaces for known multiplication facts, and 14 blank spaces for unknown multiplications facts (see Figure 14.1). Initially, the 14 blank spaces represented each of the seven unknown multiplication facts for Set A, listed twice. No answers were written on any racetrack space, and a timer was used to monitor fluency. Once students mastered Set A, seven unknown problems from Set B were written twice in the 14 blank racetrack spaces, and three of the mastered problems from Set A were written into the three blank spaces for known problems. Once students mastered Set B, seven unknown problems from Set C were written twice in the 14 blank racetrack spaces, and three of the mastered problems from Set B were written into the three blank spaces for known problems. If students answered the unknown problem in the board space correctly, the teacher provide positive reinforcement, repeating both the fact and correct answer ("Great, 8 times 4 is 32"), and the students continued to the next board space. If students answered incorrectly, the teacher provided a negation and both the fact and correct answer ("No, 8 times 4 is 32"), followed by the students repeating the multiplication fact and correct answer and labeled teacher feedback, then moving to the next board space. If no student response occurred within five seconds on moving into a new board space, the teacher provided both the fact and correct answer ("8 times 4 is 32"), followed by the student repeating the multiplication fact and correct answer and labeled teacher feedback, then moving to the next board space.

High-Probability Instructional Sequence

A second academic strategy for increasing academic success, specifically when student noncompliance results in academic failure, is using a *high-probability instructional sequence* (HPIS). HPIS is an antecedent strategy conceptually based on behavioral momentum (Nevin & Grace, 2000; Nevin et al., 1983), whereby a series of brief, highly complied-with commands precede a single, less-complied-with command. For example, after empirically establishing single-digit multiplication problems as high-probability (high-p) for completion and one-times six-digit digit multiplication problems as low-probability (low-p) for completion for two elementary grade students with a history of academic noncompliance enrolled in an urban school, Hutchinson and Belfiore (1998) created four-row worksheets where each row had two to three 1-by-1 digit problems followed by one 1-by-6 digit problem (e.g., 2 × 9 = __; 4 × 6 = __; 3 × 7 = __; 287,529 × 7 = __). Overall, when multistep, low-p academic problems are preceded by a series of single-step, high-p academic problems, results have shown increases in rate of completion, increases in percentage of engagement, and/or decreases in latency to initiate (e.g., Belfiore et al., 1997; Belfiore et al., 2002; Hutchinson & Belfiore, 1998; Lee et al., 2012; Wehby & Hollahan, 2000). Academic worksheets embedding a high-p sequence increase the level of reinforcement available (problem completion), resulting in increased academic success.

Generalization

Teaching to skill mastery is only the start of fostering academic success for at-risk students enrolled in high-poverty urban schools. Once academic mastery (i.e., acquisition or accuracy) has been reached, teachers must plan for and execute strategies for *generalization* over time and across novel instructional stimuli and settings. Generalization over time may be described as response maintenance. Does the learned academic response remain learned when assessed a week later or after holiday break? The simplest strategy for response maintenance is to provide additional opportunities for practice. For example, homework, independent instructional time, peer tutoring, and classwide review sessions should embedded opportunities to practice those academic skills previously mastered.

Generalization across novel instructional stimuli and settings requires teachers to determine the next environment for the learned skill. For example, after mastery of mathematics computation, students solve relevant word problems requiring previously mastered mathematics computation. When students master weekly sight or spelling words, teachers can ask students to write sentences or stories using the mastered words. After using an embedded mnemonics strategy in which flashcards with the written letter was embedded into a mnemonic (e.g., the letter /c/ was part of the caterpillar) to teach consonant letter names and sounds, Sener and Belfiore (2017) asked students to name words that began with or ended with that consonant letter sound. When asked prior to intervention, none of the four students could identify any words. Postintervention, all four students could identify words beginning with the mastered consonant sounds (range three to nine novel words), while three of the four students could produce words ending with the mastered consonant sound (range one to two novel words).

Culturally Relevant Curriculum

Culturally relevancy is less about instructional strategies and more about instructional content. Freire (1998) suggested students have a right to dream differently, and, as such, a one-size-fits-all, mass-produced curriculum requires augmentation. In the "Assessing Student Preferences" section earlier, conducting a student preference assessment gives the teacher some context of the student's lived experience, and the legitimacy of those experiences can be woven into the fabric of the curriculum. In doing so, the augmented curriculum now connects to the student in a way that a mass-produced published curriculum cannot. This connectedness of curriculum increases student engagement, and student engagement increases academic success (Cabrera et al., 2014). For example, writing prompts that include culturally relevant images, photos, essays, music, artifacts, and/or art may produce a richer writing sample than a commercially produced prompt (e.g., "write a paragraph describing an exotic animal you'd like to have as a pet"). In the second prompt, students who do not own pets, do not comprehend the word "exotic," and/or have never been to a zoo may produce a writing sample with few sentences, or none at all. Repeated failure when provided with such commercial writing prompts may in turn result in students engaging in behaviors nonconducive to learning, resulting in less academic time and fewer opportunities. Additionally, required reading of the *March* trilogy (Lewis et al., 2016), the graphic novel of the civil rights movement as witnessed by the late John Lewis, may provide a richer cultural context and increased time on reading task resulting in increased academic success for Black students enrolled in urban schools than *Old Yeller* (Gipson, 1956).

Linking educational planning and behavioral-based academic instructional strategies reconstructs the classroom environment. This new classroom pedagogy now establishes increased levels of academic success by directly teaching in small groups embedding culturally relevant content. Student success is further enhanced by using individual and classwide self-monitoring checklists, in-seat assignments constructed from behavioral concepts of behavioral momentum, and strategies that teach for academic generalization over time and across novel academic stimuli. All of this occurs in a classroom where teachers and students set high behavioral expectations, resulting in a consistently safe place to learn.

Increase Positive Classroom Regard, Reinforcement, and Resilience

Nevin et al. (1983) showed that behavioral persistence (resistance to change) is a function of both response-dependent reinforcement and response-independent reinforcement. When some disruption occurs in the environment, behaviors associated with richer schedules of reinforcement (antecedent and consequent to the behavior) show more persistence following that disruption. In the context of the classroom, where students are constantly faced with challenging school demands (i.e., unknown materials, substitute teacher, novel assignments), instructional staff delivering stimuli with known reinforcing properties (e.g., teacher verbal praise) contingently on the occurrence of school behaviors, as well as delivering stimuli with known reinforcing properties noncontingently on some time-based schedule, may increase the persistence of those school behaviors when classroom challenges arise. Delivering consistent contingent and noncontingent reinforcement requires the development of a time-based (interval) or response-based (ratio) schedule. Those schedules should also include whether the reinforcers (e.g., verbal praise, tokens) are delivered at a fixed time interval or a varied time interval, or whether the reinforcers are delivered following a fixed number of responses or following a varied number of responses.

High-Probability Request Sequence

Whereas an HPIS, discussed earlier in this chapter, has been defined as an academic strategy that increases compliance with low-compliance instructional tasks, the *high-probability request sequence (HPRS)* is defined as an intervention that increases compliance with low-compliance activity requests (Cooper et al., 2020). Identical to the HPIS, the HPRS is an antecedent strategy, conceptually based on behavioral momentum (Mace et al., 1988; Nevin et al., 1983), whereby a series of two to four brief, highly complied-with requests precedes a single, less-complied-with request. For example, when faced with a situation where a first-grade student who has a history of noncompliance when asked to return to his desk, a teacher has two options: (a) ask the student to return to his seat, which typically results in student noncompliance, or (b) present a series of highly complied-with, brief requests (e.g., "give me five, give me a high five, fist pump") immediately before asking the student to return to his seat. Choosing the first option often requires a repeat of the request (which may result in continued student noncompliance or behavioral escalation) or a teacher-delivered punishing consequence (e.g., verbal reprimand, loss of token/points, or removal from class), whereas the second option, the HPRS, has been shown to be highly effective in increasing compliance with requests typically not complied with (e.g., Belfiore et al., 2008; Mace et al., 1988; Riviere et al., 2011).

Implementing an HPRS requires a preassessment prior to intervention to determine request compliance. Belfiore et al., (2008) allowed for a series of typical classroom requests to be assessed over a three- to four-day period. The outcome of that preassessment resulted in a set of requests with a low probability of compliance (less than 40% compliance) and a set of requests with a high probability of compliance (greater than 80% compliance). Low probability of compliance requests (low-p) included "sit down," go to your desk," and "get work from the box." High probability of compliance requests (high-p) included "give me a high five," "raise your hand," and "clap your hands." The low-p requests served as the dependent variable, and the high-p requests served as the intervention. Whereas baseline was the delivery of only low-p commands ("return to your seat"), intervention was the delivery of two to four high-p commands ("give me a high five," raise your hand," and "clap your hands") prior to delivering the low-p command ("return to your seat"). The HPRS increased student percentage of compliance with low-p requests and the rate of reinforcement (e.g., teacher saying "That's great giving me five") to high-p requests, antecedent to the low-p request. The persistence of student compliance prior to the low-p request demonstrated a momentum-like effect increasing the probability of compliance with the low-p request ("return to your seat"). The HPRS is a proactive strategy, increasing the level of reinforcement available, resulting in increased classroom compliance and a richer history of success.

Token Economy and Lottery as a Classwide Strategy

A *token reinforcement system* defines an interconnected set of contingencies among (a) token-earning behavior, (b) tokens, (c) exchange opportunities, and (d) back-up reinforcers (Hackenberg, 2018). Tokens may be manipulable objects (e.g., tickets, coins) or nonmanipulable objects (e.g., stickers, marks on the chalkboard). Tokens are neutral stimuli that can be earned, accumulated, and exchanged for back-up reinforcers during scheduled exchange opportunities. Tokens derive their value as conditioned reinforcers from repeated pairings with the back-up reinforcers for which they are exchanged (Hackenberg, 2018). Back-up reinforcers may be unconditioned reinforcers (e.g., food, water) or conditioned reinforcers (e.g., privileges, opportunities, preferred tangibles).

A variation of a token reinforcement system is a consequent-based *lottery* or raffle, where students earn tokens (e.g., tickets) that are entered into a drawing for the opportunity to obtain a back-up reinforcer. Working with a group of eight students enrolled in an urban K-8 school, Glascott and Belfiore (2019) instituted a lottery system where students earned tickets on a Variable Momentary Time sampling-Differential Reinforcement of Other behavior schedule (VMT-DRO 150 seconds), where tickets were delivered contingent on the absence of noncompliant behavior only at the end of each cued interval. Students could earn up to 12 tickets per 30-minute session, and 2 tickets were drawn at the end of each intervention session. Using a single case ABAB design, results showed the token reinforcement, in the form of a groupwide lottery system, was successful at decreasing noncompliant behaviors during the guided reading group sessions (Glascott & Belfiore, 2019).

Fairness and Equity

Freire (1998) states teachers and students have educational roles, but each should show respect for the other. Building *fairness and equity* in the classroom is predicated on the teacher's ability to be humble, allowing for genuine dialog between teacher and student, and to be respectful of the lives of each child, with an understanding of what each child brings to the table. Freire (2014) asks: How can we teach without respecting our students? Assessing student preferences, setting behavioral expectations for the classroom through teacher–student dialog, and augmenting curriculum with culturally relevant curriculum all establish a condition of fairness and equity in the classroom. A classroom that is consistently fair and equitable for all builds reinforcement, resilience, and positive regard.

Specifically speaking of the Black male student, Edmin (2012) designed the 5 Cs of reality pedagogy. The 5 Cs include (a) Cogenerative dialog, brief end-of day conversations with students about the positive and negative outcomes of the class day and solutions; (b) Coteaching, encouraging students to lead the lesson while the teacher observes: teacher as learner and learner as teacher (Freire, 1998); (c) Cosmopolitanism, establishing class expectations that require responsibility of all for all; (d) Context/Cultural relevancy, using artifacts to connect the life of the student to the in-class lesson; and (e) Content, listening to our students; teacher humility (Edmin, 2012).

When working with students, brief, end-of-day conversations may only include a discussion of the positive outcomes observed that day. For example, the teacher brings students together for 10 to 15 minutes before dismissal, refreshing students as to the classroom behavioral expectations posted around the room. Next the teacher calls on each student allowing them to give examples of positive behaviors they witnessed that day. Points may be awarded to the student who "caught" the good behavior occurring and reported on it and to the student who was "caught" engaging in the good behavior. Both Edmin's 5 Cs and catching good behavior become classroom routines that build teamwork and respect for others, while reinforcing positive behavioral expectations. These strategies require students and teachers to take ownership of their behavior, as well as the collective behavior of the classroom team.

Summary

Students enrolled in high-poverty urban schools face both academic and disciplinary challenges (Noltemeyer & Mcloughlin, 2010), and as a result, this places them more at risk for academic failure than those students enrolled in low-poverty, nonurban schools (National Center for Education Statistics, 2019). In this chapter the behavior analytic premise put forward has been that when students are repeatedly exposed to aversive school situations, they engage in behaviors nonconducive to learning as a means to escape the aversiveness of the condition. Engaging in such behaviors results in disproportionately higher rates of school-based sanctions, reinforcing those escape-maintained behaviors. Additionally, in this chapter we have provided a number of applied, evidence-based strategies for use with at-risk students in high-poverty urban schools:

- Strategies for fostering academic success:
  - Curriculum-based assessment;
  - Assessing student preferences;
  - Classwide expectations;
  - Self-management;
  - Teacher-directed instruction;
  - High-probability instructional sequence;
  - Generalization;
  - Culturally relevant curriculum.
- Strategies for increasing positive classroom regard, reinforcement, and resilience:
  - High-probability request sequence;
  - Token economy and classwide lottery;
  - Fairness and equity.

Redesigning the academics through planning and instructing, while concurrently increasing positive regard, reinforcement, and resilience creates a school environment where academic success and social success are optimized, altering the valance of the environment from aversive to positive. In the end, Hilliard (2003) strongly suggests that the educational community has the pedagogical expertise to reduce the gap of academic proficiency in students enrolled in high-poverty, urban schools—now it is a matter of will.

References

Banks, T. (2015). Teacher education reform in urban preparation programs. *Journal of Education and Learning, 4*, 60–71. https://doi.org/10.5539/jel.v4n1p60

Belfiore, P. J., Auld, R., & Lee, D. L. (2005). The disconnection in poor urban education: Equal access and a pedagogy of risk-taking. *Psychology in the Schools, 42*, 855–863. https://doi.org/10.1002/pits.20116

Belfiore, P. J., & Lee, D. L. (2018). The role of evidence-based practices, and the potential for success in urban classrooms. *Journal of Evidence-Based Practices for Schools, 17*, 162–173.

Belfiore, P. J., Lee, D. L., Scheeler, M. C., & Klien, D. (2002). Implications of behavioral momentum and academic achievement for students with behavioral disorders: Linking theory with practice. *Psychology in the Schools, 39*, 171–180. https://doi.org/10.1002/pits.10028

Belfiore, P. J., Lee, D. L., Vargas, A. U., & Skinner, C. H. (1997). Effects of high preference, single digit mathematics problem completion on multiple digit mathematics problem performance. *Journal of Applied Behavior Analysis, 30*, 327–330. https://doi.org/10.1901/jaba.1997.30-327

Belfiore, P. J., Pulley-Basile, S., & Lee, D. L. (2008). Using a high probability command sequence to increase classroom compliance: The role of behavioral momentum. *The Journal of Behavioral Education, 17*, 160–171. https://doi.org/10.1007/s10864-007-9054-x

Black, M. M., & Krishmakumar, A. (1998). Children in low income urban settings: Interventions to promote mental health and well-being. *American Psychologist, 53*, 635–646. https://doi.org/10.1037/0003-066x.53.6.635

Blanchett, W. J., Mumford, V., & Beachum, F. (2005). Urban school failure and disproportionality on a post-Brown era. *Remedial and Special Education, 26*, 70–81. https://doi.org/10.1177/07419325050260020201

Blicha, A., & Belfiore, P. J. (2013). The effects of automated prompting and self-monitoring on homework completion for a student with Attention Deficit-Hyperactivity Disorder. *Journal of Education and Learning, 2*, 51–60. https://doi.org/10.5539/jel.v2n3p51

Bradshaw, C. P., Mitchell, M. M., O'Brennan, L. M., & Leaf, P. J. (2010). Multilevel exploration of factors contributing to the overrepresentation of black students in office disciplinary referrals. *Journal of Educational Psychology, 102*, 508–520. https://doi.org/10.1037/a0018450

Cabrera, N. L., Milem, J. F., Jaquette, O., & Marx, R. W. (2014). Missing the (student achievement) forest for all the (political) trees: Empiricism and the Mexican American Studies program in Tucson. *American Educational Research Journal, 51*, 1084–1118. https://doi.org/10.3102/0002831214553705

Carroll, R. A., Joachim, B. T., St. Peter, C., & Robinson, N. (2015). A comparison of error-correction procedures on skill acquisition during discrete-trial instruction. *Journal of Applied Behavior Analysis, 48*, 257–273. https://doi.org/10.1002/jaba.205

Cooper, J. O., Herron, T. E., & Heward, W. L. (2020). *Applied Behavior Analysis* (pp. 628–653). Pearson.

Edmin, C. (2012). Yes, black males are different, but different is not deficient. *Kappan, 93*, 13–16. https://doi.org/10.1177/003172171209300504

Engelmann, S., Becker, W. C., Carnine, D., & Gersten, R. (1988). The direct instruction follow through model: Design and outcomes. *Education and Treatment of Children, 11*, 303–317.

Fantuzzo, J., LeBoeuf, W., Rouse, H., & Chen, C. (2012). Academic achievement of African American boys: A city-wide, community-based investigation of risk and resilience. *Journal of School Psychology, 50*, 559–579. https://doi.org/10.1016/j.jsp.2012.04.004

Freire, P. (1998). *Pedagogy of freedom: Ethics, democracy, and civic courage*. Rowman and Littlefield.

Freire, P. (2014). *Pedagogy of commitment*. Paradigm Publishers.

Gipson, F. (1956). *Old yeller*. Harper.

Glascott, T., & Belfiore, P. J. (2019). The effects of token reinforcement, in the form of a lottery, on noncompliance in an urban third grade classroom. *Psychology and Behavioral Science International Journal, 13*(5), 555874. https://doi.org/10.19080/PBSIJ.2019.13.555874

Gregory, A., Skiba, R. J., & Noguera, P. A. (2010). The achievement gap and the discipline gap: Two sides of the same coin? *Educational Researcher, 39*, 59–68. https://doi.org/10.3102/0013189x09357621

Gregory, A., & Weinstein, R. S. (2008). The discipline gap and African Americans: Defiance or cooperation in the high school classroom. *Journal of School Psychology, 46,* 455–475. https://doi.org/10.1016/j.jsp.2007.09.001

Hackenberg, T. D. (2018). Token reinforcement: Translational research and application. *Journal of Applied Behavior Analysis, 51,* 393–435. https://doi.org/10.1002/jaba.439

Hilliard, A. (2003). No mystery: Closing the achievement gap between Africans and excellence. In T. Perry, C. Steele, & A. Hilliard (Eds.), *Young, gifted and black: Promoting high achievement among African-American students* (pp. 131–166). Beacon Press.

Hutchinson, J. M., & Belfiore, P. J. (1998). Adding a sequence of high-preference mathematic problems to increase low-preference mathematics problems performance. *Proven Practices, 1,* 12–16.

Kim, T., & Axelrod, S. (2005). Direct Instruction: An educators' guide and plea for action. *The Behavior Analyst Today, 6,* 111–120. https://doi.org/10.1037/h0100061

Lee, D. L., Belfiore, P. J., & Budin, S. G. (2008). Riding the wave: Creating a momentum of school success. *Teaching Exceptional Students, 40,* 65–70. https://doi.org/10.1177/004005990804000307

Lee, D. L., Lylo, B., Vostal, B., & Hua, Y. (2012). The effects of high-preference problems on the completion of nonpreferred mathematic problems. *Journal of Applied Behavior Analysis, 45,* 223–228. https://doi.org/10.1901/jaba.2012.45-223

Lewis, J., Aydin, A., & Powell, N. (2016). *March* (Trilogy). Top Shelf Productions.

Mace, F. C., Hock, M. L., Lalli, J. S., West, B. J., Belfiore, P. J., Pinter, E., & Brown, D. K. (1988). Behavioral momentum in the treatment of noncompliance. *Journal of Applied Behavior Analysis, 21,* 123–141. https://doi.org/10.1901/jaba.1988.21-123

McKinney, S. E., Campbell-Whately, G. D., & Kea, C. D. (2005). Managing student behavior in urban classrooms: The role of teacher ABC assessments. *The Clearing House, 79,* 16–20. https://doi.org/10.3200/tchs.79.1.16-20

Mucci, M., See, A., & Belfiore, P. J. (2018). Increasing opportunities to respond: The use of flash cards and mathematic racetrack on multiplication fact computation. *Journal of Evidence-Based Practices for School, 17,* 195–219.

National Center for Education Statistics. (2019). *The Nation's Report Card.* U.S. Department of Education and the Institute of Education Sciences.

Nevin, J. A., & Grace, R. C. (2000). Behavioral momentum and the law of effect. *Behavioral Brain Science, 23*(1), 73–90. https://doi.org/10.1017/a0140525x00002405

Nevin, J. A., Mandell, C., & Atak, J. R. (1983). The analysis of behavioral momentum. *Journal of the Experimental Analysis of Behavior, 39,* 49–59. https://doi.org/10.1901/jeab.1983.39-49

Noltemeyer, A., & McLoughlin, C. S. (2010). Patterns of exclusionary discipline by school typology, ethnicity, and their interaction. *Perspectives on Urban Education, Summer,* 27–40.

Payne, L. D., Marks, L. J., & Bogan, B. L. (2007). Using curriculum-based assessment to address academic and behavioral deficits of students with emotional and behavioral disorders. *Beyond Behavior, Spring,* 3–6.

Peterson, S. M., & Neef, N. A. (2020). Functional behavior assessment. In J. O. Cooper, T. E. Herron, & W. L. Heward (Eds.), *Applied behavior analysis* (pp. 628–653). Pearson.

Riviere, V., Becquet, M., Peltret, E., Facon, B., & Darcheville, J. (2011). Increasing compliance with medical examination requests directed to children with autism: Effects of a high-probability request procedure. *Journal of Applied Behavior Analysis, 44,* 193–197. https://doi.org/10.1901/jaba.2011.44-193

Sener Akin, U., & Belfiore, P. J. (2017). Mnemonic strategy: Improving letter-sound correspondence for students with dyslexia enrolled in an EFL program in Belgium. *Journal of Evidence-Based Practices for Schools, 16,* 23–45.

Simmons-Reed, E. A., & Cartledge, G. (2014). School discipline disproportionality: Culturally competent interventions for African American males. *Interdisciplinary Journal of Teaching and Learning, 4,* 95–109.

Skiba, R. J. (2014). The failure of zero reject. *Reclaiming Children and Youth, 22,* 27–33.

Skiba, R. J., Simmons, A. B., Ritter, S., Rausch, M. K., Cuadrado, J., & Chung, C. (2008). Achieving equity in special education: History, status, and current challenges. *Exceptional Children, 74,* 264–288. https://doi.org/10.1177/001440290807400301

Warren, S. R. (2002). Stories from the classrooms: How expectations and efficacy of diverse teachers affect the academic performance of children in poor urban schools. *Educational Horizons, 80,* 109–115.

Wehby, J. H., & Hollahan, M. S. (2000). Effects of high-probability requests on the latency to initiate academic tasks. *Journal of Applied Behavior Analysis, 33,* 259–262. https://doi.org/10.1901/jaba.2000.33-259

15
ADVANCES IN THE USE OF TECHNOLOGY AND ONLINE LEARNING TO IMPROVE OUTCOMES FOR STUDENTS WITH DISABILITIES

Sean J. Smith, Maggie A. Mosher, and K. Alisa Lowrey

In today's 21st-century classroom, technology is increasingly viewed as a tool that can further individualize the growth and development of students with disabilities (SWDs). When designed for the variability of the learner, technology can customize the learning experience, extending the strengths of the learner while further supporting the needs in order to develop the necessary academic, social, emotional, and behavioral skills (Edyburn, 2020). Over the past two decades, initiatives like one-to-one computer (e.g., laptops) and device (e.g., iPads) adoption programs have significantly increased access to and use of technology in K-12 instruction. Integrating these technologies into classroom instruction has featured variations of blended learning, gamification, educational apps, and efforts to embed the technology as a vital part of the instructional day (Smith & Basham, 2016a). With the onset of the 2020–2021 pandemic, technology's role in K-12 education dramatically increased with an urgency not seen before. The COVID-19 pandemic solidified the day-to-day instructional reliance on technology. Classroom teachers and building leaders went from the use of technology tools to facilitate aspects of instruction to the use of technology in order to access, direct, and conduct instruction on a daily basis. The trajectory of this change in the use of technology's impact on learning is unknown. Even so, due to the significant economic investment in educational technology, the role of technology in the education of all K-12 students, including SWDs, has been meaningfully altered.

Historical Context

Incorporating technology into content-area instruction for students with and without disabilities dates as far back as the 1970s (Woodward & Rieth, 1997). And yet technology for SWDs has often been limited to what we call assistive technology (AT) and tied to a designated support need within individualized education plans (IEPs; Adebisi et al., 2015). AT is defined as "any item, piece of equipment, or product system, whether acquired commercially off the shelf, modified, or customized, that is used to increase, maintain, or improve functional capabilities of a child with a disability" (Assistive Technology Act, 2004, p. 4). AT was first included in the Individuals with Disabilities Education Act (IDEA) (1997) under Related Services clarifying students' right to AT in their IEP. In the 1997 amendments to IDEA, Congress specifically required that AT be considered for every student with a disability as part of the annual IEP process, as part of the student's special education service delivery, a related service, or as a supplementary aid or service. The intent was to broaden student access to AT devices supported by accompanying services and to further empower IEP teams in the consideration of AT in the lives of SWDs. And yet placing AT within the context of the IEP has served as a double-edge sword. While it is a requirement tied to the IEP, the focus on the student and the individualized nature of the technology have led to the development of a time-intensive, formalized process. For example, over the past several decades, the selection of AT has often been determined through a consideration process, which has led to a specialized team of educators (e.g., speech and language pathologist, AT specialist) tasked with conducting an AT evaluation. While this process has led to successful AT determination, the required time and expertise entailed with the AT process, has led to a limited number of SWDs being considered for AT (Edyburn, 2020). As a result, the explosion of educational technology across K-12 classrooms is often underutilized due to the AT process (Edyburn, 2020).

In today's postpandemic world, viewing technology for SWDs through the lens of AT is limiting. With many commonly used digital devices having built-in assistive features, SWDs increasingly have access to the tools needed to promote a level of independence. The onset of the pandemic and the reliance on digital technologies throughout the 2020–2021 academic school year have changed the role of technology for all educational stakeholders. Teachers, and the students they serve, had limited choice in technology adoption. Students, educators, and even family members were forced to use various technology tools. Zoom, learning management systems (e.g., Google Classroom, SeeSaw), and other technology tools have become ubiquitous to remote, distant, online, or hybrid learning. Complicating the infusion of this technology tools and solutions into the instruction of SWDs is the fact that only a small portion of technology apps, programs, environments, and devices have been subjected to formal analysis in use for SWDs (Benavides-Varela et al., 2020). While frameworks like Universal Design for Learning (UDL) have increasingly been adopted to facilitate the design and planning of this new 21st-century classroom, those impacts are not clear either (Ok et al., 2017).

Although the 2020–2021 academic year led to a significant infusion of various technologies and their use within instructional design, there is a limited understanding of the growing research on these innovations and the implications on practice, as well as future research. For SWDs, this limited understanding of online learning existed prior to 2020–2021 and has, most likely, only increased since then (Smith et al., 2016). While this is expected to change with the dramatic implementation of various forms of online learning (e.g., hybrid, blended) during the 2020–2021 academic year, the current state of these limited investigations presents a number of unknowns as the educational field looks for direction, guidance, and information from which to make the instructional, behavioral, and social-emotional decisions vital for the growth and development of SWDs in the K-12 classroom.

In this chapter we discuss current empirical studies regarding the use and application of technologies in the education of SWDs particularly aligned to innovations supportive of online, hybrid, or distance education. To that end, we will highlight the current state of research focused on technology innovations aligned with online learning and its use for SWD by (a) examining recent empirical studies specific to technology and SWDs, highlighting technology aligned with online instruction; (b) considering implications of this research for practitioners through frameworks such as UDL; and (c) offering considerations for future research to foster further implementation of effective technology practice into the educational experiences of SWDs, particularly directed to online formats expected to be essential to individualizing instruction through flexible means in the postpandemic learning environment.

Technology Solutions for Students With Disabilities

Determining what we know is foundational to identifying future steps for both practitioners seeking to operationalize technologies in their instructional efforts within the K-12 classroom and for researchers seeking to further determine the impact of technologies in the lives of SWDs. To provide information on technology to meet current practitioner needs to support online learning as well as hybrid and face-to-face models, empirical research is presented here organized by educational technologies. Again, the technologies we have identified are innovations that align with the demands of online or hybrid instruction, taking into consideration the need for a level of student independence, limited direct teacher intervention, and tools that facilitate a further personalized or individualized nature of instruction often required in online or hybrid learning experiences (Smith & Basham, 2016).

Multimedia

Multimedia and its use in education often refers to the integration of text, data, images, graphics, audio, and video in a digital form (Ault et al., 2017). Investigations feature studies on behavior, instruction, and learning, as well as social-emotional development (Bouck et al., 2017). Although featuring a number of digital elements, video and the combination of audio with visuals has been at the forefront of multimedia interventions (e.g., video podcasting; Green et al., 2020). Embedding meaningful illustrations, detailed narrative, and making purposeful visual connections to instruction, video-based multimedia has shown to be particularly useful for teaching, maintaining, and generalizing student understanding. This is especially evident in the anchor, or the situated context multimedia fosters within the learner. Establishing connections between what the student knows and what the instruction seeks to further introduce, researchers have shown the ability, particularly through video, of improving student knowledge, comprehension, and ability to apply to subsequent instruction (Romig et al., 2018). Overall, research supports the use of the various interactive features of multimedia, particularly video, to assist SWD knowledge and skill development, and more important, students' ability to generalize to understanding and application (Romig et al., 2018).

Educational Apps

With the growth of one device for every child (e.g., one-to-one initiatives), investments in mobile devices (e.g., iPad), and the proliferation in the development of educational apps, a series of empirical students have examined the impact of these apps on the growth and development of SWDs. Ranging from investigations on behavior (Holcomb et al., 2020), literacy (Alison et al., 2017), writing, mathematics (Bouck et al., 2018), social-emotional (Esposito et al., 2017), and life skills (Jimenez & Alamer, 2018), researchers have sought to understand the role and subsequent impact of these apps on SWD outcomes. Regardless of the purpose, these educational app studies explored an array of issues, and yet used the app in one of two primary ways: (a) as a stand-alone app investigating its impact as an instructional, behavioral, or social emotional intervention or (b) in combination with an educational practice or effective interventions to determine the power of the combined approach.

Researchers have investigated the impact of apps combined with interventions or practices focused on behaviors, including applied behavioral analysis (Esposito et al., 2017), functional communication training (Muharib et al., 2019), and behavioral intervention plans (Holcomb et al., 2020). In the area of instruction, apps have been used with varied practices, including (a) learning strategies to promote reading comprehension, (b) systematic instruction to teach literacy skill development (Ault et al., 2017), (c) math manipulatives (Bouck et al., 2018), and (d) writing interventions and a variety of other classroom-based interventions (e.g., skill development to foster independent responses) (Jimenez & Alamer, 2018).

The majority of educational app studies featured investigations on the impact of the specific app. Overall, these studies either compared the educational app with a face-to-face or a traditional intervention (teacher-directed instruction) and/or measured the impact of student outcomes after the app intervention (e.g., learned skill, reduce inappropriate behaviors). Findings suggest educational apps have a positive impact on student development (Bouck et al., 2019). Although studies have varied in questions and methodology, outcomes suggest educational apps have a significant positive effect on student learning, their ability to learn, and their ability to complete independent tasks associated with their education (e.g., vocabulary, spelling, writing organization) (Esposito et al., 2017). Although sample sizes were small, with many studies featuring a multiple baseline methodology featuring fewer than ten participants, findings repeatedly indicate educational apps improve student development. These findings were regardless of the instructor's role. And yet many of these findings did not employ traditional instruction, so little comparison data are available (Evmenova et al., 2019). Further research is needed to determine how effective educational apps are in comparison with traditional instruction (e.g., student outcomes, time spent in the development).

Video Modeling

Based on Bandura's Social Learning Theory (1977), video modeling (VM) uses audio-visual technology (i.e., iPhone, iPad) to teach students through watching and imitating others' actions. This process allows educators to utilize students' visual strengths and removes extraneous stimuli. Studies conducted by Plavnick and Hume (2014) list VM as a cost-efficient and useful tool in teaching social skills to SWDs. VM's use ranges from increasing verbal social interactions (Oh-Young et al., 2018), to improving independent living skills (Wynkoop et al., 2018), to facilitating student self-instruction in daily scheduling, to reducing inappropriate behaviors. Student- and teacher-created VM, as well as online and television-produced VM (i.e., meTV, PEERS Role Play Videos), are effective means for teaching prosocial behaviors to SWDs (Naylor et al., 2019).

VM has been successful in both targeting skill development (e.g., food preparation) and increasing independence. Overall, findings continue to suggest VM is a technology-based solution to support SWDs to develop and do so at an increasing level of independence. The growing research illustrates technology-based options that are specific to the student needs, often independent of an educator, and lead to a desired skill (Oh-Young et al., 2018).

Digital Game-Based Learning

Digital game-based learning (DGBL) provides a combination of in-class lessons and educational gameplay where teachers present new concepts and students practice these concepts through digital games. Through focusing on students' motivation and engagement, DGBL differs from gamification, which utilizes game elements (i.e., levels, trophies) and infuses them within lessons to increase student engagement. For example, Byun and Joung (2018) reviewed 33 empirical studies analyzing the effects of DGBL on students' mathematic achievement in K-12 classrooms and found only small effect sizes on student learning. Additionally, they found DGBL predominately used in elementary grades and within math content, such as learning numbers and operations, measurement, and geometry. They did find DBGL widely used and highly engaging for students. While DGBL is engaging, it does not always lead to higher student outcomes. Therefore, other instructional methods directly connected to improved learning outcomes may provide a better use of resources.

Computer-Assisted Instruction

Computer-assisted instruction (CAI) encompasses all instruction or remediation presented on a computer. CAI has been used to provide initial instruction, additional practice with content, and remediation to support many SWDs. While CAI is seen as an effective instructional approach, researchers note that prerequisite skills are often identified as necessary for effective CAI use and that a prerequisite assessment should be conducted to determine additional support needs when using CAI.

Specific aspects of CAI have been studied to include virtual manipulatives/virtual models, multiple representations, and visual displays. The immediate feedback and interactive and engaging content within CAI (i.e., virtual manipulatives, multiple representations) encourage active engagement in learning for SWDs (Satsangi & Bouck, 2015). For example, embedding virtual, visual mathematical models within instruction and guided practice in strategic, rigorous, and explicit teaching has been shown to improve instruction for struggling learners (Bryant et al., 2016). In fact, virtual manipulatives alone have been shown to be useful tools for teaching, maintaining, and generalizing mathematical skills (i.e., area, perimeter, word problems) to students with learning disabilities (Satsangi & Bouck, 2015). Overall, research supports the use of interactive visual models (i.e., virtual manipulatives) within CAI to assist SWDs.

Intelligent Tutoring System

Intelligent tutoring systems (ITSs) aim to provide immediate and customizable feedback and instruction within the digital learning system and thus, without outside teacher support. ITS differs from CAI and DBGL. For instance, most ITSs utilize step-based interaction, whereas CAIs utilize answer-based user interfaces. ITS's adaptive nature to student needs and differences (e.g., prior knowledge, motivation levels) lends itself to having more favorable outcomes for SWDs. A meta-analysis by Kulik and Fletcher (2016) compared conventional instruction to problem-centered instructional models and found ITSs with computer-based scaffolding positively affected students' learning. These findings were regardless of the instructor's effects, study types, and region. While there is strong evidence that ITS can accurately scaffold problem-solving practices by providing adaptive guidance within problems (VanLehn, 2006), the limited inclusion of SWDs requires further research to determine how it specifically influences SWDs.

Virtual Reality

Virtual reality (VR) provides digital simulations of a real-world environment through varying computational devices (i.e., laptops, tablets, head-mounted displays) and exists on a continuum from non to fully immersive based on the type of technology used to display the environment (Carreon et al., 2020). For example, head-mounted displays (HMDs) are fully immersive, as users do not experience outside stimuli. In contrast, the same VR software (i.e., Unity, Unreal) presented through a computer screen would be regarded as nonimmersive. A descriptive review of 25 research studies conducted in K-12 settings examined the use of VR for content acquisition and found VR to be a promising instruction mode, particularly for SWDs (Carreon et al., 2020). VR can provide instruction with reduced verbal demands, visually appealing animations, and a user sense of embodied social presence, which contribute to increased learning motivation and attainment for struggling students (Howard & Gutworth, 2020). Likewise, VR-based interventions provide deliberate practice to improve student knowledge and skill performance autonomously.

Miller and Bugnariu (2016), as well as Bellani and colleagues (2011), found immersive VR to be a promising method of instruction for expressive communication and social reciprocity due to the ability to provide practice within an environment that closely mimics the real world while allowing for focus on targeted content. An educator's ability to select specific social-emotional learning (SEL) skills within a VR-delivered intervention allows for a more specialized and individualized environment for K-12 students (Howard & Gutworth, 2020). Overall, with the increased capacity of VR to offer immersive learning experiences, current findings suggest the further ability to independently support learner development. Besides SEL, the ability to create virtual learning environments suggests promise in content-based instruction, the development and practice of appropriate behavioral expectations, and further practice in skills critical for learning (e.g., executive functioning) (Carreon et al., 2020).

Augmented Reality

Augmented reality (AR) provides a digital overlay onto a real environment (i.e., HP Reveal) through mobile devices (i.e., iPads) or glasses (i.e., Thinkpad A3 Smart Glasses). Radu's (2014) meta-analysis found AR in educational settings improved motivation and learning for struggling students at a low to no financial cost. Educators can develop and implement AR forms (Bacca et al., 2014) through QR codes, interactive 3-D models, and specific content into physical objects with embedded codes (i.e., merge cubes). Of particular relevance is the flexibility of the AR tools (e.g., QR codes) that vary in cost, tool requirements, and similar flexible features. While AR can involve visuals, audio, interactive graphics, and other digital formats, it can also be simplified to an image and access to a variety of mobile devices. This flexibility offers variance in access and use by the educators and their students.

Online Learning

Providing instruction through inclusive online environments is a dynamic, multifactorial, and complex process that involves the student's and the educator's participation. Despite the increase in online learning in recent years, there is little evidence on this medium's effectiveness for SWDs (Dahlstrom-Hakki et al., 2020; Vasquez & Straub, 2016). Although online learning provides the ability to customize instructional design and delivery for the individual needs of SWDs, these same students are also influenced by the deficiencies of online educational environments. Studies have shown that educational technology can individualize learning for SWDs in some online settings (Dahlstrom-Hakki et al., 2020). Other studies suggest SWDs have increased difficulty in online learning compared to their neurotypical peers (Smith & Basham, 2016a). For success in online instruction, SWDs often require executive functioning and self-regulation skills (i.e., goal planning, organization, working memory, task initiation, impulse control), which are often areas of deficit (Basham et al., 2020).

It is critical to integrate supports and encourage metacognition within technology-delivered interventions (Basham et al., 2016a). For over a decade, researchers in K-12 online programs have identified that synchronous learning activities and web conferencing assist in supporting at-risk students' learning (Smith & Basham, 2016b). Research suggests deficits in executive functioning and self-regulation skills are significant predictors for lack of perseverance in online courses. Providing SWDs intensive support throughout online learning through methods such as executive function coaching support and real-time online dynamic social interactions (Ybarra & Winkielman, 2012) has the potential for decreasing these barriers (Dahlstrom-Hakki et al., 2020) Madaus and colleagues' (2011) needs assessment determined that a critical impediment to online learning for students with learning disabilities and attention deficit hyperactivity disorder (ADHD) was the lack of face-to-face interactions. However, instructor- and peer-mediated synchronous discussions significantly improve students' online learning outcomes (Means et al., 2013; Vasquez & Slocum, 2012).

Implications for Practice and Research

Implications for Practitioners

The rapid pace of technology innovations causes gaps between the use of technology for SWDs and empirical research (Kennedy & Boyle, 2017). Educators have focused on selecting tools to make instruction accessible for specific individuals with disabilities who may need a specific support to overcome a barrier within the instructional environment (Hall et al., 2012). However, recent trends in instructional design present an opportunity for practitioners to reimagine their use of technology in their curricular design. Thomas and colleagues (2019) present four considerations educators must make daily for the continued success of SWDs. These include (a) the match of the technology to the student, (b) the intervention or curriculum delivered through the technology, (c) the guidance required for successful use (i.e., guided practice), and (d) technology's impact on students.

Educators struggle to assist SWDs in online settings primarily due to struggles in supporting the digital environment's pedagogical design rather than the actual technology use (Carter & Rice, 2016). Teacher involvement facilitated through professional development on both the technology and intervention had a more significant effect on student learning outcomes.

Technology's individualized experience and reinforcement have the potential to assist educators in increasing students' motivation to continue using the intervention. For example, Lorenzo and colleagues (2016), utilizing HMDs for 20 students with autism spectrum disorder (ASD) and desktop VR for the remaining 20 students, found students using immersive VR maintained improvements in self-control, empathy, and emotion recognition for two years. The more immersive environment displayed more effortless transfer of the acquired skills into the real school environment than the desktop display. Both technologies ultimately taught the targeted social skills, which were independently maintained for students as they progressed through the school year. In fact, immersive technology has been shown to be so rewarding that teachers no longer need to provide students with external reinforcers for the intervention's continued use. Didehbani and colleagues (2016) discovered that the natural rewarding of appropriate social interactions by the immersive technology allowed teachers to stop providing physical rewards (i.e., cookies and stickers). Playing in the environment with the interactive objects became rewarding in itself.

It is imperative when selecting technology to ensure immersion levels and technology interaction requirements fit the student's sensory thresholds, ability levels, and areas of need. For example, Parsons (2015) found that participants with ASD who had lower verbal and executive abilities were more exploratory in the virtual environment and required more prompting to stay on task. Mantziou and colleagues (2015) also found the immersive technology was only useful when it matched the student's sensory seeking and avoiding behaviors.

Additionally, designing technology as a part of the curriculum must be considered. The UDL framework offers a design structure that posits technology at the very forefront of how we make decisions about teaching and learning (Rose & Meyer, 2002). Focused on the curriculum rather than an individual student, the UDL framework supports practitioners to incorporate technology that enhances representation, engagement, action, and expression by removing barriers. While not synonymous with UDL, technology can be used proactively through the UDL framework to design curriculum that embraces the variable needs of all learners (Rose et al., 2005). Intentionally designing curriculum to incorporate options for learners that include tools like text-to-speech, computer-assisted learning options, readability options, etc., can create a more engaging, active curriculum that supports universal useability of technology (Edyburn, 2020). For educators, this is different from selecting a technology to support one student based on the inaccessibility of the curriculum (i.e., AT). The expanded use of the UDL framework through the Every Student Succeeds Act of 2015 (ESSA) and the Higher Education Act of 2008 has identified the UDL framework as an educational innovation that is here to stay. Paired with the explosion of online/hybrid learning environments enabled through the COVID-19 pandemic, the UDL framework is beneficial in bringing technology into the initial curriculum design decisions. Shifting the mindset of educators to view the selection, implementation, and evaluation of technology as something that must be considered alongside educational goals, methods, materials, and assessments for the entire class comes with implementations for practice. This directly affects teacher preparation and training.

Since the passage of ESSA, states have increasingly identified UDL as an initiative area for preservice and in-service teacher training. Models of professional development have been implemented to support teachers in using the framework for curriculum decision-making. These models include seminars (Lowrey et al., 2019), online learning modules (Lee & Griffin, 2021), online coursework (Evmenova, 2018), and embedding UDL in teacher preparation, to name a few. To better understand the impact of the UDL framework on the selection and use of technology within the classroom, states with UDL as an ESSA initiative area must collect outcomes related to the selection, implementation, and evaluation of technology by educators. State systems should be transparent about their utilization of the UDL framework in curriculum decisions, including those decisions that use technology from a universal useability perspective (Edyburn, 2020). Transparently codifying systems change through initiatives in teacher preparation and professional development, curriculum decisions, technology decisions, and purchasing will effectively support the field of education to make better decisions about implementation of the UDL framework as it applies to technology. Additionally, district innovations that demonstrate the use of technology through the UDL framework as a method to enhance the learning experience should be shared. Finally, individual teacher experiences in using the UDL framework to select, implement, and evaluate technology would be beneficial to understanding, replicating, and/or improving teacher experiences with UDL and technology. The UDL reporting criteria may be useful to support these endeavors (Rao et al., 2020).

Implications for Future Research

When considering technology interventions, it is essential to reflect upon the design (Jarrold et al., 2013), teaching strategies utilized, research-based principles, and students' active engagement (Satsangi & Bouck, 2015). Researchers and programmers must consider how technology can be leveraged to provide continuity of instruction and the successful acquisition of knowledge for each user's unique needs. Future research must consider not only the student's understanding of the technology but also key stakeholders who will be assisting students with implementation. The needs of these key stakeholders must be examined beyond basic professional development in how to effectively use the technology. Schaaf (2018) found that even when teacher professional development was found to be satisfactory in improving teacher understanding and their ability to generally apply technology for SWDs, trouble persisted in (a) the inability to problem-solve technology implementation, (b) identifying errors in selection and how to correct efforts to apply technology, and (c) choosing alternatives to the technology when the tool was determined to be ineffective. Researchers must consider potential instructional techniques that can assist practitioners in problem-solving technology implementation and effective application.

Implementing the UDL framework as a path to engage technology use directly related to the instructional goals, methods, materials, and assessments has implications for future research as well. Researchers must continue to investigate the in-service and preservice models of teacher professional development utilizing a UDL system (Evmenova, 2018; Lee & Griffin, 2021; Lowrey et al., 2019). Additionally, closer analysis of the universal useability of technology as it fits within the UDL framework in face-to-face, hybrid, and online learning should be measured, as well as the continued use of technology as AT for individual learners. Helpful here is the nationwide research agenda proposed by Smith and colleagues in 2019, tweaked specifically to include the analysis of technology use within the UDL frame. A plethora of research methodologies as suggested by Saffar (2019), Basham et al. (2020), and Ok et al. (2017) are necessary to establish how the UDL framework can support the implementation of technology as part of the curriculum design rather than as an addendum or retrofitted tool. Research must be conducted at the systemic level of states, districts, schools, and classrooms. Individual teacher experiences must be explored to better understand the decision-making of educators as they select technology to support the curriculum goals, methods, and assessments. Stakeholders (families, students) must be included in the research if we are to learn from the issues of 2020 remote learning. Finally, the implementation of the UDL reporting criteria in these research endeavors would further validate the findings for replication in practice (Rao et al., 2020).

Box 15.1 Additional Readings and Resources

Recognizing that the parameters of a chapter offer certain restrictions in what we can and cannot include within a defined space, there are a number of excellent readings and resources to suggest in order for one to learn more about the trends oriented around technology and SWDs. Following is an initial list for consideration:

1. National Council on Learning Disabilities (2020). *Inclusive technology in a 21st century learning system*. Washington, DC: NCLD.
2. Rao, K., Smith, S. J., Edyburn, D., Grima-Farrell, C., Van Horn, G., Yalon-Chamovitz, S. (2018). *UDL Reporting Criteria*. Report developed by a working group of the Universal Design for Learning Implementation and Research (UDL-IRN) Research Committee. Retrieved from https://udl-irn.org/udl-reporting-criteria/
3. Smith, S. J., Rao, K., Lowrey, K. A., Garder, J., Moore, E., Coy, K. Marino, M. T., & Wojcik, B. (2019). Recommendations for a national research agenda in Universal Design for Learning (UDL): Outcomes from the UDL-IRN Preconference on Research. *Journal of Disability Policy Studies*, *30*(3), 174–185. https://doi.org/10.1177/1044207319826219

References

Adebisi, R. O., Liman, N. A., & Longpoe, P. K. (2015). Using assistive technology in teaching children with learning disabilities in the 21st century. *Journal of Education and Practice*, *6*(24), 14–20.

Alison, C., Root, J. R., Browder, D. M., & Wood, L. (2017). Technology-based shared story reading for students with autism who are English-language learners. *Journal of Special Education Technology*, *32*(2), 91–101. https://doi.org/10.1177/0162643417690606

Amend Assistive Technology Act of 1998, Pub. L. No. 108–364, § 2, 118 Stat. 1701 (2004).

Ault, M. J., Baggerman, M. A., & Horn, C. K. (2017). Effects of an app incorporating systematic instruction to teach spelling to students with developmental delays. *Journal of Special Education Technology*, *32*(3), 123–137. https://doi.org/10.1177/0162643417696931

Bacca, J., Baldiris, S., Fabregat, R., & Graf, S. (2014). Augmented reality trends in education: A systematic review of research and applications. *Journal of Educational Technology & Society*, *17*, 133.

Basham, J. D., Blackorby, J., & Marino, M. T. (2020). Opportunity in crisis: The role of universal design for learning in educational redesign. *Learning Disabilities: A Contemporary Journal*, *18*(1), 71–91.

Basham, J. D., Hall, T. E., Carter, R. A., Jr., & Stahl, W. M. (2016a). An operationalized understanding of personalized learning. *Journal of Special Education Technology*, *31*, 126–136. https://doi.org/10.1177/0162643416660835

Bellani, M., Fornasari, L., Chittaro, L., & Brambilla, P. (2011). Virtual reality in autism: State of the art. *Epidemiology and Psychiatric Sciences*, *20*(3), 235–238. https://doi.org/10.1017/S2045796011000448

Benavides-Varela, S., Callegher, C. Z., Fagiolini, B., Leo, I., Altoè, G., & Lucangeli, D. (2020). Effectiveness of digital-based interventions for children with mathematical learning difficulties: A meta-analysis. *Computers & Education*, *157*, 103953. https://doi.org/10.1016/j.compedu.2020.103953

Bouck, E. C., Bassette, L., Shurr, J., Park, J., Kerr, J., & Whorley, A. (2017). Teaching equivalent fractions to secondary students with disabilities via the virtual—representational—abstract instructional sequence. *Journal of Special Education Technology*, *32*(4), 220–231. https://doi.org/10.1177/0162643417727291

Bouck, E. C., Park, J., Satsangi, R., Cwiakala, K., & Levy, K. (2019). Using the virtual-abstract instructional sequence to support acquisition of algebra. *Journal of Special Education Technology*, *34*(4), 253–268. https://doi.org/10.1177/0162643419833022

Bouck, E. C., Shurr, J., Bassette, L., Park, J., & Whorley, A. (2018). Adding it up: Comparing concrete and app-based manipulatives to support students with disabilities with adding fractions. *Journal of Special Education Technology*, *33*(3), 194–206. https://doi.org/10.1177/0162643418759341

Bryant, B. R., Bryant, D. P., Porterfield, J., Dennis, M. S., Falcomata, T., Valentine, C., . . . Bell, K. (2016). The effects of a Tier 3 intervention on the mathematics performance of second grade students with severe mathematics difficulties. *Journal of Learning Disabilities*, *49*(2), 176–188. https://doi.org/10.1177/0022219414538516

Byun, J., & Joung, E. (2018). Digital game-based learning for K—12 mathematics education: A meta-analysis. *School Science and Mathematics*, *118*(3–4), 113–126. https://doi.org/10.1111/ssm.12271

Carreon, A., Smith, S. J., Mosher, M., Rao, K., & Rowland, A. (2020). A review of virtual reality intervention research for students with disabilities in k-12 settings. *Journal of Special Education Technology*. https://doi.org/10.1177/0162643420962011

Carter, R. A., Jr., & Rice, M. (2016). Administrator work in leveraging technologies for students with disabilities in online coursework. *Journal of Special Education Technology*, *31*, 137–146. https://doi.org/10.1177/0162643416660838

Dahlstrom-Hakki, I., Alstad, Z., & Banerjee, M. (2020). Comparing synchronous and asynchronous online discussions for students with disabilities: The impact of social presence. *Computers & Education*, *150*, 103842. https://doi.org/10.1016/j.compedu.2020.103842

Didehbani, N., Allen, T., Kandalaft, M., Krawczyk, D., & Chapman, S. (2016). Virtual reality social cognition training for children with high functioning autism. *Computers in Human Behavior*, *62*, 703–711. https://doi.org/10.1016/j.chb.2016.04.033

Edyburn, D. L. (2020). Universal usability and universal design for learning. *Intervention in School and Clinic*, *56*(5). https://doi.org/10.1177/1053451220963082

Esposito, M., Sloan, J., Tancredi, A., Gerardi, G., Postiglione, P., Fotia, F., Napoli, E., Mazzone, L., Valeri, G., & Vicari, S. (2017). Using tablet applications for children with autism to increase their cognitive and social skills. *Journal of Special Education Technology*, *32*(4), 199–209. https://doi.org/10.1177/0162643417719751

Evmenova, A. S. (2018). Preparing teachers to use universal design for learning to support diverse learners. *Journal of Online Learning Research*, *4*(2), 147–171.

Evmenova, A. S., Graff, H. J., Genaro Motti, V., Giwa-Lawal, K., & Zheng, H. (2019). Designing a wearable technology intervention to support young adults with intellectual and developmental disabilities in inclusive postsecondary academic environments. *Journal of Special Education Technology*, *34*(2), 92–105. https://doi.org/10.1177/0162643418795833

Green, K. B., Stuckey, A., Towson, J. A., Robbins, S. H., & Bucholz, J. L. (2020). Special education preservice teacher knowledge of mathematics methods: The effects of content acquisition podcasts (CAPs). *Journal of Special Education Technology*, *35*(3), 145–154. https://doi.org/10.1177/0162643419854494

Hall, T. E., Meyer, A., & Rose, D. H. (2012). *Universal design for learning in the classroom: Practical applications*. Guilford Press.

Holcomb, C., Baker, J. N., & More, C. (2020). Digital behavior intervention plans: Effects on general education teacher fidelity of implementation. *Journal of Special Education Technology*, *35*(3), 155–166. https://doi.org/10.1177/0162643419854502

Howard, M. C., & Gutworth, M. B. (2020). A meta-analysis of virtual reality training programs for social skill development. *Computers & Education*, *144*, 103707. https://doi.org/10.1016/j.compedu.2019.103707

Individuals with Disability Education Act Amendments of 1997 [IDEA], Pub. L. No. 105-17 Stat. 37 (1997). https://www.congress.gov/105/plaws/publ17/PLAW-105publ17.pdf

Jarrold, W., Mundy, P., Gwaltney, M., Bailenson, J., Hatt, N., . . . Swain, L. (2013). Social attention in a virtual public speaking task in higher functioning children with autism. *Autism Research*, *6*(5), 393–410. https://doi.org/10.1002/aur.1302

Jimenez, B. A., & Alamer, K. (2018). Using graduated guidance to teach iPad accessibility skills to high school students with severe intellectual disabilities. *Journal of Special Education Technology*, *33*(4), 237–246. https://doi.org/10.1177/0162643418766293

Kennedy, M., & Boyle, J. R. (2017). The promise and problem with technology in special education: Implications for academic learning. In J. M. Kauffman, D. P. Hallahan, & P. Pullen (Eds.), *Handbook of special education* (pp. 606–614). Routledge. https://doi.org/10.4324/9781315517698-46

Kulik, J. A., & Fletcher, J. D. (2016). Effectiveness of intelligent tutoring systems: A meta analytic review. *Review of Educational Research, 86*(1), 42–78. http://doi.org/10.3102/0034654315581420

Lee, A., & Griffin, C. C. (2021). Exploring online learning modules for teaching universal design for learning (UDL): Preservice teachers' lesson plan development and implementation. *Journal of Education for Teaching*. https://doi.org/10.1080/02607476.2021.1884494

Lorenzo, G., Lledó, A., Pomares, J., & Roig, R. (2016). Design and application of an immersive virtual reality system to enhance emotional skills for children with autism spectrum disorders. *Computers & Education, 98*, 192–205. https://doi.org/10.1016/j.compedu.2016.03.018

Lowrey, K. A., Classen, A. I., Sylvest, A. E. (2019). Exploring ways to support preservice teachers' use of UDL in planning and instruction. *Journal of Educational Research and Practice, 9*, 261–281.https://doi.org/10.5590/JERAP.2019.09.1.19

Madaus, J. W., Banerjee, M., McKeown, K., & Gelbar, N. (2011). Online and blended learning: The advantages and the challenges for students with learning disabilities and attention deficit/hyperactivity disorder. *Learning Disabilities: A Multidisciplinary Journal, 17*(2), 69–76.

Mantziou, O., Vrellis, I., & Mikropoulos, T. A. (2015). Do children in the spectrum of autism interact with real-time emotionally expressive human controlled avatars? *Procedia Computer Science, 67*, 241–251. https://doi.org/10.1016/j.procs.2015.09.268

Means, B., Toyama, Y., Murphy, R., & Baki, M. (2013). The effectiveness of online and blended learning: A meta-analysis of the empirical literature. *Teachers College Record, 115*(3), 1–47.

Miller, H., & Bugnariu, N. L. (2016). Level of immersion in virtual environments impacts the ability to assess and teach social skills in autism spectrum disorder. *Cyberpsychology, Behavior, and Social Networking, 19*(4), 246–256. https://doi.org/10.1089/cyber.2014.0682

Muharib, R., Correa, V. I., Wood, C. L., & Haughney, K. L. (2019). Effects of functional communication training using GoTalk Now™ iPad® application on challenging behavior of children with Autism Spectrum Disorder. *Journal of Special Education Technology, 34*(2), 71–79. https://doi.org/10.1177/0162643418783479

Naylor, A., Spence, S., & Poed, S. (2019). Using video modelling to teach expected behaviours to primary students. *Support for Learning, 34*, 389–403. https://doi.org/10.1111/1467-9604.12274

Oh-Young, C., Filler, J., Kucskar, M., Buchter, J., O'Hara, K., & Gelfer, J. (2018). A comparison of peer network and peer video modeling to increase positive verbal social interactions in young children with disabilities. *Journal of Special Education Technology, 33*(4), 270–283. https://doi.org/10.1177/0162643418776631

Ok, M. W., Rao, K., Bryant, B. R., & McDougall, D. (2017). Universal design for learning in pre-k to grade 12 classrooms: A systematic review of research. *Exceptionality, 25*(2), 116–138. https://doi.org/10.1080/09362835.2016.1196450

Parsons, S. (2015). Learning to work together: Designing a multi-user virtual reality game for social collaboration and perspective-taking for children with autism. *International Journal of Child-Computer Interaction, 6*, 28–38. https://doi.org/10.1016/j.ijcci.2015.12.002

Plavnick, J. B., & Hume, K. A. (2014). Observational learning by individuals with autism: A review of teaching strategies. *Autism, 18*(4), 458–466. https://doi.org/10.1177/1362361312474373

Radu, I. (2014). Augmented reality in education: A meta-review and cross-media analysis. *Personal and Ubiquitous Computing, 18*(6), 1533–1543. https://doi.org/10.1007/s00779-013-0747-y

Rao, K., Ok, M. W., Smith, S. J., Evmenova, A. S., & Edyburn, D. (2020). Validation of the UDL reporting criteria with extant UDL research. *Remedial and Special Education, 41*(4), 219–230. https://doi.org/10.1177/0741932519847755

Romig, J. E., Sundeen, T., Thomas, C. N., Kennedy, M. J., Philips, J., Peeples, K. N., Rodgers, W. J., & Mathews, H. M. (2018). Using multimedia to teach self-regulated strategy development to preservice teachers. *Journal of Special Education Technology, 33*(2), 124–137. https://doi.org/10.1177/0162643417746373

Rose, D. H., Hasselbring, T. S., Stahl, S., & Zabala, J. (2005). Assistive technology and universal design for learning: Two sides of the same coin. In *Handbook of special education technology research and practice* (pp. 507–518). Knowledge By Design.

Rose, D. H., & Meyer, A (2002). *Teaching every student in the digital age: Universal design for learning.* ASCD.

Saffar, O. A. (2019). Using the pragmatic approach with special education and universal design for learning (UDL). *Journal of Education and Practice, 10*, 124–135.

Satsangi, R., & Bouck, E. C. (2015). Using virtual manipulative instruction to teach the concepts of area and perimeter to secondary students with learning disabilities. *Learning Disability Quarterly, 38*, 174–186. https://doi.org/10.1177/0731948714550101

Schaaf, D. N. (2018). Assistive technology instruction in teacher professional development. *Journal of Special Education Technology*, *33*(3), 171–181. https://doi.org/10.1177/0162643417753561

Smith, S. J., & Basham, J. B. (2016a). K-12 online learning: Leadership considerations for the 21st century classroom. *Journal of Special Education Leadership*, 67–69.

Smith, S. J., & Basham, J. B. (2016b). The emerging field of online special education. *Journal of Special Education Technology*, *31*, 123–125. https://doi.org/10.1177/0162643416660839

Smith, S. J., Basham, J. B., Rice, M., & Carter, R. (2016). Preparing special educators for the K-12 online learning environment: A survey of teacher educators. *Journal of Special Education Technology*, *31*, 170–178.

Thomas, C. N., Peeples, K. N., Kennedy, M. J., & Decker, M. (2019). Riding the special education technology wave: Policy, obstacles, recommendations, actionable ideas, and resources. *Intervention in School and Clinic*, *54*(5), 295–303. https://doi:10.1177/1053451218819201

VanLehn, K. (2006). The behavior of tutoring systems. *International Journal of Artificial Intelligence in Education*, *16*(3), 227–265.

Vasquez, E., & Slocum, T. (2012). The evaluation of synchronous online tutoring for students at-risk of reading failure. *Exceptional Children*, *78*, 221–235. https://doi.org/10.1177/001440291207800205

Vasquez, E. I., & Straub, C. (2016). Online writing instruction for children with disabilities: A review of the empirical literature. *Reading & Writing Quarterly: Overcoming Learning Difficulties*, *32*(1), 81–100. https://doi.org/10.1080/10573569.2014.951502.

Woodward, J., & Rieth, H. (1997). A historical review of technology research in special education. *Review of Educational Research*, *67*, 503–536. https://doi.org/10.3102/00346543067004503

Wynkoop, K. S., Robertson, R. E., & Schwartz, R. (2018). The effects of two video modeling interventions on the independent living skills of students with Autism Spectrum Disorder and intellectual disability. *Journal of Special Education Technology*, *33*(3), 145–158. https://doi.org/10.1177/0162643417746149

Ybarra, O., & Winkielman, P. (2012). On-line social interactions and executive functions. *Towards a Neuroscience of Social Interaction*, *188*. https://doi.org/10.3389/fnhum.2012.00075

16
ENHANCING THE SOCIAL LIVES OF STUDENTS WITH DISABILITIES
Effective Practices and Improved Outcomes

Erik W. Carter, Hilary E. Travers, and Michael Tuttle

Education is a substantially social endeavor. Each day, hundreds of students with and without disabilities enter their school to learn alongside their peers from scores of committed educators. Classrooms are dominated by academic discussions and collaborative projects. Cafeterias reverberate with chatter among friends. Recess provides a reprieve of play with schoolmates. Hallways are filled with locker conversations and passing exchanges. And extracurriculars connect students around shared interests and common pursuits. Nearly every moment of the school day is spent in the company of others. The extent to which students can successfully navigate—and enjoy—these myriad interactions and multiple relationships can substantially affect their learning and engagement in school (Bukowski et al., 2020; Zins et al., 2007). In other words, students' social experiences are not an incidental aspect of schooling; they can have a major influence on educational outcomes.

Yet many students with disabilities struggle with the social dimensions of schooling. Students may be unsure of how to interact successfully with their peers or with adults, or they may lack the skills needed to do so effectively and consistently across contexts. Some students have complex communication needs that require augmentative and alternative communication (AAC) supports. Others experience significant difficulties regulating their emotions and managing their interpersonal behaviors. Indeed, social and communication challenges are named among the eligibility criteria for multiple special education categories (e.g., autism, deaf-blindness, emotional disturbance, intellectual disability, speech-language impairment). However, social-related needs can still be evident among students regardless of the disability label they receive (Wiley & Siperstein, 2015).

The social challenges students with disabilities encounter are often reflected in the outcomes they experience. Hundreds of descriptive, observational, and intervention studies illustrate the paucity of social interactions or positive peer relationships within or beyond the school day (e.g., Biggs et al., 2018; Carter et al., 2010; Garrote et al., 2017). Likewise, nationally representative studies of elementary and secondary students report wide variations in friendships and interpersonal competence within and across disability categories (Blackorby et al., 2005; Wagner et al., 2003). For example, Table 16.1 highlights six social-related measures collected as part of the most recent National Longitudinal Transition Study-2012 (Lipscomb et al., 2017). Such studies present a complex portrait of the social experiences of students with disabilities. Although some students are thriving socially, many more are struggling in this area.

Table 16.1 Example Social Outcomes of Adolescents With Disabilities

Disability Category	Gets Together With Friends Weekly[a]	Knows How to Make Friends[a]	Can Make Friends in New Situations[a]	Chooses to Do Activities With Friends[a]	Has Trouble Communicating by Any Means[b]	Has Trouble Understanding What Other People Say[b]
Autism	29%	76%	67%	45%	50%	70%
Deaf-blindness	16%	97%	85%	51%	75%	84%
Emotional disturbance	58%	88%	80%	60%	17%	41%
Hearing impairment	47%	91%	82%	56%	44%	70%
Intellectual disability	42%	92%	86%	48%	60%	69%
Multiple disabilities	35%	91%	80%	53%	62%	61%
Orthopedic impairment	35%	95%	87%	61%	41%	33%
Other health impairment	57%	94%	86%	57%	21%	46%
Specific learning disability	56%	93%	89%	57%	20%	35%
Speech or language impairment	53%	95%	89%	57%	39%	35%
Traumatic brain injury	48%	91%	91%	59%	40%	53%
Visual impairment	47%	90%	91%	61%	13%	20%
All students with IEPs	52%	92%	86%	56%	29%	44%

Source: Data are derived from Lipscomb et al. (2017).
[a]Student report. [b]Parent report.

A well-rounded education must devote serious attention to the social needs of students with disabilities. In the absence of meaningful assessment and focused intervention, students may miss out on the skills, knowledge, supports, and opportunities needed to develop socially and academically. This chapter addresses the roles that educators can play in enhancing the social skills, participation, and relationships of students with disabilities. We begin by describing six types of social outcomes educators might work to promote. We then review ten research-based practices that contribute to noticeable changes in one or more of these areas. Next, we detail the roles educators should play in addressing the social dimensions of their students' lives. Finally, we conclude by offering recommendations for research focused on improving the social outcomes of students with and without disabilities.

The Aims of Interventions

Equipping students with disabilities to thrive socially is a complex endeavor. Indeed, the social domain is multifaceted and—as illustrated in the opening paragraph—it is experienced in numerous ways throughout each school day. Enhancing the social success of students with disabilities often requires attending to multiple dimensions of their social experiences. In this section, we describe six primary outcome areas that can be addressed within social-focused interventions for students with disabilities. Each of these outcomes are prominent within the research literature and/or are emphasized in prevailing frameworks (e.g., Bukowski et al., 2020; Carter, 2018). Each area is closely related to the others and comprises a potential outcome for intervention efforts.

Social Skills

Social skills refer to the collection of verbal and nonverbal interpersonal behaviors students use in the midst of their daily interactions with peers, teachers, and others (McDaniel et al., 2018). Knowing how to communicate effectively, work collaboratively, resolve conflict, and establish friendships can be key to developing and navigating satisfying and valued relationships. Moreover, such skills can contribute to academic success within the classroom. Although the importance of specific social skills should always be considered in light of context, chronology, and culture, studies have identified an array of social skills that are highly valued by teachers, employers, parents, and peers (e.g., Agran et al., 2016; Lane et al., 2006). These include controlling one's temper in conflict situations, following directions, getting along with people who are different, and listening to others. The degree to which students are familiar with and fluent in the use of these skills can affect the quality of their interactions, as well as shape how others evaluate their social competence. Educators often draw upon social skill checklists or an array of formal assessments to decide which social skills to address and to evaluate the impact of their instruction.

Social Interactions

Social interactions are the communicative exchanges students have with other people throughout the school day. Such interactions can range from brief greetings to extended conversations, and they are a primary avenue through which students access social support from others. Within the classroom, social interactions regularly take place as part of small-group projects, during whole-class discussions, when seeking assistance, or after instruction has concluded. Outside of the classroom, other peers are usually the primary interaction partners in cafeterias, clubs, homerooms, hallways, playgrounds, and buses. For students who are socially isolated or who are supported primarily by one-to-one paraprofessionals, promoting interactions with peers can increase access to the general curriculum and set the stage for friendship formation. Educators usually rely on direct observation to examine the frequency, focus, and reciprocity of students' interactions with different conversation partners (e.g., peers, adults).

Social Participation

Social participation entails having ongoing involvement in inclusive activities alongside other same-age students at one's school. This could involve being part of the same array of extracurricular activities, after-school events, school programs, field trips, or academic and elective classes as anyone else. Many students with disabilities—particularly those with autism, intellectual disability, and multiple disabilities—have restricted access to general education courses and limited involvement in other school programming (Lipscomb et al., 2017; Williamson et al., 2020). Absence from typical school activities affects the degree to which students with disabilities come to be known by others, have opportunities to interact, and feel like a full member of the school community. Moreover, friendships typically emerge from regular participation in shared activities with peers over time.

Documenting changes in social participation is one way educators can evaluate the impact of social-focused interventions.

Social Relationships

Social relationships are the personal connections students develop and maintain with others over time. These relationships can range from casual acquaintances to close friendships to romantic partners. Moreover, students can develop valued relationships with both adults (e.g., teachers, assistants, mentors, coaches, supervisors) and similar-age peers (e.g., classmates, clubmates, teammates, tutors, coworkers, neighbors). Each of these social relationships can serve different functions and hold varied importance to a student at particular points in time. For example, friendships—which are marked by close companionship, mutual affection, and reciprocity—are often prioritized by children and youth. The constellation of relationships students develop is considered to be their social network. Among students with disabilities, the size, composition, and quality of these social networks can vary widely (Lipscomb et al., 2017). For example, friendships are often quite limited for students with severe disabilities, whereas prosocial peer relationships may be less common for students with emotional disturbance. Educators often rely on student self-report, peer nominations, or observations when characterizing the social networks of their students with disabilities.

Social Acceptance

Social acceptance refers to the extent to which students are viewed positively by others in the school community. The experience of being accepted or rejected by one's peers can directly affect overall well-being and school engagement (Bukowski et al., 2020). Although views about disability have improved dramatically over the last few decades (Siperstein et al., 2007), some students still hold negative attitudes or display unwelcoming postures toward their schoolmates with disabilities. This may be especially pronounced when students with disabilities have extensive support needs, exhibit problem behaviors, or interact in unconventional ways. Social acceptance can be influenced by multiple factors, including the social skills of students with disabilities, the nature of their interactions with others, or the attitudes others hold about disability. Although a variety of attitude scales and climate surveys can be used to assess broader acceptance of certain student groups within a school, educators often examine the actions of peers (e.g., positive and negative interactions, bullying) within a particular setting when gauging the degree of social acceptance for a student with disabilities.

Belonging

Belonging is the assurance of acceptance, value, and membership within a particular community. Although belonging has been defined in quite varied ways, its importance is widely affirmed (Baumeister & Leary, 1995). When belonging is experienced, relationships and learning may be more likely to flourish. In contrast, the absence of belonging is associated with a host of deleterious outcomes (e.g., Korpershoek et al., 2020). Although students with disabilities have experienced increased involvement in the life of their school over the past few decades, belonging is not an automatic outcome of inclusion. Instead, Carter (2021) argues that belonging is most likely to be experienced when students with disabilities are present, invited, welcomed, known, accepted, supported, heard, befriended, needed, and loved. These ten dimensions of belonging can be used by educators to examine the experiences of their students in this area.

Approaches to Intervention

Research addressing the social outcomes of students with disabilities has spanned more than five decades. Over this time, hundreds of studies have examined a multitude of approaches for improving social competence and peer relationships within and beyond the school. Recognizing that an exhaustive review of every intervention approach and configuration is beyond the scope of this chapter, we instead present a broader overview of interventions that have some evidence of both impact and feasibility. In other words, we highlight interventions that have produced improvements in valued social outcomes (see prior section) and that can be readily implemented by educators in ordinary schools.

We organize available interventions into two primary categories: support-based and skill-based approaches (Carter & Hughes, 2007). Support-based approaches emphasize the creation of socially supportive environments in which peer interactions and social skills are actively promoted, prompted, or supported. In other words, they involve changing the educational contexts in ways that enhance social opportunities and outcomes. Skill-based approaches emphasize providing instruction that improves the quality of students' interactions and relationships. They teach students relevant skills that will enhance their social competence. The most impactful interventions, however, may be those that integrate aspects of both approaches.

Support-Based Approaches

Five widely used and extensively researched interventions incorporate support-based approaches for improving social outcomes: peer support arrangements, peer networks, cooperative learning groups, peer partner programs, and adult facilitation strategies. The first four can be characterized as peer-mediated interventions, in which students with disabilities receive ongoing support from fellow students without similar disabilities (called "peer partners"). To date, these five support-based approaches have been evaluated primarily with students who have autism, intellectual disability, or multiple disabilities.

Peer Support Arrangements

Peer support arrangements involve equipping and supporting peers to provide ongoing social, behavioral, and/or academic support to a student with disabilities within inclusive classrooms (Carter, 2017). One or two peer partners are recruited from the same classroom and then participate in an initial orientation session focused on practical and appropriate ways they can support their classmate with disabilities in various large- and small-group activities. For example, peer partners encourage their classmates' contributions to ongoing discussions, model age-appropriate communication and social skills, prompt use of an AAC device, promote proximity to and interactions with other classmates, and offer needed academic assistance. As the students work together throughout the semester, they receive ongoing guidance, assistance, and social facilitation from a paraprofessional, special educator, or related services provider. These staff gradually fade back their direct support as the students gain experience and confidence working together independently. These interventions are usually implemented as an alternative to an exclusive reliance on one-to-one paraprofessional support models used so widely for students with severe disabilities.

Peer support arrangements are an evidence-based practice for substantially increasing social interactions and participation for students with disabilities (Brock & Huber, 2017). In addition, students with disabilities tend to maintain or increase their academic engagement in ongoing instruction as one-to-one adult support is reduced. Working closely alongside peer partners increases the amount of individualized assistance, interaction opportunities, and corrective feedback students with disabilities receive. Moreover, these interdependent arrangements ensure students with disabilities are participating in instructional activities that align more closely with those of their classmates.

Peer Networks

Peer networks involve creating a core social group around a student with disabilities that meets regularly outside of the classroom (Asmus et al., 2017). An adult facilitator—typically a general educator, school counselor, or special educator—organizes and supports the network throughout the semester or school year. Peer networks typically involve three to six peers without disabilities who are selected on the basis of shared interests or other commonalities. Weekly or biweekly network meetings can take place in the cafeteria during lunch, on the playground at recess, in an empty classroom during an advisory period, or as part of extracurricular or after-school events. During each meeting, students engage in a mutually enjoyable shared activity (e.g., eating a meal, playing a game, completing a service project, participating in a leisure activity). The peer partners also schedule times to connect with the focus student outside of formal meetings (e.g., walking together to class, hanging out during break, attending a club meeting, getting together outside of school). Over time, the adult facilitator gradually turns responsibility for network meetings over to the students.

Peer networks are an evidence-based practice for substantially increasing social interactions, peer relationships, and school participation of students with disabilities during noninstructional times of the day (Carter, 2021). Peer networks establish a regular context for students with and without disabilities to meet one another in a group setting, discover common interests, and interact socially. During regular group meetings, students with disabilities are able to practice and receive feedback on the use of social-communication skills (e.g., initiating, commenting, turn taking, sharing) within enjoyable shared activities. Specifically, social skills are addressed incidentally through peer modeling and feedback, rather than taught explicitly through direct instruction. Peer networks are used with students with limited social networks.

Cooperative Learning Groups

Cooperative learning groups are small-group classroom arrangements designed to promote collaborative and interdependent interactions among group members with and without disabilities. This class of interventions involves dividing a classroom of students into heterogeneous groups (e.g., four to five students), establishing common learning goals for each group, delineating the specific roles each student in the group will assume (e.g., checker, facilitator, recorder, timekeeper), and establishing expectations all group members must accomplish together (i.e., group accountability). Students often benefit from receiving clear instruction on how to work together and provide feedback effectively. To involve students with severe disabilities, one or more fellow group members can be provided additional information and guidance on how to support their active participation in collaborative activities (e.g., peer support arrangements).

Cooperative learning groups can have positive effects on both social interactions and social acceptance of students with disabilities (Garrote et al., 2017). These inclusive interventions provide ongoing opportunities for teacher-sanctioned interactions during class, establish interdependent contingencies that reward collaborative work, and create a socially supportive environment for all group members. They offer a promising instructional alternative for teachers who rely heavily on lectures, large-group discussions, and independent seatwork.

Peer Partner Programs

Peer partner programs refer to a collection of formal interventions that teach peers without disabilities more about their schoolmates with disabilities and pair them together during particular periods of the school day (Ziegler et al., 2020). Peer partner programs differ from other support-based interventions in their focus on creating group-based opportunities for students with and without disabilities to spend time together. Schools usually establish peer partner programs as credit courses or formal clubs, which creates consistent times each day or week for students to connect with one another. Peer partner programs are referred to by a variety of names (e.g., Peer Buddy Programs, Peer to Peer, Best Buddies) and vary widely in their particular configurations. For example, some peer partner programs adopt "reverse mainstreaming" models (i.e., peer partners provide support in self-contained classrooms), whereas others are used to create inclusive school activities. In many schools, peer partner programs provide a structure for delivering the other individualized interventions discussed in this chapter (e.g., peer support arrangements, video modeling, peer networks).

Research examining peer partner programs has been mostly evaluative (Carter, 2018). By design, they create opportunities for peer interaction and social participation that did not otherwise exist. However, available studies have focused primarily on changes in the views of participating peer partners. Peers regularly report substantial improvements in their knowledge about, attitudes toward, and comfort around students with disabilities, suggesting these programs may contribute to greater social acceptance.

Adult Facilitation Strategies

Adult facilitation is implemented when paraprofessionals, special educators, or other school staff actively encourage or prompt interactions among students with and without disabilities (Carter et al., 2010). Each of the four interventions discussed previously incorporate active facilitation by adults to some degree. For example, a special education teacher might assign collaborative tasks, initiate a peer network, or encourage shared work within a peer support arrangement—all in an effort to increase peer interaction. At the same time, adult facilitation has also been evaluated as a stand-alone intervention. For example, paraprofessionals have been asked to call attention to the interests and experiences students with and without disabilities have in common, redirect interactions away from adults and toward other classmates, interpret the communicative intent of atypical behaviors, model positive and respectful interactions for peers, provide needed information to students, and directly prompt interactions.

Adult facilitation is an effective way of increasing the occurrence of social interaction within general education classrooms and other inclusive school settings (Brock & Anderson, 2020). However, paraprofessionals and special educators must find the right balance between providing just enough facilitation to spur social connections without their presence and involvement inadvertently stifling peer interactions. Furthermore, the extent to which these interactions will continue in the absence of ongoing facilitation is uncertain, as is the degree to which greater acceptance or new relationships are likely to develop.

Skill-Based Approaches

Five research-based interventions incorporate skill-based approaches for improving social outcomes: social skills training, AAC use, self-directed intervention strategies, social narratives, and video modeling. These interventions have been evaluated extensively with students who have both high- and low-incidence disabilities, as well as across school levels.

Social Skills Training

Social skills training is a collection of intervention practices used to teach social interaction, prosocial behavior, and social-cognitive skills that facilitate interpersonal interactions (Gresham, 2015). Instruction focuses on one or more of the following goals: facilitating the acquisition of new skills (e.g., using social amenities, turn taking, problem-solving), improving the performance of existing skills, addressing competing problem behaviors, and/or promoting generalized use of social skills. Although an array of instructional strategies can be used, social skills lessons often incorporate a rationale, direct instruction, modeling, prompting, reinforcement, role playing, and/or performance feedback. The focus and format of social skills training are flexible and should be aligned with the assessed needs of individual students with disabilities and the settings in which the skills will be used. Moreover, social skills training can be provided individually or in groups, as well as incorporate peer-mediated tactics.

Research addressing the efficacy of social skills training has produced divergent findings depending on the training approach, target outcomes, focus population, and time frame (e.g., Mostert, 2012; Gresham, 2015). While it is clear that students with disabilities can learn critical social skills when provided strong instruction marked by high fidelity and careful assessment, the generalized impact of these interventions is less certain. The extent to which improvements in social skills affect the subsequent social interactions, friendship formation, and belonging of students with disabilities warrants much closer attention.

Augmentative and Alternative Communication

AAC interventions are designed to equip students with a reliable and relevant means of interacting with others (Biggs et al., 2018). For students with complex disabilities who may have limited speech, the absence of an effective communication system can be a primary barrier to valued social outcomes in school. Providing individualized AAC systems and teaching their use across settings can provide students with disabilities a way of collaborating with classmates, connecting socially with friends, or making their needs and preferences known. Two categories of AAC have been evaluated in schools: unaided systems (e.g., use of gestures, facial expressions, sign language) and aided systems (e.g., use of basic tools or high-tech devices). As with social skills training, the ways in which instruction is provided should be individualized, usually based on the needs of the student, the type of AAC system selected, and the contexts in which it will be used. However, systematic instruction (e.g., least-to-most prompting, time delay) is the most common approach. Moreover, many AAC interventions can be enhanced by providing collateral instruction to peers or other communication partners.

Implementation of AAC is an evidence-based practice for increasing communication skills and peer interactions among students with complex communication needs (Biggs et al., 2018; Morin et al., 2018). Evaluations of these interventions usually focus on device use, introductory communication functions, and conversational exchanges with peers. The degree to which use of AAC affects social acceptance and leads to the development of new peer relationships has received much less consideration in the literature.

Self-Directed Strategies

Self-directed strategies involve teaching students with disabilities to manage their own social behaviors within and beyond the classroom. Students learn to apply one or more self-management strategies (e.g., goal setting, self-prompting, self-instruction, self-monitoring, self-evaluation) to prompt and reinforce desired social-communicative behaviors. For example, students with intellectual disability have been taught to (a) initiate interactions with classmates by using a picture book comprising various conversational cues, (b) self-monitor the extent to which they greet fellow schoolmates, (c) use self-instruction to rehearse and start conversations during extracurricular activities, and (d) self-monitor their use of relevant interaction skills with their classmates. These self-directed strategies are highly portable and can be applied within a variety of school settings and social contexts.

Self-directed strategies can positively affect students' use of discrete social skills (e.g., initiations, eye contact) across settings and the occurrence of peer interactions within the classroom (Carter et al., 2010). Moreover, increased student involvement in the instruction of skill-based social skills also promotes important self-determination skills (e.g., setting goals, problem-solving, decision-making). These strategies increase a student's independence and decrease their reliance on adults to initiate or facilitate conversations. Empowering students with a more prominent role in their social development may lead to more generalized outcomes.

Social Narratives

Social narratives are story-based interventions that describe specific social situations, highlight relevant cues, and share examples of appropriate responding (Leaf et al., 2020). They are designed to make expected behaviors more explicit and salient for students with disabilities who have difficulty discerning when and how to respond in various situations. Social narratives are individualized based on the needs of each student and are often quite short. The narratives are read to or by students with disabilities just prior to encountering the social situation described in the narrative. Examples of social narrative interventions include social stories, cartooning, social scripts, and power cards.

Research support for these interventions has been quite mixed (Leaf et al., 2020; Zimmerman & Ledford, 2017), with some studies showing some evidence of impact and many others offering no such evidence. To date, these studies have focused primarily on students with autism. Although some reductions in inappropriate behaviors have been evident, increases in social-communication skills have been more equivocal. Because social narratives appear to be more helpful for some students or social skills than for others, educators should apply these interventions with caution and only when accompanied by ongoing data collection.

Video-Based Instruction

Video-based instruction entails using video footage to teach specific social or academic skills to students with disabilities (Boon et al., 2020). Video modeling involves showing students a short video depicting a set of targeted social behaviors, asking them to imitate those behaviors in an actual setting, and providing performance feedback. Video prompting breaks down a complex situation into a sequence of individual behaviors that are modeled step-by-step on video. Both video modeling and video prompting rely on observational learning from an exemplar model to supplement relying solely on spoken instruction. Variations in video-based instruction usually involve the source of the model (e.g., self, peers, adults), the perspective depicted in the video (e.g., point of view, third person), and the time when skills must be performed (e.g., simultaneous, delayed).

Video-based instruction is effective for teaching an array of social skills, such as social initiations, commenting, asking questions, and using social amenities (Boon et al., 2020; Qi et al., 2018). Most studies indicate video-based instruction produces moderate to strong results on social outcomes. One reason may be that video-based instruction provides a convenient means for repetition and reuse of models to extend practice of skills. Moreover, many video-based instruction interventions report high levels of social validity, suggesting that educators believe the procedures of these interventions can be practically integrated into school routines.

Implications for Practitioners

Attention to the social-related needs of children and youth should have a prominent place within the overall school curriculum and in the individualized education programs of students with disabilities. Indeed, the new "three Rs" emphasize fostering supportive *relationships* alongside promoting *rigor* and *relevance* (Test et al., 2014). In the absence of serious attention to this critical domain, noticeable improvements in the social lives and learning of students with disabilities are unlikely to arise. The following guidance is offered for educators, related services providers, and other school staff.

First, effective interventions should be always aligned directly with the social-related needs of students. Each of the ten intervention approaches described earlier in this chapter were designed to address particular—and sometimes quite different—aspects of students' social lives. Thus, practitioners should assess each student's strengths and needs in this domain using the best available and most relevant assessments (e.g., ratings scales, direct observations), as well as consider carefully the specific social contexts in which students currently (or will) participate. In other words, interventions should be selected to match students' needs and also fit well within all performance contexts. Moreover, each of these ten interventions should be applied with specific students in very individualized ways. Although each intervention has core components that are essential to implement, many aspects of the intervention must still be individually tailored to meet the needs of each student and setting.

Second, the power of peers within social-focused interventions should not be overlooked. Peers already play a prominent role in many of the evidence-based practices addressed in this chapter. Indeed, their involvement as social models, instructors, supports, collaborators, and conversational partners makes them an active component of most interventions. Practitioners should determine which peers will be involved, the manner in which they will be invited, the ways they will be prepared for their roles, and the supports needed to ensure their success. When interventions focus on increasing peer interaction and fostering friendships, decisions related to the engagement of peers can take on even greater importance. When appropriate, the preferences and perspectives of students with disabilities regarding which peers to involve and how they should be sought out should be prioritized. Moreover, efforts to connect students with and without disabilities should take into consideration factors like age, peer dynamics, and cultural factors.

Third, ongoing evaluation is needed to determine whether social-focused interventions are working well or need further refinement. Practitioners should collect both summative and formative data focused on the implementation and outcomes of their intervention efforts. Approaches identified as "evidence-based practices" within the literature are still never guaranteed to have the same effects for your students; local impact must always be evaluated using data-based decision-making. An array of data collection approaches can be used to provide valuable insights. For example, direct observations can provide objective information on the skills students are using, the interactions they are having, the supports they are receiving, the participation they are experiencing, and the relationships they are enjoying. Social skill assessments can help gauge how others assess the social competence of students. Finally, conversations with students, peers, parents, and other practitioners can provide a unique perspective on how they view the intervention approaches and their impact on recipients.

Fourth, the interventions reviewed in this chapter have typically been evaluated one at a time, with a small number of students at a given school, for a fairly short duration, and primarily by (or in collaboration with) external researchers. In contrast, local schools adopting these interventions in actual practice must determine how to deliver a wide variety of social-focused interventions to a very large number of students with disabilities in multiple school settings across every single semester. This can feel like a daunting task when considered alongside the host of other academic and behavioral interventions described throughout this handbook. Coordination and collaboration among special educators, general educators, paraprofessionals, related services providers (e.g., speech-language pathologists, occupational therapists), and other school staff will be essential to making this work. To support this work, school leaders should allocate sufficient planning time, professional development, and priority to addressing the social dimensions of students' lives.

Implications for Research

Research addressing the social lives of students with disabilities has a long and impactful history. Although much is now known about promising pathways for enhancing the social outcomes of elementary and secondary students, additional work is needed to expand the knowledge base. This section highlights four important areas for future research.

First, the social lives of students develop and deepen over time. Likewise, their social skills, interactions, participation, relationships, acceptance, and experience of belonging each take time to emerge and constantly evolve. For some students with disabilities, their progress may even proceed at a somewhat different pace and path. Yet most social-focused intervention studies have adopted a fairly short time horizon for evaluation. Longer-term studies are needed to examine the impact of most interventions beyond a single semester or school year. For support-based approaches, an enduring question is whether pronounced social outcomes will still maintain when effective supports (e.g., peer partners, adult facilitation, proximity to others) are removed. For skill-based approaches, it is unclear whether the skills students do acquire ultimately contribute to subsequent improvements in social interactions and relationships.

Second, more comprehensive interventions may be needed to substantially change the social landscape for many students with disabilities. Carter (2018) describes how five factors—those related to students, peers, supports, opportunities, and context—can each interact, or all coalesce, to hinder the social outcomes of students with disabilities. Unfortunately, most of the interventions reviewed in this chapter focus on just a subset of these barriers. For example, social skills training addresses relevant student-related factors (e.g., acquisition and performance deficits), but does not increase interaction opportunities among students or tackle the attitudes of peers. Similarly, peer support arrangements focus on the preparation of peers and the provision of needed social supports, but do not usually embed explicit instruction on social skills. Combining support- and skill-based interventions in clever ways may provide the field with more robust interventions that yield broader impact.

Third, documenting the diverse dimensions of students' social lives is incredibly difficult work. A host of measurement challenges become evident when attempting to (a) establish a portrait of the social-related strengths and needs of students with disabilities and (b) document changes in their social outcomes as a result of intervention. Although strong measures of social skills and peer interaction are now available, outcomes related to relationships, acceptance, and belonging are often more subjective and complex to capture. Moreover, so many aspects of students' social lives—including their interactions and relationships with peers—take place away from the watchful eye of educators and other adults (Farmer et al., 2011). This is increasingly the case with the advent of new technologies that connect students virtually. Much more work is needed to develop a portfolio of rigorous and relevant measures that researchers and educators alike can use to examine this important aspect of schooling and student development. This is likely to require both qualitative and quantitative approaches that integrate information drawn from multiple vantage points (e.g., students, peers, educators, families).

Fourth, social outcomes are inherently reciprocal. For example, social skills are both used with and shaped by peers, interactions involve ongoing exchanges among students, friendships are marked by a bond of mutual affection, and belonging entails a strong interconnectedness within a particular community. It is impossible to fully understand the social experiences of students with disabilities in isolation of others in their school environment. Future studies should examine more closely the dynamic ways in which the social behaviors and relationships of students with disabilities and their peers interact with and influence each other. Likewise, researchers should explore the impact of social-focused interventions—particularly support-based approaches—on participating peer partners. Available studies suggest peers may benefit substantively from working alongside and supporting their schoolmates with disabilities (Travers & Carter, in press).

Additional Readings and Resources

The following online resources expand on the intervention approaches described in this chapter:

- *Overview of Peer-Mediated Interventions*: www.ksdetasn.org/resources/2124
- *Steps for Implementing Peer Networks and Peer Support Arrangements*: www.kypeersupport.org/how-to-modules/
- *TIES Center Resources on Peer Engagement*: https://tiescenter.org/peer-engagement
- *NPDC Evidence-Based Practices Modules Addressing Social Skills Training, Peer-Mediated Instruction and Intervention Module, and Video Modeling*: https://autismpdc.fpg.unc.edu/evidence-based-practices
- *Natural Peer Supports Modules*: www.pattan.net/Supports/Inclusive-Practices/Other-Projects-and-Trainings

References

Agran, M., Hughes, C., Thoma, C. A., & Scott, L. A. (2016). Employment social skills: What skills are really valued? *Career Development and Transition for Exceptional Individuals, 39*(2), 111–120. https://doi.org/10.1177/2165143414546741

Asmus, J. M., Carter, E. W., Moss, C. L., Biggs, E. E., Daniel, M., Born, T. L., Bottema-Beutel, K., Brock, M. E., Cattey, G. N., Cooney, M., Fesperman, E. S., Hochman, J. M., Huber, H. B., Lequia, J. L., Lyons, G. L., Vincent, L. B., & Weir, K. (2017). Efficacy and social validity of peer network interventions for high school students with severe disabilities. *American Journal on Intellectual and Developmental Disabilities, 122*(2), 118–137. https://doi.org/10.1352/1944-7558-122.2.118

Baumeister, R. F., & Leary, M. R. (1995). The need to belong: Desire for interpersonal attachments as a fundamental human motivation. *Psychological Bulletin, 117*(3), 497–529. https://doi.org/10.1037/0033-2909.117.3.497

Biggs, E. E., Carter, E. W., & Gilson, C. B. (2018). Systematic review of interventions involving aided AAC modeling for children with complex communication needs. *American Journal on Intellectual and Developmental Disabilities, 123*(5), 443–473. https://doi.org/10.1352/1944-7558-123.5.443

Blackorby, J., Wagner, M., Cameto, R., Davies, E., Levine, P., Newman, L., Marder, C., & Sumi, C. (2005). *Engagement, academics, social adjustment, and independence: The achievements of elementary and middle school students with disabilities*. SRI International.

Boon, R. T., Urton, K., Grünke, M., & Ko, E. H. (2020). Video modeling interventions for students with learning disabilities: A systematic review. *Learning Disabilities: A Contemporary Journal, 18*(1), 49–69. https://eric.ed.gov/?id=EJ1264341

Brock, M. E., & Anderson, E. J. (2020). Training paraprofessionals who work with students with intellectual and developmental disabilities: What does the research say? *Psychology in the Schools*. Advance online publication. https://doi.org/10.1002/pits.22386

Brock, M. E., & Huber, H. B. (2017). Are peer support arrangements an evidence-based practice? A systematic review. *The Journal of Special Education, 51*(3), 150–163. https://doi.org/10.1177/0022466917708184

Bukowski, W. M., Laursen, B., & Rubin, K. H. (Eds.) (2020). *Handbook of peer interaction, relationships, and groups* (2nd ed.). Guilford Press.

Carter, E. W. (2017). The promise and practice of peer support arrangements for students with intellectual and developmental disabilities. *International Review of Research in Developmental Disabilities, 52*, 141–174. https://doi.org/10.1016/bs.irrdd.2017.04.001

Carter, E. W. (2018). Supporting the social lives of secondary students with severe disabilities: Critical elements for effective intervention. *Journal of Emotional and Behavioral Disorders, 26*(1), 52–61. https://doi.org/10.1177/1063426617739253

Carter, E. W. (2021). Dimensions of belonging for individuals with intellectual and developmental disabilities. In A. W. Harrist & S. M. Wilson (Series Eds.), J. L. Jones & K. L. Gallus (Vol. Eds.), *Belonging and resilience in individuals with intellectual and developmental disabilities: Community and family engagement* (pp. 13–34). Springer.

Carter, E. W. (2021). Peer-mediated support interventions for students with autism spectrum disorders. In P. A. Prelock & R. McCauley (Eds.), *Treatment of autism spectrum disorders: Evidence-based intervention strategies for communication and social interactions* (2nd ed., pp. 310–329). Brookes Publishing.

Carter, E. W., & Hughes, C. (2007). Social interaction interventions: Promoting socially supportive environments and teaching new skills. In S. L. Odom, R. H. Horner, M. Snell, & J. Blacher (Eds.), *Handbook on developmental disabilities* (pp. 310–329). Guilford Press.

Carter, E. W., Sisco, L. G., Chung, Y., & Stanton-Chapman, T. (2010). Peer interactions of students with intellectual disabilities and/or autism: A map of the intervention literature. *Research and Practice for Persons with Severe Disabilities, 35*, 63–79. https://doi.org/10.2511/rpsd.35.3-4.63

Farmer, T. W., Lines, M. M., & Hamm, J. V. (2011). Revealing the invisible hand: The role of teachers in children's peer experiences. *Journal of Applied Developmental Psychology, 32*(5), 247–256. https://doi.org/10.1016/j.appdev.2011.04.006

Garrote, A., Dessemontet, R. S., & Opitz, E. M. (2017). Facilitating the social participation of pupils with special educational needs in mainstream schools: A review of school-based interventions. *Educational Research Review, 20*, 12–23. https://doi.org/10.1016/j.edurev.2016.11.001

Gresham, F. (2015). Evidence-based social skills interventions for students at risk for EBD. *Remedial and Special Education, 36*(2), 100–104. https://doi.org/10.1177/0741932514556183

Korpershoek, H., Canrinus, E. T., Fokkens-Bruinsma, M., & de Boer, H. (2020). The relationships between school belonging and students' motivational, social-emotional, behavioural, and academic outcomes in secondary education: A meta-analytic review. *Research Papers in Education, 35*(6), 641–680.

Lane, K. L., Wehby, J. H., & Cooley, C. (2006). Teacher expectations of student's classroom behavior across the grade span: Which social skills are necessary for success? *Exceptional Children, 72*(2), 153–167. https://doi.org/10.1177/001440290607200202

Leaf, J. B., Ferguson, J. L., Cihon, J. H., Milne, C. M., Leaf, R., & McEachin, J. (2020). A critical review of social narratives. *Journal of Developmental and Physical Disabilities, 32*, 241–256. https://doi.org/10.1007/s10882-019-09692-2

Lipscomb, S., Hamison, J., Liu, A., Y., Burghardt, J., Johnson, D. R., & Thurlow, M. (2017). *Preparing for life after high school: The characteristics and experiences of youth in special education* (Vol. 2). U.S. Department of Education.

McDaniel, S., Zaheer, I., & Scott, T. M. (2018). Teaching social skills. In J. McLeskey, L. Maheady, B. Billingsley, M. Brownell, & T. Lewis (Eds.), *High leverage practices for inclusive classrooms* (pp. 120–130). Taylor & Francis.

Morin, K. L., Ganz, J. B., Gregori, E. V., Foster, M. J., Gerow, S. L., Genç Tosun, D., & Homng, E. R. (2018). A systematic quality review of high-tech AAC interventions as an evidence-based practice. *Augmentative and Alternative Communication, 34*(2), 104–117. https://doi.org/10.1080/07434618.2018.1458900

Mostert, M. P. (2012). Social skills training and students with learning disabilities. In J. P. Bakken, F. E. Obiakor, & A. F. Rotatori (Eds.), *Learning disabilities: Practice concerns and students with LD* (pp. 87–112). Emerald Group.

Qi, C. H., Barton, E. E., Collier, M., & Lin, Y. (2018). A systematic review of single-case research studies on using video modeling interventions to improve social communication skills for individuals with autism spectrum disorder. *Focus on Autism and Other Developmental Disabilities, 33*(4), 249–257. https://doi.org/10.1177/1088357617741282

Siperstein, G. N., Norins, J., & Mohler, A. (2007). Social acceptance and attitude change: Fifty years of research. In J. W. Jacobson, J. A. Mulick, & J. Rojahn (Eds.), *Handbook of intellectual and developmental disabilities* (pp. 133–154). Springer.

Test, D. W., Smith, L., & Carter, E. W. (2014). Equipping youth with autism spectrum disorders for adulthood: Promoting rigor, relevance, and relationships. *Remedial and Special Education, 35*, 80–90. https://doi.org/10.1177/0741932513514857

Travers, H. E., & Carter, E. W. (in press). A systematic review of how peer-mediated interventions impact students without disabilities. *Remedial and Special Education* https://doi.org/10.1177/0741932521989414.

Wagner, M., Cadwallader, T., & Marder, C. (2003). *Life outside the classroom for youth with disabilities.* SRI International.

Wiley, A. L., & Siperstein, G. N. (2015). SEL for students with high-incidence disabilities. In j. A. Durlack, C. E. Domitrovich, R. P. Weissberg, & T. P. Gullotta (Eds.), *Handbook of social and emotional learning: Research and practice* (pp. 213–228). Guilford Press.

Williamson, P., Hoppey, D., McLeskey, J., Bergmann, E., & Moore, H. (2020). Trends in LRE placement rates over the past 25 years. *The Journal of Special Education, 53*(4), 236–244. https://doi.org/10.1177/0022466919855052

Ziegler, M., Matthews, A., Mayberry, M., Owen-De Schryver, J., & Carter, E. W. (2020). From barriers to belonging: Promoting inclusion and relationships through Peer to Peer programs. *TEACHING Exceptional Children, 52*(6), 426–434. https://doi.org/10.1177/0040059920906519

Zimmerman, K. N., & Ledford, J. R. (2017). Beyond ASD: Evidence for the effectiveness of social narratives. *Journal of Early Intervention, 39*(3), 199–217. https://doi.org/10.1177/1053815117709000

Zins, J. E., Bloodworth, M. R., Weissberg, R. P., & Walberg, H. J. (2007). The scientific base linking social and emotional learning to school success. *Journal of Educational and Psychological Consultation, 17*(2–3), 191–210. https://doi.org/10.1080/1047441070141314

17
THEORETICALLY AND EMPIRICALLY SUPPORTED INTENSIVE INTERVENTIONS FOR STUDENTS' SOCIAL-EMOTIONAL AND BEHAVIOR NEEDS

Eric Alan Common, Kathleen Lynne Lane, Wendy Peia Oakes, and Katie S. Austin

Teachers are remarkably committed professionals, willing to meet students' academic, behavioral, and social-emotional needs. This is a complicated endeavor, given the broad range of students' performance patterns. Although some students come to school with the full set of skills to interact well with others and follow school rules, others struggle substantially (Walker et al., 2004). Students who are eligible for special education services, such as those under the disability category of emotional disturbance (ED), have access to a free and appropriate public education (FAPE) in the least restrictive environment (Individuals with Disabilities Education Improvement Act [IDEA], 2004). Unfortunately, ensuring the provision of FAPE to students with ED has been controversial and challenging. It has been controversial because many leaders and professional organizations have criticized the definition as vague and lacking empirical support (Algozzine, 2017; Mattison, 2015). It has been challenging in that research has shown consistent concerns related to underidentifying students with ED. Between 12% and 20% of school-age youth in the United States demonstrate behavioral challenges to meet criteria for a mental health disorder, while less than 1% of the total school population are found eligible for and receive services under the ED category (Kauffman & Landrum, 2018; Merikangas et al., 2010). This suggests most students who engage in challenging behavior receive their K-12 schooling in general education settings. As such, in this chapter, we emphasize working beyond special education contexts and more broadly into service delivery models such as preventative tiered systems of support.

Educators need access to theoretically and empirically validated practices for supporting students with or at risk for emotional and behavioral disorders (EBDs), including ED. Fortunately, many environmental and instructional behavior change strategies have been empirically tested and found to be effective in meeting the needs of students with EBD. Examples include (a) creating structure and predictability (e.g., physical environment, routines, active supervision); (b) promoting a positive classroom climate (e.g., behavior-specific praise, high-probability requests); (c) using effective instructional strategies (e.g., high rates of opportunities to respond, direct instruction, instructional feedback); (d) group contingencies (e.g., good behavior game); (e) incorporating assessment in data-based decision-making (e.g., screening and progress monitoring, assessment-based interventions, arranging practices within tiered systems); and (f) positive behavior interventions and supports (e.g., self-management and otherwise modifying antecedent and consequence events; Mitchell et al., 2019).

Historical Context

Over the last two decades, schools have adopted a variety of tiered systems, including positive behavior interventions and supports (PBIS; Sugai & Horner, 2002); response to intervention (RTI; Fuchs & Vaughn, 2012); interconnected systems framework (ISF; Barrett et al., 2017); and comprehensive, integrated, three-tiered (Ci3T) models of prevention (Lane et al., 2019). Across tiered systems, primary (Tier 1) prevention efforts have the awesome charge to meet most students' needs. Secondary (Tier 2) interventions are additive and provide for the needs of approximately 10% to 15% of students. Tertiary (Tier 3) interventions are intended for students with intensive intervention needs or multiple risk factors, about 3% to 5% of students.

For students with intensive intervention needs, two theoretically and empirically supported practices include functional assessment-based intervention (FABI, Umbreit et al., 2007) and individualized de-escalation plan (IDP; Colvin & Scott, 2015). FABIs refer to interventions based on the function of the target (e.g., problem) behavior, as determined by a functional assessment. IDPs refer to interventions based on matching strategies specific to students' behavioral characteristics associated with each phase of the acting-out cycle (described subsequently). Both FABI and IDP are guided by the theory and application of applied behavior analysis and prevention science (Lane et al., 2013). In tiered systems of support, Tier 3 efforts are additive, building on primary prevention efforts.

Purpose

In this chapter, we review two theoretically and empirically supported practices at Tier 3 to prevent and respond to challenging behavior of students with intensive intervention needs. At this level of assessment and intervention delivery, data-based decision-making permeates every step. It is imperative that intervention components (e.g., strategies, practices, and programs) are socially valid and founded on empirical evidence and implemented in ways that support sustained implementation. First, we examine John Umbreit and colleagues' model for designing, implementing, and evaluating FABI (Umbreit et al., 2007). Umbreit et al. developed a model to systematically plan, implement, and evaluate FABI with attention to addressing feasibility and social validity issues in authentic educational settings (Blair et al., 1999; Lane et al., 1999; Umbreit, 1995, 1996, 1997; Umbreit & Blair, 1997; Umbreit et al., 2004). Second, we examine Geoff Colvin and colleagues' (2015) model for designing, implementing, and evaluating IDP. Colvin et al. developed a model to systematically plan, implement, and evaluate IDP with attention to proactive procedures that are both systematic and straightforward (Colvin et al., 1993; Colvin & Sugai, 1988). Both practices offer ways of organizing theory and practice and offer tools and other technologies that fit well within school systems to guide various educators across many roles to support students with intensive intervention needs who engage in challenging behavior. In the sections that follow, we first examine the development of FABI and IDP, including descriptions of practices and underlying theoretical and empirical support. Second, we evaluate the empirical support of these intensive interventions for student behavior. We conclude by discussing the breadth and scope of rigorous research undergirding each intervention's foundation and address implications for practitioners and future research.

Current State of Research

Functional Assessment-Based Interventions

The Umbreit model for FABI involves a systematic and coordinated approach to design, implement, and evaluate multicomponent intervention packages based on why the challenging behavior (hereby referred to as problem behavior) occurs. This model has extensive empirical support demonstrating positive effects in reducing problem behavior and/or increasing replacement or desired behaviors (e.g., Common et al., 2017; Gage et al., 2012; What Works Clearinghouse, 2016; Wood et al., 2015).

Developing Effective Practices

DEFINITION AND DESCRIPTION

FABIs involve the coordinated process of gathering information (i.e., functional behavioral assessment) to identify the function and develop behavior intervention plans. Functions of behavior are categorized by accessing (positive reinforcement) or escaping (negative reinforcement) attention, tangible/activity, or sensory experiences. The assessment is composed of direct (e.g., observation) and indirect (e.g., interviews, rating scales) measures. Information is gathered and analyzed using a function matrix (described subsequently) to determine antecedents (a) that set the stage for behavior(s) (b) to occur and the consequences (c) which follow the behavior. Functional behavior assessment results are used to develop a behavior intervention plan promoting functionally equivalent (usually) replacement behaviors as a new way of meeting their needs (Umbreit et al., 2007). FABIs are informed by assessment data and data-based decision-making guided by the function matrix and function-based intervention decision model (described subsequently) to guide what skills to teach or promote through the use of environmental changes and adjustments in behavioral contingencies (Cooper et al., 2020). Unique aspects include FABI's emphasis on recognizing the communicative intent of behavior (e.g., function) and use of intervention components, including antecedent adjustments, reinforcement adjustments, and extinction components, tailored to meet an individual student's needs.

Umbreit et al. (2007) developed a unique five-step process, which provides a practitioner-friendly, systematic approach to design, implement, and evaluate FABIs in school contexts (Lane, Oakes, et al., 2015). Unique features include the *function matrix, function-based intervention decision model*, and the application of *A-R-E components* (A = antecedent adjustments, R = reinforcement adjustments, and E = extinction procedures; described subsequently).

Function Matrix   The function matrix is a tool used to organize and analyze functional behavior assessment data related to consequences maintaining the targeted behavior of concern (e.g., problem behavior). The 2 × 3 matrix is organized by possible function: type of reinforcement (columns: positive reinforcement [access], negative reinforcement [avoid]) and by type of reinforcer (rows: attention, tangibles/activities, sensory). Data across functional assessment (i.e., record review, interviews, rating scales, ABC data collection) are reviewed and placed into the corresponding cell or cells of the type of reinforcement and reinforcer indicated (Umbreit et al., 2007). For example, in an ABC observation, if the teacher responds to the student leaving the learning location by asking them to sit at the back table until the lesson is over, the observation would be recorded in the cell for avoiding an activity, suggesting the behavior in that instance was maintained by negative reinforcement.

Function-Based Intervention Decision Model The function-based intervention decision model with two action axioms (IF <this> is true, THEN do <that>) is guided by two questions: (a) Can the student perform the replacement behavior? and (b) Do antecedent conditions represent effective practices? Answers to these questions lead to one of four intervention options. These include Method 1: Teach the replacement behavior; Method 2: Improve the environment; Method 3: Adjust the contingencies; and Methods 1 and 2: Teach the replacement behavior and improve the environment (Umbreit et al., 2007). Once the appropriate intervention method is determined, the specific A-R-E components are developed for consideration.

A-R-E Intervention Components A-R-E intervention components are designed and guided by the maintaining function as determined by the function matrix analysis and the intervention method as determined by the function-based intervention decision model. The following components are included in the behavior intervention plan: (a) teach or modify antecedents, (b) reinforce the occurrence of the replacement behavior, and (c) place the target behavior on extinction (withhold reinforcement). The hypothesized function and method inform tactics embedded within and across the A-R-E intervention package.

Five-Step Process To facilitate implementation, Lane, Oakes, et al. (2015) developed a five-step systematic approach for educators to work in tandem—as part of a team-based approach to design, implement, and evaluate FABI (Umbreit et al., 2007; see Figure 17.1). In *Step 1: Identify students who need a FABI*, teams identify students as part of regular school practices such as identifying and supporting students with Tier 3 needs using systematic screening data (Oakes et al., 2014) or as part of an individual education plan (guided by IDEA, 2004). After communicating with the parent and student and securing permissions, the process begins with conducting the functional assessment. In *Step 2: Conduct the functional assessment*, teams review student records and use functional behavioral assessment tools (e.g., interviews, rating scale, A-B-C data) to identify and operationally define the targeted problem behavior and determine the maintaining function(s) of the problem behavior. Next, data are entered into the function matrix and analyzed to develop a functional hypothesis statement. Next, a replacement behavior is identified and operationally defined. In *Step 3: Collect baseline data*, teams identify the behavior of interest (i.e., target or replacement behavior) and determine the dimension of interest (e.g., frequency) and appropriate behavior measurement system (e.g., time sampling) aligned to the dimension. Data recording procedures are planned, taught, and practiced to criterion (e.g., 90% interobserver agreement across three consecutive trial sessions) across observers. Baseline data are collected by those trained to criteria, with interobserver agreement data collected for approximately 25% of the observations. Baseline data are graphed and monitored regularly (e.g., daily; Ledford & Gast, 2018) to inform phase change decisions (e.g., introduction of the intervention).

In *Step 4: Design the intervention*, teams design the behavior intervention plan using the function-based intervention decision model with attention to ensure alignment between identified function(s) and the resulting behavior intervention plan. Each intervention includes teaching or modifying A-R-E components specific to the intervention method. Treatment integrity forms listing each specific plan tactic are designed and materials prepared. These suggested components are first reviewed by the teacher (and student as appropriate) and assessed in terms of social validity. If there are serious concerns for any stakeholder (e.g., student embarrassed or teacher does not feel behavior intervention plan is feasible), procedures are revisited and modifications are made or additional training is provided (Common & Lane, 2017). The teacher and student are then trained in the procedures with checks for understanding (e.g., modeling, role play) collected prior to beginning the intervention.

Theoretically and Empirically Supported

Step 1: Identify students who need a FABI
- Select student for functional assessment-based intervention (e.g., as part of individual education plan, as part of tiered prevention model)
- Communicate with parents and secure permissions

Step 2: Conduct the functional assessment
- Records review
- Conduct parent, teacher, and student interviews
- Operationally define target and replacement behavior
- Complete Social Skills Improvement System - Rating Scales
- Collect A-B-C data
- Organize data using the function matrix to identify the function of the behavior

Step 3: Collect baseline data
- Select dimension of behavior and select an appropriate measurement system that aligns with the dimension
- Primary and secondary observers trained to reliability in data collection procedures
- Begin data collection, including plans for assessing interobserver agreement (IOA)

Step 4: Design the intervention
- Select intervention method using the function-based intervention decision model
- Draft and finalize intervention using A-R-E components
- Create treatment integrity form
- Collect pre-intervention social validity

Step 5: Test the intervention
- Introduce intervention and continue data collection, including IOA and treatment integrity data
- Withdraw intervention an continue data collection
- Reintroduce intervention and continue data collection
- Collect post-intervention social validity
- Review ethical procedures at each step in the process

Figure 17.1 Five-Step Overview of the Umbreit Model
Source: Adapted from Lane, Oakes, et al. (2015). Social Skills Rating Scales (Gresham & Elliott, 1990)

Finally, in *Step 5: Test the intervention*, teams implement and evaluate the behavior intervention. Data are collected to answer three questions (Lane, Oakes, et al., 2011): (a) Was the intervention implemented as planned (i.e., treatment integrity)? (b) Was a functional relation established between the introduction of the intervention and changes in student behavior, and did these outcomes generalize or maintain (i.e., monitoring student outcomes to determine a functional relation)? (c) What did stakeholders (e.g., teachers, parents, students) think about the social significance of the intervention goals, the social acceptability of the intervention procedures, and the effects of the intervention after concluding the intervention? For this, teams (a) implement a validated single-case research design to monitor student outcomes (e.g., $A\text{-}B_k$, changing criterion), (b) collect treatment integrity data regularly and throughout the intervention, and (c) administer social validity surveys prior to and after the intervention. Across the Umbreit model, highly individualized and data-informed FABIs are designed, implemented, and evaluated, which promote prosocial behavior and reduce targeted problem behavior while acknowledging the communicative intent of the behavior.

Individualized De-escalation Plans

IDPs involve the systematic and coordinated approach to select research-based intervention strategies, practices, and programs aligned with each phase of the acting-out cycle. Unlike FABIs, there has been less experimental research evaluating IDPs explicitly, although there are studies of individual components (e.g., offering choices; Royer et al., 2017). Next we summarize salient features recommended for each phase of the acting-out cycle and highlight supporting research.

Developing Effective Practices

DEFINITION AND DESCRIPTION

IDPs involve a continuum of preventative and reactive strategies for responding to students' acting-out behaviors at each stage of the acting-out cycle. Acting-out behaviors refer to a series of behaviors within an escalating *behavior chain* (i.e., sequence of behaviors and successive interactions) and the presence of *successive interactions between one or more persons* (Colvin & Scott, 2015). Across fields, professional–student interactions are a frequent antecedent to more severe behavior (Duxbury & Whittington, 2005). For example, student behaviors displayed as part of acting-out behavior are followed by a specific teacher behavior, either escalating or de-escalating the student's subsequent behavior.

Colvin and colleagues proposed a seven-phase model of the acting-out cycle, including calm, triggers, agitation, acceleration, peak, de-escalation, and recovery. From an applied behavior analytic perspective, each response serves as both the consequence of the previous behavior and the antecedent for the next behavior in the chain. IDPs are an intervention for students requiring intensive intervention (e.g., Tier 3 support). Teachers can either independently or as part of a team-based process identify patterns by assessing a student's classroom environment, escalating behavior chain, and history of successive interactions between individuals (e.g., acting-out behavior cycle summary checklist). For each phase, teams select specific class-wide and student-level strategies (see Figure 17.2).

De-escalation techniques are widely recommended across education and other helping professions. While the evidence base is broad and rapidly expanding—particularly in the areas of mental health, healthcare, and community settings—gaps remain in the literature, particularly in working with children and adolescents (National Collaborating Centre for Mental Health, 2015). In the subsequent paragraphs, we describe each stage of the acting-out cycle and highlight the research base associated with recommended intervention components.

Theoretically and Empirically Supported

Phase	Characteristics of Student Behavior	Intervention Agent's Primary Objectives	Student-Level Strategies
Calm	– Cooperative and acceptable	– Facilitate and maintain student engagement with instruction and learning – Prevent the triggering and escalation of problem behaviors	Classwide strategies – Classroom management practices (e.g., designing a physical space, behavior expectations, Simonsen et al., 2008) – Low-intensity strategies to promote academic engagement and prevent disruption (e.g., active supervision, behavior-specific praise; high-probability request sequence, instructional choice, instructional feedback, opportunities to respond, precorrection; Lane et al., 2015) Student-level strategies – Proactive strategies to promote academic engagement and prevent disruption (e.g., antecedent adjustments; behavior contract, differential reinforcement; noncontingent reinforcement; self-monitoring; Cooper et al., 2020; Simonsen et al., 2008)
Triggers	– Involves series of unresolved problems (e.g., school-based or non-school-based triggers). See also motivating operation (Cooper et al., 2020).	– Facilitate resolving the issue and appropriate behavioral responses – Develop strategies for student to self-manage trigger	Classwide strategies – Expectations visible – Direct instruction in behavior expectations and social-emotional learning Student-level strategies – Precorrection, active supervision, and instructional feedback (Allen et al., 2020; Ennis et al., 2017; Lane, Menzies, et al., 2015) – Coaching (e.g., direct instruction, modeling, prompting; Cooper et al., 2020) – Direct instruction in self-regulation (Menzies & Lane, 2011) – Direct instruction in social skills (Cook et al., 2008) – Functional assessment-based interventions (Common et al., 2017; Gage et al., 2012; WWC, 2016)
Agitation	– Unfocused and distracted – Some behaviors increasing – Some behaviors decreasing	– Prevent further escalation	Student-level strategies – Show empathy – Provide highly contextualized accommodations – Redirect student behavior (e.g., job or errand) – Instructional choice (Lane, Menzies, et al., 2015; Royer et al., 2017) – Self-management (Maggin et al., 2013) – High-probability request sequence (Common et al., 2019; Lane, Menzies et al., 2015) – Two-phase intervention – Increase teacher proximity

Figure 17.2 Some Characteristics and Research-Based Strategies Across the Acting-Out and Individualized De-escalation Plans

Source: Source across columns: Colvin and Scott (2015) with citations within including summaries and/or evaluations of research support.

Phase	Characteristics of Student Behavior	Intervention Agent's Primary Objectives	Student-Level Strategies
Acceleration	– Eliciting staff engagement (e.g., teacher) leading to further negative interactions	– Prevent severe behavior – Diffuse situation	Student-level strategies – Avoid escalating prompts – Maintain calmness, respect, and detachment – Delay responding to minor disruptive behavior – Nonthreatening, limit-setting procedures and debriefing Classwide strategies – Crisis or emergency response plans at the district, school, and classroom level (Kerr & King, 2018)
Peak	– Out of control	– Maintain safety – Preserve student's dignity	Student-level strategies – Remain calm – Maintain safety – Maintain student's dignity – If nonsafety concern, prompt other students to remain on task – If safety concern, use emergency procedures (e.g., room clear)
De-escalation	– Confusion or lack of focus	– Facilitate bringing the student to a calmer state	Student-level strategies – Allow isolated space – Determine if student will remain in class/school or be sent home – Re-engage classroom activities with an independent activity with exit criteria – Determine consequences (and restore environment; as applicable) – Nonjudgmental discussion (e.g., avoid discussing "blame")
Recovery	– Eagerness for busy work – Reluctance to interact	– Avoid triggers – Increase student opportunities for success	Student-level strategies – Follow through with consequences for nondisruptive behavior – Resume and follow regular schedule – Debrief with problem-solving routine – Provide positive reinforcement for student's appropriate behaviors

Figure 17.2 (Continued)

Phase One: Calm   The student's behaviors are cooperative and acceptable. Characteristics of student behavior in phase one may include being goal-directed, compliant, and cooperative. The key objective is to facilitate and maintain student engagement with instruction to prevent the escalation of problem behaviors. Recommendations emphasize proactive practices for establishing a positive and structured learning environment that supports quality instruction and prevents problem behaviors from occurring (Colvin & Scott, 2015; Scott et al., 2011). Evidence-based classroom management practices include designing a physical space, developing a practical classroom schedule, establishing classroom expectations, implementing classroom routines, utilizing behavior management practices, and assessing student skill level to determine the curriculum (Simonsen et al., 2008). They also include the delivery of effective lesson planning that productively engages students. Other low-intensity strategies to facilitate classroom management include opportunities to respond (Common et al., 2020), behavior-specific praise (Royer et al., 2019), active supervision (Allen et al., 2020), instructional feedback (Oakes, Lane, et al., 2018), high-probability request sequence (Common et al., 2019), precorrection (Ennis et al., 2017), and instructional choice (Royer et al., 2017). These proactive, evidence-based, low-intensity strategies are associated with increasing student engagement and decreasing disruptive behavior (Lane, Menzies, et al., 2015).

Phase Two: Triggers   The student's overall behavior involves unresolved problems or concerns left unaddressed. Such concerns can occur either within or beyond the school day and can include events that happened in the more distant past (e.g., divorce of parents; Cooper et al., 2020) rather than more immediate antecedents observed before the problem behavior (Colvin & Scott, 2015). Examples of non-school-based triggers may include unpredictable schedules, health problems, nutrition needs, inadequate sleep, substance abuse, and gangs and deviant peer groups, whereas examples of school-based triggers may include denial of something needed, something negative inflicted, changes in routine, peer provocations, ineffective problem-solving, facing errors in instruction, and receiving correction procedures (Colvin & Scott, 2015). The key objective is to identify triggers that set off the problem behavior, develop strategies for managing the triggers, resolve the issue, and establish appropriate behavioral responses. Recommended practice is to manage triggers with precorrection (Colvin & Scott, 2015), an evidence-based proactive strategy to provide the student with an opportunity for success and sustain engagement with the lesson (Ennis et al., 2017). This often involves teaching social skills or self-management strategies (Cook et al., 2008).

Phase Three: Agitation   The student's overall behavior is unfocused and distracted. Certain student behaviors will increase or decrease in comparison to the student's behavior in the calm phase. Examples of increasing behaviors are darting eyes, busying with hands, moving in and of groups, and engaging in off-task behavior. Behaviors that may decrease are staring into space, veiling eyes, containing hands, or withdrawing (Colvin & Scott, 2015). The key objective is to prevent further escalation. Recommended practices include showing empathy, providing reasonable options or choices, and allowing students a moment or two to choose how to move forward. The approach for moving forward is highly contextualized. For example, a teacher might say, "I see you are having a hard time right now" to show empathy and offer the student two options for getting started, followed by one minute for the student to decide. While waiting for the student's response, the teacher might step away to acknowledge other students and return to hear what the student decided and recognize them for moving forward (Colvin & Scott, 2015).

Phase Four: Acceleration The student's behaviors in this phase may include questioning/arguing; displaying off-task, noncompliant, or defiant behavior; provoking others; whining or crying; avoidance and escape; threatening or intimidating others; verbal abuse; or destroying property. These behaviors often elicit educator engagement, leading to further negative interactions. This is the last phase in which the educator has an opportunity to avoid peak behavior in this particular response cycle. The key objective is to prevent severe behavior and diffuse the situation. Practices include avoiding escalating prompts; maintaining calmness, respect, and detachment; utilizing nonconfrontational limit-setting procedures; and debriefing (Colvin & Scott, 2015).

Phase Five: Peak The student's behaviors may include serious destruction of property, physical attacks, self-abuse, severe tantrums, or running away (Colvin & Scott, 2015). The behaviors are characterized as out of control and the prevention of problem behavior no longer possible, necessitating the teacher to respond. The key objective is to maintain safety and to preserve dignity. Emergency procedures require swift, efficient, effective, and flexible response actions that are feasible and transparent enough to be implemented across all stakeholders. Practices include developing and implementing effective crisis or emergency response plans (Kerr & King, 2018). Faculty and staff should be oriented and have ready access to school and district policies (Colvin & Scott, 2015). Lane, Menzies, et al. (2011) recommend including emergency procedures as part of the behavior intervention plan. If peers' safety is a concern, use emergency procedures (e.g., room clear); if safety is not a concern, prompt other students to remain on task. This would not be the time to offer choices, as doing so would likely further escalate the student.

Phase Six: De-escalation The student's overall behaviors show confusion and lack of focus. Characteristics may include confusion, reconciliation, withdrawal, denial, responsiveness to directions, and avoidance of discussion or debriefing (Colvin & Scott, 2015). The key objective is for the educator to bring the student back to a calmer state. Recommended practices include a seven-step process involving teacher decisions and actions based on student behaviors to guide students to the recovery and calm phases gradually. These steps include (a) isolate the student; (b) decide to retain or send the student home; (c) engage in independent work with clear exit criteria; (d) complete exit paperwork (as appropriate); (e) determine consequences; (f) restore the environment (as applicable); and (g) continue the regular schedule (Colvin & Scott, 2015). Each subsequent step of this seven-step process is designed to obtain higher levels of cooperation so that when the student exits this phase and resumes normal activity, there is a greater chance the student will be cooperative (Colvin & Scott, 2015).

Phase Seven: Recovery In phase seven, the student's overall behavior shows an eagerness for busy work and a reluctance to interact. Characteristics of student behavior may include eagerness for independent work or activity, subdued behavior in group work or whole-class discussion, and defensive behaviors. The key objective is to avoid triggers and increase student opportunities for success. Recommended practices in phase seven include transition steps and debriefing, even though the student may not want to revisit the situation. Transitional efforts continue to build on the compliance and engagement re-established in phase six and focus on student engagement in regular routines. The teacher is encouraged to refrain from negotiating consequences with the student and instead is encouraged to provide instructional feedback with attention to problem-solving behaviors and communicate support. The debriefing or feedback session should include opportunities for the student to review the context of important events that may have contributed to serious acting-out behavior and discuss problem-solving activities the student can be equipped with to manage and respond to similar events in the future (Colvin & Scott, 2015). Across the Colvin model, highly contextualized and data-informed IDPs are designed, implemented, and evaluated to promote a student's engagement and cooperation while preventing and having a plan in place to respond efficiently and effectively to problem behaviors.

Evaluating Effective Intensive Interventions for Student Behavior

Over the last three decades, researcher and teaching communities have partnered to understand better the effectiveness of intensive interventions to prevent and respond swiftly to students' social-emotional and behavioral needs. This includes a broad range of rigorous scientific inquiry examining the design, implementation, and evaluation of student-level interventions (Lane, Menzies, et al., 2015). Concurrently, the evidence-based practice movement in education has led to an accumulation of knowledge in what works (What Works Clearinghouse, 2016). Evidence-based practice, as a noun, refers to specific strategies, practices, or programs that are empirically supported based on examination and syntheses of extant literature. As a verb, evidence-based practice refers to the process practitioners use to select a strategy, practice, or program based on their professional expertise, student and other key stakeholder preference, and empirical support (Cook et al., 2020). Once a strategy, practice, or program is identified, it can vary substantially between one context and the next. For intensive interventions for behavior, such as FABI and IDP, challenges can arise in accumulating sufficient evidence to be labeled as an evidence-based practice. One challenge is the breadth of assessment tools, procedures, and ultimate interventions used across intensive interventions (Lane et al., 2009). Second, studies at this level of intensity often have insufficient samples to meet methodological quality indicators (Common et al., 2017).

To date, functional behavioral assessment-based interventions are considered an evidence-based practice for promoting engagement and social-emotional competencies and reduce problem behavior (Gage et al., 2012; What Works Clearinghouse, 2016). Common et al. (2017) reviewed 18 studies examining the efficacy of the Umbreit model supporting students with and at risk for high-incidence disabilities. While this review found insufficient evidence to classify FABI as evidence-based due to a small number of participants within ($n \geq 3$) and across studies ($n \geq 20$), the magnitude effect sizes were substantial. This review was consistent with similar reviews demonstrating the quality and rigor showing the Umbreit model as empirically supported across early childhood (Wood et al., 2015) and secondary settings (Lane et al., 2009). At this time, IDPs have not yet been systematically evaluated as an intensive (Tier 3) intervention. However, they are supported by behavior analytic principles (Cooper et al., 2020) and incorporate high-leverage and evidence-based practices for preventing and responding to problem behavior across phases (McLeskey et al., 2017; Simonsen et al., 2008).

Across the intensive interventions described in this chapter, emphasis is placed on systematic and coordinated approaches to design, implement, and evaluate multicomponent interventions in education settings. As such, research to date has formally evaluated (e.g., methodological evaluation, synthesis of effects) FABIs but not yet IDPs. As conceptually systematic and technically described, both FABI and IDP describe the evidence-based practice process practitioners use based on their professional expertise, student and other key stakeholder preference, and empirical support (Cook et al., 2020).

Implications for Practitioners

Multicomponent, intensive interventions for behavior—such as FABI and IDP—are theoretically and research supported due to the highly ideographic process involved in the design, implementation, and evaluation of behavior intervention plans to prevent and respond to problem behavior. While intensive intervention efforts may be time-consuming, we encourage those practitioners working with students with the most intensive intervention needs to work in coordination as part of a school-wide system (Lane et al., 2019). In addition, we encourage practitioners to engage in team-based, practice-based, professional learning models to learn how to effectively, efficiently design, implement, and evaluate these intensive interventions (Lane, Oakes, et al., 2015).

As we consider implications for practitioners, it is important to consider issues of capacity and sustainability in building educators' capacity to detect and respond to students whose multiple needs warrant Tier 3 supports. In optimal conditions, school systems would have clearly articulated, integrated, tiered systems to meet the whole child. Intensive supports, such as FABI and IDP, would be provided for students for whom Tier 1 (and often Tier 2) efforts are insufficient. These most intensive supports would ideally build upon the foundational elements of Tier 1 practices (e.g., school-wide expectations taught, practiced, and reinforced; school-wide instruction of social skills). If Tier 3 interventions are decoupled from Tier 1, newly acquired skills developed from intensive intervention efforts are unlikely to generalize (Lane et al., 2020). To build educators' capacity at Tier 3, this charge must be considered beyond the individual team or school, including district and state. This is a formidable task and one that could benefit from future practitioner–researcher partnerships. For practitioners, this will include attending to educators' capacity building with attention to professional learning and coaching, as well as organization capacity with attention to systems-level coordination and teaming.

Faculty and Staff Capacity Building

Throughout the design, implementation, and evaluation of intensive interventions for behaviors, practitioners need skills to analyze multiple sources of data to guide intervention design, evaluation, and, as necessary, intensification (Lane, Oakes, et al., 2015; Lemons et al., 2019). Emphasis on professional learning and coaching to build the capacity and coordination of team-based approaches is an important consideration when supporting students with intensive intervention needs. We encourage a selection of intervention components well-aligned for individualization and intensification, such as antecedent-based interventions, reinforcement, extinction, skill acquisition (e.g., self-regulation, social-emotional learning), low-intensity strategies (e.g., precorrection), and self-management (e.g., self-monitoring), which are effective as part of individualized data-based interventions. During the implementation process, educators need the knowledge and confidence to implement procedures consistently, collect repeated measures on individual performance, and monitor treatment fidelity (Lane, Oakes, et al., 2015). During the evaluation process, teams need skills to analyze data and make intervention decisions (Ledford & Gast, 2018). This requires knowledge and experience to engage in assessment, intervention selection, implementation, and evaluation. One way to respond to this challenge is through coordinated and data-informed professional learning, incorporating practice and team approaches to support building capacity and sustained service delivery (Common et al., 2021; Oakes et al., 2020). For example, Lane and colleagues, as part of a systematic line of practice-based professional learning and preservice education around the Umbreit model, developed the five-step task analyzed process (see Figure 1; Lane, Oakes, Power, et al., 2015) to train school-site teams with an emphasis on coordinating theory with practice using district-sustaining procedures (Common et al., 2021; Lane, Oakes, et al., 2015; Oakes, Schellman, et al., 2018).

Organizational Capacity

In addition to the skills needed to analyze multiple sources of data to guide data-based decision-making, educators need the organizational capacity to coordinate and collaborate effectively. Across assessments and interventions, teams are more effective if they have the skills to analyze data and select research-based intervention components that are well aligned with the unique needs of the student, related stakeholders, and environment (Common et al., 2021). This can be a formidable charge, given the breadth and responsibilities of educators within a building. In some school systems, one challenge to school-level implementation of intensive interventions for behavior is the absence of school-level teams dedicated to designing, implementing, and evaluating Tier 3 supports (Lemons et al., 2019). Educators working in a school utilizing a tiered prevention model can coordinate and integrate expertise and other resources within a building (e.g., empowering classroom teachers to identify and respond to students needing Tier 3 supports).

Implications for Future Research

Additional Inquiry Needed

First, we encourage future inquiry in intensive intervention data-based decision-making, problem-solving, and intervention component selection. For example, FABI and IDP would benefit from additional inquiry around demonstration and comparison research designs, examining the efficacy of FABI and IDP behavior intervention plans guided by the Umbreit and Colvin models, respectively. Further research is needed examining the initial training (preservice and in-service) and coaching of authentic intervention agents (e.g., teachers and other educators) in the use of FABI and IDP and student outcomes associated with these intervention plans. Across these related inquiries, single-case, group design, and systematic reviews with relevant research questions are well-suited to answer these and future research questions.

Intensive Intervention in Education Contexts

Second, the field needs additional inquiry on how intensive intervention for students fits into education broadly (Braun et al., 2020). This may include issues of leadership support, pragmatic and feasibility issues (e.g., scheduling and resource allocation), and potential need and complications associated with wrap-around services (e.g., coordination, time; Lemons et al., 2019). Fuchs et al. (2017) offer the Taxonomy of Intervention Intensity to (a) select or evaluate an intervention or (b) guide the adaptation of intervention intensification. Research questions across descriptive, qualitative, and mixed methods are all well-suited in understanding issues related to problem-solving models at this level of intervention intensity and explore issues of implementation knowledge utilization and adaptation.

Summary

In this chapter, we reviewed two highly effective intensive interventions for students' social-emotional and behavior needs: FABI and IDP. We provided an overview of the current state of research and discussed implications for practitioners and researchers. For extended connections and resources for learning about and supporting the implementation of FABI and IDP, Table 17.1 summarizes seminar resources, including a practitioner article, research article, learning modules, websites, and books related to FABI and IDPs.

Table 17.1 Additional Readings and Resources

Type of Resource	Resource	Rational
Practitioner article	Lane, K. L., Oakes, W. P., & Cox, M. (2011). Functional assessment-based interventions: A university-district partnership to promote learning and success. *Beyond Behavior, 20*(3), 3–19.	Describes university partnership, unique features of Umbreit model, and its systematic approach.
Research article	Gann, C. J., Ferro, J. B., Umbreit, J., & Liaupsin, C. J. (2014). Effects of a comprehensive function-based intervention applied across multiple educational settings. *Remedial and Special Education, 35*(1), 50–60. https://doi.org/f5mw7k	FABI demonstration (multiple baseline design) across inclusive settings.
Learning modules	*Iris Center (2019). Addressing Disruptive and Noncompliant Behaviors (Part 1): Understanding the Acting-Out Cycle. https://iris.peabody.vanderbilt.edu/module/bi1/	One of two-part series on acting-out cycle and disruptive and noncompliant behavior.
	*Iris Center (2019). Addressing Disruptive and Noncompliant Behaviors (Part 2): Behavioral Interventions. https://iris.peabody.vanderbilt.edu/module/bi2/#content	Two of two-part series on acting-out cycle and disruptive and noncompliant behavior.
Websites	*Collaborative for Academic, Social, and Emotional Learning (CASEL, n.d.) CASEL. https://casel.org/	CASEL supports educators and policy makers in promoting social-emotional learning.
	*Comprehensive, Integrated, Addressing Disruptive and Noncompliant Behaviors (Part 2): Behavioral Interventions Three-tiered Models of Support (n.d). Professional learning. www.ci3t.org/pl	Materials to include IDP within Ci3T Intervention Grid and implementation materials.
	*Comprehensive, Integrated, Three-tiered Models of Support (2016). Functional Assessment-based Interventions. www.ci3t.org/fabi	Materials to design, implement, and evaluate FABI. Resources include professional learning aids, video modules, and implementation materials.
	*Intensive Intervention. (n.d.) Intensive intervention. https://intensiveintervention.org	Professional learning and recommendations for intensive intervention for behavior.
Books	Colvin, G., & Scott, T. M. (2015). *Managing the cycle of acting-out behavior in the classroom*. Corwin Press.	Most recent textbook on IDP following the Colvin model.
	Cooper, J. O., Heron, T. E., & Heward, W. L. (2020). Applied behavior analysis (3rd ed.). Pearson.	Discusses principles and technologies related to behavior analysis used across FABI and IDP.
	Umbreit, J., Ferro, J., Liaupsin, C., & Lane, K. L. (2007). Functional behavioral assessment and function-based intervention: An effective, practical approach. Prentice Hall.	Seminal textbook on FABI following the Umbreit model.

Note. *Includes freely available materials.

References

Algozzine, B. (2017). Toward an acceptable definition of emotional disturbance: Waiting for the change. *Behavioral Disorders, 42*(3), 136–144. https://doi.org/fp9d

Allen, G. E., Common, E. A., Germer, K. A., Lane, K. L., Buckman, M. M., Oakes, W. P., & Menzies, H. M. (2020). A systematic review of the evidence base for active supervision in pre-K—12 Settings. *Behavioral Disorders, 45*(3), 167–182. https://doi.org/fqff

Barrett, S., Eber, L., & Weist, M. (2017). *Advancing education effectiveness: Interconnecting school mental health and school-wide positive behavior support*. www.pbis.org/resource/advancing-education-effectiveness-interconnecting-school-mental-health-and-school-wide-positive-behavior-support

Blair, K. S. C., Umbreit, J., & Bos, C. S. (1999). Using functional assessment and children's preferences to improve the behavior of young children with behavioral disorders. *Behavioral Disorders, 24*(2), 151–166. https://doi.org/fp9f

Braun, G., Kumm, S., Brown, C., Walte, S., Hughes, M. T., & Maggin, D. M. (2020). Living in Tier 2: Educators' perceptions of MTSS in urban schools. *International Journal of Inclusive Education, 24*(10), 1114–1128.

Colvin, G., & Scott, T. M. (2015). *Managing the cycle of acting-out behavior in the classroom*. Corwin Press.

Colvin, G., & Sugai, G. (1988). Proactive strategies for managing social behavior problems: An instructional approach. *Education and Treatment of Children*, 341–348.

Colvin, G., Sugai, G., & Patching, B. (1993). Precorrection: An instructional approach for managing predictable problem behaviors. *Intervention in School and Clinic, 28*(3), 143–150.

Common, E. A., Bross, L. A., Oakes, W. P., Cantwell, E. D., Lane, K. L., & Germer, K. A. (2019). Systematic review of high probability requests in K-12 settings: Examining the evidence base. *Behavioral Disorders, 45*(1), 3–21. https://doi.org/fqfh

Common, E. A., & Lane, K. L. (2017). Social Validity Assessment. In J. K. Luiselli (Ed.), *Applied behavior analysis advanced guidebook: a manual for professional practice* (pp. 73–92). Elsevier.

Common, E. A., Lane, K. L., Cantwell, E. D., Brunsting, N. C., Oakes, W. P., Germer, K. A., & Bross, L. A. (2020). Teacher-delivered strategies to increase students' opportunities to respond: A systematic methodological review. *Behavioral Disorders, 45*(2), 67–84.

Common, E. A., Lane, K. L., Oakes, W. P., Schellman, L. E., Shogren, K., Germer, K. A., & Quell, A. E. (2021). Building site-level capacity for functional assessment-based interventions: Examining a practice-based professional learning series. *Manuscript in Preparation*.

Common, E. A., Lane, K. L., Pustejovsky, J. E., Johnson, A. H., & Johl, L. E. (2017). Functional assessment-based interventions for students with or at-risk for high-incidence disabilities: Field-testing single-case synthesis methods. *Remedial and Special Education 38*(6), 331–352. https://doi.org/gdcdrk

Cook, B. G., Collins, L. W., Cook, S. C., & Cook, L. (2020). Evidence-based reviews: How evidence-based practices are systematically identified. *Learning Disabilities Research & Practice, 35*(1), 6–13. https://doi.org/10.1111/ldrp.12213

Cook, C. R., Gresham, F. M., Kern, L., Barreras, R. B., Thornton, S., & Crews, S. D. (2008). Social skills training for secondary students with emotional and/or behavioral disorders: A review and analysis of the meta-analytic literature. *Journal of Emotional and Behavioral Disorders, 16*(3), 131–144. https://doi.org/fn2ghf

Cooper, J. O., Heron, T. E., & Heward, W. L. (2020). *Applied behavior analysis* (3rd ed.). Pearson.

Duxbury, J., & Whittington, R. (2005). Causes and management of patient aggression and violence: Staff and patient perspectives. *Journal of Advanced Nursing, 50*(5), 469–478.

Ennis, R. P., Royer, D. J., Lane, K. L., & Griffith, C. E. (2017). A Systematic Review of Precorrection in PK-12 Settings. *Education and Treatment of Children, 40*(4), 465–495.

Fuchs, L. S., Fuchs, D., & Malone, A. S. (2017). The taxonomy of intervention intensity. *Teaching Exceptional Children, 50*(1), 35–43.

Fuchs, L. S., & Vaughn, S. (2012). Responsiveness-to-intervention: A decade later. *Journal of learning disabilities, 45*(3), 195–203. https://doi.org/f3w84w

Gage, N. A., Lewis, T. J., & Stichter, J. P. (2012). Functional behavioral assessment-based interventions for students with or at risk for emotional and/or behavioral disorders in school: A hierarchical linear modeling meta-analysis. *Behavioral Disorders, 37*(2), 55–77.

Gresham, F. M., & Elliott, S. N. (1990). *Social skill rating scale*. Pearson Assessments.

Individuals with Disabilities Education Improvement Act of 2004 (IDEA 2004). Public Law 108–446; 20 U.S.C. §§ 1400 et seq.

Kauffman, J. M., & Landrum, T. J. (2018). *Characteristics of emotional and behavioral disorders of children and youth with disabilities*. Pearson.

Kerr, M. M., & King, G. (2018). *School crisis prevention and intervention*. Waveland Press.

Lane, K. L., Bruhn, A. L., Crnobori, M. L., & Sewell, A. L. (2009). Designing functional assessment-based interventions using a systematic approach: A promising practice for supporting challenging behavior. In T. E. Scruggs & M. A. Mastropieri (Eds.), *Advances in learning and behavioral disabilities* (Vol. 22, pp. 341–370). Emerald.

Lane, K. L., Menzies, H., Bruhn, A., & Crnobori, M. (2011). *Managing challenging behaviors in schools: Research-based strategies that work*. Guilford Press.

Lane, K. L., Menzies, H. M., Ennis, R. P., & Oakes, W. P. (2015). *Supporting behavior for school success: A step-by-step guide to key strategies*. Guilford Press.

Lane, K. L., Oakes, W. P., Cantwell, E. D., & Royer, D. J. (2019). *Building and installing comprehensive, integrated, three-tiered (Ci3T) models of prevention: A practical guide to supporting school success* (v1.3). KOI Education.

Lane, K. L., Oakes, W. P., & Cox, M. (2011). Functional assessment-based interventions: A university-district partnership to promote learning and success. *Beyond Behavior, 20*(3), 3.

Lane, K. L., Oakes, W. P., Powers, L., Diebold, T., Germer, K., Common, E. A., & Brunsting, N. (2015). Improving teachers' knowledge of functional assessment-based interventions: Outcomes of a professional development series. *Education and Treatment of Children, 38*(1), 93–120. https://doi.org/fp9k

Lane, K. L., Oakes, W. P., Royer, D. J., Buckman, M. M., Common, E. A., Allen, G. E., & Cantwell, E. D. (2020). Supporting the installation of Comprehensive, Integrated, Three-tiered (Ci3T) Models of Prevention: Educator perspectives. *Manuscript in Review*.

Lane, K. L., Umbreit, J., & Beebe-Frankenberger, M. (1999). A review of functional assessment research with students with or at-risk for emotional and behavioral disorders. *Journal of Positive Behavioral Interventions, 1*(2), 101–111.

Lane, K. L., Walker, H., Cronbori, M., Oliver, R., Burhn, A., & Oakes, W. (2013). Strategies for decreasing aggressive, coercive behavior: A Call for preventative efforts. In B. G. Cook & M. Tankersley (Eds). *Research-based practices in special education* (pp. 192–212). Pearson.

Ledford, J., & Gast, D. (2018). *Single case research methodology: Applications in special education and behavioral sciences*. Routledge.

Lemons, C. J., Sinclair, A. C., Gesel, S., Danielson, L., & Gandhi, A. G. (2019). Integrating intensive intervention into special education services: Guidance for special education administrators. *Journal of Special Education Leadership, 32*(1), 29–38.

Maggin, D., Briesch, A. M., & Chafouleas, S. M. (2013). An application of the What Works Clearinghouse Standards for evaluating single-subject research: Synthesis of the self-management literature base. *Remedial and Special Education, 34*(1), 44–58. https://doi.org/10.1177/0741932511435176

Mattison, R. E. (2015). Comparison of students with emotional and/or behavioral disorders as classified by their school districts. *Behavioral Disorders, 40*(3), 196–209. https://doi.org/10.17988/0198-7429-40.3.196

McLeskey, J., Barringer, M-D., Billingsley, B., Brownell, M., Jackson, D., Kennedy, M., Lewis, T., Maheady, L., Rodriguez, J., Scheeler, M. C., Winn, J., & Ziegler, D. (2017, January). *High-leverage practices in special education*. Council for Exceptional Children & CEEDAR Center. https://ceedar.education.ufl.edu/high-leverage-practices/

Merikangas, K. R., He, J. P., Burstein, M., Swanson, S. A., Avenevoli, S., Cui, L., Benjet, C., Georgiades, K., & Swendsen, J. (2010). Lifetime prevalence of mental disorders in US adolescents: Results from the National Comorbidity Survey Replication—Adolescent Supplement (NCS-A). *Journal of the American Academy of Child & Adolescent Psychiatry, 49*(10), 980–989. https://doi.org/bz9v5v

Mitchell, B. S., Kern, L., & Conroy, M. A. (2019). Supporting students with emotional or behavioral disorders: State of the field. *Behavioral Disorders, 44*(2), 70–84.

National Collaborating Centre for Mental Health (UK) (2015). *Violence and aggression: Short-term management in mental health, health and community settings: Updated edition* (NICE Guideline). British Psychological Society www.ncbi.nlm.nih.gov/books/NBK356325/

Oakes, W. P., Lane, K. L., Cox, M. L., & Messenger, M. (2014). Logistics of behavior screenings: How and why do we conduct behavior screenings at our school? *Preventing School Failure, 58*(3), 159–170. https://doi.org/10.1080/1045988X.2014.895572

Oakes, W. P., Lane, K. L., Menzies, H. M., & Buckman, M. M. (2018). Instructional feedback: An effective, efficient, low-intensity strategy to support student success. *Beyond Behavior, 27*(3), 168–174. https://doi.org/gfz3sr

Oakes, W. P., Lane, K. L., Royer, D. J., Buckman, M. M., Common, E. A., Allen, G. E., & Cantwell, E. D. (2020). Supporting the installation of comprehensive, integrated, three-tiered (Ci3T) models of prevention: Educator perspectives. *Manuscript in Review*.

Oakes, W. P., Schellman, L. E., Lane, K. L., Common, E. A., Powers, L., Diebold, T., & Gaskill, T. (2018). Improving Educators' knowledge, confidence, and usefulness of functional assessment-based interventions: Outcomes of professional learning. *Education and Treatment of Children, 41*(4), 533–565. https://doi.org/gfjsrt

Royer, D. J., Lane, K. L., Cantwell, E. D., & Messenger, M. L. (2017). A systematic review of the evidence base for instructional choice in K—12 settings. *Behavioral Disorders, 42*(3), 89–107. https://doi.org/fqfg

Royer, D. J., Lane, K. L., Dunlap, K. D., & Ennis, R. P. (2019). A systematic review of teacher-delivered behavior-specific praise on K—12 student performance. *Remedial and Special Education, 40*(2), 112–128. https://doi.org/frg9

Scott, T. M., Anderson, C. M., & Alter, P. (2011). *Managing classroom behavior using positive behavior supports.* Pearson.

Simonsen, B., Fairbanks, S., Briesch, A., Myers, D., & Sugai, G. (2008). Evidence-based practices in classroom management: Considerations for research to practice. *Education and Treatment of Children, 31*(1), 351–380. https://doi.org/db8769

Sugai, G., & Horner, R. (2002). The evolution of discipline practices: School-wide positive behavior supports. *Child & Family Behavior Therapy, 24*(1–2), 23–50.

Umbreit, J. (1995). Functional assessment and intervention in a regular classroom setting for the disruptive behavior of a student with attention deficit hyperactivity disorder. *Behavioral Disorders, 20*(4), 267–278. https://doi.org/fp9m

Umbreit, J. (1996). Assessment and intervention for the problem behavior of an adult at home. *Journal of the Association for Persons with Severe Handicaps, 21*(1), 31–38.

Umbreit, J. (1997). Eliminating challenging behaviors in multiple environments throughout the entire day. *Education and Training in Mental Retardation and Developmental Disabilities, 32*(4), 321–330. www.jstor.org/stable/23879207

Umbreit, J., & Blair, K. B. (1997). Using structural analysis to facilitate the treatment of noncompliance and aggression in a young child at-risk for behavioral disorders. *Behavioral Disorders, 22*(2), 75–86 https://doi.org/fp9q

Umbreit, J., Ferro, J., Liaupsin, C., & Lane, K. L. (2007). *Functional behavioral assessment and function-based intervention: An effective, practical approach.* Prentice Hall.

Umbreit, J., Lane, K. L., & Dejud, C. (2004). Improving classroom behavior by modifying task difficulty: The effects of increasing the difficulty of too-easy tasks. *Journal of Positive Behavior Interventions, 6*(1), 13–20. https://doi.org/dfnpdc

Walker, H., Ramsey, E., & Gresham, F. M. (2004). *Antisocial behavior in school: Evidence-based practices* (2nd ed.). Wadsworth.

What Works Clearinghouse, U.S. Department of Education, Institute of Education Sciences. (2016). *WWC intervention report: Functional behavioral assessment-based interventions: Children identified with or at risk for an emotional disturbance.* Author. https://ies.ed.gov/ncee/wwc/EvidenceSnapshot/667

Wood, B. K., Oakes, W. P., Fettig, A., & Lane, K. L. (2015). A review of the evidence base of functional assessment-based interventions for young students using one systematic approach. *Behavioral Disorders, 40*(4), 230–250. https://doi.org/gdz3h2

18
THE BEHAVIORAL, ACADEMIC, AND SOCIAL ENGAGEMENT (BASE) MODEL OF SOCIAL INCLUSION

Thomas W. Farmer, Heartley B. Huber, David L. Lee, Jill V. Hamm, and Brittany Sterrett

Promoting the social inclusion of students with disabilities in general education settings has been a special education priority for several decades (Siperstein & Parker, 2008). Although many advances have been made in terms of supporting the social experiences and relationships of students with both high- (e.g., Klang et al., 2020) and low-incidence (e.g., Carter, 2018) disabilities, students receiving special education services continue to experience elevated rates of social difficulties in inclusive classrooms. Interventions to support social adjustment and enhance peer experiences of students with disabilities include individual competence-focused approaches such as social skills training and social and emotional learning programs (e.g., Bierman & Sanders, 2021; Daley & McCarthy, 2020) and peer-focused strategies to foster supportive peer networks (e.g., Sreckovic et al., 2017). Although strong individual and peer-orientated strategies may enhance social inclusion, there remains a need to manage social dynamics and the moment-to-moment experiences of students with disabilities to promote their social roles, relationships, and adaptation within the classroom community (Farmer et al., 2019; Hymel & Katz, 2019).

The Behavioral, Academic, and Social Engagement (BASE) model was created to help address this need. Building on a dynamic developmental-ecological systems perspective and the concept of correlated constraints, the BASE model integrates socially relevant interventions and supports across the academic, behavioral, and social domains (see Farmer et al., 2013, 2019; Farmer, Bierman, et al., 2021, Farmer, Sterrett, et al., 2021). Reflecting a person-in-context perspective of social development and adaptation, the BASE model aims to create classroom ecologies aligned with and responsive to the characteristics, strengths, and needs of individual students. In this chapter, we outline the theoretical foundations of the BASE model, summarize the BASE delivery framework and intervention components, present preliminary findings of BASE, and consider implications for practitioners and future research needs.

Conceptual Foundations of the BASE Model

Children and youth develop as an integrated whole within the dynamic-ecological systems in which they are embedded (Bronfenbrenner, 1996). This means that discrete domains of functioning (e.g., behavioral, cognitive, emotional, physical, social) do not develop or adapt independent of each other within the individual, nor are they divorced from the continuous contributions of the relevant contexts that help to shape their expression (Magnusson & Cairns, 1996). On the contrary, multiple developmental factors are bidirectionally linked, influencing and influenced by each other, as well as the circumstances, affordances, and limitations of the contexts and ecologies that operate as buffers and catalysts in development (Cairns, 2000).

This phenomenon, known as correlated constraints, has the potential to foster both stability and adaptation in the functioning and characteristics of individuals (Magnusson & Cairns, 1996). On one hand, because developmental factors are bidirectionally linked, stability in functioning is likely to occur when changes in one domain are short-lived and prior states of functioning are returned to and maintained because the other factors or domains within the system do not adapt in correspondence with the changes in the focal domain. On the other hand, if changes in the focal domain are strong enough to foster change in other factors, the developmental system may reorganize (i.e., various factors change to correspond with each other), and the individual will experience sustained adaptation and new patterns or trajectories of functioning (Farmer, Bierman et al., 2021; Magnusson & Cairns, 1996).

The concept of correlated constraints is a critical but often overlooked aspect of intervention. Interventions often are designed to address a focal issue and not the other factors in the developmental system, including the ecology, that contribute to the student's functioning in the domain of interest. When implementing an evidence-based program (EBP), teachers commonly claim an intervention worked for a short period of time, only for the student to return to prior behaviors and levels of functioning. In such cases, it is likely that correlated constraints are in action. The intervention may effectively affect the focal issue, but other factors contributing to the student's functioning do not change, limiting the EBP's effectiveness. Dynamic intervention frameworks attuned to correlated constraints help guide adaptive, data-driven strategies, which are responsive to developmental factors and processes, including the student characteristics, classroom dynamics and functioning, and broader ecological factors (Farmer, 2020; Darling-Hammond et al., 2020).

The BASE model is designed to leverage correlated constraints and natural developmental processes by focusing on the moment-to-moment management of ongoing classroom structure and activities contributing to students' social opportunities, experiences, and adaptation. BASE focuses on creating a classroom ecology aligned with other intervention approaches (e.g., individual skill building, peer support strategies) and complements and reinforces their impact by fostering teachers' awareness of the social impact of various classroom tasks, instructional approaches, and management strategies (Farmer et al., 2016; Farmer, Dawes et al., 2018). With support, teachers can learn to use and adapt specific strategies to establish a context that contributes to students' positive social experiences, roles, and relationships (Norwalk et al., 2020), with the overarching goal to promote and sustain the long-term social adaptation of children and youth with disabilities.

As the *American Heritage Dictionary* defines *society* as a "community of interdependent individuals" characterized by their "mutual interests, participation in characteristic relationships, shared institutions, and a common culture," the classroom society reflects the functioning of the teacher and students as they collectively contribute to an environment that influences and is influenced by the adaptation and inclusion of specific students (see also Farmer et al., 2011, 2019). Figure 18.1 depicts the classroom society as being composed of six factors: (a) students' social opportunities (i.e., social experiences and activities afforded to them); (b) the social roles (i.e., reputations, influence, centrality) students develop within the classroom; (c) the specific peer groups (i.e., cliques and social networks) and affiliations students form; (d) the intragroup dynamics of each peer group in the class characterizing the group's identity and interactions of its members; (e) the intergroup dynamics characterizing the interactions and relationships between distinct groups and their members; and (f) the overall social structure (i.e., how groups and individuals are organized in the social system in relation to each other) and climate and norms (i.e., general culture, beliefs, values) students collectively negotiate and develop to guide their interactions and relationships. Bidirectional arrows indicate

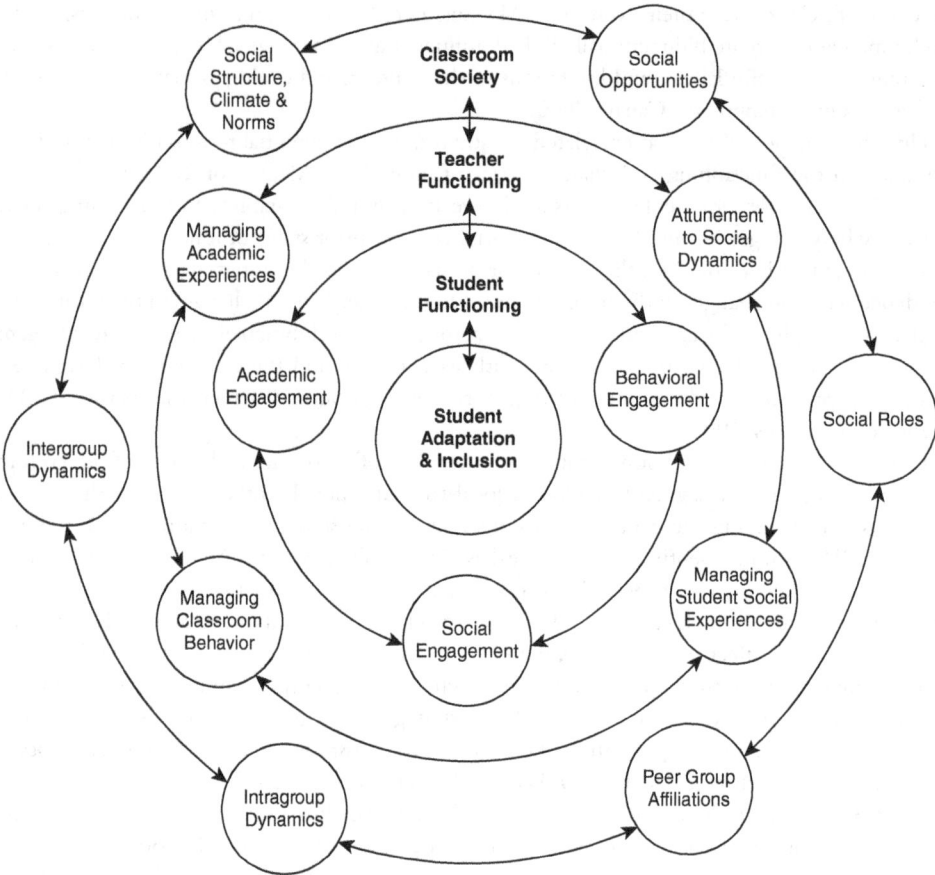

Figure 18.1 Conceptual Foundations of the BASE Inclusion Model

each factor influences and is influenced by the others. Likewise, teacher- and student-level factors are bidirectionally linked in their respective rings and collectively contribute to each student's social adaptation, inclusion, and overall adjustment in the classroom and school social system (Farmer, Dawes, et al., 2018; Farmer, Talbott, et al., 2018). Given the interconnected nature of these relevant factors, teachers must go beyond single focused approaches to support an individual student's social development, foster supportive peer networks, or create a positive general classroom climate to more effectively support inclusion. The ways these various factors operate together in the system and how all relevant factors can be aligned to foster students' inclusion and adaptation also matter.

Understanding peer group dynamics is a critical aspect of managing classrooms and supporting socially vulnerable students (Trach et al., 2018). However, teachers' knowledge and support of students' social relations varies considerably (Gest et al., 2014; Hendrickx et al., 2020; Ryan et al., 2015). Some teachers are very attuned to their classroom social system and are aware of distinct peer groups, students' social roles in the classroom, and the general culture and beliefs guiding how students engage with each other (Hamm et al., 2011). Yet many teachers are not as well attuned to the classroom society, and their understanding of students' social vulnerabilities may be affected by how they perceive specific students' social characteristics (Dawes et al., 2017; Marucci et al., 2020; Wilbert et al., 2020). In addition, many teachers do not believe that addressing students' social relationships is their responsibility (Gest et al., 2014). When teachers understand classroom social dynamics and work to foster egalitarian social structures, students who are socially vulnerable are more likely to feel included and perceive the classroom and peer culture as positive and supportive (Chen et al., 2015; Gest et al., 2014; Hamm et al., 2010; Norwalk et al., 2016). Fortunately, teachers can learn to be attuned to social dynamics (Farmer et al., 2010; Hamm et al., 2011) and incorporate this information in their general management of moment-to-moment daily activities, including academic instruction and classroom behavior (Farmer et al., 2019; Motoca et al., 2014).

The BASE Delivery Framework and Intervention Components

Because classroom social systems depend on the composition of the peer ecology and dynamic interchanges at the individual, peer group, and social structural levels (Ahn & Rodkin, 2014; Bronfenbrenner, 1943), the management of classroom social dynamics varies from class to class and depends on the characteristics and resources of the teacher. Therefore, establishing a manualized intervention for classroom social dynamics management that can be implemented by teachers with fidelity in a lock-step fashion is not feasible. To be responsive to the dynamic aspects of peer social systems, classroom behavior management, and students' distinct instructional needs, the BASE model uses a delivery framework called directed consultation (DC) to help general education teachers in their classrooms. The DC process is typically conducted by an intervention specialist with advanced training in special education, school psychology, or school mental health. A critical aspect of DC and the activities of the intervention specialist center on a progress monitoring framework known as the scouting report.

Directed Consultation

To address the widely varying culture, ecology, and sociopolitics affecting the efficacy of social inclusion in school communities, the BASE model centers on being responsive to the strengths, needs, resources, and opportunities of students and teachers within the specific contexts they are embedded in. Consistent with advances in managing and adapting EBPs in child and adolescent mental health (Chorpita, 2019; Southam-Gerow, 2020), DC is aimed at utilizing knowledge and practice elements from the extant evidence base and tailoring relevant intervention strategies to specific ecologies and developmentally meaningful circumstances (Farmer, Sterrett, et al., 2021; Motoca et al., 2014). The DC process consists of four integrated delivery mechanisms: ongoing data collection, tailored universal training, ongoing training of tailored EBPs, and targeted intervention adaptation based on progress monitoring data.

Ongoing Data Collection

DC utilizes observations, interviews, and data use consultation to assess resources, strengths, needs, and current practices. The aim is to understand the overall classroom culture, determine what is working, clarify the perspectives of key stakeholders (e.g., students, parents, teachers, administrators) and determine the degree to which stakeholder viewpoints converge or diverge, and identify potential intervention leverage points at multiple levels (i.e., student, teacher, social structure) within the classroom society. Typically, this occurs prior to any intervention efforts as part of the scouting report (see later) and continues across the DC and intervention implementation training period. Over time, the collection of data shifts from a process led by the intervention specialist to the establishment of a data collection and data use system that special educators, school administrators, and other school personnel can use independently to support teachers to implement and adapt tailored interventions.

Tailored Universal Training

Through our experiences implementing the BASE model across the nation (e.g., Farmer, et al., 2013; 2019; 2020; Farmer, Sterrett et al., 2021), we have found significant variation in social dynamics students experience in important and impactful ways across districts, schools, and even classrooms. Before conducting workshops or consultation activities, data collected as part of the previous step is used to identify practice elements and strategies included the BASE training materials that are most relevant to the current circumstances and ecology. Developing examples from classroom observations and using positive examples of teachers in the school who already use BASE model concepts and strategies help lay a foundation for how this approach may positively affect their classroom culture and ecology and their students. Furthermore, we individualize workshop and training activities around issues teachers are currently addressing, and we frame dialog to encourage teachers to become problem-solving partners as we work to identify strategies and modifications to address their needs. We link these efforts back to data and help teachers think through what information they need to understand if an intervention is working or if adjustments are needed. Although the universal training is tailored to the context and culture of the school, initial workshops and training activities are designed around the core principles and strategies of the BASE intervention components described next.

Ongoing Training of Tailored EBPs

Building from ongoing data collection activities and teachers' responses to and uptake of the tailored universal training strategies and processes, we provide ongoing training of tailored EBPs through online instructional modules focused on intervention practice elements to target key developmental leverage points and address specific classroom and student needs. In essence, this step involves deciding which aspects of the general training should be extended further with more detail and which elements are not relevant to the current and immediate needs and should be discontinued. As this phase focuses on the general use of tailored strategies, teacher implementation data are necessary to clarify issues of fidelity and the effective use of strategies. Teachers are offered guidance to determine whether tailored EBPs are effective or if a more individualized intervention is necessary.

Targeted Intervention Adaptation

During the targeted intervention adaptation phase of the DC process, an implementation consultation approach focuses more closely on specific students or needs that may not have been addressed through general implantation of tailored EBPs. Consultation can be conducted with individual teachers or with teams or groups of teachers who share students or have similar concerns. An intervention or inclusion specialist uses local data collected through the scouting report to guide a structured problem-solving process designed to identify possible mismatches between strategies and specific needs or contextual factors. They may also identify potential adaptations to existing strategies or guide the use of new strategies to better support positive trends in the progress monitoring data.

The Scouting Report

The scouting report is designed to generate data about intervention needs and leverage points that can be used to help guide the general DC process and inform the delivery of specific professional development and consultation support activities. The goal of the scouting report is to identify factors contributing to students' school adjustment such as the general functioning of the classroom/school; the values, systems, and practices that influence the climate and culture of the focal ecology;

community strengths and constraints; current teacher capacities, strengths, and support needs; resources and supports available to the teacher; and the intervention support needs of focal students (Farmer et al., 2016; Farmer and Hamm, 2016).

Conducting sociometric assessments to clarify the classroom social dynamics is a useful initial step (Farmer et al., 2012; McKown, 2019). Further data collection should focus on clarifying the perspectives of key stakeholders (i.e., school adults, classmates, parents) and how they may be contributing to the overall classroom environment and social functioning of the student. To do this, it is helpful to conduct pre-observation interviews; observations of the general focal context; observations of synchronous interactions between the focal student and teachers/school adults; observations of synchronous interactions between the focal student and classmates who key adults (i.e., teachers, parents) and/or the social dynamics data indicate have roles and relationships that influence the student; and post-observation interviews with stakeholders to further clarify what was observed (Farmer et al., 2016; Farmer, Dawes, et al., 2018).

The BASE Components

Academic engagement enhancement (AEE) centers on creating a classroom culture that promotes productive academic engagement of all students. The context is structured to provide adaptive supports tailored to promote the routine daily functioning of each student, whatever their needs (Farmer, Sterrett, et al., 2021; Sutherland et al, 2018). The AEE component aims to promote a positive and engaged climate, promote a peer culture that supports academic engagement, and use data to guide the adaptation of routine daily strategies to meet the needs of individual students. To achieve this, the AEE component is organized into three distinct but complementary categories of instructional management strategies: academic context management, pacing activities for success, and reinforcing desired behaviors (see Farmer, Hamm, et al., 2019, 2020; Farmer, Sterrett, et al., 2021).

Competence enhancement behavior management (CEBM) involves managing the classroom context, student behavior, and interplay between students and contexts to normalize differences and make behavioral supports nonstigmatizing (Farmer et al., 2006; McLesky & Waldron, 2007). This requires using EBPs and data to adapt strategies to balance the needs of specific students and the classroom ecology (Sutherland et al., 2018). Teachers learn to approach behavior management with a positive mindset, have high expectations for students, use problems as opportunities to teach desired behaviors, and communicate to students that they are important (Farmer et al., 2006; Milner, 2018). The goal is to foster a climate of productive and supportive behavior. To accomplish this, CEBM is organized into three categories: behavioral context management, eliciting and reinforcing desired behavior, and positive behavior redirection (see Farmer, Hamm, et al., 2019, 2020; Farmer, Sterrett, et al., 2021).

Social dynamics management (SDM) centers on harnessing the power of the peer group to manage the instructional and behavioral context while fostering students' positive social roles and relationships. Classroom social dynamics refers to how classrooms are socially structured and how this structure affects and is affected by student interactions (Farmer et al., 2019). Students coordinate their behaviors with each other, sort themselves into groups, create social hierarchies, and develop social roles (Ahn & Rodkin, 2014; Trach et al., 2018). Although social dynamics are peer driven, teachers can facilitate students' social experiences, opportunities, and roles (Gest et al., 2014; van den Berg and Stoltz, 2018). The goal of SDM is to create a climate of peer support. SDM involves three categories: social context management, attunement and management of group processes, and supporting students' social roles and relations (see Farmer, Dawes, et al., 2018; Farmer, Hamm, et al., 2019, 2020; Farmer, Sterrett, et al., 2021). In the following section, we detail the research base for the BASE model.

Empirical Foundations of the BASE Model

BASE has been evaluated in intervention development and pilot investigations, as well as two large cluster randomized trials (CRTs) in rural (36 schools; 2,453 students; 188 teachers) and metropolitan (24 schools; 2,925 students; 220 teachers) areas. Teachers who receive BASE training are more likely to manage the classroom in ways that promote a general classroom context supportive of youth who are at risk of being socially marginalized. Structured observations and ratings of classroom management indicate that BASE teachers use more effective communication strategies, provide encouragement to motivate students, manage classroom social dynamics to promote positive social opportunities and experiences, and use more positive feedback and less negative feedback/redirection (Motoca et al., 2014). Further, BASE teachers are more likely to be attuned to students' social relations, and they report greater efficacy in supporting students (Farmer et al., 2010, 2011; Hamm et al., 2011).

In turn, students in BASE classrooms report more positive social experiences and classroom engagement. For example, significant intervention effects moderated by students' sex, race/ethnicity, and economic status were found for self-reported social anxiety, defiance, willingness to protect peers from being bullied, and emotional problems (Dawes et al., 2020). Students with exceptionalities (e.g., students with disabilities, academically gifted students) tend to perceive less peer support for bullying directed toward them (Chen et al., 2015), while students with behavioral risks in BASE classrooms are more likely to affiliate with prosocial peers (Farmer, Hamm, et al., 2010). Likewise, students are more likely to perceive that the peer culture is supportive of positive academic effort and achievement (Hamm et al., 2014), and they tend to report a greater sense of belonging and support in the classroom (Hamm et al., 2011).

Students from racial and ethnic minority groups also report more positive experiences in BASE classrooms. Indigenous early adolescents in BASE schools were more likely to view the peer culture as less socially risky and more supportive of academic engagement and achievement, and they demonstrated improved grades and test scores as compared to Indigenous students in control schools (Hamm et al., 2010). Black and Latinx students in BASE schools were more likely to report that they would protect peers from being bullied, and they endorsed lower rates of defiance toward teachers (Dawes et al., 2020). Further, Black and Latinx students in BASE schools perceived less discrimination from peers or teachers (Marraccini et al., 2021).

Implications for Practice: Integrating BASE With Other Social/Peer Support Interventions

Classroom social dynamics often serve as setting events for social behavior and relationships and are a critical component for social interventions (Hamm et al., 2020). When the social dynamics of the classroom do not consistently support a positive, inclusive social context, it is not uncommon for an evidence-based social intervention to have an immediate impact, and yet those improvements in social behavior may not maintain over time, even though the intervention is maintained (Lee, 2018). Given the dynamic system of factors contributing to students' social inclusion and their social adaptation in the classroom, a temporary or short-lived impact of a social intervention may not mean the intervention is not effective. Rather, it is possible other factors in the system are operating as setting events to maintain interfering behavior and the student's social difficulties in the classroom (Farmer, Talbott, et al., 2018). To promote the social inclusion of students with disabilities, it is necessary to support individual-focused (e.g., social skills training) and relationship-focused (e.g., peer network) interventions along with efforts to manage general classroom social dynamics (Farmer, Dawes, et al., 2018; Farmer, Hamm, et al., 2019). When we view social dynamics as conditions that contribute to social adaptation and the corresponding impact of evidence-based practices, we are better positioned to tailor interventions to specific issues, contexts, and circumstances.

The BASE Model of Social Inclusion

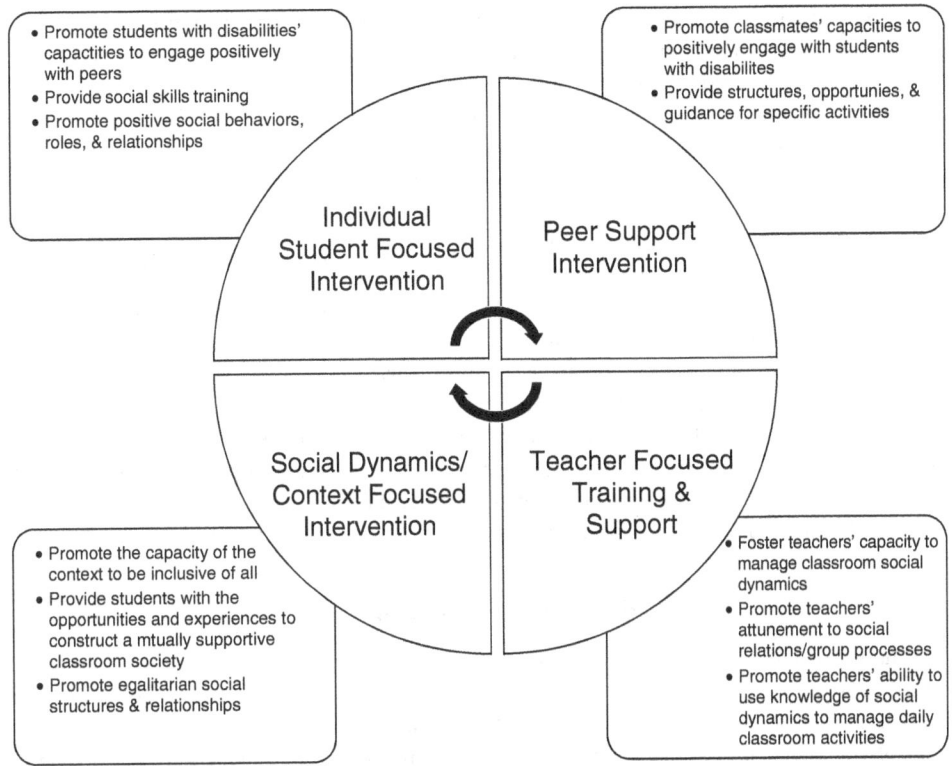

Figure 18.2 The BASE Multidomain, Integrated Model for Fostering Social Inclusion

We propose that social inclusion interventions should include an emphasis on adaptive, data-driven, nested models of support that work across the three tiers of the Multi-Tiered Support System (MTSS; Farmer, Bierman, et al., 2021). Reflecting the integrated and dynamic approach of the BASE model, such efforts should include bridging the social support needs and competencies of students with disabilities, with careful management of their day-to-day and moment-to-moment activities, opportunities, and experiences in the classroom social ecology (Garrote et al., 2020; Juvonen et al., 2019; Hymel & Katz, 2019; Trach et al., 2018). An integrated and dynamic approach for promoting social inclusion should (a) view the focal student, classroom peers, teacher practices, and the classroom context as distinct but bidirectionally linked levels in the social inclusion process (Farmer et al., 2016) and (b) aim to bring these levels into synergistic alignment to sustain positive and productive social behaviors and relationships for all students across the classroom.

Figure 18.2 illustrates the aims and capacities an inclusion or intervention specialist can use to guide their efforts in providing integrated and comprehensive supports for social inclusion in general education classrooms across each of the four domains (i.e., focal student, peer support, teacher support, context support). At the student level, the focus is on social skills training and other individually focused supports to promote the student's positive social behaviors, roles, and relationships. The aim is to provide universal (Tier 1), as well as more individualized (Tier 2) and targeted (Tier 3) supports, with the goal of enhancing the student's social competence and expand their ability to engage in mutually gratifying interactions and seek out meaningful relationships. At the peer support level, practitioners should promote classmates' positive attitudes and social behaviors toward all peers, including those who are different from themselves, while structuring opportunities and experiences designed to encourage social connections with classmates with disabilities (e.g., partner activities, small-group work; see Carter, 2018; Trach et al., 2018). At the teacher support level, the role of the interventionist may focus on gathering data and information to help general educators choose new strategies or change their current approaches to positively influence the social dynamics in their classrooms. Given their responsibility to meet the instructional, behavioral, and social needs for diverse groups of students, general education teachers may find it challenging to see how the whole classroom functions together and how this affects specific students. Intervention specialists can conduct scouting reports to collect information about classroom social dynamics. They can become the eyes and ears for teachers, support data analysis, and offer objective insight (see Farmer et al., 2016). With this support, teachers can learn to become more attuned to classroom social dynamics and use this information to more effectively manage daily activities. At the context level, teachers can provide ground rules and expectations and model the types of interactions they would like to see among students. Utilizing social dynamics data, teachers can also facilitate experiences and opportunities that help students to develop their own social system and peer social structures that are egalitarian, cooperative, and supportive of all (Farmer, Hamm, et al., 2019; Furrer et al., 2020; Garrote et al., 2020; Gest et al., 2014; Hymel et al., 2019; Juvonen et al., 2019).

Direction for Future Inquiry

While the BASE model has a strong theoretical grounding and robust research base, future research can further strengthen our understanding of the impact of specific intervention components and provide important insight for implementation. First, much of the extant research is focused on the impact of the BASE model on students' perceptions and relies on student self-rating. Including perspectives and measures from other stakeholders, including teachers, administrators, and families, would offer important insight into the intervention's impact on the perceptions of other stakeholders, as well as the social validity of the intervention.

Second, future research is needed to understand the impact of specific BASE model mechanisms on student outcomes. The differential positive effects on the outcomes of students whose teachers were trained in the BASE model as compared to students in control groups supports the conclusion that BASE model–trained teachers more effectively managed and fostered engaged, productive, and supportive classroom environments. However, additional research is needed to examine which academic, behavioral, and social dynamic strategies or processes affected which student outcomes.

Third, additional research is needed to examine the effectiveness of the BASE model when implemented in conjunction with individualized Tier 3 interventions. Given the influential nature of the social context on individualized social and behavioral interventions, we anticipate the improved social dynamics associated with implementation of the BASE model may enhance the impact of individual and peer-mediated interventions in multiple different ways, such as increasing over effects of the intervention, decreasing the time necessary to see improvements, and improving maintenance of positive changes in social and adaptive behavior over time. However, research is needed to evaluate the effectiveness of the BASE model when paired with individualized, targeted interventions, as well as whether the effectiveness of targeted evidence-based interventions is maintained, enhanced, or reduced.

Summary

In conclusion, several advances have been made in promoting the social inclusion of students with disabilities. Efforts to enhance the social skills and competencies of students with disabilities continues to be a cornerstone of this work. So, too, are strategies that focus on peer supports. Dynamic-ecological systems approaches to social development suggest that individual and peer support strategies can be enhanced by including a focus on teachers' attunement to classroom peer group processes and the use of social dynamics support strategies in the day-to-day and moment-to-moment management of classroom activities. The BASE model provides one framework for accomplishing this. However, we suggest that as work on social dynamics management in inclusive classrooms moves forward, there is a need for additional research that explicitly focuses on working across student, peer, teacher, and context support perspectives.

Authors' Note

This work was supported by grants from the Institute of Education Sciences (R305A040056; R305A160398; R305A120812). The views expressed in this chapter are those of the authors and do not reflect the views of the granting agency.

Compliance With Ethical Standards

The authors declare that they have no conflict of interest.

References

Ahn, H.-J., & Rodkin, P. C. (2014). Classroom-level predictors of the social status of aggression: Friendship centralization, friendship density, teacher—student attunement, and gender. *Journal of Educational Psychology, 106*, 1144–1155. https://doi.org/10.1037/a0036091

Bierman, K. L., & Sanders, M. T. (2021). Teaching explicit social-emotional skills with contextual supports for students with intensive intervention needs. *Journal of Emotional and Behavioral Disorders, 29*, 14–23. https://doi.org/10.1177/1063426620957623

Bronfenbrenner, U. (1943). A constant frame of reference for sociometric research. *Sociometry, 6*, 363–397. https://doi.org/10.2307/2785218

Bronfenbrenner, U. (1996). Foreward. In R. B. Cairns, G. H. Elder, & E. J. Costello (Eds.), *Developmental science* (pp. ix–xvii). Cambridge University Press.

Cairns, R. B. (2000). Developmental science: Three audacious implications. In L. R. Bergman, R. B. Cairns, L-G. Nilsson, & L. Nystedt (Eds.), *Developmental science and the holistic approach* (pp. 49–62). LEA.

Carter, E. W. (2018). Supporting the social lives of secondary students with severe disabilities: Considerations for effective intervention. *Journal of Emotional and Behavioral Disorders, 26*, 52–61. https://doi.org/10.1177/1063426617739253

Chen, C-C., Hamm, J. V., Farmer, T. W., Lambert, K., & Mehtaji, M. (2015). Exceptionality and peer victimization involvement in late childhood: Subtypes, stability, and social marginalization. *Remedial and Special Education, 36*, 312–324. https://doi.org/10.1177/0741932515579242

Chorpita, B. F. (2019). Commentary: Metaknowledge is power: Envisioning models to address unmet mental health needs: Reflections on Kazdin (2019). *Journal of Child Psychology and Psychiatry 60*, 473–476. https://doi.org/10.1111/jcpp.13034

Daley, S. G., & McCarthy, M. F. (2020). Students with disabilities in social and emotional learning interventions: A systematic review. *Remedial and Special Education*, Early Access. https://doi.org/10.1177/0741932520964917

Darling-Hammond, L., Flook, L., Cook-Harvey, C., Barron, B., & Osher, D. (2020). Implications for educational practice of the science of learning and development. *Applied Developmental Science, 24*, 97–140. https://doi.org/10.1080/10888691.2018.1537791

Dawes, M., Chen, C-C., Zumbrunn, S. K., Mehtaji, M., Farmer, T. W., & Hamm, J. V. (2017). Teacher attunement to peer-nominated aggressors. *Aggressive Behavior, 43*, 263–272. https://doi.org/10.1002/ab.21686

Dawes, M., Farmer, T. W., Hamm, J. V., Lee, D., Norwalk, K., Sterrett, B., & Lambert, K. (2020). Creating supportive contexts during the first year of middle school: Impact of a developmentally responsive multi-component intervention. *Journal of Youth and Adolescence, 49*, 1447–1463. https://doi.org/10.1007/s10964-019-01156-2

Farmer, T. W. (2020). Reforming research to support culturally and ecologically responsive and developmentally meaningful practice in schools. *Educational Psychologist, 55*, 32–39. https://doi.org/10.1080/00461520.2019.1698298

Farmer, T. W., Bierman, K. L., Hall, C. M., Brooks, D. S., & Lee, D. L. (2021). Tiered systems of adaptive supports and the individualization of intervention: Merging developmental cascades and correlated constraints perspectives. *Journal of Emotional and Behavioral Disorders, 29*, 3–13. https://doi.org/10.1177/1063426620957651

Farmer, T. W., Chen, C-C., Hamm, J. V., Moates, M. M., Mehtaji, M., Lee, D., & Huneke, M. R. (2016). Supporting teachers' management of middle school social dynamics: The scouting report process. *Intervention in School and Clinic, 52*, 67–76. https://doi.org/10.1177/1053451216636073

Farmer, T. W., Dawes, M., Hamm, J. V., Lee, D., Mehtaji, M., Hoffman, A. S., & Brooks, D. S. (2018). Classroom social dynamics management: Why the invisible hand of the teacher matters for special education. *Remedial & Special Education, 39*, 177–192. https://doi.org/10.1177/0741932517718359

Farmer, T. W., Goforth, J. B., Hives, J., Aaron, A., Hunter, F., & Sgmatto, A. (2006). Competence enhancement behavior management. *Preventing School Failure, 50*, 39–44. https://doi.org/10.3200/PSFL.50.3.39-44

Farmer, T. W., & Hamm, J. V. (2016). Promoting supportive contexts for minority youth in low-resource rural communities: The SEALS model, directed consultation, and the scouting report approach. In L. J. Crockett & G. Carlo (Eds.), *Rural ethnic minority youth and families in the United States* (pp. 247–265). Springer.

Farmer, T. W., Hamm, J. V., Dawes, M., Barko-Alva, K., & Cross, J. R. (2019). Promoting inclusive communities in diverse classrooms: Teacher attunement and social dynamics management. *Educational Psychologist, 54*, 286–305. https://doi.org/10.1080/00461520.2019.1635020

Farmer, T. W., Hamm, J. V., Lee, D., Lane, K. L., Sutherland, K. S., Hall, C. M., & Murray, R. M. (2013). Conceptual foundations and components of a contextual intervention to promote student engagement during early adolescence: The supporting early adolescent learning and social success (SEALS) model. *Journal of Educational and Psychological Consultation, 23*, 115–139. https://doi.org/10.1080/10474412.2013.785181

Farmer, T. W., Hamm, J. V., Lee, D. L., Sterrett, B., Rizzo, K., & Norwalk, K. (2020). An adaptive, correlated constraints model of classroom management: The behavioral, academic, and social engagement (BASE) program. In T. W. Farmer, M. Conroy, E. M. Z., Farmer, & Sutherland (Co-editors), *Handbook of research on emotional & behavioral disorders: Interdisciplinary developmental perspectives on children and youth* (pp. 227–242). Routledge.

Farmer, T. W., Hamm, J. L., Petrin, R. A., Robertson, D. L., Murray, R. A., Meece, J. L., & Brooks, D. S. (2010). Creating supportive classroom contexts for academically and behaviorally at-risk youth during the transition to middle school: A strength-based perspective. *Exceptionality, 18*, 94–106.

Farmer, T. W., Lane, K. L., Lee, D. L., Hamm, J. V., & Lambert, K. (2012). The social functions of antisocial behavior: Considerations for school violence prevention strategies for students with disabilities. *Behavioral Disorders, 37*, 149–162. https://doi.org/10.1177/019874291203700303

Farmer, T. W., Lines, M. M., & Hamm, J. V. (2011). Revealing the invisible hand: The role of teachers in children's peer experiences. *Journal of Applied Developmental Psychology. 32*, 247–256. https://doi.org/10.1016/j.appdev.2011.04.006

Farmer, T. W., Sterrett, B., Norwalk, K., Chen, C-C., Dawes, M., Hamm, J. V., Lee, D. L., & Farmer, A. G. (2021). Supporting the inclusion of socially vulnerable early adolescents: Theory and illustrations of the BASE model. *Frontiers in Education*. https://doi.org/10.3389/feduc.2020.587174

Farmer, T. W., Talbott, B., Dawes, M., Huber, H. B., Brooks, D. S., & Powers, E. (2018). Social dynamics management: What is it and why is it important for intervention? *Journal of Emotional and Behavioral Disorders, 26*, 1–10. https://doi.org/10.1177/1063426617752139

Furrer, V., Valkanover, S., Eckhart, M., & Nagel, S. (2020). The role of teaching strategies in social acceptance and interactions: Considering students with intellectual disabilities in inclusive physical education. *Frontiers in Education, 5*, 200. https://doi.org/10.3389/feduc.2020.586960

Garrote, A., Felder, F., Krähenmann, H., Schnepel, S., Sermier Dessemontet, R., Moser Opitz, E. (2020). Social acceptance in inclusive classrooms: The role of teacher attitudes toward inclusion and classroom management. *Frontiers in Education, 5*, 198. https://doi.org/10.3389/feduc.2020.582873

Gest, S. D., Madill, R. A., Zadzora, K. M., Miller, A. M., & Rodkin, P. C. (2014). Teacher management of elementary classroom social dynamics: Associations with changes in student adjustment. *Journal of Emotional and Behavioral Disorders, 22*, 107–118. https://doi.org/10.1177/1063426613512677

Hamm, J. V., Farmer, T. W., Dadisman, K., Gravelle, M., & Murray, R. A. (2011). Teachers' attunement to students' peer group affiliations as a source of improved student experiences of the school social-affective context following the middle school transition. *Journal of Applied Developmental Psychology, 32*, 267–277. https://doi.org/10.1016/j.appdev.2010.06.003

Hamm, J. V., Farmer, T. W., Lambert, K., & Gravelle, M. (2014). Enhancing peer cultures of academic effort and achievement in early adolescence: Promotive effects of the SEALS intervention. *Developmental Psychology, 50*, 216–228. https://doi.org/10.1037/a0032979

Hamm, J. V., Farmer, T. W., Robertson, D., Dadisman, K., Murray, A. R., Meece, J., & Song, S. (2010). Effects of a developmentally based intervention with teachers on Native American and White early adolescents' schooling adjustment in rural settings. *Journal of Experimental Education, 78*, 343–377. https://doi.org/10.1080/00220970903548038

Hamm, J. V., Granger, K. L., & Van Acker, R. A. (2020). Classroom peer ecologies and cultures, and students with EBD. In T. W. Farmer, M. Conroy, E. M. Z., Farmer, & Sutherland (Co-editors), *Handbook of research on emotional & behavioral disorders: Interdisciplinary developmental perspectives on children and youth* (pp. 125–139). Routledge.

Hendrickx, M. M. H. G., Mainhard, T., Cillessen, A. H. N., & Brekelmans, M. (2020). Teacher behavior with upper elementary school students in the social margins of their classroom peer group. *Frontiers in Education, 5*, 189. https://doi.org/10.3389/feduc.2020.568849

Hymel, S., & Katz, J. (2019). Designing classrooms for diversity: Fostering social inclusion. *Educational Psychologist, 54*, 331–339. https://doi.org/10.1080/00461520.2019.1652098

Juvonen, J., Lessard, L. M., Rastogi, R., Schacter, H. L., & Smith, D. S. (2019). Promoting social inclusion in educational settings: Challenges and opportunities. *Educational Psychologist, 54*, 250–270. https://doi.org/10.1080/00461520.2019.1655645

Klang, N., Olsson, I., Wilder, J., Lindqvist, Fohlin, N., & Nilholm, C. (2020). A cooperative learning intervention to promote social inclusion of heterogeneous classrooms. *Frontiers in Psychology, 11*, 3485. https://doi.org/10.3389/fpsyg.2020.586489

Lee, D. L. (2018). Social dynamics management and functional behavioral assessment. *Journal of Emotional and Behavioral Disorders, 26*, 62–64. https://doi.org/10.1177/1063426617750142

Magnusson, D., & Cairns, R. B. (1996). Developmental science: Principles and illustrations. In R. B. Cairns, G. H. Elder Jr., & J. Costello (Eds.), *Developmental science* (pp. 7–30). Cambridge University Press.

Marraccini, M. E., Hamm, J. V., Lambert, K., & Farmer, T. W. (2021). *Perceived ethnic-racial discrimination in middle school: Latent transitions over time.* Submitted for publication.

Marucci, E., Oldenburg, B., Barrera, D., Cillessen, A. H. N., Hendrickx, M., & Veenstra, R. (2020). Halo and association effects: Cognitive biases in teacher attunement to peer-nominated bullies, victims, and prosocial students. *Social Development* (early access). https://doi.org/10.1111/sode.12455

McKown, C. (2019). Challenges and opportunities in the applied assessment of student social and emotional learning. *Educational Psychologist, 54*, 205–221. https://doi.org/10.1080/00461520.2019.1614446

McLesky, J., & Waldron, N. L. (2007). Making differences ordinary in inclusive classrooms. *Intervention in School and Clinic, 42*, 162–168. https://doi.org/10.1177/10534512070420030501

Milner, H. R. (2018). Development over punishment: An unhealthy fixation on punishment hurts underserved students. *Educational Leadership, 75*(6), 93–94.

Motoca, L., Farmer, T. W., Hamm, J. V., Byun, S-Y., Lee, D., Brooks, D. S., Rucker, N., & Moohr, M. (2014). Directed consultation, the SEALS Model, and teachers' classroom management. *Journal of Emotional of Behavioral Disorders, 22*, 119–129. https://doi.org/10.1177/1063426614521299

Norwalk, K. E., Dawes, M., Hamm, J. V., & Farmer, T. W. (2020). Improving middle school teachers' self-reported use of social dynamics management practices. *Journal of Applied School Psychology.* Published online: 04 August, 2020. https://doi.org/10.1080/15377903.2020.1799129

Norwalk, K. E., Hamm, J. V., Farmer, T. W., & Barnes, K. L. (2016). Improving the social context of early adolescence through teacher attunement to victimization: Effects on school belonging. *Journal of Early Adolescence, 36*, 989–1009. https://doi.org/10.1177/0272431615590230

Ryan, A. M., Kuusinen, C. M., & Bedoya-Skoog, A. (2015). Managing peer relations: A dimension of teacher self-efficacy that varies between elementary and middle school teachers and is associated with observed classroom quality. *Contemporary Educational Psychology, 41*, 147–156. https://doi.org/10.1016/j.cedpsych.2015.01.002

Siperstein, G. N., & Parker, R. C. (2008). Toward an understanding of social integration: A special issue introduction. *Exceptionality, 16*, 119–124. https://doi.org/ 10.1080/09362830802194921

Southam-Gerow, M. A., Cox, J. R., & Kinnebrew, A. (2020). Managing and adapting practice. In T. W. Farmer, M. Conroy, E. M. Z., Farmer, & Sutherland (Co-editors), *Handbook of research on emotional & behavioral disorders: Interdisciplinary developmental perspectives on children and youth* (pp. 321–340). Routledge.

Sreckovic, MA, Hume, K., & Able, H. (2017). Examining the efficacy of peer network interventions on the social interactions of high school students with autism spectrum disorder. *Journal of Autism and Developmental Disorders, 47*, 2556–2574. https://doi.org/10.1007/s10803-017-3171-8

Sutherland, K. S., Farmer, T. W., Kunemund, R. L., & Sterrett, B. I. (2018). Learning, behavioral, and social difficulties within MTSS: A dynamic perspective of intervention intensification. In N. D. Young, K. Bonanno-Sotiropoulos & T. A. Citro (Eds.), *Paving the pathway for educational success: Effective classroom interventions for students with learning disabilities.* Rowman & Littlefield.

Trach, J., Lee, M., & Hymel, S. (2018). A social-ecological approach to addressing emotional and behavioral problems in schools: Focusing on group processes and social dynamics. *Journal of Emotional and Behavioral Disorders, 26*, 11–20. https://doi.org/10.1177/1063426617742346

van den Berg, Y. H. M., & Stoltz, S. (2018). Enhancing social inclusion of children with externalizing problems through classroom seating arrangements: A randomized control trial. *Journal of Emotional and Behavioral Disorders, 26,* 31–41. https://doi.org/10.1177/1063426617740561

Wilbert, J., Urton, K., Krull, J., Kulawiak, P. R., Schwalbe, A., & Hennemann, T. (2020). Teachers' accuracy in estimating social inclusion of students with and without special educational needs. *Frontiers in Education, 5,* 243. https://doi.org/10.3389/feduc.2020.598330

19
MULTILINGUAL LEARNERS
Testing, Assessment, and Evaluation

Julie Esparza Brown and Terese C. Aceves

Introduction

In 1968, Lloyd Dunn published his seminal article asking why special classes for children with mild intellectual disabilities served mainly Black students. He estimated that between 60% and 80% of students in special education were from low socioeconomic (SES) backgrounds or an ethnic minority. In the ensuing decades, much research has focused on disproportionality in special education (both over- and underrepresentation of minority students, referred to here as multilingual learners or MLs, defined later), yet this phenomena remains widespread in specific special education eligibility categories (e.g., specific learning abilities, emotional disturbance, autism, language disorders) and in more restrictive settings (Artiles, 2011; Artiles et al., 2010; Harry & Klingner, 2014; Losen et al., 2015; Oswald et al., 1999; Snyder et al., 2016). More specifically, research highlights underrepresentation of MLs in early elementary years and overrepresentation in upper elementary schools (Park, 2020). As the student population in the United States becomes increasingly culturally and linguistically diverse and given the historic and current trends, disproportionality is likely to increase unless educators carefully examine the complex causal factors and focus on ameliorating the problem (Park, 2020; Umansky et al., 2017). In addition to school structure, policies, curriculum, and assessment practices continue to privilege White and middle-class students, assuming broad mainstream cultural knowledge that diverse populations may not possess (Sciuchetti, 2017). This perceived "deficit" often triggers a "blame the child" attitude and a focus on within-child deficits for academic challenges rather than first examining contextual factors. While some educators believe that special education placement can help close achievement gaps (Hurwitz et al., 2020; Schwartz et al., 2021), data from the National Assessment of Educational Progress (NAEP) show achievement disparities with fourth-grade students with disabilities scoring 40 points below peers on national reading assessments (National Center for Education Statistics, 2017). Thus, an unfortunate and somewhat common practice of placing struggling ML students into special education programs merely because general education academic supports are unavailable continues to feed an inequitable and stratified system (Becker & Deris, 2019). One answer to these challenges is relying less on this traditional assessment paradigm focused on within-student factors to instead examining students' context or ecology and alignment to curricular assumptions as a first step. One such model is the Multi-Tiered System of Support (MTSS).

The current chapter will outline a research-based MTSS that nests students' ecologies within the testing, assessment, and evaluation continuum to support teams in developing more equitable decision-making processes. We later present new reconceptualizations of normative samples for multilingual students and conclude with considerations for future research in this area. This chapter will not, however, include discussion of special education eligibility assessment for MLs. The reader is referred to the work of Flanagan et al. (2007) and the Culture-Language Interpretive Matrices for a discussion regarding discerning cultural and linguistic differences versus disability during eligibility determination.[1] We first begin the chapter by defining important terms as we consider the fair evaluation of students who speak multiple languages, including English.

Defining Diverse Learners

The ever-growing diversity in our schools necessitates that every educator understand the wealth of perspectives MLs bring with them to school and the ways in which students from diverse backgrounds may need unique support and scaffolding. Here, we focus primarily on those students from homes where English is not the primary language. This group of students has been defined by many labels, including limited English speakers, English language learners, English learners, emergent bilinguals, and recently, multilingual learners. Here we chose the term multilingual learners (MLs) to emphasize that bilingualism and multilingualism are assets that should be leveraged and celebrated. In pre-K–12 public schools, there are close to 5 million MLs (Hussar et al., 2020). Data indicate that 14.7% of these students are enrolled in special education programs, with the majority identified with a specific learning disability.

Context Matters

Historically, the concept of disability has been rooted in a medical model focused on within-individual differences with little or no consideration of outside factors or ecologies. In response, many scholars have reconceptualized disability as a social phenomenon that "reflects the biases, self-interests, and moral evaluations of those in a position to influence policy" (Albrecht & Levy, 1981, p. 14). This reconceptualization, then, is used as a tool to analyze the ways society pathologizes individuals with disabilities and other differences to instead view an individual as a product of their systems (Annamma et al., 2013). As Annamma and Morrison (2018) conclude, "When one is viewed as different from the ideal normative and that difference is viewed as deficit, there are a plethora of impacts" (p. 116). For students with multiple intersectionalities (e.g., minority, English learners, immigrant), school teams may view diverse students from a deficit perspective and attribute differences to a within-individual disability. To combat this deficit-based perspective, using a sociocultural lens prevails on us to view children's development in relation to their "participation in the everyday practices and settings of their lives" (Rogoff et al., 2018, p. 6). Thus, it is incumbent upon evaluation teams to first understand students' everyday lives or ecologies, cultural and language practices, family/community assets, and developmental processes and their alignment with assumptions about school readiness and the developmental sequence of cognitive constructs. "[L]earning and development occur in the process of people's participation in the activities and events of their cultural communities" (Rogoff et al., 2018, p. 6).

Clarifying Evaluation, Assessment, and Testing

Both educational research and school practice have brought significant attention to the challenges involved in the evaluation, assessment, and testing of students from culturally and linguistically diverse backgrounds (Linan-Thompson & Ortiz, 2009; King Thorius & Sullivan, 2013; Ortiz,

2019). These challenges include using data from measures developed for norming populations that do not represent the experiences and knowledge of ML students (Ortiz, 2019). Additionally, making high-stakes and eligibility instructional decisions using such data adds further concern regarding the appropriateness of these decisions (Richards-Tutor et al., 2016). When inaccurate, the most harmful of these decisions involve those leading to eligibility for special education identification. While students may receive individualized support through special education instruction, they generally receive these services in more restrictive settings, and their access to the general education curriculum may be minimized. Consequently, special education should be reserved for students with innate disabilities rather than those for whom the general education has not met their needs.

Although the terms testing, assessment, and evaluation are sometimes used interchangeably, they are distinct concepts. Testing includes "administering a predetermined set of questions or tasks for which predetermined types of behavioral responses are sought, to an individual or group of individuals, to obtain a score" (Salvia et al., 2017, p. 5). Assessment involves the "process of systematically gathering multiple sources of data, evaluating the data, using them to make instructional decisions, and planning future instruction" (Haas & Brown, 2019, p. 65). Evaluation, on the other hand, is the process of using data collected through testing and assessment to determine to what extent the educational objectives are being met. Both the terms "assessment" and "evaluation" are referenced in federal law (e.g., 20 U.S. Code 1414[1]) when describing initial and ongoing eligibility determination of students for special education services, while the term "testing" is largely absent (CASP, 2020).

MTSS for ELs: Culturally and Linguistically Responsive Data-Based Decision-Making

The processes of evaluation, assessment, and testing, embedded within preventive-focused, multitiered support, provide the field with potentially more appropriate alternatives to traditional practices. MTSS provides increasing levels of focused support for students not meeting grade-level benchmarks in core academic areas. MTSS involves (a) conducting universal screening three to four times per year, (b) providing evidence-based instruction and intervention, (c) conducting ongoing progress monitoring, (d) engaging in data-based decision-making, (e) involving a collaborative team approach, and (g) adhering to fidelity of implementation (U.S. OSEP, 2018). For students from more diverse language and cultural backgrounds, culturally responsive assessment and testing practices consider ML students' strengths and needs and provide primary and/or English language literacy instruction and intervention based on individual needs and ongoing progress monitoring (August et al., 2015). To better understand the origin of individual and/or similar groups of students' learning problems, professionals determine whether this is a result of one or more instructional, curricular, environmental, or learner (ICEL) factors and gather multiple data sources (records, interviews, observations, testing [RIOT]; Leung, 1993) with an intentional focus on recognizing context when making data-based decisions. [Refer to Haas and Brown (2019) for a greater description of culturally and linguistically responsive assessment and data-based decision-making practices within an MTSS framework.]

Currently, a large proportion of districts across the country use an MTSS process to identify students early in the learning process whose screening data suggest a level of "riskness." This "riskness" may be primarily due to a school's inability to appropriate teach ML learners to successfully learn to read, write, or do math. Increasingly intense support across multiple tiers of MTSS may or may not lead to special education referrals. Two crucial dangers, however, are inherent in any support and referral process—the same biased practices and assumptions found in traditional assessment and evaluation practices can be transferred to MTSS if teams do not sufficiently consider a student's contexts and lived experiences. Second, if interventions and support are not linguistically and culturally responsive, they may be ineffective for MLs. Next, we highlight initial work from two federally funded U.S. model implementation projects focused on culturally and linguistically responsive MTSS models and their testing, assessment, evaluation, and data-based decision-making processes.

Implementation Studies

To investigate improvements to implementing culturally responsive MTSS models for MLs with and without disabilities, the U.S. Department of Education's Office of Special Education Programs (OSEP) has funded three model demonstration research projects. The purpose of these research projects is to support ML students' language and literacy outcomes (see www.mtss4els.org), specifically Projects ELITE², ELLIPSES, and LEE. Project ELITE² (Project ELITE Report, 2012–2015) focuses on implementation efforts to provide MTSS for ML students initially in kindergarten through third grade while recently extending its work for students in grades 3 to 5. Projects ELLIPSES and LEE focus on providing effective culturally and linguistically responsive teaching practices for MLs in grades 3 to 5. Project LEE's focus and structure will be described in greater depth to provide an example of these investigations.

Project LEE

Project lectura para excelencia y éxito (Project LEE) at Portland State University also received funding from OSEP to establish a model demonstration center. They partnered with a school district in the Pacific Northwest that had a well-established MTSS process but wanted to refine practices for MLs. Over three years, Project LEE staff worked closely with teams at three schools to specifically address the literacy achievement of MLs, particularly those in the two dual-language schools. Within Project LEE's partner schools, regular testing, assessment, data collection, and team meetings ensured that all students were either achieving benchmarks or receiving the support they needed to progress towards them. Here, we review the structure of the four types of data team meetings (100%, 20% Intervention, and Individual Problem Solving) the schools implemented. Data team membership included administration, classroom teachers, instructional specialists (e.g., reading specialist), English language development teacher, counselor/psychologists, speech and language specialists, and special education teachers.

100% MEETINGS: EVALUATING THE EFFECTIVENESS OF CORE INSTRUCTION

Each quarter, grade-level teams convened to review data (achievement, behavior, and attendance) to determine if core instruction was benefitting all students. In dual-language schools, reading data were analyzed across both English and Spanish using DIBELS (University of Oregon, 2020) and IDEL (University of Oregon, 2006) curriculum-based measures (CBMs). Research, though limited, suggests screening measures have predictive validity across students from different linguistic groups and with varying English proficiency levels (Baker et al., 2007; Kim et al., 2016). Research on Spanish CBMs is extremely limited but also suggests technical adequacy (Baker et al., 2007; Keller-Margulis et al., 2012; Ramirez & Shapiro, 2006, 2007). Given that MTSS models are predicated upon the concept that about 80% of students should be meeting grade-level benchmarks, the team kept this target in mind. The fall benchmarking scores for oral reading fluency (ORF) and Fluidez en la lectura oral (FLO) the team used are presented in Table 19.1.

Table 19.1 DIBELS 8th Edition Third-Grade Benchmark Goals (DIBELS English: ORF) and (IDEL Spanish: FLO)

DIBELS Fall Benchmarking

105+	Negligible risk
104	Core support/minimal risk
73	
72	Strategic support/some risk
55	
54	Intensive support/at risk
0	

Available at: https://dibels.uoregon.edu

IDEL Fall Benchmarking

60 and above	Core support/minimal risk
59	Strategic support/some risk
50	
49	Intensive support/at risk
0	

Available at: https://dibels.uoregon.edu

As an example, during fall 100% meetings, the team reviewed data from one third-grade classroom including data from 24 dual-language students' ORF and FLO scores. In this program, students have received the majority of their reading instruction in Spanish until third grade, when they transition to a greater percentage of instruction in English. The first level of analysis was to determine the efficacy of core instruction using the assumption that about 80% of students should be at benchmark. Examining the ORF data, they noted 58% of the class were at benchmark, 17% were in the strategic range, and 25% were in the intensive range. Given the dual-language status of the classroom's program, data were reviewed for the second language as well. The data for FLO indicated 50% of all students were at benchmark, 33% at the strategic level, and 17% were in the intensive range. Figure 19.1 shows the side-by-side English/Spanish assessment data, English learner status and English proficiency level, and if they were identified as a student receiving special education services.

Looking closely at the data indicated that less than 80% of students were meeting benchmarks in either language. To further understand the problem, the team disaggregated the data by student population (ML, special education, economically disadvantaged, race) to examine student group progress. Figure 19.1 indicates there were ten ML students. Of those, 30% were at benchmark in English, 20% in the strategic range, and 50% in the intensive range. This closer analysis clearly showed that core instruction was not meeting the needs of 70% of EL students in the classroom. Conducting this same analysis for English-only students showed that 79% of students were at benchmark, 14% at the strategic level, and 7% in the intensive range—much more in line with achievement expectations. Therefore, class-wide intervention needed to target ML students' English reading instruction. The team discussed the instruction, curriculum, and environment (ICE) and culturally and linguistically responsive strategies to bolster core instruction. This same process of analysis was also conducted using the IDEL data. In this case, 50% of ML students were at the benchmark in Spanish instruction, 40% in the strategic range, and 10% in the intensive range. For the English-only group in Spanish instruction, 50% were at the benchmark, 28% in the strategic range, and 21% in the intensive range. This analysis indicated that core Spanish instruction was not conferring expected benefits in either the ML or English-only student populations, and the intervention needed was to carefully examine both the Spanish and English core instruction. During the winter term data team members reviewed winter data to examine overall class-wide progress, particularly with the ML group.

Student	Oral Reading Fluency (ORF)	Fluidez en la lectura oral (FLO)	EL Status/Prof Level*	IEP
A	100	71	4	
B	35	50	3	X
C	107	68		
D	74	60		
E	68	46		
F	76	67	4	
G	53	44	2	X
H	99	58		
I	53	68	3	
J	101	44		
K	78	53	4	
L	92	66		
M	106	58		
N	49	53	2	
O	62	36		X
P	98	61		
Q	72	60	4	
R	45	53	3	
S	96	71		
T	84	63		
U	87	66		
V	68	75	3	
W	52	58		
X	88	56		

*Level 1 = Beginning, Level 5 = Fluent English proficiency.

Key

| Above benchmark | Benchmark | Strategic | Intensive |

Figure 19.1 Example of Third-Grade Fall Data for Oral Reading Fluency in a Dual-Language Setting—DIBELS and IDEL

INTERVENTION MEETINGS: DETERMINING INITIAL SUPPORT NEEDS

The second set of meetings determined which individual learners required intervention support (generally the lowest 20%). Universal screening data, classroom assessments, and students' background information and context were examined. In a dual-language program, teams analyzed data across languages by reviewing DIBELS and IDEL data side by side to determine the appropriate type of and language of intervention. Using Figure 19.1, the classroom teacher and team examined the data to look for the following patterns: (a) above benchmark/benchmark across both languages; (b) above benchmark/benchmark in one language, strategic in the other language; (c) strategic across both languages; (d) strategic in one language and intensive in the other language; and (e) intensive across both languages. Each of these scenarios suggests a different intervention focus. Figure 19.1 showed that nine students either were meeting or were above benchmarks across both languages. However, five students scored within the benchmark range in one language and strategic in the other language. In this case, the intervention should include instruction on how to use the skills they have acquired in one language and apply them to the second language (teach for transfer). The same strategy would likely be helpful to the two students in the benchmark in one language and intensive in the second language but with an emphasis on language development. For example, sounds not found in students' first language will need more focus, since these will be much harder for students to discern. Students scoring within the strategic range across both languages, or strategic and intensive range across the languages, likely need interventions that target foundational reading skills, as well as language development in both languages. For students in the intensive range across both languages, they will need intensive foundational skill instruction using the same principles just discussed. Intervention in their stronger language may prove to be most beneficial. In general, the language of intervention should match the language of instruction, but language proficiency should also be considered.

20% MEETINGS: PROGRESS MONITORING

Each quarter, teams also met to review progress monitoring data for all students receiving interventions and students in special education. The group analyzed growth by reviewing aim lines, trend lines, and grade-level norms, again examining any student group differences (Deno, 1985, 2013). For students whose progress was well below their "true peers" (Brown & Doolittle, 2008), or students with similar backgrounds and characteristics, the intervention may need adjusting. For ML students, interventions must provide cultural relevance and linguistic support in order for them to access the skill instruction. When students have not made adequate growth over more than one quarter, the team may consider a referral to individual problem-solving, although teams are reminded not to make hasty decisions about referral while at the same time making timely referrals based on patterns of response (Ryder, 2016).

INDIVIDUAL PROBLEM SOLVING MEETINGS

During individual problem solving (IPS), the team gathered information to determine the root cause of the student's difficulties and plan intensive interventions targeting the student's specific and unique needs. Another possible outcome of IPS is a referral for a special education evaluation, again after adequate time and data demonstrate the need. If an ML student is referred for a special education evaluation, special education law includes what is commonly referred to as an "exclusionary clause," which directs multidisciplinary teams to rule out that the primary reason for difficulties is caused by (a) a visual, hearing, or motor disability; (b) limited English proficiency; (c) inadequate instruction; (d) cognitive disability; (e) emotional disturbance; (f) cultural factors; or (g) environmental or economic disadvantages (IDEA, 2004). It is helpful during IPS for teams to reconceptualize the "exclusionary clause" and to instead reframe it as "inclusionary factors" because information on all of the listed factors is key in determining appropriate support and intervention. Additionally, if the student is later referred for a special education evaluation, teams have documented evidence that these items have been addressed throughout the support process. "Determining whom to refer for a special education evaluation and/or when to do so is not a single event, but rather a process" (Haas & Brown, 2019, p. 108). As a step in this process, standardized testing tools are often used in special education evaluations and may also be used throughout the data-gathering process to support teaching and learning. Next, we shift our focus to standardized tools and examine the ongoing challenges in their use with MLs, particularly the adequacy of current practices regarding normative samples.

Assessing MLs: Reconceptualizing Normative Samples

There is no shortage of research on test bias and the challenges of testing diverse learners with inconsistent findings. Warne et al. (2014) assert this variability lies in how bias is defined. Perhaps the most salient factors affecting test performance, however, are a student's developmental language level (in the language of the test) and acculturative knowledge acquisition, which are seldom thoroughly examined (Ortiz & Wong, 2020).

In an effort to conduct fair and valid assessments, native language assessments are used. Little attention has been paid to the fact, though, that these tests are often based on the assumption that all multilingual students are proficient or at least near proficient in their heritage/home language. In 2018, the Pew Research Center reported that 72% of MLs were born in the United States as compared to 28% foreign-born MLs (Bialik et al., 2018), meaning that the majority of our ML students are exposed to at least two languages from birth. Similarly, there are a wide range of instructional programs that either rely or do not rely on the native language, which also creates large differences in the language development and experiences of the students. Consequently, whether due to societal factors, such as the devaluation of a language other than English, or other sociocultural factors, many U.S.-born MLs and long-term MLs possess vastly different levels of proficiency and development in their heritage language, as well as English. By definition, English learners who enter the school system in the United States are "bilingual" and not "monolingual" speakers. They are no more comparable to native English speakers than they are to monolingual, heritage language speakers (Ortiz & Wong, 2020). But this issue has not been adequately considered in the construction of normative samples used in native language assessments. For example, one commonly used Spanish language assessment battery is normed exclusively on monolingual Spanish speakers, not individuals who live in two language worlds here in the United States, and therefore the validity of assessment results is subject to the same issues as English assessments, as highlighted in the study discussed next.

Native Language Assessments and Multilingual Learners

Research on native language assessments when used in the United States is surprisingly scarce, but one such study was conducted by this chapter's first author. Brown (2007) examined the performance of average-achieving third-grade to fifth-grade U.S.-born MLs on the *Batería III Woodcock-Muñoz: Pruebas de habilidades cognitivas* (Muñoz-Sandoval et al., 2005). Two groups were assessed—those who had received English-only instruction throughout their schooling and those who had received native language instruction in literacy and math in a dual-language program since kindergarten. The data and teacher reports indicated that none of the participating students experienced academic difficulties. Participants were given the Language Acquisition Scales assessment (DeAvila & Duncan, 2005) in both Spanish and English to measure their language proficiency. Language scores indicated that all but one student in each language were not considered proficient in either Spanish or English, nor were they monolingual speakers of either language. Fourteen subtests of the *Batería III Woodcock-Muñoz: Pruebas de habilidades cognitivas* were administered to the students to yield an overall general intellectual ability (GIA) score and seven broad ability scores. The GIA mean score for the English-only instructional group was 84.44, while the GIA man score for the native language instructional group was 90.81. Thus, neither group performed at the expected level for average overall ability (i.e., SS = 100). Figure 19.2 presents the results of the mean broad ability scores of these two groups arranged by specific cluster score. With the exception of the mean score for auditory processing (which cannot be translated from one language to another and simply highlights the structural differences between English and Spanish), all other broad ability scores revealed a progressive decline as the language demands of the tasks increased. Since all of the students were average achieving with no history of academic difficulties, it would be reasonable to expect they would have scored close to the test's normative mean (SS = 100) on all domains measured. However, this was not the case. More-

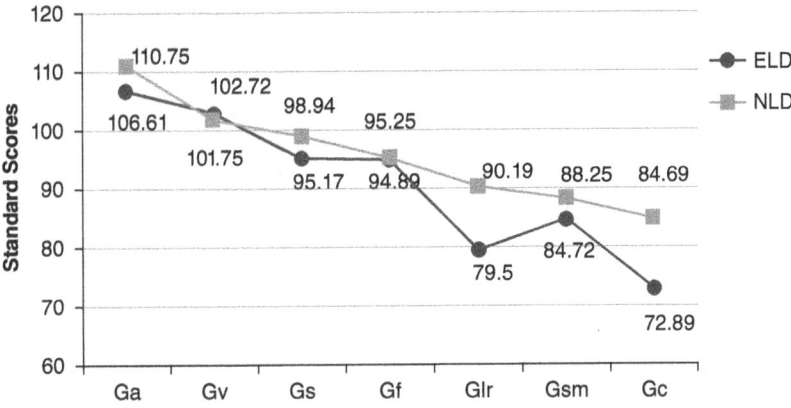

Figure 19.2 Comparison of Cluster Scores for Native Language Development and English Language Development

over, even when native language instruction was being provided, the decline in performance relative to language development was still quite marked and highlights the fact that ML students, who may or may not be stronger in their native language, do not possess the same level of language development as do the monolingual, Spanish-speaking individuals in the norm group. Consequently, if evaluators consider the scores valid from this heritage/native language test as they are generated from normal administration, they may be misidentifying students for special education. The results here suggest that using a test with monolingual norm samples in heritage/native language (in this case Spanish) for ML students can be as problematic as administering a standardized test in English to MLs, and scores likely *underpredict students' true abilities* in both circumstances.

Reconceptualizing Normative Samples

In recognition of the inadequacy of monolingual norm sampling and in response to these long-standing concerns about differences in language development among MLs, new tests for ML students have recently been developed that focus on norm sample construction as it relates to variable language development across all ages. The first test, the Bilingual English-Spanish Assessment (BESA; Peña et al., 2018) measures overall language functioning and ability for children ages 4:0 to 6:11 but is intended for use only with MLs who are Spanish-English speakers/learners. The goal of the BESA is to provide a comprehensive measure of language competency by examining the combination of both languages rather than measuring only one or the other. The assessments are not completely parallel, nor are items mere translations across the languages. The BESA contains five different normative samples that include (a) functional monolingual: English; (b) bilingual dominant: English; (c) balanced bilingual; (d) bilingual dominant: Spanish; and (e) functional monolingual: Spanish. Thus, bilinguals are compared in terms of language development based on a categorical system that takes into account the differences in proficiency and functioning that characterize the variable experiences of each. This represents a significant advance in terms of fairness in decision-making, as it begins to narrow the comparison group in a way that makes it more accurate than the use of a single norm sample that does not account at all for language development differences.

The second test, the Ortiz Picture Vocabulary Acquisition Test (Ortiz PVAT; Ortiz, 2018) takes this notion further and treats language development differences as a continuum that ranges from as little as 1% lifetime exposure on up to 99% exposure. At 100% exposure to English, the individual is essentially a monolingual speaker, and a separate norm sample composed only of monolingual English speakers is utilized. Thus, the Ortiz PVAT contains two norm samples: one for monolingual, native English-speaking students and the second for all others who are learning English but not exclusively. The language exposure norms for English learners were carefully stratified across the entire range of language development (from as little as one week exposure to nearly full lifetime exposure) and across each age level in the test from 2:6 to 22:11. The Ortiz PVAT is perhaps the first test of language that demonstrates no significant differences in performance as a function of race/ethnicity (Ortiz & Wong, 2020). Further, because the test is designed to evaluate only in English, it is useful with any individual regardless of their heritage language. A second analysis of the English learner norm sample indicated that performance among speakers of various languages did not differ significantly and highlighted the premise that English language acquisition is a largely invariant process that is not affected by the first language learned or when English learning begins (Ortiz & Wong, 2020).

While there are limited data on the use of these two assessments, they represent a new paradigm of tests that finally attempt to create fair and valid assessments specifically for bilingual populations that represent the type of individuals on whom testing in the United States is typically conducted. As Wiggins (1998) stated, the goal of assessment should be "to educate and improve student performance, not merely to audit it" (p. 7). To this end, more accurate and informed decisions can be made for MLs when we use appropriate tests that consider their unique learning characteristics along with multiple data sources.

Considerations for Future Research

Research investigating appropriate testing, assessment, and evaluation practices for students from diverse linguistic and cultural backgrounds continues to require greater consideration and critical inquiry. Preliminary findings from promising initial studies focused on improving culturally responsive MTSS structures for MLs will provide the field with a greater understanding regarding how to more appropriately address testing, assessment, and evaluation practices with this growing population of students. Researchers should continue to investigate critical questions around the appropriateness of nonstandardized and standardized measures, concerns around validity and reliability, students' primary and second language status and needs, and how these and numerous other factors contribute to or do not contribute to disability identification and special education determination. In the current chapter we discussed testing, assessment, and evaluation practices as they informed data-based, instructional decision-making practices. We conclude this chapter by drawing attention to three areas of consideration necessary for supporting appropriate instructional and assessment practices for MLs and future work in this area, specifically (a) monitoring the progress of MLs and "ever Els," (b) making the appropriate comparisons, and (c) collaborating with a broad range of professionals.

When examining classroom-, school-, and district-level data to make informed decisions about individual and groups of ML students, school/district teams should take into account the needs, development, and overall trajectory of these students over time. An ever English learner framework has been used within educational accountability discussions (Umansky et al., 2017) and for longitudinal research purposes tracking ML students at the school, district, and state level (Dynarski & Berends, 2015; Umansky et al., 2017). Specifically, ever English learners include all ML students who enter school regardless of whether or not these students reclassify as fluent English proficient at a future time. Using this framework is an important accountability measure that will allow systems to track the long-term outcomes for ML students, whether or not they exit ML/EL status at some point in their education. In Richard-Tutor and colleagues' (2016) review of empirical studies involving ML learners, the authors recommend teachers and specialists continue monitoring students' progress even after students exit from ML/EL status. Specifically, progress in language and skill development should continue to be measured after redesignation. Along these lines, currently there is a dearth of evidence and guidance on appropriate accommodations for MLs with disabilities on state-approved English language proficiency assessments. Without appropriate accommodations,

MLs with reading disabilities, for example, may never meet reclassification criteria for exiting English language development services and may remain a long-term English learner, limiting access to the mainstream curriculum. Of the four language domains assessed on proficiency tests (reading, writing, speaking, and listening), reading and writing scores tend to be more heavily weighted than listening and speaking on composite scores (Board of Regents, 2016).

In order to better understand the learning needs and progress of ML students, more appropriate comparisons should be made regardless of when students reclassify out of ML/EL status. Specifically, making important instructional decisions for ML students across tiers of support should be made by comparing students' progress with similar *true peers*, that is students from comparable backgrounds (August et al., 2015; Keller-Margulis et al., 2012; Richards-Tutor et al., 2016). True peers are "students who have the same or similar levels of language proficiency, acculturation, and educational backgrounds" (Brown & Doolittle, 2008, pg. 6). They provide a fairer standard of reference when making decisions regarding progress and/or need for added support. Although standards for progress and growth rates are well established for native English speakers, no such standards yet exist for ML speakers (Brown & Sanford, 2011).

Finally, future research investigating testing, assessment, and evaluation practices supporting MLs must analyze effective methods of collaboration with professionals having a broad array of skills, training, and expertise (García & Ortiz, 2008; Linan-Thompson & Ortiz, 2009; Martinez et al., 2014). The current chapter provided several examples where joint analysis by qualified professionals and stakeholders regarding a wide range of data will provide greater accuracy in data-based decision-making for MLs. Ultimately, decisions regarding identification, progress, and support should not remain in the hands of a few privileged professionals. Each individual, particularly parents, has unique expertise to bring to the table, and their contributions should be valued and heard.

In closing, much has been accomplished in the last 20 years since the President's Commission on Excellence in Special Education report (2002) calling for significant changes to the landscape of identification and special education service provision for students with disabilities. The commission called for elevating the importance of demonstrating gains and positive outcomes in student achievement over mere bureaucratic compliance. Since the report, there has been increased momentum in research and school implementation around improving identification and monitoring practices, including introducing multitiered systems and frameworks, with the goal of providing early intervention and support for all students with and without disabilities. In the last ten years we have witnessed growing interest and research, though insufficient, around meeting the needs of students with disabilities from more diverse cultural and linguistic communities. The landscape has begun to shift here as well, bringing greater attention to increasing the validity and reliability of standardized measures specifically for MLs; prioritizing student-level information when making decisions; reconsidering exclusionary factors as necessary inclusionary factors (e.g., culture, language proficiency, appropriate instruction); and intentionally addressing these factors through more robust and culturally responsive instruction, testing, assessment, and evaluation practices. These considerations will further improve the academic achievement and postsecondary outcomes of a growing number of multilingual children and youth with disabilities. Readers are encouraged to explore the following resources for further reference.

- Aceves, T. C., & Orosco, M. J. (2014). *Culturally responsive teaching* (Document No. IC-2). Retrieved from University of Florida, Collaboration for Effective Educator, Development, Accountability, and Reform Center website: http://ceedar.education.ufl.edu/tools/innovation-configurations/
- Haas, E. M., & Brown, J. E. (2019). *Supporting English learners in the classroom: Best practices for distinguishing language acquisition from learning disabilities.* Teachers College Press.
- Richards-Tutor, C., Aceves, T., & Reese, L. (2016). *Evidence-based practices for English Learners* (Document No. IC-18). Retrieved from University of Florida, Collaboration for Effective

Educator, Development, Accountability, and Reform Center website: http://ceedar.education.ufl.edu/tools/innovation-configurations/

Note

1 C-LIM categorizes individual tests from English cognitive assessments on two factors: cultural loading and linguistic demand. While there continues to be limited empirical validation (Cormier et al., 2014), this framework can be useful as one data source within a comprehensive evaluation.

References

Albrecht, G., & Levy, J. (1981). Constructing disabilities as social problems. In G. Albrecht (Ed.), *Cross national rehabilitation policies: A sociological perspective* (pp. 11–32). Sage Publications.

Annamma, S. A., Connor, D., & Ferri, B. (2013). Dis/ability critical race studies (DisCrit): Theorizing at the intersections of race and dis/ability. *Race Ethnicity and Education, 16*(1), 1–31.

Annamma, S., & Morrison, D. (2018). Identifying dysfunctional education ecologies: A DisCrit analysis of bias in the classroom. *Equity & Excellence in Education, 51*(2), 114–131.

Artiles, A. J. (2011). Toward an interdisciplinary understanding of educational equity and difference: The case of the racialization of ability. *Educational Researcher, 40*(9), 431–445. https://doi.org/10.3102/0013189X11429391

Artiles, A. J., Kozleski, E. B., Trent, S., Osher, D., & Ortiz, A. (2010). Justifying and explaining Disproportionality, 1968–2008: A critique of underlying views of culture. *Exceptional Children, 76,* 279–299.

August, D., Artzi, L., Kuchle, L., & Halloran, C. (2015). *Quality of English language proficiency assessments.* https://ncela.ed.gov/files/15_2037_QELPA_ELSWD_ Summary_final_dla_5–15–15_508.pdf

Baker, S. K., Cummings, K. D., Good, R. H., & Smolkowski, K. (2007). *IDEL: Indicadores Dinamicos del Éxito en la Lectura: Summary of decision rules for intensive, strategic and benchmark instructional recommendations in kindergarten through third grade (Technical Report No. 1).* https://dibels.uoregon.edu/docs/techreports/IDEL_Instructional_Rec.pdf

Becker, G. I., & Deris, A. R. (2019). Identification of Hispanic English language learners in special education. *Education Research International, 2019,* 1–9. https://doi.org/10.1155/2019/2967943

Bialik, K., Scheller, A., & Walker, K. (2018). *6 facts about English language learners in U.S. public schools* [Report]. Pew Research Center. www.pewresearch.org/fact-tank/2018/10/25/6-facts-about-english-language-learne rs-in-u-s-public-schools/

Board of Regents of the University of Wisconsin System. (2016). *ACCESS for ELLs 2.0: Interpretive guide for score reports.* WIDA.

Brown, J. E. (2007). *The impact of cultural loading and linguistic demand on the performance of English/Spanish bilinguals on Spanish language cognitive tests.* (Unpublished manuscript). Portland State University.

Brown, J. E., & Doolittle, J. (2008). A cultural, linguistic, and ecological framework for Response to Intervention: A preliminary guide. *Practitioner Brief Series.* National Center for Culturally Responsive Educational Systems.

Brown, J. E., & Sanford, A. (2011). *RTI for English language learners: Appropriate using screening and progress monitoring tools to improve instructional outcomes.* National Center on Response to Intervention.https://mtss4success.org/resource/rti-english-language-learners-appropriately-using-scree ning-and-progress-monitoring-tools

California Association of School Psychologists. (August 2020). *CASP school psychology practice during COVID series—#1: Assessment guidance.* Sacramento, CA.

Cormier, D. C.,. McGrew, K. S., & Ysseldyke, J. E. (2014). The influence of linguistic demands and cultural loading on cognitive test scores. *Journal of Psychoeducational Assessment, 32*(7), 610–625.

DeAvila, E., & Duncan, S. (2005). *Language assessment scales.* McGraw-Hill.

Deno, S. L. (1985). Curriculum-based measurement: The emerging alternative. *Exceptional Children, 52*(3), 219–232.

Deno, S. L. (2013). Problem-solving assessment. In R. Brown-Chidsey & K. J. Andren (Eds.), *Assessment for intervention: A problem-solving approach* (2nd ed., pp. 10–36). Guilford Press.

Dynarski, S., & Berends, M. (2015). Introduction to Special Issue. *Educational Evaluation and Policy Analysis, 37*(1 suppl), 3S–5S.

Flanagan, D. P., Ortiz, S. O., & Alfonso, V. C. (2007). *Essentials of cross-battery assessment with C/D ROM* (2nd ed.). John Wiley.

García, S. B., Ortiz, A. A. (2008). A framework for culturally and linguistically responsive design of response to intervention models. *Multiple Voices for Ethnically Diverse Exceptional Learners, 11*(1), 24–41.

Haas, E. M., & Brown, J. E. (2019). *Supporting English learners in the classroom: Best practices for distinguishing language acquisition from learning disabilities*. Teachers College Press.

Harry, B., & Klingner, J. (2014). *Why are so many minority students in special education? Understanding race and disability in schools* (2nd ed.). Teachers College Press.

Hurwitz, S., Perry, B., Cohen, E. D., & Skiba, R. (2020). Special education and individualized academic growth: A longitudinal assessment of outcomes for students with disabilities. *American Educational Research Journal, 57*(2), 576–611.

Hussar, B., Zhang, J., Hein, S., Wang, K., Roberts, A., Cui, J., Smith, M., Bullock Mann, F., Barmer, A., & Dilig, R. (2020). *The condition of education 2020* (NCES 2020–144). U.S. Department of Education. National Center for Education Statistics. https://nces.ed.gov/pubsearch/pubsinfo.asp?pubid=2020144.

Individuals with Disabilities Education Improvement Act [IDEA], 20 U.S.C. §§ 1400 et seq. (2004).

Keller-Margulis, M. A., Payan, A., & Booth, C. (2012). Reading curriculum-based measures in Spanish: An examination of validity and diagnostic accuracy. *Assessment for Effective Intervention, 37*(4), 212–223.

Kim, J. S., Vanderwood, M. L., & Lee, C. Y. (2016). Predictive validity of curriculum-based measures for English Learners at varying English proficiency levels. *Educational Assessment, 21*(1), 1–18.

King Thorius, K., & Sullivan, A. L. (2013). Interrogating instruction and intervention in RTI research with students identified as English language learners, *Reading & Writing Quarterly: Overcoming Learning Difficulties, 29*(1), 64–88.

Leung, B. (1993). Assessment is a R.I.O.T.! *Communiqué, 22*(3), 1–6.

Linan-Thompson, S., & Ortiz, A. (2009). Response to intervention and English-language learners: Instructional and assessment considerations, *Seminars in Speech and Language, 30*(2), 105–120. https://doi.org/10.1055/s-0029-1215718

Losen, D. J., Hodson, C., Ee, J., & Martinez, T. (2015). Disturbing inequities: Exploring the relationship between racial disparities in special education identification and discipline. In D. J. Losen (Ed.), *Closing the school discipline gap: Equitable remedies for excessive exclusion*. Teachers College Press.

Martinez, R. S., Harris, B., & McClain, M. B. (2014). Practices that promote English reading for English learners (ELs). *Journal of Educational and Psychological Consultation, 24*(2), 128–148.

Muñoz-Sandoval, A. F., Woodcock, R. W., McGrew, K. S., & Mather, N. (2005). *Batería III Woodcock-Muñoz Pruebas de Habilidades Cognitivas*. Riverside Publishing.

National Center for Education Statistics., National Assessment of Educational Progress, Educational Testing Service., & United States. (2017). *NAEP mathematics & reading assessments report card for the nation and the states*. National Center for Education Statistics, Office of Educational Research and Improvement, U.S. Dept. of Education.

Oswald, D. P., Coutinho, M. J., Best, A. M., & Singh, N. N. (1999). Ethnic representation in special education: The influence of school-related economic and demographic variables. *The Journal of Special Education, 32*(4), 194–206.

Ortiz, S. O. (2018). *Ortiz picture vocabulary acquisition test (Ortiz PVAT)*. Multi-Health Systems.

Ortiz, S. O. (2019). On the measurement of cognitive abilities in English learners, *Contemporary School Psychology, 23*, 68–86.

Ortiz, S. O., & Wong, J. (2020). Advances in the measurement of language ability in English Learners. *The Score*, APA Division 5 (Quantitative and Qualitative Methods) Newsletter.

Park, S. (2020). Demystifying disproportionality: Exploring educator beliefs about special education referrals for English Learners. *Teacher College Record, 122*(5), 1–34.

Peña, E. D., Gutierrez-Clellen, V., Iglesias, A., Goldstein, B., & Bedore, L. M. (2018). *Bilingual English-Spanish assessment (BESA)*. Brookes Publishing.

President's Commission on Excellence in Special Education. (2002, July). *A new era: Revitalizing special education for children and their families*. https://ectacenter.org/~pdfs/calls/2010/earlypartc/revitalizing_special_education.pdf

Project ELITE Report. (2012–2015). *Implementing a multitiered instructional model for English learners*. www.elitetexas.org/files/downloads/ELITE_Project_Report.pdf

Ramirez, R. D., & Shapiro, E. S. (2006). Curriculum-based measurement and the evaluation of Reading skills of Spanish-speaking English language learners in bilingual education classrooms. *School Psychology Review, 35*, 356–369.

Ramirez, R. D., & Shapiro, E. S. (2007). Cross-language relationship between Spanish and English oral reading fluency among Spanish-speaking English language learners in bilingual education classrooms. *Psychology in the Schools, 44*, 795–806.

Richards-Tutor, C., Aceves, T., & Reese, L. (2016). *Evidence-based practices for English learners* (Document No. IC-18). Retrieved from University of Florida, Collaboration for Effective Educator, Development, Accountability, and Reform Center website: http://ceedar.education.ufl.edu/tools/innovation-configurations/

Rogoff, B., Dahl, A., & Callanan, M. (2018). The importance of understanding children's lived experience. *Developmental Review, 50*(Part A), 5–15. https://doi.org/10.1016/j.dr.2018.05.006

Ryder, R. (2016, April 29). A response to intervention process cannot be used to delay-deny an Evaluation for preschool special education services under the Individuals with Disabilities Education Act. U.S. Department of Education, Office of Special Education and Rehabilitative Services.

Salvia, J., Ysseldyke, J. E., & Bolt, S. (2017). *Assessment in special and inclusive education.* Cengage Learning.

Schwartz, A. E., Hopkins, B. G., & Stiefel, L. (2021). The effects of special education on the academic performance of students with learning disabilities. *Journal of Policy Analysis and Management, 00*(1), 1–41.

Sciuchetti, M. B. (2017). Addressing inequity in special education: An integrated framework for culturally responsive social emotional practice. *Psychology in the Schools, 54*, 1245–1251.

Snyder, T. D., de Brey, C., & Dillow, S. A. (2016). *Digest of education statistics 2015.* Institute of Education Sciences, National Center for Education Statistics.

Umansky, I. M., Thompson, K. D., & Diaz, G. (2017). Using an ever-English learner framework to examine disproportionality in special education. *Exceptional Children, 84*(1), 76–96.

University of Oregon. (2006). *Indicadores dinámicos del éxito de la lectura* (7a ed). University of Oregon. http://dibels.uoregon.edu

University of Oregon. (2020). *8th Edition of Dynamic indicators of basic early literacy skills (DIBELS®): Administration and scoring guide.* University of Oregon. https://dibels.uoregon.edu

U.S. Office of Special Education Programs. (2018). *Meeting the needs of English learners with and without disabilities: Brief 1, Multi-Tiered instructional systems for ELs.*

Warne, R., Yoon, M., & Price, C. J. (2014). Exploring the various interpretations of "test bias". *Cultural Diversity and Ethnic Minority Psychology, 20*(4), 570–582. DOI: 10.1037/a0036503

Wiggins, G. (1998). *Educative assessment: Designing assessments to inform and improve student performance.* Jossey-Bass.

20
TEACHING CHILDREN HOW TO PLAY
More Than Just a Context

Erin E. Barton and Justin Lane

Play is an important early milestone for children, as it supports healthy growth and learning throughout childhood. Children should have time to engage in meaningful play throughout the day, as it is essential to their well-being (Ginsburg, 2007). Play promotes independent engagement across settings and allows children to become active members of their social contexts (Lifter, Mason, et al., 2011). The development of increasingly complex play skills is important to all children, including children with disabilities (Barton et al., 2020).

In nurturing and responsive environments, play can provide children with meaningful and sufficient opportunities and developmentally appropriate and contextually relevant contexts to learn and practice motor skills, language skills, cognitive skills, and social skills (Barton et al., 2020; Lifter, Mason, et al., 2011). Playful interactions with caregivers, peers, and teachers are a primary context for practicing and generalizing skills and provide important information about the child's learning and development (Lifter, Mason, et al., 2011). Play has been shown to be correlated with social and communication skills (Mills et al., 2014), physical and mental health (Hirsh-Pasek et al., 2009), healthy attachments with caregivers (Cohn, 1990), and friendships with peers (Coolahan et al., 2000). Given its developmental importance, we believe play should be a developmental domain and an instructional goal (Lifter, Foster-Sanda, et al., 2011b).

Overview of Play Types

There are two primary categories of play: social play (Parten, 1932) and object play (Barton, 2016; Smilansky, 1968). These categories are represented across various play taxonomies, all of which propose an increasingly complex sequence of play behaviors across specific categories (see Table 20.1). These categories are exhaustive but not mutually exclusive. When children play, they use multiple different behaviors simultaneously, although each might require unique developmental repertoires.

Social Play

Social play includes play behaviors defined relative to how the child is interacting (or not) with other adults or children in their environments. In 1932, Parten developed a social play taxonomy for young children that remains ubiquitous. Parten used the following categories to define social play: (a) onlooker, (b) solitary, (c) parallel, (d) associative, and (e) cooperative (see Table 20.1). She also

Table 20.1 Definitions of Social and Object Play

Social Play Taxonomy[b]	Object Play Taxonomy[a]
Unoccupied behavior: Watching people and things with momentary interest rather than playing with them.	**Sensorimotor play**: Exploring materials by touching, mouthing, biting, smelling, banging, kicking, lifting, stretching, and balancing them.
Solitary play: Playing alone with toys that are different from those of peers near him or her.	**Relational play**: Combining objects through building, grouping, or associating objects in different ways.
Onlooker play: Watching other children play and occasionally talking to them.	
Parallel play: Playing near other children with similar toys, but rarely interacting.	**Functional play**: Using objects in the manner in which they are supposed to be used.
	Pretend play
Associative play: Playing near other children, with the same materials, and talking about their play and the materials.	**Functional pretend play**: Nonliterally using actual or miniature objects in the manner they are supposed to be used without the reality-based outcome.
	Symbolic play
Cooperative play: Playing together with the same toys, assigning roles, and following the same common goal or topic.	**Object substitution**: Using objects as if they were something else.
	Imagining absent objects: Performing a motor action that suggests using an object in the object's absence.
	Assigning absent attributes: Assigning roles, emotions, or attributes to the self, objects, or others.

documented a sequential emergence of qualitatively different social play behaviors, which support a developmental sequence of play. For example, in solitary play, the child plays alone or proximal to peers but with different toys or using different play behaviors than their proximal peers. In parallel play, the child plays proximal to peers, with the same toy or a similar toy, but independently and with no interactions. In associative play, the child plays near peers *and* interacts with peers using similar, if not identical, objects.

Object Play

Object play taxonomies define play relative to the child's behaviors in relation to objects, toys, or materials. There are numerous object play taxonomies and most include the following play types: (a) sensorimotor, (b) relational, (c) functional, and (d) symbolic or pretend. Across most taxonomies, these object play categories encompass a multitude of behaviors that require distinct skills and are not mutually exclusive. Also, the object play categories typically demonstrate increasing complexity—much like Parten's social play taxonomy—and suggest a developmental progression of object play (Belsky & Most, 1981). For example, sensorimotor play is first observed in infancy and includes mouthing or banging objects in a restrictive or repetitive manner (Van Berckelaer-Onnes, 2003). As toddlers develop better motor skills, they often start to engage in relational play, which includes the nonfunctional but purposeful combination of two or more objects (Lifter et al., 2005).

Although all most object play taxonomies include symbolic or pretend play categories, the definitions vary (Barton, 2010). These behaviors require an inference on the part of the observer or clear secondary indicators, which children might not always provide. For example, the child might hold the cup up to her mouth, and we could use her gestures to infer that she is pretending to drink. Or she might hold the cup up to her mouth and say, "This juice is good," which clearly tells us she is pretending to drink from the cup. Across object play taxonomies these symbolic behaviors are nonliteral in nature, but they are not consistently defined. Barton and Wolery (2008, 2010) developed a pretend play taxonomy to address the inconsistencies in defining and measuring these nonliteral object play behaviors. In their taxonomy they deduced four categories of pretend play from the pretend play intervention literature and included two major categories of play: functional play with pretense and symbolic play (see Table 20.1).

Pretend play does not require another individual and can be solitary or involve social interactions with others. Social pretend play is characterized by sustained interactions with others around a nonliteral theme or the use of common toys in a nonliteral manner and represents a complex and sophisticated form of play. Social pretend play requires children to have both complex pretend play and social skills in their repertoire (Pierce-Jordan & Lifter, 2005). We focus this chapter on object play skills, given that object play tends to receive less attention in research and practice than social skills.

Rationale for Teaching Play

The are many empirically supported reasons to teach children to engage in increasingly complex object play. We will discuss three of these. First, play is flexible; occurs across settings, materials, peers, and skills; and provides an ideal context for teaching, practicing, and assessing multiple skills (Lifter, Mason, et al., 2011). Multiple evidence-based practices for teaching children use play as the context for instruction (e.g., embedded instruction [Snyder et al., 2018], enhanced milieu teaching [Kaiser & Hampton, 2017], and peer-mediated strategies [Joseph et al., 2016]).

Second, play is predictive and might be a behavioral cusp for other important skills. Developmentally, play and language often are said to parallel each other due to the simultaneous advances in complexity (Lifter, Mason, et al., 2011; Lifter & Bloom, 1989). This is supported by intervention research; researchers have demonstrated simultaneous increases in play and language even when play was the primary target (Barton, 2016). Play also has been shown to be related to advancements in social skills, particularly for young children with autism spectrum disorder (ASD) (Freeman et al., 2015).

Third, play has a practical benefit in that it provides a meaningful context for participation and engagement. Further, when children are independently engaged in play, it frees up time for their caregivers to complete other important tasks. Play also is incompatible with challenging or maladaptive behaviors, which makes it ideal as an instructional goal for young children. If we teach children to engage in sustained and independent play behaviors with or near their peers, they might be less likely to engage in challenging or stereotypic behaviors (Machalicek et al., 2009; Nuzzolo-Gomez et al., 2002).

Fourth, although providing time for unstructured play and interactions with nurturing, responsive adults and socially competent peers is sufficient for facilitating increasingly complex play for many children, children with disabilities engage in less complex and fewer play behaviors than their typically developing peers (Williams et al., 2001). These play deficits are likely to have lasting and deleterious impacts on learning for young children. Play deficits can be particularly debilitating for young children because play is a typical context for interactions with caregivers and peers, independently engaging with their environments, and learning and practicing skills (Strain et al., 2008). Children with disabilities are less likely to demonstrate the play skills necessary to engage in meaningful interactions with others or create learning opportunities. Children with disabilities will require intentional, systematic instruction to learn appropriate play skills (Barton et al., 2020). Thus, it is critically important to intentionally teach children with disabilities to play.

Promoting Object Play

A number of research- and evidence-based interventions are recommended for promoting object play in children in typical contexts. Regardless of the intervention, instruction should be forward focused, with the long-term goal that the presence of age-appropriate toys and materials serves as the cue and motivation for a child to actively engage in object play—beginning with early exploration of materials to more advanced forms of symbolic play (e.g., object substitution, assigning absent attributes) (Barton, 2016; Barton & Wolery, 2008). Initially, children may require structured supports. Some supports, such as visual schedules, may continually be incorporated into the day to promote object use, while other supports, such as prompts, are typically introduced and removed over time (Ledford et al., 2019). Interventions to promote object play can be introduced in isolation until a child displays generalized improvements in targets skills or as a multicomponent treatment package. We have outlined common instructional practices ordered by degree of difficulty and planning (see Table 20.2).

Visual Supports

Visual supports refer to providing a static depiction or symbolic representation of an item or action that serves as a cue or support for displaying a target behavior. Visual supports can take the form of pictures, written words, schedules, task analyses, and any related symbolic representation of items or activities (Cooper et al., 2019). Incorporating visual supports into instruction is considered relatively low effort, since the majority of preparation involves creating materials prior to providing instruction. Visual supports may be used as a standalone assistance or as part of more complex instructional procedures (e.g., response prompting procedures; Ledford et al., 2019). Considerations for selecting appropriate visual supports include the extent to which a child understands the depiction or representation of an item or action, visual acuity, and attending to stimuli in the environment (Meadan et al., 2011). Consider providing a match-to-sample task where the child is asked to match the target stimuli to similar visuals, or ask the child to expressively identify the item or action. If needed, visual supports can take the form of objects that are affixed to a card or board or created to accommodate children with low vision.

Promoting attention is a common consideration that is not unique to visual supports and should be considered as needed to ensure a child is attending to stimuli in their environment (Wolery et al., 1992). Thus, we recommend providing an attending cue and obtaining an attending response. An attending cue refers to an adult behavior that ensures the child is oriented toward the adult or target stimuli (general attending cue) or draws a child's attention to the critical features of a stimulus (specific attending cue). An attending response is a child behavior that serves as a proxy for attention (e.g., orientation, eye gaze shift, matching like items) (Ledford et al., 2019). With consideration of each of these, there are a variety of approaches for incorporating visuals into instruction. A number of visual supports are appropriate for promoting object play, ranging from line drawings or photographic depictions of an action or multiple actions to reinforcement-based systems for promoting actions on objects.

Table 20.2 Summary of Interventions

Intervention	Description
Visual supports	Providing a readily accessible representation of an action on objects in the form of objects affixed to a card or board, photographs, pictures, written directions, etc., to promote object play in children.
• Object, pictorial, and text-based supports	A static representation of play behaviors; children must understand what each visual represents.
• Task analyses	Representing multistep play behaviors as a series of images; the goal is that children have a referent that clearly communicates expectations for engaging with toys and related materials.
• Structured systems	Utilization of reinforcement-based systems that provide a method for visually outlining a contingency and the reinforcement that will follow contingent on an attempt to or successfully engaging in object play. Examples include if/then boards and token boards.
Environmental arrangement	Curating the immediate setting to promote engagement, interactions, and play.
• Physical arrangement	Consideration of how the physical layout of a space can promote engagement with toys and related materials.
• Temporal arrangement	Planning the day with regard to the schedule, length of activities, and opportunities to engage in object play.
• Social arrangement	Providing adult or peer models and supports to encourage object play in children, with additional training and coaching recommended for adults and children who require support to learn how to encourage and reinforce children to engage in object play in context.
Video modeling	Similar to other visual support systems, video modeling presents examples of play behaviors via a video. The child has an opportunity to watch the video at least once and is then presented with the same or similar materials for purposes of engaging in the same or similar actions observed in the video. It may be necessary to include prompts and reinforcement to encourage a child to attend to video models and to engage with toys and related materials.
Response prompting procedures	Systematic teaching focused on initially providing a prompt or series of prompts following presentation of a stimulus, with that support delayed in time until a child responds to the target stimulus alone.
• Single-prompt procedures	During instruction, a single controlling prompt is provided to promote independent levels of responding.
• Prompting hierarchies	During instruction, a series of prompts, concluding with a controlling prompt, is presented as part of a hierarchy to promote independent levels of responding.

OBJECTS, PICTORIAL SUPPORTS, OR TEXT-BASED SUPPORTS

Objects, line drawings, photographs, or written descriptions or instructions associated with object play may be used to promote novel or expanded forms of a child's action on objects. Such supports are typically intended to represent a single play action (or discrete behavior) and, in turn, encourage object play. You must first determine if a child understands what each support represents (Ledford et al., 2019). For example, if a child is unaware of the connection between a line drawing and an associated play action, then it will not benefit the child. It might be necessary to teach the association of visual supports and related actions using adult supports such as modeling.

TASK ANALYSES

Oftentimes, during play-based instruction we are focused on teaching multistep behaviors for the purpose of promoting complex play sequences, such as a feeding a doll or character, or building a garage to store and repair miniature vehicles. Thus, a play sequence composed of varied physical actions on objects would consist of a series of pictorial or text-based supports presented in sequential order, beginning with the first action to the final action (e.g., horizontally along a picture board) (Cooper et al., 2019). A larger play sequence may be broken down into multiple task analyses. For example, arranging blocks to build a tower or garage, gathering and driving miniature vehicles into the tower or garage, and engaging in symbolic play behaviors related to repairing the vehicles could represent three separate task analyses that are related to the concept of vehicle-based object play.

STRUCTURED SYSTEMS

Reinforcement-focused visual supports can be utilized to increase the likelihood a child will engage in object play during similar situations in the future. The environmental change associated with the reinforcement, also known as the reinforcer, is delivered contingent on the target action occurring in context. Reinforcers may (e.g., descriptive praise, continuation of an activity) or may not (e.g., stickers, edibles) be directly related to the immediate activity. Reinforcer value should be regularly tested and adapted as needed. It is important to deliver reinforcers that are potent enough to promote long-term behavior change. Reinforcers can be systematically removed from the instructional context as the child is successful, but might need to be used during maintenance when the prompts or other supports are faded (Alberto & Troutman, 2012; Sulzer-Azaroff & Mayer, 1991). Examples of reinforcement-focused visual supports include if/then or token boards. If/then boards are tools for visually presenting expectations in the form of an expected action and subsequent reinforcing outcome. An if/then board highlights the relation between an action and reinforcement and promotes early discrete behaviors and participation. A token board involves establishing a clear contingency with the child (e.g., engaging in pretend play results in you earning tokens) followed by an opportunity to earn tokens (an item or object that serves as a placeholder for later accessing a reinforcer) (Cooper et al., 2019). Token boards have a long-standing history in the literature for promoting behavior change.

Environmental Arrangement

Environmental arrangement refers to the extent to which the (a) physical layout of a space, (b) temporal ordering of the child's day, and (c) social supports are planned for or made available for purposes of promoting socially meaningful behavior change in children.

PHYSICAL ARRANGEMENT

The physical layout of the environment refers to how items, including furniture and materials, like toys, are arranged in a space. Related to object play, age-appropriate materials and items should be readily accessible to children (Grisham-Brown & Hemmeter, 2017). Given the natural cue for playing with toys is the presence of those items, it is imperative that careful consideration be given to the selection and availability of toys and related items. For example, in a classroom there could be designated spaces for construction toys and dramatic play materials; materials should be placed in easily accessible spaces such as bins, on tables or the floor, or on shelves. Relatedly, it is important to have a variety of materials and a plan for rotating materials to promote continued engagement. Also, children should be allowed to intermix items across categories or specified locations, since more advanced forms of play can include a variety of contextually related (e.g., miniature vehicles and a garage play set) and unrelated items (e.g., blocks as a train; pipe cleaner as a water hose) (Division for Early Childhood, 2014; Lane & Brown, 2016). Physical arrangement involves curating spaces that are inviting to children and promotes item use (e.g., enough space to build and play). In addition, proper arrangement of the physical space creates additional opportunities to properly plan for the temporal and social aspects of the child's environment.

TEMPORAL ARRANGEMENT

The temporal arrangement of the environment refers to the classroom schedule, time allowed for activities, and instructional opportunities. When planning instruction, children require adequate amounts of time throughout the day to choose and engage with objects. The length of activities can vary based on the specific instructional objective for each child. Given the extent to which challenging behavior, cognition, and motor delays can moderate engagement and object play, some children may require additional instructional time to select and begin to engage with objects. Ideally, such decisions should be based on the child's learning history (i.e., formative and summative evaluation of observational data and instructional data) (e.g., a child is more actively engaged with objects in the morning instead of the afternoon).

Some children will actively and independently explore a variety of materials and objects across the day, while others may play with a single item each day and play in the same area. To address this potential issue, a visual schedule across or within activities could be introduced. If a child is not actively engaged with a variety of items, it decreases the likelihood of generalized object use, which has long-term implications for early language use and social interactions. Finally, dosage requires consideration when planning instruction. Dosage refers to the number of opportunities (or trials) a child requires to make progress on instructional objectives (McConnell & Rahn, 2016). Again, adults must consider a child's learning history relative to the target skill when identifying an adequate number of instructional opportunities.

SOCIAL ARRANGEMENT

The social arrangement of the environment is composed of adults and peers in the child's immediate setting.

Adult Supports and Models Engaging in responsive interactions with a child in the form of attending to, imitating, and expanding on a child's play actions encourages positive adult–child interactions and provides meaningful input to a child in the form of modeling other play actions (Lane & Brown, 2016). If a child pauses during play or displays difficulty engaging in play, the adult can initiate a play action and then wait for the child to respond. In general, whether expanding on a child's play or initiating a play action, it is important to wait for the child to respond (Kaiser & Hampton, 2017). Some children may require additional time to process and respond to environmental input (e.g., a child with a physical disability may require 10 to 15 seconds before beginning to imitate another person's actions), and, as such, adults should adjust their expectations accordingly (Wolery et al., 1992). If a child imitates an action, adults should provide descriptive praise and continue the play sequence. If a child does not, the adult should continue with the sequence of attending to, imitating, and expanding on object play.

Although responsive interactions are commonly recommended as the foundation for adult–child interactions, adults may require specific training and coaching on how to actively engage in responsive interactions with children, especially around how to model multiple and varied play behaviors (Barton & Wolery, 2010). A number of standalone and combined approaches to training and coaching adults are available in the literature. Of those approaches, performance-based feedback is one of the most commonly recommended and effective approaches for improving adult outcomes (Artman-Meeker et al., 2015). Performance-based feedback involves providing constructive and informative comments about instructional outcomes for adults either in the moment (e.g., bug in ear, text messaging) or following an observation (at the end of a session or after viewing a recording; e.g., email) (Barton et al., 2016, 2018). Additional practices for training and coaching adults includes modeling, role playing, and practicing procedures. Spending time training and coaching adults to implement interventions with fidelity is associated with short- and long-term positive outcomes for children.

Peer Supports and Models Same-aged or similarly aged peers serve as a natural model for how to play with toys and related items. One relatively easy approach to promote object play is to ensure children are near peers who typically display multiple and varied play behaviors. Thus, children who actively observe and imitate peers will likely benefit from peer models alone, without any additional feedback or external supports. Relatedly, assigning peer buddies within or across activities increases the likelihood that children will remain proximal to one another. If a child does not reliably observe and imitate peers, additional feedback and supports should be introduced and, in turn, a child will likely display therapeutic improvements in object play (Ledford & Pustejovsky, 2021). First, consider providing reinforcement in the form of related (e.g., praise) or unrelated actions or items (e.g., stickers) for all children who engage in attending behaviors or those who imitate peers. For children who do not readily attend to or imitate peers, adults can train peers to gain a child's attention, model play behaviors, and then deliver subsequent reinforcement. The extent to which a peer can be taught to engage in these behaviors will likely be dependent on the peer's age and attention (Grisham-Brown & Hemmeter, 2017).

Video Modeling

Video modeling is a commonly used and popular intervention to promote a variety of behaviors (Wong et al., 2015), including object play, in children (Palechka & MacDonald, 2010). A task analysis of a play sequence is presented via video in its entirety followed by an opportunity for the child to imitate the observed actions with the same or similar materials. Alternatively, the video may be played on a continuous loop while the child has an opportunity to engage with items. Video models may be presented on a laptop, tablet, or other mobile device. Instructors can record themselves, other adults or peers, or the child engaging in the target play actions. Oftentimes, if peers or the child is videoed, adult prompts, reinforcement, and subsequent editing of videos are required to produce a video model. A video model may be filmed from various perspectives, including point of view or self-modeling, but the extent to which the perspective influences outcomes seems to be inconsequential. If the child has a history of responding well to one type of perspective, use that as a guide for planning instruction. If a video model alone is unsuccessful, additional adult supports are typically added to instructional sessions, including a partial or full physical prompt and reinforcement.

Response Prompting

Response prompting procedures have a long-standing history for promoting socially meaningful behaviors, including object play, in children with or at risk for disabilities (e.g., Barton & Wolery,

2010; Barton et al., 2020). Response prompting procedures are typically referred to as errorless or near-errorless teaching procedures and can be divided into single-prompt strategies (e.g., constant time delay or progressive time delay—CTD and PTD, respectively) or prompting hierarchies (e.g., system of least prompts—SLP). In addition, prompts are typically categorized as controlling or noncontrolling. A controlling prompt refers to an adult behavior or environmental modification that ensures a correct response (e.g., partial physical prompt, modeling a target behavior with the same or similar materials). In contrast, a noncontrolling prompt essentially serves as a hint or additional cue for the child to display the target behavior, but does not guarantee a correct response. The goal is for the child to respond to the natural cue or antecedent for a target behavior. Initially, the procedures are designed to draw the child's attention to the natural cue, show the child how to display the behavior in context, and transfer responding from an adult prompt to the natural cue alone.

Single-prompt strategies, like PTD, involve presenting the natural cue for target behavior and initially immediately providing a controlling prompt (e.g., Liber et al., 2008). The presentation of the controlling prompt is followed by a delay interval that is held constant across the intervention (e.g., four seconds to respond to an adult's model for object play). In contrast, the time between the natural cue for a behavior and the controlling prompt is systematically or progressively increased within or across sessions (e.g., zero-second prompt delay, one-second prompt delay, two-second prompt delay, and finally reaching a terminal delay of four seconds). The plan for increasing the prompt delay is typically dependent on the child's behavior (e.g., the child responded independently or to the controlling prompt at 100% of opportunities until reaching a terminal delay), with the option for decreasing the prompt delay if a child is making errors. Children are reinforced in the form of naturally occurring consequences, such as adult attention or continued actions on items. Additionally, some children may require further unrelated reinforcers (e.g., stickers, edibles). Although ideally we want a child to maintain a behavior in response to the natural consequence, it may not be feasible during the early stages of teaching. Some children might need additional support to understand the relation between their actions and pleasant changes in the environment (cf. Ledford et al., 2019; Wolery et al., 1992).

In contrast to single-prompt strategies, prompting hierarchies allow the child to essentially select what level of support they need to engage in the target behavior, with the controlling prompt provided at the end of a teaching trial (Barton & Pavilanis, 2012; DiCarlo et al., 2004). Prompting hierarchies, like SLP, typically refer to procedures that initially involve providing the natural cue for a target behavior and then waiting a set delay for a child to provide an independent response (e.g., materials in front of child [cue], wait four seconds, with the goal of the child placing a plastic bottle to a doll's mouth [target behavior] within that delay). If the child does not display the target behavior, the adult provides an intermediate prompt (noncontrolling prompt). A prompting hierarchy may include one to three intermediate prompts, with each level providing increasing amounts of support. Unless a child commonly displays challenging behaviors in response to adult prompts, a single intermediate prompt will likely suffice. The final step is providing a controlling prompt (cf. Ledford et al., 2019; Wolery et al., 1992).

Response prompting strategies are more complex than using visual depictions of actions on objects alone, meaning that multiple steps are required to implement the procedures as intended. Although complex relative to other procedures, response prompting procedures are well-established practices for showing a child when to display a behavior and how to reliably demonstrate that behavior in context. They have been shown to be implemented with fidelity by endogenous practitioners with support and feedback (Barton & Wolery, 2010; Barton, 2016).

Recommendations for Practice

We provide the following recommendations for practices when teaching play to young children using the instructional procedures described in the previous section.

Individual Considerations

Children with or at risk for disabilities oftentimes require systematic supports to recognize when and how to play. A number of strategies were suggested in this chapter, but additional considerations warrant attention. First, it is important to establish clear expectations and routines for all children (e.g., rules, transitions). This increases the predictability of the day and allows a child to focus on learning new skills or expanding their current repertoire of skills instead of trying to learn how to navigate the environment. In addition, we cannot discount the importance of reinforcement. Adults should plan to conduct preference assessments (e.g., multiple stimulus without replacement) to identify potential reinforcing stimuli or activities (e.g., toys, edibles, social attention). Once identified, reinforcers should be delivered immediately and contingently (i.e., child should understand what behavior is being reinforced).

Initially, praise alone may not serve as a reliable reinforcer for promoting long-term improvements, but descriptive praise should be paired with tangible and activity reinforcers. This pairing process will likely eventually lead to praise alone serving as a social reinforcer. It is not necessary to praise each and every action, but instead descriptive praise should be delivered to teach. Such systematic planning should not be confused with continually engaging in positive interactions in general; it is important to display positive affect, actively engage with children, and respond contingently to all attempts to communicate. Devoting planning time to creating a supportive and reinforcing environment is key to promoting success in object play. Third, when children play, they often use repetitive actions or themes with an occasional novel play behavior. Novel play behaviors are play actions that have not previously been used by the child within the activity. This means we should support children in using new play behaviors with new toys, new play behaviors with the same toys, or the same play behaviors with different toys. Children also often use sequential, related play behaviors, which means when teaching we should continue teaching until the child can use multiple varied and sequential play behaviors. Finally, children often use speech or other verbalizations during play. When teaching, we should incorporate related verbalizations and ensure we are using a mode of communication that the child can imitate. We should teach words, phrases, or signs related to the child's play behaviors.

Including Peers

Few object play intervention studies have included peers within the instructional sessions, which limits our understanding of play interventions. However, we know that when children play, they are often play near their peers. Thus, we recommend teaching object play in contexts with or near peers. Although we focused this chapter on object play, social play and object play occur simultaneously in young children and are not mutually exclusive. It might be important to set up the instructional sessions to include children who play at similar levels or have similar play interests. Once children are engaging in increasingly complex play, teach them to interact with each other using play behaviors that they have mastered (Pierce-Jordan & Lifter, 2005).

Defining Play

Teaching children to play requires clear operationalized definitions. One major limitation in the object play intervention research is the inconsistency with which play is defined and measured (Barton, 2010). This makes it hard to synthesize across research studies and provide recommendations for practice. Further, there is limited research on the normative rates of play for young children—likely due to the idiosyncratic nature of play. Although individualization and variation in play goals across children is expected, consistency in broad categories might be necessary for advancing the research on play interventions and linking practices to specific outcomes. We recommend using clearly defined play categories when developing play goals that allow for more depth than breadth.

Teaching Generalized Play

We want children to use multiple and varied play behaviors across settings and activities. Thus, we recommend focusing on teaching children to use a variety of different play behaviors across materials, settings, and friends, rather than focusing on rigid or specific play targets (e.g., feed the baby with the bottle, race the cars around the track, use the blocks as a road). Play goals can focus on types or categories of play to ensure children use different behaviors within and across teaching opportunities. Varying targets, teaching across activities and materials, and including different play partners supports children's generalized play skills, which increases the likelihood that they will engage in increasingly complex play over time and across settings.

Long-Term Maintenance of Play Outcomes

Sustained and independent play should be a primary goal for young children. However, there is a dearth of research examining maintenance of play skills over time, including complexity of play. We recommend teaching play using instructional prompts that can be systematically faded to ensure children continue to play once prompts are removed. It might be important to continue to reinforce independent play after prompts are removed. As children develop other new skills, their play also should evolve and show an increased sophistication. However, for some children, increasingly complex play will have to be systematically taught.

Promoting Communication During Play

A child typically learns reliable and meaningful methods for communicating wants, interests, and feelings during early interactions with adults and peers, such as using speech, gestures, or a speech-generating device to share with others in conversation (Paul & Norbury, 2012). Social interactions typically occur around age-appropriate activities, including object play, where a child receives input in the form of how to say words and phrases and the rules for how to communicate during such interactions. Play serves as a natural context for modeling words and associated play behaviors. Adults should plan to model varied examples of language at the child's target language level when (a) the child is playing with toys or related materials or (b) when taking a turn during play-based activities (Lane & Brown, 2016; Ledford et al., 2019).

Planning Instructional Opportunities

Classrooms are dynamic environments and require flexibility and adaptability when planning how to improve socially meaningful behaviors in all children. Providing universal supports, as well as individualized services to all children, can be a daunting task for any educator or related service provider (Wolery & Hemmeter, 2011). Specifically, finding time to provide an adequate number of opportunities for learning can be an ongoing challenge (see dosage considerations discussed in the "Temporal Arrangement" section). Matrices are a feasible approach to plan when, how, and who will provide instruction on object play and other instructional goals and objectives (Grisham-Brown & Hemmeter, 2017; Ledford et al., 2019). Matrices can be organized into an (a) objective-by-strategy, (b) objective-by-activity, or (c) activity-by-instructor matrix. Matrices also are effective communication tools to share expectations across adults.

Conclusion

Play is a primary form of engagement for young children and should be regularly assessed and taught. In this chapter, we provided guidelines for identifying play goals and teaching play to young children. Given the clear and replicated research highlighting the benefits of play for young children, research should continue to examine and identify effective and efficient practices that support children's play, and practitioners should continue to teach play to young children.

References

Alberto, P. A., & Troutman, A. C. (2012). *Applied behavior analysis for teachers* (9th ed.). Pearson.

Artman-Meeker, K. M., Fettig, A., Barton, E. E., Penney, A., & Zeng, S. (2015). Applying an evidence-based framework to the early childhood coaching literature. *Topics in Early Childhood Special Education, 35*(3), 183–196.

Barton, E. E. (2010). Development of a taxonomy of pretend play for children with disabilities. *Infants & Young Children, 23*(4), 247–261.

Barton, E. E. (2016). Critical issues and promising practices for teach play to young children with disabilities. In B. Reichow, B. A. Boyd, E. E. Barton, & S. L. Odom (Eds.), *Handbook of early childhood special education* (pp. 267–286). Springer International Publishing.

Barton, E. E., Fuller, E., & Schnitz, A. (2016). The use of email to coach preservice early childhood teachers. *Topics in Early Childhood Special Education, 36*(2), 79–90.

Barton, E. E., Murray, R., O'Flaherty, C., Sweeney, E. M., & Gossett, S. (2020). Teaching object play to young children with disabilities: A systematic review of methods and rigor. *American Journal on Intellectual and Developmental Disabilities, 125*(1), 14–36.

Barton, E. E., & Pavilanis, R. (2012). Teaching pretend play to young children with autism. *Young Exceptional Children, 20*, 1–13.

Barton, E. E., Pokorski, E. A., Gossett, S., Sweeney, E., Qiu, J., & Choi, G. (2018). The use of email to coach early childhood teachers. *Journal of Early Intervention, 40*, 212–228.

Barton, E. E., & Wolery, M. (2008). Teaching pretend play to children with disabilities: A review of the literature. *Topics in Early Child Education, 28*, 109–125.

Barton, E. E., & Wolery, M. (2010). Training teachers to promote pretend play in young children with disabilities. *Exceptional Children, 77*, 85–106.

Belsky, J., & Most, R. K. (1981). From exploration to play: A cross-sectional study of infant free play behavior. *Developmental Psychology, 17*(5), 630–639.

Cohn, D. A. (1990). Child-mother attachment of six-year-olds and social competence at school. *Child Development, 61*(1), 152–162.

Coolahan, K., Fantuzzo, J., Mendez, J., & McDermott, P. (2000). Preschool peer interactions and readiness to learn: Relationships between classroom peer play and learning behaviors and conduct. *Journal of Educational Psychology, 92*(3), 458–465.

Cooper, J. O., Heron, T. E., & Heward, W. L. (2019). *Applied behavior analysis* (3rd ed.). Merrill/Prentice Hall.

DiCarlo, C. F., & Reid, D. H. (2004). Increasing pretend toy play of toddlers with disabilities in an inclusive setting. *Journal of Applied Behavior Analysis, 37*, 197–207.

Division for Early Childhood of the Council for Exceptional Children. (2014). *DEC recommended practices in early intervention/early childhood special education*. www.dec-sped.org/recommendedpractices.

Freeman, S. F., Gulsrud, A., & Kasari, C. (2015). Brief report: Linking early joint attention and play abilities to later reports of friendships for children with ASD. *Journal of autism and developmental disorders, 45*(7), 2259–2266.

Ginsburg, K. R., the Committee on Communications, & the Committee on Psychosocial Aspects of Child and Family Health. (2007). The importance of play in promoting healthy child development and maintaining strong parent—child bonds. *Pediatrics, 119*, 182–191.

Grisham-Brown, J., & Hemmeter, M. L. (2017). *Blended practices for teaching young children in inclusive settings* (2nd ed.). Brookes.

Hirsh-Pasek, K., Golinkoff, R. M., Berk, L. E., & Singer, D. (2009). *A mandate for playful learning in preschool: Applying the scientific evidence*. Oxford University Press.

Joseph, J. D., Strain, P., Olszewski, A., & Goldstein, H. (2016). A consumer reports-like review of the empirical literature specific to preschool children's peer-related social skills. In B. Reichow, B. Boyd, E. E. Barton, & S. Odom (Eds.), *Handbook of early childhood special education* (pp. 179–197). Springer.

Kaiser, A. P., & Hampton, L. H. (2017). Enhanced milieu teaching. In R. J. McCauley, M. E. Fey, & R. B. Gillam (Eds.), *Treatment of language disorders in children* (2nd ed.) (pp. 87–119). Brookes.

Lane, J. D., & Brown, J. A. (2016). Promoting communication development in young children with or at-risk for disabilities. In B. Reichow, B. A. Boyd, E. E. Barton, & S. L. Odom (Eds.), *Handbook of early childhood special education* (pp. 199–224). Springer International Publishing.

Ledford, J. R., Lane, J. D., & Barton, E. E. (2019). *Methods for teaching in early education*. Routledge.

Ledford, J. R., & Pustejovsky, J. E. (2021). Systematic review and meta-analysis of stay-play-talk interventions for improving social behaviors of young children. *Journal of Positive Behavior Interventions*. Advance online publication. https://doi.org/10.1177/1098300720983521.

Liber, D. B., Frea, W. D., & Symon, J. B. G. (2008). Using time delay to improve social play skills with peers for children with autism. *Journal of Autism and Developmental Disorders, 38*, 312–323.

Lifter, K., & Bloom, L. (1989). Object knowledge and the emergence of language. *Infant Behavior and Development, 12*(4), 395–423.

Lifter, K., Ellis, J., Cannon, B., & Anderson, S. R. (2005). Developmental specificity in targeting and teaching play activities to children with pervasive developmental disorders. *Journal of Early Intervention, 27*(4), 247–267.

Lifter, K., Foster-Sanda, S., Arzamarski, C., Briesch, J., & McClure, E. (2011). Overview of play: Its uses and importance in early intervention/early childhood special education. *Infants & Young Children, 24*(3), 225–245.

Lifter, K., Mason, E. J., & Barton, E. E. (2011). Children's play: Where we have been and where we could go. *Journal of Early Intervention, 33*(4), 281–297.

Machalicek, W., Shogren, K., Lang, R., Rispoli, M., O'Reilly, M. F., Franco, J. H., & Sigafoos, J. (2009). Increasing play and decreasing the challenging behavior of children with autism during recess with activity schedules and task correspondence training. *Research in Autism Spectrum Disorders, 3*(2), 547–555.

McConnell, S. R., & Rahn, N. L. (2016). Assessment in Early Childhood Special Education. In B. Reichow, B. A. Boyd, E. E. Barton, & S. L. Odom (Eds.), *Handbook of early childhood special education* (pp. 89–106). Springer International Publishing.

Meadan, H., Ostrosky, M. M., Triplett, B., Michna, A., & Fettig, A. (2011). Using visual supports with young children with autism spectrum disorder. *Teaching Exceptional Children, 43*, 28–35.

Mills, P. E., Beecher, C. C., Dale, P. S., Cole, K. N., & Jenkins, J. R. (2014). Language of children with disabilities to peers at play: Impact of ecology. *Journal of Early Intervention, 36*(2), 111–130.

Nuzzolo-Gomez, R., Leonard, M. A., Ortiz, E., Rivera, C. M., & Greer, R. D. (2002). Teaching children with autism to prefer books or toys over stereotypy or passivity. *Journal of Positive Behavior Interventions, 4*(2), 80–87.

Palechka, G., & MacDonald, R. (2010). A comparison of the acquisition of play skills using instructor—created video models and commercially available videos. *Education & Treatment of Children, 33*, 457–474.

Parten, M. B. (1932). Social participation among pre-school children. *The Journal of Abnormal and Social Psychology, 27*(3), 243–269.

Paul, R., & Norbury, C. F. (2012). *Language disorders from infancy through adolescence: Assessment and intervention* (4th ed.). Mosby Elsevier.

Pierce-Jordan, S., & Lifter, K. (2005). Interaction of social and play behaviors in preschoolers with and without pervasive developmental disorder. *Topics in Early Childhood Special Education, 25*(1), 34–47.

Smilansky, S. (1968). *The effects of sociodramatic play on disadvantaged children: Preschool children*. Wiley.

Snyder, P., Hemmeter, M. L., McLean, M., Sandall, S., McLaughlin, T., & Algina, J. (2018). Effects of professional development on preschool teachers' use of embedded instruction practices. *Exceptional Children, 84*(2), 213–232.

Strain, P. S., Schwartz, I. S., & Bovey, E. H. (2008). Social competence interventions for young children with autism. In *Social competence of young children: Risk, disability, and intervention* (pp. 253–272). Paul H. Brookes Publishing.

Sulzer-Azaroff, B., & Mayer, G. R. (1991). *Behavior analysis for lasting change*. Holt, Rinehart & Winston.

Van Berckelaer-Onnes, I. A. (2003). Promoting early play. *Autism, 7*(4), 415–423.

Williams, E., Reddy, V., & Costall, A. (2001). Taking a closer look at functional play in children with autism. *Journal of Autism and Developmental Disorders, 31*(1), 67–77.

Wolery, M., Ault, M. L., & Doyle, P. M. (1992). *Teaching students with moderate to severe disabilities: Use of response prompting strategies*. Longman.

Wolery, M., & Hemmeter, M. L. (2011). Classroom instruction: Background, assumptions, and challenges. *Journal of Early Intervention, 33*(4), 371–380.

Wong, C., Odom, S. L., Hume, K. A., Cox, A. W., Fettig, A., Kucharczyk, S., . . . Schultz, T. R. (2015). Evidence-based practices for children, youth, and young adults with autism spectrum disorder: A comprehensive review. *Journal of Autism and Developmental Disorders, 45*, 1951–1966.

21
ADDRESSING THE WHOLE YOUTH
Characteristics and Evidence-Based Practices and Programs for Systems-Involved Youth

Kristine Jolivette, Skip Kumm, Sara Sanders, and Sarup R. Mathur

Many school-age youth receive their education and other services outside the purview of typical pre-K–12 school settings and have had contact with outside entities to meet their unique needs. Such youth may be referred to as *systems-involved*. Systems-involved youth generally means a youth who is involved in some way with either the juvenile justice system or child welfare system. These youth may live at home and receive services and supervision (e.g., community therapy, probation) from these entities or they may physically reside outside of their home to receive their services and supports (e.g., shelter care, therapeutic group home, foster care, residential treatment facility, juvenile justice facility). Additionally, some of these youth may be multisystem-involved. Vidal et al. (2019) defined multisystem-involved as "children or adolescents who are *concurrently* served in more than one service; specifically, the child welfare system, the juvenile justice system, or the behavioral health system" (p. 17). For those in a residential program, they are provided with "a structured temporary living environment that provides both predictability and controllability in which youth can learn to prosocially influence what happens to them" (Elson et al., 2020, p. 2).

Characteristics of Systems-Involved Youth

No matter where a youth receives their services, supervision, and supports, systems-involved and multisystem youth present multiple and complex needs across domains with comorbidity issues to be addressed, including histories of (a) education needs (e.g., eligible for special education services; e.g., Leone & Weinberg, 2012); (b) mental health problems (e.g., Bender, 2010); (c) prior exposure to trauma (e.g., Baglivio et al., 2014); (d) substance abuse histories (e.g., Ford & Blaustein, 2013); (e) past victimization (e.g., emotional, physical, sexual; e.g., Finigan-Carr et al., 2018); (f) school or community aggression and/or delinquency (e.g., Hirsch et al., 2018); (g) maltreatment (e.g., Stone & Zibulsky, 2014); and/or (h) placement instability, homelessness, or out-of-home placements (e.g., Doyle, 2007). Systems-involved youth require a comprehensive and integrated set of programming, supports, and services rooted in empirical evidence to address *all* their needs (e.g., Vidal et al., 2019). However, evidence suggests the contrary—systems-involved youth are not being provided with scientific treatment and programming (e.g., Chuang & Wells, 2010). These youth are at an increased risk for challenges in establishing positive relationships, maintaining employment, and producing desirable outcomes in life (Courtney et al., 2019), as well as continued, prolonged contact with such systems. We briefly describe the characteristics of systems-involved youth.

Educational Characteristics

Many systems-involved youth experience educational challenges resulting in compromised or hindered performance in school, thus affecting their postschool success. Many of these youth demonstrate splintered skills in reading or math as well as processing deficits when compared with their peers who are not systems-involved (Krezmien et al., 2014) and demonstrate lower-than-expected academic achievement (Balfanz & Byrnes, 2013). These youth may not have histories of role models to support positive and productive study habits, may not come from environments where school was valued or emphasized, and may lack access to persons to aid in studying or answering questions related to academic content. Some systems-involved youth have been found to be chronically absent from instruction, fallen behind with the curriculum, dropped out of school entirely, or engaged in criminal behavior (e.g., Wang et al., 2005). Several factors contribute to these youth missing school (e.g., transportation, parent's physical or mental health condition, economic hardship, substance abuse, child care needs, or child abuse or neglect; Courtney et al., 2019). Further, systems-involved youth are disproportionally eligible for special education services. Estimates of disabilities of youth who are in foster care as compared to their counterparts (Slayter, 2016) span from three times to between one-third and one-half of youth (Cheatham et al., 2020); these estimates persist for justice-involved youth (e.g., Kincaid, 2017).

Mental Health Characteristics

Researchers consistently identify systems-involved youth as experiencing mental health concerns at a much higher rate than their peers. For example, Abram et al. (2013) found that 70% of justice-involved youth have one or dual types of a mental health diagnosis, while others have found these youth to have higher diagnosed mental health disorders than comparable peers (e.g., Development Service Group, 2017). More recently, Dierkhising et al. (2019) found that at the time of arrest half of the youth were receiving mental health services (Development Services Group, 2017). For youth in foster care, Turney and Wilderman (2016) found that they were more likely to have diagnosed anxiety issues (five times), behavioral issues (six times), and depression (seven times) as compared to their peers; all of these were statistically significant.

Trauma Characteristics

Many systems-involved youth have been exposed to potentially traumatizing events at points in their lives with long-term negative impact on their trajectories and experiences. Oftentimes, diagnoses and symptoms may develop in response to adverse childhood experiences and traumatic events (Baglivio et al., 2016); thus, this relationship between trauma and systems (i.e., juvenile justice) is not surprising. For example, Rosenberg et al. (2014) found correlational significance between trauma exposure and posttraumatic stress disorder for these youth. For youth in residential facilities, estimates prevail that half to almost three-fourths of youth will have experienced trauma prior to placement (e.g., Jaycox et al., 2004). It is hypothesized that gender differences exist with female youth who are systems-involved and who have higher percentages of exposure to trauma (e.g., Collin-Vezina et al., 2011). Across these systems, youth have higher percentages of trauma exposure related to neglect, physical/emotional/sexual abuse, domestic violence, and out-of-home placements, or combinations of them (e.g., Briggs-Gowan et al., 2012) as compared to their peers. For a significant proportion of youth involved in these systems, traumatizing experiences are associated with their behavior problems. For example, exposure to trauma for justice-involved youth can make it difficult for them "effectively [manage] emotions physical reactions, impulses, attention, consequential thinking (i.e., problem-solving and decision-making based on an awareness of and accurate evaluation of consequences), and involvement in interpersonal relationships (i.e., ranging from extreme isolation to enmeshment in dangerous or exploitive relationships)" (National Child Traumatic Stress Network, 2017, p. 2).

Addressing the Needs of Systems-Involved Youth

Systems-involved youth are school-aged youth who have their entire lives ahead of them, no matter the circumstances that brought them into a system or their specific placement location. For example, the Council of Juvenile Correctional Administrators (2017) has adopted a positive youth development approach for addressing the needs of youth who are involved in the juvenile justice system. There have been calls for interagency collaboration and for the unification of a common set of outcomes for which such systems are to strive for in enriching the lives of youth. Katz and colleagues (n.d.) put forth seven outcome domains that include youth (a) social-emotional well-being, (b) connectedness, (c) health, (d) healthy and safe environment, (e) youth contribution and engagement, (f) education, and (g) employability and economic opportunity. To realize these outcomes, a wide range of evidence-based practices are warranted to promote positive youth development across domains so these youth may thrive.

Evidence-Based Practice Guidance for Systems-Involved Youth

Several entities exist with empirical guidance for system service providers as to what practices have been deemed evidence-based for systems-involved youth, no matter the specific delivery location of those services (e.g., shelter care, group homes, hospital school and clinic, residential treatment center, juvenile justice facility) or area to address (e.g., academics, behavior, social-emotional learning, mental health, trauma, substance abuse). A description of a few examples of these entities by type of system, each with searchable databases, include (a) *justice*—the Office of Juvenile Justice Delinquency Prevention, Department of Justice (https://ojjdp.ojp.gov/model-programs-guide/home), Crime Solutions, National Institute of Justice (https://crimesolutions.ojp.gov/), and Blueprints for Healthy Youth Development (www.blueprintsprograms.org/); (b) *welfare*—the California Evidence-Based Clearinghouse for Child Welfare (www.cebc4cw.org) and the Child Welfare Information Gateway (www.childwelfare.gov/library/); (c) *trauma*—the National Child Traumatic Stress Network (www.nctsn.org/treatments-and-practices/trauma-treatments/interventions); (d) *education* across all systems—the What Works Clearinghouse, Department of Education (https://ies.ed.gov/ncee/wwc/); and (e) *mental health and substance abuse*—the Evidence-Based Practices Resource Center, Substance Abuse and Mental Health Services Administration (www.samhsa.gov/resource-search/ebp). This list is not meant to be exhaustive, but instead highlights some of the reputable sites from which system entities may look for guidance on evidence-based practices across need areas.

Evidence-Based Practices for Systems-Involved Youth Across Need Areas

School-aged systems-involved youth have the same potential as their peers to achieve their goals and improve their skill sets across all areas of need. Thus, it is critical they be afforded the same experiences, opportunities, and "developmentally- and age-appropriate, scientifically validated services" (e.g., Jolivette, 2016, p. 1) fostered within a physically and emotionally safe environment (de Azua, 2018). For example, the U.S. Departments of Education and Justice (2014) put forth five guiding principles to positively improve the high-quality education youth in juvenile justice facilities receive. The first, second, and fourth principles speak to evidence-based practices (i.e., a safe, healthy, facility-wide climate that prioritizes education; necessary funding to support educational opportunities for all youth . . . comparable to opportunities for peers who are not systems-involved; rigorous and relevant curricula, respectively). Further, the integration of treatment, programming, and educational services provided in residential care is critical. For example, the Association of Children's Residential Centers states that

> residential intervention and schools are complementary and not competing for importance. Youth in residential treatment should not be denied a solid educational experience because their life experiences and/or development/mental health concerns may be acute. High quality education fosters the development of self-regulatory, relational, and cognitive skills, and is empowering.
>
> (Lieberman et al., 2018, p. 3)

Given the characteristics and varied needs across domains these youth experience, it is important to consider multiple areas to target for both habilitation and rehabilitation while accounting for child and adolescent development principles. Based on the positive youth development framework, guidance from the U.S. Departments of Education and Justice, and the Association of Children's Residential Centers, the focus of treatment, programming, and education should be positive, strengths-based, forward thinking, and anchored to empirical support. Also important is the recognition that some systems-involved youth are afforded other protections or guidance per legislation (e.g., educational disabilities, the Individuals with Disabilities Education Act; Juvenile Justice and Delinquency Prevention Act). Given that many systems-involved youth are adolescent aged, marked by "an intense period of physical, emotional, intellectual and social development" (Coalition for Juvenile Justice, 2006, p. 4), we first define habilitation and rehabilitation to capitalize on a growth mindset. Then, we highlight a few evidence-based practices in several focal areas in which improvements in skill sets have been achieved for these youth.

Habilitation and Rehabilitation

Since systems-involved youth are school-age and continually developing, it is important to anchor evidence-based practices from the lens of habilitation and rehabilitation. In the broadest sense, habilitation means the acquisition of new skills, content knowledge, and experiences. Given the foundational holes in exposure, experiences, and skill sets presented by many systems-involved youth due to their out-of-home placements and disruptions in their education (Lieberman et al., 2018), all need habilitation in critical skill sets across domains (Liddell et al., 2014), while others also may need rehabilitation in specific areas. Rehabilitation means providing opportunities to regain skills, content knowledge, and experiences. Whether habilitative or rehabilitative in focus, the treatment, programming, and education of systems-involved youth should promote the acquisition of goals, positive outcomes, and healthy child and adolescent development (Liddell et al., 2014). Additionally, the focus should include a broad range of outcome domains to fully measure youth progress. Katz et al. (n.d.) suggest a seven-outcome domain framework to be measured for these youth across systems: (a) social-emotional well-being, (b) connectedness, (c) health, (d) healthy and safe environment, (e) youth contribution and engagement, (f) education, and (g) employability and economic opportunity.

Education

Education is critical for the health and well-being and long-term success of systems-involved youth. The skills gleaned from their education can open career pathways as they re-enter the community, no matter what system they were served in. Lieberman et al. (2018) urges "the field to prioritize education equally with treatment and to ensure that educational practices are of the highest quality. It is not only a basic right for the youth, it is also necessary for them to achieve long term positive outcomes" (p. 6). The urgency and call for appropriate educational services, and especially for those systems-involved youth with disabilities, has been voiced by many (e.g., Every Student Succeeds Act of 2015, Individuals with Disabilities Education Act, The Uninterrupted Scholars Act, U.S. Departments of Education and Justice). The Title I, Part D of the Every Student Succeeds Act details how systems are to provide prevention and intervention services for systems-involved youth. These youth enter and move between systems educationally well behind their peers across content areas with fewer educational experiences and opportunities (American Youth Policy Forum, 2017). However, from a habilitation and rehabilitation lens, a system can positively address these issues. For justice-involved youth, O'Cummings et al. (2010) state that "academic outcomes achieved during incarceration have an important impact on the achievements of youth after their release and have shown to reduce recidivism" (p. 1). The education provided to systems-involved youth, no matter the time in the system (e.g., short term or long term), need to be the same educational services and opportunities as their peers who are not systems-involved. Although this is the goal, it is not always a reality. For example, the Council of State Governments Justice Center (2015) found only eight states that provided equal services and opportunities. Beyond legislative acts calling for quality education for systems-involved youth, some systems have created curriculum and tools to augment training for teachers in these systems. For example, an educator's curriculum was created for preservice and in-service juvenile justice teachers consisting of nine modules (i.e., trends and issues in juvenile justice and education, institutional culture, student assessment, curriculum, teaching and learning, behavior management, social skills, transition, and program and classroom evaluation; Brooks & White, 2000). The Legal Center for Youth Justice and Education (2020) created the Blueprint for Change: Education Success for Youth in the Juvenile Justice Systems. For example, Goal 5 (quality education in facilities) and Goal 6 (supportive school environments) provide benchmarks related to (a) evidence-based practices; (b) equity, inclusiveness, and fairness of educational experiences and opportunities; (c) specific mention of meeting the needs of youth with disabilities; and (d) family involvement as a meaningful and planned part of the youth's education. In another example, The Legal Center for Foster Care & Education (2014) created a Blueprint for Change: Education Success for Children in Foster Care with eight goals and 56 benchmarks, with Goals 4 and 5 (youth have the support to fully participate in school and youth have support to prevent school dropout, truancy, and disciplinary actions, respectively) focusing on access to mental health services, disability protections, and youth voice in all aspects of their educational programming. As our science on systems-involved youth needs evolves, so do our instructional approaches. The U.S. Departments of Education and Justice (2014) state that we must "employ current instructional methods and materials appropriate to a student's age, grade placement, development, and culture" (p. 17). Two literacy-based methods have been consistently implemented with systems-involved youth that incorporate scaffolded and explicit instruction to mastery and include a) strategy instruction—in particular, the self-regulated strategy development instructional approach in the areas of reading and writing with embedded self-regulation components (i.e., goal setting, self-reinforcement, self-statements) and varying intensifications (e.g., Ennis et al., 2014; Sanders et al., 2021); and b) direct instruction—in particular the Corrective Reading curricula (e.g., Allen-DeBoer et al., 2006).

Behavior

Systems-involved youth display a wide range of behaviors just as their non-systems-involved peers. The difference is that systems-involved youth may display higher frequencies and intensities of problem behaviors based on prior traumatic experiences, unintentional facility triggers, and deficits in self-regulation skill, thus resulting in the youth becoming dysregulated. Self-regulation is a pivotal skill for all youth, and part of their treatment, programming, and education must focus on teaching and modeling self-regulation skills through a variety of strategies, staff reinforcing youth for engaging in self-regulatory behaviors, and supporting youth in re-regulating after displays of problem behaviors. Ford and Blaustein (2013) posit that self-regulation

> involves the ability to: (a) consciously focus attention, (b) be aware of the environment and one's own physical and emotional body states; (c) draw on memory in order to learn from the last and adapt effectively in the present; and, (d) maintain or regain emotion states that provide a genuine sense of well-being and lead to further self-regulation.
>
> *(p. 669)*

For systems-involved youth, it is important to address their problem behaviors early on, using effective methods including routines and in a positive rather than a punitive manner (Gonsoulin et al., 2012). Also, it is important for the behavior management system to be consistent across all treatment, programming, and educational aspects; thus, a facility-wide approach is recommended for and employed by many systems (e.g., U.S. Departments of Education and Justice, 2014). Facility-wide positive behavior interventions and supports is one framework systems have adopted to address the unique behavioral needs of youth and as a means to organize their practices, with Tier 1 supports provided to all youth (universal), Tier 2 supports for some youth who need additional supports in addition to Tier 1 (targeted), and Tier 3 supports for a few youth who need intensive supports alongside Tier 1 and 2 supports (intensive) (Myers & Farrell, 2008). This framework allows systems to define their facility-wide behavioral expectations for all youth across all facility environments and recurring activities with a coordinated plan to teach and model the expectations across all treatment, programming, and education hours as implemented by all staff (Jolivette, Kimball, et al., 2016). Some systems have adapted this framework to better organize all their practices across all youth domains. The specific practices selected are based on youth data (e.g., intake, case files) and aim to improve overall behavioral health and self-regulation. Examples of behavioral and prosocial tiered strategies employed by these systems include (a) motivational interviewing, (b) check in/check out, (c) restorative justice practices, (d) merging two worlds, (e) cognitive behavior therapy, and (f) de-escalation strategies (e.g., Jolivette et al., 2020).

Social-Emotional Learning

Behavioral and social-emotional learning (SEL) challenges can go hand-in-hand, yet purposefully planned and executed SEL practices and programs are often a missing component in the treatment and programming of systems-involved youth (Beyer, 2017). As Glenn and colleagues (2020) state,

> juvenile justice researchers and practitioners can use SEL as a tool for addressing delinquent behavior . . . despite its clear potential to address the behavioral and social challenges generally often found for youthful offenders, there remains a dearth of research on the use of SEL-informed interventions for justice-involved youth.
>
> *(p. 1)*

SEL is predicated on five elements: self-management, self-awareness, social awareness, relationship skills, and responsible decision-making (CASEL, 2020). Osher et al. (2016) state that "SEL creates a foundation for academic achievement, maintenance of good physical and mental health, parenting, citizenship, and productive employment" (p. 11). Even though systems-involved youth can benefit from SEL programming directly related to their behavioral self-regulation needs, this is an emerging area. While a number of SEL practices have been recommended for use with these youth, few have been systematically examined for feasibility and effectiveness. For example, Positive Action is a curriculum for school-age populations that (a) promotes a healthy lifestyle using six themes (self-concept, positive actions for your body and mind, managing yourself responsibly, treating others the way you like to be treated, telling yourself the truth, and improving yourself continually); (b) addresses many youth outcomes (e.g., academics, behavior, violence, mental health, gang prevention, substance abuse); (c) is delivered in short conversation sessions; and (d) is recognized by U.S. Departments of Education, Health and Human Services, and Justice as an evidence-based practice; however, it has only recently been employed with systems-involved youth in an exploratory manner (e.g., Jolivette et al., 2021).

Mental Health

Given the high percentages of systems-involved youth experiencing acute mental health issues, it is imperative that these issues be directly addressed through a comprehensive and integrated approach across all aspects of programming (e.g., interconnected systems framework, Barrett et al., 2017). This is especially important as researchers cite that the juvenile system (Amani et al., 2018) is the de facto mental health provider for youth in crisis. Bilchik and colleagues (2017) offer seven strategies for promoting the mental health abilities and skills of systems-involved youth (i.e., those in the juvenile system), which could easily be adopted and, if need be, adapted across other systems. These strategies include (a) strengthen programming and policies around evidence-based practices aimed toward rehabilitation and positive youth development; (b) engage and empower families to play an active role in their children's treatment; (c) create facility environments that are safe and conducive for learning and personal growth; (d) break down "staff silos" and encourage information sharing and cross-training opportunities; (e) provide staff with training on adolescent development, cultural competency, and trauma sensitivity, and create environments of staff wellness; (f) track mental health data within facilities and develop targeted strategies to address deficiencies; and (g) create a model of transition for the re-entry process to ensure stability for youth and to discourage recidivism. Within the foster care system, mental health can be addressed with an emphasis on placement stability, family involvement, and emphasis on school completion (e.g., high school diploma, GED). With many systems-involved youth experiencing mood disorders, anxiety disorders, self-harm, and disruptive behavior disorders, it is imperative that a variety of mental health–focused interventions be provided. Some common mental health interventions implemented in these systems include (a) thinking for a change, (b) dialectical behavior therapy, (c) multisystemic therapy, (d) cognitive behavior therapy, (e) Coping Cat, and (f) aggression replacement therapy (e.g., Kumm et al., 2020).

Trauma-Informed Programming

As the Substance Abuse and Mental Health Services Administration (SAMHSA, 2014) stated, "there is an increasing focus on the impact of trauma and how service systems may help to resolve or exacerbate trauma-related issues" for systems-involved youth (p. 3). SAMHSA (2014) suggests six key principles (i.e., safety; trustworthiness and transparence; peer support; collaboration and mutuality; empowerment, voice, and choice; and cultural, historical, and gender issues) be present when entities, families, and practitioners are adopting and implementing a trauma-informed approach. As such, many system-serving entities are cultivating and implementing trauma-informed environments for the youth served. The Association of Children's Residential Centers calls for residential programs to provide trauma-informed programmatic predictability to support the neurodevelopment of youth and to address the adverse childhood experiences so many systems-involved youth experience (Elson et al., 2020). To achieve trauma-informed programmatic predictability, trauma-informed interventions need to (a) include youth-guided practices; (b) be family driven; (c) address equity, diversity, and inclusion; (d) incorporate daily routines and rituals; (e) include sensory strategies; (f) be rooted in individual planning; (g) emphasize relational interactions; and (h) have consistent expectations (Elson et al., 2020). For the justice system, the National Child Traumatic Stress Network (2015) details eight essential elements of a trauma-informed juvenile justice system spanning aspects of policies and procedures to screening and assessment staff education with prevention of secondary traumatic stress, directly partnering and collaborating with youth, families, and cross-systems to practices that directly address concepts of disparity and diversity. Some common trauma-informed programs implemented with systems-involved youth that produce positive outcomes and promote self-regulation include (a) Sanctuary Model; (b) Trauma Affect Regulation Guide for Education and Therapy; (c) Trauma Focused-Cognitive Behavioral Therapy; (d) Attachment, Regulation and Competency; (e) Trauma-Adapted Multidimensional Treatment Foster Care; (f) Trauma and Grief Components Therapy for Adolescents; and (g) collaborative problem-solving (e.g., Bailey et al., 2019).

Transition Planning and Practices for Systems-Involved Youth

An area of critical importance for systems-involved youth is transition planning and practices, as these youth often move from placement to placement and will reintegrate into their community. For example, a youth may reside in a residential treatment center and then transition back to their home, while others may reside in a juvenile facility and then transition to a step-down placement (e.g., group home, foster home). To ensure that the skill gains made transfer to their next placement, purposeful and carefully crafted transition protocols need to be in place. For example, foster care–involved youth ages 18 to 21 years may receive supports to prepare them for transition out of foster care and into adulthood in some states through the Fostering Connections to Success and Increasing Adoptions Act of 2008 (Dworsky et al., 2014). Several transition toolkits have been created for specific use with systems-involved youth per the research and support the highlighted domain areas noted earlier. For justice-involved youth, Griller Clark et al. (2016) created a comprehensive toolkit predicated on six practices (transition team, efficient records transfer, transition plan, research-based programming, regular monitoring and tracking, adequate funding) and four stages (entry into the juvenile justice system, residency, exit from secure care, aftercare to best support youth leaving the justice system).

Implications for Practitioners for Future Research

Moving forward, it is imperative for stakeholders, including practitioners, policy makers, and researchers, to support the adaptation of evidence-based practices used with typically developing peers for specific application in the systems that serve systems-involved youth (e.g., residential treatment facilities, juvenile justice facilities). Many of these systems have unique contextual factors given the 24/7 treatment, programming, and education services they provide, necessitating adaptations of evidence-based practices to fit daily operations and youth needs (Jolivette, 2016). These adaptations should be systematically researched and reported, adding to the current literature base used by policy makers to choose effective practices to address the needs of systems-involved youth. Furthermore, as evidence-based practices are adapted and investigated, it is critical that a variety of tiered practices for Tiers 2 and 3 be investigated across the domains (e.g., academic, behavioral, social-emotional, mental health). Most systems-involved youth present with multifaceted and complex needs across the domains that require evidence-based practices and supports (Leone & Weinberg, 2012; Vidal et al., 2019). Adapting and implementing a variety of Tier 2 and 3 practices will provide facilities serving systems-involved youth with a toolbox of effective practices to individualize in tandem with the recommendations of systems-involved entities (see section on evidence-based guidance). As evidence-based practices are adapted and implemented within facilities serving systems-involved youth, common outcomes should be used across facilities to evaluate youth progress and growth. Common outcomes will allow for a more rigorous evaluation of a practice's effectiveness across systems-involved youth. Finally, there is a need for cross-discipline support within and across systems in treatment and programming, as facilities layer in evidence-based practices. Coordination between all disciplines within a facility and across facilities (e.g., mental health, corrections, education) on the implementation and evaluation of an evidence-based practice may increase the effectiveness of the practices and its impact on systems-involved youth in their care.

Summary

Given the complex and comorbid needs of systems-involved youth, it is imperative that evidence-based programming across domains to address the "whole child" or "whole youth" be employed to afford them the same growth and outcomes as their peers. One method to do so is to provide evidence-based practices across all daily treatment, programming, and education activities in tandem with the characteristics of this population. Lieberman et al. (2018) urges "the field to prioritize education equally with treatment and to ensure that educational practices are of the highest quality. It is not only a basic right for the youth, it is also necessary for them to achieve long term positive outcomes" (p. 6). As we continue to refine our science and empirical foundation to improve the services which systems-involved youth should be afforded to meet their complex needs, it is clear that we need to focus on "communication and coordination among these two systems" (Goodkind et al., 2013, p. 267) not only while these youth are systems-involved but also as they transition back to their community.

References

Abram, K. M., Teplin, L. A., King, D. C., Longworth, S. L., Emanuel, K. M., Romero, E. G., McClelland, G. M., Dulcan, M. K., Washburn, J. J., Welty, L. J., & Olson, N. D. (2013). *PTSD, trauma, and comorbid psychiatric disorders in detained youth*. Juvenile Justice Bulletin. U.S. Department of Justice, Office of Justice Programs, Office of Juvenile Justice and Delinquency Prevention.

Allen-DeBoer, R. A., Malmgren, K. W., & Glass, M. (2006). Reading instruction for youth with emotional and behavioral disorders in a juvenile correctional facility. *Behavioral Disorders, 32*, 18–28. https://doi.org/10.1177/019874290603200101

Amani, B., Milburn, N. G., Lopez, S., Young-Brinn, A., Castro, L., Lee, A., & Bath, E. (2018). Families and the juvenile justice system: Considerations for family-based interventions. *Family & Community Health, 41*, 55–63. https://doi.org/10.1097/FCH.0000000000000172

American Youth Policy Forum. (2017, September). *Supporting pathways to long-term success for systems-involved youth: Lessons learned*. www.aypf.org/wp-content/uploads/2017/09/Brief-Supporting-Pathways-to-Long-Term-Success.pdf

Baglivio, M. T., Epps, N., Swartz, K., & Huq, M. S. (2014). The prevalence of adverse childhood experiences (ACES) in the lives of juvenile offenders. *Journal of Juvenile Justice, 3*(2). www.prisonpolicy.org/scans/Prevalence_of_ACE.pdf

Baglivio, M. T., Wolff, K. T., Piquero, A. R., & Epps, N. (2016). The relationship between adverse childhood experiences (ACE) and juvenile offending trajectories in a juvenile offender sample. *Journal of Criminal Justice, 43*, 229–241. https://doi.org/10.1016/j.jcrimjus.2015.04.012

Bailey, C., Klas, A., Cox, R., Bergmeier, H., Avery, J., & Skouteris, H. (2019). Systematic review of organization-wide, trauma-informed care models in out-of-home care (OoHC) settings. *Health and Social Care in the Community, 27*, 10–22. https://doi.org/10.1111/hsc.12621

Balfanz, R., & Byrnes, V. (2013). *Meeting the challenge of combating chronic absenteeism: Impact of the NYC mayor's interagency task force on chronic absenteeism and school attendance and its implications for other cities*. Everyone Graduates Center, Johns Hopkins University School of Education. http://new.every1graduates.org/resources/reports

Barrett, S., Eber, L., & Weist, M. (2017). *Advancing education effectiveness: Interconnecting school mental health and school-wide positive behavior support*. https://assets-global.website-files.com/5d3725188825e071f1670246/5d76c6a8344facab50085275_final-monograph.pdf

Bender, K. (2010). Why do some maltreated youth become juvenile offenders? A call for further investigation and adaptation of youth services. *Children and Youth Services Review, 32*, 466–473. https://doi.org/10.1016/j.childyouth.2009.10.022

Beyer, L. N. (2017). *Social and emotional learning and traditionally underserved populations.* American Youth Policy Forum. www.aypf.org/wp-content/uploads/2017/10/SEL-Special-Populations_Final.pdf

Bilchik, S., Umpeirre, M., & Lenhoff, C. (2017). *A roadmap for change: How juvenile justice facilities can better serve youth with mental health issues.* Regional Research Institute for Human Services, Portland State University. https://drive.google.com/file/d/1JVqrXmH3yQXCvv3FzFklDvs35iNJYrO8/view

Briggs-Gowan, M. J., Carter, A. S., & Ford, J. D. (2012). Parsing the effects violence exposure in early childhood: Modeling development pathways. *Journal of Pediatric Psychology, 37,* 11–22. https://doi.org/10.1093/jpepsy/jsr063

Brooks, C. C., & White, C. (March, 2000). *Curriculum for training educators of youth in confinement.* U.S. Department of Justice, Office of Justice Programs, Office of Juvenile Justice and Delinquency Prevention.

Cheatham, L., P., Randolph, K. A., & Boltz, L. D. (2020). Youth with disabilities transitioning from foster care: Examining prevalence and predicting positive outcomes. *Children and Youth Services Review, 110,* 10477. https://doi.org/10.1016/j.childyouth.2020.104777

Chuang, E., & Wells, R. (2010). The role of interagency collaboration in facilitating receipt of behavioral health services for youth involved with child welfare and juvenile justice. *Children and Youth Services Review, 32,* 1814–1822. https://doi.org/10.1016/j.childyouth.2010.08.002

Coalition for Juvenile Justice. (2006). *What are the implication of adolescent brain development for juvenile justice? Emerging Concept Brief.* Washington, DC. Retrieved from https://www.juvjustice.org/sites/default/files/resource-files/resource_134.pdf

Collaborative for Academic, Social, and Emotional Learning. (2020). *CASEL framework.* https://casel.org

Collin-Vezina, D., Coleman, K., Milne, L., Sell, J., & Daigneault, I. (2011). Trauma experiences, maltreatment-related impairments, and resilience among child welfare youth in residential care. *International Journal of Mental Health & Addiction, 9,* 577–589. https://doi.org/10.1007/s11469-011-9323-8

Council of Juvenile Correctional Administrators. (2017). *A toolkit for positive youth development.* www.cjca.net

Council of State Governments Justice Center. (2015). *Locked out: Improving educational and vocational outcomes for incarcerated youth.* www.njjn.org/uploads/digital-library/CSG-LOCKED_OUT_Improving_Educational_and_Vocational_Outcomes_for_Incarcerated_Youth_Nov-2015.pdf

Courtney, M. E., Valentine, E. L., & Skemer, M. (2019). Experimental evaluation of transitional living services for system-involved youth: Implications for policy and practice. *Children and Youth Services Review, 96,* 396–408. https://doi.org/10.1016/j.childyouth.2018.11.031

de Azua, R. (2018). *Professional development: Safe and supportive learning environments in juvenile justice systems.* American Institutes for Research, National Technical Assistance Center for the Education of Neglected or Delinquent Children and Youth.

Development Service Group. (2017). *Intersection between mental health and the juvenile justice system: Literature review.* Office of Juvenile Justice and Delinquency Prevention.

Dierkhising, C. B., Herz, D., Hirsch, R. A., & Abbott, S. (2019). System backgrounds, psychosocial characteristics, and service access among dually involved youth: A Los Angeles case study. *Youth Violence and Juvenile Justice, 17*(3), 309–329. https://doi.org/10.1177/1541204018790647

Doyle, J. J. (2007). Child protection and child outcomes: Measuring the effects of foster care. *American Economic Review, 97,* 1583–1610. https://doi.org/10.1257/aer.97.5.1583

Dworsky, A., Smithgall, C., & Courtney, M. E. (2014). *Supporting youth transitioning out of foster care, Issue Brief 1: Education programs.* OPRE Report #2014-66. Office of Planning, Research and Evaluation, Administration for Children and Families, U.S. Department of Health and Human Services.

Elson, S., Foltz, R., Lieberman, R. E., & Sisson, K. (April, 2020). *Redefining residential: Trauma-informed practice: The importance of predictability in residential interventions.* Association of Children's Residential Centers. https://togetherthevoice.org/wp-content/uploads/2020/04/Paper-16-final.pdf

Ennis, R. P., Jolivette, K., Terry, N. P., Fredrick, L. D., & Alberto, P. A. (2014). Classwide teacher implementation of self-regulated strategy development for writing with students with E/BD in a residential facility. *Journal of Behavioral Education, 24,* 88–111.

Finigan-Carr, N., Steward, R., & Watson, C. (2018). Foster youth need sex ed, too!: Addressing the sexual risk behaviors of system-involved youth. *American Journal of Sexuality Education, 13,* 310–323. https://doi.org/10.1080/15546128.2018.1456385

Ford, J. D., & Blaustein, M. E. (2013). Systematic self-regulation: A framework for trauma-informed services in residential juvenile justice programs. *Journal of Family Violence, 28,* 665–677. https://doi.org/10.1007/s10896-013-9538-5

Glenn, J. W., Mitchell, D., Williams, S., & Taylor, L. C. (Summer, 2020). *Leveraging social & emotional learning (SEL) for justice-involved youth.* Juvenile justice Institute Research & Policy Brief. NC Central University. https://legacy.nccu.edu/formsdocs/proxy.cfm?file_id=4660

Gonsoulin, S., Darwin, M. J., & Read, N. W. (2012). *Providing individually tailored academic and behavioral support services for youth in the juvenile justice and child welfare systems*. National Evaluation and Technical Assistance Center for Children and Youth Who Are Neglected, Delinquent, or At-Risk.

Goodkind, S., Shook, J. J., Kim, K. H., Pohlig, R. T., & Herring, D. J. (2013). From child welfare to juvenile justice: Race, gender, and system experiences. *Youth Violence and Juvenile Justice, 11*, 249–272. https://doi.org/10.1177/1541204012463409

Griller Clark, H., Mathur, S. R., Brock, L., O'Cummings, M., & Milligan, D. (2016). *Transition toolkit 3.0: Meeting the educational needs of youth exposed to the juvenile justice system*. National Evaluation and Technical Assistance Center for the Education of Children and Youth Who Are Neglected, Delinquent, or At Risk.

Hirsch, R. A., Dierkhising, C. B., & Herz, D. C. (2018). Educational risk, recidivism, and service access among youth involved in both the child welfare and juvenile justice systems. *Children and Youth Services Review, 85*, 72–80. https://doi.org/10.1016/j.childyouth.2017.12.001

Jaycox, L. H., Ebener, P., Damesek, L., & Becker, K. (2004). Trauma exposure and retention in adolescent substance abuse treatment. *Journal of Traumatic Stress, 17*, 113–121. https://doi.org/10.1023/B:JOTS.0000022617.41299.39

Jolivette, K. (2016). *Multi-tiered systems of support in residential juvenile facilities*. The National Technical Assistance Center for the Education of Neglected or Delinquent Children and Youth (NDTAC).

Jolivette, K., Kimball, K. A., Boden, L. J., & Sprague, J. R. (2016). The utility of a multi-tiered behavioral system in juvenile corrections: The positive behavior interventions and supports (PBIS) framework. *Corrections Today, 78*, 42–47. https://doi.org/10.1177/0198742918763946

Jolivette, K., Swoszowski, N. C., Sanders, S., Ennis, R. P., & Sprague, J. R. (2020). Facility-wide positive behavior interventions and supports: Concrete visuals for all staff within juvenile facilities. *Corrections Today, April/March*, 20–26. https://doi.org/10.1177/0741932519865258

Jolivette, K., Virgin, A. S., Sanders, S., Kumm, S., Kearley, A., Hackney, A., & Pitzel, A. (2021, March). *An adapted social-emotional learning curriculum for use in juvenile justice facilities: Positive Action*. Paper presented at the International Council for Exceptional Children.

Katz, J., Osher, D. M., Thorngren, M., Hoffman, C., & Oberlander, S. (n.d.). *Interagency collaboration and the development of a common outcomes framework to advance positive youth development*. https://youth.gov/sites/default/files/IWGYP-Common-Outcomes-Brief_508.pdf

Kincaid, A. (2017). *Prevalence of youth with disabilities in the juvenile justice system*. https://conservancy.umn.edu/bitstream/handle/11299/190546/Kincaid_umn_0130E_18289.pdf?sequence=1&isAllowed=y

Krezmien, M. P., Leone, P. E., & Wilson, M. G. (2014). Marginalized students, school exclusion, and the school-to-prison pipeline. In W. T. Churchill, D. W. Springer, & A. R. Roberts (Eds.), *Juvenile justice sourcebook* (pp. 267–288). Oxford University Press.

Kumm, S. A., Mathur, S. A., Cassavaugh, M., & Butts, E. (2020). Using the PBIS framework to meet the mental health needs of youth in juvenile justice facilities. *Remedial and Special Education, 41*, 80–87. https://doi.org/10.1177/0741932519880336

Legal Center for Foster Care & Education. (2014). *Blueprints for children: Education success for children in foster care*. https://fostercareandeducation.org/DesktopModules/Bring2mind/DMX/Download.aspx?EntryId=1624&Command=Core_Download&method=inline&PortalId=0&TabId=124

Legal Center for Youth Justice and Education. (2020). *Blueprint for change: Education success for youth in juvenile justice systems*. https://jjeducationblueprint.org/

Leone, P., & Weinberg, L. (2012). *Addressing the unmet educational needs of children and youth in the juvenile justice and child welfare systems*. Center for Juvenile Justice Reform.

Liddell, W., Clark, P., & Starkovich, K. (2014). Effective programs and services. In *Desktop guide to quality practice for working with youth in confinement*. National Partnership for Juvenile Services and Office of Juvenile Justice and Delinquency Prevention. https://info.nicic.gov/dtg/node/16

Lieberman, R. E., Kon, D., Myers, P., Maccarry, D., Hughes, A., Burton, L., & Sisson, K. (2018, March). *Redefining residential: Integrating education in residential interventions*. Association of Children's Residential Centers. https://togetherthevoice.org/wp-content/uploads/2020/02/ACRC_position-paper-14.pdf

Myers, D. M., & Farrell, A. F. (2008). Reclaiming lost opportunities: Applying public health models in juvenile justice. *Children and Youth Services Review, 30*, 1159–1177. https://doi.org/10.1016/j.childyouth.2008.03.002

National Child Traumatic Stress Network. (2015). *Essential elements of a trauma-informed juvenile justice system*. www.nctsn.org/resources/essential-elements-trauma-informed-juvenile-justice-system

National Child Traumatic Stress Network. (2017). *Complex trauma: In juvenile justice system-involved youth*. www.nctsn.org/sites/default/files/resources//complex_trauma_in_juvenile_justice_system_involved_youth.pdf

O'Cummings, M., Bardack, S., & Gonsoulin, S. (2010). *The importance of literacy for youth involved in the juvenile justice system*. National Evaluation and Technical Assistance Center for the Education of Children and Youth Who Are Neglected, Delinquent, or At Risk (NDTAC).

Osher, D., Penkoff, C., Sidana, A., & Kelly, P. (2016). *Improving conditions for learning for youth who are neglected or delinquent: Second edition*. National Technical Assistance Center for the Education of Neglected or Delinquent Children and Youth (NDTAC).

Rosenberg, H. J., Vance, J. E., Rosenberg, S. D., Wolford, G. L., Ashley, S. W., & Howard, M. L. (2014). Trauma exposure, psychiatric disorders, and resiliency in juvenile-justice involved youth. *Psychological Trauma: Theory, Research, Practice, and Policy, 6*, 430–437. https://doi.org/10.1037/a0033199

Sanders, S., Harris, C., & Jolivette, K. (2021). Improving the reading comprehension skills of systems-involved youth: Using the TRAP strategy. *Manuscript Submitted for Publication*.

Slayter, E. (2016). Youth with disabilities in the United States child welfare system *Children & Youth Services Review, 64*, 155–165. https://doi.org/10.1016/j.childyouth.2016.03.012

Stone, A., & Zibulsky, J. (2014). Maltreatment, academic difficulty, and systems-involved youth: Current evidence and opportunities. *Psychology in the Schools, 52*, 22–39. https://doi.org/10.1002/pits.21812

Substance Abuse and Mental Health Services Administration. (2014). *SAMHSA's concept of trauma and guidance for trauma-informed approach*. HHS Publication No. (SMH) 14-4884. Rockville, MD: Substance Abuse and Mental Health Services Administration.

Turney, K., & Wilderman, C. (2016). Mental and physical health of children in foster care. *Pediatrics, 138*(5). https://doi.org/10.1542/peds.2016-1118

U.S. Departments of Education and Justice. (2014). *Guiding principles for providing high-quality education in juvenile justice secure care settings*. Washington, DC.

Vidal, S., Connell, C. M., Prince, D. M., & Tebes, J. K. (2019). Multisystem-involved youth: A developmental framework and implications for research, policy, and practice. *Adolescent Research Review, 4*, 15–29. https://doi.org/10.1007/s40894-018-0088-1

Wang, X., Blomberg, T. G., & Li, S. D. (2005). Comparison of the educational deficiencies of delinquent and nondelinquent students. *Evaluation Review, 29*(4), 291–312. https://doi.org/10.1177/0193841X05275389

22
BULLY PREVENTION AND SOCIAL AND EMOTIONAL LEARNING

Impact on Youth With Disabilities

Nikita McCree, Monica Romero, Stephanie Hopkins, Lindsey Mirielli, and Chad A. Rose

With increasing societal and scientific attention focused on bullying, coupled with the growth in bully prevention initiatives designed to reduce bullying within our nation's schools, students continue to struggle with the development and mastery of the social and emotional skills necessary to effectively recognize, respond to, and report bullying (Rose et al., 2019). With the nation's schools composed of students from diverse backgrounds, including those with disabilities, some students struggle with social and emotional skill acquisition, while others are simply not taught. Social and emotional learning (SEL) is a skill acquisition process that is not only important for lifelong success in and out of the classroom, but the skills developed through the SEL process are critical to reducing bullying involvement risk, especially for youth with disabilities (Domitrovich et al., 2017; Rose & Gage, 2017). However, research demonstrates that SEL combined with the Multi-Tiered System of Support (MTSS) is a promising framework for bully prevention (NASEM, 2016; Rose et al., 2019).

Bullying is a multidimensional, complex, and aversive experience that continues to negatively affect students across the world, including the United States. Over the course of the last half-century, bullying has garnered much attention and has been the source of increased research and scientific inquiry (Swearer et al., 2010). The perception and interpretation of bullying has gone through many iterations, erroneously at first as a "rite of passage" (Popp et al., 2014), suggesting that bullying is unavoidable because it is entrenched within the school culture and climate. Presently, it has been labeled a public health concern for school-aged youth (Bradshaw, 2013; Harbin et al., 2019), where experiences and exposure may be more fluid than initially hypothesized (Gumpel et al., 2014; Rose et al., 2015; Ryoo et al., 2015). Specifically, Rose and colleagues (2015) argued that historically, bullying was conceptualized as a linear interaction between a "bully" and "victim," but more contemporary research suggests that students may move in and out of roles based on time and context. To understand bullying from a theoretical perspective, many bully prevention scholars have drawn upon Bronfenbrenner's (1977) *Ecological Systems Theory*, which suggests that bullying is a function of children's interactions over time with more complex social and environmental systems, including individual, familial, peer group, school, community, and societal factors (Hong & Espelage, 2012; Rose et al., 2015). From this lens, it is important to note that bullying involvement is rarely a static process, but rather a series of more dynamic interactions that are grounded in peer-to-peer socialization and communication.

DOI: 10.4324/9781003156888-22

The Centers for Disease Control and Prevention defines bullying as

> any unwanted aggressive behavior(s) by another youth or group of youths who are not siblings or current dating partners that involves an observed or perceived power imbalance and is repeated multiple times or is highly likely to be repeated. Bullying may inflict harm or distress on the targeted youth including physical, psychological, social, or educational harm.
>
> *(Gladden et al., 2014, p. 7)*

In short, bullying is defined by an imbalance of physical or emotional power, there is an intent to cause physical or emotional harm, and the behaviors are repeated or likely to be repeated over time. Recent national data suggest that approximately one in five students ages 12 to 18 report experiencing school-based bullying, which represents more than 5 million school-aged youth nationwide (Musu-Gillette et al., 2018). Unfortunately, the negative outcomes associated with bullying involvement span across multiple domains, including psychosomatic, psychosocial, behavioral, social, and educational. Given that almost 20% of American youth report experiencing bullying, it is imperative for scholars and practitioners to continue to implement interventions and strategies designed to reduce detrimental long- and short-term outcomes by further understanding risk characteristics and effective prevention approaches within a school context. The overall purpose of this chapter is to examine these critical constructs for youth with disabilities, who are at escalated risk for bullying involvement.

Bullying Involvement of Youth With Disabilities

While involvement in bullying is a concern for many school-aged youth, students with disabilities are disproportionately involved in bullying when compared to their peers without disabilities. This discrepancy often begins in preschool (Son et al., 2012) and persists over time (Rose & Gage, 2017). For example, Rose and Gage (2017) determined that students with disabilities were significantly more likely to experience victimization and engage in bully perpetration over time when compared to their peers without disabilities in grades 3 through 12. Unfortunately, involvement in bullying among youth with disabilities is also associated with disproportionate effects, where students with disabilities who are victimized tend to report higher levels of psychological distress, physical harm, and emotional trauma when compared to their peers without disabilities (Hartley et al., 2015).

Evaluation of bullying involvement among youth with disabilities has evolved over the past decade. For example, early reports dichotomized disability status, which established the disproportionate involvement among youth with disabilities (McLaughlin et al., 2010; Rose et al., 2011). More recent studies, however, have examined the disproportionate rates among specific subgroups of youth with disabilities. From a prevalence perspective, a majority of subgroups of youth with disabilities, including youth with emotional behavior disorders (EBDs), autism spectrum disorder (ASD), other health impairment (OHI), speech or language impairments, intellectual disabilities (IDs), and learning disabilities (LDs), tend to report greater rates of victimization than their peers without disabilities (NASEM, 2016; Rose et al., 2015). Youth with ASD (Bear et al., 2015; Symes & Humphrey, 2010; Twyman et al., 2010; Zablotsky et al., 2012) and youth with ID tend to have the highest rates of victimization comparatively, where youth with behavioral-oriented disabilities, such as EBD and OHI, tend to engage in higher rates of aggressive behaviors that may be construed as bullying (Rose & Espelage, 2012; Rose & Gage, 2017; Ryoo et al., 2015).

In addition to specific disability labels, the relationship between bullying involvement and educational placement of students with disabilities has been examined within the context of inclusive versus self-contained services. While a free appropriate public education (FAPE) within the least restrictive environment (LRE) is a right of all students with disabilities, and schools are required to provide students with disabilities a continuum of services (IDEA, 2004), environmental factors may place some students at greater risk of bullying involvement. For example, studies that have dichotomized disability status and examined environmental variables suggest that students with disabilities in a more restrictive environment experience and engage in higher rates of bullying when compared to their peers in inclusive environments (Rose et al., 2009; Rose et al., 2012; Thompson et al., 1994). However, when specific disabilities are considered in combination with educational placement, some discrepancies exist. For instance, Zablostky and colleagues (2013) found that students with ASD who were served within inclusive environments experienced higher rates of victimization than their peers who were served in self-contained classrooms.

So, the question remains: What places students with disabilities at greatest risk for bullying involvement? Rose and Espelage (2012) argued that involvement in bullying may likely be predicted by characteristics associated with the disabilities (e.g., inappropriate behaviors under normal circumstances, social skills deficits), not the presence or absence of a disability. From a social-ecological perspective, disability identification, and subsequent bullying involvement, may result from "ineffective interactions between a person's capabilities and the demands of his or her environments" (Luckasson & Schalock, 2012, p. 3). In reality, the disproportionate rates at which students with disabilities are involved in bullying are likely a combination of multiple factors. Specifically, the intersectionality of disability status (i.e., presence or absence of a disability), disability label, disability severity, characteristics of a specific disability, comorbidity of multiple disabilities, special education services, educational placement, gender, and skill deficits all serve as compounded predictors of bullying involvement among youth with disabilities.

While all of the factors should be considered when crafting the individualized education program (IEP) for youth with disabilities, one consistent predictor has emerged in relation to the disproportionate representation of youth with disabilities within the bullying dynamic. In early reviews, both McLaughlin and colleagues (2010) and Rose and colleagues (2011) reported that students with disabilities are more likely to be involved in bullying if they have social and communication skill deficits. For example, it has been argued that the disproportionate representation of students with disabilities in the bullying dynamic may be due to deficits in social information processing, which is associated with communicative deficits, withdrawal, and/or aggressive responses that can lead them to "misinterpret social cues and not understand age appropriate verbal and nonverbal communication" (Rose & Gage, 2017 p. 300) With that said, what has demonstrated promise in improving social and communication skill acquisition among students with disabilities is an increased focus on the development of social and emotional competence (Greenberg et al., 2017). Therefore, intervention approaches designed to support this subset of youth should be implemented school-wide, include multiple components, be implemented across a variety of settings, and be grounded in skill development (NASEM, 2016; Preast et al., 2020).

Multi-Tiered System of Support

One promising approach to school-wide implementation of bully prevention practices that includes multiple components and allows for interventions to be situated across a variety of settings is MTSS. MTSS is a prevention and intervention delivery framework that stems from a public health model and is designed to prevent academic failure and challenging behavior within the school environment through the implementation of scaffolded interventions and systems (Sailor et al., 2021). Sailor and colleagues (2021) argued that MTSS has been transformative in schools because the framework applies to all students, is grounded in measurement and data-based decisions, allows for the integrations of behavioral and academic interventions, is scaffolded to proactively address academic or behavioral concerns, is grounded in a team approach allowing for increased collaborations, and embraces the principles of Universal Design for Learning (UDL). As an intervention delivery framework, MTSS is viewed as a tiered approach, including universal or primary prevention (Tier 1), selective or secondary interventions (Tier 2), and indicated or tertiary interventions (Tier 3), which provides a continuum of support (Bradshaw, 2013, 2015; Lewis et al., 2010). The overall premise of MTSS is to provide scaffolded supports that are data-driven in order to proactively support the academic, behavioral, and functional needs of all students within an educational environment (Bradshaw, 2013, 2015; Lewis et al., 2010; Sailor et al., 2021).

Positive Behavioral Intervention and Supports

While MTSS is the overarching framework for supporting all school-aged youth, positive behavioral interventions and supports (PBIS) is an MTSS that is specific to supporting behavioral and functional needs. As with MTSS, PBIS is not a curriculum or a single intervention—it is a comprehensive and proactive framework for intervention delivery designed to reduce challenging behavior, promote student success, and improve the school's overall climate (Pugh & Chitiyo, 2012). The foundation of PBIS relies on the interaction between foundational school-based systems, ongoing data collection and progress monitoring, and implementation and intervention practices to support student outcomes (Sugai & Horner, 2006). Therefore, PBIS is a collaborative problem-solving framework, where data are used to identify skill deficits, determine appropriate and scaffolded supports, and evaluate the success and outcomes of specific tiered interventions and practices. As with MTSS, PBIS is typically viewed as a three-tiered framework for implementing universal or school-wide (Tier 1), small-group or targeted (Tier 2), and individualized (Tier 3) supports (Sugai & Horner, 2006). In the following section, we provide detail about each of these tiers within PBIS.

Tier 1: Universal Prevention

Tier 1 represents the foundation of PBIS, where school-wide expectations and behaviors are established and strategies by which the students are taught are implemented and monitored. Expectations and behaviors are framed from a positive perspective, where students are objectively taught, and subsequently reinforced, for engaging in appropriate behaviors. In turn, common language, behaviors, and expectations are entrenched within the school climate and culture, which remains consistent between classrooms and educational environments throughout the school. A majority of students, between 80% and 85%, receive appropriate levels of support in Tier 1 (Lewis et al., 2010; Sugai & Horner, 2006).

Tier 2: Selective or Targeted Interventions

For students who do not respond adequately to Tier 1 supports or have an identified skill deficit, they may benefit from targeted (Tier 2) interventions. This typically includes 10% to 15% of students, and interventions are generally implemented in small groups (Lewis et al., 2010). School personnel use data to identify students who have specific behavioral needs, including social and communication skill deficits (Rose et al., 2019). Tier 2 instruction includes increased precorrection, opportunities to respond, behavior-specific praise, and increased focus on behavioral function. Tier 2 instruction is designed to bolster a student's skills in a specific area, and when the skill is demonstrated and mastered, the student can return to Tier 1 (Lewis et al., 2010; Sugai & Horner, 2006).

Tier 3: Individualized or Indicated Preventative Interventions

Students who do not respond adequately to Tier 2 supports and require more intensive behavioral interventions, typically between 1% and 5% of the student population, may receive Tier 3, or individualized supports. This tier represents the most intensive and comprehensive supports, where intervention delivery is grounded in multiple sources of data, including function-based assessment (e.g., functional behavior assessment). Tier 3 supports are individualized, where a specific behavior, or set of behaviors, are targeted; socially appropriate behaviors are taught, modeled, and monitored; and specific reinforcement techniques are implemented. Typically, intervention implementation and success at Tier 3 is actively monitored by a multidisciplinary team (Lewis et al., 2010; Rose et al., 2019; Sugai & Horner, 2006).

Social and Emotional Learning

SEL is designed to help youth acquire "the skills, attitude, mindset or the aptitude that allows you to develop social and emotional competence, which allows you to successfully manage life tasks, such as learning, solving problems, forming relationships, and becoming empathetic" (Elias et al., 1997, p. 2). SEL is composed of five domains, including self-awareness, self-management, responsible decision-making, relationship skills, and social awareness (CASEL, 2012), which are critical for reducing bullying involvement among youth (Espelage et al., 2013; Espelage, Low, et al., 2015). It has been demonstrated that when students are directly taught skills in these substantive domains, they are able to recognize and manage emotions, self-monitor their performance, negotiate and manage conflict appropriately, be more empathetic, and establish and maintain healthy relationships (Elias, 2004; Smith & Low, 2013). Unfortunately, the skills within these domains, including the ability to build and maintain healthy relationships, are often areas of concern for students with disabilities, where this subset of youth tends to struggle with social and communication skill acquisition (Espelage et al., 2016; Rose et al., 2019; Swearer et al., 2012). The inability to establish healthy relationships, build and maintain friendships, and cultivate a supportive peer network is associated with social and communication skill deficits, where children with fewer friends have a lack of social support, making them more likely to be victimized and more susceptible to emotional harm. On the other hand, students who develop these skills are more likely to be accepted by their peers, less likely to be involved in bullying, and more likely to intervene when they witness bullying (Espelage, Rose, et al., 2015, 2016; Smith & Low, 2013). Additionally, students who are exposed to SEL report a decrease in aggressive behavior, school absences, disciplinary referrals, and increases in academic achievement and prosocial skills (Smith & Low, 2013). Given the positive outcomes associated with SEL, an increasing number of schools are incorporating evidence-based SEL interventions into their curriculum (Preast et al., 2020).

Intersection of SEL and Bully Prevention

SEL programs designed to increase skill acquisition and decrease challenging behaviors, such as bullying, are centered around the belief that academic skills and social and emotional behaviors are interconnected (Durlak et al., 2011; Espelage et al., 2016). Specifically, as students' ability to manage and regulate their emotions, make responsible decisions, and establish quality relationships increases, their socially appropriate behaviors and academic achievement improve (Zins et al., 2004), which is critically important for youth with disabilities (Rose et al., 2011). However, lack of exposure to social and emotional skill development among school-aged youth may exacerbate externalizing and internalizing behaviors such as aggression and bullying (Preast et al., 2020). For example, in a study detailing the social-emotional development of kindergarten youth exposed to SEL, young children who did not achieve or were not exposed to developmentally appropriate social and emotional competencies engaged in higher levels of challenging behavior and were viewed as antisocial (Raver & Knitzer, 2002). Raver and Knitzer (2002) argued that the challenging behaviors and social skills deficits, without intervention, may persist into elementary school, resulting in decreased academic achievement and performance and long-term risks such as grade retention, increased likelihood of school withdrawal, and exacerbated social and communication skill deficits (Raver & Knitzer, 2002). Fortunately, there is emerging evidence that SEL improves behavior and academic outcomes for school-aged youth (Low et al., 2015; Taylor et al., 2017), such as significant decreases in self-reported delinquency, risk-taking, and problem behavior, including decreases in bullying, cyberbullying, and homophobic name-calling (Espelage, Low, et al., 2015), especially among youth with the most intensive support needs (Low et al., 2015). Espelage, Rose, and Polanin (2015, 2016) further demonstrated the benefits of SEL for students with high-intensity needs, where, in a randomized clinical trial, they found that SEL programming reduces bullying involvement among youth with disabilities while increasing academic outcomes and a willingness to intervene in situations perceived as bullying. Therefore, SEL has demonstrated a relationship between increased levels of prosocial skills, decreases in bullying involvement, and improvements in academic outcomes for many youth, including those with disabilities.

Embedding SEL Within a Multitiered Framework

Recently, scholars have addressed the utility of embedding SEL within a multitiered framework such as PBIS (NASEM, 2016; Rose et al., 2019; Sailor et al., 2021). Since PBIS is a problem-solving and intervention delivery framework (Oakes et al., 2021; Sugai & Horner, 2006), it is imperative to design, adopt, and implement interventions that meet all students' needs, including strategies for bully prevention (Rose & Monda-Amaya, 2012; Rose et al., 2019). It should be noted that PBIS alone may not be enough to reduce bullying within a school environment, especially for youth with disabilities. For example, Gage and colleagues (2019) found no significant difference in student perceptions of bullying when comparing schools that implement PBIS with fidelity versus schools that are not implementing and have not been trained to implement PBIS. While PBIS has been found to address behavioral issues such as decreased office disciplinary referrals and suspensions (Gage et al., 2017, 2018), Gage and colleagues (2019) argued that bully prevention, specifically strategies for social and communication skill development, should be implemented within the PBIS framework to directly address concerns related to bullying, especially among youth with disabilities (see Figure 22.1).

Establishing the Foundation

Although many scholars are recommending the integration of SEL within PBIS, the logistics require planning and preparation. Specifically, the planning requires establishing a school-based team, conducting a school-wide needs assessment, evaluating existing practices and programs, frequently assessing the prevalence of bullying within a given school environment, conducting behavioral risk screeners, adopting tiered SEL interventions and approaches, and establishing a plan for ongoing evaluation (Lewis & Rose, 2013; Preast et al., 2020; Rose et al., 2019; Sugai & Horner, 2006). Ultimately, the success of integration and reduction in bullying hinges on collaboration and planning.

Establishing a School-Based Team

Collaborative practices are key to the successful implementation of SEL within a PBIS framework. Therefore, establishing a school-based team that includes multiple perspectives, is decision and

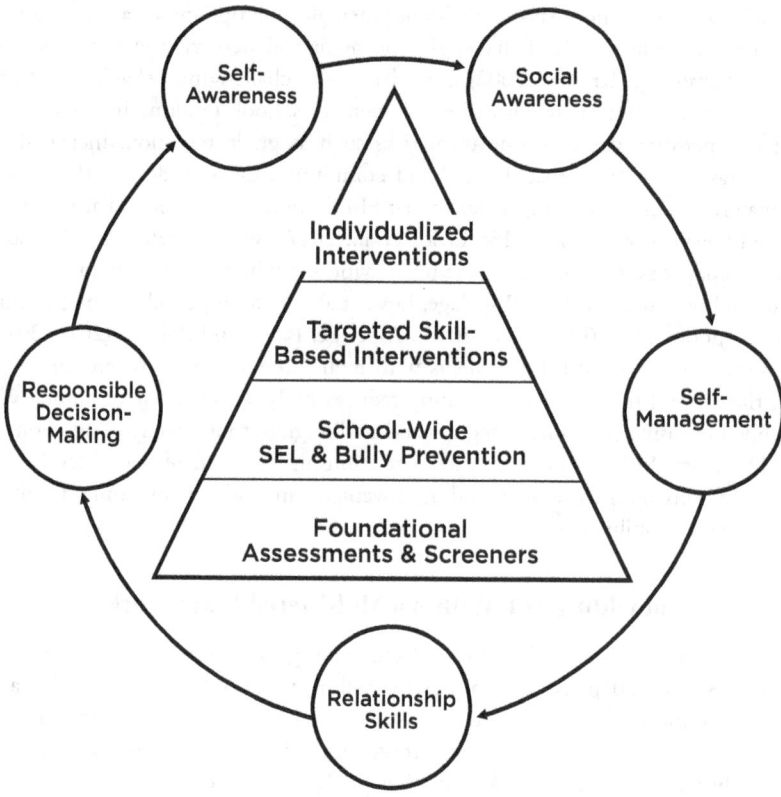

Figure 22.1 Embedding SEL Within a PBIS Framework for Bully Prevention

process driven, maintains shared leadership, and has a strong understanding of risk factors associated with bullying involvement is essential for improving school climate and culture (Preast et al., 2020; Rose et al., 2019; Sugai & Horner, 2006). This team could include but is not limited to special and general education teachers, administrators, counselors, school psychologist, behavior specialist, home-school coordinator, social worker, and school resource officer. Additionally, soliciting input from parents, caregivers, and community members can help inform practices and implementation procedures, but the core team should only include school staff that has authority to review student records and discuss student data and outcomes. To support all students within the school environment, the charge of this team could include but is not limited to establishing a bully prevention action plan and implementation protocol, establishing a process for reporting and conducting investigations, identifying and monitoring interventions, reviewing data and making data-based decisions, and providing oversight related to the tiered bully prevention approach (see Figure 22.2).

School-Wide Climate Assessments

Conducting a school-wide climate assessment is critical to bully prevention due to the social complexity of bullying. The difficulty is often associated with objectively defining, measuring, and contextualizing bullying among diverse student populations, which often results in complications for schools' and districts' ability to provide impactful and meaningful bully prevention interventions, especially for youth who are most at risk (Casper et al., 2015). Therefore, it is recommended for

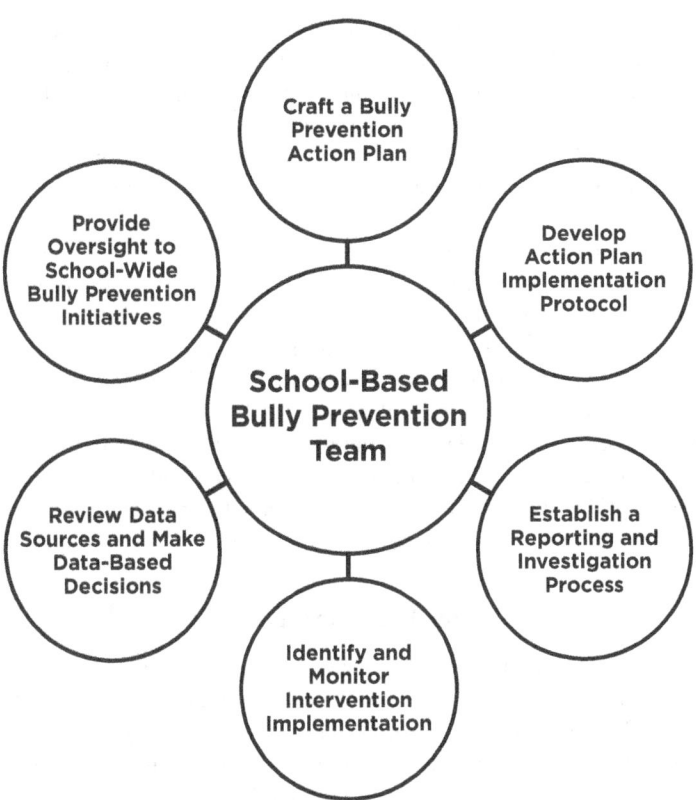

Figure 22.2 Roles and Responsibilities for a School-Based Bully Prevention Team

schools to conduct frequent school-wide climate assessments (Lewis & Rose, 2013; Lewis et al., 2010) that are based on the school's or district's identified need and evaluate school-related constructs such as perceptions of school climate, school belongingness, social supports, peer involvement, empathy, bullying involvement, and supportive attitudes towards bullying (Rose et al., 2019).

To meet these needs, the school-based bully prevention team should be trained to examine multiple sources of data collected (e.g., disciplinary data, bullying reports, academic achievement, attendance, anecdotal records) in connection with the school-wide climate assessment data to determine challenges, deficits, areas to target for improvement, and specific subpopulations who may need additional supports within the school context (Lewis & Rose, 2013). The purpose of this process should be to drive data-based decisions regarding interventions and establish a sustainable bully prevention approach that is specific to the school environment; supports the diverse learning and behavioral needs of all students; and increases as buy-in from teachers, administrators, students, parents, and community members increase (Rose et al., 2017).

Behavioral Risk Screeners

Given that social and communication skill deficits are two of the most notable predictors of bullying involvement, especially among youth with disabilities (McLaughlin et al., 2010; Rose et al., 2011), it is recommended that schools conduct annual systematic behavior risk screeners to proactively identify youth who may benefit from targeted or individualized instruction (Eklund & Dowdy, 2014; Preast et al., 2020; Rose et al., 2019). Systematic behavioral risk screeners are brief assessments, generally completed by a student's teacher, that identify risk factors, skill deficits, warning signs, and areas for improvement (Brock, 2015; Jenkins et al., 2007). While disciplinary records and teacher referrals are often used to identify students with more significant support needs (Eklund et al., 2009; Sugai et al., 2000), these approaches are often reactionary and subject to teacher bias (Eklund et al., 2009; Miller et al., 2015). Systematic behavioral risk screeners establish a proactive measure of student performance in critical areas that allow for identification and implementation of necessary and individualized supports.

One widely used systematic behavioral risk screener is the Social, Academic, and Emotional Behavior Risk Screener (SAEBRS; Kilgus et al., 2013), a 19-item teacher-completed rating scale that takes approximately 10 to 20 minutes to complete per classroom. The screener is used to identify youth who are at risk for social (i.e., interpersonal functioning, externalizing behaviors), academic (i.e., academic readiness behaviors), and emotional (i.e., affective behaviors) behavior deficits through three separate subscales (von der Embse et al., 2016; Whitley & Cuenca-Carlino, 2020). The higher a student's score on the SAEBRS, the more acceptable the rater deems their behavior. This screener has been used with youth in kindergarten through grade 12, with high internal consistency (Kilgus et al., 2015). By using a systematic behavioral risk screener, schools can effectively identify students who could benefit from targeted or individualized interventions.

Tier 1: Universal SEL

As previously stated, the National Academies of Sciences, Engineering, and Medicine (NASEM, 2016) recommends implementing bully prevention within a multitiered framework, such as PBIS, with an emphasis on skill development and social and emotional learning. The national emphasis on school-wide bully prevention stems from recent national data that suggest almost 20% of the student population reports being victimized at school in the past 12 months (Musu-Gillette et al., 2018), and students are more likely to engage in bullying when they view the school climate as unhealthy (Wang et al., 2013). Success within a multitiered framework centers on the implementation of universal-level systems such as behavior expectations that are framed positively, direct instruction on expectations, and reinforcement strategies for engaging in socially appropriate behaviors (Gage et al., 2017; Scott et al., 2019; Sugai et al., 2000). However, PBIS alone may not be sufficient for reducing bullying with a school environment (Gage et al., 2019).

School-wide efforts to prevent bullying and victimization are predicated on the assumption that reducing these behaviors must include a universal focus on critical skill development (Espelage, 2014), such as social and communication skills, through social and emotional learning (Gage et al., 2019; McLaughlin et al., 2010; Preast et al., 2020; Rose et al., 2019). SEL curricula that includes instruction in self-awareness, social awareness, self-management, responsible decision-making, and relationship skills (CASEL, 2012) are designed to support the acquisition of critical social and communication skills necessary for navigating the complex social and environmental systems extant within the bullying dynamic (Hong & Espelage, 2012). By embedding universal SEL within a PBIS framework, all students are exposed to the benefits of MTSS (e.g., universal expectations, teacher-directed instruction), as well as direct instruction in critical SEL skills. To date, several SEL programs have been developed, evaluated, and demonstrated positive outcomes for school-aged youth, including reductions in bullying involvement (Durlak et al., 2011; Gaffney et al., 2019). We describe several of these programs in the following section.

Second Step Social and Emotional Learning Program

A number of school-wide SEL interventions are available that could be seamlessly embedded within a PBIS framework. The *Second Step Social and Emotional Learning Program* (Committee for Children,

2008) is one of the most common and has one of the largest evidence bases for positive student outcomes (Brown et al., 2011; Espelage, Low, et al., 2015; Espelage et al., 2013; Gaffney et al., 2019; Taylor et al., 2017), including reductions in delinquency, risk taking, problem behaviors, bullying and cyberbullying, and homophobic name-calling (Espelage, Low, et al., 2015), especially among youth with demonstrated skill deficits (Low et al., 2015). The *Second Step* curriculum is a comprehensive, school-wide program that focuses on empathy, emotion management, problem-solving, and self-monitoring designed to improve social and emotional skills, including social and communication skill acquisition (Committee for Children, 2008). The curriculum includes weekly classroom lessons that are scaffolded by grade level (kindergarten through eighth grade), interactive daily practice activities, parental communication letters, and adaptation and modification recommendations to meet the individual needs of all students. Weekly lessons and daily practice activities are grounded in sound learning principles and include a consistent structure of review, model, demonstrate, reinforce, and reflect (Committee for Children, 2008, 2011). In addition to *Second Step*'s promise for all school-aged youth, Espelage, Rose, and Polanin (2015, 2016) demonstrated the utility among youth with disabilities in a large-scale randomized clinical trial of middle school youth, where students with disabilities who were exposed to *Second Step* reported less bullying, improved academic marks, and an increased propensity to intervene in bullying situations when compared to youth with disabilities who did not have access to *Second Step*.

Second Step: Bullying Prevention Unit

The *Second Step: Bullying Prevention Unit* (Committee for Children, 2013) is a supplement to the elementary-level *Second Step Social and Emotional Learning Program* (Committee for Children, 2008, 2011). This supplemental unit includes four lessons per grade level and is designed to be situated within the universal program, following the empathy and being assertive units, through sequential and scaffolded lessons. Overall, the unit provides direct instruction in recognizing, reporting, and refusing bullying; bystander responsibilities; and cyberbullying awareness and prevention. The goal for this supplemental unit is for teachers to provide direct instruction in bully prevention within the context of social and emotional learning.

Steps to Respect

Steps to Respect (Committee for Children, 2009) is a 12- to 14-week universal SEL curriculum that specifically targets bully prevention among elementary-aged youth. As with *Second Step*, *Steps to Respect* is a scaffolded curriculum that focuses specifically on the social and emotional skills necessary to recognize, report, and respond to bullying; establish social and communication skills; and cultivate positive peer relationships (Brown et al., 2011; Swearer et al., 2010). Initial studies that have examined *Steps to Respect* have found reductions in bullying, rumor spreading, and general aggressive behaviors; increases in willingness to intervene in bullying situations; and improved perceptions of the overall school climate (Brown et al., 2011; Frey et al., 2005).

Strong Start, Strong Kids, *and* Strong Teens

The *Strong Start* (Merrell et al., 2007, 2009), *Strong Kids* (Merrell et al., 2007a, 2007b), and *Strong Teens* (Merrell et al., 2007c) program is a comprehensive SEL curriculum that is scaffolded to meet the needs of students in kindergarten through 12th grade. The impetus of the *Strong Start, Kids, and Teens* program is to improve emotional regulation and internalizing behaviors (Carrizales-Engelmann et al., 2016; Merrell, 2010). Each program includes 10 to 12 classroom lessons designed to promote interpersonal and intrapersonal relationships, establish emotional well-being, improve critical SEL skills, improve self-awareness and self-management, and increase health strategies for dealing with stress (Merrell, 2010). Studies examining the various iterations of the *Strong Start, Kids,* and *Teens* program have found decreased internalizing behaviors, increased social skills, and improved SEL knowledge (Kramer et al., 2010; Marchant et al., 2010; Merrell et al., 2008; Neth et al., 2020), especially for youth at greatest risk (Caldarella et al., 2009). This program is unique in that it spans all grade levels, focuses on internalizing behaviors and emotion regulation, and can be implemented school-wide or used as a targeted intervention for youth who demonstrate internalizing behavior challenges or social and communication skill deficits.

Blueprint for Homegrown SEL Situated Within a PBIS Framework

While SEL implemented within a PBIS framework is a recommended approach for bully prevention (NASEM, 2016; Rose et al., 2019), especially for youth with disabilities, school-level budgets to purchase such programs may be limited. To address this concern, Lewis and Rose (2013) provided guidance for developing a bully prevention action plan that is grounded in SEL and can be situated within a PBIS framework. In addition to establishing a school-based team, conducting a school-wide climate assessment, and using systematic behavioral risk screeners to identify students who are at risk for bullying involvement, Lewis and Rose (2013) outlined a framework for developing a homegrown bully prevention protocol. This protocol hinges on initial data collection and school-based needs assessments, where appropriate prosocial behaviors are determined, bystander roles are outlined, strategies for increased supervision in high-risk locations are identified, lesson plans for teaching prosocial skills are developed, and a hierarchy of consequences, including targeted skill development, is established. Ultimately, this action plan and protocol centers on the recommendation that students need to know what to say, what to do, and who to tell if they witness or experience bullying, and adults need to know how to support the victim, respond to the bullying behaviors, and protect reporters (see Figure 22.3; Ievers-Landis et al., 2019; Ross & Horner, 2009; Yasuda et al., 2016)

Overall, the strength of a universal bullying prevention approach is that all students and staff are immersed in the curriculum to improve the school climate while reducing the prevalence of bullying among the entire student body. Within the classroom, lessons about bullying prevention and social and emotional learning are key elements in program effectiveness (Low et al., 2014). Students should be actively engaged in dialogue and problem-solving associated with bullying prevention

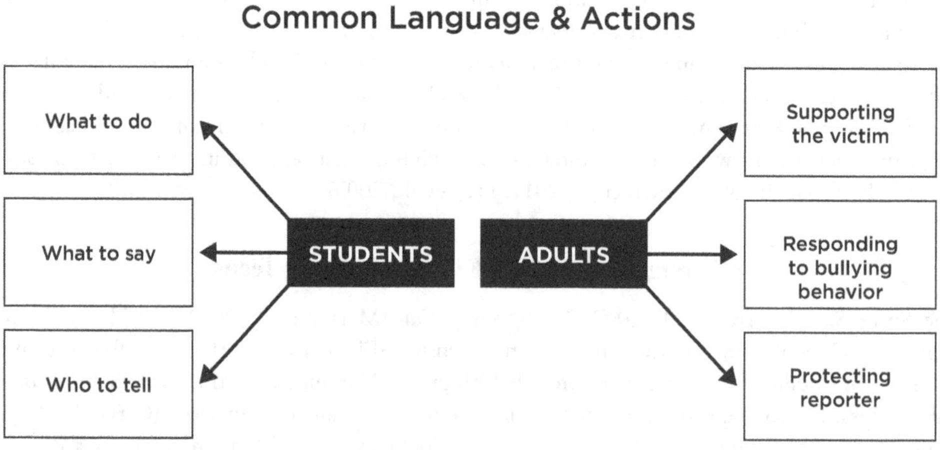

Figure 22.3 Establishing School-Wide Common Language and Actions for Students and School Personnel

(Shriberg et al., 2015). By incorporating social skills throughout the universal curriculum, students get the opportunity to learn, practice, and validate their skills within a natural environment, thereby decreasing bullying involvement (Rose et al., 2011).

Tier 2: Targeted Interventions

In addition to universal bully prevention interventions, schools should implement more targeted skills interventions. Targeted interventions are implemented for students who continue to display social and communication skill deficits and emotional concerns or do not respond to universal prevention efforts. The systematic behavioral risk screener can be used as an initial tool to identify students who could benefit from Tier 2 instruction (Preast et al., 2020; Rose et al., 2019). Tier 2 interventions typically happen in small groups and are designed as more intensive, direct instruction on a specific subset of skills (Mitchell et al., 2011; Rose et al., 2019). Many Tier 2 approaches address critical elements of bully prevention (Espelage et al., 2011) and have demonstrated promise for youth with disabilities (Rose & Monda-Amaya, 2012). Now, we discuss several of these approaches.

Social Skills Improvement System: Classwide Intervention Program

The *Social Skills Improvement System: Classwide Intervention Program* (Gresham & Elliot, 2007) is a targeted social skills intervention designed to be implemented in small groups that has demonstrated success in increasing social skills and decreasing internalizing behaviors among elementary youth (DiPerna & Volpe, 2005). The program is scaffolded and appropriate for students in kindergarten through eighth grade who have demonstrated deficits in social and communication skills. Overall, ten critical social skills are targeted across ten separate units that include lesson plans focusing on teaching, demonstrating, reinforcing, and generalizing skills across multiple environments (Gresham & Elliot, 2007). Since social and communication skill deficits are two of the most notable predictors of bullying involvement, especially among youth with disabilities, the *Social Skills Improvement System: Classwide Intervention Program* has promise for this subset of youth; yet some adaptations and modifications may be necessary for students with the most intensive needs (Preast et al., 2020).

Cool School

Cool School (The Language Express, Inc., 2016) is an interactive SEL curriculum designed to specifically address situations related to bullying. The program is developmentally appropriate for elementary-aged youth, especially for those at greatest risk of bullying involvement. *Cool School* includes 20 webisodes and accompanying lessons that are approximately 30 minutes in length. The webisodes are grounded in responsible decision-making related to bullying scenarios that students may face in elementary school. Each webisode lesson follows five distinct steps, including a review and follow-up from the previous lesson, introduction to the weekly skill and social dilemma, presentation of the webisode that illustrates the social dilemma, discussion of appropriate and alternative responses to the webisode, and a concluding activity (The Language Express, Inc., 2016). While several investigations of *Cool School* are being conducted, data from a preliminary pilot study of elementary-aged youth documented decreases in victimization and increases in prosocial behaviors, emotional regulation, academic self-efficacy, and competence (Rose et al., *prep*).

Check-in/Check-out

Check-in/Check-out (CICO; Crone & Horner, 2003; Crone et al., 2010) is a Tier 2 strategy commonly implemented within a PBIS framework that addresses a skill deficit for an individual student.

CICO employs a systematic process where the behavioral focus is identified, the student and supervising teacher meet to discuss program expectations, the student is provided with a *Daily Progress Report* that outlines the daily expectations, the student "Checks In" with the mentor teacher at the beginning of the day to ensure the student is prepared for the day or upcoming activities and understands the expectations, the student's teacher(s) provide written feedback on the *Daily Progress Report* throughout the day, and at the end of the day, the student "Checks Out" with the teacher. During check-out, the teacher reviews the *Daily Progress Report*, determines if the student met expectations, and provides them with a predetermined reinforcer coupled with behavior-specific praise (Crone et al., 2010). After "Check Out," the student has their parent/guardian sign the *Daily Progress Report* and returns the signed document the next day (Crone et al., 2010; Drevon et al., 2018). If the student did not meet expectations, the teacher reminds the student of the expectations and outlines strategies for improvement. In a recent meta-analysis, Drevon and colleagues (2018) determined that CICO significantly reduced problem behavior and increased academic engagement. Given the strong evidence base for CICO, it is plausible that this intervention could be used to increase social and communication skills, while decreasing involvement in bullying.

Blueprint for Homegrown Social and Communication Skill Lessons

Using the systematic behavioral risk screener to identify students who have social and communication skill deficits is an important strategy to bully prevention, especially among youth with disabilities (Rose et al., 2019). However, once these students are identified, specific interventions should be implemented to increase skill acquisition and reduce risk for bullying involvement (Preast et al., 2020; Rose et al., 2019). Preast and colleagues (2020) suggested that in addition to using the behavioral risk screener to identify deficits, teachers should assess the presentation of the deficit by using Kauffman and Kinnealey's (2015) social skills taxonomy, which includes an assessment of verbal and nonverbal presentation, emotional response, collaborative skills, and interpersonal and intrapersonal relationships. Preast and colleagues (2020) also argued that in addition to presentation, the specific social and communication skill deficit should be identified (e.g., conversations, emotion regulation, seeking help, cultivating relationships). Once identified, the teacher can design step-wise lessons that include introducing the skill, demonstrating the skill, role-playing the skill, reinforcing the skill through behavior-specific praise and predetermined reinforcers, and generalizing the skill by employing reinforcement strategies within the natural environment. This approach, based on foundational behavioral principles of prompting, providing opportunities to respond, and providing behavior-specific praise, can improve skill acquisition, while reducing bullying involvement (Preast et al., 2020).

Tier 3: Individualized Interventions

Students who do not respond adequately to Tier 1 or Tier 2 intervention, including those who are chronically victimized or those who engage in chronic levels of challenging behaviors, may require more intensive supports (Rose & Monda-Amaya, 2012). These supports are provided in Tier 3 and are highly individualized. Between 1% and 5% of the student population may require this intensive level of support (Horner et al., 2010; Sugai & Horner, 2006). Generally, individualized supports at Tier 3 begin with a functional behavior assessment (FBA), which is consistent with the PBIS framework and subsequent interventions (Crone & Horner, 2003) and, at a minimum, includes a review of existing data, teacher reports, and systematic observations. The FBA helps the multidisciplinary team and the school-based bully prevention team operationalize the behavior, identify antecedents, and pinpoint maintaining consequences (O'Neill et al., 1997). Once the FBA is complete, a behavior intervention plan and supporting annual, measurable goals are developed to outline individualized interventions for socially appropriate skill acquisition (Fairbanks et al., 2008; Rose & Monda-Amaya, 2012).

While few studies have examined Tier 3 interventions for bully prevention, Rose and Monda-Amaya (2012) argued that Tier 3 bully prevention interventions should be designed to increase social competence, independence, and understanding personal values. For example, a social narrative can be used for specific skill acquisition by identifying a target skill, creating an appropriate and complete scenario, presenting the scenario to the student, discussing implications from the scenario, teaching the student to self-monitor based on the scenario, and implementing a reinforcement strategy for demonstrating the skill within the natural environment (Xin & Sutman, 2011). Similarly, for students who struggle with help-seeking behaviors or do not want to appear dependent on adult support, an attention signaling strategy could be implemented by identifying when the student needs the most support, establishing an appropriate covert signal that is known by the teacher and student, and ensuring the teacher will promptly respond when the student engages in the predetermined signal (Rose & Monda-Amaya, 2012). This approach will allow the student to develop a stronger sense of independence. Additionally, as part of the behavior intervention plan, the multidisciplinary team could elect to teach the student self-determination skills to improve intrapersonal values and independence by providing the student with opportunities for decision-making, teaching the student problem-solving skills, incorporating self-management strategies, and fostering goal setting and attainment skills (Wehmeyer et al., 1996). However, it should be noted that Tier 3 strategies are individualized to meet the specific needs of the student. Because social and communication skills are two of the strongest predictors of bullying involvement among youth with disabilities, individualized instruction for social and communication skill acquisition should be considered with crafting Tier 3 interventions (Rose et al., 2019).

Recommendations and Moving Forward

Given that students with disabilities are disproportionately involved within the bullying dynamic (Rose & Gage, 2017) and social and communication skill deficits are two of the most notable predictors of bullying involvement (Rose et al., 2011), school leaders should consider implementing a multitiered bully prevention approach that is grounded in social and emotional learning (Preast et al., 2020). By situating SEL within an MTSS framework, such as PBIS, schools can proactively address school-based bullying, while modeling, teaching, and reinforcing critical life skills for all students. Most importantly, schools can demonstrate the importance of social and communication skill development by embedding these skills into the daily curriculum, thereby prioritizing both academic achievement and social development among all students.

References

Bear, G. C., Mantz, L. S., Glutting, J. J., Yang, C., & Boyer, D. E. (2015). Differences in bullying victimization between students with and without disabilities. *School Psychology Review, 44*, 98–116. https://doi.org/10.17105/SPR44-1.98-116

Bradshaw, C. P. (2013). Preventing bullying through Positive Behavioral Interventions and Supports (PBIS): A multitiered approach to prevention and integration. *Theory into Practice, 52*(4), 288–295. https://doi.org/10.1080/00405841.2013.829732

Bradshaw, C. P. (2015). Translating research to practice in bullying prevention. *American Psychologist, 70*(4), 322. https://doi.org/10.1037/a0039114

Brock, S. E. (2015). Mental health matters. *Communiqué, 43*(7), 1–15.

Bronfenbrenner, U. (1977). Toward an experimental ecology of human development. *American Psychologist, 32*, 513–531. https://doi.org/10.1037/0003-066x.32.7.513

Brown, E. C., Low, S., Smith, B. H., & Haggerty, K. P. (2011). Outcomes from a school-randomized controlled trial of Steps to Respect: A Bullying Prevention Program. *School Psychology Review, 40*, 423–443. https://doi.org/10.1080/02796015.2011.12087707

Caldarella, P., Christensen, L., Kramer, T. J., & Kronmiller, K. (2009). The effects of Strong Strat on second grade students' emotional and social competence. *Early Childhood Education Journal, 37*(1), 51–56. https://doi.org/10.1007/s10643-009-0321-4

Carrizales-Engelmann, D., Feuerborn, L. L., Gueldner, B. A., & Tran, O. K. (2016). *Merrell's strong teems, grades 9–12: A social and emotional learning curriculum* (2nd ed.). Paul H. Brookes Publishing Co.

Casper, D. M., Meter, D. J., & Card, N. A. (2015). Addressing measurement issues related to bullying involvement. *School Psychology Review, 44*(4), 353–371. https://doi.org/10.17105/spr-15-0036.1

Collaborative for Academic, Social, and Emotional Learning (CASEL). (2012). *2013 CASEL guide: Effective social and emotional learning programs—Preschool and elementary school edition.* Author.

Committee for Children. (2008). *Committee for Children Second Step: Student success through prevention program.* Author.

Committee for Children. (2009). *Steps to respect.* Author.

Committee for Children. (2011). *Second step social and emotional learning program.* Author.

Committee for Children. (2013). *Second step: Bullying prevention unit.* Author.

Crone, D. A., Hawken, L. S., & Horner, R. H. (2010). *Responding to problem behavior in schools: The behavior education program* (2nd ed.). Guilford Press.

Crone, D. A., & Horner, R. H. (2003). *Building positive behavior support systems in schools: Functional behavioral assessment.* Guilford Press.

Diperna, J. C., & Volpe, R. J. (2005). Self-report on the social skills rating system: Analysis of reliability and validity for an elementary sample. *Psychology in the Schools, 42*(4), 345–354. https://doi.org/10.1002/pits.20095

Domitrovich, C. E., Durlak, J. A., Staley, K. C., & Weissberg, R. P. (2017). Social-emotional competence: An essential factor for promoting positive adjustment and reducing risk in school children. *Child development, 88*(2), 408–416. https://doi.org/10.1111/cdev.12739

Drevon, D. D., Hixson, M. D., Wyse, R. D., & Rigney, A. M. (2018). A meta-analytic review of the evidence for check-in check-out. *Psychology in the Schools, 56*(3), 393–412. https://doi.org/10.1002/pits.22195

Durlak, J. A., Weissberg, R. P., Dymnicki, A. B., Taylor, R. D., & Schellinger, K. B. (2011). The impact of enhancing students' social and emotional learning: A meta-analysis of school-based universal interventions. *Child Development, 82*(1), 405–432. https://doi.org/10.1111/j.1467-8624.2010.01564.x

Eklund, K., & Dowdy, E. (2014). Screening for behavioral and emotional risk versus traditional school identification methods. *School Mental Health, 6*(1), 40–49. https://doi.org/10.1007/s12310-013-9109-1

Eklund, K., Renshaw, T. L., Dowdy, E., Jimerson, S. R., Hart, S. R., Jones, C. N., & Earhart, J. (2009). Early identification of behavioral and emotional problems in youth: Universal screening versus teacher-referral identification. *The California School Psychologist, 14*(1), 89–95. https://doi.org/10.1007/bf03340954

Elias, M. J. (2004). The connection between social-emotional learning and learning disabilities: Implications for intervention. *Learning Disability Quarterly, 27*(1), 53–63. https://doi.org/10.2307/1593632

Elias, M. J., Zins, J. E., Weissberg, R. P., Frey, K. S., Greenberg, M. T., Haynes, N. M., Kessler, R., Schwab-Stone, M. E., & Shriver, T. P. (1997). *Promoting social and emotional learning: Guidelines for educators.* ASCD.

Espelage, D. L. (2014). Ecological theory: Preventing youth bullying, aggression, and victimization. *Theory into Practice, 53*(4), 257–264. https://doi.org/10.1080/00405841.2014.947216

Espelage, D. L., Green, H., & Polanin, J. R. (2011). Willingness to intervene in bullying episodes among middle school students: Individual and peer-group influences. *The Journal of Early Adolescence, 32*, 776–801. https://doi.org/10.1177/0272431611423017

Espelage, D. L., Low, S., Polanin, J., & Brown, E. (2013). The impact of a middle-school program to reduce aggression, victimization, and sexual violence. *Journal of Adolescent Health, 53*(2),180–186. https://doi.org/10.1016/j.jadohealth.2013.02.021

Espelage, D. L., Low, S., Van Ryzin, M. J., & Polanin, J. R. (2015). Clinical trial of second step middle school program: Impact on bullying, cyberbullying, homophobic teasing, and sexual harassment perpetration. *School Psychology Review, 44*(4), 464–479. https://doi.org/10.17105/spr-15-0052.1

Espelage, D. L., Rose, C. A., & Polanin, J. R. (2015). Social-emotional learning program to reduce bullying, fighting, and victimization among middle school students with disabilities. *Remedial and Special Education, 36*(5), 299–311. https://doi.org/10.1177/0741932514564564

Espelage, D. L., Rose, C. A., & Polanin, J. R. (2016). Social-emotional learning program to promote prosocial and academic skills among middle school students with disabilities. *Remedial and Special Education, 37*(6), 323–332. https://doi.org/10.1177/0741932515627475

Frey, K. S., Nolen, S. B., Edstrom, L. V. S., &Hirschstein, M. K. (2005). Effects of a school based social—emotional competence program: Linking children's goals, attributions, and behavior. *Journal of Applied Developmental Psychology, 26*, 171–200. https://doi.org/10.1016/j.appdev.2004.12.002

Fairbanks, S., Simonsen, B., & Sugai, G. (2008). Classwide secondary and tertiary tier practices and systems. *Teaching Exceptional Children, 40*(6), 44–52. https://doi.org/10.1177/004005990804000605

Gaffney, H., Ttofi, M. M., & Farrington, D. P. (2019). Evaluating the effectiveness of school-bullying prevention programs: An updated meta-analytical review. *Aggression and violent behavior, 45*, 111–133. https://doi.org/10.1016/j.avb.2018.07.001

Gage, N. A., Lee, A., Grasley-Boy, N., & George, H. P. (2018). The impact of school-wide positive behavior interventions and supports on school suspensions: A statewide quasi-experimental analysis. *Journal of Positive Behavior Interventions, 20*(4), 217–226. https://doi.org/10.1177/1098300718768204

Gage, N. A., Leite, W., Childs, K., & Kincaid, D. (2017). Average treatment effect of school-wide positive behavioral interventions and supports on school-level academic achievement in Florida. *Journal of Positive Behavior Interventions, 19*(3), 158–167. https://doi.org/10.1177/1098300717693556

Gage, N. A., Rose, C. A., & Kramer, D. A. (2019). When prevention is not enough: The distal effect of School-Wide Positive Behavior Interventions and Supports on students' perceptions of bullying. *Behavioral Disorders, 45*(1), 29–40. https://doi.org/10.1177/0198742918810761

Gladden, R. M., Vivolo-Kantor, A. M., Hamburger, M. E., & Lumpkin, C. D. (2014). *Bullying surveillance among youths: Uniform definitions for public health and recommended data elements, version 1.0*. National Center for Injury Prevention and Control, Centers for Disease Control and Prevention and U.S. Department of Education.

Greenberg, M. T., Domitrovich, C. E., Weissberg, R. P., & Durlak, J. A. (2017). Social and emotional learning as a public health approach to education. *The Future of Children*, 13–32. https://doi.org/10.1353/foc.2017.0001

Gresham, F., & Elliott, S. N. (2007). *Social skills improvement system (SSIS) rating scales*. Pearson Education Inc.

Gumpel, T. P., Zioni-Koren, V., & Bekerman, Z. (2014). An ethnographic study of participant roles in school bullying. *Aggressive Behavior, 40*(3), 214–228. https://doi.org/10.1002/ab.21515

Harbin, S. M., Kelley, M. L., Piscitello, J., & Walker, S. J. (2019). Multidimensional bullying victimization scale: Development and validation. *Journal of school violence, 18*(1), 146–161. https://doi.org/10.1080/15388220.2017.1423491

Hartley, M. T., Bauman, S., Nixon, C. L., & Davis, S. (2015). Comparative study of bullying victimization among students in general and special education. *Exceptional Children, 81*(2), 176–193. https://doi.org/10.1177/0014402914551741.

Hong, J. S., & Espelage, D. L. (2012). A review of research on bullying and peer victimization in school: An ecological system analysis. *Aggressive and Violent Behavior, 17*, 311–322. https://doi.org/10.1016/j.avb.2012.03.003

Horner, R. H., Sugai, G., & Anderson, C. M. (2010). Examining the evidence base for school-wide positive behavior support. *Focus on Exceptional Children, 42*(8). 1–14. https://doi.org/10.17161/foec.v42i8.6906

Individuals with Disabilities Education Improvement Act (IDEA), Pub. L. No.108–446, 118 Stat. 2647 (2004).

Ievers-Landis, C. E., Dykstra, C., Uli, N., & O'Riordan, M. A. (2019). Weight-related teasing of adolescents who are primarily obese: Roles of sociocultural attitudes towards appearance and physical activity self-efficacy. *International Journal of Environmental Research and Public Health, 16*(9), 1540. https://doi.org/10.3390/ijerph16091540

Jenkins, J. R., Hudson, R. F., & Johnson, E. S. (2007). Screening for at-risk readers in a response to intervention framework. *School Psychology Review, 36*(4), 582–600. https://doi.org/10.1080/02796015.2007.12087919

Kauffman, N. A., & Kinnealey, M. (2015). Comprehensive social skills taxonomy: Development and application. *The American Journal of Occupational Therapy, 69*(2), 1–10. https://doi.org/10.5014/ajot.2015.013151

Kilgus, S. P., Chafouleas, S. M., Riley-Tillman, T. C., & von der Embse, N. P. (2013). *Social, academic, & emotional behavior risk screener*. Author.

Kilgus, S. P., Sims, W. A., von der Embse, N. P., & Riley-Tillman, T. C. (2015). Confirmation of models for interpretation and use of the Social and Academic Behavior Risk Screener (SABRS). *School Psychology Quarterly, 30*, 335–352. https://doi.org/10.1037/spq0000087

Kramer, T. J., Caldarella, P., Christensen, L., & Shatzer, R. H. (2010). Social-emotional learning in kindergarten classrooms: Evaluation of the Strong Start curriculum. *Early Childhood Education Journal, 37*(4), 303–398. https://doi.org/10.1007/s10643-009-0354-8

Lewis, T. J., Jones, S. E., Horner, R. H., & Sugai, G. (2010). School-wide positive behavior support and students with emotional/behavioral disorders: Implications for prevention, identification, and intervention. *Exceptionality, 18*(2), 82–93. https://doi.org/10.1080/09362831003673168

Lewis, T., & Rose, C. A. (2013). Addressing bullying behavior through school-wide positive behavior supports. *Council for Exceptional Children: Education Week, Arlington, VA*.

Low, S., Van Ryzin, M. J., Brown, E. C., Smith, B. H., & Haggerty, K. P. (2014). Engagement matters: Lessons from assessing classroom implementation of Steps to Respect: A Bully Prevention Program over a one-year period. *Prevention Science, 15*(2), 165–176. https://doi.org/10.1007/s11121-012-0359-1

Low, S., Cook, C. R., Smolkowski, K., & Buntain-Ricklefs, J. (2015). Promoting social-emotional competence: An evaluation of the elementary version of Second Step©. *Journal of School Psychology, 53*, 463–477. https://doi.org/10.1016/j.jsp.2015.09.002

Luckasson, R., & Schalock, R. L. (2012). Human functioning, supports, assistive technology, and evidence-based practices in the field of intellectual disability. *Journal of Special Education Technology, 27*(2), 3–10. https://doi.org/10.1177/016264341202700202

Marchant, M., Brown, M., Caldarella, P., & Young, E. (2010). Effects of Strong Kids curriculum on students with internalizing behaviors: A pilot study. *Journal of Evidence-Based Practices for Schools, 11*, 124–143.

McLaughlin, C., Byers, R., & Vaughn, R. P. (2010). *Responding to bullying among children with special educational needs and/or disabilities*. Anti-Bullying Alliance.

Merrell, K. W. (2010). Linking prevention science and social-emotional learning: The Oregon Resiliency Project. *Psychology in the Schools, 47*(1), 55–70. https://doi.org/10.1002/pits.20451

Merrell, K. W., Carrizales, D., Feuerborn, L., Gueldner, B. A., & Tran, O. K. (2007a). *Strong Kids—grades 3–5: A social and emotional learning curriculum*. Paul H. Brookes Publishing.

Merrell, K. W., Carrizales, D., Feuerborn, L., Gueldner, B. A., & Tran, O. K. (2007b). *Strong Kids—grades 6–8: A social and emotional learning curriculum*. Paul H. Brookes Publishing.

Merrell, K. W., Carrizales, D., Feuerborn, L., Gueldner, B. A., & Tran, O. K. (2007c). *Strong Teens—grades 9–12: A social and emotional learning curriculum*. Paul H. Brookes Publishing.

Merrell, K. W., Juskelis, M. P., Tran, O. K., & Buchanan, R. (2008). Social and emotional learning in the classroom: Impact of Strong Kids and Strong Teens on students' social-emotional knowledge and symptoms. *Journal of Applied School Psychology, 24*, 209–224. https://doi.org/10.1080/15377900802089981

Merrell, K. W., Parisi, D., & Whitcomb, S. (2007). *Strong Start—Grades K-2: A social and emotional learning curriculum*. Paul H. Brookes Publishing.

Merrell, K. W., Whitcomb, S., & Parisi, D. (2009). *Strong Start—Pre-K: A social and emotional learning curriculum*. Paul H. Brookes Publishing.

Miller, F. G., Cohen, D., Chafouleas, S. M., Riley-Tillman, T. C., Welsh, M. E., & Fabiano, G. A. (2015). A comparison of measures to screen for social, emotional, and behavioral risk. *School Psychology Quarterly, 30*(2), 184. https://doi.org/10.1037/spq0000085

Mitchell, B. S., Stormont, M., & Gage, N. A. (2011). Tier two interventions implemented within the context of a tiered prevention framework. *Behavioral Disorders, 36*(4), 241–261. https://doi.org/10.1177/019874291103600404

Musu-Gillette, L., Zhang, A., Wang, K., Zhang, J., Kemp, J., Diliberti, M., & Oudekerk, B. A. (2018). *Indicators of school crime and safety: 2017 (NCES 2018–036/NCJ 251413)*. National Center for Education Statistics, U.S. Department of Education, and Bureau of Justice Statistics, Office of Justice Programs, U.S. Department of Justice. Washington, DC.

National Academies of Sciences, Engineering, and Medicine (NASEM). (2016). *Preventing bullying through science, policy, and practice*. The National Academies Press. https://doi.org/10.17226/23482

Neth, E. L., Caldarella, P., Richardson, M. J., & Heath, M. A. (2020). Social-emotional learning in the middle grades: A mixed-methods evaluation of the Strong Kids program. *Research in Middle Level Education, 43*(1), 1–13. https://doi.org/10.1080/19404476.2019.1701868

Oakes, W. P., Lane, K. L., Royer, D. J., Menzies, H. M., Buckman, M. M., Brunsting, N., Cantwell, E. D., Schatschneider, C., & Lane, N. A. (2021). Elementary teachers' self-efficacy during initial implementation of comprehensive, integrated, three-tiered models of prevention. *Journal of Positive Behavior Interventions, 23*(2), 93–105. https://doi.org/10.1177/1098300720916718

O'Neill, R. E., Horner, R. H., Albin, R. W., Storey, K., & Sprague, J. R. (1997). *Functional assessment and program development for problem behavior: A practical handbook* (2nd ed.). Brooks/Cole Publishing.

Popp, A. M., Peguero, A. A., Day, K. R., & Kahle, L. L. (2014). Gender, bullying victimization, and education. *Violence and victims, 29*(5), 843–856. https://doi.org/10.1891/0886-6708.vv-d-13-00047

Preast, J. L., Bowman, N., & Rose, C. A. (2020). Creating inclusive classroom communities through social and emotional learning to reduce social marginalization among students. In *Accessibility and diversity in education: Breakthroughs in research and practice* (pp. 102–120). IGI Global. https://doi.org/10.4018/978-1-7998-1213-5.ch006

Pugh, R., & Chitiyo, M. (2012). The problem of bullying in schools and the promise of positive behaviour supports. *Journal of Research in Special Educational Needs, 12*(2), 47–53. https://doi.org/10.1111/j.1471-3802.2011.01204.x

Raver, C. C., & Knitzer, J. (2002). *Ready to enter: What research tells policymakers about strategies to promote social and emotional school readiness among three-and four-year-old children*. Harris School of Public Policy Studies, University of Chicago, Working Papers. https://doi.org/10.7916/D82V2QVX

Rose, C. A., Cohen, D., Owens, S., Hopkins, S., Graves, K., & Reinke, W. (prep). *A pilot evaluation of a web-based social and emotional learning program to reduce bullying among elementary-aged youth*. Manuscript in preparation, University of Missouri.

Rose, C. A., & Espelage, D. L. (2012). Risk and protective factors associated with the bullying involvement of students with emotional and behavioral disorders. *Behavioral Disorders, 37*(3), 133–148. https://doi.org/10.1177/019874291203700302

Rose, C. A., Espelage, D. L., & Monda-Amaya, L. E. (2009). Bullying and victimization rates among students in general and special education: A comparative analysis. *Educational Psychology, 29*(7), 761–776. https://doi.org/10.1080/01443410903254864

Rose, C. A., & Gage, N. A. (2017). Exploring the involvement of bullying among students with disabilities over time. *Exceptional Children, 83*(3), 298–314. https://doi.org/10.1177/0014402916667587

Rose, C. A., Hopkins, S., McGillen, G., & Simpson, J. (2019). Current trends in bully prevention: Maintaining a positive school climate and culture. In D. Bateman, J. Cline, & M. Yell (Eds.), *Current trends and legal issues in special education* (pp. 155–174). Corwin Press. https://doi.org/10.4135/9781071800539.n11

Rose, C. A., & Monda-Amaya, L. E. (2012). Bullying and victimization among students with disabilities: Effective strategies for classroom teachers. *Intervention in School and Clinic, 48*(2), 99–107. https://doi.org/10.1177/1053451211430119

Rose, C. A., Monda-Amaya, L. E., & Espelage, D. L. (2011). Bullying perpetration and victimization in special education: A review of the literature. *Remedial and special education, 32*(2), 114–130. https://doi.org/10.1177/0741932510361247

Rose, C. A., Simpson, C. G., & Moss, A. (2015). The bullying dynamic: Prevalence of involvement among a large-scale sample of middle and high school youth with and without disabilities. *Psychology in the Schools, 52*, 515–531. https://doi.org/10.1002/pits.21840

Rose, C. A., Slaten, C. D., & Preast, J. L. (2017). Bully perpetration and self-esteem: Examining the relation over time. *Behavioral Disorders, 42*(4), 159–169. https://doi.org/10.1177/0198742917715733

Rose, C. A., Swearer, S. M., & Espelage, D. L. (2012). Bullying and students with disabilities: The untold narrative. *Focus on Exceptional Children, 45*(2), 1–10. https://doi.org/10.17161/fec.v45i2.6682

Ross, S. W., & Horner, R. H. (2009). Bully prevention in positive behavior support. *Journal of Applied Behavior Analysis, 42*, 747–759. https://doi.org/10.1901/jaba.2009.42-747

Ryoo, J. H., Wang, C., & Swearer, S. M. (2015). Examination of the change in latent statuses in bullying behaviors across time. *School Psychology Quarterly, 30*, 105–122. https://doi.org/10.1037/e618372013-001

Sailor, W., Skrtic, T. M., Cohn, M., & Olmstead, C. (2021). Preparing teacher educators for statewide scale-up of Multi-Tiered Systems of Support (MTSS). *Teacher Education and Special Education, 44*(1), 24–41. https://doi.org/10.1177/0888406420938035

Scott, T. M., Gage, N. A., Hirn, R. G., Lingo, A. S., & Burt, J. (2019). An examination of the associations between MTSS implementation fidelity measures and student outcomes. *Preventing School Failure: Alternative Education for Children and Youth, 63*(4), 308–316. https://doi.org/10.1080/1045988x.2019.1605971

Shriberg, D., Burns, M., Desai, P., Grunewald, S., & Pitt, R. (2015). A multiyear investigation of combating bullying in middle school: Stakeholder perspectives. *School Psychology Forum: Research in Practice, 9*(2), 143–161.

Smith, B. H., & Low, S. (2013). The role of social-emotional learning in bullying prevention efforts. *Theory Into Practice, 52*(4), 280–287. https://doi.org/10.1080/00405841.2013.829731

Son, E., Parish, S. L., & Peterson, N. A. (2012). National prevalence of peer victimization among young children with disabilities in the United States. *Children and Youth Services Review, 34*, 1540–1545. https://doi.org/10.1016/j.childyouth.2012.04.014

Sugai, G., & Horner, R. R. (2006). A promising approach for expanding and sustaining school-wide positive behavior support. *School Psychology Review, 35*(2), 245–259. https://doi.org/10.1080/02796015.2006.12087989

Sugai, G., Sprague, J. R., Horner, R. H., & Walker, H. M. (2000). Preventing school violence: The use of office discipline referrals to assess and monitor school-wide discipline interventions. *Journal of Emotional and Behavioral Disorders, 8*(2), 94–101. https://doi.org/10.1177/106342660000800205

Swearer, S. M., Espelage, D. L., Vaillancourt, T., & Hymel, S. (2010). What can be done about school bullying? Linking research to educational practice. *Educational Researcher, 39*, 38–47. https://doi.org/10.3102/0013189x09357622

Swearer, S. M., Wang, C., Maag, J. W., Siebecker, A. B., & Frerichs, L. J. (2012). Understanding the bullying dynamic among students in special and general education. *Journal of School Psychology, 50*, 503–520. https://doi.org/10.1016/j.jsp.2012.04.001

Symes, W., & Humphrey, N. (2010). Peer-group indicators of social inclusion among pupils with autistic spectrum disorders (ASD) in mainstream secondary schools: A comparative study. *School Psychology International, 31*(5), 478–494. https://doi.org/10.1177/0143034310382496

Taylor, R. D., Oberle, E., Durlak, J. A., & Weissberg, R. P. (2017). Promoting positive youth development through school-based social and emotional learning interventions: A meta-analysis of follow-up effects. *Child Development, 88*(4), 1156–1171. https://doi.org/10.1111/cdev.12864

The Language Express, Inc. (2016). *Cool school bully prevention program* [Online Computer Program]. Author.

Thompson, D., Whitney, I., & Smith, P. K. (1994). Bullying of children with special needs in mainstream schools. *Support for Learning, 9*(3), 103–106. https://doi.org/10.1111/j.1467-9604.1994.tb00168.x

Twyman, K. A., Saylor, C. F., Saia, D., Macias, M. M., Taylor, L. A., & Spratt, E. (2010). Bullying and ostracism experiences in children with special health care needs. *Journal of Developmental & Behavioral Pediatrics, 31*(1), 1–8. https://doi.org/10.1097/dbp.0b013e3181c828c8

Von der Embse, N. P., Pendergast, L. L., Kilgus, S. P., & Eklund, K. R. (2016). Evaluating the applied use of a mental health screener: Structural validity of the Social, Academic, and Emotional Behavior Risk Screener. *Psychological Assessment, 28*, 1265–1275. https://doi.org/10.1037/pas0000253

Wang, C., Berry, B., & Swearer, S. M. (2013). The critical role of school climate in effective bullying prevention. *Theory Into Practice, 52*(4), 296–302. https://doi.org/10.1080/00405841.2013.829735

Wehmeyer, M. L., Kelchner, K., & Richards, S. (1996). Essential characteristics of self determined behavior of individuals with mental retardation. *American Journal on Mental Retardation, 100*(6), 632–642.

Whitley, S. F., & Cuenca-Carlino, Y. (2020). Examining the technical adequacy of the Social, Academic, and Emotional Behavior Risk Screener. *Assessment for Effective Intervention, 46*(1), 67–75. https://doi.org/10.1177/1534508419857225

Xin, J. F., & Sutman, F. X. (2011). Using the smart board in teaching social stories to students with autism. *Teaching Exceptional Children, 43*(4), 18–24. https://doi.org/10.1177/004005991104300402

Yasuda, P. M., Ievers-Landis, C. E., & Rose, C. A. (2016). *Say NO bullying: A resource book for children and teens with disorders of short stature.* Human Growth Foundation.

Zablotsky, B., Bradshaw, C. P., Anderson, C., & Law, P. (2012). Involvement in bullying among children with autism spectrum disorders: Parents' perspectives on the influence of school factors. *Behavioral Disorders, 37*(3), 179–191. https://doi.org/10.1177/019874291203700305

Zablotsky, B., Bradshaw, C. P., Anderson, C. M., & Law, P. (2013). Risk factors for bullying among children with autism spectrum disorders. *Autism, 18*, 419–427. https://doi.org/10.1177/1362361313477920

Zins, J. E., Weissberg, R. P., Wang, M. C., & Walberg, H. J. (2004). *Building academic success on social and emotional learning; What does the research say?* Teachers College Press.

INDEX

Note: Page locators in **bold** indicate a table. Page locators in *italics* indicate a figure.

ABA *see* applied behavioral analysis
Abram, Karen M. (et al. 2013) 261
absenteeism 43
academic engagement enhancement (AEE) 225
academic failure 163–165, 168, 171, 175, 274
acceleration 208, 212
Aceves, Terese C. 3, 156
Adolf, Suzanne M. (et al. 2017) 86
Agitation 208, 211
augmented reality (AR) 183
AIMSweb (academic screener) *24*, 85
Al Otaiba, Stephanie 1
Allinder, Rose M. 61
Anderson, Eric J. 98, 107
Annamma, Subini 234
Ansley, Brandis M. (et al. 2016) 65
Antisocial Behavior in School: Strategies and Best Practices (Walker) 6
applied behavior analysis (ABA) 2, 5, 7, 13, 20, 25, 204, 208
area under the curve (AUC) 86, 94
Arizona 9, 151
assessment data 2, 48, 99, 143, **170**, 205, 236–237, 279
Assessment Schedule 6, *24*, 47, 51
assessments: diverse backgrounds, challenges of 234–235; Language Acquisition Scales 240; mathematics 138, *139*, 144, 147; multiple screening 85–86, 138; sociometric 225; speed-power 85, 87; writing 111, 113
assistive technology (AT) 178–179, 185
at-risk students: 5 C's of reality 175; academic strategies 163, 168–169, 171–172, 173–174; academics, gaps in 164–165; behaviors nonconductive for learning 164; cultural relevance 172–173; curriculum based assessment 165–166; disciplinary actions 164; expectations 167; fairness and equity 174–175; generalization (strategy) 169, 172–173, 175; positive reinforcement 173, 174; self-monitoring 167, 168, **168**; student preferences 167; teacher-directed instruction (SMART) 169, **170**, 170–171
attention deficit hyperactivity disorder (ADHD) 35, 72, 76, 183
audio feedback 116
augmentative and alternative communication (AAC) 190, 194, 196, 197
Austin, Christy R. (et al.) 75
autism spectrum disorder (ASD) 184, 249, 273–274
autonomy 35, 46–47, 51, 58–59, 157, 159

Baker, Doris Luft (et al. 2016) 155, **153**, 157
Bandura's Social Learning Theory 181
Barth, Amy E. 77
Barton, Erin E. 3, 249
Basham, James D. (et al. 2020) 186
BAU *see* business as usual
behavior: academic 6, 44, 167; acting out 204, 208, 212; behavior specific praise 5, 9, 12, 24, 203, *209*, 211, 275, 284; challenging **11**, 19, 98, 204–204, 253, 274–275, 277; criminal 261; emotional 37; management 56, 98, 101, 104, *107*, 108, 211, 223, 264–265; problem 3 7, 205–206, 208, 211, 277, 284; prosocial 50; risk screeners 279–280, 282, 284; student 43, 50, 108, 204, 208, *209*, *210*, 213; target behavior 10, 20, 167, 206, 250, 255
Behavioral, Academic, and Social Engagement (BASE) model: correlated constraints concept

220–221; effective communication, enhanced 226; intervention components 223–225; research based 228–229; social inclusion 220, *227*; social intervention practice 226–228
Belfiore, Phillip J. 2, 167, 172, 174
Bellani, Marcella (et al. 2011) 182
Berninger, Virginia W. 111
Berry, Ann B. (et al. 2011) 63
Bilingual English-Spanish Assessment (BESA) 241
Billingsley, Bonnie S. 62
Blicha, Amy 167
Bos, Samantha E. 2
Bowers, Peter N. 75
British Dyslexia Association (BDA) 83
Brock, Matthew E. 98, 107
Bronfenbrenner, Urie 272
Buckman, Mark Matthew 1, 4
Bugnariu, Nicoleta L. 182
bullying: critical skill development 280; perception/interpretation 272–274
bullying prevention 277–278, *279*, 281–282
burnout *see* teacher
business as usual (BAU): condition 35–36, 38–39, 99; school 34
Byun, Jae Whan 181

Calhoon, Mary Beth 141
California 4, 151, 262
calm 208, 211–212
Carter, Erik W. 2, 97, 103, 193
Castro-Olivo, Sara M. (et al. 2018) **153**, 157
Catellano, Marisa 46
Catts, Hugh (et al. 2001) 86, 94
CBA *see* curriculum-based assessment
CEEDAR Center *see* Collaboration for Effective Educator Development, Evaluation and Reform
Check-in/Check-out (CICO) 283–284
child welfare system 260
children: pretend play time 247, 248
Ci3T (comprehensive, integrated, three-tiered model): intensive intervention needs (Tier 3) 10, 204, 214; intervention grids 8, 47, 51; leadership teams 6, 11–12; partnerships 7–8; positive behavioral interventions 19, 44, **52**; teacher empowerment (Tier 2) 9, 47, 52; treatment integrity 24, 28
classroom: management 3–4, 44, 49, 51, 97, *209*, 211, 226
Clemens, Nathan 2
cluster randomized trials (CRTs) 226
computer-assisted instruction (CAI) 182
codebook/coding procedures 100
cognitive behavior therapy 265–266
Coker, David L. (et al. 2018) 114
collaboration: expectations for 57–58, 62; peer intervention 157, 159; structures for 46–47, 51, **154**

Collaboration for Effective Educator Development, Evaluation and Reform (CEEDAR) Center 117, 120
collegial: relationships 43, 51; support 57, 59–60; trust 46, 52
Colvin, Geoffrey 204, 208, 215
Common Core State Standards 110
common formative assessments (CFAs) 143
Common, Erik Alan 2, 213
competence enhancement behavior management (CEBM) 225
Compton, Donald L. (et al. 2014) 73, 74, 78, 86
computation: mathematical 129–130, 140, 141–142, **166**, 172
computer adaptive assessments (CAA) 85, 88
Concept Oriented Reading Instruction (CORI) 34–35
conservation of resources (COR) theory 57, 59, 62, 65–66
Cool School 283
COR *see* conservation of resources theory
Council for Exceptional Children (CEC) 21, 104
Council of Juvenile Correctional Administrators 262
COVID-19 14, 51, 99, 103, 150, 178, 185
critical mathematics content 125–126
Cronbach's alpha 87
Cuenca-Carlino, Yojanna 117
culturally responsive and sustaining pedagogies (CRSPs): effective intervention practices 152–155, 156–158; evidence-based instructional strategies 157, 158–159
culture: school 43, 56, 59–60, 272
Culture-Language Interpretive Matrices 234
Cumming, Michelle M 2
curricular materials 45, 60, 61, 63
curriculum-based assessment (CBA) 140, 165–167, 169
curriculum-based measurements (CBMs) 85, 88, *139*, 141, *145*
Cutting, Laurie E. 85

Daily Progress Report 284
data systems 14, 50
data-based individualization (DBI) 138, *139*, 141, 144–145, *146*, 147
data-informed learning 10–11, 13, 23, 47, 50, 52, 214
Datchuk, Shawn M. (et al. 2020) 117
Datnow, Amanda 46
DBI *see* data-based individualization
de-escalation techniques 208, *209–210*, 211–212
Dennis, Minyi Shih (Knight, et al. 2016) 131
digital game-based learning (DGBL) 181
Diagnostic Online Mathematics Assessment (DOMA) 142, 143, 146
dialectical behavior therapy 266
DIBELS **153**, 236, **237**, 238

Didehbani, Nyaz (et al. 2016) 184
Dierkhising, Carly B. (et al. 2019) 261
Direct Behavior Ratings 14
directed consultation (DC) 223–224
diverse learners 132, 158, 234, 239
diversity 93, 98, 234, 266–267
DOMA *see* Diagnostic Online Mathematics Assessment
dosage (attempts) 253
dyslexia: prevalence of 35–36, 72; universal screening 83–84, 86, 90–91

EBDs *see* emotional behavioral disorders
ecological systems theory 57, 59, 272
ecosystems (school) 57, 77, 159
Edmin, Christopher 175
effectiveness intervention (EI) 93
effectiveness of core instruction (ECI) 92–93
Elleman, Amy M. 77, 78
emotional disturbances (EDs) 5, 203
emotional behavior disorders (EBDs) 5, 56, 59, 63, 66, 203, 273
Empowering Teachers with Low-Intensity Strategies to Support Instruction 9, 211, 214
English language learners 2, 117, 234
English learners: academic achievement, current 151–152; instruction models 158; intervention studies 160; motivational strategies 155, 157; peer interaction, benefits from 157, 196, 199–200; reading interventions 152, 155
English proficiency 236–237, 239
Enhanced Core Reading Instruction (ECRI) 74
Ennis, Robin Parks 9
environmental arrangement 252
Esparza Brown, Julie 3, 240
Espelage, Dorothy L. 274, 277, 281
ethnic minority 226, 233
Every Student Succeeds Act (ESSA) 97, 103, 184–185
evidence-based practice: academic instruction 56; guidance for systems involved youth 262; implementing 117, 221
explicit instruction: attribution retention 37; mathematical 127, 129–130, 132; reading interventions 71, 79, 98; writing instruction 113, 118
externalizing 5, 8, 20, 276, 280

FABI *see* functional assessment-based interventions
Farmer, Thomas W. 2
First Step Act (dyslexia screening) 83
FitzPatrick, Erin 2
Fletcher, J.D. 182
Flower, Linda 111
fluency: mathematical 127, 129–130; reading 14, 73–74, 88, 152, **153** *see also* reading fluency
Fluhler, Sally K. 2
Fluidez en la lectura oral (FLO) 236

foundational reading skills 36, 72, 152, 238
free and appropriate public education (FAPE) 97, 203, 273
Freeman-Green, Shaqwana (et al. 2015) 131
Freire, Paulo 172, 174
Fuchs, Lynn S. (et al. 2017) 140, 141, 215
function matrix 205–206, *207*
functional assessment-based interventions (FABI): definition/description 205; evidence based intervention 213–214; five-step process 206, *207*, 208; student behavioral/academic interventions 2, 7, 10

Gage, Nicholas 273, 277
Garwood, Justin D. (et al. 2019) 115
Gates-MacGinitie Reading Comprehension 85
general intellectual ability (GIA) 240
Gersten, Russell (et al. 2009) 130
Giangreco, Michael F. (et al. 2001) 98, 104
Glascott, Taylor 174
Goldhaber, Dan (et al. 2018) 63
Gough, Phillip B. 111
Graff, Cristina Santamaría 158
Graham, Steve 111–112, 113, 114, 116
Grant, Adam 3
Gray Oral Reading Test (GORT) 84–84
Griffith, Priscilla L. 111
Guin, Kacey 44

Hanushek, Erik A. (et al. 2016) 44
Hawaii 63, 115
Hayes, John R. 111
head-mounted displays (HMDs) 182
Hebert, Michael 114
Herman, Keith C. (et al. 2018) 49
high-poverty schools 43, 60, 63, 94
high-probability instructional sequence (HPIS) 171, 173
Higher Education Act of 2008 184
Hilliard, Asa 176
Hitchcock, Caryl H. (et al. 2016) 115
Horner, Robert H. 48
Hume, Kara 181

IDDs *see* intellectual and developmental disabilities
IDEA *see* Individuals with Disabilities Education Act
IEP *see* individualized education program
IES *see* Institute of Education Sciences
IES Early Career Development and Mentoring Grant 9
iMTSS Network projects 13
individualized de-escalation plan (IDPs) 208, 213, 215
individualized education program (IEP): goals 62, 97, 108; specialized instruction 90, 144, 178–179, *238*

Individuals with Disabilities Education Act (IDEA, 2004) 45, 56, 98, 178
Institute of Education Sciences (IES) 8, 45, 163
instruction, curriculum, and environment (ICE) 237
intellectual and developmental disabilities (IDDs) 98
interconnected systems framework (ISF) 6, 45, **52**, 204
internal consistency 87–88, 280
internalizing 5, 8, 12, 14, 20, 276, 281–282
International Dyslexia Association (IDA) 83
intervention: A-R-E intervention 206, *207*; critical elements of 155–157 (visual charts); culturally responsive 132, 150; evidence-based 126, 132, 157–158, 228, 250; function-based 98, 205–206, *207*, 276; individualized 284–285; intensive (student behavior) 213–214, 215; mixed-method designs 159; multicomponent 132; multicomponent (problem behavior) 205; peer support 3, 46; positive behavior 6, 204, 265; pre-referral 4–5; reading comprehension 76–78; research 152; semantic information 74–75; social focused 192–194; social-focused 2, 192, 199–200; supplemental reading 37, 74; targeted 283–284; Triple Focus 73; word reading 71
intelligent tutoring systems (ITSs) 182
iPad 116

Jackson, C. Kirabo 60
Jitendra, Asha K. (et al. 2018) 132
Jolivette, Kristine 3
Joung, Eunmi 181
Jozwik, Sara 117
Juel, Connie 111
juvenile justice system 260, 262, 267

Katz, Jason (et al.) 262, 263
Katz, Jennifer (et al.) 262, 263
Kauffman, Nancy A. 284
Keenan, Janice M. 84
Ketterlin-Geller, Leann R. 143
Kinnealey, Moya 284
Kirby, John R. 75
Kissel, Brian T. (et al. 2019) 110
Klingbeil, David (et al. 2019) 94, 147
Klingner, Janette 159
Knitzer, Jane A. 277
Kulik, James A. 182
Kurasaki, Karen S. 100

Lane, Justin 3, 206
Lane, Kathleen Lynne 1
Latino families **153**, 157
leadership team: meetings 12; stakeholders 46
Leko, Melinda M. (et al. 2018) 58, 59
Lembke, Erica S. 2
Lewis, Tim 282

Lieberman, R. (et al. 2018) 263, 268
lines of inquiry 13
long-term English learners (LTELs) 151, 152, 155
Lorenzo, Gonzalo (et al. 2016) 184
Lovett, Maureen W. (et al. 2020) 38, 73

Makarin, Alexey 60
mathematics: assessments 138, 140, 142, 147; case study, assessment 144–146; diagnostics 142; fluency 129–130; interventions 126, 132; language of 127–128; manipulatives 129, 180; multiple representations 128–129; progress monitoring 141; research base 131–133, 147; screening 138, *139*, 140; targeted support 125; universal screening measures 138, 144, 147; word-problems 130–131
mathematics difficulty (MD) 125
McCree, Nikita 3
McLeskey, James 62
McLoughlin, Caven S. 164
Meenan, Chelsea E. 84
mental health: disorders 203, 208, 247, 260–261; support 6, 45, 223, 263–264, 266
Menzies, Holly M. 8
Messick, Samuel 88
meta-analyses3 1, 57, 76, 114, 152
Miller, Haylie L 182
Montague, Marjorie (et al. 2011) 131
Morrison, Deb 234
Mucci, M. (et al. 2018) 166, 171
Multi-Tiered Systems of Support in Reading (MTSS-R) 91
multilingual learners 3, 45, 233–234, 240
multimedia (technology) 115, 180
Multi-tiered System of Supports (MTSS) 1, 125, 151, 157, 227, 233, 272, 274

National Academies of Sciences, Engineering, and Medicine (NASEM) 272, 280
National Assessment of Educational Progress (NAEP) 163, 233
National Center for Systemic Improvement (NCSI) 93
National Center on Improving Literacy (NCIL) 93
National Center on Intensive Intervention's 87, 93
National Center on Intensive Interventions (NCII) 93, 138
National Commission on Writing 110
National Council of Teachers of Mathematics 126, 142
Nelson, Gena1 32
Nevin, John A. (et al. 1983) 173
New York City, New York 4, 62
Noltemeyer, Amity 164

O'Brien, Kristen Merrill (et al. 2019) 58, 59, 66
Oakes, Wendy Peia 1, 49, 206
object play **248**, 248–250, **251**, 252–256

ODRs *see* office discipline referrals
office discipline referrals (ODRs) 8, 12, *24*, 47
Office of Juvenile Justice Delinquency Prevention 262
Office of Special Education Model Demonstration Projects 151
Office of Special Education Programs (OSEP) 63, 236
Ok, Min Wook (et al. 2017) 186
oral reading fluency (ORF) 236, *238 see also* fluency
orthography (correct spelling) 73
Ortiz Picture Vocabulary Acquisition Test (Ortiz PVAT) 241

paraprofessionals (paras): coding procedures 100–103; demographics (case study) 100; experience (job) 101, 103; research data, effectiveness 106, *107*, 107–108; responsibilities 98, 101; support staff 97; teacher support 104–105; training/coaching 99–100, 104
Parsons, Sarah 184
Parten, Mildred B. 247
PBIS *see* positive behavior intervention and supports
Peabody Individual Achievement Test (PIAT) 84
peak 208, 212
Peer Assisted Learning Strategies (PALS) 158
peer networks 194, 196, 220, 222
peer partner programs 195–196
peer support 35, 46, 194–196, 200, 225–228
Pennsylvania System of School Assessment (PSSA) 85
Petscher, Yaacov 86, 94
phonemic awareness *see* reading difficulties
phonics instruction 37, 72–75, 78, 118, 152, **153**
physical arrangement 252–253
pictorial representations 128–129
Plavnick, Joshua B. 181
Portland State University 158, 236
positive behavioral interventions and supports (PBIS): meeting student needs 44–46; supports behavioral/functional needs 275
Powell, Sarah R. 2
practice-based professional development (PBPD) 117
Preast, June L. (et al. 2020) 284
pretend play **248**, 249
professional development (PD): paraprofessional support staff 97; poor experiences with 43, 48, 104; social validity 117–118, 184–185, 199, 224
professional learning opportunities 46, 48, 50
Project Elite 2 158, 236
Project Ellipses 158, 236
Project ENHANCE 7, 11
Project FUNCTION 7, 10
Project Lee 158, 236
Project SCREEN 7, 12

Project Support and Include 9
Project WRITE 7–8

Qualitative Reading Inventory–3 (QRI) 84

Radu, Iulian 183
randomized control trials (RCTs) 7, 8–9, 152, **154**
Raver, C. Cybele 277
RCT *see* randomized control trials
reading achievement 1, 31, 33–34, 38–39
reading comprehension: language building skills/vocabulary knowledge 76–77, 114; speech-language disability 75–76; strategies 77–78
reading difficulties: consequences of (possible) 71, 264; phonemic awareness 36, 72; pronunciation 72–74; students with 31, 71; vowel alert 73–74
reading fluency 36–37, 39, 75, 79
reading interventions: best practices 2, 22; elementary grade 34–35, 39; meta-analysis, writing impact 114; word-level 72–73, 74 *see also* English learners
reading program 22, 34–35, 37, 44
recovery 208, 212–213
Reed, Deborah K. 75
regression discontinuity designs (RDDs) 119
reinforcement-focused visual supports 252
Reinke, Wendy M. (et al. 2013) 49
reliability (screening) 87–88
Research practice partnerships (RPPs) 160
response-to-intervention (RTI)1 9, 45, 125, 204
Riccomini, Paul J. (et al. 2015) 128
Richards-Tutor, Cara (et al. 2016) 242
Richards-Tutor, Catherine 2
Ronfeldt, Matthew (et al. 2013) 44
Rose, Chad A. 272, 273, 274, 277, 281, 282, 285
Rosenberg, Harriet (et al. 2014) 261
Ross, Scott W. 48, 49
RTI *see* response to intervention

Saffar, Ohud Adnan 186
Sailor, Wayne (et al. 2021) 274
SAMHSA *see* Substance Abuse and Mental Health Services Administration
Scarborough, Hollis S. 85
Schaaf, David N. 185
schema (word problem) 131
school: inequities 150; organizational health 43–44
school-wide climate assessment 278–279, 282
School-wide Expectation Matrix for Specific Setting Survey (SESSS) 6
School-wide Positive Behavioral Interventions and Supports (SW-PBIS) 19
Second Step (bully prevention) 281
Second Step: Bullying Prevention Unit 281
Seethaler, Pamela M. 140
self-advocacy 104, 110–111, 114, 117
self-determination 111, 198, 285
self-efficacy 8, 31, 33, 39, 49, 112, 119, 283

self-regulated strategy development (SRSD) 8, 14, 112–116, 159–160
self-regulation 111, 116, 183, 264–265
Shapiro, Edward S. (et al. 2015) 85
Siuty, Molly Baustien (et al. 2018) 61
Skiba, Russell J. 164
small-group: instruction 97, 168–169; intervention 39, 74
SMART *see* Supplemental Mathematics and Reading Tutoring
Smith, Sean J. 2, 115, 185
social and emotional learning (SEL) 3, 183, 265, 272, 276, *278*
social cognitive theory 5, 66
social dynamics management (SDM) 225
social inclusion 2, 220, 223, 226–228
social play 247, 248, **248**, 256
Social Skills Improvement System: Class wide Intervention Program 283
social skills training 196, 197, 200, 220, 227, 284
social validity 6, 19–21, *24*, 25, 28
Social, Academic, and Emotional Behavior Risk Screener (SAEBRS) 280
Solari, Emily J. 2
SOLVE 131
special education teachers (SETs): administrative support 64; emotional exhaustion 48–49, 61–62; informational resources 57–59, 64; instructional effectiveness 60, 62; logistical resources 57, 59–60, 66; mentoring 5 7, 59, 65; paraprofessional support 57, 59, 97, 117, 194; shortage of 63; social resources 58–59, 62; stress management plan 65; workforce 2, 50, 52, 56, 59, 62–64; working conditions 56–58, 59–60, 61–62, McLeskey 64–66
specific reading comprehension deficit (S-RCD) 84–85
speech recognition 115
speech-to-text/text-to-speech 115
spelling patterns 73–74
SRSD *see* self-regulated strategy development
STAR-Math (academic screener) 85, 144
statistical learning 73–75
Steacy, Laura M. (et al. 2019) 73, 74
Steps to Respect 281
Stevens, E. (et al. 2017) 75
stressors 43
Strong Start, Kids, and Teens 281–282
student: behavioral needs, meeting 45, 213, 265, 275, 279; engagement 44; learning outcomes 43, 45, 56, 127, 159, 181, 184; social-emotional well-being 44–45, 262–263
Student Risk Screening Scale for Internalizing and Externalizing (SRSS-IE) 12, *24*
students with disabilities (SWDs): computer-assisted learning 182; cooperative learning groups 195; educational apps 180–181; game-based learning 181; online learning 178, 183; peer support 194–196; role of technology 178–180, 183–185; screening procedures 83; self-directed strategies 197–198; social interaction 190, 192; social relationships/acceptance 193, 198; social skills, improving 190, 192, 196; written communication challenges 110–111
Study of Personnel Needs in Special Education (SPeNSE) 66
Substance Abuse and Mental Health Services Administration (SAMHSA) 262, 266
Supplemental Mathematics and Reading Tutoring (SMART) 166, **166**, 169, **170**, 171
system-level support 5
systems-involved youth: behaviors of 264–265; characteristics of 260–262; definition 260, 262; educational needs 263–264; future research implications 267–268; mental health concerns 261, 266; social-emotional learning challenges 265–266; special needs of 262; transition planning/practices 267; trauma, impacts and exposure 261, 266

Taxonomy of Intervention Intensity 215
teacher: burnout 43–44, 48–49; confidence 45; decision-making involvement 46; efficacy 43, 45, 48–49; installation/sustainability 11; participation 46; retention 43; turnover, negative effect of 44; well-being 1, 43, 44–46, 48–49, 52
teachers: new/onboarding 50; special education 43; stressed/low coping 50–51
TeenACE (writing intervention) 115
temporal arrangement 253, 257
Think Again (Grant) 3
Thomas, Cathy Newman (et al. 2019) 184
Thorius, Kathleen A. King 158
tiered systems: for all students (Tier 1) 5, 47; provide clear vision and purpose 45; secondary (Tier 2) 6, 8, 14, 19, 47, 204, 275; support teacher well-being 46, 48, 52; tertiary (Tier 3) 6, 8, 19, 47, 204, 275; *see also* Ci3T
transparency (creating) 47
trends 66
Trial Urban District Assessment (TUDA) 2019 163
triggers 208, 211–212, 233, 264
Turney, Kristin 261

U.S. Department of Education 119
U.S. Departments of Education and Justice 262, 263, 264, 265
Umbreit, John (et al. 2007) 204, 205, 208, 213–215
Universal Design for Learning (UDL) 179, 184–186, 275
universal screening: who should be present 92
universal screening 83, 85, 93, 144, 147; assessments 93, 138, 144, 147; classification

accuracy 90–91; consistency/reliability 87–88; procedures 35, 45, 83, 235; univariate/multivariate 85–86; validity 88–90; where should we be going 93–94

Valerio, N. 65
van Garderen, Delinda 131
VanDerHeyden, Amanda M. 94
Variable Momentary Time sampling-Differential Reinforcement of Other behavior schedule (VMT-DRO) 174
Vidal, Sarah (et al. 2019) 260
video based learning 198
video modeling (VM) 181
vocabulary: mathematics 128
virtual reality (VR) 182–183

Wagner, Rick (et al. 2020) 94
Walker, Hill 5–6
Warne, Russell (et al. 2014) 239
Weschler Individual Achievement Test 85
Wharton School, The 3
What Works Clearinghouse (WWC) 112–113, 117, 119, *209*
Wiggins, Gran t242
Wijekumar, Kausalai (et al. 2018) 116
Wilderman, Christopher 261
Wilson, Joshua 115–116
Winn, William D. 111
Wolery, Mark 249
Wong, Venus (et al. 2017) 62
Woodcock-Johnson Passage Comprehension-3 (WJPC) 84–85
word-level automaticity: text-reading fluency 72, 79
word-level reading difficulties (WLRDs): common occurrence 71–72; comprehension instruction 78–79; explicit phonics instruction 72, 78; five word identification strategies 73; interventions 74–75
working conditions: precursor to stress 43, 52
World Health organization (WHO) 83
Writer(s) Within Community (Graham) 111–112
writers: environmental/social motivations 111–112; struggling 112, 114
writing: genre knowledge 112; performance 119; research 112–113; student recommendations 111–112; web based programs 116
written communication: barriers to 110; content area instruction 114–115; evidence-based practices, implementing 117–118; performance of students with disabilities 111, 114, 116–117; writing outcomes 115; writing process, research findings 112–113, 114, 119
WWC *see* What Works Clearinghouse

Xin, Yan Ping 131

youth: connectedness 172, 262–263; multisystem-involved 260, 262; social-emotional well-being 44–45, 262–263; trauma exposure 261
Yovanoff, Paul 143

Zablotsky, Benjamin 274
Zoom (Zoom Video Communications, Inc.) 100, 179